A Chaos of Delight

A Chaos of Delight

**SCIENCE, RELIGION AND MYTH
AND THE SHAPING OF WESTERN THOUGHT**

Geoffrey P. Dobson

LONDON   OAKVILLE

Published by
Equinox Publishing Ltd.
UK: Unit 6, The Village, 101 Amies St., London SW11 2JW
www.equinoxpub.com

British Library Cataloguing-in-Publication Data
A catalogue record for this book is available from the British Library.

ISBN 1 84553-018-7 (hardback)
     1 84553-019-5 (paperback)

Library of Congress Cataloging-in-Publication Data

A chaos of delight : science, religion and myth, and the shaping of western thought / Geoffrey P. Dobson.– 1st ed.
    p. cm.
Includes bibliographical references and index.
ISBN 1-84553-018-7 (hardcover) -- ISBN 1-84553-019-5 (pbk.)
1. Religion and science. 2. Mythology. I. Title.
BL240.3.D63 2005
140--dc22   2005001884

Typeset by Kate Williams, Swansea.
Printed and bound in Great Britain by Antony Rowe Ltd., Chippenham.

Contents

Contents

*Let each one examine his thoughts, and he will find them all
occupied with the past and the future.* Blaise Pascal (1623–1662)[1]

Preface

A Chaos of Delight has been a labour of love for over ten years. The title is taken from the words of Charles Darwin when he witnessed the natural magnificence and extraordinary diversity of life in a Brazilian rainforest. On 28 February 1832, he wrote in his diary: "The mind is a chaos of delight, out of which a world of future & more quiet pleasure will arise."[2] My inspiration came around 1986 when I was working as a research scientist at the National Institutes of Health (NIH), Maryland, USA. Ironically, the idea was not seeded in the intensely stimulating workplace at NIH with its thousands of scientists and medical discoveries, but when my neighbours in Highwood Road, Rockville asked what I did during the day and why science was important. When I look back on those enjoyable years chatting about the "news and views" of the day, usually over a beer, I don't think I ever offered satisfactory answers.

Over the years, as I became more interested in promoting the understanding of science, I realized that any meaningful effort must include an *understanding of what science is not*. What began as a story about science grew into something much larger and more difficult than I had first imagined: a history of the different ways human beings have sought meaning and made sense of the world. The tantalizing fact that underpins our story is that despite human beings sharing 98.5 per cent of our 32 000 genes with the chimpanzee (differing only in about 500 genes), we are the only species to seek meaning by imposing order and process on external stimuli, and expressing it in language, art, history, myth, religion and science. Human beings are, as cultural anthropologist Clifford Geertz (*b*.1926) claims, "symbolising, conceptualising, meaning-seeking animals", who possess the "drive to make sense out of experience, to give it form and order".[3] This drive by different peoples in different places and at different times is a major factor responsible for the cultural parallels and differences that exist today.

A Chaos of Delight was written for a general readership with two principal aims: to understand how different cultures have looked at the same world and devised totally different explanations ranging from deeply mythopoeic existential–metaphysical reflections to purely physical ones; and to provide a history of Western ideas in which the reader can place their own worldview, and better understand its origins and development. The book is a guided tour into the succession of ways human beings have constructed order and meaning over the past 5000 years. At a time in history when our knowledge-base is doubling every ten years or so, there is a growing concern that the general public are being left behind. It is my hope that this book will help to bridge this ever-widening gap.

It is further hoped that the book will help to promote a better understanding of the changing roles that science, religion and myth have played in shaping the images of ourselves and our place in the wider universe. For much of the last century, despite ongoing efforts to reconcile the differences between science and religion, deeper chasms appear to have formed. One school argues that there is no conflict because religion is completely in accordance with reality, and *within* its theological framework science is its servant not its master. Another school argues that science and religion are incompatible because each system relies on different methodologies, and disunity may arise when both seek to explain the same phenomena with different answers. In the public arena, religion is often associated with barrier-building, violence and wars, and science with mischief and mistrust. In my view, greater harmony between science and religion can be reached from a deeper understanding of their respective origins, intersections and divergence through the history of ideas. Much benefit can be gained by appropriating the past in the present and future. In this context, I agree with the sentiments of Danish philosopher Søren Kierkegaard (1813–1855) when he wrote: "Life can only be understood backwards, but it must be lived forward."[4]

As we move through the Sumerian, Egyptian, Greek, early Christian, Medieval and Renaissance periods to the present, one unifying feature that stands out above all others as the most certain thing about human knowledge in general, and science, religion or myth in particular, is its uncertainty. From a cross-cultural perspective, one's religious views are framed by articles of faith derived from history, and within their highly prescribed boundaries there exists a system that is just as dynamic as modern-day science. In all likelihood, you will come away from the journey with a cache of historical biases and legacies that frame and underpin your worldview. For me, one great legacy from the ancient Greeks, and befitting of the twenty-first century, is that you could be wrong in your thinking and still be highly productive in society by advancing knowledge through endless creativity and discovery. An important lesson for the third millennium is that diversity of opinion is healthy and essential; it is blind acceptance of dogma that impedes understanding and progress.

Lastly, and in accordance with my broader theme of appropriating the past in the present and future, I invite you to ponder the question on how human beings 2000 years from now might view progress in the twentieth and twenty-first centuries. Just as the ancient Greeks reflected on older cultures, and we reflect on all of them today, what do you think peoples of the future will write of our recent history? I asked this question of Nobel Laureate Sir John Cornforth (*b.*1917) early in 1993 and in his reply (23 June 1993) he wrote: "I think it is possible that our posterity 2000 years on might say something like this: *These people had the first opportunity to secure the earth's future, and they squandered it. That might have been expected: they were imprisoned by the past, and they did not live long enough to break free.*" I sincerely hope Cornforth is wrong, as I am sure he himself does. The ball is in our court to make the changes we wish to see.

Acknowledgements

I should like to thank the many specialists who took time out of their hectic schedules to comment on the very early draft chapters and who have helped steer the enterprise. Warm thanks go to John T. Edsall and Brian Davies for their guiding comments on Chapter 1, John Baines for his comments on the ancient Near Eastern chapters and Edward F. Wente for his helpful criticisms; Edward Hussey and Lloyd Gerson for their commentaries on the Presocratic chapter, Venerable Edward Byford and Rosemary Dunn for commenting on the early and medieval Christian chapters and Oliver Leaman for clarifying Averroes. I should also like to thank John Hedley-Brooke for his fathomless scholarship on Copernicus, Kepler, Galileo and Newton. Thanks also go to Ian Whittingham for his early comments on the origins of the universe, and to my good friend, the late Peter Hochachka for his comments on the origins of life. No person is expert in all the areas covered in this book, and I take full responsibility for any obscurities and errors that remain.

I should also like to thank my mentors and colleagues over the years; John Baldwin, Peter Hochachka, David Randall, Britton Chance, Richard Veech, Janet Passonneau, and the late Eldo Wiebe. Special thanks go to Kirk Jensen for his editorial criticism and friendship over the years, and to Joe Wisnovsky and Richard O'Grady for their continual encouragement. Thanks also go to my past coworkers at the National Institutes of Health, in particular Walter Teague and the late Ming-ta Huang, to my colleagues at James Cook University and to my present and past students. I should also like to thank Sir Gustav Nossal for his wisdom, encouragement and advice, and the Equinox team, Janet Joyce and Valerie Hall, and Kate Williams for their professionalism, flexibility and constructive comments on the text, layout and referencing. I should also like to thank Karla Pincott for her editorial suggestions, the library staff at James Cook University and Jean Dartnall for providing the index. Lastly, I should especially like to thank my parents Bev and Des, Dianne and Tim Donovan, Bill and Nora Green, their respective progeny and, most of all, my very patient and loving wife, Louise, and daughters, Georgia, Caitlin and Ashley. Without your resolute love, support, and sense of humour, Louise, this book would have never been completed.

We gaze up at the same stars, the sky covers us all, the same universe compasses us. What does it matter what practical system we adopt in our search for the truth? Not by one avenue only can we arrive at so tremendous a secret. Symmachus (c.345–c.402)[1]

CHAPTER 1

Science, religion and myth: making sense of the world

The universe, sense-experience and reality

For it is owing to their wonder that men both now begin and at first began to philosophize; they wondered originally at the obvious difficulties, then advanced little by little and stated difficulties about great matters, for example, about the phenomena of the moon and those of the sun, and about the stars and about the genesis of the universe. Aristotle[2]

Imagine for a moment that you and a small group of friends were dropped off in some remote area of the country with all your memories and accumulated knowledge erased. Overnight your world would be transformed from one of global information to one of local experiences. Each day would be a survival adventure with every sensory encounter exposing another deep mystery wanting explanation. Like our early ancestors, you would wonder about day and night, the changing phases of the moon, the positions of the shimmering stars, the daily and seasonal movements of animals, the seasons and the mystery of life and death. Superimposed on these regular patterns you may experience a thunderstorm, a tsunami, a torrential flood, a bush fire, an earthquake, a solar eclipse, a sudden injury, sickness or premature death. How might you and your group explain these events, and in what forms might those stories appear?

Our journey begins further down a path of cultural advancement, around 3500 BC. The place is the ancient Near East and the people are the Sumerians and Egyptians. As in our mind game, we shall assume that all the events in space and time were once deep mysteries to these people. We shall further assume that the five basic senses have remained the same over time; for example, a reed growing along the Euphrates or Nile Rivers five thousand years ago would have possessed sensible qualities similar to those of a reed today. The major differences between now and then are how we imagine and reflect upon a reed. The ancient Sumerians or Egyptians believed that as soon as a reed was fashioned into a basket or musical instrument, or used as a writing tool, it appropriated magical powers of divine origin. This mythopoeic way of thinking dominated human thought for thousands of years until the Greek philosophers used new methods of reasoning and logic to seek alternative explanations involving physical objects and their relations. Mythopoeic belief still exists today in many of the hunter–gatherer cultures of Australasia, Africa, the Americas, the Arctic and the Pacific Rim.

Over the millennia, not only has our thinking about world events changed, but so also has the stratum of our perceptions (apprehension of an idea of sense). For example, in the sixteenth century the telescope extended the human senses far beyond their "normal" physiological limits, as did the microscope in the seventeenth century, which unveiled countless new worlds within worlds never before experienced by human beings. In recent years, with the aid of science and technology, our perceptions have extended from the smallest of subatomic particles that exist for only fractions of a second to the largest of distant galaxies that are billions of years old.

What we perceive as real, therefore, is something actual or experienced as part of developed *knowledge* of objects of sense and not merely an idea.[3] Experience links us to the wider world and the society in which we live; it defines who we are as individuals through community, ownership, self and identity. Thus we are not impartial spectators, but active participants who seek meaning in the things we experience around us. As societies change, human thought patterns change and so do our perceived realities. The most we can know singly or collectively is the sum of our reflections and perceptions cultivated through art, crafts, music, mythology, religion, literature, science, technology, medicine and history. How the external world is experienced by the common chimpanzee, family pet or bird is another question altogether.

Science, religion and myth as "truth-seeking" systems

Wisdom is the daughter of experience, truth is only the daughter of time.

Leonardo Da Vinci[4]

Like aspects of reality, truth is an extremely elusive concept. Truth can be a verifiable fact such as the earth being roughly spherical, or it can be a feeling such as loving someone, or it can be the belief (or disbelief) in God. Truth can also be a moral judgement that is beyond the reach of verifiability or logical proofs. The moral judgement that murder is a hanging offence is held as a "truth" by some people, but that "truth" may or may not be part of contemporary civil law and ethical standards. In broad terms, truth is the product of knowledge manifest in statements, arguments, practices and beliefs considered to be true. The difficulty is that what you consider true, another may consider wrong or downright offensive. Disagreement or controversy, however, does not mean that the truth is out of human reach, only that there is a lack of consensus about what is considered true.

Since time immemorial human beings have perceived the sun rising in the east, moving across the sky during the day and setting in the west at night. It was not until many thousands of years later that the truth emerged: day and night were produced by the earth rotating about its axis every 24 hours, and the seasons by the earth revolving around the sun once a year. Similarly, for thousands of years heaven was believed to be above the earth and the underworld (or hell) below it. On a flat earth, the concepts "up" and "down" were relatively straightforward. However, when the earth was found to be spherical these directions became more problematic. "Up" for people living in the northern hemisphere would be "down" for people living on the opposite side of the globe. Belief in a flat earth by the Sumerians, Babylonians, Egyptians and most ancient Greeks – and perpetuated by members of the Flat Earth Society – is now generally considered to be wrong. Reasons for groups such as the Flat Earth Society deviating from the norm relate to an unwillingness to let go of tradition and a refusal to accept new knowledge from science and technology. The moon landing on 20 July 1969 and spectacular pictures of Earth sent back by Apollo 11 astronauts were believed by some to have been a complete fraud sanctioned by the US government.

Whatever the belief, its truth evokes a sense of rightness in a person, cultural group, state or nation. Over the millennia, a rich diversity of worldviews has arisen in part from a different mix of mythopoeic, religious and scientific truths, and each system still profoundly influences Western thinking today.

Myth: early mode of explanation

[Myth] is not a mere mass of unorganized and confused ideas; it depends upon a definite mode of perception. If myth did not *perceive* the world in a different way it could not judge or interpret it in its specific manner. We must go back to this deeper stratum of perception in order to understand the character of mythical thought.

Ernst Cassirer[5]

Myths: from stories to a way of life

Most of us associate myths with stories,[6] fun, fantasy and fabrications. Western children believe in the myths of Santa Claus, the Easter Bunny, the Tooth Fairy and Little Red Riding Hood. These stories are larger than life in our early years. They only become less significant as we grow older and learn that the world is not make-believe and whimsical but highly ordered and intelligible. As we age, realities change and so do our myths. Myths are also associated with our identity. Some urban myths include America's Wild West, Ground-Hog Day and Halloween, and Australia's Waltzing Matilda and Man from Snowy River, and the list goes on. Each country has its own stories that assist in providing national identity: America, "the land of the free" and "land of opportunity"; Australia, the land of sun-bronzed Aussies, Gallipoli and "mate-ship". Each myth may have some seed of truth but has become stylized over the years to take on "larger than life" status.[7]

Other forms of myth help appropriate and personalize history. As stories of major events such as a flood, fire, drought, sickness or war are passed down from one generation to the next they can enlarge out of proportion and no longer represent objective accounts of history. Historical myths can also be used to incite despotism and hatred against others. A chilling example in the twentieth century was Adolf Hitler's use of the Aryan myths of superiority to inspire the German peoples to sacrifice themselves for the Fatherland. Unfortunately, the myth lives on today in the white supremacy movement and other splinter groups. There are many other examples of myths used by individuals and groups that violate human rights. Indeed, myths are so intricately woven into the fabric of modern society that it is often difficult to recognize them as such. Nevertheless, despite this difficulty, modern myths are all used in different ways to construct order and meaning in our lives.

Our journey through time will reveal other functions of myths. In ancient times, they provided our ancestors with a way to explain complex events and relations going on around them. Thus from a modern perspective ancient myths should not be trivialized but should be explored and understood within their cultural contexts.[8] The study of ancient myths is an enormous subject because of the diverse roles they play in society, roles that range from Bronislaw Malinowski's "social charter", Ernst Cassirer's "organ of revelation", Clive Staples Lewis's "fable and fact" and Claude Lévi-Strauss's "mediator between culture and nature" through to Sigmund Freud's "repressed libido".[9] Myth expert Joseph Campbell (1904–1987) proposed four main functions of myth:[10]

- **Metaphysical**: Myths dealing with the wonders of the ever-changing world. In early cultures, they provided a way of explaining a flood, a thunderstorm, life and death, and so on.
- **Social**: Myths helping to give meaning to an established social order in a world of unpredictable outcomes.
- **Cosmogonical and cosmological**: Myths providing a symbolic image of the creation, structure and maintenance of the universe and an explanation of its workings
- **Harmonizing "pedagogical"**: Myths about the human condition and how best to harmonize one's life in the face of personal loss and suffering.

Myths possess authority by presenting themselves

Myth was an intellectual tool used by the ancients to order their everyday experience, including their place in the world. Symbolic linkages helped explain "the way of animal powers", "the way of the seeded earth", "the way of celestial lights" and the "way of man".[11] Every myth possessed authority not by proving itself but by presenting itself as a symbolic narrative, usually involving the deeds of different animals, gods, superhuman beings and heroes. Myths were recounted over and over again, often in dramatic form, from one generation to the next. Over time, variations arose from place to place on the explanation of a thunderstorm, a flood, the creation of the universe, a disease, famine or unexpected death.[12] While the subject matter of myths remained the same over many millennia, the early Greek philosophers, with their new ways of thinking, questioned myth's authority and explanatory power (see Ch. 4). Consequently, in the West many myths slipped down the intellectual scale to become fanciful outdoor allegorical plays and orations.

Animism and anthropomorphism

Since our early ancestors did not write, today's anthropologists have a difficult task in trying to reconstruct the ancient mindset. Around the campfire, the ancients probably told stories of the day's hunt, and other survival experiences, which passed down through the generations. Paleolithic peoples probably saw the world as an extension of themselves in the form of more powerful animal or human spirits. As knowledge grew, traditions and "binding" relations between humans and supernatural beings[13] were established. The spirits could be praised in the good times and appeased during the bad, not unlike the stories of the hunter–gatherer cultures in parts of the world today.[14] Their "book of knowledge" grew from the traditions of their forefathers supplemented with life experiences.

Over time, as human beings shifted from hunter–gatherer communities to a more settled agricultural existence, anthropologists believe the main story themes changed from being animistic to being more anthropomorphic.[15] In the first river-valley civilizations (Chs 2 and 3), and later in Homeric Greece (Ch. 4), the gods became invisible extensions of human beings but differed by possessing immortality and superhuman powers.

Mythopoeic symbolism as a mode to thinking

Eminent Mesopotamian scholar Henri Frankfort (1897–1954) provides a good example of mythopeic symbolism as a mode of thinking:

> [Modern human beings] would explain, for instance, that certain atmospheric changes broke a drought and brought about rain. The Babylonians observed the same facts but experienced them as the intervention of the gigantic bird Imdugud which came to their rescue. It covered the sky with the black storm clouds of its wings and devoured the Bull of Heaven, whose hot breath had scorched the crops.[16]

Contrast this account with the more objective, physical explanation of the Greek Anaximenes, who lived in Miletus around the middle of the first millennium BC (Ch. 4). Anaximenes claimed that air was the atmosphere in its most evenly distributed state, fire was air's most rarefied state, water was its more condensed state, and earth and rock its most condensed state. Anaximenes wrote:

> The form of air is as follows: when it is most uniform it is invisible to sight [atmospheric air]; but it is made manifest by cold and heat and moisture and motion. [Air] moves continually; for it would not change as much as it does if it were not in motion. As [air] thickens or rarefies it appears as different. For when [air] spreads out into rarer form it becomes fire; winds on the other hand are air as it thickens; air cloud is produced by compression; and water still by more compression; when further thickened it becomes earth and in its thickest form stones.[17]

A more modern scientific explanation of atmospheric changes did not appear until the late-eighteenth and nineteenth centuries. Today, we know that air comprises mostly nitrogen, oxygen, carbon dioxide and water vapour. As an air mass rises from the earth's surface, the lower atmospheric pressure causes it to expand and subsequently cool. If the water vapour cools below a critical temperature, or dew point, the moisture in the air mass condenses into droplets on microscopic atmospheric particles, giving rise to clouds. And when the combination of temperature, humidity and droplet size is just right, rain falls. It has been estimated that about $1400 \, km^3$ of water per day is evaporated from land and ocean surfaces, and returns to the earth as rain.

Despite improvements in our understanding of world phenomena such as cloud formation, rain, thunder and lightning, it is important to stress that the older highly mythologized explanations of the Sumerians, Babylonians, Egyptians and later Homeric societies (and other ancients) provided perfectly "reasonable" ways of ordering experience given the intellectual framework and boundaries from which they built their knowledge. The Near-Eastern and Homeric reality was a world full of gods and divine manifestations, not a world of physical objects, as we believe today.

Religion: cosmic and social order in a moral framework

[Religion] is the positive human response to experience in thought (myth and theology) and action (cult and worship) .   T. Jacobsen[18]

In ancient times, religious practices appear to have grown out of a class of myths that primarily dealt with the "binding" linkages between human beings, spirits and their gods.[19] These mythopoeic linkages told of a creation, maintenance of world order, life and death, happiness and future success. Use of myths in the different religions seems to have provided a wider authority and wholeness in worldview at a time in history when all knowledge was bounded by divine causation.[20]

Genesis, for example, presents a world created by the Hebrew God in six days: a three-layer cake with heaven on top, flat motionless earth in the middle and the dark underworld at the bottom. This description was not unique to the Hebrews but had precedents dating back at least to 3000 BC. The Hebrew version was compiled around 800–900 BC and gave the Hebrew writers a more complete picture with deeper explanatory significance of historical events.[21] Importantly, the association of myth with religion does not mean a worldview is right or wrong, but only that the mythical content requires identification, clarification and interpretation. Truth does not emerge full-blown on the literal surface, but is contained deep within the layers of the ancient mind's literary genre.[22] The story of Adam and Eve, the creation of Adam from clay, the creation of Eve from Adam's rib, and the flood that wiped out humankind are not considered true today in the literal sense but were the ancient Hebrew's attempt to convey meaning about deep mysteries. We shall see the same in ancient Sumer and Egypt in Chapters 2 and 3. The stories reflect an honest, highly imaginative, culturally conditioned consciousness involving mystery, myth and religiosity.

Attempts to define religion

Most early civilizations had no words for religion as we have today. Religion's etymology[23] comes from the Latin *religio*, meaning "a mutual binding obligation" or "oath" and emphasizes a relationship between human beings and their god(s).[24] Greater interest in the meaning of religion (and myth) did not occur until the nineteenth century, when history and anthropology became disciplines in their own right. Anthropologist Edward B. Tylor (1832–1917) defined religion as "the belief in spiritual beings".[25] James Frazer (1854–1941) believed religion was "a propitiation or conciliation of powers superior to man which are believed to direct and control the course of nature and of human life".[26] Myth expert Joseph Campbell argued that religion was a way of "bringing inner experience into the outer life of the people themselves".[27] And philosopher and mathematician Alfred North Whitehead (1861–1947) wrote that religion was "what an individual does with his own solitariness".[28]

In the early twentieth century, French sociologist Émile Durkheim (1858–1917) added a social dimension by defining religion as "a system of beliefs and rituals with reference to the sacred which binds people together into social groups".[29] The purpose of a "binding" ritual, he argued, was to reaffirm an individual's social identity, shared values and way of life among a group, community or nation. Durkheim's emphasis on religion's social function was a turning point. We shall see that over the past 5000 years, the social "binding" of human beings to gods in the West has changed dramatically from a nationalistic duty within a "corporate" structure to a more voluntary one based on choice. Today, Western beliefs in god(s) range from radical fundamentalism to atheism.[30]

Religion as a vital and pervasive feature of human life

> Religion, then, can be defined as a system of beliefs and practices by means of which a group of people struggles with the ultimate problems of human life. It expresses their refusal to capitulate life to death. To give up in the face of frustration, to allow hostility to tear apart their human aspirations.
> J. M. Yinger[31]

A truly remarkable fact is that no society has been discovered without some form of religiosity, meaning a belief in spirits, supernatural powers or gods.[32] Human burial sites in the Middle East as early as 90 000 to 120 000 years ago,[33] and in Europe around 40 000 years ago, imply heightened ritual and death awareness. The ritual interment of the dead may[34] have been part of a wider symbolic enactment of the separation of life and death.[35] The discovery of small carved figurines of a Mother Goddess of fertility[36] (birth and regeneration) from Minoan Crete to China, and the appearance of spectacular cave art[37] in parts of Europe, the Americas and Australasia adds to the hypothesis of a new "cultural" awareness and heightened religiosity.[38]

Baring and Cashford have further suggested that the new awareness followed two main myth themes:[39] a wider search for meaning beyond everyday experience such as linking life and death to a higher power, the Mother Goddess; and the symbolic representation of local hunting experiences in cave art that could be talked about, reflected upon and worshipped. In part, Baring and Cashford base their claims on the Mother Goddess, heavenly bodies, the sun, moon or the stars not widely depicted in Paleolithic cave art; and animals not symbolized as carved figurines.[40] Although controversial, the idea does appear to have support in the Bradshaw rock paintings scattered over about 50 000 km^2 of the rugged Kimberley region of northern Western Australia. The Bradshaw rock art represents animals and hunting scenes dated to around 20 000 years ago although they may extend as far back as 60 000 years.

Given the solitude of human beings living in small groups, it is not hard to imagine the changes that took place when the Paleolithic lifestyle slowly transformed from pack hunting to living in small temporary villages, then to larger agricultural settlements and finally grand civilizations. Religiosity must have also changed, presumably, from simple myth-based belief and ritual systems involving shaman-like individuals[41]

7

to a more complex hierarchical system of people management with a hierarchy of gods.[42] Archaeologist Colin Renfrew writes on this possibility: "This notion of a hierarchy of divinities is one which comes more easily to a society which is itself hierarchically structured, for instance to a state society. It is difficult to imagine such a feature in an egalitarian society organised at the band level."[43] Chapters 2 and 3 will show this close binding between human activities on earth and divine activities in heaven. With the invention of writing, codified rules gradually replaced memory in all aspects of urban life, including myth-based rituals and religious practices.

Another dramatic turning point in religious thinking occurred in the Middle East, India and China between 800 BC and 500 BC. This extraordinary fertile period gave rise to today's major world religions. In Israel, the Hebrew prophets taught a mono-theistic faith from which Judaism, Christianity and Islam developed. In India, the teachings of Buddha (c.563–483 BC) gave rise to Buddhism,[44] and in China, the teachings of Confucius (c.551–c.479 BC) founded an ethical system that grew into Confucianism.[45] At around the same time, another extraordinary revolution had began in Ionian Greece among the ancient Presocratic philosophers (600–400 BC). This period of heightened abstraction is called the "Axial Age" and the major worldviews that exist today were shaped at that time.[46]

Multi-dimensional features of religion
Religion is a multi-dimensional activity comprising at least six major components: spiritual, experiential, mythical, social, ritual and doctrinal. Each will be discussed briefly below to help put our story in its proper context.

1. The spiritual dimension and ultimate reality
All religions have an ultimate reality. It may be an eternal source, truth or principle that governs the universe, an impersonal transcendent God who created everything or a more personal God who must be kept separate from his creations.[47] Aspects of Hindu Vedanta, Buddhist Mahayana and Taoism have an impersonal ultimate reality, which is the creator principle and eternal truth of the universe.[48] The Tao, for example, is the eternal and unchanging source in which originate and return all the manifestations of the universe. All the gods, human beings, plants, animals and insects, everything in the universe, including the universe itself, came from the Tao.[49] Confucianism, albeit a more secular doctrine of worldly social-mindedness, has as its ultimate reality the moral law that is omnipresent, hidden from the senses and eternal.[50]

The ultimate reality in the monotheistic traditions of Christianity, Judaism and Islam is a personal God. The God of the Old Testament is different from any god of the Hindu pantheon, ranging from the oldest supreme Varuna to Brahman of the Upanishads. The concept of divinity is also different because the God of the Jews, Christians and Muslims created the world only once, not many times, as described in the ancient Hindu literature. However, it would be wrong to think that the God of the Old Testament is similar for Jews, Christians and Muslims, as differences of interpretation have occurred over the centuries.

The Christian God, for example, involves the notion of Christ as *logos*, who affects the entire meaning of the creation and world order. Similarly, the Muslim God, Allah, is placed into the Islamic context with special meanings and acts of symbolism, but without the Christian Trinity.[51] Notwithstanding many similarities among the world religions, we have to recognize that each operates within its own set of boundaries and historical truths.

2. The experiential dimension

The experiential dimension is the foundation of the origin and development of all religious traditions. It may involve an enlightened interaction with the super-sensory world or with some divine manifestation in the sensory world. The experience and its truth may be realized through revelation, prophecy, doctrine, dreams, trances, songs, orations, oracles or waking visions.

Buddhism grew from Buddha's enlightenment in the sixth century BC as he sat in meditation beneath the Bo-Tree. Judaism developed from the Mosaic doctrine and the inaugural visions of the prophets (c.550 BC). Christianity developed from a small breakaway Jewish sect who believed that Jesus by his resurrection had brought about the beginnings of final salvation.[52] The message spread to the Gentile world via St Paul after he had a conversation with the resurrected Christ on the road to Damascus. And Islam was finalized after a series of revelations from the Arabian Prophet Muhammad (AD c.570) and God's angel, Gabriel. As a general conclusion most, if not all, religions and their developed philosophies are based on the experience of some "enlightened" person or persons. The problem for historians is sorting out the relationship between the religious experience, its mythical content and the facts of history.

3. The mythical dimension

Every religion contains some form of myth. Myths are recorded in the ancient literature as if they actually occurred in history. The Passover, for example, re-enacts the exodus of the children of Israel from bondage in Egypt back to the Promised Land. The historical event may be true, partly true or fabricated, but nonetheless is appropriated through myth, ritual and service. The story provides a framework for understanding the individual and personal journey through life. Catholic baptism is another example. Although Jesus appears not to have taught baptism, Paul taught that it symbolized a believer's union with Christ in his death, burial and resurrection. The believer finds solace and validation of personal rites of passages in the historical and cultural myths of the community in which he or she lives.

4. The social dimension

The social dimension of religion helps to support and validate an individual's place within a particular group sharing a common belief system. Religion imposes order on an ever-changing, often perilous, world and helps to provide deeper meaning to the human condition in the grander scheme of things. Davis and Moore give a penetrating account of the social function of religion:

> The reason why religion is necessary is apparently to be found in the fact that human society achieves its unity primarily through the possession by its members of certain ultimate values and ends in common. Although these values and ends are subjective, they influence behaviour, and their integration enables this society to operate as a system ...

In an extremely advanced society built on scientific technology, the priesthood tends to lose status, because sacred tradition and supernaturalism drop into the background ... [but no] society has become so completely secularized as to liquidate entirely the belief in transcendental ends and supernatural entities. Even in a secularized society some system must exist for the integration of ultimate values, for their ritualistic expression, and for the emotional adjustments required by disappointment, death and disaster.[53]

5. The ritual and service dimension

Ritual and prescribed service are essential features of religion. They involve a myriad of devotional activities including worship (prayer), ritual, sacrifices and offerings.[54] In the earliest civilizations services were performed at selected communal sites, such as on a mound, in a cave or on a mountaintop. Ancient Mesopotamians built ziggurats,[55] Egypt had the pyramids[56] and China had a mythical peak in the Thai Shan cult.[57] Ancient India had its golden mansion of the god Varuna at the sky's zenith. Homeric Greece had Mount Olympus near Athens and Israel had Mount Sinai, where God revealed the Covenant to Moses.[58] In the Old Testament, the prophet Isaiah wrote of a time when "the mountain of the house of the Lord shall be established as the highest of mountains".[59] In Muslim history, the Arabian prophet Mohammed had a mountain cave for devotional purposes where he heard a voice saying to him: "Mohammed, you are God's messenger."

A recurring theme in ancient times is a preoccupation with "high places" providing privileged access to heaven and the divine. In early Mesopotamia, one of the highest rooms in the towering ziggurats was a dark bedchamber frequented by the priestess, who became the bride of the gods.[60] This "mythical" marriage each year renewed the fertility of the soil and the strength of the king's arms.[61] Such rituals illustrate the strong ties between early human beings and their gods upon which life and death depended.

6. The doctrinal dimension

Doctrine underpins the narratives of all world religions. The Hindus have their sacred scriptures of Vedic (c.1000 BC), writings of Upanishads (800–400 BC) and philosophy of Buddha (c.500 BC). The Chinese have the Analects of Confucius, teachings of Lao Tse (founder of Taoism) and variations of Buddhism. Similarly, Judaism, Christianity and Islam have their books of religion, with their own individual style, inner dynamic and historical meaning.

The narrative and doctrinal dimensions contain many stories and moral laws that bind a people to their gods. In Judaism it is not only the Ten Commandments, but also over 600 rules imposed on the Jewish community by God. The books of Christianity and Islam are also heavily codified revelations with answers to profound existential questions. The central ethic for Christian faith is love founded in the life, death and resurrection of Jesus Christ.

However, within any doctrine there is not always agreement on the nature of a religious truth. In Chapter 6, we discuss the Christian doctrine of Trinity and the heated debates that ensued among religious scholars. History is full of examples where consensus could not be reached and religious sects have formed and split off from the mainstream. According to the *World Christian Encyclopedia*, there are around 35 000 denominations of Christianity, each differing on some fundamental interpretation of central dogma or past events.[62] The "single truth" of a sacred text may have many interpretations.

Religion defined

Taking account of its multi-dimensional structure, religion may be defined as a social response to a world of predictable and unpredictable outcomes involving an "enlightened" spiritual leader, human beings and their god(s). Religion is a way of ensuring a meaningful, happy and purposeful life and a possible means to the afterlife. It provides consolation for personal and community tragedy, often through prayer, divine revelation, stories, imagery and moral teachings. All major religions have been culturally conditioned. Most of us are born into at least one system of codified beliefs and service, which we continually grapple with, modify or reject throughout our lives as part of an ongoing and personal search for deeper meaning and purpose.

World religions today

> The belief in God has often been advanced as not only the greatest, but the most complete of all the distinctions between man and lower animals ... I am aware that the assumed instinctive belief in God has been used by many persons as an argument for His existence ... The idea of a universal and beneficent Creator does not seem to arise in the mind of man, until he has been elevated by long-continued culture.
>
> Charles Darwin[63]

Today about 35 per cent of the world's population is Christian, 22 per cent is Muslim, 15 per cent is Hindu, 6 per cent is Buddhist, 1 per cent is Confucian, 0.3 per cent is Jewish, 0.1 per cent is Baha'i and a fraction of a per cent of the world's population holds primal religions.[64] Older religions include those defunct in early Mesopotamia, Egypt and Greece, and those still existing in Australasia, Africa, the Americas, the Arctic and the Pacific Rim. With the exception of Judaism, the popularity of the world religions has steadily increased over the past 20 years. About 20 per cent of the world population is non-religious (agnostic, secular humanist and atheist) (Fig. 1.1).

Science: seeking relationships among physical objects

> Nam et ipsa scientia potestas est
> [Knowledge itself is power]
>
> Francis Bacon[65]

The universe is ordered and explainable

Natural science provides a very different way of making sense of the world. Natural science began in ancient Greece with the Presocratic philosophers of the sixth century BC. As will be discussed in Chapter 4, this group single-handedly invented a physical cosmos and a new system of reasoning, logic and validity to explain the wondrous workings of the world. Their fundamental tenet was that the physical universe was ordered and explainable: there was no longer any need for hundreds of gods to carry out specific duties or have complex interactions with human beings. After many stops and starts over the next

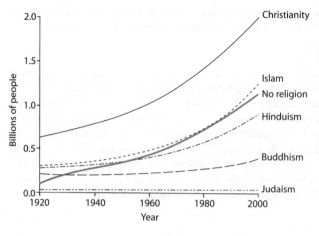

Figure 1.1 Comparative growth of world religions (1920–2000). The data show a steep rise in the popularity of the major world faiths, with the exception of Judaism. The rise reflects both population expansion and increased recruitment. Non-belief has increased steeply over the past 40 years. (Adapted version of Ch. 19, Figure 1, by John Taylor in McManners (1990:634), by permission of Oxford University Press.)

two millennia, natural science grew in the seventeenth century to become the most powerful problem-solving and knowledge-seeking system ever invented.

The word "science" comes from Latin *scientia* (to learn or to know) and entered the English language in the Middle Ages around 1340 as a French import equated with learning and knowledge.[66] The word "scientist" is more recent and was coined in 1833 by English scientist and philosopher William Whewell (1794–1866) to describe a person who was "a cultivator of science", by making an analogy with the word "artist".[67] Modern natural science can be defined as the sociohistoric process of understanding the physical universe and our place in it.[68] The system is built on scientific facts interwoven into conceptual schemes as they relate to perceptible, verifiable (or falsifiable) sense-experience. It is self-correcting and, for the most part, self-perpetuating, with no absolutes; science begins with a question and ends with a question.[69]

Growth of Western science

> [Individuals who break through by inventing a new paradigm are] almost always …
> either very young or very new to the field whose paradigm they change … These are
> the [people] who, being little committed by prior practice to the traditional rules of
> normal science, are particularly likely to see that those rules no longer define a
> playable game and to conceive another set that can replace them.   T. S. Kuhn[70]

For most of its history, Western science has passed through six main stages. The first stage was a pre-scientific stage (3500–650 BC), when knowledge was generally sought for some practical good of a social collective. It was followed by an originative stage (in Greece, 650–30 BC), when Greek philosophers sought to understand the workings of the world largely for advancing knowledge itself using new methods of interrogation. The second stage was at odds with the older Near Eastern and contemporary Homeric religions with their hundreds of gods, although the concept of the divine was not dismissed altogether (Ch. 4). At the third stage, a "desenile" stage (AD 300–1200), natural philosophy was avoided in the West because it distracted the mind from contemplation of God and scriptural writings. This was typical of the early Roman and Western Latin Christendom periods until the Islamic "revival" of philosophy in the ninth century.

The fourth stage was a "revival" stage (1200–1450) during the "great age of literary translation" and "institutionalization of reason" in the universities. Studying nature was endorsed by a number of highly influential theologian-philosophers as a genuine road to understanding God's creation. The fifth stage was a more techno-mathematical "experimental" stage (1450–1850) involving free-thinkers of the likes of Copernicus, Kepler, Galileo, Newton and many others who viewed the workings of the world more mechanistically. The sixth stage of Western science was a "maturation" phase (1850–), when it increasingly combined with technology to become an enormous social, intellectual and economic benefit. The homes we live in, the water we drink, the clothes we wear, the medicines with which we heal the sick and prolong life, transport, communications, space exploration, computers and the Internet are all products and refinements of modern science and technology.[71] The informational revolution of the twenty-first century promises to accelerate discovery in all areas; it will solve many deep mysteries about ourselves and generate many more that we haven't yet contemplated. Indeed, the twenty-first century appears to be the beginning of a new seventh "translational" stage of science, where the spectacular diversity of life is increasingly recognized to involve surprisingly fewer changes to a primitive genetic master plan than previously thought. Understanding the unifying principles underpinning life's grand design will, I believe, translate into new approaches to repair damaged or diseased organs including nerves, further delay the ageing process, lead to the first "cookbook" creation of life from raw materials, and continue to unveil the deep mysteries of life, the universe and its composition (see Chs 9, 10 and 11).

Five major features of modern science

- **Science's function is to help understand the physical universe and our place in it**. It does so by extending, ordering and bringing sensory experience into a logical system of thought and assembly.[72] The facts of science (observations and measurements) are not only the raw materials of scientific enquiry, but the proof of its results.
- **Science seeks knowledge by objectifying natural phenomena from the smallest of particles to the largest of distant galaxies**. Science breaks the event or entity of interest into pieces and describes it operationally by linking concepts and formulating conceptual schemes and natural laws. The conceptual schemes and laws are verified (or falsified) by observation, experiment and measurement. Scientific reductionism does not do away with the thing being explained as asserted by some critics of science.
- **Science is a never-ending cycle of questions and answers with no absolutes**. Authority in science is self-corrective because the scientific process generates many more new questions than answers. Conceptual schemes and laws are only as valid as the assumptions and methods used to derive them. Over time the truths may be subtly modified or completely abandoned. One of the most misunderstood features of science is that it does not answer "first causes", such as

13

the "cause" of gravity or questions about God's existence. However, there is no limit to science's ability to solve problems within its reach.

- **There is no "one" method of science**. Science is a process that is built on a connected series of logical and practical operations involving an idea, a test or experiment and some kind of measurement. The scientific process is characterized by rules of logic and methods of experiment and measurement.

- **Basic or curiosity-driven science is full of surprises**. Scientific discovery and innovation underwrite human quality of life in profound ways. Many people and politicians fail to realize that most scientific, medical and technological discoveries are mere "accidents" of the process, with their benefits not realized until many years or decades later. Basic or curiosity-driven science[73] is a proven economic, practical and social success that has paid for itself over and over again. X-rays, the transistor, clinical imaging modalities, penicillin, computers, lasers, optical fibres, nanotechnology, DNA fingerprinting and bionic implants are just a few examples of the "accidental" spin-offs of basic research. The development of the World Wide Web in 1990 was yet another "surprise" in a long chain of invention involving basic science. CERN computer scientist Tim Berners-Lee wanted to improve communications between physicists in universities and research institutions around the world. Today the Web drives the largest informational revolution ever in history; and it would not have been possible without the invention of the transistor in 1948 and basic research into the quantum mechanical properties of crystalline solids decades earlier. Supporting basic research is our lifeline to the future because the future is invented, not predicted. There is a wonderful story from the early nineteenth century, when a cynical member of the British government asked Faraday about the relevance of his ongoing work converting electrical energy to a force. Faraday's terse but farsighted reply was: "One day, Sir, you may tax it."

The language of science

Concepts

Concepts are abstract terms used every day to generalize categories or groups of particular objects and their parts, events or operations. According to philosopher Rudolf Carnap (1891–1970), the concepts of modern science fall into three broad groups: classificatory, comparative and quantitative.[74]

Classificatory concepts place an object in a given class. For example, cloud, lightning, rain, animal, plant, gene, head, hot, cold, dry, wet and species are all classificatory concepts. The second type of concept, the comparative concept, differs from a classificatory concept by being more descriptive, and gives more information about the object studied. Instead of classifying an object as hot or cold, dry or wet, comparative concepts would describe objects as hotter or colder, drier or wetter. Comparative concepts play an important role in science because they are more effective in describing sense-experience.

The third kind of concept is the quantitative concept. It is an outgrowth of the classificatory and comparative concept, and relies on some kind of measurement of quantity. The following example shows the progression of ideas from a classificatory to a quantitative concept:

| classificatory | → | comparative | → | quantitative concepts |
| e.g. hot, cold | → | hotter, colder | → | temperature and heat |

Importantly, quantitative concepts are usually defined in terms of a set of operations that lead to their measurement.[75] Temperature, for example, did not have a precise meaning until Gabriel Fahrenheit (1686–1736) and Anders Celsius (1701–1744) introduced a defined scale on a thermometer. Likewise, heat did not have a precise meaning until James Prescott Joule (1818–1889) accurately measured the unit quantity of heat, or calorie, in a calorimeter. One calorie is defined as the heat required to raise the temperature of 1 gram of water 1 °C, from 14.5 °C to 15.5 °C. However, quantification through standardization did not begin with science, but with technology dating back to the Sumerians and Egyptians (see Chs 2 and 3).

Conceptual schemes

The great value of a concept is how it relates to other concepts. Concepts can be likened to letters of the alphabet and conceptual schemes help narrate the scientific stories. An example of a conceptual scheme is Newton's law of gravitation. The law relates the quantitative concepts of force, mass and distance. It is expressed mathematically:

$$F = G\frac{m_1 m_2}{d^2}$$

where F is the mutual force of gravitational attraction in newtons (N), m_1 and m_2 are the masses of two bodies in kilograms (kg) separated by distance d in metres (m). The constant G is the gravitational constant, equal to 6.672×10^{-11} N m^2 kg^{-2}.

Newton's law, expressed in words, states that any two bodies attract each other with a gravitational force directly proportional to the product of their masses and inversely proportional to the square of the distance between them at their centres. If the Earth had half its present mass, the gravitational force between the Earth and the moon would be half because, all else being equal, force is proportional to mass. Similarly, if the Earth's mass remained the same but the distance between the Earth and the moon doubled, the gravitational force would become a quarter of today's value. What Newton further demonstrated was that gravity is not just a property of the solar system but a universal property of matter. The law of gravitation helps explain how the universe is stuck together, and why there is a high tide when there is a full moon. It describes the trajectory of the planets around the sun and how satellites orbit around the Earth.

Another different type of conceptual scheme is one formulated against large sets of independent criteria. The best example is Darwin's theory of natural selection and human descent. Natural selection is not something we can readily see or measure directly, but is inferred from different kinds of observations and measurements.[76] Darwin knew only too well that he could not "directly" observe the origin of a new species, much less evolutionary trends.[77] He went about his search not by formulating and testing a hypothesis through some repeatable experiment and measurement or mathematical model, but by comparing large sets of independent geological, embryological, morphological and anatomical data.[78] He reasoned that if all the sources pointed to the same result (and disproved all others), his theory should be received.[79] Darwin wrote to his botanist friend Joseph Hooker in 1861: "The doctrine must sink or swim according as it groups and explains phenomena. It really is curious how few judge this way, which is clearly the right way."[80] Darwin's approach is similar to how a modern historian judges and weaves past events into history or how a Greek philosophy scholar pieces together early Greek thought from the extant fragments and commentaries from ancient texts.

Power of prediction

The clarity, rigidity and elegance of a conceptual scheme or theory is often expressed in a mathematical formula (e.g. Newton's law of gravitation) or a non-mathematical statement (e.g. Darwin's theory of natural selection and human descent).[81] In general, a scientific theory is valuable in three ways: first, in its universality to describe and explain what has been carefully observed; secondly, in its ability to endure criticism as new knowledge is found; and thirdly, in its ability to predict what has not been observed, but is still within the bounds of known physical laws. Prediction is an extremely powerful aspect of scientific enquiry because it extends beyond what is known, or at least beyond what is supported by scientific facts. Here are four brief examples of how scientists have used a theory for prediction.

- **The bending of light rays around large gravitating bodies.** Albert Einstein's special theory of relativity, published in 1911,[82] predicted that light rays approaching the sun (or any gravitating body) would be deflected near the surface. He based his theory on the assumption that light has energy, and energy has mass.[83] On 29 May 1919, English astronomer Arthur S. Eddington (1882–1944), while on an astronomical expedition to the island Principe in equatorial Africa to observe a 6–8-minute total solar eclipse, confirmed Einstein's prediction. He calculated that the deflection of light caused by the gravitational field of the sun was on average 1.64 seconds of arc (as opposed to Einstein's calculated 1.75 seconds of arc).[84] The agreement between theory and measurement gave Einstein's principle of mass–energy equivalence, with respect to the speed of light, scientific verifiability.[85]
- **The expansion of the universe.** An equally ingenious prediction from Einstein, but this time from his 1916 theory of general relativity and field equations, was that the universe was not "standing still" but expanding in all directions.[86] This most remarkable mathematical prediction, which incidentally Einstein originally thought preposterous, gained support in 1929 with the observations of astronomers Edwin Hubble (1889–1953) and Milton Humason (1891–1972) (see Ch. 9).
- **The existence of black holes.** Einstein's theory of general relativity also predicted the idea of black holes: regions of space-time that not even light can escape because gravity is so strong.[87] For a long time many physicists were highly sceptical and thought the existence of black holes was pushing relativity theory too far. Today black holes are considered to be real phenomena created out of the collapse of stars. As the star becomes smaller and smaller, the gravitational field at the surface becomes stronger and stronger to a point where nothing escapes, not even light.[88] Black holes are detected by the things they swallow up,

such as neighbouring stars or whole galaxies. More recently, they have been seen to emit faint x-rays and are believed to be located in the centres of galaxies, including our own Milky Way.

- **The theory of cosmic wormholes.** The fourth example of the predictive power of a scientific theory is cosmic wormholes. Cosmic wormholes may provide rapid interstellar transport without exceeding the speed of light. They represent severe distortions in the fabric of space in the universe caused by extremely powerful gravitational fields such as black holes. Some theoretical physicists hypothesize that by moving the mouth of a wormhole and collapsing it, the system could potentially turn into a time machine that would permit human beings to visit the past.[89] While the wormhole theory has no experimental support, its formulation, according to theoretical physicists, still lies within the bounds of existing physical laws.[90] Such "thought experiments" may seem totally contrived and fanciful, but they are extremely powerful in challenging scientists to think beyond the present and forage the path of future discovery. The key point is that while science must operate within the province of human experience it must also be encouraged to extend beyond it.

Another recent example of the predictive power of science comes from the analysis of the six universal physical constants. Astronomer Royal Martin Rees discusses the consequences of making the constants slightly higher or lower.[91] Rees explains that if the constant describing the amount of energy produced in the stars were 10 per cent higher there would be no hydrogen left in space, and if it were 10 per cent lower there would be no heavy elements. If the force of gravity were 10 per cent higher the planets would spiral into the sun, and if it were weaker they would spiral out into space. If any of these cases actually existed, life on earth would have been impossible. Importantly, Rees's examination is not metaphysics but solid science within the realm of current physical theory, and one day may bear fruit with new discoveries.

A self-correction process with no absolutes

That Western science is a dynamic, self-correcting process with no absolutes is one of the most difficult aspects of science to convey to the non-scientific layperson. The statement *with no absolutes* simply means that science's conceptual schemes and laws are valid only in relation to the methods and assumptions used to derive them.[92] In general, a conceptual scheme in science, unlike the observations, is not a perceived action but an inferred one formulated from the experimental data at hand.

For example, although Newton's law of gravitation has gained wide consensus, it is not an "absolute" law. The law was formulated when Newton applied the laws of motion to two spherical bodies placed in an abstract or idealized system that had been isolated from all other influences. One of the fundamental assumptions he made was that gravitational force acted instantaneously across empty space between two bodies, whether they be the Earth and the moon or the Earth and distant planets. By combining the law of gravitation with his fundamental laws of motion, he was able to prove mathematically that the path of a planet orbiting around the sun was an ellipse.

Newton's physical law holds generally true for all celestial bodies in the solar system (and wider universe), but exceptions to the rule do exist. It does not accurately describe orbits of artificial satellites around Earth. For that we must appeal to classical

Newtonian mechanics, which takes into account the deviation of the Earth's non-spherical shape, density and atmospheric drag.[93] Similarly, Newton's law does not accurately describe the precession of the orbit of the planet Mercury around the sun and physicists must incorporate Einstein's relativistic mechanics. Put simply, Newton's law of gravitation represents *a generalization or an over-simplification* of what actually occurs in nature. It is the best Newton could do with the information and methods he had available. Today, Newton's concepts of absolute time, space and mass have all been replaced by Einstein's four-dimensional space-time continuum (see Ch. 9).

The important point is that science can only postulate functional dependencies or relations, not absolutes. A fundamental error made by many non-scientists writing about science is to imply the existence of absolute laws.[94] A "cause" in twentieth- and twenty-first-century science is generally a statistical change in an independent variable, while an "effect" is a statistical change in a dependent variable. Physicist Ernst Mach (1838–1916) clearly understood this difference when he wrote:

> There is no cause nor effect in nature; nature has but an individual existence; nature simply is. Recurrences of like cases in which A is always connected with B, exist but in the abstraction which we perform for the purpose of mentally reproducing the facts. Cause and effect, therefore are things of thought, having an economical office. It cannot be said why they arise.[95]

Nineteenth-century causality and/or determinacy, in the strictest meaning of cause-and-effect, have no place in today's science because science never reaches finality; each problem begins and ends with a question. Thus the very essence of science does not lie in its permanence, but in its development toward greater learning and understanding.

Is mathematics an exception to the rule?

If there are no absolutes in science, what about the rules and laws in mathematics? In one sense, the rules and laws in mathematics are absolute. However, mathematics of its own accord gives no account of reality; it is a symbolic language, a tool of formal logic *par excellence* used by theoretical and experimental scientists to order, explore and predict interrelationships. Alongside the spoken word, art, writing and music, mathematics is one of the purest forms of language abstraction invented by human beings. Mathematics is not concerned with a description of phenomena *per se* but with a specific language of relations among concepts.[96] In other words, mathematics does indeed provide science with "certain" answers,[97] but the discipline of mathematics by itself is not a science.

What is a scientific truth?

If we say that there are no absolutes in science, what, then, is a scientific truth or proof? This question is at the very heart of understanding the scientific process. Today a scientific "truth" is defined as that relation derived by careful observation and some form of verifiable experimentation, usually involving measurement.[98] The "truths" (or relations) are those observational theory-laden statements as part of the "method" that have been scrutinized and agreed upon by the scientific community. As knowledge advances, the "truths" undergo continual refinement; they may be subtly changed or completely abandoned.

Understanding science through its methodology

> Generally, researchers don't shoot directly for a grand goal. Unless they are geniuses (or cranks) they focus on bite-sized problems that seem timely and tractable. That is the methodology that pays off for most of us.
>
> M. Rees[99]

The nature of a scientific truth is best understood through its methodology. For many decades textbooks have often talked about "one" method in science. However, I know of no professional scientist who would subscribe to "one" method. Scientists simply do not carry out their business in this way. Instead, scientists use curiosity, intuition and common sense and a whole arsenal of strategies to interrogate natural phenomena. These operations are broadly summarized in Figure 1.2.

After forming an idea or hypothesis,[100] scientists perform a preliminary test or experiment (usually with institutional infrastructure support). If the hypothesis fails the first test, the initial idea and founding assumptions are re-evaluated. Having preliminary data at hand, a scientist usually seeks external funding to continue the research. The funding process is peer-driven and assesses the novelty of the idea, and the methodology and competency of the scientists. If successful, the idea can be more fully tested using an appropriate sample size and statistical test. When a tentative hypothesis is affirmed by a scientist and later by others, it may be general enough to become a theory.

However, most hypotheses turn out to be wrong, which is why Popper argued for falsification and not verification as the driving force of science.[101] That is, no finite number of positive tests can prove a scientific hypothesis, but one negative case can prove it false. While I understand Popper's idea of falsification driving science[102] on a broad scale, and as a criterion for separating science from pseudoscience, it does not drive science daily. In practice, what drives science is the fun, and excited anticipation that your experiment "will work" and "will lead" to a new discovery or interpretation. Popper's falsification can really do no better (or no worse) at driving science than verification. As Jacob Bronowski (1908–1974) pointed out, both falsification and verification offer evidence for or against a conceptual scheme, and no more.[103]

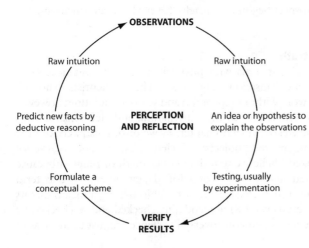

Figure 1.2 Simplified scheme showing the process of scientific discovery. There is no one scientific method, only a number of operations and criteria that must be adhered to before an enquiry can be called scientific.

Science, religion and myth: similarities and differences

It is not to be expected that there should be agreement about the definition of
anything until there is agreement about the thing itself.   J. S. Mill[104]

We have now reached an important stage of our analysis. As a general conclusion, science, religion and myth are different dimensions of the human experience in response to the unknown. All three attempt to demystify the world in different ways: myth and religion use more prescriptive methods with metaphysical or transcendental origins, whereas science is more descriptive, operating exclusively in the physical domain, which may or may not be bounded by the divine. Each system involves an outward expression of thought, language and practice with truth packaged in symbolic or conceptual form. Notwithstanding pathological deranged mind-states, the symbolic representations are not patchwork illusions, but a meaning-seeking and purpose-driven correspondence between the external world, experience and language. If there is no correspondence, each system as we know it would cease to exist.

Myth and religion: prescriptive roads to truth

Mythopoeic and religious truths largely deal with deep personal reflection involving emotional, moral and cosmic qualities. Spirituality appears to be a common denominator that can be expressed in many forms, ranging from a reflective act involving animal and human-like spirits to a deeply binding personal relationship with hundreds of gods or one god exclusively (Fig. 1.3). The truths are usually prescribed by an authority within a social collective and involve opposing passions such as love and hate, fear and hope, life and death, good and evil. The authority may be a spiritually enlightened person such as a priest, prophet, shaman, witch, sorcerer, medicine man, seer, magician or diviner, using revelation, oracular utterances, song, spirit possessions, incarnations, dreams, trances, hypnosis, divinations, magic, visions or prayers. From the study of early cultures, religion appears to have developed from piety of worship with myth as a major mode of explanation through symbolic imagery and linkages. Historically, religion arose within a moral and cosmic framework and provided the believer with a promise and prospect beyond the reach of everyday affairs, including the possibility of afterlife.

Science: descriptive road to truth

Western science is very different; it deals with physical objects without necessarily invoking mythopoeic or divine causation (Fig. 1.3). Those scientists who are highly religious carry on their work without separation and self-contradiction; however, how the world of physical objects relates to the supernatural and vice versa remains problematic. This will become clearer in later chapters as we distinguish between the "objects" of myth and religion and the "objects" of science. The practice of science involves a more "impersonalized" belief system than either myth or religion because its operations can be repeated and verified (or falsified) by others.[105] The term "impersonalized" does not mean that science is free of "subjectivity"; it means that its procedures, experiments and results can be independently checked and re-checked by independent parties. Disagreements and controversy in science are just as lively as in

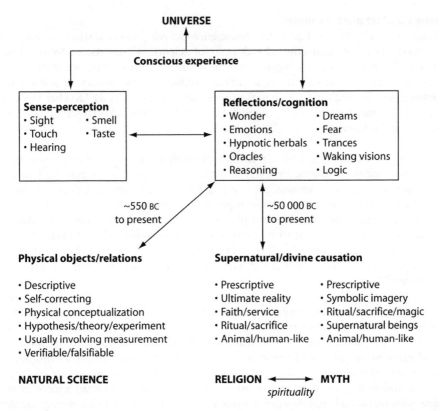

Figure 1.3 Schematic showing the possible conceptual developments leading to science, religion and myth. Each cognitive system responds to questions about the mysteries of the universe and our place in it. Natural science is a Greek invention and deals with conceptual relations among physical objects. Historically, religion and myth deal with knowing based on personal and/or societal feelings and beliefs derived from sensory and super-sensory inputs. Myth and religion are linked via spirituality, which may range from a reflective act involving animal or human-like spirits to deeply binding personal relationships with hundreds of gods or one God exclusively.

religion and may range from emotional outbursts to healthy criticism involving methodologies, analysis or interpretation of data, which all help drive the process.

One of the biggest misconceptions today is to equate religious faith with a scientist's attitude to a hypothesis, theory or law.[106] For the believer, despite periodic moments of doubt, God is absolute and unwavering, whereas a scientist's attitude to a hypothesis, theory or law is most definitely not. Authority in science is always being challenged by new ideas, criticism and revision. No scientific idea is free from criticism, and those scientists who think they are absolutely correct are in the minority. Nineteenth-century physiologist Claude Bernard (1813–78) put the issue into its proper perspective when he wrote: "Men who have excessive faith in their theories or ideas are not only ill prepared for making discoveries; they also make very poor observations."[107]

When subject matter collides

Many of the conflicts that arise between science and religion occur when the mythical components of religion enter the domain of science. If the results from science repeatedly oppose religious dogma, then the dogma becomes untenable from a scientific perspective. One of the most famous conflicts in the history of science was between Galileo and the Church in the seventeenth century. On 31 October 1992, an official statement was made by Pope John Paul II on the Church's position[108] on science and religion:

> From the Galileo affair, we can learn a lesson that remains valid in relation to similar situations that occur today and that may occur in the future … There exists two realms of knowledge, one that has its source in revelation and one that reason can discover by its own power. To the latter belong especially the experimental sciences and philosophy. The distinction between the two realms of knowledge ought not to be understood as opposition. The two realms are not altogether foreign to each other; they have points of contact. The methodologies proper to each make it possible to bring out different aspects of reality.[109]

Conflict and confusion may also arise when science and scientists enter the realm of religion and talk about the existence of God. Those scientists who continue to associate God either directly or metaphorically with the scientific process are committing a fatal error in judgement. Science deals with relations among physical objects, not super-sensory phenomena. As discussed earlier in this chapter, all we can ask of science is to postulate functional interrelationships, not "first causes". Nor can science answer questions on moral issues. Science has often been charged with undermining morality and ethics but science does no such thing; human beings do.[110] Today the scientific enterprise has to meet strict ethical standards that are overseen by internal institutional and external national and international regulatory bodies. A significant ongoing controversy surrounds stem cell research and its ethical and deep religious implications, including the cloning of animals and human beings.

Having completed the general introduction to our story, we shall now enter the extraordinary world of the Sumerians and Egyptians, explore the roles myth and religion have played in framing their worldviews, and ask why natural science was not part of their innovation and discovery. Unfortunately, we can only touch on the equally fascinating Indian and Chinese traditions with their parallel discovereies, intersections and contributions to Western thought; to do otherwise would be an entirely new undertaking. Our story will concentrate on the contributions of Near Eastern, Greek, Christian, Islamic and Renaissance thought. Western traditions only became distinctive after the West experienced renewed stimulus from a number of literary revivals of classical antiquity between the twelfth and sixteenth centuries. This is true for the rise of modern science and the expansion of western Christianity, even if today a high proportion of their practitioners are not from the West.

It was not God but the hard-working Sumerians who created the
"land between the rivers".   V. Gordon Childe

CHAPTER 2
LIFE AMONG THE GODS, PART I:
the Sumerians – service and supplication

The birth of civilization

Civilization, taken in its wide ethnographic sense, is that complex whole which includes knowledge, belief, art, morals, law, custom, and any other capabilities and habits acquired by [a person] as a member of society.   E. B. Tylor[1]

At the end of the last Ice Age (about 10 000 BC), the massive ice sheets that had once covered most of Europe slowly retreated northwards towards their existing polar limits.[2] The earth's surface warmed by 10–15 °C and the sea level rose by some 100–150 m.[3] The large "non-migratory" cold weather animals such as the woolly mammoth and woolly rhinoceros followed the glaciers northwards and eventually became extinct from hunting pressure and lack of food. By comparison, "migratory" animals such as reindeer, caribou and musk ox survived, but exist today in vastly diminished numbers. North Africa, formerly cool and well-watered under glacial influence, began to dry up, leaving vast savannas fringed with small isolated pockets of lush forest vegetation in the northeastern corner.[4] Continental Europe, in contrast, supported a prolific growth of dense forests and vegetation. The profound warming of the earth and rising sea level set in motion unprecedented increases in the world population.[5]

For a long time the increase in world population was thought to be due to waves of small hunter-gatherer groups migrating and diffusing *into* these new areas of opportunity.[6] While some migrations must have occurred, a more likely reason for the increase in world population appears to have been "pre-existing" groups changing from a nomadic hunter-gatherer to a more sedentary food-producing lifestyle.[7] The transition marked the beginning of the New Stone Age or Neolithic[8] agricultural revolution (*c.*10 000–*c.*4000 BC).

This new farming culture was not a widespread phenomenon but developed independently in different places at different times. In the Near East, it was well underway in southern Levant (the western part of the Fertile Crescent) around 8000 BC.[9] By 6500 BC, farming had appeared in Europe[10] and parts of South Asia, and by 5000 BC, it was evident in the Huang Ho valley.[11] In the Americas, the new farming culture began in Peru around 8000 BC and in Mesoamerica by 6000 BC. The term "culture" is used here in its broadest meaning of "cultivation of human potentiality".[12] Culture is social; it is the learned and shared understandings that guide behaviour among people rather than a property of the individual.

Urbanization was the next major development in the cultivation of human potentiality. It was not simply a change in settlement type but a total restructuring of society linked to a developing agriculture-based economy,[13] with grain surplus and trade. With urbanization came more well-defined occupational and class distinctions, a change from pictographic to phonetic writing, new forms of art and crafts, and new myths and religious practices. Technology, too, reached new heights, with the appearance of monumental architecture, complex irrigation networks, time-keeping and more accurate ways of measuring, weighing and counting.

Foremost in the development of these large urban centres were highly complex *state societies*, now called civilizations.[14] Civilizations first appeared in southern Mesopotamia about 3500 BC (in the Sumerian cities Ur, Uruk (Erech) and later Babylon), in Egypt around 3000 BC, and in India's Indus valley around 2500 BC.[15] On the western side of the Mediterannean, civilizations began on the island of Crete with the Minoans (*c.*2600–1600 BC) and on the Greek mainland with the Mycenaeans (*c.*2200–1100 BC). Civilizations also appeared in China some time before 1500 BC (the Shang Dynasty) as well as in Mesoamerica (the Maya, the Zapotecs, the Toltecs and the Aztecs) (see Fig. 2.1). From around 10 000 BC to the birth of Christ, the world population rose from 10 million to around 150 million.[16] Our story begins with the Sumerians and Babylonians of ancient Mesopotamia.

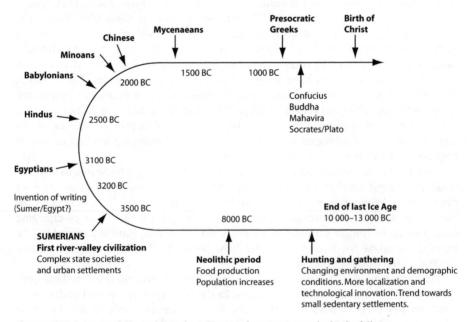

Figure 2.1 Schematic of the world's early civilizations from 3500 BC to the birth of Christ.

Mesopotamia: the home of the Sumerians

The Sumerians invented writing; they possessed the most amazing creation and cosmological myths; they invented the wheel, plough and ox-cart; they invented the 60-minute division of the hour, 60-second division of the minute and 360 parts to a circle to map their skies; they practised metallurgy and experimented with the arts and crafts. However, they never invented natural science. Why not?

According to the Greek translators of the Old Testament, early Mesopotamia was the home of Abraham.[17] It was the region located between the Tigris and Euphrates Rivers, hence called the "land between the rivers" (*mesos* means "middle" and *potamos* "river"). Today archaeologists associate the name Mesopotamia[18] with modern-day Iraq in the Persian Gulf, and a part of Syria (see Fig. 2.2).[19] In ancient times, it contained two kingdoms: Assyria to the north, and the fertile plain of Babylonia[20] to the south.[21]

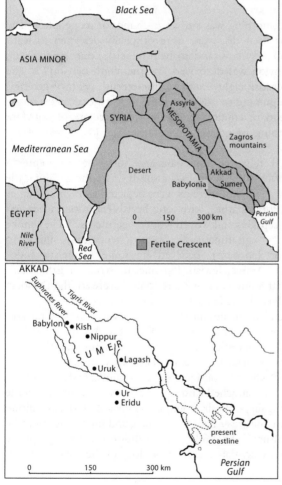

Figure 2.2 Ancient Mesopotamia and Sumerian city-states. Mesopotamia was approximately 480 km long and 240 km wide. It was located between the Tigris and Euphrates Rivers, which flowed into the Persian Gulf. The word "Mesopotamia" means "land between the rivers". The "Fertile Crescent" (shaded) was so named by ancient Near Eastern expert James Henry Breasted in 1916 to represent a great cultivable semicircle linking the southeastern corner of the Mediterranean (Palestine) to the northern corner of the Persian Gulf (Sumer). A large part of the region is bordered by mountains to the north and the desert to the south.

Babylonia was itself divided into two geographical areas: Akkad to the north and Sumer to the south (Fig. 2.2). The biblical name for the southern area was the "plain of Shinar",[22] later called the Euphrates valley, approximately between modern Baghdad and the Persian Gulf.[23] The Sumerians lived towards the south and the Akkadians to the north.

Who were the Sumerians?

Archaeological discoveries made in Egypt and in the Near East in the past hundred years have opened our eyes to a spiritual and cultural heritage undreamed of by earlier generations. What with the unearthing of civilizations buried deep in dirt and dust, the deciphering of languages dead for millenniums, and the recovery of literatures long lost and forgotten, our historical horizon has been widened by several millenniums.

S. N. Kramer[24]

One hundred and fifty years ago, nothing was known of Sumer or its people.[25] The early excavations responsible for their discovery were originally designed to learn more about the Babylonians and Assyrians, and to help to settle, once and for all, whether, as the Bible states, Babylon was destroyed "by the wrath of God".[26] The project was of some urgency because eighteenth- and nineteenth-century geology, archaeology and biology were beginning to question some of the literal truths of the Old Testament. However, instead of confirming or denying the fate of Babylon, archaeologists discovered something of greater importance: the lost world of the Sumerians.

Although the information is sketchy, the Sumerians are thought to have entered "the land between the rivers" about 5000 BC from the south or southeast, along the Iranian coast on the Persian Gulf.[27] The Sumerians were depicted in their statues as "dark, bullet-headed people" of short stature, with long beards (no moustache) and large curved noses, clothed in sheepskins and woven woollen garments.[28] They spoke predominantly a monosyllabic or agglutinative[29] tongue (structurally similar to Turkish, Mongolian, Finnish or Japanese), believed by some to be of Indo-European[30] origins (not Semitic – Arabic, Jewish, Phoenician, Syrian or Ethiopian). There has been the suggestion that Sumerian may share some features of the Davidian languages of southern India.[31] Overall, the language has no close cognates.

Around 5000 BC, a separate semi-nomadic cultural group appeared in the same area as the Sumerians. These people are known as the Akkadians (the Assyrians and later Babylonians) and are linguistically of Semitic origins.[32] The Sumerians and Akkadians existed as two politically distinct cultures for tens of centuries with apparently few territorial and economic disputes.[33] This relationship changed around 2350 BC when the Akkadians, led by Sargon I of Akkad, launched a number of devastating attacks on the south. The Sumerians were never again politically dominant as a people and their culture was absorbed into the Babylonian culture (c.2350–1200 BC), and much later into the Neo-Babylonian or Chaldean culture (c.884–539 BC).[34] All direct knowledge of the Sumerians had disappeared by the Christian era. A chronology of the major events is presented in Table 2.1.

Table 2.1 Early Mesopotamian chronology. Adapted from Oppenheim (1977: 335–48), Bottero (1992: vii), Postgate (1992: 1–5) and Sasson *et al.* (1995: vi–vii).

*c.*8000–4000 BC	Appearance of village farming. Simple irrigation methods. Distinctive pottery. The "Ubaid people" were growing crops by diverting the waters from the alluvial fans of the smaller watercourses of the Euphrates River (and to a lesser extent the Tigris). First permanent agricultural settlements appeared about 5000 BC in the **early Ubaid period** (5000–4000 BC).
*c.*4000–3200 BC	**Uruk period.** Rise of Sumerian culture, culminating in city-states with temple as dominant institution. Metallurgy. Originally ruled by priestly class. Writing invented around 3200 BC; earliest found at Eanna Temple at Uruk.
*c.*3200–2750 BC	Sumerian civilization reached its zenith around 2900 BC. **Early Dynastic I period** (2900–2750 BC). Political structure of city-states established with long list of ruling kings. Each city had a favourite ruling god of the pantheon: Ur had Nanna/Sin (moon god); Uruk had Ishtar/Inanna (goddess of love and war) and sky god Anu; Nippur had Enlil (father of the gods) and Eridu had Ea.
*c.*2750–2350 BC	Strong Semitic influence with warfare between city-states. Sumerian spoken mostly in the south and Semitic in the north. Characterized by **Early Dynastic II period** (2750–2600 BC) and **Early Dynastic III period** (2600–2350 BC).
*c.*2350–2150 BC	Sumer was no longer politically dominant; overtaken by the Akkadian Empire, dynasty of Sargon of Akkad. City-state decline.
*c.*2150–1800 BC	**Neo-Sumerian period** (Transitional period). Rise of Babylon. Third Dynasty of Ur (2150–2000 BC) and Isin-Larsa dynasties (2000–1800 BC). By 1800, Sumerian ceased to be spoken. Hammurabi reunited the country in a single kingdom under the authority of the monarch of Babylon (kingdom lasted some 700 years).
*c.*1800–1600 BC	**Babylonian period** (2000–1600 BC). Babylonian Empire, ruled by King Hammurabi. Language: Semitic Akkadian. Old Indo-European invasions of Near East.
*c.*1600–745 BC	Invasion by the Kassites. Widespread cultural disintegration. Babylonian revival from 1100 BC.
*c.*745–539 BC	Era of empires: Assyrian, Neo-Babylonian, Persian. Akkadian was replaced by Aramaic.
331 BC	Overthrow of the Persian Empire by Alexander the Great of Macedonia (356–323 BC).

Who discovered them?

I must admit that I was tempted more than once to abandon the study of the Assyrian inscriptions because I despaired of ever obtaining a satisfactory result.

H. C. Rawlinson[35]

The story of the discovery of the Sumerians is fascinating. It was the result of a process involving a number of archaeological and scriptural anomalies, painstaking scholarship and a lot of luck. The excitement began around 1843–45, when French consular agent Paul E. Botta at Mosul, and later British counterpart Austen H. Layard, began digging in mounds north and south of Mosul on the east bank of the Tigris.[36] The sculptural reliefs and small clay tablets unearthed led to the discovery of three ancient Assyrian capital cities, referred to in the Old Testament as Khorsabad, Nimrud and Nineveh.

In the 1850s, Botta and Layard were followed by two Englishmen, W. K. Loftus and H. A. Churchill, who became intrigued with the older ruins to the south in

Babylonia.[37] Rawlinson later identified the two mounds at Tell Mukayyar and Tell-Abu-Shahrein as the ancient lost cities of Ur of Chaldees and Eridu (once a major seaport of Sumer and Babylonia).

The second line of evidence for the discovery of a lost people came from a number of linguistic anomalies in the cuneiform script. In the late eighteenth century, and early part of the nineteenth century, three languages were identified as cuneiform: Semitic-Babylonian, Indo-European Persian and Elamite.[38] Despite Georg Grotefend's (1775–1853) belief that he had discovered the key to cuneiform, something wasn't quite right. In 1850, Irish philologist Edward Hincks noticed that the Semitic language of the Babylonians and Assyrians was transcribed by syllables,[39] a feature contrary to their basic language structure.[40] A possible explanation was that the Semites had *borrowed* and adapted the script from another people. This proposal, together with the excavation of mounds in southern Babylonia, raised the level of excitement.

However, there remained the question of accuracy of translation of the texts. The issue appears to have been settled in 1857 when the British Museum in London asked Rawlinson to translate an inscription on a cylinder from the reign of the Assyrian King Tiglath-pileser I (1116–1076 BC).[41] After some discussion, three independent experts, W. H. Fox Talbot, Hincks and Julius Oppert, were also asked by the British Museum to submit their translations. The four translations were signed, sealed and delivered to the President of the Royal Asiatic Society, who had them examined by their Select Committee.[42]

The committee found that the four translations were in broad agreement, with Hincks and Rawlinson's versions nearly identical,[43] and concluded that there was no doubt that the key to "Babylonian" cuneiform decipherment had been discovered.[44] On 17 January 1869, after a decade of intense debate, and following Hincks's earlier suggestion, Oppert named the people and their language "Sumerian". The name "Sumerian" was chosen after the word for southern Babylonia, *Sumer*, or more accurately *Shumer*.[45] The discovery of cuneiform meant that all the wedge-shaped characters that had adorned the tens of thousands of baked clay tablets in the world's museums were not decorations, but the life history of a lost civilization.

Building of the city-states

By 3500 BC, the Sumerians, through unbridled creativity and tireless effort, slowly transformed the flat, hot, dry, treeless and stoneless "plain of Shinar" into a vast assembly of city-states with agricultural surplus and a trade economy.[46] At its peak Sumer had between 15 and 20 city-states, with one capital at any given period.[47] Each city-state was an independent sociopolitical entity with its own government, economy and laws, patron-god,[48] ruling temple priests,[49] nobles, free citizens, farmers, crafts-men, merchants and slaves.[50] The people saw themselves as citizens of city-states rather than nationals of Sumer.[51]

The major Sumerian cities were at Ur, Uruk (Erech), Kish, Lagash and Nippur; each supported populations of up to 100 000 inhabitants.[52] As each city-state became larger and more complex, priestly rule was joined by military rule.[53] The military leaders became the kings and lived in palaces separate from the temples. Although kingship became hereditary, the priests never lost their power. The priests remained the overseers of organized trade, taxation and learning, assembled codes of law and owned a major part of the surrounding farmlands. Sumerian politics was therefore, like every other facet of Mesopotamian life, intimately tied to their religion, which will be discussed later.

Each city-state had its own fortified temple with a tower called a ziggurat, an anglicized form of the Akkadian word for a stepped "temple tower".[54] The ziggurat is believed to have been built to support the stairway to be used by the gods to travel from one realm to the other and provide them with the amenities required along the way (food, a place to rest, etc.). The ziggurat was also the chief organizing centre run by the priestly class, who dealt with social, economic and legal affairs.[55] It was often referred to as god's house; it was located on the highest ground, and could be seen by farmers who worked great distances outside the city walls.[56] The ziggurat was also the place of priestly worship, sacrifice and ceremony. Every year the Sumerians held their most sacred sacrificial ritual to assure the success of the new season's crop.[57] According to British archaeologist Glyn Daniel, a young priest and priestess had sexual intercourse in the tower in the presence of an officiating priest, after which they were both sacrificed and buried.[58]

Within this urbanized social framework, the Sumerians invented the most amazing things. They invented a number system to measure, weigh and count that eventually gave rise to mathematics and geometry. They invented ways to tell the time using a water clock. They observed the changing phases of the moon and the position of the stars, from which astronomy and astrology developed. They invented new industrial arts and crafts (including metallurgy), from which chemistry developed. They invented the wheel (c.3700 BC) and the ox-driven plough, which transformed agricultural practices and crop yields for millennia. And, last but not least, the Sumerians invented perhaps the greatest of human symbolic abstractions: phonetic writing.

The invention of writing

Blessed be he who invented writing.

Jean Paul (from a pious saying of the ancient Indians)[59]

From pictures to symbols

Writing permitted the transfer of a large body of knowledge in an organized, accurate and convenient manner. Knowledge was no longer restricted to one locality, such as a large immovable rock or a cave wall, but could be catalogued, studied, stored and modified to meet the changing needs of a people. Sumerian writing was not of the picture type but a symbolic form, which expressed the spoken sound as a written sign.[60] A *picture* of a human head now stood for the *word* "ka", the *sound* "ka" and the *idea* of mouth.[61] From a simple picture,[62] "ka" had a sound "value" and a sound "sign", which was used in combination with other "signs" to communicate meaning between the external and mental worlds.[63] The Sumerian idea of going from a picture to a sound to a sign was a sea-change in the history of communication and dissemination of ideas.

The earliest Sumerian writing appeared around 3200 BC.[64] The script is thought to have developed out of the needs and necessities of a growing economy and administration.[65] Before this time, tokens were used as a record-keeping device, a practice believed to date back millennia.[66] In 1700, Hebrew scholar Thomas Hyde (1636–1703) called the wedge-shaped signs "cuneiform" from the Latin *cuneus*, meaning a wedge. Hyde thought the characters were of an Old Persian script that served as decorations and ornaments.[67] He had no idea the signs were intended to convey meaningful speech.

Writing permitted the Sumerians to log their astronomical observations, record their long traditions, codify their laws, preserve their agricultural and animal husbandry techniques, document their medical information, list their battles, and document their creation stories and other important social events. Writing also provided a means for the ruling priests and kings to communicate with their gods in sacred texts and on monuments. The human brain, remarkable as it is, could not have developed a high civilization without first inventing writing.

The Sumerians wrote on clay

Writing was a highly skilled art restricted to scribes, who belonged to the social elite.[68] Like the Egyptians, most of the people of Mesopotamia were illiterate, which meant that knowledge was in the hands of the powerful rulers rather than the people.[69] It was not until the later culture of Greece that writing and reading became freely available to the people through education.

Since stone was scarce in Mesopotamia, clay was the principal medium for writing until about 500 BC. The Sumerian writer or scribe[70] used soft clay tablets that were hardened by baking and firing at 1100–1200 °C.[71] The heating procedure made the tablets virtually indestructible. The characteristic wedge-shaped impressions were formed from the oblique tilt of the square-tipped stylus or reed punch in soft clay. The tablets varied in size but most commonly were 15 cm long, 5 cm wide and 2.5 cm thick. They were kept in libraries.[72] Those tablets of special importance were sometimes baked once, covered again with a thin coating of clay, and written over again in duplicate, and baked again.[73] This was the ancient version of a modern photocopying machine. If the outer writing was defaced by accident or by design, the top layer could be removed to expose the original copy.

Structure and origin of the universe

> In Sumer, a good millennium before the Hebrews wrote down their Bible and the Greeks their Iliad and Odyssey, we find a rich and mature literature consisting of myths and epic tales, hymns, lamentations and numerous collections of proverbs, fables, and essays.
>
> S. N. Kramer[74]

The Sumerian (and later Babylonian) worldview was a mythopoeic construction where most phenomena were considered to be caused by, or to be manifestations of, a divine presence or being (i.e. a god).[75] Life was a lengthy continuous struggle against a harsh, unforgiving world, that nevertheless each year supplied an annual flood to support the Sumerians' agricultural needs. Without a flood, which was a gift to human beings from the gods, there was no agriculture, no grain surplus, no economy, no trade, no prosperity, no gods and no existence. According to their myths, the gods created human beings for the sole purpose of service and supplication; it was the job of human beings to supply them with food, drink and shelter.[76] Satisfactory service was rewarded with a long happy life and unsatisfactory service was punished by hardship, disease and early death.[77] There was no afterlife, no messiahs, no resurrections and no last judgement.[78]

The Sumerian gods were organized in an elaborate hierarchy reflecting the Sumerian political system. The most powerful were the creator-gods, followed by hundreds of lesser gods ranked according to the everyday phenomena they controlled.[79] The people saw their universe as "divine" in all its manifestations.[80] Daily and seasonal meteorological sense-phenomena and events were explained using myths that were absolute and not to be questioned.[81] Mythopoeic symbolism was the language of Sumerian religion. Symbolic imagery was used because the gods were invisible, and their divine manifestations were depicted through sense-phenomena.[82] The gods interacted with human beings like absentee parents. Everything in the universe, including human civilization and all its products, belonged to the realm of the gods.[83]

Sumerian cosmogony and cosmology

The Sumerians appeared to show little interest in the origin of the universe.[84] The undifferentiated primeval (or primordial) sea presumably had been around for ever.[85] The creation of heaven, earth, the waters and underworld from the primeval sea occurred simultaneously with the gods, who maintained world order.[86] The four powerful creator-gods[87] were: An, the sky or heaven god; Ki (later changed to Ninhursag or Ninmah), the earth goddess; Enlil, the air god; and Enki (Ea in Akkadian), the water god, who was also the moon god and god of wisdom.[88]

The earth was generally perceived as a flat disc floating in a boundless sea with heaven above in the shape of a dome (Fig. 2.3). Separating heaven and earth was the expanding atmosphere called the *lil*. *Lil* possessed unique properties of movement and expansion and was also responsible for the formation of the "heavenly bodies"

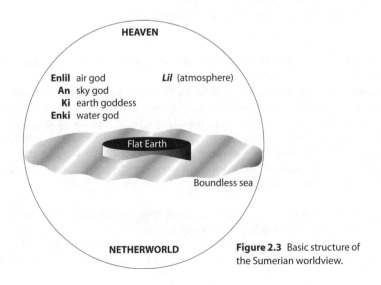

Figure 2.3 Basic structure of the Sumerian worldview.

(the sun, moon, planets, and stars) and their luminosity. Surrounding the fixed and immovable heaven–earth was the boundless or infinite sea. Below earth was the netherworld, which some claim was the ancient way of giving symmetry to the world.[89] While most of the gods lived in heaven, there is some mention that a few lived "below", presumably meaning in the netherworld.

After the basic structure was in place, the world was ready for the plants, animals and human beings and other necessary things required to sustain the gods.[90] The major events from the birth of the gods to the appearance of the world and human beings is summarized below.[91]

- **First there was a primeval sea, presumably thought to have existed for ever.** It appears that the Sumerian world was created from the primeval sea, which was represented as the goddess Nammu (or Namma).[92] From an early tablet on a list of Sumerian gods, the goddess Nammu, written with a pictograph for primeval "sea", was described as "the mother, who gave birth to Heaven and Earth".[93] Heaven and earth were apparently seen as the created products of the primeval sea. It appears that the Sumerians never asked what existed in either time or space before the primeval chaos.[94]
- **From the primordial sea arose the cosmic mountain consisting of a united heaven and earth.** The idea that heaven and earth were once united is implied from the first line of a "Cattle and Grain" story, which reads "On the mountain of Heaven and Earth." Presumably earth was at the bottom of the mountain and heaven at the peak.
- **Some gods existed before the separation of heaven and earth.** This notion was deduced by Kramer from the following five lines:

  > After Heaven had been moved away from Earth,
  > After Earth had been separated from Heaven,
  > After the name of man had been fixed,
  > After An (Heaven-god) carried off Heaven,
  > After Enlil (air-god) carried off Earth …

  Kramer concluded that the heaven and air gods must have existed *before* the separation of heaven and earth.[95]
- **Heaven and earth were separated by the god Enlil before the creation of heavenly bodies, man, animals and plants.** Enlil, the air god, was the product of the union of An, the male heaven god, and Ki, the female earth god. In some versions Enlil carried off his mother, earth, An carried off heaven, and earth and heaven were separated by the *lil*, or air.[96] In other myths the powerful creator-gods only had to speak the word, or pronounce the name, and separations and structures would come into being.[97]

The stage now was set for the creation of man, animals and plants and the establishment of civilization. The mother of all living things on earth, according to Sumerian belief, was the all-powerful creation goddess Ninhursag (formerly the earth goddess, Ki).[98] Three literary myths concern the creation of human beings, who were fashioned from clay and divine blood.[99] The first is the Enki–Ninhursag myth (*c*.2800 BC), the second is the Babylonian *Atrakhasis Epic* (*c*.1800 BC) and the third is the *Enuma Elish* (*c*.1500 BC). There is one other version of human beings growing out of the ground like plants.[100] The common thread running through all these myths was that human beings were created to serve the gods by providing food, clothing and shelter, a task that used to be performed by the lesser gods. When humanity multiplied, death was decreed by the gods to keep the population in check, and "kingship was lowered from heaven" to coordinate the events.[101] The gods endowed mortal humans with mind (or intelligence).[102]

The Enki–Ninhursag creation myth and biblical parallels

One of the major achievements of all this archaeological activity in "Bible lands" is that a bright and revealing light has been shed on the background and origin of the Bible itself. We can now see that this greatest of literary classics did not come upon the scene full-blown, like an artificial flower in a vacuum; its roots reach deep into the distant past and spread wide across the surrounding lands.   J. J. Glassner[103]

Broad structure of the creation myth
The Sumerian Enki–Ninhursag creation myth is dated to around 2800 BC, but probably began much earlier. The 278-line, six-column tablet begins with the separation of heaven and earth, proceeds through divine procreations and marriages and then narrates how the creation goddess, Ninhursag, brought "green things" on to the earth in the Garden of Dilmun. It continues with Ninhursag condemning her brother Enki to death for eating the forbidden plants, creating the goddess Ninti from the rib of dying Enki and creating man from clay (or dust) under the direction of Enki and his mother Nammu (the primeval sea).[104] The 5000-year-old story was first published in 1915, but its fascinating parallels with the Genesis story were not appreciated until about 1945.[105] The following is the Enki–Ninhursag myth according to Kramer's translation.[106]

Condemnation for eating the forbidden plants
After the water god Enki ordered the sun god Utu to bring fresh water "from the earth", the powerful goddess Ninhursag proceeded to bring life to the Garden of Dilmun.[107] Ninhursag had created eight special plants in the garden and the myth narrates how Enki asked a messenger god, Isimud, to collect these precious plants and bring them to him. Enki proceeded to eat the eight plants. Ninhursag was furious and cursed her brother to death, whereupon eight of his body organs instantly became sick and began to waste away.

Ninhursag left the garden because she could not bear to witness the death of her brother. After a while she was coerced back to the garden by a messenger of Enlil (the air god and king of all the Sumerian gods) to help save her brother. She placed her dying brother near her vulva, and after asking which of his eight organs were affected, she proceeded to bring him back to life by creating a special god to heal each afflicted organ. Enki survived as the Sumerian god of wisdom and was put in charge of maintaining the earth's organization according to Enlil's plans.

The first parallel is the remarkable similarity between Enki's action in eating the eight green plants, and the subsequent curse cast upon him by the powerful goddess Ninhursag, and the Adam and Eve story in Genesis. Adam and Eve ate the forbidden fruit from the "Tree of Knowledge" and were reprimanded by God for committing such a sinful act of disobedience, after which the whole of humanity suffered.[108]

Location of the Garden of Dilmun and watering "from the earth"

Dilmun, which was also known as the "paradise of the gods", was a sacred place, "pure", "clean" and "bright", that knew no sickness or death, and where "the lion kills not, the wolf snatches not the lamb", and "the pain of childbirth does not exist".[109] The second parallel is the location of the Garden of Dilmun and the Garden of Eden. According to the Sumerian story Dilmun was located to the east of Sumer. It was in the same location as the Babylonian "land of the living" or "home of the immortals".[110]

The Garden of Eden in Genesis was the garden planted by God in the east, from which a river flowed to form the four world rivers, two of which were the Tigris (Hiddekel), which flowed east of Assyria, and the Euphrates.[111] This geographical description in Genesis would put the location of the Garden of Eden very close to the Garden of Dilmun.[112] Biblical scholars concede that the Garden of Eden was associated with the Tigris and the Euphrates. Many Assyriologists believe that the other two rivers referred to in the Bible, namely the Pishon and Gihon, may be the Hebrew names for two of the principal canals that joined the great waterways.[113]

A third parallel between the stories relates to the watering of the Garden of Dilmun. There was a lack of fresh water and Enki ordered the sun god, Utu, to bring water up "from the earth". Dilmun was thus turned into a divine garden with food aplenty. This passage in the Enki–Ninhursag myth has a parallel in the Old Testament. Noteworthy human beings had not yet been created to do the work when the Lord "brought up a mist from the earth, and watered the whole face of the earth". Genesis (2:5–8) states:

> And every plant of the field before it was in the earth, and every herb of the field before it grew: for the Lord God had not caused it to rain upon the earth and *there was not* a man to till the ground.
>
> But there went up a mist from the earth, and watered the whole face of the earth.
>
> And the Lord God formed man *of* the dust of the ground, and breathed into his nostrils the breath of life and man became a living soul.
>
> And the Lord God planted a garden eastward in Eden; and there he put the man whom he had formed.[114]

Goddess Ninti from Enki's rib

Another fascinating parallel relates to the creation of the goddess Ninti from Enki's rib and the biblical passage describing the fashioning of Eve from the rib of Adam. The Genesis passage states:

> And the Lord God caused a deep sleep to fall upon Adam, and he slept: and he took one of his ribs, and closed up the flesh instead thereof. And the rib, which

the Lord God had taken from man, made he a woman, and brought her unto the man. And Adam said, This *is* now bone of my bones, and flesh of my flesh: she shall be called a Woman, because she was taken out of man.[115]

During the course of bringing Enki back to life, the goddess Ninhursag asked, "What hurts you?" Enki replied, "My rib hurts me." Ninhursag responded, "To the goddess Ninti I have given birth for you."[116] Ninti, the goddess of childbirth, cured Enki's rib and Enki survived as one of the pantheon. There are interesting associations between the Sumerian name Ninti and the Hebrew name Eve. Ninti means "the Lady of the rib" from *ti*, the Sumerian word for rib.[117] However, *ti* also means "to make live" and therefore an alternative for Ninti in Sumerian is "the Lady who makes live".[118] According to Strong's concordance of the Bible[119] Eve is defined as "life-giver" or "she who makes live" from the Hebrew root *hayah* "to live".[120] It seems likely that the compilers of Genesis were aware of the double meaning from earlier Sumerian mythology, because by choosing the "rib" automatically they assumed "the act of birth" and therefore "rib" was appropriate to the name "Eve" as "mother of all living human beings".

Creation of man from clay or dust

A fifth parallel, again of profound interest in the history of religion, is the comparison between the Enki–Ninhursag myth and the Hebrew creation of Adam from clay (or dust from the ground as described in Genesis 2–3). According to Genesis (1:1–31), God created (through the word) the universe and all life on earth within six days: on the first day, time and the separation of light from darkness; on the second day, the heavenly bodies; on the third day, the earth, water and plants; on the fourth day, the sun and the moon, from which light ruled the day and night on earth; on the fifth day, all animals, "the fish in the sea and the fowl in the air"; and on the sixth day, human beings in God's own image: the first man, Adam, who was moulded from dust or clay; then woman, Eve, who was fashioned from Adam's rib.[121]

The relevant passage of the Enki–Ninhursag myth begins with a problem of procuring bread for the gods, who required regular meals; many myths talk about how the great gods organized the world after the separation of earth and heaven and made the lesser gods dig rivers and canals and grow food. Over time the lesser gods went on strike and demanded to be relieved of duty, which led to the creation of a substitute, man.[122] At first Enki, the water god and god of wisdom, did not hear of the gods' difficulties in procuring bread as he was asleep in the abyss. Enki's mother, Nammu, the primeval sea, contacted her son to alert him of the problem. She said to him:

O my son, rise from your bed, from your (?) work what is wise,
Fashion servants of the gods, may they produce their doubles (?)[123]

Enki proceeded to tell his mother that the problem would be solved by the creation of man from the "clay that is over the abyss". It will be man who can be the provider of food, clothing and shelter for the gods. The passage continues:

O my mother, the creature whose name you uttered, it exists,
Bind upon it the image (?) of the gods;

35

Mix the heart of the clay that is over the abyss,
The good and the princely fashioners will thicken the clay,
You, do you bring the limbs into existence;
Ninhursag (Ninmah) will work above you,
The godesses (of birth) ... will stand by you at your fashioning;
O my mother, decree its (the new-born's) fate,
Ninhursag (Ninmah) will bind upon it the mold (?) of the gods,
It is man ...[124]

The Enki–Ninhursag myth was not the only creation myth of man. Another myth tells how human beings spontaneously sprouted from the ground like plants (similar to the creation myths in Egypt), while another version describes how man was formed from the blood of two Lagma gods sacrificed for that purpose (later revived and reinterpreted in the famous Babylonian cosmogonic poem, *Enuma Elish*).[125]

A word of caution

Despite fascinating parallels between the stories of the 5000-year-old myth and Genesis, differences do exist. Genesis has only one God who acts and creates *ex nihilo* ("out of nothing") (although not explicitly stated until 2 Maccabees 7:28).[126] In the Sumerian Enki–Ninhursag myth there was one primeval god (Nammu) and many lesser gods, and the creation was not "out of nothing" because the primeval sea had been around for ever. Another difference is the rise of civilization in Genesis was a human endeavour blessed by God (human beings were blessed, not the inventions) whereas in Sumer, civilization and all its products were the result of their gods' creative actions.[127] And lastly, Genesis (1–11) is a more recent compilation of the late fifth century BC, and many of its stories received literary form around 800–900 BC.[128]

The Sumerian flood myth

> Kramer [1944] ... has demonstrated that almost every section of the Gilgamesh saga exists as a separate entity in Sumerian – including the Flood. This independent Sumerian form of the story of the Flood has particular significance for Genesis 6–9 inasmuch as in it creation precedes the Flood. The conjunction of creation and Flood in the biblical story has a precedent.
> C. Westermann[129]

Most of us are familiar with Noah and the Flood,[130] where the waters rose for 40 days from the "great deep" and covered the tops of the highest mountains. We are told in Genesis (8:3–4) that the Flood waters abated after 150 days and the Ark came to rest on the mountains of Ararat. However, less widely known are the parallels with the older myths of ancient Mesopotamia.[131]

The single Sumerian "Flood" tablet was one of 30 000 tablets discovered by the expeditions of the University of Pennsylvania to Nippur between 1889 and 1900.[132] It was not until 1914 that epigrapher Arno Poebel translated the six-column tablet and published his findings in English. The exact date of the original myth is not known, but it was probably written down not long after the invention of writing.[133] Unfortunately, only one-third of the "Nippur Tablet" exists. The first section about the Flood (some 37 lines into the myth) concerns the creation of man, plants and animals:

> My mankind, in its destruction I will …,
> To Nintu I will return the … of my creatures,
> I will return the people to their settlements,
> Of the cities, they will build their places of the divine laws,
> I will make restful their shade,
> Of our houses, they will lay their bricks in pure places,
> The places of our decisions they will be found in pure places.
> He directed the pure fire-quenching water,
> Perfected the rites and the exalted divine laws,
> On the earth he …d, placed the … there.
> After An, Enlil, Enki, and Ninhursag,
> Had fashioned the blackheaded people,
> Vegetation luxuriated from the Earth,
> Animals, four-legged (creatures) of the plain,
> were brought artfully into existence.[134]

After an unintelligible section of about 37 lines, the myth continues with the heavenly origin of kingship and the founding of the five cities: Eridu, Badtibira, Larak, Sippar and Shuruppak:

> After the … of kingship had been lowered from heaven,
> After the exalted tiara and the throne of kingship had been lowered from heaven,
> He perfected the rites and the exalted divine laws,
> Founded the five cities in … pure places,
> Called their names, apportioned them as cult centers.
> The first of these cities, Eridu, he gave to Nudimmud, the leader,
> The second, Badtibira, he gave to …,
> The third, Larak, he gave to Endurbilhursag,
> The fourth, Sippar, he gave to the hero Utu,
> The fifth, Shuruppak, he gave to Sud.
> When he had called the names of these cities, approportioned them as cult centers,
> He brought …,
> Establishing the cleaning of the small rivers as …[135]

There is another unintelligible section followed by a story of how the gods became angry about a decision by a more powerful god to bring down a flood to destroy humankind. Presumably the previous unreadable section relates to why the supreme god was unhappy and the need to start the creation all over again.

Next is the appearance of the Sumerian hero called Ziusudra (or Ziusdra). Ziusudra was the Sumerian equivalent of the Akkadian Utnapishtim and the biblical Noah.[136] Ziusudra was portrayed as a pious, humble, god-fearing king of the city-state

Shuruppak (around 2900 BC). He is depicted standing by a wall when he learned through revelation of the decree of the gods "to destroy the seed of mankind".[137]

> All the windstorms, exceedingly powerful, attacked as one,
> At the same time, the flood sweeps over the cult centers.
> After, for seven days and seven nights,
> The flood had swept over the land,
> And the huge boat had been tossed about by the windstorms on the great waters,
> Utu came forth, who sheds light on heaven and earth,
> Ziusudra, opened a window on the huge boat,
> The hero Utu brought his rays into the giant boat.
> Ziusudra, the king,
> Prostrated himself before Utu,
> The king kills an ox, slaughters a sheep.[138]

Again, after another unreadable section, the last existing lines of the myth tell of the deification of Ziusudra. He was given "life like a god" and breath eternal as he prostrated himself before An and Enlil.

> Ziusudra, the king,
> Prostrated before An and Enlil,
> An and Enlil cherished Ziusudra,
> Life like a god they gave him:
> Breath eternal like a god they bring down for him.
> Then, Ziusudra, the king,
> The preserver of the name of vegetation and of the seed of mankind,
> In the land of crossing, the land of Dilmun, the place where the sun rises, they
> caused to dwell.[139]

The remainder of the tablet (about 39 lines) is lost so it is not known what happened to Ziusudra with his new god-like powers in the paradise of the Garden of Dilmun. According to Norman Cohn, the Sumerian flood myth appears to have been composed for a political purpose designed to strengthen the established order of kingship (and priesthood) being established *by* the gods.[140]

The Babylonian version of the flood myth: the Epic of Gilgamesh

> I am the first man to read this text after two thousand years of oblivion.
>
> George Smith[141]

There were two Babylonian versions of the flood myth.[142] The first is the myth of Utnapishtim (or Atrakhasis) where a flood was brought about *before* human beings were created in mythic times after the lesser gods went on strike and refused to work for the senior gods.[143] The second version of the same story is one of 12 tablets collectively known as the Epic of Gilgamesh.[144] The Sumerian King List indicates that Gilgamesh was a ruler of Uruk during the First Dynasty (around 2700 BC) for 126 years.[145] The King List is also of interest as it mentions the flood specifically: "the deluge overthrew the land".[146] We shall now consider the Gilgamesh myth.

Discovery and broader meaning of the Epic of Gilgamesh

The larger epic was discovered on a tablet in the nineteenth century and translated in 1872 by the English Assyriologist George Smith. George Smith was a young assistant at the British Museum[147] when he reported his discovery and translation to the Society of Biblical Archaeology on 3 December 1872. He began his address:

> A short time back, I discovered among the Assyrian tablets in the British Museum, an account of the Flood; which under the advice of the President, I now bring before the society … On reviewing the evidence it is apparent that the events of the Flood narrated in the Bible and the Inscriptions are the same, and occur in the same order.[148]

Not surprisingly, Smith's presentation received mixed opinions ranging from total disdain to believing it to be one of the most spectacular discoveries in biblical archaeology.[149]

The Epic of Gilgamesh begins with a brief declaration of Gilgamesh's heroic deeds and fortunes as "two-thirds god and one-third man".[150] The myth is intricately woven into a deeper problem of life and death, and the pursuit of the supernatural, which gives the whole story its meaning and unity.[151] What began as a search for knowledge and wisdom ended in a search for immortality. Gilgamesh failed to obtain immortality, which, after much reflection, he accepted with quiet resignation. The individual dies but not humanity. The epic was so profoundly rich in meaning that it spread in various written forms throughout western Asia, including Syria and Asia Minor.[152] It was known to the Canaanites, the Hittites, the Greeks[153] and Romans, and to the compilers of the Old Testament in the fifth century BC, where it has survived in Jewish, Christian and Muslim traditions.[154]

The flood myth in the Epic of Gilgamesh

The Babylonian flood on Tablet 11 was originally written[155] in the Akkadian language some time between 2500 BC and 2000 BC.[156] The story begins with Gilgamesh meeting Utnapishtim, an old Akkadian man who had obtained immortality. Gilgamesh wondered why he and Utnapishtim looked the same although he was mortal and Utnapishtim was not.

Utnapishtim told Gilgamesh a story in which the gods became angry at humanity and decided to send a flood to destroy all living things. Utnapishtim's life was spared because he was a good and humble man. The god Ea, who broke rank from the other gods, warned Utnapishtim of the impending doom and commanded him to build a boat. The boat had to be constructed to very precise dimensions, sealed with bitumen and then filled with "the seed of all living creatures".[157] Utnapishtim built the boat and, as he entered the vessel, a devastating storm fell upon the earth.

The wind blew for "six days and seven nights … The downpour, the tempest, and the flood overwhelmed the entire land." On the seventh day the storm and flood subsided. The world was deathly silent and all mankind had returned to clay.[158] The myth continues to talk about how the boat came to rest on Mount Nisir[159] in the

Zagros mountains (Mount Nisir and Mount Ararat are about 480 km apart). After seven days Utnapishtim sent out a dove, then a swallow in search for land but both birds returned. Finally, he sent out a raven, which did not return (in Genesis 8:7 Noah sends out the raven first, followed by two doves).

Utnapishtim eventually found a way out by deciding to make a sacrifice to the great gods. Despite Enlil's initial disbelief and anger that some mortal had survived the deluge ("No man was to survive the destruction"), after counsel with the other gods, he finally awarded Utnapishtim and his wife immortality.[160] The story ends with Utnapishtim telling Gilgamesh that he must begin his journey to immortality by trial. The trial was to sleep for six days and seven nights, the length of time of the deluge. Gilgamesh failed the test, and met the decision with quiet resignation and acceptance.

Was there a flood in Sumer that devasted humankind?

The story of the Flood, which we know from Genesis and associate with Noah, originated in Mesopotamia. Right down to the first half of the present century large areas of what used to be Mesopotamia and is now Iraq were frequently devastated by flood. When torrential rain combined with the melting snows in spring, the Tigris and Euphrates could burst their banks; then the country would be submerged under hundreds of miles of lakes. In ancient times this phenomenon gave rise to powerful tradition: it was believed that there had once been a flood so overwhelming that nothing was ever the same again.   N. Cohn[161]

Excavations of the city at Ur[162] have partially substantiated the view that a flood devastated Sumer.[163] In the late 1920s archaeologist Sir Leonard Woolley (1880–1960) was among the first to discover material evidence of a great flood. In one excavation site, he found up to 3.7 m of silt, which sealed strata containing painted pottery of the Ubaid period (c.5000 BC), the earliest known phase of occupation in southern Mesopotamia. The flood was estimated to be around 8 m in depth, 480 km long and 160 km across, which would have covered much of the fertile valley between the high Syrian desert and the Elamite mountains.[164] It may not have wiped out all humankind but, from the perspective of local Mesopotamian experience, most survivors probably thought it had. In the London newspaper *The Times* (16 March 1929), Woolley claimed credit for the discovery of the Ur flood without mentioning another flood discovered earlier in the northern portion of the floodplain of Kish. The Kish excavators felt that Woolley had cheated them of credit for their discovery, even though it was a different flood at a different time. Today, most archaeologists doubt that the Ur, Kish or even Shuruppak floods could be the *source* of the Mesopotamian flood narratives but agree that many were catastrophic and responsible for the loss of tens of thousands of lives.[165]

More recently, attention has shifted from searching for a Noahic flood in the "land between the rivers" to the Black Sea (see Fig. 2.2). In the 1990s, two marine geologists at Columbia University in New York, William Ryan and Walter Pitman, proposed that there was an enormous transfer of water from the Mediterranean Sea into a freshwater lake that formed the Black Sea about 5600 BC; this violent flooding may have inspired the Noahic flood stories. Drawing on findings of geology, archaeology, agriculture, genetics, language and the development of textiles and pottery, these two scientists postulate that by about 9000 BC, various tribes came to the shores of the Euxine Lake, where water supply was fresh and plentiful.[166] As vast continental glaciers melted and rainfall increased, the Mediterranean Sea level rose up to 150 m higher than the landlocked freshwater Euxine Lake.

Eventually the Mediterannean Sea carved out rivulets inland that dramatically enlarged and flowed into the Euxine Lake to form the Black Sea. The basin filled at an extraordinary rate of 42 km³ of water per day, which would be equivalent to a force of over 200 times the flow of Niagara Falls and heard at least 190 km away. The inundation continued for nearly a year. The water level has been estimated to have risen about 15 cm a day. The shoreline expanded by up to 1.6 km each day until it reached an area of about 414 000 km² and a maximum water depth of 2210 m.[167] Unbelievably, it has been estimated that the volume of water that formed the Black Sea accounted for a lowering of the world's oceans by as much as 30 cm. The effect of the inundation on farming communities must have been catastrophic. Ryan and Pitman propose that over the next few hundred years the flood may have contributed to the spread of farming and language throughout Europe, Central Asia and the Middle East.[168] It may also have led to the Ubaid people entering lower Mesopotamia and forming permanent agricultural settlements (Table 2.1).

Ryan and Pitmans's tantalizing proposal of a catastrophic flood has received some support. In 1999 Robert Ballard, the explorer who discovered the wreck of the *Titanic* in 1985, confirmed the presence of an ancient coastline some 168 m below the present sea level. In the following year, using state-of-the-art underwater video search equipment and a fleet of submarine robots, the team further uncovered a large wooden building 19 km offshore at a depth of more than 90 m. Organic material such as wood is well preserved in the oxygen starved waters of the Black Sea. Carbon dating of some of the artifacts found near the ancient coastline show variable ages, but none yet around 7600 years old. Many artifacts could not be raised with the expedition's equipment. The team also found shells of freshwater and saltwater creatures that, when dated, largely confirm the timing Ryan and Pitman set for the massive flood. Although it is early days, it appears that there was an apocalyptic flood north of Turkey that could have inspired the Mesopotamian and later Genesis account of a great flood. Whether or not the cumulative evidence will challenge Mesopotamia (or Egypt) as the cradle of Western civilization remains to be determined.

Search for Noah's ark

The familiar Bible story of Noah's Ark is not an original Hebrew story at all; it was taken over by the Hebrews from Mesopotamia and incorporated, with suitable emendations, in their own sacred canon; it is exactly the same tale as we find on tablets written before the time of Abraham, and not only the incidents but even much of the phrasing is identical.   Sir Leonard Woolley[169]

Notwithstanding growing scepticism regarding parts of the Genesis story in the nineteenth and twentieth centuries, the lure of finding evidence of the "single" flood and Noah's ark on the mountains of Ararat has been enticing.[170] Authentication of the

Bible was (and still is) a major preoccupation of many scholars, explorers and entrepreneurial businessmen. As early as 1902, a German boy and his uncle claimed to have seen the ark during an eight-day hike, but unfortunately nothing was found. In 1949, a US spy plane flew over mountains in northern Turkey and photographed what appeared to be the outline of an ancient vessel on the side of a glacier. On many occasions between 1952 and 1969, French explorer Fernand Navarra visited Mount Ararat and eventually found an old piece of wood thought to have belonged to the ark. The piece of wood was radiocarbon-dated some years later and found to be about 1000 years old.[171] The timber is now thought to be part of a religious memorial erected prior to the Muslim conquest to commemorate the landing site of the ark.[172]

In the 1960s, American businessman John Libi funded seven expeditions to Mount Ararat after seeing Noah's ark in a dream. Again, his attempt proved unsuccessful. In 1986, former US Apollo 15 astronaut and moon explorer James Irwin led another expedition in search of the ark, but he and his team were arrested by the Turkish authorities, who suspected that he was spying in a politically sensitive area.[173] In 1989, two people in an aircraft reportedly sighted the remains of Noah's ark on snow-capped Mount Ararat, but nothing was found above the timber line. In the same year, an interesting and highly controversial book was published called *The Ark of Noah,* in which author David Fashold reported the presence of a boat-shaped object near Mount Ararat.

Seeking authenticity, a few years later Fashold teamed up with Australian geologist Ian Plimer and, after visiting the site, Fashole was convinced by Plimer that the object was nothing more than a geological deposition that had formed millions of years ago.[174] Allen Roberts, an ordained Christian minister and fundamentalist creationist, remained unconvinced. He appears to have reproduced Fashold's diagram of the object and included it in his public speaking engagements and lectures, claiming that the structure was indeed part of Noah's ark.[175] In June 1997, Fashold and Plimer won an Australian Federal Court case against Roberts for infringement of copyright, but failed on the larger charge of misleading or deceptive conduct "in trade or commerce".[176]

In short, the chances of finding evidence of a "single" Hebrew flood of cataclysmic proportions and a biblical wooden ark measuring 300 cubits long (1 cubit is approximately 0.5 m) and 50 cubits wide with three decks 30 cubits high are small. The problem is compounded when you imagine that to fulfil its purpose the ark would have had to have contained some 30 million species ranging from the smallest of single cells to the largest of elephants (and including some 20 000 species of termites). There is also heated debate on where the ark actually rests.[177] Sites range from mountains in Turkey, Arabia, Armenia, Kurdistan and Iran, depending upon whether you are Christian, Jewish or Muslim.

Sumerian religion: the virtue of obedience

Their religion was boldly polytheistic and anthropomorphic. A multitude of testimonies about it, extraordinarily varied and difficult to penetrate, are preserved for us. They are from all periods of a long history but separated by large lacunae.

J. Bottero[178]

Religion: a social instrument to guide and control human activities

Religion in early Mesopotamia appears to have been a hierarchical organization of the gods in heaven, which closely matched the political organization of human beings on earth.[179] Religion in Sumer was an institution of social solidarity that provided a moral and practical means to guide and control human activities on earth. All sense-phenomena (the trees, birds, insects, wind, sea, sun, moon, and so on) were perceived as divine "personalities" with "powers".[180] As soon as a reed was taken from a marsh and crafted into a basket, a hut, a pipe, a pen or a musical instrument it came under the direct power of the reed goddess Nidaba.[181] It was Nidaba who produced the reeds, taught the herdsman his tunes and inspired the scribe to write his inventories, stories and poems.[182] The goddess's power only came into being as the basket, a hut, a pipe or pen was made; her job was to make it work well and fulfil its purpose.[183]

The Sumerians (and later Babylonians) believed that if the binding and mutual obligation between themselves and their gods were severed, all life would be destroyed and world order would return to chaos. Life was a continuous struggle to maintain the status quo, a fateful drama centring on the annual flood. The belief that the flood was a gift from the gods was sanctioned and perpetuated by the priests and king. In the Sumerian pantheon, there were at least 50 "great gods", seven "fate-decreeing gods" and hundreds of other gods, including a person's own personal gods (some 2000 gods have been listed, most with Sumerian names).[184] Below the lesser gods in the hierarchy was another class of supernatural hybrid beings (animals and personages).[185] These were evil spirits or daemons, who lurked in the streets at night bringing misfortune.[186] This basic pantheon design has many parallels to those in neighbouring Egyptian religion and in later Greek popular religion.

Even though nobody actually saw the gods, they were envisaged as being immortal and intelligent and having human-like or anthropomorphic features and behaviours; they planned and acted, ate and drank, married and raised families and were subject to other human passions and weaknesses.[187] The people of early Mesopotamia did not believe in the afterlife, as the following passage from the Epic of Gilgamesh indicates:

When the gods created mankind,
They gave them death.
But (endless) life they kept for themselves![188]

Assyriologists remind us that the early Mesopotamians had no words for heaven and hell, as in later Jewish traditions.[189] Neither did the early Mesopotamians believe in the transmigration of souls from one body to another, as in ancient Hindu cultures or in the later Orphic religions of archaic Greece. Upon death, the Sumerians believed that their spirits descended "below" to the netherworld.[190] To facilitate the journey, travel items such as food, sandals (or, if a king, a chariot), weapons, toiletries and jewellery were placed in grave coffins or tombs.[191]

Mythologized carriers of self: *ilu, istaru, lamassu* or *sedu*

There appear to have been four "guardian" spirits or souls individualized and mythologized in ancient Mesopotamia. This concept of personal spirits meant that every person could understand who he or she was as an individual and through prayer could seek protection from personal misfortune, illness or hardship. Beyond this, very little is known. According to Leo Oppenheim the two features uniting the four spirits were luck, and the world of daemons and the dead.[192] These four "guardian" spirits, Oppenheim writes, "are individualized and mythologized carriers of certain specific psychological aspects of one basic phenomenon, the realization of the self, the personality, as it relates the ego to the outside world and, at the same time, separates one from the other".[193]

The most frequently mentioned spirit in the Mesopotamian prayers was *ilu*; a person who had the *ilu* was a happy or lucky person. The idea appears to have been borrowed by the later Greeks, who used the word *daemon*.[194] Socrates, for example, was frequently seen in the marketplace talking to people about virtue and good, but also speaking to his friendly daemon (see Ch. 5). Good luck in Mesopotamia was attained through prayers and offerings to the gods. Daily prayer (with offerings) was also practised by the people in their homes, which in Old Babylonian times (after the Ur III period) included personal shrines.[195] People used a vast number of spells and incantations to promote a "binding" to their personal and patron gods, and in this way promoted a two-way harmony. One had to be vigilant in never taking these deities for granted and had to thank them at every opportunity otherwise one's personal life would suffer. The other protective spirits or souls were *istaru*, *lamassu* or *sedu*. The basic meanings of the four "guardian" spirits are summarized in Table 2.2.

The priesthood: linking the people to their gods

The temple priest's job in ancient Mesopotamia was to communicate with the gods and protect the world order by sanctioning the gods to prevent the evil forces looming beyond the organized borders.[196] As far as is known, no one would have ever dreamed of arguing with the priests or telling them they exercised superstitious nonsense. The temple priests also acted as the managers, keepers and mediators of knowledge. Secrecy played an important role in the acquisition of knowledge.[197] There is an old Zuni proverb: "Power told is power lost."

Table 2.2 The four "guardian" spirits or souls of early Mesopotamia (adapted from Oppenheim 1977: 198–206).

Ilu	This personal spirit or deity (male) imparted luck, happiness and good fortune to those who requested protection, and may form the basis of human spirituality.
Istaru	A companion spirit or deity (female) who was mentioned in prayers and linked to one's protection, fate or destiny. Oppenheim (1977) believes the term has some similarities with the Greek *tyche* (chance, luck or fate).
Lamassu	This protective spirit (female) was often mentioned in prayers referring to one's individual characteristics and aptitudes, and may be an extension of some external soul manifested in the likeness of the individual, and similar to the Egyptian concept of *ka* (see Ch. 3; Oppenheim 1977: 200). The term in Old Babylonian times was taken literally to mean "angel" and has been compared to the later Greek word *eidolon*, which means statue and likeness of an individual. *Lamassu* has also been compared to *angelos* of the New Testament (Acts 12:15), where the "angel" of Petrus appears looking and speaking like himself.
Sedu	A protective spirit who was the male counterpart of *lamassu*. In Akkadian, *sedu* is connected to the spirits of the dead or one's ancestors. The word may also refer to vitality and sexual potency. In the Old Testament *sedu* refers to idols, whereas in the Old Testament the term refers to daimons (or demons).

By cataloguing and learning about the gods' creation (and will), the temple priests could praise the gods when good fortune occurred and appease them when things went wrong. During and after a drought, famine or flood it was the high priests who determined the appropriate time for ritualistic ceremonies and sacrifices to the gods through prayer, magic and divination.[198]

An animal was often sacrificed in the temple as a substitute for man as the following liturgy explains: "The lamb is the substitute for humanity; he hath given up a lamb for his life, he hath given up a lamb's head for the man's head."[199] Most sacrifices were thought to serve as the gods' "meals". Another sacrifice was designed to renew the earth's fertility.[200] In short, the priests, in conjunction with the kings, were the authority and intellectual backbone of the Sumero-Babylonian city-states and responsible for people's knowledge of the gods.

Sumerian (and Babylonian) science and technology

> All their sciences were structured not according to axioms that were revealed and demonstrated, according to laws that were deduced and articulated, but they were based on accumulations of concrete and individual cases that were enumerated in the way of Lists.
>
> J. Bottero[201]

The early Mesopotamians were so successful at agriculture that specialist groups slowly began to develop within the city walls. These specialist groups, under the guidance of the priestly class, became the inventors, creators and sustainers of "civilized" life. Within their mythopoeic–religious mindset, the Sumero-Babylonians found better ways to count, weigh and measure; to tell the time and predict the future; to heal the sick and afflicted; and to work with metals, glass and ceramics. The early Mesopotamian quest for knowledge was mostly practical, not theoretical. It was strongly interwoven into their agricultural lifestyle of work, play, ritual, war and artistic endeavour. For our purposes, Sumero-Babylonian science and technology was *organized practical knowledge*.

Mathematical language

> Mesopotamian evidence affords the earliest glimpse into the interaction between metrology, the science of measurement (or approximation *par excellence*), and the exact sciences.
>
> M. A. Powell[202]

The first Institute of Standards

The Sumerian system of standards with units was revolutionary.[203] Imagine a craftsman using his fingers, palm or forearm to measure prescribed lengths of wood or stone for a building without some reference standard. Imagine the problem of employing hundreds of craftsmen using individual fingers, palms or arm lengths to map their fields, construct or repair their dykes, or erect their monumental temples with towering ziggurats. The "personal" cubit from the elbow to the middle finger was replaced with a standard measure of a length made out of either metal, rope or wood.[204] The Sumerians were also the first to engineer self-supporting arches, columns, ramps, inclined walkways, domes and tunnel-shaped vaults.[205]

The idea of standardization applied to any quantity such as weights and volumes.[206] Picture the confusion at the marketplace if silver was used as a unit of commodity, accounting or money exchange without some kind of standard. The first Sumerian "Institute of Standards" probably used reference weights made of hard stone.[207] A simple barrel shape was the most common, but weights shaped in the form of a duck, with its neck resting along its back, were also prevalent. Apparently there were harsh penalties for those who used false weights in conducting business. Beale and Carter claim there is a hint of standardization in the protoliterate Uruk period (4000–3200 BC),[208] but it was not until writing had been invented that the first Sumerian "Institute of Standards" was possible.[209] It would be nearly impossible to write an inventory if there were no concept of number, magnitude, order or form.

The need for mathematics

> Probably the single most impressive aspect of Mesopotamian mathematics is its use of algebraic logic with strong geometric overtones. Assessing its limitations is more difficult. Trigonometry is missing … It seems Mesopotamian mathematics remained essentially elementary, but the nature of our source material – tables and textbooks whose age of origin remains in doubt – will continue to make assessment of the outer limits of mathematical thought elusive.
>
> M. A. Powell[210]

A system of measures, units and standards is of no value without the fixed relations between them. Sumerian tablets show the basics of addition, subtraction, multiplication and division. In addition they had mathematical tables[211] with reciprocals, multiplications, squares and square roots, cubes and cube roots to help with calculations using quadratic equations and exponential functions.[212] The Babylonians in particular even applied the algebraic method to areas of geometry, something the early Greek philosophers never accomplished.

The Sumerians may have known that a triangle inscribed into a semicircle contained a right angle, and that the sum of the squares of the two shorter sides equals the square of the hypotenuse (Pythagoras's theorem).[213] This latter relation was known by the early Babylonians[214] and widely used around the end of the second millennium BC. The Babylonians also had an accurate value for pi (π, or the ratio of the circumference of a circle to its diameter) of 3⅛ (correct to about 0.6 per cent),[215] but they commonly rounded the value to 3.

The Sumerian sexagesimal number system

> Numerical terms – expressing some of "the most abstract ideas which the human mind is capable of forming", came only slowly into use.
>
> Adam Smith[216]

The Sumerians originated a number system called "sexagesimal". This system was a mixture of a decimal (base 10 system) and a base 60 system. Instead of using our present system of units in tens, the Sumerians used 1, 10, 60, 600, 3600 and so on.[217] Some of the numerical signs are presented in Figure 2.4.

The concept of zero was not known to the Sumerians, Egyptians or Greeks.[218] Instead of using a different symbol for each higher unit, the Sumerians used the same symbol but indicated its value *by its position*.[219] This was an ingenious step forwards. For example, the number 11 in our modern Arabic decimal system has a place value notation of $(1 \times 10) + 1$, and 311 has a place value notation of $(3 \times (10 \times 10)) + (1 \times 10) + 1$. In the Sumerian system, 1 followed by 1 was not 11 but $(1 \times 60) + 1 = 61$ and 3 followed by 1 followed by 1 was not 311 but $(3 \times (60 \times 60)) + (1 \times 60) + 1 = 10\,861$.[220] The Sumerians considered the number 60 a complete number assigned to the god Anu, and it was also their basis for expressing fractions.[221]

Figure 2.4 Sumerian numerical signs. The Sumerians originated a "sexagesimal" number system, which was a mixture of a decimal (base 10) system and a base 60 system: thus based on 1, 10, 60, 3600, 36 000, and so on. The signs shown were used by the Sumerians around 2500–2000 BC and were made with a square-ended stylus. Before this they were incised with a reed or wooden spike with rounded ends (not shown) (Kramer 1963:92).

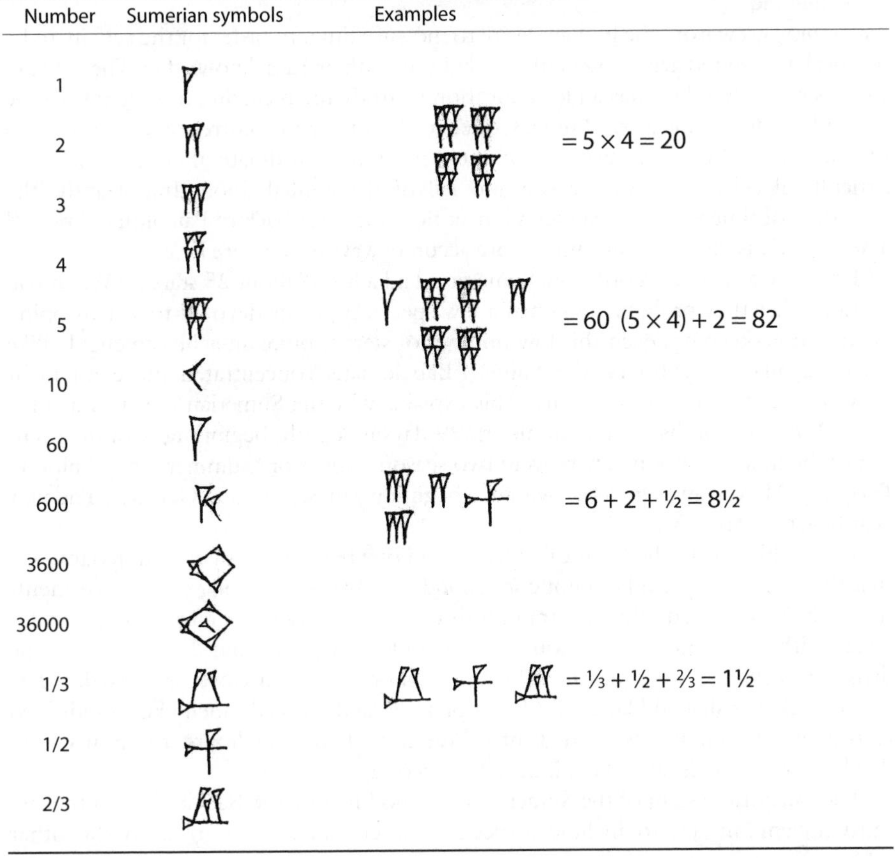

Number	Sumerian symbols	Examples
1		
2		$= 5 \times 4 = 20$
3		
4		
5		$= 60\ (5 \times 4) + 2 = 82$
10		
60		
600		$= 6 + 2 + \frac{1}{2} = 8\frac{1}{2}$
3600		
36000		
1/3		$= \frac{1}{3} + \frac{1}{2} + \frac{2}{3} = 1\frac{1}{2}$
1/2		
2/3		

The introduction of the unit 60 appears to have been the Sumerian attempt to unify their different systems of measures such as time-keeping, measuring and weighing.[222] The division of an hour into 60 minutes, a minute into 60 seconds and the circle into 360 degrees were all Sumerian inventions. Using this system the shift in position of a heavenly body could be measured in degrees or parts thereof, as astronomers do today. One degree is $\frac{1}{360}$ of the circuit around the sky; each degree is split into 60 minutes of the arc, and each minute into 60 seconds of the arc. Similarly, the number 360 can be divided by 12, 10, 9, 8, 6, 5, 4, 3 and 2 as opposed to the number 100, which can be divided by 10, 5, 4, and 2. This new mathematical language vastly improved time-keeping and marked the birth of astronomy and astrology.

Sumerian and Babylonian astronomy

Inquiry into the heavens, which took such diverse forms as celestial omens, horoscopes and descriptive and mathematical astronomy occupies a central place in the cultural and intellectual history of ancient Mesopotamia.   F. Rochberg[223]

Time-keeping
Astronomy grew from the human desire to measure time. In order for the activity to be practical, it required great observational skill and mathematical knowledge. The flat land with its clear blue skies was an ideal location to study the recurring movements of the heavenly bodies. A measure of time, sequence, duration and recurrence was essential to the Sumero-Babylonians because of their need to coordinate their religious and agricultural activities with the rise and fall of the annual flood. Importantly, the recording of time was not a Sumerian invention but dates back to Paleolithic times.[224] The Sumerians, however, invented more accurate ways to measure it.

From the available records, the Sumerians had a list of about 25 stars.[225] When you consider that they probably only had a few specialist priests devoted to star mapping beyond time-keeping, even this low number of stars is quite an achievement. Unlike their Egyptian neighbours, the Sumero-Babylonians concentrated more on lunar movements than solar movements. This explains why the Sumerian year was divided into 12 moon-months, with each month 29 days in length, beginning with the evening of the new full moon. There were two seasons: *emesh* or "summer", beginning in February–March; and *enten* or "winter", beginning in September–October. The new year began in April–May.[226]

The problem with the lunar calendar,[227] and one recognized by the Sumerians, was that the 12-month period did not correspond exactly with the solar year. Adjustments had to be made by adding an extra month to the calendar every few years. Their day began with sunset and was 12 double-hours in length (hence our 24-hour day). The divisions of the day were measured by a sundial or by a water clock or clepsydra. The water clock was shaped like a cylinder or prism[228] and worked much like a sand-filled egg-timer. The night was divided into three periods of four hours, the hours were divided into minutes, and the minutes into seconds.

The calendric system of the Sumerians was modified by the Babylonians in the late third millennium BC to include a week of seven days. In contrast to the other recurring celestial phenomena, the week does not correspond to any astronomical cycle and appears to have first been established for religious reasons.[229] The seven-day week was based on the subdivision of the moon-month of 28 days and calculated by dividing 28 days by the four lunar phases (new moon, first quarter, full moon, and last quarter). Of these 28 days, the 7th, 14th, 21st and 28th were special days where people had to refrain from some activities and observe rituals.[230] The day of each full moon bore the name *shapatu*, from which the Hebrew "Sabbath" was derived. The Sabbath was later applied to the last day of the week, a sacred rest day that was subsequently adopted by most Western cultures.[231]

The number seven, while not part of the sexagesimal system, had special significance in Sumer and Babylonia. The duration of the Sumerian flood was seven days, and the number seven was commonly used in Sumerian rituals and medical practices.[232] There were also seven planetary bodies (counting them in order from Earth were the Moon, Mercury, Venus, the Sun, Mars, Jupiter and Saturn).[233] Each of the seven planets was believed to be a powerful god who eventually became responsible for one day of the week. They were also used by the later Greco-Romans in the naming of their days of the week.[234]

Astrology

> This second-millennium astrology was limited to the interpretation of celestial omens, whereby a sign in the sky was associated with a terrestrial event, usually concerning the king or the country as a whole.　　　　　F. Rochberg[235]

The Sumero-Babylonians extended their celestial observations to include future predictions of the gods. Originally astrology meant the same as astronomy – "the knowledge of stars" – but as more knowledge was obtained, astrology later became restricted to the art of interpreting celestial events and predicting future events on earth.[236] Astronomers and astrologers initially were of the same group or, at the very least, worked very closely together in the main temples or the king's royal palace.[237]

Ancient astrology was intimately connected with religion and provided a channel of communication between the people and their gods.[238] The different phases of the moon, for example, influenced human health, vitality and sexual power; moonlight was thought to influence beauty, as well as insanity, hence our word "lunatic". Some of the ritual acts during a sacrifice were intended to prompt a god to exercise power to promote or prevent a future event.[239] The purpose of later Babylonian horoscopes was primarily to record the position of the seven known planets on the date of a birth.[240]

The importance attached to astrology is further illustrated from the hymnal narrative poems on two clay cylinders excavated from the city of Lagash (*c*.2130–2000 BC).[241] One of the poems was named "Gudea's dream" because it commemorated the actual construction of a temple in Lagash by Gudea (who ruled the city around 2120 BC). In his dream, Gudea found guidance from many gods. Nidaba, the goddess of writing and learning, was depicted holding a golden stylus and studying a clay tablet upon which the starry heavens were drawn. Nidaba directed Gudea in the dream to build the temple in accordance with the position of the "holy stars".[242]

Astrology seems to have reached its zenith in southern Babylonia around 600 BC.[243] The Neo-Babylonians or Chaldeans (c.884–539 BC)[244] provided elaborate mathematical descriptions for the motions of the sun, moon and planetary systems.[245] Their descriptive charts were later referred to by the Greeks as the Zodiac (the Greek word *zodiakos* means "circle of animals"), which was a circle divided into 12 equal parts of 30°.[246] Each 30° part of the circle was given a "star" sign that named the star constellations in each quadrant as seen from the earth.[247] Similar systems were developed by the Egyptians, Indians and Chinese and are still widely practised in the West today.[248]

Medicine

Mystery, magic, and medicine: in the beginning they were one and the same … For primitive, or ancient, medicine is the expression of a philosophy that grows from the natural reactions of all ignorant men placed in hazardous surroundings.

H. W. Haggard[249]

Sumerian medicine

Like every other facet of Sumerian life, medicine was closely interwoven with religion, magic and astrology.[250] The kind of treatment depended upon the severity of the injury or disease. The first physician in Sumer was a practitioner named Lulu; reference to him was discovered by Sir Leonard Woolley on a tablet excavated at Ur dating back to around 2700 BC.[251] Earlier Sumerian medical texts do exist but they refer to doctors of animals such as a "doctor of donkeys" or a "doctor of oxen", with no mention of human subjects or specific names of a practitioner.[252]

One of the oldest Sumerian medical texts lists some 145 medical cases, but the tablet is so badly damaged that only the remedies, not the specific ailments, have been recovered.[253] Each of the prescriptions on this tablet begins with a list of ingredients, followed by a method of how to pulverize and mix the ingredients with a liquid to create a paste. Directions of how to apply the paste to the sick part of the body are given. Oil was often used as a carrier to prevent the paste from permanently sticking to the body. One prescription included use of an alkali plant (*Salicornia fruticosa*), salt, cassia oil and powdered asafoetida together with other ingredients.[254] These were mixed, after which fine beer and boiling water were added. The solution was sprinkled on the patient and was followed by a rub with tree oil.

Another prescription directs the pharmacist to pulverize the fur of an animal and the skin of a water snake, add the root of myrtle, alkali ash, barley, powdered resin, kusibu plant and water, mix all the ingredients then boil. This mixture was filtered and the filtrate poured on to the patient, followed again by a rub with tree oil.[255] The Sumerians believed that the use of oils extracted from botanicals would assist in the cure and this may have been their substitute for our modern antiseptic agents.

Sumerologists stress that the oldest documented medical procedures were free from magical spells, incantations and lamentations.[256] On these tablets, common medical complaints such as colds, upset stomachs, cuts and abrasions seem to be considered part of normal human existence and required only "household" herbal remedies, such as potions, bandages, cataplasms (pastes made of purified clay and other oils), suppositories, enemas and purgatives. In contrast, more life-threatening illnesses were considered to be of supernatural origin and could only be treated by appeasing the god(s) in question. The Sumerians believed that when a particular god became angry he or she could project something into the body of a human victim. By this method the gods could inflict suffering and misfortune upon their human servants on earth. This idea dominated much of ancient medical thinking for thousands of years, from Sumer to Homeric Greece.[257]

In more severe cases, evil spirits were removed by elaborate exorcisms, sacrifices and rituals carried out by the most powerful priesthood magicians, astrologers and diviners.[258] The diviners were specialists who solicited omens from the gods and interpreted the signs sent by the gods. One common practice was to foretell the course of a disease by inspecting the liver of a sacrificial animal (often a sheep),[259] performing a rite in close proximity to the human patient, and, after consulting a medical tablet or handbook, providing the diagnosis.[260] In contrast to exorcists, diviners did not generally belong to the priesthood but were attached to the king's palace, local governments or army.[261]

Babylonian medicine

> While Mesopotamian medicine is among the best documented in the ancient world, and is of interest in its own right, it cannot be claimed that it was a precursor to the "scientific" medicine now practiced in most parts of the world.   R. D. Biggs[262]

Most of these Babylonian medical texts are from the late third and second millennium BC but still contain Sumerian words and phrases.[263] Most Babylonian tablets recorded minor everyday ailments and their cures. The following account provides the description and cure of a patient with a burning stomach:[264]

> If a man's stomach is hot, you shall bray (grind) together the seven drugs [names were not identifiable]. Then strain, steep in beer, bring to a boil, strain again, and cool. Add barley water and sprinkle with rose water. Introduce this brew into his anus [by means of an enema] and the sick man will recover.[265]

The role of the Babylonian physician[266] (and presumably Sumer) was more as an artist than a priest or magician/astrologer. The physician's tools were botanical, zoological and mineralogical, with only a few incantations and conjurations.[267] The *materia medica* used included salt, river bitumen, crude oil, wool, milk, turtle shell and water snake. By far the major ingredients were botanical – thyme, mustard, plum tree, pears, figs, willow, fur and pine – and processed products like beer, wine and vegetable oil.[268] Regardless of skill, the physician's profession was not endowed with high social status as in modern Western society. There is one cuneiform passage that places the physician at the same level as the innkeeper and the baker.[269]

Surgery in Babylonian times (unlike in ancient Egypt) was limited. While physicians were not subject to legal sanctions in the normal course of their work, a surgical operation was a different matter.[270] Operations were hazardous events and subject to the strictest code of ethics and regulations.[271] The most famous document containing the laws and penalties for human misconduct is the Code of

Hammurabi,[272] named after King Hammurabi (*c*.1810–1750 BC), who ruled Babylon in the first half of the eighteenth century BC.[273] The basic principle behind Hammurabi's Code was to protect the public against social injustices; "an eye for an eye", "a tooth for a tooth", and "a limb for a limb".[274] One Babylonian law pertaining to the practice of medicine states: "If the doctor shall treat a gentleman and shall open an abscess with a bronze knife and shall preserve the eye of the patient, he shall receive ten sheckels of silver. If the patient is a slave, his master will pay two sheckels of silver." However, "If the doctor shall open the abscess with a bronze knife and shall kill the patient or shall destroy the sight of the eye, his hands shall be cut off." In the case of the death of a slave the doctor should "replace the slave with a new slave".[275]

Such an extreme system of laws governing surgical medicine, if widespread, undoubtedly would have impeded medical progress in the fields of medicine, anatomy, biology and physiology.

Chemical arts and crafts: harnessing the mystery of fire

> What we do not know, and probably can never learn, is how principles from one science were transferred and applied in another, although we can be certain that this did happen.
>
> M. A. Powell[276]

The chemical arts and crafts probably originated from experimenting with fire. Imagine the mystery surrounding the chemical conversion of a powdery green or blue ore into a bright red copper metal. Or imagine the addition of two or more compounds ending in a spectacular explosion; a dramatic colour change or transformations from a solid to a liquid and back again by simply changing the temperature. Chemical phenomena must have conjured up the most wondrous explanations involving the fire god Gibil.

Metallurgy, commodity exchange and coinage

Copper metallurgy dates as far back as 6500 BC, although most of the metalwork activity in Sumer appears in the mid-fourth millennium.[277] The metals used were copper, tin, gold, silver, electrum, lead and iron. Sumerian metallurgy appears to have developed from a combination of five major discoveries and observations:

- that a kiln furnace was capable of extraordinary high temperatures, believed to be in excess of 1100 °C;[278]
- that some metals like copper were capable of being shaped with hammering;
- that certain metals were capable of being melted but only at high temperatures (the melting point of copper is 1083 °C);
- that metals could be extracted from their native ores[279] by removing the non-metallic elements; and
- that metals could be mixed or alloyed in the molten state to produce a new metal with different properties.[280]

Alloying involved extracting two or more metals, mixing and annealing, then casting into a variety of moulds for farming, cooking and other domestic purposes. The alloy bronze is a mixture of copper and tin and much harder than either metal by itself, and was known to the Sumerians.[281] Gold was often referred to as gold dust, suggesting its source was from alluvial deposits.[282] Gold was used for jewellery and adorning statuettes, and it was also alloyed with silver to produce a pale-yellow metal known in later Greek times as *electrum*.[283] Silver had at least three purposes in Sumer/Babylonia: as a standard for accounting; as a medium of exchange; and, eventually, for currency.[284]

The monetary value of a commodity is thought to have been measured against some standard of grain.[285] Later, copper was used as a medium for exchange and this metal was followed by silver. A money economy using silver alone was not in use during the fourth and third millennia.[286] The use of silver for exchange was largely accomplished by weight, and in the city of Ur they used rings of silver with standardized weight in units of *minas* and *shekels*.[287]

In later Babylonian times the silver content of currency was standardized, with the minimum content assured by the stamp "GIN".[288] It was a crime for a person to melt the silver pieces marked "GIN". One shekel was equivalent to one GIN (about 8 g).[289] Silver manufacture and distribution were controlled or overseen by the priesthood. It may seem odd given their amazing genius, but Mesopotamia as a country did not embrace the simplicity brought about by coinage.[290] Coinage in the conventional meaning of money was invented in the Near East in Lydia (now western Turkey).

Why "natural" science never appeared in Sumer

> As they were polytheists and saw the world as an enchanted place teeming with gods and goddesses, it was through myth and in reference to deities that they developed solutions to the problems with which they were faced … Mythmaking was an intellectual device that could express both symbolically and in concrete terms a conceptual system that considered the political and the social order as well as nature and the cosmos. Myth conferred validity on institutions, practices, or customs through their power to organise experience.
>
> J. J. Glassner[291]

Sumerian science remained a "list", science with long lists of plants, animals, metals and stones. The lists were written in the form of appearance, type of material and their practical uses.[292] In addition, the Sumerians classified things by "clustering" them into pairs. In agriculture, the list pairs were summer and winter, cattle and grain, bird and fish, tree and reed, silver and bronze, pick-axe and plough, shepherd and farmer.[293] In cosmology there were lists of male and female gods involved with the creations; heaven and counter-heaven (netherworld); wet (water) and dry (earth); and life and death. The method of describing reality as a system of opposites helped the Sumero-Babylonians explain order in a world of change. The same "clustering" was also apparent in ancient Egypt and much later in Presocratic and classical Greece, demonstrating a possible exchange and borrowing of ideas in these early times.

Notwithstanding the importance of list and clustering classifications to systematize knowledge, the process falls short of "natural" science because it lacks the conceptual formulation of more impersonalized relationships among the phenomena. A possible exception might be Babylonian astronomy, which was by far the most advanced of any ancient culture.[294] A form of objectivity[295] seems to have been developed very early in the sense that the Babylonians separated themselves from the celestial objects they observed. However, the conceptual *framework* from which they developed their astronomical knowledge was far removed from that employed in "natural" science today, as there was no concept of the physical object, or concept of physical relations to explain sensible phenomena. The Sumero-Babylonians used their astronomical observations and mappings to tell the time and to drive their myth-based astrology, not for "natural" science. All their explanations and inventions started and ended with their gods as the master governors or controllers of the universe.

The Sumero-Babylonians therefore appear to have had no equivalent term for wider "nature" meaning the "physical world". Although Oppenheim suggested that the meaning for *simtu* (Sumerian *nam*), one of the four Mesopotamian protective souls (or spirits), could be associated with Greek *physis* (*natura* in Latin) as the "nature of things", there was no word in the Mesopotamian language for "nature" meaning the "physical" world. One meaning for *simtu* was that it originated *"from an agency endowed with the power to act and to dispose"*.[296] The Sumero-Babylonian god Ninurta, god of thunderstorms and the plough, declared that the *simtu* of all precious stones was their intrinsic qualities, which Oppenheim interpreted as "the *nature* of these stones".[297] As we shall see in Chapter 4, *physis* in Homeric Greece also meant "origin" or "growth", but later, in Presocratic Greece, it came to mean the "physical world".[298] The physical world in ancient Greece comprised physical objects and was increasingly distanced from the gods or other divine agencies.

Similarly, the term "nature" appears to have no equivalent to the "physical world" in ancient Hebrew or early Christian literature. Theologian and scientist Arthur Peacocke believes this is because Greek *physis* relates to something centred in itself, which diminishes its dependence on the creator-god.[299] Instead, the New Testament uses the word "creation" and the verb "create". Peacocke argues that Greek "physis" implies *subsistence and autonomy* whereas "creation" possesses a more theological *sourcehood and dependence* on God.[300] However, some degree of caution should be exercised with this kind of analysis. Lacking a word by itself in either the Sumero-Babylonian or ancient Hebrew literature is not sufficient evidence to conclude that a people were not aware of materiality or physicality. Words and concepts do not map easily in the obscure and often fragmentary extant ancient literature. In ancient times, there is no word for religion but we know from the Sumero-Babylonian writings, art and adornments that these people were highly religious and bound to their gods.

Despite the caution, it is difficult to imagine how the Sumero-Babylonians could have invented a concept like the physical object and "natural" science given their highly mythopoeic-religious mindset and worldview. Their intellectual framework appeared to be more practical than theoretical. Sense-phenomena with divine "supernatural" powers and manifestations were not to be tampered with outside the religious directives from the priesthood. Everything in the universe, including human civilization and all its extraordinary products, belonged to the realm of the gods, not the people. We shall see a similar worldview in ancient Egypt, but with a fascinating twist.

Do not raise your voice in the house of god / He abhors shouting;
Pray by yourself with a loving heart / Whose every word is hidden.
He will grant your needs / He will accept your offerings.
Libate for your father and mother / Who are resting in the valley;
When the gods witness your action / They will say: "Accepted."

Maxims of Ani[1]

CHAPTER 3

LIFE AMONG THE GODS, PART II:
ancient Egyptians – optimism and opportunity

Introduction

Concerning Egypt itself ... there is no country that possesses so many wonders, nor
any that has such a number of works which defy description.   Herodotus[2]

Most of us have grown up with the wonders of ancient Egypt. They were first
popularized in the West by Greek historian Herodotus, who lived in the fifth century
BC. He was so captivated with what he learned in Egypt that, on return to his home in
Asia Minor, he read what was to become his famous "history" to the general public.
They showed little interest, so a despondent Herodotus moved to Athens, where his
stories were more warmly embraced. A few years later, the Athenian citizens awarded
him a prestigious prize of ten talents (about $15 000) for his literary achievements.[3]

Over the years the Egyptian way of life and their monumental architecture have
captivated Western imagination. This chapter explores this fascination by examining
their cultural ethos and worldview; their society's structure; and the role myth,
religion and science played in shaping their thinking. As in Mesopotamia, the world of
the Egyptians was a world of gods and powers, where the individual always surrendered to the will of the social organization. Despite this common mindset, there
were major differences in daily life, creation stories, concepts of life and death, science,
medicine and technology.

Ancient Egypt: the "Black Land"

Ancient Egypt was named by its people Kemi(t) or Chemi(t),[4] which literally means
"Black Land", from the colour of the sediment deposited after the river floods.[5] The
physical geography of Egypt afforded the Egyptians great prosperity and protection
for many millennia. The Egyptians nestled along the Nile River in between the
forbidding deserts to the east and west, mountain ranges to the south and the

Mediterranean Sea to the north (Fig. 3.1). Upper Egypt (valley proper) was known as *ta-shema*, "the land of the *shema* or reed", and Lower Egypt (pastoral triangular delta) was known as *ta-mehu*, "the land of the papyrus plant".[6] Upper and Lower Egypt were so-named because the Nile flowed from the south to the north (Upper → Lower), which is why the Egyptian word "to go south" meant "to go upstream".[7]

The Nile River,[8] one of the world's longest rivers, winds its way from central Africa to the Mediterranean Sea. Every year for over ten thousand years it has overflowed its banks from the high summer monsoon rainfalls in Ethiopia and the East African Plateau.[9] The water level began to rise in late June or early July (beginning at the summer solstice), reached its maximum at Cairo towards the end of September and subsided in November.[10] The rich alluvium silt that reached the 15 000 km² northern triangular delta was ideally suited for agriculture (80 per cent clay and 20 per cent sand).[11] Because of the extraordinary amount of silt, the Egyptians referred to the Nile as the river of the earth not of the heavens. The distinction implies the river itself was not a god but a manifestation of a god.[12] The Nile river valley and its annual flood was the Egyptian's lifeline for over 3000 years.

Figure 3.1 Ancient Egypt can be visualized as a vibrant green strip of land on average 16 km wide running some 1210 km in a south–north direction along the Nile river valley. The desert on either side formed a natural barrier against invasions for over 3000 years. Three principal cities of ancient Egypt were Thebes, Memphis (biblical Noph) and Heliopolis (biblical On). Thebes was located in the heart of Upper Egypt (southern Egypt) and Memphis in Lower Egypt (23 km from present-day Cairo). Founded around 3000 BC, Memphis was the capital city of the Old Kingdom. Thebes was the southern religious capital of the New Kingdom. Heliopolis, located about 10 km northeast of Cairo, was a famous religious city of Lower Egypt. Heliopolis was so named by the Greeks because it was the home of Egyptian sun worship.

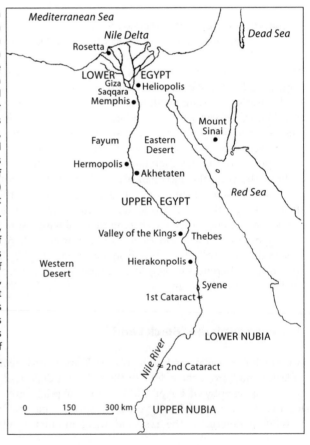

Beginnings of Egyptian archaeology

In the eighteenth century very little, if anything, was known of predynastic Egypt. The landmark event that changed all this was Napoleon Bonaparte's (1769–1821) sea invasion of northern Egypt in 1797–98.[13] Napoleon took with him a scientific team of geographers, mineralogists, botanists and artists whose job it was to record all flora, fauna and history. Napoleon's military staff called the scientific team "the donkeys", but as it turned out they were essential in establishing Egyptian archaeology and provided the West with an important link that opened a window into Egypt's past.

Following Napoleon's crushing military defeat in 1798 by the British naval commander Lord Horatio Nelson (1758–1805), the scientific team was permitted to remain in Egypt until 1802. The team founded the famous French Institute of Egyptian Antiquities in Cairo.[14] One of their greatest discoveries was the Rosetta Stone,[15] a black basalt stele bearing three different scripts: Greek, Demotic and Egyptian hieroglyphs. The stele was accidently discovered in 1799 by a French working party which was rebuilding a fort at Rosetta near Alexandria.[16] It provided the key to unlocking one of the greatest Egyptian mysteries: their hieroglyphic language.

In the decades following, large numbers of opportunistic travellers and collectors visited Egypt in search of fame and fortune. Egyptology became a popular pursuit for the rich and famous. In an effort to preserve Egyptian antiquity, a Museum and Antiquities Service of Egypt formed in 1858. Its members, with the help of many distinguished scholars from all around the world, were instrumental in transforming the field of Egyptology from the collection of a few bits and pieces to the highly systematized knowledge-seeking venture it is today.[17] A summary of Egyptian prehistory and civilization is presented in Table 3.1.

Table 3.1 Summary of Egyptian prehistory and civilization. The chronology was adapted and modified from Baines & Malek (1984: 8–9), Shafer (1991: 201–3) and Shaw & Nicholson (1995: 89, 159, 226).

c.7500 BC	Early people of unknown origin.
c.5000 BC	Earliest Neolithic settlements in Lower Egypt (c.5200 BC) in the Faiyum (60 km from Cairo). Predynastic **Badarian** culture in Upper Egypt at Asyut (c.5000–c.4000 BC) and wider spread. **Naqada I** (Amratian) culture (c.4500–c.3500 BC) to the south.
c.3500–3110 BC	Building of ancient Egypt: **Naqada II** (3500–3300 BC) and **Naqada III** (Gerzean A) (3300–3110 BC). Both cultures spread across the entire river valley. Possibility of Mesopotamian influence in Late-predynastic period. Writing – Narmer Palette (c.3100 BC).
c.3110–2665 BC	**Early Dynastic period**. Egyptian civilization reached high maturity.
c.2664–2155 BC	**Old Kingdom**
c.2040–1640 BC	**Middle Kingdom**
c.1550–1070 BC	**New Kingdom**
c.1070–332 BC	**Late period.** Conquered by the Persians in 525 BC (~200 years of Persian rule). Camels first used in Egypt (c.650 BC).
c.332 BC–30 BC	Hellenization of Egypt under Ptolemies.
c.30 BC–AD 395	**Greco-Roman period**

The Egyptian people and their lifestyle

Predynastic Egypt (10 000–3110 BC)

10 000–5000 BC

Archaeologists know very little about who occupied the Nile valley between about 10 000 BC and 7500 BC. Low population numbers, and the accumulation of silt and the shifting of the Nile bed have obliterated the early human activity.[18] These early people appear to have lived along the banks of the Nile in mud or reed huts. They dressed in animal skins, and fished and hunted along the Nile and in the dense forests that fringed the river valley.

By 5000 BC, a wave of people migrated into the valley from southern Arabia and eastern Africa.[19] The earliest farming cultures developed in Badari, a southern town located southeast of Asyut (Badarian culture), and in the area of Fayum (Al-Faiyum), located in northern Upper Egypt about 110 km southwest of Cairo.[20] Egypt was eventually divided into the south (Upper) and north (Lower) (see Fig. 3.1).[21] There is little information on the different political organizations of the two regions.[22]

4500–3500 BC

A few centuries later, another wave of immigrants entered the Nile valley, but this time from Asia.[23] These peoples were also farmers and responsible for a higher small-scale village culture known as Naqada (Naqada was a town located on the west bank of the Nile in Upper Egypt just north of Karnak) (Fig. 3.1): divided into Naqada I and Naqada II. Unlike the older Badarian culture, Naqada I culture spread over much of southern Upper Egypt. They domesticated cattle and donkeys, and used mud bricks to build homes. Decorated white pottery, war maces, bone figurines of women and artistic and refined stonecutting of limestone, granite and basalt all characterized the Naqada I culture.[24] Linguistically, the peoples of Naqada are believed to be of Semitic descent, but the evidence is far from convincing.[25]

Most archaeologists believe the Naqada II culture was locally developed, possibly from Mesopotamian roots.[26] Egyptian mud-brick architecture (e.g. the Great Tomb of Naqada), cylinder seals (excavated at Naqada), and the famous Egyptian slate palettes and stone mace heads with votive (or dedicative) inscriptions and recessed and panelled brick are unmistakably Mesopotamian in design.[27] Given the distance of about 1450 km east to west between Egypt and Mesopotamia, the question is not whether exchange occurred, but how much. A major route is believed to be via Syria and Palestine.

3500–3110 BC

By 3000 BC, Egypt was divided into agricultural districts called *nomes* formed under the influence of the Naqada II and III[28] cultures. Each *nome* had its own civil government, social traditions and centre of worship, much like a "mini" Sumerian city-state.[29] Each "town" was located on the highest ground to protect it from the rising waters during the flood, and was separated by boundary stones. The population of Late-predynastic Egypt has been estimated to be around 100 000 to 200 000 people.[30] If Herodotus's estimate of 20 000 *nomes* in Egypt is correct there were, on average, 300 people per town or district.[31]

The Egyptians were a very mixed group of Caucasoid (light-coloured skin) and Negroid (dark-skinned) people who spoke an Afro-Asiatic tongue.[32] Their art reveals a "dynastic race" depicted as slender, dark-haired individuals with working men wearing loincloths, and women wearing long sheaths with wide shoulder straps usually attached just below their breasts.[33] It appears that children wore no clothes until adolescence.[34]

Pharaonic Egypt: unification and birth of a nation

No high Egyptian civilization existed in the middle to late fourth millennium BC. There was no hieroglyphic script and little or no metallurgy (with the exception of perhaps copper). Around 3110 BC, the Upper and Lower Kingdoms[35] were united. Three main factors were involved in the unification process:

- coordinated spread of uniform culture under one Pharaonic rule;
- synchronization of religious statesmanship; and
- centralization of military power.

The unification of Egypt brought about a new social optimism. In a few centuries, the Egyptian culture changed from a subsistence economy to a grain surplus and trade economy.[36] Between the Old and Middle Kingdoms the population increased from about two million to three million.[37] The people had a greater sense of autonomy, stability and permanence. In contrast to the people of Sumer, the Egyptians were not citizens of a state but nationals under pharaonic rule.[38]

The word "pharaoh" is the Hebrew construct of the Egyptian *Per-a'o*, meaning "the great house". It was originally applied to the seat of government at the royal palace but later came to apply to the king himself.[39] All authority was derived from the gods, and since the pharaoh was a self-proclaimed god, all power belonged to him. It was not the "divine" nature of the king himself that held the country together, but the people's belief that the *divine nature of society and its well being* were expressed through the king.[40]

The Pharaoh's power as *god incarnate as king* can be read in the words of Egyptian King Ramesses III (*c*.1184–1153 BC):

Give heed to my utterances / hearken to them.
I speak to you / I make you aware
That I am the son of Re [sun god] / who issued from his body.
I sit upon his throne rejoicing / since he established me as king
as lord of this land.
My councils are good / my plans come to pass.
I protect Egypt / I defend it.[41]

Again, this self-proclamation was very different from the power of the rulers of Mesopotamia, who considered themselves divine *representatives* of their gods, *never* the gods themselves.

The job of the Egyptian pharaoh was to maintain and uphold the social and world order or *ma'at*. The *ma'at* was both an abstract principle and a goddess (Ma'at, daughter of the sun god).[42] The reward for a person supporting the pharaoh was success in life and the afterlife after judgement. The divine link from the gods to pharaoh to the people was ensured through a highly prescribed personal and community ritual, which will be discussed later. Below the pharaoh and the priests were the royal traders and soldiers; next in line came the shepherds, farmers and peasants; and finally the slaves (mostly prisoners of war).[43] The peasants who worked in the fields gave a portion of their growing crops to the government as taxes. Genesis (47:24) tells us that a fifth of all the food was grown to support the pharaonic government.

The Egyptian outlook: optimistic yet conservative

The Egyptians' outlook on life differed from that of the Sumerians. A glass of water was half-full not half-empty, or at least, this was the impression the Egyptians portrayed. They spent more time worshipping and requesting their gods *to act on their behalf,* rather than supplicating themselves, as appeared in Sumer. However, on a deeper level, the Egyptians remained "cautiously" optimistic in an ever-changing world that in one season could produce bumper crops and in another death and destruction. In addition, the Egyptians had a superior national "confidence" and considered all foreigners barbarous, uninitiated and backward. The following story told by a Syrian prince reflects Egyptian superiority:

> For (the imperial god) Amon founded all lands. He founded them, but first he founded the land of Egypt, from which thou has come. For skilled work came forth from it to reach this place where I am, and teaching came from it to reach this place where I am.[44]

There was also more of an "equal opportunity" social mobility in Egypt than Mesopotamia, because a son was not bound by law to follow his father's occupation.[45] The most talented individuals were selected for a given profession and provided the population with a very progressive system for continued learning and self-improvement within the boundaries set down by the pharaoh and the priesthood officials.[46]

The gift of the Nile

Egypt's success can be traced to the taming of the Nile River. The Nile provided the Egyptians with water for drinking, agriculture and a means of transportation in a culture that appears to have made little use of the wheel.[47] Free access to the river meant that the Egyptian traders could travel to Mediterranean countries and barter their goods for commodities. Unlike the Sumerians, who built canals *above* their growing fields, the Egyptians ingeniously devised a system of dykes to regulate water flow and let the force of the Nile do all the work. The Egyptians were so successful at damming and releasing water that only about 10 per cent of the total Nile floodwater reached the Mediterranean Sea during the months of June, July and August.

The average height of the flood at its peak was around 6 m.[48] The Egyptians measured the height of the flood using a "Nilometer": a vertical gauge made of a series of lines carved into natural rocks or the stone walls of their monumental buildings. Nilometers with graduated lines in cubits have been found at Memphis, Luxor and Edfu.[49] Late period texts (712–332 BC) reveal that the preferred flood height was 16 cubits (6.5 m).[50]

Above 16 cubits, flood damage was imminent and below about 12 cubits (4.9 m), famine would occur in the upcoming year.[51] This reinforces again the fine balance between life and death along the Nile valley in ancient Egypt.

Hieroglyphic writing

Independent invention or imported from the Near East?

Writing helped shape Egypt into a single nation. No matter how good a country's damming or irrigation skills were, without written communication there would be little or no scope for advancement beyond small agricultural towns. The invention of phonetic writing was attributed to the Egyptian god Thoth. Writing began as pictographic signs and developed into a new ideographic script sometime around 3100 BC.[52] It is not known whether the Egyptians invented writing independently or borrowed the idea from the Sumerians.[53]

The "import" hypothesis is partially supported by the finding that no developmental stage of writing has been uncovered in predynastic Egypt.[54] Hieroglyphs appeared to be fully developed during the final stages of the predynastic Naqada III culture on funerary artifacts from Abydos.[55] Whether hieroglyphs were an independent invention in Egypt is unknown because the textual evidence is scanty. Most modern Egyptian scholars have never thought the Egyptians had priority over phonetic writing, but the possibility can't be excluded either.

Hieroglyphic, hieratic and demotic scripts

Hieroglyphs are those "sacred carvings graven on stone" of temple walls, public monuments and the pharaohs' tombs.[56] The first recorded use of the word "hieroglyph" is attributed to Greek historian Diodorus Siculus of Agyrium (c.80 BC) who wanted to separate the ancient Egyptian carvings from the local script used in the Greco-Roman times.[57]

Hieroglyphs, like cuneiform writing, express mental images such as a tree or a bird as ideas that also stand for sounds of speech.[58] The Egyptian signs had consonantal sound value (words with only two or three consonants) but no vowels; whereas Sumerian cuneiform writing possessed syllabic value (one consonant plus one vowel for each sign) giving its "agglutinative" qualities.[59] The Egyptian script had an alphabet that contained some 24 individual signs for consonant sounds, which allowed greater flexibility in the language. A consonant-based alphabet and its elaborate pictorial character was the novelty behind hieroglyphs.[60]

Hieroglyphic script was not the only script in Egypt. Two other shorthand versions, "hieratic" (c.3200 BC) and "demotic" (or "enchorial", i.e. "local script", c.700 BC), were employed for literature and everyday record-keeping in business, but only hieroglyphs were used for religious or monumental/ornamental writings.[61] The hieroglyphic, hieratic and demotic scripts survived for over 3000 years until the later Christian rulers outlawed their use.[62] The hieroglyphic script ceased to be understood after about AD 250.[63] All three scripts were replaced by a Coptic script (Coptic being the language of Christian Egypt), which was an adaptation of the Greek alphabet (24 letters plus seven Egyptian hieratic characters).[64]

Writing on paper

In addition to writing on stone and clay, the Egyptians wrote on paper fashioned from the inner pith of the papyrus plant (*Cyperus papyrus*).[65] The word "paper" is derived from the Greek *papyros* (Latin *papyrus*), possibly from *pa-per-aa*, the "material of Pharaoh".[66] The Greeks also called papyrus *byblos*,[67] and a strip of *byblos* was known as a *byblion* (or *biblion*), from which the Bible derived its name. Papyrus paper was prepared by laying longitudinal strips side by side to a required width, then placing another layer of strips at right angles across the first for added strength.[68] The strips and layers were then pasted together using glue possibly prepared from the glutinous material of the papyrus plant mixed with water.[69] Any roughness was smoothed out using ivory or a smooth shell and the sheet was dried under heavy pressure. The completed sheets (up to 20 sheets) were then attached to each other to create rolls of scapus or paper.[70] Papyrus paper had the advantage of being easy to transport from place to place, unlike carvings on heavy rock or cumbersome clay tablets. The major problem was the paper's fragility and susceptibility to dampness, which explains why the best preserved scripts have been found in dry desert tombs.[71]

The Rosetta Stone: the key to hieroglyphic decipherment

The decipherment of hieroglyphs, like cuneiform writing, is a fascinating detective story. The solution was found by deciphering the inscriptions on the black basalt commemorative Rosetta Stone.[72] The inscriptions were in two languages (Egyptian and Greek) and three scripts (hieroglyphic, demotic and Greek).[73] The hieroglyphic carvings were located at the top (14 lines survived), popular demotic in the middle (32 lines), and Greek at the bottom.[74] Greek was included because it was the language of the ruling Ptolemic government during the Hellenistic period. The major difficulty was how to decipher the hieroglyphic "carvings".

The first clues came from independent scholars: the arabist Silvestre de Sacy (1758–1838), the Swedish archaeologist David Akerblad and English scientist and part-time Egyptian enthusiast Thomas Young (1773–1829).[75] It was De Sacy who drew attention to the different characters written in demotic and Akerblad who transliterated some of the Greek names and produced a 16-letter demotic alphabet. However, Thomas Young attacked the problem from another direction. Young cleverly questioned the validity of the long-held assumption that *hieroglyphic* = *ideographic* and *demotic* = *alphabetic*. Through exacting perseverance, Young correctly identified the names Ptolemy and Cleopatra in both demotic and Greek. In the twentieth century, Sir Wallis Budge (1857–1934), curator of Egyptian and Assyrian antiquities at the British Museum, wrote about Young's achievements:

> Young came to the conclusion that if a foreign conqueror of a certain country caused inscriptions commemorating his conquest to be drawn up in the native language of that country, and that language was written with pictorial characters similar to the Egyptian hieroglyphs, the scribes would, in writing the conqueror's name, make use of the PHONETIC values of a number of pictorial characters without any regard for the actual meanings of these characters as pictures.[76]

Unfortunately for Young, his discovery was soon eclipsed by French Egyptologist Jean François Champollion (1790–1832). Champollion had also begun with the assumption that *the hieroglyphs were not ideograms, but phonetic.*[77] Champollion recognized also that the sounds of 12 hieroglyphic signs on the Rosetta Stone were part of an alphabet itself. He deduced the hieroglyphic signs in the names of Cleopatra and Ptolemy. From this amazing connection he was able to transliterate the hieroglyphs from the Greek names. The names Cleopatra and Ptolemy provided the phonetic value that he transcribed from Greek to demotic and the hieroglyphs.

On 27 September 1822, Champollion announced his discovery in a letter to the French Academy of Science. Soon thereafter, the Academy publicly credited him with the decipherment. Between 1822 and 1824, Champollion continued his work and developed a complete alphabet and the rudimentary principles of Egyptian grammar, which were published in his *Precis du Systeme Hieroglyphique.*[78] With the decipherment of hieroglyphs, archaeologists could now delve into the minds of the ancient Egyptians in a more accurate way.

How did ancient Egyptians perceive the world?

To the Egyptians, the world of experience was a finite "box" of light, space, and order within an infinite expanse of dark, formless waters.... What lies outside the biosphere of earth, sky and Duat (a region accessible to the world yet inaccessible to the living) is not "nothingness" but a universe that is the antithesis of all that defines the world. It is infinite, where the world is bounded; formless and chaotic, where the world is shaped and ordered; inert where the world is active; and wholly uniform in substance (water) where the world is materially diverse ... The universe beyond the biosphere is not merely the negation of existence; it is also existence waiting to happen.   J. P. Allen[79]

The ancient Egyptian worldview was deeply rooted in myth and religion. Like the early Mesopotamians, the Egyptians lived in a world of divine "beings" and manifestations. Creation and existence were products of a myriad of interactions involving the wills and actions of the gods.[80] Each major city (Heliopolis, Hermopolis, Memphis or Thebes) had slight variations of how the world was created and maintained, reflecting the nation's past cultural traditions prior to unification.[81]

However, most of the creation myths began with a single act of creation using a variety of means followed by a series of divine births manifest in the structure of the world (or universe).[82] There are five recurring themes:

- the world existed before the creation as an undifferentiated watery substance called the primeval waters or Nun (or Nu);[83]
- all existence (or being) was derived from a single primordial source (or Monad), conceptualized in most cases as the creator-god Atum;[84]
- the world arose from a primeval hill or mound out of the Nun (making the distinction between the hill and the surrounding waters);[85]
- the process from a single primordial source to world structure and life on earth was a slow, not a catastrophic one;[86] and

- the creation myths were closely connected with the Egyptian wider views on rebirth, renewal and immortality.[87]

The three major Egyptian creation myths are the Heliopolis creation myth, the myth in Memphite theology and Hermopolis magna.

- **The Heliopolis creation myth** centred around sun worship in the chief city Heliopolis. The myth involves the supreme god, Atum (or Re), and four generations of gods comprising the Ennead, or "the nine".[88] The Ennead dominated ancient Egyptian religious thought from the Old Kingdom to the Greco-Roman period and described the interrelationships between nine fundamental divine "forces".[89] The world creation was an emanation of god; the myth reveals how the creator-god transformed the "one into the many", which eventually led to human society. It is one of the earliest creation myths and influenced many others,[90] and possibly the later Neoplatonic Plotinus (see Ch. 6).
- **Memphite "theology"** is an alternative but compatible creation myth using the spoken word.[91] In contrast to the Heliopolis creation myth, Memphite theology postulated a world creation according to a plan of a demiurge or craftsman.[92] Ptah was the god of artists, sculptors and craftsmen. He was not manifest "in the phenomena" but beyond them.[93] Each entity in the world was a divine thought, and then a word. Creation was therefore an act of separation with the heart "planning", the tongue "formulating" and the spoken word "creating". Memphite theology has been interpreted as the closest Egyptian parallel to the biblical Genesis through the spoken word.[94] A major difference, however, is that the act of speaking only comes *after* "thinking" with the heart and "speaking" with the tongue, although Egyptologist Jan Assmann believes that the spoken word refers equally to writing as much as to speaking.[95] Notwithstanding the biblical parallels, the notion of a separate craftsman is also a theme seen in Plato (see Ch. 5).
- **Hermopolis magna.** This creation myth dealt with the problem of how "being" came from "non-being". How did the structure of the universe form out of the primeval sea? The story involves eight primeval gods or Ogdoad (Hermopolis means the eight), and these four divine couples represent the infinite Flood, the Waters, Darkness and Chaos.[96] Some believe the Hermopolitan creation myth developed from incorporating the creation theology of Heliopolis and Memphis.[97] The question of how structure and form came from "non-being" is one of the great mysteries that entertained later Greek philosophers and early Christian theologians (see Chs 5 and 6).

In an attempt to simplify a complex subject, we shall concentrate on the Heliopolitan creation myth found in the many scattered texts and artifacts dating back to around 2700 BC,[98] but first we shall look at the structure of the Egyptian universe.

Structure of the universe

The ancient Egyptians viewed the earth as a flat disk floating in water surrounded by the "Nun", "Great Circuit", "Great Green" or "Great Encircler".[99] The Nun was the

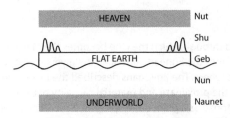

Figure 3.2 Ancient Egyptian cosmology (adapted from Wilson 1951b: 55).

primeval uncontrolled liquid "element" that contained the *potential seeds* of world structure and life itself.[100] It was "non-being", ready to be fashioned into structure and form. The Nun retreated to the edges encircling the sea and organized world after the creation (see Fig. 3.2).

The Nun was the place where the sun god, Re, re-emerged every day after his nightly journey through the underworld. It was also where the negative forces lived that, from time to time, ventured out and tormented humanity. The Nun was where distressed souls who had not been granted the appropriate funeral rites were found, and where the souls of condemned people or stillborn babies returned.[101]

The Egyptian gods formed the constitutive parts of the universe. The flat earth was a manifestation of the god Geb. Geb was separated from his consort Nut (the goddess of the sky) by his father Shu (god of air and light). Pyramid and Coffin Texts[102] speak of "keeping the sky clear of the Earth and the Waters", an image that also appears in Genesis (1:6–7).[103] Nut often appeared as an inverted pan or sky vault and was the interface between the surface of the waters and the dry atmosphere.[104] One version had the sun sailing on these waters just as people sail on the Nile (see below).

The sky vault contained heaven and the "heavenly bodies" suspended from it. According to one myth, the vault was supported by four enormous posts extending upwards from earth.[105] Another version replaces the posts with the air god, Shu: "The arms of Shu are under Nut, that he may carry her."[106] The sky goddess Nut was also represented as a naked woman bending face-down over earth with her fingers and toes touching the ground, with the sun, moon and stars adorning her body.[107] Every evening, the sky goddess swallowed the setting sun and every morning she gave birth to him from her womb. Depictions of this myth are common on the ceilings of temples as well as royal tombs and the lids of coffins.[108] Nut has even been represented as a celestial cow with a track on her underbelly to permit the daily east–west journey of the sun god's boat across the sky. These different manifestations of the sky goddess offered no problem to the ancient Egyptian mindset, as their way of thinking did not appear to demand the same logical consistency as that later developed in Greek philosophy and transmitted to the West.

Directly under the earth was the underworld, called the counter-heaven or "Naunet", and represented by the watery abyss.[109] Thus, the myth created an abstract idea that represented symmetry and spatial limits.[110] The idea of symmetry of opposites (heaven and counter-heaven; life and death; light and dark; air and moisture; hot and dry, male and female; water and earth) was a theme that dominated the ancient mindset for thousands of years.

Origins of the world

> Creation is the process through which the One becomes the Many – through which
> the Monad developed into the Ennead, sum of all the diverse forces and elements
> that constitute the biosphere. The Egyptians described the process in generational
> terms, reflecting both the proximate and material causality of the creation. The world
> developed from the Monad as a plant develops from a seed. Each of its numberless
> constituent parts derives both its substance and its energy from the one original
> source … In creation, the Monad is not disintegrated but realised. Atum continues to
> exist, both as the sum of all creation ("the total of the gods' forms") and as its
> continuing source of life.
> J. P. Allen[111]

Atum as the primeval creator-god

According to the Heliopolitan creation myth of the Pyramid Texts, the supreme god
Atum (or Re) created the world. In contrast, in Sumer it was the goddess Nammu (or
Namma) "the mother, who gave birth to Heaven and Earth", not a male.[112] The
Egyptian god Atum said that, in his own pre-creation state, he was alone (literally
meaning "one") with the formless Nun.[113] His creations built a theogony (creation of
gods) from the "primeval mound" that appeared out of the formless Nun. After the
world creation, it was the responsibility of a supreme god and the hundreds of lesser
gods to maintain its structure, balance and harmony. Again, in ancient Near Eastern
cosmogonical thinking, the world was not created "out of nothing" as in Hebrew
Genesis but out of the "formless" Nun that had been around forever.

Atum and "high places"

In another Pyramid Text, Atum (or Re) was said to have emerged "high on the hill".
The hill formed part of the temple of the sun, who "came into being from the Nun
before Heaven and earth were separated".[114] The Egyptians believed, as did the early
Mesopotamians, that "high places" provided a privileged access to the gods.[115] The
idea of a "primeval mound of creation" and "high ground" may have also influenced
the building and shape of their great pyramids.[116] Some Pyramid Texts make direct
references to the ascent of the pharaoh to heaven by way of pyramid steps (the step
pyramid being the forerunner to the true pyramids).[117] Moreover, the idea of the
creation mound itself may have arisen from observations that new life "spontaneously" emerged from the high ground after a Nile flood.

Atum and the Ennead

A number of Old Kingdom Pyramid Texts identify Atum as the sun god. He was the
supreme creator on the primeval hillock, who spat out, coughed up or ejected the first
two creator-gods, Shu (god of air or dryness) and Tefnut (goddess of moisture or
humidity).[118] The inscription on the Pyramid Text translates: "Thou didst spit
what was Shu; thou didst sputter out what was Tefnut".[119] While it is generally
accepted that the meaning of Tefnut is to "eject" or "spit", some also associate it with
the act of masturbation to create a pair of gods.[120] Here, again, the Egyptians abstract
the origin of things from associations consistent with their own observations and
experience.[121]

From the union of Shu (dry air) and Tefnut (moisture), a second divine couple was created, the sky goddess Nut (a woman) and the earth god Geb (a man),[122] who had four children: Isis and Osiris, Seth and Nephthys. It was Shu who separated heaven (Nut) from earth (Geb). Collectively, the Ennead represented four generations as follows:

Atum (or Re) (creator-god)
Shu (air god) – **Tefnut** (moisture god)
Geb (earth god) – **Nut** (heaven god)
Osirus, Isis, Seth, Nephthys

Several "versions" of the Heliopolitan cosmogony from different periods exist. To give an idea of an early reference to the Ennead and the creation, the following translation of Pyramid Text Utterance 600 is by Leonard H. Lesko:

Atum Kheprer, you have come to be high on the hill, you have arisen on the Benben stone in the mansion of Benben in Heliopolis, you spat out Shu, you expectorated Tefnut, and you put your two arms around them as the arms of a *ka* symbol, so that your *ka* (personality) might be in them. O Atum, place your arms around the king, around his edifice, around this pyramid as the arms of *ka*, so that the King's *ka* can be in it, firm forever and ever. O Atum, place your protection over this king, over this pyramid of his, over this edifice of the king, so that you may guard against anything happening evilly against him forever and ever, just as your protection was placed over Shu and Tefnut.

O great Ennead which is in Heliopolis – Atum, Shu, Tefnut, Geb, Nut, Osiris, Isis, Seth, Nephthys – children of Atum, extend his heart (goodwill) to his child (the king) in your name of None Bows. Let his back be turned from you toward Atum, so that he may protect this king, so that he may protect this pyramid of the king, so that he may protect this edifice of his from all his gods [and] from all the dead, and so that he may guard against anything happening evilly against him forever and ever.[123]

Another variation of the creation of Shu and Tefnut comes from a compilation of mortuary texts better known as *The Book of the Dead*,[124] dated at around 1600 BC.[125] Instead of violently ejecting or spitting Shu and Tefnut, Atum is portrayed as creating the eight gods by the creative power of thought, and naming eight of his body parts. Each body part had a separate power, existence and character.[126] The act of creating a god by "thinking" and "speaking" a name after a body part has parallels with the Sumerian creation myth of Enki and Ninhursag discussed in Chapter 2 (pp. 33–6).

Creation and the fate of humankind

Egyptian creation myths are nearly always identified with the creation of the world, not human beings.[127] However, one Egyptian text does explain how human beings were created in the "image of god" and emphasizes the goodness of the creator-god in caring for his human creations, which has some parallels with Hebrew Genesis.[128] The following excerpt emphasizes the gentleness and kindness of the creator-god in caring for human beings, but also paradoxically in making the purposes of creation the interests of human beings. The account has strong moral overtones including severe penalties for disobedience.

> Well tended are men, the cattle of god. He [creator-god] made Heaven and Earth according to their [human] desire, and he repelled the water monster [at creation]. He made the breath [of] life [for] their nostrils. They are his images that have issued from his body. He arises in Heaven according to their desire. He made for them plants and animals, fowl and fish, in order to nourish them. He slew his enemies and destroyed [even] his [own] children when they plotted rebellion [against him].[129]

A second version of the myth comes from a more recent text and explains how human beings were created from the tears of Atum or the sun god.[130] The story begins with the creator-god losing his eye and sending his children, Shu and Tefnut, to find the lost eye and the person responsible for his loss. During the delay the creator-god decides to replace his missing eye with a substitute (represented as a goddess). When his original eye is finally found and learns of its substitute, it begins to weep with rage, and its tears give birth to human beings.[131] This link between tears and the origin of human beings is further implied by the similarity in the Egyptian words for tears and human beings: *remut* and *remet*.[132] As Egyptologist Erik Hornung points out,[133] it also provides a way of linking human beings to the divine.

Once created, human fate was dependent on the "binding" relationships with their gods. In contrast to the gentleness and kindness of most gods, there were a number of gods who believed human beings were not to be trusted because they possessed weaknesses of betrayal and deceit.[134] Some Egyptian myths, not unlike the Sumerian, Babylonian and later Hebrew traditions, addressed the continual struggle and suffering of human life. One famous myth begins with the assassination of the King Osiris[135] (son of Geb and Nut) by his brother Seth who then assumed the throne. After the assassination, Osiris's widow, Isis, gave birth to Horus (falcon-like ruler of earth) on Osiris's dead body. Horus grew up with contempt for his Uncle Seth, and eventually convinced his grandfather Geb and the tribunal of gods to denounce him. Horus eventually became the King of Egypt by way of inheritance.[136] Osiris later became ruler of the netherworld. If the "binding" relations with the gods were not adhered to as part of a social collective, personal betrayal and deceit were punished severely, including possible barring of entry into the afterlife (see "The concept of immortality", p. 72).

To sum up, notwithstanding the many variations on the creation from one grand city to the next in Egypt, there was one overarching conceptual theme. That theme was a temporal sequence of events:

primeval water $\rightarrow$ gods $\rightarrow$ universe structure, symmetry, order and harmony $\rightarrow$ plants, animals and human beings

And it was from the two- and three-dimensional manifestations of the hundreds of gods that the Egyptians understood the workings of the world and their place in it.

Pre-eminence of Atum or sun god, Re

In the grand conceptual scheme that formed their reality, the ancient Egyptians were preoccupied with the sun.[137] In ancient Mesopotamia the focus was on the moon (hence their adherence to a lunar calendar). The Heliopolitan sun god Atum was also referred to as Khepri,[138] who was a manifestation of a dung beetle (or scarab) rolling its dung-ball through the heavens, day after day.[139] The sun god was also the sun itself and source of all light, heat and regeneration. By about 2500 BC the sun god became the national god of Egypt. Later, he was joined by other deities to form new gods such as Re-Horus and Amun-Re (who was also known as the "king of gods").[140] The sun god in his creator role took the name Re-Atum.[141]

Every day the sun travelled westwards underneath the sky vault and was swallowed up at night by the Nun. One story tells how the sun god travelled by boat at night and was constantly under attack from the evil forces of the underworld. The trip was depicted in paintings, with Horus at the front protecting the sun god against attacks from a serpent led by Apophis (personification of negative forces). A partial or full eclipse of the sun was explained by the successful conquest by the serpent (snake, or dragon), which swallowed the sun.[142] In spite of the formidable power of the negative evil forces, the sun god always fought back to re-emerge triumphantly the next day out of the Nun, bringing life back to earth once again.[143]

Another story to explain the nightly disappearance of the sun was that Re was swallowed up by the sky goddess Nut who then spat him out again in the morning after traversing the realm of the dead.[144] A version already mentioned had the sky formed by the body of the goddess Nut, with her head on a level with the western horizon and her genitalia on the eastern horizon. The sun god was consumed by her every evening and traversed her body during the night to be reborn at sunrise.[145] The perils and triumphs of these cyclical journeys have been described in detail in the royal *Underworld Books*.[146] In another version the sun god had wings like the falcon, and soared effortlessly in the sky.[147]

All these stories about the life and death and immortality of the sun might seem quite fantastic to our modern minds. However, they were acceptable to the ancient Egyptians as part of their reality. There apparently was no conflict, no questioning on what was true or false: they all were accepted "as is". Perhaps the diversity of ideas and stories reflect the ever-changing world they were trying to understand. We shall see the same thing again in their religious beliefs and rituals.[148]

Monotheism, Moses and the Egyptians

> Just what led Akhenaten (originally Amenhotep IV) to equate the deity with a sole
> God is not easy to determine; nor is there sufficient evidence to reach any firm
> conclusions. J. L. Foster[149]

Although most Egyptian myths have a pantheon of gods led by the sun god, there is one New Kingdom variation surrounded by intrigue and mystery. During the reign of King Akhenaten (*c*.1352–*c*.1336 BC), the sun god, Aten, was considered the universal god of whom all other gods were a manifestation.[150] This remarkable abstraction was the closest the Egyptians ever came to monotheism, but is the notion supported by the facts?

Monotheism: fact or fiction?

In his fifth regnal year, Akhenaten decided to change his birth name from Amenhotep (incorporating the god Amun's name, and meaning "Amun is content") to Akhenaten (meaning "glory of the Aten or sun disk"). Akhenaten disbanded the priesthood that had determined tradition for over 1500 years, and began to build a new city at El-Amarna to replace the old religious capitals of Memphis and Thebes.[151]

Scholars have long debated whether Akhenaten was a monotheist. There was, certainly, a clear monotheistic tendency in his notion of the multiplicity of the divine as one Aten.[152] Akhenaten's famous *Hymn to Aten* claims: God is one; God is alone; God is the creator of the universe; God is universal; God is love; God is light; God is beauty; God is father; and God is within.[153] The *Hymn of Aten* is carved on a wall in the tomb of Eye at Tell el-Amarna, and was a major statement of a new faith.[154]

Could Akhenaten have borrowed the idea of monotheism from the Hebrews, or was it the other way around? Could the monotheism of Abraham, Isaac, Jacob and Moses have been derived from worship of Akhenaten's Aten or sun god? Striking parallels have been drawn between the *Hymn of Aten* and Psalm 104, which deals with praise of the "splendour and multifariousness" of Yahweh's creation.[155] Some experts argue for a direct borrowing because of the similar tone and the closeness of the hymn, particularly to verses 20–26 in Psalm 104.[156] Others argue against direct borrowing, believing that each belongs to a common literary tradition, perhaps with Near Eastern roots.[157]

Akhenaten's purpose in equating one god to the sun disk is not known. It may have been his response to the increasing threat to his sovereignty from the all-powerful priesthood of Amun, which he quickly disbanded, switching Egyptian worship from Amun exclusively to Aten.[158] Secondly, Akhenaten may have taken full advantage of a resurgence of the sun cult from Heliopolis. Thirdly, Akhenaten himself may have wanted to become what Breasted termed "the first individual in human history".[159] In other words, Akhenaten was the first individual to challenge the status quo. Perhaps Egyptologist Erik Hornung was nearer the truth when he wrote: "The new creed could, indeed, be summed up in the formula, there is no god but Aten, and Akhenaten is his prophet."[160]

Moses the Egyptian?

Perhaps even more surprising is the suggestion that Akhenaten was associated with the biblical Moses. The extraordinary proposal is based on the claim that both were in the same place at the same time, and shared the belief in one god. The controversy came to a head when Sigmund Freud, in his famous book *Der Mann Moses und die monotheistische Religion*,[161] argued that the legendary Moses was really an Egyptian, perhaps a noble in Akhenaten's court.[162] Freud also talked about the similarities between the Egyptian Aten and the historical God of Israel (*Adonai*).[163]

Moses the Egyptian may not be as far-fetched as it first appears. The name Moses, for example, is a form of the Egyptian *mose* meaning "child of".[164] The real question therefore is: the child of "whom"? The Old Testament itself recounts that Moses was raised as an Egyptian prince: "And the child grew, and she brought him to the Pharaoh's daughter, and he became her son; and she named him Moses".[165] But it also states that Moses was the son of a Hebrew of the house of Levi, although the identity of his father remains vague.[166] Some scholars have even equated the biblical Moses with Akhenaten himself.[167] The main problem is that Moses and the Exodus took place during the reign of Ramesses II (*c*.1290–*c*.1224 BC), some 50–100 years after Akhenaten's reign.[168] From the reign of Ramesses II there is simply no extant text that mentions Moses or the children of Israel. The first mention of Israel and the Exodus was during Ramesses' successor Merneptah's reign (1224–1214 BC), and was discovered on a stele by Flinders Petrie (1853–1942) in 1896.

What are we to make of this? I think it is fair to say that most Egyptian scholars do not see a connection between Moses and Akhenaten because of incompatible chronology.[169] Other than putative monotheism, there is simply no other aspect of Akhenaten's life, or in the cult of Aten, that remotely resembles the Old Testament's account of Moses or liberation of the children of Israel from Egypt.[170] Before one tries to seek a connection between Moses and Akhenaten, it seems more prudent to first establish the historicity of Moses. The most likely scenario to emerge is that monotheism grew independently; belief in one god was short-lived in Egypt but long-term in Israel (see Chs 6 and 7).

Dynastic religion

> Among no people ancient or modern has the idea of life beyond the grave held so
> prominent a place as among the ancient Egyptians.   J. H. Breasted[171]

Although there was no word for religion in ancient Egypt analogous to the Latin *religio*, meaning "to bind", there is little doubt of a "binding" relationship between the people and their gods.[172] For ordinary Egyptians, the "binding" was observing the rites sanctioned by the pharaoh and priesthood officials.[173] Without continued service, all life would come to an end.[174] Reality in ancient Egypt, as in Sumer, was built on absolute, mythopoeic, full-blown, guaranteed, "divine" truths.[175] Sense-phenomena like the annual flood, the quaking of the earth, the movement of the heavenly bodies or other meteorological phenomena were explained by divine causation involving one or more gods. This feature of ancient Egyptian thinking will be the topic of later discussion.

The gods did not live close to the Egyptian people but exerted governance from the heavens.[176] Since ordinary Egyptians had limited access to the temples,[177] they communicated with their gods through daily rituals,[178] dreams and prayer. In addition, they had small amulets, stelae and votives as images[179] of the district gods to worship.[180] Religion in ancient Egypt was a national affair, not a personal one. There was no such thing as a personal religion as we understand it today, only private worship or prayer as part of the social collective.

Animism and anthropomorphism
The Egyptian worldview contained gods depicted symbolically as animals and human beings, and later hybrids.[181] Scholars of comparative religion believe that animal/human imagery was the ancient way to merge past myths with present religious beliefs and service. Some of the animal forms included the god Horus as the falcon, Thoth as an ibis or baboon and Anubis as a jackal.[182] Other animals worshipped included the bull

for its strength and fertility, the cow for its milk and hide, sheep for their wool, dogs for hunting and guarding and the wolf for its wisdom and cunning. The cat was worshipped for its stealth, the ibis for removing serpents from the water, the crocodile for its strength and the egg-eating mongoose for controlling the crocodile population.[183] The dung beetle or scarab, which was believed to come to life spontaneously in pellets of dung, was a symbol of eternal life. To kill or hurt a sacred beetle, or other sacred animals, resulted in severe torment, penalty and even death if the act was heinous or deliberate. Roman statesman Marcus Tullius Cicero (106–43 BC) once wrote of these ancient practices in Egypt: "for many shrines have been rifled, and images of the Deities have been carried from their most sacred places by us; but we never heard that an Egyptian offered any violence to a crocodile, an ibis, or a cat".[184] The gods were also worshipped in human forms, from at least around 3000 BC.[185] It was not until the New Kingdom (c.1550–1070 BC) that the gods were represented as a mixture of animal and anthropomorphic parts.[186]

The concept of immortality

> I cannot conceive that [God] could make such a species as the human merely to live and die on this Earth. If I did not believe in a future state, I should believe in no God.
> John Adams in a letter to Thomas Jefferson[187]

The people of Egypt planned for the afterlife much as we plan for our retirement: we save money and the Egyptians maintained social and world harmony (*ma'at*). An ancient Egyptian adage said: "The man who lives by *ma'at* will live forever, but the covetous has no tomb."[188] *Ma'at* also stood for righteousness, truth or social justice, an idea adopted and extended by the ancient Greeks,[189] and for "the renewal and rejuvenation of the life of the world".[190]

From the end of the Old Kingdom each person was judged after death by King Osiris, who ruled the underworld.[191] Before this time justice, we are told, was unchallenged.[192] If Osiris's verdict was favourable, a person would live a good life in the Kingdom of the Dead; if not, he or she could be abandoned to a monster, sometimes depicted as part crocodile and part hippopotamus.[193] The Egyptian idea of heaven was a rural paradise or "Fields of the Reeds": a place where the sun shone and people worked in the fields, just as in Egypt during mortal life.[194] Reincarnation was not part of the Egyptian afterlife.[195]

Information on death awareness comes from three main texts: The Pyramid and Coffin Texts; *The Book of the Dead*; and an assortment of ritual and magical texts, and funerary equipment such as amulets and statuettes.[196] The Pyramid Texts are of greatest antiquity, comprising some 800 spells or "utterances" written on the walls of the corridors and burial chambers of the pyramids.[197] *The Book of the Dead* is a much later document (dated at around 1600 BC) and represents a "democratization" of funerary religion with some 200 "utterances".[198] Every word or phrase had great magical power in the afterlife, measured in direct proportion to its usefulness in the living world.[199] *The Book of the Dead* was often placed in the coffin of the dead person.

One of the most famous utterances in *The Book of the Dead* was the last judgement before Osiris, where a person had to prove their worthiness to enter the afterlife.[200] The judgement took the form of weighing the heart of the dead person, representing the individual's entire earthly existence, against a feather, the symbol of the goddess Ma'at, representing order, harmony, justice and truth.[201] The ritual also included reciting the relevant confessions such as "I have not stolen", "I have not slain anyone treacherously", "I have not slandered anyone or made false accusation", "I have not committed adultery" and so on.[202]

Human beings possessed a body and three spiritual elements

> To the Egyptians the heart was the organ that steered the will, thought and feelings. It determined the human character, and in the scenes of judgment it often substituted for the whole personality, being weighed on scales against the symbol of truth or order or Ma'at (as a goddess or feather). In its capacity of "free will" (and aspect of the Egyptian heart), it determined whether an individual has conformed to Ma'at.
>
> E. Hornung[203]

In Egypt, the living and dead were of the same community. This meant that the dead could intervene positively or negatively among the living.[204] The most important parts of a person's make-up were the body and three spiritual elements: the *ka*, *ba* and *akh* (see Table 3.2). In addition, everyone had a name and a shadow. The name had to be assigned immediately at birth, or the person would not properly come into existence or be able to enter the afterlife; a person's shadow protected them from harm.[205] The Egyptians firmly believed in luck or good "fortune" (*renenet*). They were not only answerable to their gods, but their fate was apparently fixed at birth, and their death was in the hands of a particular god.[206]

To enter the afterlife, the three elements had to be in harmony. If a person had led an "ordered" life, their *ka* and *ba* were transfigured into a third spiritual element: the *akh* or enlightened spirit. The *akh* was the essence of each person's immortality.[207] If a person's *ba* failed the test, and was not deemed suitable for the afterlife, it would not return and the person was condemned to death and known as *mut*, or a dead person (Table 3.2). When the *ba* or soul returned, the person would live for ever. The Egyptians did not believe in transmigration of the soul or *ba*.[208] The ancient Egyptians wanted to live for ever and believed that a dead person's body had to be preserved before life could be returned. The mode of preservation was called mummification (see later).

Immortality, religion and art

> In pharaonic Egypt, there was no concept of individual creativity by the stamp of an "artist's" unmistakeable personality. Instead, other qualities were valued, such as mastery of traditional rules and their correct application and a knowledge of craft techniques that was handed down from generation to generation.   R. Drenkhahn[209]

The relationship between immortality, religion and art is a fascinating subject. Ancient Egyptian art, like religion, served as a continual reminder of the binding relationship between the people and their gods. Within the illiterate community, art was an effective way to bring the pharaoh, past and present, into the people's everyday awareness.[210]

Table 3.2 The major elements of personality linking human life with the afterlife, *ka*, *ba* and *akh*, and *mut* death (Morenz 1973:157; Baines 1991:145; Shaw & Nicholson 1995:89, 159, 226).

Ka	"Vital force" The *ka* is the force that makes the transition between life and the afterlife. It also applied to the pharaoh, but he was a special case. It came into existence during naming at the time of birth, and when the individual died the *ka* continued to live on.
Ba	Identity or the essence of a person's motivation. This has to do with freedom of movement in the next world and the ability to take on different manifestations/forms. When a person dies the *ba* is separated from the body by "coming out of the discharges from his flesh" – often represented as a bird flying away. And it can rejoin *ka* to become transformed into *akh*. Human beings had one *ba* but the gods had many. *Ba* was analogous to "soul".
Akh	Usually an individual's transfigured spirit in the next world. Known also as the immortality or enlightened spirit. If a person was judged suitable for the afterlife the *ka* and *ba* were transfigured into the *akh*. Once reunited, the *akh* was regarded as enduring and unchanging for eternity.
Mut	Dead person. If a person's *ba* failed the test because of some breach of moral conduct, he/she was condemned to death and became known as *mut* dead. In this sense *mut* means someone who has "died a second time" in judgement after death and so has suffered perpetual damnation.

Like religion, it was highly conservative. Art was not an expression of individuality as it is today. No royal artist in the Old Kingdom would have dared to change the shape of a line or contour of a body from its sacred, codified form. Neither would a scribe alter the sacred hieroglyphic signs. Statues were admired as pieces of beauty and as representations of gods and their immortality. Art was not impressionistic but informative.[211] Even the shaping of an Egyptian spoon in the form of a goddess had deep religious, political and social significance.[212] In short, monumental architecture, sculptures, paintings and pottery signified the Egyptian triumph of the world *ma'at*, which was under continual threat from external negative forces.[213]

Egyptian science (and technology)

> I'll tell you other things, So as to teach you knowledge.   Egyptian scribe[214]

So far, we have presented the Egyptian worldview and shown how myth and religion formed the intellectual framework for making sense of their experience. We have not discussed other important symbolic dimensions of their thought and action; namely the way they quantified space and time, on which their agricultural success depended. The ancient Egyptians spent much time devising better ways to count, calculate, measure and irrigate, and to build their religious monuments. They were the first to introduce a decimal number system and devise a solar calendar of 365 days to match their growing seasons. They built enduring monuments to commemorate their god-kings; practised advanced medicine and surgery; engaged in the most elaborate mummification and had advanced chemical arts and crafts. As in ancient Mesopotamia, these innovations would have never been realized without a heightened systematization of number and quantity.

Egyptian mathematics

> Mathematics is the tool specially suited for dealing with abstract concepts of any kind and there is no limit to its power in this field.   Paul Dirac[215]

The ancient Egyptians used mathematics in nearly every facet of their agricultural life. Specialist groups estimated the amount of food required to feed the growing population and the amount of beer to brew, and they used mathematics in taxation, record-keeping, designing and rebuilding irrigation channels, construction of monumental buildings, time-keeping, trade and navigation.[216] The ancient Egyptians believed that mathematics had magical divine powers, a belief that apparently had a tremendous influence on Pythagoras and other Greek philosophers. Egyptian mathematics included arithmetic (addition, subtraction, multiplication and division), trigonometry (calculation of angles, lengths and slopes), some algebra (solutions of equations) and geometry (calculation of areas and volumes).

The Moscow Papyrus and the Rhind Papyrus

Of the many hundreds of papyri found to date, only about 12 are of a mathematical type.[217] Of these 12, the principal sources of mathematical knowledge come from two mathematical papyri. The first is the Moscow (Golenishchev) Papyrus (544 × 8 cm) of about 1850 BC, which contains 25 problems. The second is the Rhind Papyrus[218] (544 × 33 cm) of about 1550 BC, with 85 problems and their solutions. Both texts are thought to date back to the early Old Kingdom (c.2600 BC), and possibly even earlier. Mathematics was revered in ancient cultures because of its problem-solving power and precision. The beginning of the Rhind Papyrus openly professes to study all things and offer the answers to many of life's inner secrets.[219] Again, as in their creation texts, the Egyptians were always striving to find wider meaning and uncover the truth; mathematics was a power that helped advance their lives and their relationships with the gods.

The Egyptian numbering system was cumbersome

Numbers were therefore not just abstractions, as we think of them today, but powers linked to the divine. The Egyptian numbering system was very cumbersome compared to ours. It was a decimal system[220] with no sign for zero but a separate sign for 1 and for each power of 10 up to a million.[221] This could be why Egyptian astronomy never advanced to the level in Babylonia, with its much easier place-value sexagesimal system (see Ch. 2, pp. 46–8). The ancient Egyptian hieroglyphic signs for 1 and multiples of 10 were as follows:[222]

1	was symbolized by a papryus leaf
10	was a tie made by bending a leaf
100	looked like a piece of rope
1000	was a lotus flower
10 000	was a snake
100 000	was a tadpole
1 000 000	was a scribe raising both his hands above his head.

The numbers 1, 5, 10, 100, 200 and 385 were written:

$$1 = \text{I} \qquad\qquad 5 = \begin{matrix}\text{II} \\ \text{III}\end{matrix} \qquad\qquad 10 = \text{I}$$

$$100 = \rho \qquad\qquad 200 = \rho\rho \qquad\qquad 385 = \begin{matrix}\rho\rho\text{IIII} \\ \rho\text{IIIIIIII}\end{matrix}$$

The signs were repeated up to the desired number of times and read from right to left (the highest values were placed on the left). Interestingly, by about 1800 BC, the Egyptians added another sign for the number 7, which was represented by a sickle.[223]

Multiplication and division

The ancient Egyptians added and subtracted numbers in much the same way as we do today. However, multiplication and division were different because the Egyptians used an additive/dyadic system and included unit fractions, with the exception of two-thirds.[224] Calculations were carried out by reducing any higher multiple into a sum of consecutive duplications.[225] The Egyptian idea of successive doubling or "additivity" is the dyadic principle of multiplication. For example, the ancient Egyptians would multiply 13 by 14 by first multiplying the number 14 by 1, then finding 14 by 2, then 28 by 2, and lastly 56 by 2. The results were written in two columns, as shown below:

Column 1	Column 2	
1	14	$(1 \times 14 = \mathbf{14})$
2	28	$(2 \times 14 = 28)$
4	56	$(4 \times 14 = \mathbf{56})$
8	112	$(8 \times 14 = \mathbf{112})$

The next step was to find the numbers in Column 1 that added to 13. In this case 13 = 1 + 4 + 8. The answer to 13 × 14 was found by adding the numbers in Column 2 that corresponded to the rows identified as adding to 13 in Column 1. Thus 13 × 14

$$13 \times 14 = 14 + 56 + 112$$
$$= 182$$

Division was also reducible by the same procedure.[226] For example, dividing 28 by 4 was found by doubling 4 until the total of 28 is reached (4 + 8 + 16 = 28).

Column 1		Column 2
1 (× 4)	=	4
2 (× 4)	=	8
4 (× 4)	=	16

By adding the corresponding numbers in Column 1, 28 ÷ 4 = 1 + 2 + 4 = 7. For more complicated calculations, the Egyptian scribe would most probably have consulted tables.

Multiplication and division carried out by successive doubling was not without its problems. If the numbers in Column 1 did not add up to the original number, other ways had to be devised. The ancient Egyptians solved the problem by introducing fractions. This can be illustrated by dividing 17 by 4:

Column 1	Column 2
1	4
2	8
4	16

Now 4 + 8 + 16 = 28, but this sum exceeds 17, so there is no solution. The sum of Column 2 is 28, which is 11 above the required 17. The ancient Egyptians solved the problem by using smaller numbers (e.g. 1 × 4 = 4) and then fractions to arrive at 17. In the above example they would divide 1 by 4, giving ¼.

Column 1	Column 2	
1 (× 4)	4	
2 (× 4)	8	(continuing increasing would exceed 17, so start decreasing again)
1 (× 4)	4	
¼ (× 4)	1	

Column 2 is now added up: 4 + 8 + 4 + 1 = 17. The answer to 17 divided by 4 is found by adding up the numbers in Column 1, giving 1 + 2 + 1 + ¼ = 4¼. Mathematical tables were widely used for such purposes.

Some specific theorems
The administration used basic arithmetic methods from everyday needs right through to the most complex engineering problems. The Rhind and Moscow papyri contain a number of examples, including many geometrical theorems. Problem 14 in the Moscow Papyrus contains the theorem to determine the volume of a frustum (a square-based pyramid with its top removed).[227] The volume can be expressed by the formula:

$$V = \tfrac{1}{3} h \left(a^2 + ab + b^2 \right)$$

where V is the volume of the frustum, h is the height of the frustum, and a and b are the lengths of the square sides of its base and its top.

Another famous theorem apparently known to the ancient Egyptians was Pythagoras's theorem.[228] Egyptian "rope stretchers" made widespread use of the relation $5^2 = 4^2 + 3^2$ to lay out the triangles for the orientation of their buildings and pyramids.[229] However there is no direct recorded evidence that the Egyptians (or Sumero-Babylonians) knew of the direct proof of Pythagoras's theorem: $c^2 = a^2 + b^2$, where a and b are the length of the shorter sides of a right-angled triangle, and c is the length of the longest side (the hypotenuse). The latest evidence from scholarship in Presocratic philosophy is that even Pythagoras had little, if anything, to do with the proof (see Ch. 4).[230]

Another area of Egyptian mathematics was their use of pi (or π), the ratio of the circumference of a circle to its diameter (see Ch. 2). The value known to the ancient Egyptians was $(^{16}/_9)^2$ or 3.1605,[231] which is an astonishing 0.6 per cent greater than the value mathematicians use today.

Ancient Egyptian weights and measures were also based on a decimal system and standard weights were originally made from stone and later from metal. Standard lengths were originally based on the "standardized" forearm, called the Royal Cubit, of approximately 50 cm and divided into seven palms (width of the palm excluding the thumb) or 28 digits (one finger's breadth). Seven palms was equal to 1 cubit and 100 cubits was equal to 1 "rod" or *khet*.[232] The importance of mathematics and a system of measures with standards was the key to the success of the Egyptians in taming the Nile and working with and pleasing their gods, as further exemplified in the construction of their magnificent pyramids.

Construction of the pyramids

Although it is not fully understood how the ancient Egyptians arrived at all their mathematical principles, no one can deny that they are implicit in the enduring magnificence of their monumental architecture. Of the 80 or so pyramids constructed during the Old Kingdom (*c.*2664–*c.*2155 BC), the most famous are the three pyramids at Giza, west of Cairo. The largest of the three, the Great Pyramid, is one of the seven wonders of the ancient world. Its construction was based on the cycle of the sun with the pharaoh god-king being its guarantor.[233] The pyramids, like their art, signified the Egyptian triumph of the *ma'at* in an ever-changing world under continual threat from external negative forces.

Twenty years to build and 100 000 workers

According to Herodotus, the Great Pyramid at Giza was commissioned by the Pharaoh Khufu (Cheops) (*c.*2480 BC).[234] One Egyptian text (Westcar Papyrus) tells how Khufu wanted a mortuary temple as an enduring monument to celebrate his reign.[235] Wanting something bigger and better than any of his predecessors, Khufu consulted the best people, including a magician named Djedi, who was described as "a man aged 110 who eats 500 loaves of bread and a side of beef for his meat, and still drinks 100 jugs of beer to this very day".[236] Djedi revealed to Khufu the secret of his destiny: the pyramids.[237]

Herodotus tells us Khufu employed some 100 000 men over a 20-year period.[238] Some experts question this estimate and believe a workforce of 10 000 men could have carried out the job in the same time, but would require specialized rollers/ ramps, rafts and levers to move and position the massive stone slabs.[239] Recent archaeological evidence also suggests that the pyramid-building workforce comprised mostly Egyptians and not slaves as once thought.

If the pyramid blocks were cut into 30 cm cubes they would extend two-thirds around the circumference of the earth

The Great Pyramid is built of limestone rock quarried locally[240] with granite passages leading into the funeral chambers where the pharaoh god-king was buried. The entire pyramid was dressed with a white, glass-smooth casing of fine-quality Tura limestone, which has since weathered. The 45-storey pyramid contained some 6.25 million tons of stone (about 2 500 000 casting blocks) and each block averaged 2.5 tons, some weighing as much as 70 tons. To give an idea of the incredible amount of stone used, if all the blocks of the Great Pyramid were cut into 30 cm cubes and placed in a row, they would cover two-thirds of the earth's circumference at the equator, or a staggering 26 717 km.[241]

History of the Great Pyramid at Giza's dimensions

In 1693 M. de Chazelles presented to the Academy of Sciences the following dimensions of the Great Pyramid at Giza:

Side of the square base	110 fathoms (1 fathom = 1.83 m)
Base (fronts are equilateral triangles)	12 100 square fathoms
Perpendicular height	77¾ fathoms
Solid content volume	313 590 cubic fathoms

These dimensions fall short by some 9.5 m of the modern estimates of the height of the pyramid. Among the first to compile a history of the dimensions of the Great Pyramid was Royal Scottish Astronomer Piazzi Smyth (1819–1900). His book is a fascinating account of the great number of theories behind the shape and construction of the Great Pyramid. For example, amateur astronomer John Taylor worked on the shape of the Great Pyramid for over 30 years (apparently without visiting the pyramid itself), and found that its height stood in the same ratio to its circumference (drawn around its base) as the radius to the circumference of a circle – that is, ½π – to an accuracy better than one in a thousand.[242] This discovery led Taylor (and later Smyth) to believe that the Great Pyramid's shape and architecture were a divinely inspired duplication of the solar system. Smyth was so much in awe of the ancients' calculations that he concluded that the Great Pyramid was "a divinely inspired Christian chronicle of man's history – past and future".[243]

Despite other attempts to measure the dimensions of the Great Pyramid at Giza, it was not until 1925 that J. H. Cole of the Egyptian Survey Department provided the most accurate measurements. Cole calculated its vertical height to be 146 m from the base, which covered some 5.3 ha (230 m × 230 m).[244] For some reason, the top 9.5 m of the pyramid had been removed in the Middle Ages, leaving only a platform at the top.[245] Earlier Smyth had remarked that the Arabs described the platform as being "large enough for eleven camels to lie down", but why it was removed remains a mystery.[246]

More like "the work of opticians than of masons"

Each casting block in the Great Pyramid at Giza was fitted to its neighbouring blocks within 0.51 mm.[247] Flinders Petrie proclaimed "The joints of the masonry are so fine as to be scarcely visible where they are not weathered, and it is difficult to insert even a knife edge between them."[248] The Egyptian accuracy and lack of geometrical errors in the construction of the Great Pyramid is nothing short of remarkable. To give an idea of the extraordinary precision, the mean error of the length of its sides of 230 m, for example, was an incredible 5.8 cm, 1 in 4000. In modern physics, this would be analogous to producing a difference in length by heating a copper bar to 15 °C.[249] Perhaps even more astonishing is the margin of error in the squareness of the pyramid itself: 0.09 per cent on the north and south sides (9 in 10 000) and 0.03 per cent on the east and west sides (3 in 10 000). The 6.25 million tons of casting blocks was set upon a dressed rock foundation, from which the opposite corners had deviated from the "true" plane by only a few centimetres (0.004 per cent).[250]

As with a great number of Early Dynastic and Old Kingdom monuments, the four sides of the Great Pyramid exactly faced the four points of the compass. The sides of the Great Pyramid, for example, deviate from true north by an average of less than three minutes of arc (0.05 degrees). The amazing thing was that the Egyptians did not yet have a compass to set true north. One possible way they achieved such accuracy was to sight a star in the northern heavens and bisect the angle formed by its rising position and its setting position.[251] This has recently been confirmed by Kate Spence,[252] who presented evidence that 4500 years ago the celestial North Pole was exactly aligned between Kochab (nestled in the Little Dipper) and Mizar of the Big Dipper constellation. But this was no mean feat as it would have required decades, if not centuries, of accurate measurements requiring sophisticated instruments to provide a sight line for alignment with the Pole Star.[253] These advanced engineering and astronomical skills to construct the Great Pyramid inspired Petrie to write in his book *Wisdom of the Egyptians*,[254] "This is more like the work of opticians than of masons."[255]

Religious significance of the pyramidal shape

The Pyramid Age (*c*.2600 BC) cannot be separated from the development of dynastic religion.[256] As mentioned, the official dynastic religion of ancient Egypt involved the solar cult that grew as part of the unification process and an attempt to systematize the many divergent beliefs of predynastic Egypt. Interestingly, one reason postulated for the shape of the pyramid has been that it represented the "primeval mound" or "hillock" referred to in the Heliopolitan creation stories.[257] In fact, the term used later for the "primeval mound" of creation was the "pyramidion".[258] The pyramid served not only as the eternal home of the pharaoh god-king but was a symbol of life itself and consistent with the Egyptians' worldview.

Astronomy and time-keeping

> The Egyptians were the first to have invented the year and to have divided it into
> twelve parts.
> Herodotus[259]

Time-keeping in Egypt, as in Sumer, developed from the practical need to match farming, politico-religious and administrative duties with natural cycles.[260] Because of its importance to agriculture, the time-keepers were members of the priesthood and they tackled formidable problems such as correlating the lunar, solar and celestial movements with the seasons, months and days. From as early as the Middle Kingdom (*c*.2040–1640 BC), the Egyptians recognized five of the planets, portraying them as deities sailing across the heavens in boats: Jupiter, Mars, Mercury, Saturn and Venus.[261] They divided the day into 24 hours: a 12-hour day and a 12-hour night.[262]

Daytime hours were measured by using a sundial (shadow clock) or alternatively a water clock, as in Sumer. Night-time hours were measured by a star clock using one star or group of stars (which are now called decans).[263]

The lunar and solar calendars

The calendar in predynastic and early pharaonic Egypt was a lunar calendar.[264] It began with the disappearance of the old moon crescent in the eastern sky just before sunrise. The Egyptian day went from sunrise to sunset, not midnight to midnight as it is measured today.[265] While the early lunar calendar was useful in regulating daily life and religious festivals (and remained so), its monthly phase-cycles (sometimes called "synodic" months) did not coincide with the agricultural seasons.

At some unknown time, the Egyptians made a very important observation that transformed time-keeping. They noticed that, every July, on around the 19th day, the rising water level of the Nile River coincided with the heliacal rising of the brightest star at sunrise. This star was called the Dog Star (Sirius, called Sothis by the Greeks) and was identified with the Egyptian goddess Sopdet.[266] The period between the two heliacal risings of this bright star closely matched the natural year.[267] The rising of the Dog Star, after being invisible for four seasons, was a very sound basis for selecting New Year's Day.[268] In the middle of the third millennium BC, the Egyptians adopted the recurring solar year of 365 days.

By encompassing the complete cycle, the priests could now plan an entire agricultural year with greater accuracy rather than planning from one lunar month to another. The next major hurdle was to relate the lunar and solar calendars. The problem was that 365 days could not easily be divided by 30 days (30 days × 12 months = 360 days). The Egyptians solved the problem by dividing the year into three major "seasons" with each season containing four lunar months, and each month having 30 days, divided into three weeks of ten days each.[269] At the end of each year, the Egyptians added five days to give 365 days. The solar calendar beginning 19 July, known as the "civil" year, was of great importance to Egypt and to later Greek astronomers. Astronomer Claudius Ptolemy (c. AD 100–170) based all his planetary and lunar tables in the *Almagest* on Egyptian years; and even Nicolas Copernicus (AD 1473–1543) used the Egyptian calendar for his calculations in his *De revolutionibus orbium coelestium*.[270]

Egyptian astronomy and the statue of Harkhebi

In general, little is known about early Egyptian astronomy.[271] Some aspects of Egyptian astronomy can be found from an inscription on a statue of Harkhebi dating back to the third century BC.[272] Harkhebi described himself as an:

Hereditary prince and count, sole companion, wise in the sacred writings, who observed everything observable in Heaven and Earth, clear-eyed in observing the stars, among which there is no erring; who announces rising and setting at their times, with the gods who foretell the future, for which he purified himself in their days when Akh [decan] rose heliacally beside Benu [Venus] from Earth and he contented the lands with his utterances; who observes the culmination of every star in the sky, who knows the heliacal risings of every ... in a good year, and who foretells the heliacal rising of Sothis at the beginning of the year. He observes her [Sothis] on the day of her first festival, knowledgeable in her course at the times of designation therein, observing what she does daily, all she has foretold is in his charge; knowing the northing and southing of the sun, announcing all its wonders [omina?] and appointing for them a time [?], he declares when they have occurred, coming at their times; who divides the hours for the two times (day and night) without going into error at night ...; knowledgeable in everything which is seen in the sky, for which he has waited, skilled with respect to their conjunction(s) and their regular movement(s); who does not disclose (anything) at all concerning his report after judgement, discreet with all he has seen.[273]

Astrology never reached the heights it reached in Babylonia

Most, if not all, celestial phenomena were associated with powerful gods. Astrology, as the practice of forecasting human and natural events from the position of the "fixed stars", sun, moon and planets, never commanded the same status in Egypt as it did in early Mesopotamia. The concept of a horoscope (belief in stars influencing human destiny) does not seem to have reached Egypt until the Ptolemaic period in the first century BC.[274] This may relate to the different relationship the Egyptians had with their gods and belief in the afterlife, thus reducing the need to forecast human and natural events. The reduced interest in horoscopes may also relate to the ancient Egyptians possessing a less sophisticated mathematics and number system than their Near Eastern neighbours.

Medicine, magic and spells

Practically every substance in the world has been used for medical treatment ... used in those days when men with magic and mystery groped blindly in their hope of overcoming their misfortunes or warding off disease.   H. W. Haggard[275]

In ancient Egypt, there was no restrictive "Code of Hammurabi" to regulate a doctor's conduct or limit future advancement. Instead, there was an unwritten law that said that if something was found beneficial, the practice would be permitted, and helps explain why Egyptian medicine was so progressive.[276] As a result, Egyptian doctors were in great numbers and held in much higher esteem than in Mesopotamia.[277] By the Late period (712–332 BC) there was so much medical knowledge, and so many specialists, that Egypt was known as the medical centre of the ancient world.[278]

Herodotus described Egypt as the home of specialists where:

Medicine is practised among them on a plan of separation; each physician treats a single disorder, and no more: thus the country swarms with medical practitioners, some undertaking to cure diseases of the eye, others of the head, others again the teeth, others of the intestines, and some those which are not local.[279]

And Homer wrote that "Egypt was teeming with drugs, the land where each is a physician, skillful beyond all men."[280]

Egypt was abounding with doctors

The first medical doctor on record was the multi-talented Imhotep[281] who lived around 2700 BC.[282] Imhotep was not only the personal doctor to King Djoser (*c.*2667–2648 BC) but also the architect responsible for the first step pyramid at Sakkara.[283] Long after his death, Imhotep was deified as the "god of healing" and worshipped for many centuries thereafter. Even the later Greeks believed their "god of healing" (Asclepius) had magical powers similar to those of Imhotep.[284]

Of the 150 estimated medical practitioners in the dynastic period, about 50 belong to the Old Kingdom.[285] The most skilful doctors were the priest-magicians who served the pharaoh.[286] Less-experienced doctors treated the public. Most doctors were highly trained in the temple schools and practised a high degree of proficiency in interrogation, inspection, diagnosis and palpation. First, they set out to discover the nature of the malevolent spirit causing the sickness; and secondly, they drove the spirit away by naming it with elaborate magical exorcisms, rites, incantations and chemical purification procedures.[287]

The doctors believed that replicating a name, image or mythical event could produce an effect in the real world.[288] Thus, command of language in the form of puns, metaphors and stories was more than just a literary skill, but if used in the right way was a powerful form of healing.[289] The combination of magic and medicine in the Old and Middle Kingdoms was superbly summed-up by the nineteenth-century French Egyptologist Gaston Maspero (1846–1916) in his book, *Life in Ancient Egypt and Assyria*:

> Often, though it [supernatural force] belongs to the invisible world, and only reveals itself by the malignity of its attacks: it is a god, a spirit, the soul of a dead man, that has cunningly entered a living person, or that throws itself upon him with irresistible violence. Once in the possession of the body, the evil influence breaks the bones, sucks the marrow, drinks the blood, gnaws the intestines and the heart, and devours the flesh. The invalid perishes according to the progress of this destructive work; and death speedily ensues, unless the evil genius can be driven out of it before it has committed irreparable damage. Whoever treats a sick person has therefore two equally important duties to perform. He must first discover the nature of the spirit in possession, and if necessary its name, and then attack it, drive it out, or even destroy it. He can only succeed by powerful magic, so he must be an expert in reciting incantations, and skilful in making amulets. He must then use medicine (drugs and diet) to content with the disorders which the presence of the strange being has produced in the body.[290]

Not all treatments involved the powers, magic and incantations. We shall now examine two main textual sources that show the beginnings of a more evidence-based medicine: the Ebers Medical Papyrus of about 1550 BC, and the Edwin Smith Surgical Papyrus,[291] of similar date.[292] Both papyri were written as working manuals for medical practitioners, and contain information believed to date back to the Old Kingdom.[293] While there is no clear mind–body distinction, as in ancient Greece, the Egyptian surgical treatises deal with minimal intervention from divine sources.

Ebers Papryus

The Ebers Papyrus is essentially a *materia medica* comprising a formulary of remedies to treat a variety of ailments and diseases.[294] The first section, "Internal medical diseases", deals with how to open and close the bowels, expel worms and alleviate fevers. Each procedure requires the recital of an incantation by a priest-physician. Other sections include diseases of the eye, skin and teeth, and gynaecological problems in women.

The vast pharmacopoeia employed must have required centuries of testing. Some of the more common drugs included opium, hemlock, bicarbonate of soda, salts of copper, squills, castor oil or animal fat (of the lion, hippopotamus, crocodile, goose and snake). Others include the flesh of lizards, blood of the bat, testicles of asses, dung of crocodile, toes of dog and ripe dates. No matter how bizarre these concoctions seem to us today, many treatments, including the blood of a bat or badger and animal urine or excrement, were widely used in London pharmacopoeias as late as the seventeenth century AD.[295]

The Edwin Smith Surgical Papyrus

The Edwin Smith Surgical Papyrus is very different because it relies more heavily on treatments of broken bones.[296] Its author was once thought to be a military surgeon, but recent opinion suggests that he may have been a doctor associated with the pyramid constructions.[297] Each of the 48 cases begins with a description of the condition followed by a diagnosis and then advice about whether the physician should treat it. If a treatment was recommended, the surgical procedures were carried out as described. The papyrus lists ten cases of wounds to the head; seven to the nose; ten to the ear, lips and jaw; six to the throat; five to the collar bone and shoulders; nine to the chest and breast; and one incomplete case of a spinal ailment.[298] A typical example is Case 25-A on a dislocation of the mandible:[299]

TITLE
Instruction concerning a dislocation of his mandible

EXAMINATION
If thou examinest a man having a dislocation in his mandible, shouldst thou find his mouth open [and] his mouth can not close for him, thou shouldst put thy thumb[s] upon the ends of the two rami of the mandible in the inside of his mouth, [and] thy two claws [meaning two groups of fingers] under his chin, [and] thou shouldst cause them to fall back so that they rest in their places.

DIAGNOSIS
Thou shoudst say concerning him "one having a dislocation in his mandible. An ailment which I will treat."

TREATMENT
Thou shouldst bind it with *ymrw*, [and] honey every day until he recovers.

In the Edwin Smith Surgical Papyrus, the use of magic and divine intervention is mentioned only once.[300] Over the centuries, doctors may have begun to rely less on "divine" or "unseen" evil forces as explanations for some injuries or sickness and more on objective accounts involving "accidental" causes. If a more empirical experienced-based medicine was practised in ancient Egypt, as seems to be the case, it predates the Hippocratic system by over a 1000 years (see Ch. 5). This proposal, however, remains highly conjectural, as Egyptian medicine was never completely separated from magical rites, gods, charms and incantations.[301]

Medical diagnosis and the heart pulse

The Edwin Smith Surgical Papyrus and Ebers Medical Papyrus both contain a treatise on the function of the heart, again illustrating the development of empirical-based medicine.[302] Although the Egyptians did not discover circulation, they knew that the heart "speaks" to various parts of the body through the pulse.[303] The Ebers Papyrus claims that "the beginning of the physician's secret knowledge of the heart and knowledge of the heart is to know the movement of the heart".[304] Diagnosing whether the heart was "speaking" too slow or too fast[305] provided doctors with valuable information about a patient's health. Another text, the Therapeutic Papyrus of Thebes, written around 1550 BC, further emphasizes the importance of the heart pulse, as well as the vessels, which again predates the Hippocratic treatises.[306] One passage states:

> There is in the heart a vessel leading to every member of the body. If the physician places his finger on the head, neck, arms, feet or body, everywhere he will find the heart, for the heart leads to every member, and speaks in the vessels to every member.[307]

The Egyptian physicians failed, however, to distinguish the blood vessels from the body's tendons and nerves. They viewed the function of the vessels collectively as vehicles for air, water, mucus, semen and other secretions.[308] The discovery of the blood circulation had to wait nearly 3000 years until the work of William Harvey in AD 1628.

Hygiene: an Egyptian way of life

Another important advance in Egyptian medicine was hygiene and public health.[309] It was not introduced, as we might expect, to prevent disease and infection.[310] The priesthood[311] introduced hygiene as part of moral cleansing during religious ceremonies. The Egyptian people bathed frequently and paid particular attention to their bowels. The art of circumcision was also practised and connected with purity and hygiene.[312] Many fragrances and cosmetics were imported, as the Egyptians associated nasty smells with impurity and sin and a good smell was considered "the fragrance of the gods". Two thousand years ago, the Roman historian Diodorus Siculus of Agyrium (c.85–20 BC) wrote on the Egyptian way of life:

> The whole manner of life in Egypt was so evenly ordered that it would appear as though it had been arranged according to the rules of health by a learned physician, rather than by a lawgiver.[313]

Mummification: preservation of the body for the afterlife

The Egyptian belief in immortality meant that a person's body had to be preserved after death.[314] In predynastic times, the dead were wrapped in a reed mat and buried on their side with a few personal belongings in a rectangle or oval pit.[315] Later, in the Old Kingdom, the Egyptians devised more elaborate methods of human preservation and burial sites, such as the monumental pyramids for the pharaoh.[316] Preservation was an essential part of funerary practice; a person's *ka* would return to find sustenance. The pyramids were built with false doors to permit the pharaoh's *ka* to move in and out among the living to ensure good fortune.[317] A mummy (or statue) had to have its mouth "opened" to ensure communication between the inanimate body and the afterlife. The Egyptians believed that if the body were decayed or unrecognizable the *ka* may go hungry and the afterlife would be jeopardized.[318]

The antiseptic procedure of body preservation is called mummification.[319] The bodies of pharaohs, priests and high officials were preserved by filling them with expensive aromatic and waxy, resinous substances and then coating them with resin-soaked bandages of linen.[320] The earliest surviving mummified body is that of Nefer, who lived around 2500 BC.[321] The embalmment process was costly. Use of waxes and perfumes was limited to the upper class and the bodies of poorer classes were salted, dried and wrapped in coarse mats and buried in shallow graves.[322] To assist the journey through the underworld, elaborate rites and spells were recited. The ancient Egyptians gained much knowledge of anatomy and physiology from the practice of mummification, which profoundly influenced later Greek medicine in the West.

The process of embalmment

Embalmment probably developed from the advanced chemical art of tanning and preserving animal hides. Herodotus described a typical procedure. The body was first positioned in the supine position. The brain was extracted through the nostrils with a long metal hook (after breaking the ethmoid bone). Next the abdominal cavity was opened along the left flank and internal organs removed and placed in a "pickling" solution with the exception of the heart. The heart was left in its place in the thoracic cavity and the insides washed with natron crystals (sodium bicarbonate) and salt water (brine) followed by a rinse with palm wine and a selection of fragrant spices.[323] The heart was considered to be the seat of life and intelligence,[324] an idea perpetuated by Aristotle in the fourth century BC (Ch. 5).

After rinsing and soaking the body for many weeks, the organs were returned to the corpse and packed tightly inside with sawdust, linen, mud, aromatic wood and flowers.[325] The body was then tightly wrapped in bandages and smeared with gum, resin, cassia and, in rare cases, bitumen.[326] Prior to the final wrapping, a funerary mask was placed over the head and shoulders to identify the mummy. The use of linen smeared with resinous products protected the body from water and other putrefactive breakdown agencies, further ensured by the extreme dryness of the desert environment. In the Ebers Medical Papyrus, in addition to mentioning conifer resins and beeswax, it also prescribes "bread in rotten condition" – a natural source of penicillin – which the Egyptians may have used for its tissue-preserving properties.

The drying of the body took about 35–40 days, and the entire embalming process, from death to burial, took about 70 days. Interestingly, Osiris, the god of death and rebirth, was also believed to have disappeared for 70 days before being resurrected as king of the dead. According to one creation myth, Osiris was the first Egyptian to be embalmed and reincarnated.[327] In the Old Kingdom, mummification was reserved for kings and those closest to them, but after Osiris became popular, from the Middle Kingdom onwards, mummification was available to anyone who could afford it.[328] Osiris offered all Egyptians the hope of an afterlife.

According to Herodotus, the process of embalmment did not proceed without problems. The most horrific reported were sexual violations carried out on women of high social status just after death. Herodotus wrote on a most loathsome form of necrophilia told to him during this travels in Egypt:

> The wives of men of rank are not given over to be embalmed immediately after death, nor indeed the more beautiful and valued women. It was not until they have been dead for three or four days that they are carried off to the embalmers. This was done to prevent indignities [carnal intercourse] from being offered to them.[329]

The practice of mummification did not occur in Sumer or Babylonia, ancient Greece, China[330] or India.[331] In India cremation was the preferred practice to facilitate the soul's migration from one existence to another and entry into the nirvana.[332]

Chemistry as craft

> Truth comes ... fully brewed in accordance with the sayings of the ancestors. Copy thy father and thy ancestors ... In this way the skilled man becomes learned.[333]

The ancient Egyptians were fascinated with the chemical arts. not only to supply their vast pharmacopoeia for treating sickness, hygiene and body preservation, but for advanced metallurgy, dyes, glazes, glass and the manufacture of pottery. Indeed, Egypt has long been recognized as the birthplace of the chemical arts, although Sumer cannot be ruled out. Indeed the words "alchemy" and "chemistry" are derived from Chemi(t) ("Black Land"). In ancient Egypt, the craftsman's job was hard and unforgiving. The lowly status of the tradesman is indicated in a section of papyrus (dated at around 1100 BC) written by a father giving some advice to his son concerning future employment.

> Put writing in your heart that you may protect yourself from hard labour of any kind, and be a magistrate of high repute. The scribe is released from all manual tasks; it is he who commands. I have seen a metal worker at his task at the mouth of his furnace, with fingers like a crocodile. He stank worse than fish-spawn. I have not seen a blacksmith on a commission, a founder who goes to the embassy.[334]

Most craftsmen worked for wealthy patrons, and the most skilled worked for the royal temple under the guidance of the priesthood. If they made new discoveries by accident or design, not all were shared with the priests, showing an independence not normally associated with the Egyptians.[335] Over time, this secrecy was in part responsible for the development of a number of specialist trades, which eventually led to the separation of the chemical from the applied arts. The most famous of chemical arts was alchemy, a quest to manufacture gold from base metals, which enjoyed a long history in medieval Europe and beyond the Renaissance.[336]

Chemical applications: the Leiden and Stockholm papyri

The earliest chemical applications in Egypt were primarily concerned with the extraction and working of metals, dyes, glazes, glass and manufacture of pottery.[337] Very few texts exist on the chemical arts. Two texts are the Leiden Papyrus and the Stockholm Papyrus,[338] which are thought to contain recipes dating back to the Middle and Old Kingdoms.[339] One feature of both papyri, and some medical texts already discussed, is that they were empirical, with few magical spells and incantations.[340]

The Leiden text contains some 75 recipes dealing with metal-working and includes the production of an alloy of gold and silver called *asem*[341] by ancient Egyptians (electrum by the Greeks).[342] There was much corruption in metal-working, illustrated by the fraudulent practice of making an alloy of gold using lead and not silver. The Leiden Papyrus states:

> One powders up gold and lead into powder as fine as flour, 2 parts of lead for 1 part of gold, and having mixed them, works them up with gum. One covers a copper ring with the mixture; then heats. One repeats several times until the object has taken *the colour*. It is difficult to detect the fraud, since the touchstone gives the mark of true gold. The heat consumes the lead but not the gold.[343]

The second text, the Stockholm Papyrus, is the larger of the two and contains about 150 recipes. The document is mostly concerned with the production of artificial gems and expensive dyes. One empirically tested recipe describes the whitening of pearls. The pearl was fed to a cockerel and left in the cockerel's gut to react chemically with its stomach acid and intestinal base; then the cockerel was killed and the pearl recovered, "when it will be found to be white".[344] Another recipe concerns the making of artificial pearls from roughened crystals (calculi developed from precipitation of calcium salts and other minerals) found in the urine of a young boy. The crystals were mixed with powdered "alum" (aluminium sulphate), and then dipped into "quicksilver" (mercury) and "woman's milk".[345] Again, these examples demonstrate that observations and experiment were part of Egyptian science and technology to achieve a practical end.

The Stockholm Papyrus also contains procedures for dyeing wool. The instructions include the cleaning and preparation of the wool with a solution made of ashes (alkaline carbonates) and the water from potter's clay (fine suspension of clay particles). Dyes of all colours were used and made from stones, flower parts, fruit juices and a vast pharmacopoeia. The recipe for setting purple dye (to be colourfast) in wool dyeing is as follows:

> After the wool has been mordanted, take twenty drachmas [one drachmas = 3.41 g] of good vinegar and add the wool. Add two of chalacanthum. Lift the wool and place it in a kettle of warm water and leave it for one hour. Take the wool out and rinse it.[346]

Metallurgy and trade

Metal harpoons have been excavated in Egypt dating back to about 3300 BC and a wide range of domestic utensils, tools, ornaments and weapons has been excavated from sites of the Old Kingdom (2664–2155 BC).[347] By the Middle Kingdom (2040–1640 BC) copper was hardened by alloying it with a small amount of tin to make bronze.[348] It is not known, however, whether tin was imported to make bronze or whether bronze itself was imported.[349] Some knowledge of bronze probably came to Egypt during the First Intermediate period (2134–2040 BC).[350]

Copper bars (or sheets) and precious metals silver, gold or electrum were used by the Egyptian traders in exchange for timber, semi-precious stones and cosmetics.[351] Money was not used in Egypt until well into the first millennium BC.[352] The other major metal of some interest was iron. Originally, iron was probably of meteoric origin because the Egyptians called it *bia-en-pet*, meaning "iron of heaven".[353] Although iron was introduced into western Asia by the third millennium BC, the Iron Age and smelting did not come to Egypt until after 525 BC while under Persian rule.[354] Before this, iron artifacts such as small daggers and the like were restricted to use in ritual practices.[355] One explanation for why the Egyptians remained in the Copper Age may relate to their social conservatism under pharaonic rule, but this is highly speculative.

Myth, religion and reality: social dimensions of the Near Eastern mindset

> We [today] have divorced philosophy, as a discipline, from religion. In the former we appreciate reality objectively, as something capable of study; in the latter we understand it subjectively, as something that can be experienced. This dichotomy did not govern ancient Near-Eastern thought. To it, appreciation of reality was subjective – "I–Thou" rather than "I–it". The results of ancient speculation are therefore communicated in the context of religion rather than science. J. P. Allen[356]

At the root of the ancient Egyptian and Sumero-Babylonian cultural success was their genius at problem-solving. Both peoples transformed their older Neolithic cultures into two of the world's first large river-valley urban settlements. This would not have been possible without a symbolic language incorporating a system of writing, mathematics, measuring, weighing and counting, and a system of units and standards to quantify. Without writing and some kind of standardization and quantification of measurement and time, critical information could not have been stored, irrigation canals could not have been built and repaired, food supplies could not have been sustained, monuments could not have been constructed, religious ceremonies could not have been coordinated, sickness and injury could not have been treated and metallurgy and trade could not have developed. Imagine building a pyramid if each worker had his own "personal" cubit as standard length. A nation simply could not have developed, or have been sustained, without the parallel development of symbolic language.

Today we take all these wonderful problem-solving operations and inventions for granted and rarely ask where they came from or the reasons behind their discovery.

Unfortunately, from the available texts and artifacts, it is not known how the Egyptians (or Mesopotamians) made their discoveries. Egyptologists know a lot about "what they did", they know a lot about "why they did it", but they are a long way from knowing "how they did it". Furthermore, the same applies to other aspects of their daily lives that are not part of their written records. A long complex vernacular or oral tradition must have existed alongside both Egyptian and Mesopotamian literary traditions.

Fortunately, considerably more is known about the intellectual framework from which the Near Eastern worldviews were constructed. Knowledge and reality in the Near East was what Frankfort termed the "I–thou" kind of structure, not the "I–it" kind, which is more in line with the way we think today.[357] While Frankfort's view is generally accepted among Near Eastern scholars,[358] some aspects of its structure have been challenged. For example, Kramer argued that the "I–thou" kind of knowledge was not representative of Near Eastern thought. It was silly, Kramer believed, to think that the ancients were unable to think reflectively or lacked the detachment of intellectual enquiry, or that the *cosmos* always appeared to them as a "thou" experienced emotionally in a dynamic reciprocal.[359]

Kramer used Frankfort's example of a Babylonian storm to illustrate his point. The Babylonians abstracted a storm as a terrifying encounter represented by a gigantic bird, Imdugud, devouring the Bull of Heaven, whose hot breath had scorched the crops.[360] Kramer argued that the ancient mindset would not have viewed a cloud in this way, but as "clouds that brought the refreshing rain".[361] Myth expert Theodor Gaster agreed with Kramer and argued that Frankfort's example of a storm "simply fails to understand the nature of *poetry*".[362] Gaster further cautioned taking a body of poetic and artistic texts, myths and tales, as representative of ancient thought. He believed that mythopoeia was more of a stylistic device.[363] While Frankfort would not have disagreed with Gaster on mythopeia as a form of poetry, his intent was to extend mythopoeia's meaning from feelings and affections *to a form of truth*.[364] Therefore Frankfort's "I–thou" analogy was largely concerned with the complex relation between language, thought and reality, with mythopeia as part of the ancients' literary genre.

Foremost in understanding the Near Eastern mindset is that most of their extra-ordinary accomplishments were made within the boundaries of a deep mythopoeic–religious worldview. The world of sense (what we call "nature") was not only interconnected, but formed a coherent and indistinguishable divine whole. The world was a grand society constructed and animated by the divine powers and manifestations of the gods, with the divine truths sanctioned by the high priests or pharaohs. This is what Frankfort was referring to when he made the analogy to "I–thou", and not a "physical" "*it*". Mythopoeia was a mode of thinking to explain relations in the world and the changing interactions between human beings and their gods. It was a way of seeking meaning, and of great explanatory significance, with its own logical structure from which the ancients built their knowledge and realities.

In summary, the Near Eastern experience was highly "mythologized" and the world was explained, almost exclusively, by divine causation using symbolic images (Fig. 3.3). The Imdugud bird in the Babylonian storm myth was a symbol of an otherwise deeply mysterious phenomenon in need of explanation. The Near Eastern experience lacked the conceptual construction of the physical world of physical objects (I–it) from which natural science depends. This is not to suggest that the mode of Near Eastern thought

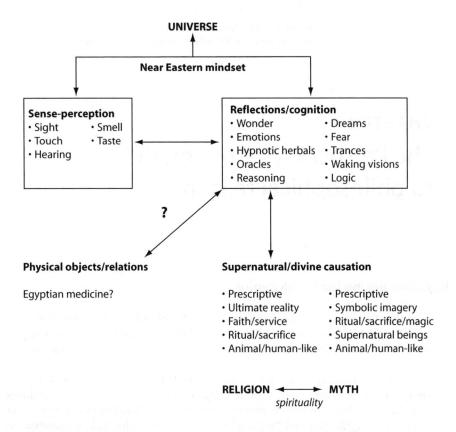

Figure 3.3 Schematic of the broad operations of the Egyptian and Sumero-Babylonian mindset leading to their divine worldviews. Both river-valley civilizations responded to questions about the universe and their place in it through myth and religion. The mythopoeic-religious mindset did not probe behind their gods' actions or ask philosophical questions about gods' existence, as in Presocratic and classical Greece. The gods were real to the people and manifest in the events going on around them such as day and night, the seasons, storms, life and death, sickness, the annual flood and so on. "Natural" science did not appear in these early cultures because the physical world comprising physical objects had not yet been abstracted.

was superstitious nonsense or lacked objectivity, only that it was framed within a "mythologized" divine worldview. To interrogate the world outside tradition, as sanctioned by the priesthood or pharaoh, would have broken the long chain of being linking self, society and the gods, and would have forfeited any chance of attaining the afterlife. The Near Eastern mindset lacked two important ingredients to break free from the past: the concept of the physical object; and a mode of reasoning and logical argument to help them explore "beyond" their traditions. In Chapter 4 we shall examine how the concept of the physical object and new modes of reasoning and argument came to the fore in ancient Greece and revolutionized Western thought, including the birth of natural science.

CHAPTER 4

The Presocratics: from myth to philosophical reason

Key to unlocking the Greek genius

The truth is that we are far more likely to underrate the originality of the Greeks than to exaggerate it, and we do not always remember the very short time they took to lay down the lines scientific inquiry has followed ever since.   John Burnet[2]

We have come to a turning point in our story. In the last two chapters, we saw that the people of Sumer and Egypt rarely ventured beyond the mythopoeic way of explaining the world around them. In this chapter we move forwards 2000 years to Greece, and show how the highly personal "I–thou" way of knowing changed dramatically to incorporate a more objective knowledge involving physical objects similar to that of today. It was truly an intellectual revolution that began in Greek epic poetry and ended in Greek philosophy: an age where distinctions were made between "myth and reason, tradition and innovation, community and individual, constraint and freedom, and error and truth".[3] The early philosophical period began around 600 BC and lasted around 200 years, and paved the way for Plato, Aristotle, Hippocratic medicine and the philosophical schools of subsequent generations.

This revolutionary way of thinking was not a widespread phenomenon but localized to small groups of independent innovators, known as the Presocratics, who lived along the Ionian coast and islands off present-day Turkey.[4] By separating nature from the gods, indeed defining nature and the physical universe for the first time, Western philosophy and science were born.[5] The Presocratics, armed with new tools of reasoning and logic, interrogated the world without the fear of retribution from the gods, ruling priestly class or god-incarnate pharaoh. The philosophical distinction between nature and the gods provided them with a key to explore everything from the creation and workings of the universe to the human mind itself. Everyday sense-phenomena such as thunder, lightning, rain, rainbows, fire, water, the stars, rivers, mountains, plants and animals were now explained by physical causes, not mythopoeic linkages to the divine.[6] The Presocratic mind-shift was a defining moment in Western history because knowledge and truth became a human responsibility without the need for divine norms sanctioned by a high priest or pharaoh, as in the Near East.

A question that has intrigued early Greek scholars for many decades is why this intellectual revolution happened in the first place. How does a new pattern of human thought arise at a particular place and time in history? The first point to make is that a change in thinking such as the one in ancient Greece rarely occurs as the result of one person or one event; rather, it is an outcome of a "process" occurring over generations with many vertical and lateral elements. Cultural historians know that a change was underway along the Ionian coast and offshore islands in the seventh century (and earlier), where there was a burgeoning cultural exchange between the region and the Near East and parts of Asia. There is also some evidence of the beginnings of a new political structure or *polis*[7] (a prelude to a democracy[8]) that appeared to nurture greater political and personal freedoms, opportunities for debate, innovation and more leisurely lifestyles.[9] Therefore, part of the reason why this intellectual revolution began in the first place appears to be because of a broad "mixing" of multicultural ideas, trade and practices, and a political system that allowed, or at least tolerated, individuals rethinking traditions and openly exploring beyond the present.

In this chapter, after introducing the epic works of Homer and Hesiod, which depicted reality more along the lines of the ancient Near East, we shall explore the worldviews of the Presocratics. How did they invent the physical object, construct a physical *cosmos* and explain the world of change? If the creator-gods were no longer useful to the philosophers, who or what became responsible for the creation of the world, ensured its harmony and prevented its collapse from evil forces? Where did the past hundreds of gods go? And who or what was left to look after the well-being of human beings? These are some of the questions that we shall examine in this chapter.

Geography and a brief history of Greece

Fostering of local independence

Greece is located about 640 km northwest of Egypt and 1900 km northwest of Sumer, across the Mediterranean Sea. The country's geography is often described as a headland broken in the middle by a huge rift with its whole eastern portion split into fragments.[10] After the demise of the Mycenaeans and subsequent Greek Dark Age (around 1000 BC), mainland Greece was divided into three parts: Northern, Central and Southern and by around 550 BC the Greeks had colonized many areas around the Mediterranean Sea, the Ionian coast being the most significant (see Fig. 4.1).

The most notable feature of Greece's geography is the absence of any great river valley. Instead, the Greeks made use of the fertile plains crisscrossing their rugged mountainous terrain. On these plains they built their cities, grew their fruit, cereals, grapes, olives and raised their sheep, goats and pigs.[11] In addition, Greece had an abundance of natural harbours, which provided its people with a gateway to Mediterranean trade and cultural exchange and, importantly, acted as a barrier against invasion.[12] The country's rugged terrain and geographical barriers promoted social independence and self-expression, but also led to fierce rivalry and hostility among neighbouring city-states and eventually conflicts. As Greece grew in power, its empire

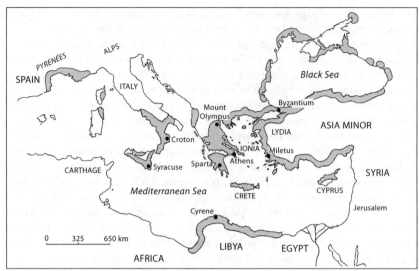

Figure 4.1 Early colonization of Greece (shaded areas) around 550 BC. Of particular significance were the Ionian coast and the offshore islands of Cos, Chios, Lesbos and Samos (not shown). This region became a major trade and intellectual exchange route and Western natural philosophy was born there. From the Ionian coast, the philosophical movement spread to mainland Greece (Abdera), southern Italy (Elea and Acragas) and Sicily.

extended from the Mediterranean Sea to the eastern side of the Aegean Sea and along the Ionian coast and offshore islands. The Ionian coast and islands became an important trade link between Europe, the Near East and Asia and allowed cross-fertilization of ideas.

Brief history of early Greece (7000–30 BC)

> We have outgrown the phase when all the arts [science and philosophy] were traced to Greece, and Greece was thought to have sprung like Pallas [virgin Greek goddess], full grown from the brain of Olympian Zeus; we have learnt how the flow of genius drew its sap from Lydians and Hittites, from Phoenicia and Crete, from Babylon and Egypt. Sir Leonard Woolley[13]

In the early nineteenth century it was customary to think of Greek history beginning around the first Olympiad (traditionally dated to 776 BC).[14] Historian George Grote (1794–1871) suggested this as a starting-point because he believed before this time history was steeped in fantasy and legend.[15] Today, Grote's view is no longer tenable and has been replaced with at least seven major periods:[16]

- Neolithic (c.7000–2600 BC)
- Minoan (c.2600–1400 BC)
- Mycenaean (c.2000–1200 BC)
- Homeric or Archaeic (c.800–600 BC)

- Presocratic (c.585–c.400 BC)
- Classical (c.469–322 BC)
- Hellenistic (c.322–30 BC)

Table 4.1 Summary of Greek prehistory and civilization (from Bury & Meiggs (1975: 501–6) and Fitton (2002: 6–7)).

*c.*7000–2600 BC	Greek **Neolithic period**. Origin unknown (Asia Minor/West Asia). Neolithic village at Knossos. Major excavation site at Thessaly and the Sesklo culture. Wood/mud-brick huts (round or rectangular). Later, appearance of first house of type called "megaron": a rectangular room with the entrance on one of the shorter sides, a central stone fireplace and a porch consisting of a roof and supported by pillars. Caves used for internments.
*c.*2600–2000 BC	Pottery in Thessaly shows a clear break away from Sesklo culture. **Early Bronze Age**. Minoan civilization appeared under local Aegean and Middle Eastern influence on the island of Crete (*c.*2600–2000 BC).
*c.*2000–1400 BC	First Minoan palaces and kingship on Crete. Potters wheel used. Hieroglyphic and Linear A writing. Strong Minoan influence on the mainland. The rise of Mycenaean culture with shaft-graves (*c.*1600 BC). Cataclysmic volcanic eruptions. Mycenaeans occupied Knossos (1450 BC). Destruction of Minoan palaces except at Knossos. The Hittites were the leading power in Asia Minor.
*c.*1400–1150 BC	**Great Age of Mycenae**. Flourishing trade with Egypt and Asia Minor. Linear B writing. Decline of Minoan culture (unknown causes). Mycenean destruction of Troy (*c.*1220 BC).
*c.*1150–800 BC	Eclipse of Mycenaean culture (drought or invasion?). Mycenae invaded and sacked by barbaric, culturally deprived Dorians from the north (*c.*1120 BC). Dorian colonization of Asia Minor. Period known as the **Greek "Dark Ages"** because archaeology reveals no new cultural traditions or written record. Mycenaean territories lapsed into cultural impoverishment.
*c.*800–600 BC	**Homeric period** (Homer's *Iliad* and *Odyssey*). Traditional date of first Olympiad (776 BC). Greek reorganization. Writing adapted from the Phoenician alphabet (*c.*750 BC). Independent city-states began to emerge (*c.*700 BC). New forms of self-government arose. Growth of sea trade and Greek colonization of Aegean Sea and Ionian coast of Asia Minor.
*c.*600–469 BC	Cultural centre of Greece shifted to Ionia on the coast of Asia Minor. **Presocratic Age**. Emergence of great thinkers, such as Thales of Miletus (*c.*624–550 BC), Anaximander (*c.*611–547 BC), Anaximenes (*c.*588–524 BC), Pythagoras (*c.*572–497 BC) to name only a few. Decay of aristocratic institutions, and subsequent rise of democracy with increasing participation of the citizens in government.
*c.*469 BC–322 BC	Democratic rule under Pericles (495–429 BC). Beginning of classical Greece with Socrates (469–399 BC). Consolidated Greece defeated Persia in the Persian Wars. Athens became the centre of Greek culture (wealth and power). Resentment from other city-states led to many internal conflicts culminating in the Peloponnesian wars (431 BC). Athens was defeated in 404 BC. Endless internal wars weakened Greek city-states, which were vulnerable to conquest. Plato (427–347 BC). Aristotle (384–322 BC). Alexander the Great (355–323 BC) founded Alexandria in Egypt (332 BC). Greece was under Macedonian rule: first King Philip II (382–336 BC) then Alexander.
322–146 BC	Great Age of Hellenic Greece under Macedonian control. Alexander the Great shifted intellectual capital from Athens in Greece to Alexandria in Egypt. Macedonian rule came under threat from the Romans. Corinthin was overthrown by Rome in 146 BC. By 44 BC, Rome controlled most of Greece, Asia Minor and northern Egypt.

To understand the dramatic influence Presocratic thought had on shaping Western thought, it is first necessary to understand the world of the epic poets Homer and Hesiod, which formed the basis of the Olympic religion practised by most Greeks for many centuries.

HOMER AND HESIOD: BRIDGING THE PAST WITH THE PRESENT

The *Iliad* and the *Odyssey* were the Old and New Testament of ancient Greece, studied by every schoolboy and cherished by Greek writers and artists as an inexhaustible source of inspiration.

C. W. Hollister[17]

Epic poetry: a staple of primary education

According to Plato and Aristotle, Homer and Hesiod[18] were among the first to "theologize" past myths into a popular Greek Olympic religion.[19] Epic poetry was the literary vehicle used by them to bridge the past, present and future. It provided an opportunity to synthesize vast amounts of past information that could not have been presented in a purely oral format.[20] Unlike Israel, Homeric Greece had no national sacred books, no secret creeds, no ancient temple documents and no need for secrecy as in Mesopotamia or Egypt.[21] The few exceptions included the sacred texts of the mystery cults of Dionysian and Orphic traditions, but these texts were not for *polis* affairs.

In the absence of sacred books, the Greeks sought to learn the will of the gods through the use of oracles and by interpreting the omens they believed were sent by the gods. The major gods lived on Mount Olympus and communicated with the Greeks by signs such as good or bad changes in health, luck, weather and so on.[22] The people responded directly through prayer, worship, ritual and sacrifice, and their thanksgiving ceremonies usually included a sacrificial meal and petitions. Each city had its own special gods and festivals. In contrast to the ancient Near East, early Greek society and thinking were built around a citizenry involving heroic Olympic traditions, not the dictates of a powerful priestly class or god-incarnate pharaoh.[23]

For centuries, Homer and Hesiod were household names and their works of epic poetry and on patterns of conduct were taught to children from a very young age.[24] Professional *rhapsodists* recited the poems in public places and attracted large audiences. Olympian religion was a national affair and Orpheus, a legendary singer in the sixth century BC (or earlier), is credited with poems containing theogonies, cosmologies and eschatological teachings.[25] Of special significance, one strand of the Orphic tradition is believed to have greatly influenced Pythagoras's (and later Plato's) views on transmigration and immortality (see later).

Homer's heroic epics: *Iliad* and *Odyssey*

Homer's *Iliad*, or "the poem about Ilios" (another name for the city of Troy) is thought to have been written in the eighth century BC. The epic describes the Trojan War of around 1250 BC between the Mycenaean Greeks and the people of Troy.[26] The attack was organized by King Agamemnon of Mycenae. His mission was to recapture Queen Helen, the abducted wife of King Menelaus of Sparta.[27] After warring for ten years and launching over a thousand ships, the Greek army finally entered Troy hidden inside an enormous wooden horse. The Greeks destroyed Troy and drove its inhabitants into exile. Homer's second poem, the *Odyssey*, is quite different but still focuses on heroes and larger-than-life themes. This epic deals with the wanderings and romantic adventures of a Greek war hero named Odysseus on his return home from the Trojan War.[28] Odysseus achieves fame not from strength and speed but from his shrewdness and ability to survive after the war and for his final restoration to family and kingship.[29]

In both poems, the Olympian gods play a pivotal role in the affairs of mortal human beings, who fight the most ferocious battles. The gods bestowed victory on their favourite heroes. Odysseus, for example, was protected during his long voyage back home to Greece after the sacking of Troy. The heroic acts of Odysseus fighting for the Greek cause were not in the absence of the gods, but in "partnership" with them.

Hesiod's *Works and Days*

Hesiod's *Works and Days* (*c*.650–675 BC) described day-to-day life in Greece and discussed how people should interact using the principles of moderation, reason and virtue.[30] According to Hesiod, moral "justice" was the main difference between humans and animals: "the fishes, beasts and birds eat one another".[31] Two famous inscriptions on the walls of the temple of Apollo at Delphi (first built around the seventh century BC) reportedly read "Know thyself" and "Nothing in excess", a theme expanded some 150 years later by Socrates. Moderation and reasonableness did not mean the Greek people had total freedom to do or say as they pleased. Crimes such as theft, murder and perjury were all punishable by law under the Code of Practices introduced by Solon[32] of Athens (*c*.640–560 BC). The lesser crimes, such as being overtly self-assertive, profane or insolent, were punishable by the wrath of god.

Hesiod's universe and its origins

According to Hesiod, the earth was a flat disk surrounded by a vast Okeanos (Fig. 4.2). The Okeanos was "the river surrounding the Earth, and source of all waters" and is believed to be of Hittite, or possibly Sanskrit, origin.[33] In addition to being the source of the oceans, the Okeanos was the origin and source of all the gods.[34] The sky was a solid hemispherical dome to which the stars were attached, and was supported on the shoulders of the mythical character Atlas. Atlas was a legendary Titan who supported the broad sky on his head and untiring arms. The underworld was the place of the dead, located below earth. Homer's *Odyssey* depicts it as a gloomy place where the souls wander around as spirits and experience no pleasure.[35] The idea of a shadowy afterlife did not appeal to all Greeks and many participated in ceremonies that gave them hope for a better afterlife.

In Hesiod's poem, the sun god crossed the sky on horses and chariots, not in a boat as in Egypt. At night, the sun god entered the Okeanos and sailed around to the east to begin another day. This symmetry implies that Hesiod (and Homer) envisaged the shape of the universe to be spherical, with a flat earth at its centre (Fig. 4.2). One cannot help noticing the extraordinary parallels between Hesiod's world structure and those of early Mesopotamia and Egypt.

Genesis according to Hesiod

For Homer and Hesiod were the first to compose Theogonies, and give the gods their epithets, to allot them their several offices and occupations, and describe their forms; and they lived but four hundred years before my time, as I believe.[36]

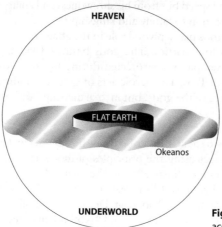

Figure 4.2 Basic structure of the world according to Homer and Hesiod.

For the origins of creation we have to turn to Hesiod's *Theogony* (*c*.700–725 BC). The *Theogony* was an attempt to relate the origin of the universe to the genealogy of the gods, and it apparently had Homer's endorsement. Homer did not write directly about the world's origin, although he did mention water as the likely element for the "essence of all things",[37] an idea that was taken up by the first Greek philosopher, Thales, some 100 years later. In the prelude to *Theogony*, Hesiod claims that the epic was revealed to him by the goddesses of literature.[38] The goddesses (or Muses[39]) appeared to Hesiod while he was tending his sheep at the foot of Mount Helicon.[40] The goddesses inspired him to sing praise to Zeus in hymn such as this:

> We know how to tell many falsehoods that sound like the truth;
> But we also know to utter the truth when we choose.

This seems to be Hesiod's way of telling his readers that he knew how to discriminate fact from fiction, truth from falsehood.[41] In contrast to the creation stories in Mesopotamia and Egypt passed down from generation to generation, the *Theogony* appears to be "one" person's account or interpretation of Greek tradition, which was eventually accepted by the people.[42] It was a literary way of linking the existing Olympian pantheon to the great mystery of the origin of the universe.[43] What follows is Francis Cornford's translation of the poem, summarized in Figure 4.3:

> First of all Chaos came into being, and next broad-bosomed Gaia [mother-earth], for all things a seat unshaken for ever, and Eros [love], fairest among the immortal gods, who looses the limbs and subdues the thought and wise counsel of all gods and of all men.
>
> From Chaos was born Erebus [male darkness] and black Night [female]; and from Night was born Bright Sky and Day [female], whom Night conceived and bore in loving union with Erebus. [Erebus and Night were the parents of Aether and later Kronos who was father of Zeus.]

And Earth first gave birth to the starry Heaven [Ouranus, sky], equal to herself, that he might cover her all about, that there might be for the blessed gods a seat unshaken for ever.

And she bore the high Hills, the pleasant haunts of the goddess Nymphs who dwell in the wooded hills. Also she bore the unharvested deep, with raging flood, the sea [Pontos], without the sweet rites of love.

And Earth lay with Heaven and bore their children the Titans; Oceanus, Hyperion, Iapetus, Themis, Memory, Phoebe, also Tethys, and the one-eyed Cyclopes and Cronus.[44]

In the beginning Hesiod[45] describes the primeval chaos "coming into being" from some primordial entity, but unfortunately he does not explain what this entity was other than to say it was gloomy. The word "chaos" meant a *separated state* out of which the present universe arose. The root meaning of the word is "gape", "gap" or "yawn", which has been translated to mean "gaping void". Chaos was therefore a "separated state of being". In modern-day cosmology, Hesiodic chaos would not be the Big Bang itself (from time zero to 10^{-43} s) but the long period between the Big Bang to just before the formation of our solar system (see Ch. 9).

From this "gaping void", the Muses told Hesiod that the earth (Gaia) and love (Eros) "came into being". Next came the earth followed by darkness (the male Erebus) and night (female), which produced a pair of opposites: air (male) and day (female). After the union of earth and heaven (or sky), the opposites began to separate; for instance light out of darkness, the heavenly fires from the stars and the land and hills from the seas, and so on. This sense of process, of cause and effect, was very different from the myths in ancient Sumer and Egypt, where the earth and heaven appeared simultaneously.[46]

But like their Near Eastern neighbours, Hesiod's gods generally behaved in a similar anthropomorhic fashion: they make love and produce offspring. Of the three creator-gods, love (Eros), was perhaps the most powerful. Love was responsible for bringing earth and heaven together, after which a long series of sexual procreations occurred, producing the universe structure. The sea, however, appeared without any apparent act of love whatsoever, so there were exceptions to gods' making love and producing structures. Hesiod's cosmogony ends with the establishment of the four elements, later

In the beginning ...?
↓
Chaos
↓
Earth – Love
↓
Darkness – Night
Sky – Day
↓
Heaven
↓
Completion of the universe

Figure 4.3 Hesiod's cosmogony from chaos to the formation of the universe.

referred to in Greek philosophy as water, air, fire and earth. The formation of the universe from chaos was now complete.

Origin of Zeus and the gods of Mount Olympus

The familiar Olympian gods emerge in the second part of the *Theogony*.[47] Their origin is the "high place" of Mount Olympus and they are headed by the sovereign deity Zeus. Zeus did not appear out of nowhere but can be traced back to Minoan times (*c*.2600–1400 BC), when Zeus was a lesser male sky god named Zagreus[48] who was the consort of the supreme Mother Goddess of fertility and earth. By 750 BC, Zagreus had grown in power to finally emerge in the epic poems of Hesiod and Homer as the almighty Zeus.[49]

The other eleven major gods were Apollo, Poseidon, Demeter, Dionysos, Athena, Hermes, Hephaistos, Hera, Ares, Artemis and Aphrodite. Each god was generally responsible for one or more of the sense-phenomena human beings experience (Table 4.2). Like Zeus, most can be traced back to earlier Greek Minoan and Mycenaean times. In addition to the major Olympian gods there were hundreds of other gods in the Greek pantheon. Unlike Sumer and Egypt, these minor gods lived all over the earth's surface, in the seas and under the earth and sometimes mingled with the people.

Hesiod claimed that after the birth of the gods, a long battle began between the Olympians and the Titans (who were bound to the world of Kronus).[50] As predicted, Zeus and his pantheon emerged victorious, bringing to an end a dynasty of dark, chaotic gods.[51] Homeric scholars suggest that the battle was Hesiod's literary abstraction of good and evil, with good representing the order of the universe, and evil the monstrous unpredictable forces that torment humans now and again. Although we are never told who the evil Titans were, they may have been an older discredited pantheon of gods from the Mycenaean period responsible for the Dark Ages.[52]

Some historians have even suggested the story of the battle was a re-enactment of an earlier conflict between two rival religions involving the Aegean and Indo-European settlers, from which the latter emerged victorious.[53] After Zeus's victory, clear separations occurred between the earth and sky and light and dark. It also heralded the

Table 4.2 Twelve major Olympian gods and divine functions.

Zeus	King of gods and responsible for thunder, with the thunderbolt as his weapon
Apollo	God of prophecy and the sun god; giver of light
Poseidon	God of the sea and shaker of the earth (earthquakes)
Demeter	Goddess of the earth and provider of grain
Dionysus	Goddess of fertility and wine
Athena	God of wisdom and knowledge and guardian of Athens (Mycenaean roots)
Hermes	God associated with vitality and cunning (even deceit)
Hephaistos	God of fire and metalworking
Hera	Goddess of marriage and goddess concerned with the life of women and guardian of children
Ares	God of war-like spirit, deified and not greatly liked among the Greeks
Artemis	Virgin goddess of nurturing, of flora and fauna and hunting (thought to be linked to older great fertility goddess)
Aphrodite	Goddess of love (Babylonian, Phoenician roots)

birth of gods responsible for world order and the health of human society.[54] The remaining portion of Hesiod's *Theogony* concerns human destiny and the continual battle to maintain world order.[55]

Human origins

A more detailed account of human origins appears in Hesiod's *Works and Days*.[56] The epic describes five successive races of humans: "the golden race of mortal men", silver race, bronze race, heroic race and iron race.[57] The first two were created by the Olympian gods at the time of Kronos "when he was king in Heaven".[58] The other three were the creations of Zeus himself. The "iron" race was the race that inhabited earth. This scheme of human succession has no parallel in either the older Mesopotamian or Egyptian literature. Hesiod makes no mention, however, of the creation of the first woman, other than a statement that the men of the silver race had mothers.[59]

Overall, *Works and Days* depicts the human condition on earth as morally wretched and depraved. In Olympian religion, there was little hope of a happy afterlife.[60] The god Hades was the ruler of the dark, bleak underworld to which all humans went after death, although there is little detail of the conditions there. Traditional Greek religion, as reflected in the epic poems, emphasized the shortness of human life compared to the immortal life of the gods.

Hesiod's separation of creator- and Olympian gods

Hesiod's creator-gods were separate from the hundreds of less powerful gods in both time and space; a similar ordering to that which appears in the extant cosmogonies of ancient Sumer and Egypt. Hesiod's creator-gods lived in the Okeanus, and were synonymous with the powers of the universe, and not with the day-to-day running of the world. In Sumer, Hesiod's Okeanus was similar to the primeval sea, and in Egypt, the Nun (see Chs 2 and 3). However, there were differences. The gods, particularly the Olympian gods, lived close to the Greek people and interacted with them. This does not appear to have been the case in ancient Sumer or Egypt. The Sumerian and Egyptian gods were involved in day-to-day affairs but exerted their influence mostly from the heavens; spatially they were more at arm's length from the people than the gods in Homeric Greece. Hesiod's cosmogony had 12 main gods (plus many lesser gods), whose main abode was Mount Olympus. This has no precedent in the ancient Near East. In 1931, Greek scholar Roy Hack described the significance of the anthropomorphic gods on Olympus and their binding relationships with human beings in the following way:

> The anthropomorphic gods [on Olympus] were now in the perilous position of being utterly dependent upon the faith of their worshippers; their lives hung by this thread; the moment any one ceased to believe in their real existence, that moment they ceased to exist. Contrast their position with the immortal powers of the universe, who will continue to exist whether any human being believes in them or not.[61]

Hesiod apparently failed to foresee the repercussions of partially separating the Greek gods from the immortal powers of the universe, and changing their location from the heavens to Mount Olympus. If a person became sceptical about a designated role of one or more of the Olympian gods to explain sense-phenomena, those gods simply vanished from the landscape. Hack and others went on to propose that this "new" awareness partially anticipated the Presocratics.[62] While there is no doubt that a change in divinity was underway, the next section shows that the literary recasting of past myths into epic poetry was very different to what the Presocratics accomplished. The Homeric stories remained a form of rationalism in mythopoeic dress, not physical relations among physical objects in a physical world.

PRESOCRATIC GREECE (c.585–c.400 BC): INVENTION OF THE PHYSICAL OBJECT

The word Presocratic ("before Socrates") first became current in English in the early twentieth century after German scholar Hermann Diels, who used it for the title of his great collection of evidence of early Greek philosophy.[63] In Greek times, Aristotle was apparently the first to distinguish between the "Presocratic" world and the older mythopoeic world of the ancients.[64] He called this new way of thinking *physiologia* to contrast it from the older *mythologia* and *theologia*, which he believed was crude, uninteresting storytelling whereby poets recited myths about heroes and gods.[65] By contrast the Greek people themselves did not consider epic poetry uninteresting; it remained a vital part of Olympic popular religion, outdoor plays and orations[66] for many centuries extending well into the Hellenistic period.[67]

The new philosophical[68] movement to which Aristotle referred developed on the Ionian coast and offshore islands near present-day Turkey (Fig. 4.1). The region had 12 major cities,[69] which had consolidated into a type of confederation (probably religious in origin) with Miletus as its main centre. During the late seventh and sixth centuries, the area became a major trade and intellectual exchange route between the East and West.[70] From the Ionian coast, the movement spread to mainland Greece (Abdera), southern Italy (Elea and Acragas) and Sicily.[71] The main groups were: the Milesians (Thales, Anaximander, Anaximenes); the Pythagoreans; the Eleatics (Parmenides and Zeno); and the Atomists (Leucippus and Democritus) (Fig. 4.4). In addition, there were a number of individuals – including Xenophanes, Heraclitus, Empedocles and Anaxagoras – who were not associated with any regular groups, but shared common intellectual interests. Unfortunately, only "fragments" of the Presocratic corpus survive and much of their thinking has been obtained from valuable excerpts, summaries and commentaries by later philosophers and historians.[72]

The Ionian Schools: the first physical reductionists

This advance in higher generalisations constitutes the essence of the new step taken by the Greeks ... It marks the advance from precepts to concepts, from the individual examples perceived by sight or touch (senses) to the universal notion which we conceive in our minds – in sculpture no longer an individual but the ideal of humanity; in geometry, no longer triangles but the nature of triangularity and the consequences which logically and necessarily flow from being a triangle.   W. K. C. Guthrie[73]

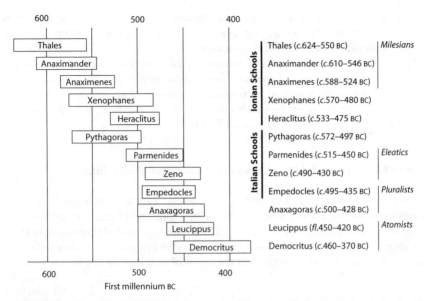

Figure 4.4 Chronology of the major Greek Presocratic philosophers. Pythagoras is generally considered the first of the "Italian philosophers", meaning those Greek thinkers who lived in southern Italy and Sicily (sometimes called "Greater Greece").

The Ionian philosophers were not interested in water to irrigate their crops but in water itself. They were not interested in air to vent their fires or kilns but with air itself. They were not interested in fire to harden their pottery or anneal their metals but in the properties of fire itself. And they were not as interested in new ways to map their lands as in number, point, line, plane and angle, and so on.[74] The Ionian philosophers were more interested in explaining everyday experience by reducing or breaking events into different parts and describing them as a series of "physical" relationships among "impersonal" objects from a single principle or *arche*.[75]

This is why the Ionian philosophers are often called the first physical reductionists. They reduced experience to interactions among physical objects, worked out the linkages or relations and then reassembled the whole. Reductionism is not doing away with the thing you are trying to explain, as is sometimes claimed. It deals with explaining everyday experience by seeking the underlying truths of that experience. This new approach of the Ionians required a new language, or at least putting old words into new contexts with new meanings.

Some scholars associate the first appearance of the Greek word *physis* with Heraclitus around 500 BC,[76] but Presocratic expert Edward Hussey discussed how it was used once by Homer to mean "essence" or "what [something] really is". Etymologically, *physis* has been connected with "to bring forth", "origin" or "genesis", and later with the "material" or "physical" source from which flows the movement detected by our senses.[77] The word *physis* was opposed to *tyche*, or chance, often conceived as mere appearance. This new use of *physis* has some parallels with the older

Mesopotamian word *simtu* (one of the four Mesopotamian protective souls or spirits). *Simtu*, as noted in Chapter 2, was associated with "originating from an agency endowed with the power to act and to dispose".[78]

Physis also became synonymous with nature (Latin *natura*), which had two distinct meanings: the sum of natural objects and events in the physical world; and the "nature" of things, the constitution, structure or essence of an object.[79] To search for the "nature" of things meant to search for the underlying or first principle, the *archē*, from which all things arose (and returned). Other new words and concepts used by the philosophers can be found in Table 4.3.

Thales of Miletus (c.624–550 BC): water as the essence of all things

> Thales, the founder of this sort of philosophy, says that it is Water (accordingly he declares the Earth rests on water), getting the idea I suppose, because he saw the nourishment of all beings is moist, and that heat itself is generated from moisture and persists in it (for that from which all things spring is the first principle of them), and getting this idea also from the fact that the germs of all beings are of a moist nature.
>
> Aristotle[80]

Very little is known about Thales' life. He reportedly travelled extensively to Mesopotamia (Babylonia) and Egypt, after which he returned and formed a group of intellectuals sharing common interests.[81] Thales is famous for proposing water[82] as the first principle (*archē*; "All things come from water, and to water all things return"[83]). Why Thales chose water is not clear. He may have borrowed the idea from the creative powers of water in Homer or Hesiod, or perhaps from the primeval sea of Mesopotamia or the Nun in Egypt. Some suggest that Thales may have been acquainted with the biblical account of the Creation, which mentions "waters under the firmament".[84] In broad structure, Thales' cosmology was a sphere with a flat earth floating in the middle of a vast water-bed: "The Earth", he reportedly said, "is supported by water on which it rides like a ship."[85]

Thales further reasoned that the air (either as steam or invisible vapour) was produced by the expansion of water (accompanying heating), and the earth was a result of the cooling and contraction of water.[86] He also explained earthquakes as caused by "physical" wave tremors that led to rifts and earth tremors.[87] There was no need to invoke the Olympian god of the sea, Poseidon, or any other god to explain the annual flooding of the Tigris, Euphrates and Nile.

Thales as a geometrician and astronomer

Thales was among the first to bring geometry and arithmetic to Ionia.[88] While in Egypt, Thales reportedly used geometry to estimate the height of a pyramid. Selecting the time of day when his shadow was equal to his own height, he ingeniously paced out the shadow cast by the pyramid and calculated its vertical height by simple geometry.[89] Thales also devised a way to calculate the distance of ships from land. He advised Greek sailors on navigational routes (via knowledge from Phoenicia), and he played an instrumental role in reforming the Greek calendar by introducing four distinct seasons of the solar year.

Table 4.3 Definitions of Greek terms.[90]

Aether	The *aether* or the fifth element was so-named by Empedocles. It is a purified form of Anaximenes' "air", which surrounded the world/universe. It was pure, everlasting, alive and intelligent; all the attributes of the divine, which is why it is referred to as "divine air".
Archē	The word *archē* was used by Homer and by Presocratic Anaximander to denote the first principle or essence of things. Plato sometimes adopted the word "archetypes" to describe his "ideas" or "Forms". Aristotle described *archē* as a primary substance or element. The word usually conveys a starting-point or beginning, or an originating and underlying "cause". In the theological sense, *archē* is also often translated to mean "a beginning" or "starting-point". The word has been preserved today in the English language as "archetype".
Cosmos	The finite world as opposed to the wider universe (which may be finite or infinite). Many worlds are called *cosmoi*. It is often claimed that Pythagoras was among the first to coin the term *cosmos* for the intelligibility, harmony and order of the world. Only after Aristotle were the terms *cosmos* and universe used interchangeably.
Dialectic	*Dialectic* originally meant "art of conversation or debate", but then adopted a more specific meaning in the language of philosophy for the type of reasoning that seeks to develop truth. The term was generally applied by Socrates and later in Plato's Academy to describe Socrates' mode of argument. Plato and later Aristotle accredited its invention to Zeno of Elea (*c*.490–430 BC). Aristotle used the intellectual process of "dialectic", as opposed to "science" for that department of mental activity that examines the presuppositions on which the sciences are based. Where Aristotelian science aims at general laws, dialectic investigates the logical construction of those laws, including their strengths and limitations.
Divine	In the beginning, the idea of the "divine" was probably conceived as a belief in an external spiritual power or force. Later it became synonymous with the gods. The word "divine" did not appear before Anaximander, and was not widely used as a substitute for god until the middle of the fourth century BC.
Logos	There is no English word to adequately convey the meaning of *logos*, in its Greek context. In Homer's epic the word *logos* is often translated as something "spoken" from the verb *legein*, "to say" or "to state": not mere talk, prayer, story-telling or commands but a significant statement, narrative or discussion. Later, with Heraclitus, *logos* was associated with "law", "reason" and "principle" and the process of linking thought to reality. *Logos* may also have been based on the Hebrew *memra*, but this theory is controversial. In Christian theology, after Philo Judaeus, *logos* has been associated with "divine reason" manifest in the creation of the world. In philosophy, *logos* is "discourse" and "general principle", and in mathematics, with "proportion". The English word "logic" is derived from *logos* from Greek *logikos*.
Nous	*Nous* appears to have been borrowed from earlier writings as it was a favourite word of Homer to describe "mental seeing" or "planning". The big difference was that Anaxagoras added a creative and cosmic ordering component to *nous* by specifically invoking mind-intelligence (pure reason). Anaxagoras's *nous* was the cosmic organizing principle that first set the universe in motion and continued thereafter to play a key role in the animations of living forms, which Aristotle likened to the cosmic Mind. It existed in a pure state, unmixed with matter and organized the world into its present form from an undifferentiated mass.
Psyche	Generally equates with soul: inner soul or cosmic soul. The word appears to be related to the Homeric *thymos* (the conscious, emotional self) which was the seat of passions, courage and love. In Homer's *Iliad*, *psyche* was used in the sense of "breath" (as was the later Latin *anima*), which then came to mean "breath of life" or life principle. The *psyche* in Homer is mentioned only when it leaves the body after death; it is the life breath or animating spirit that departs as a ghost. Pythagorean *psyche* was also immortal and temporarily on loan to a human beings or animals during life; it left after death and returned in new life. Pythagorean *psyche* has a fuller notion of personality and more intimate sense of identity than Homer's *psyche*. Thus, *psyche* came to be an intellectual element associated with life and, after Anaximenes, developed a cosmic dimension of which all human beings were a part. In other contexts, *psyche* can be taken to mean a cause of motion or a self-mover.
Pneuma	Anaximenes gave Homer's "life-breath" the new name *pneuma*, which, in the fifth century, was changed to *aether* by Empedocles. Interestingly, the term *pneuma theu* was also used in the Old Testament (Genesis 1:2) and is commonly interpreted as the "Spirit of God". It also appears in the later New Testament and is often translated to mean "Holy Ghost". Finally, the word *pneuma* came to be synonymous with mind itself, soul or spirit (sometimes immortal).

Herodotus and Xenophanes further reported that Thales predicted the solar eclipse of 28 May 585 BC.[91] Thales is said to have rejected the claim that the eclipse was due to "Zeus darkening the Sun at noon".[92] Eclipses were a part of natural cycles and could be predicted from mathematical astronomy, something he probably learned from the high priests of Babylonia.[93]

Static electricity and magnetism

Thales reportedly knew that when amber was rubbed it had a "certain degree of animation".[94] Today this phenomenon is known as "static electricity". Thales is also credited with the idea that a magnet had animation or a life-force because it attracted iron.[95] He claimed that magnets had a soul and could move other bodies without being moved themselves, which led some later commentators to link this power with the human soul and soul of the universe.[96] Aristotle wrote: "Thales, judging by what they report, seems to have believed that the soul was something that produces motion, inasmuch as he said that the magnet has a soul because it moves iron ... Some say that the soul is mixed in the whole universe."[97] Cicero and Aetius (fl. c. AD 100) went one step further and linked Thales with the idea that god was soul (mind), who fashioned all things from water.[98]

Thales as the first philosopher

Despite the scanty nature of the evidence, if we accept Aristotle's account,[99] Thales' way of thinking was revolutionary. Although he appears to have relied on past mythopeic representations for the broad construction of his world, he did not rely on mythical explanations for its workings, and this alone justified the claim that he was the first natural philosopher.[100] Sense-phenomena were now explained using a new conceptual framework involving physical manifestations linking all things to one irreducible element, water. The hundreds of gods and their manifestations were no longer required.

Anaximander of Miletus (c.610–546 BC): *apeiron* as the essence of all things

> It [his book *Concerning Nature*] effectively defined the shape and contents of Greek philosophical cosmology for centuries to come, establishing a tradition which might be regarded as culminating in Plato's *Timaeus* or – translated to Rome – in Lucretius' *On the Nature of Things*.   M. Schofield[101]

Anaximander[102] shared Thales' idea that one could explain the world in physical terms but rejected water as the underlying principle from which the world and everything in it arose. "How could fire come from water?", he asked. Anaximander's "first principle" was something more abstract and hidden from the human senses: the *apeiron*.

The apeiron

No one really knows how Anaximander viewed the *apeiron*. Simplicius (c. AD 525) states it was "neither water nor any of the so-called elements".[103] The *apeiron* is often translated as "unlimited",[104] "without boundaries", "formless", "unrestricted", "eternal", "inexhaustible" and "indeterminate".[105] According to Aristotle, it was the initial substance into which "everything takes rise and to which everything returns ... It encompasses all things and governs all things".[106] Aristotle also believed the *apeiron* was divine from its association with the immortal, eternal, indestructible, all-encompassing and all-governing.[107] It was the highest divine principle that guided the interplay between the conflicting opposites and rhythmic cycles of the visible world.[108]

The *apeiron* was the eternally moving, inexhaustible reservoir surrounding the world, out of which everything came and returned. The idea has some parallels with Thales' water, Homer's *Okeanos*, the Sumero-Babylonian primeval sea and the Egyptian Nun, from which the world "came into being". Having something "surrounding" the world with creative functions is a recurring theme in ancient cosmological thinking. From what Anaximander wrote and later commentators conjectured, the *apeiron*:

- makes up the unlimited universe;
- possesses eternal motion;
- lies outside the world and is beyond human experience;
- is the first principle from which the world was created;
- is immortal, eternal, indestructible and all-encompassing; and
- governs or steers all things, that is, world order.

The physical world of Anaximander

Anaximander's world was physical. It was an intelligible series of dynamic cycles between opposing properties; hot and cold, wet and dry.[109] The four physical opposites were not made of the *apeiron*, but were *products*. Each separated very early during the world formation from intrinsic "eternal" motion (see "Anaximander's cosmogony and cosmology", below). The "four opposites" and the concept of "separating out" formed the basis of explanation of physical change.[110]

The winds were not a manifestation of the gods but were produced when the finest vapours of the air separated and then moved together in one mass.[111] Lightning occurred when the wind leaped forth and separated the clouds. Thunder was explained by Anaximander: "when (wind) is imprisoned in a dense cloud and escapes with violence, the disruption of the cloud produces the noise, and the rest appears luminous in contrast with the dark of the cloud".[112] Rain was formed from vapour raised by the sun and concentrated in the clouds, which then fell to the ground.[113]

Anaximander explained the motions of the heavenly bodies as caused by currents of air (wind) that acted like bellows to fuel the fire, giving them brightness. Reality was a world built from physical states detected by the human senses (seeing, hearing, smelling, touching and tasting). Such physical explanations extended beyond meteorological phenomena and were adopted by the Hippocratic doctors later to diagnose and treat human sickness (Ch. 5).

Anaximander's cosmogony and cosmology

The *cosmos* and its major features, including life on earth, are conceived as the outcome of evolving interactions between two fundamental but opposed physical forces. It emerges somehow from something infinite and eternal which surrounds and controls it.

M. Schofield[114]

Anaximander's *Concerning Nature* began with a cosmogony and ended with a geometric description of a finite world that he called a *cosmos* (see Table 4.3).[115] The *cosmos* was physical, intelligible and ordered by immanent law. Only the *cosmos* was created, not the *apeiron*, which had been around for ever.[116] The idea of an eternal universe, as opposed to a finite world, was similar to the cosmologies of ancient Mesopotamia, Egypt and Homeric Greece. The most significant difference was the absence of a powerful pre-creator or creator-gods.

In the beginning there was a cosmic "seed" or "egg", which rapidly expanded to form the *cosmos*. The seed began as a portion of the rotating[117] *apeiron*, split away and was set in motion by two opposing qualities, hot and cold.[118] As the hot and cold "separated", the flame (hot and dry) formed a spherical sheath around the air (cold–wet). From the action of the flame, the core further separated into air and a kind of mud that dried to form the earth and sea.[119] Fire was therefore the active agent for the expansion from a seed to a *cosmos*. Note how Anaximander begins to build the world from a logical intellectual process of successive "cause and effect" stages, not unlike Hesiod and the ancient Near East peoples, but without any mention of gods making love and begetting offspring.[120] Instead the approach is more naturalistic.

The earth (cold and dry) remained at the centre with the less dense water (cold and wet) partly covering it. Above the earth was the air (warm and wet) and the least dense fire (hot and dry) of the fixed stars.[121] The fixed stars remained the closest to the earth, next was the moon, and the sun was outermost (highest concentration of fire) (see Fig. 4.5).[122] The daily movements of the heavenly bodies were explained by the wind driving the "invisible" concentric rings of fire, which had "breathing holes" through which the stars, moon and sun shone.[123]

Anaximander calculated the diameters of the cosmic rings in multiples of three; the outermost sun wheel was 27 times the earth's diameter; the moon wheel 18 times; and the closest fixed stars and planets 9 times.[124] The flat cylindrical earth had a depth of one-third its diameter, but no one knows why he chose this ratio.[125] Anaximander was the first to give cosmology a mathematical basis without divine causation. No Sumerian, Babylonian, Egyptian or Greek had ever done this before. Mathematizing the cosmic order led to the idea of cosmic intelligence.

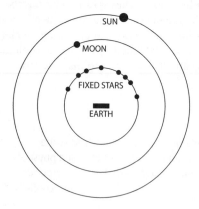

Figure 4.5 Schematic of Anaximander's cosmology. According to Hippolytus (d. *c.* AD 235) "The heavenly bodies came into being as a circle of fire separated off from the fire in the world, and enclosed by air. There are breathing-holes, certain pipe-like passages, at which the heavenly bodies show themselves; accordingly eclipses occur when the breathing holes are blocked up. The moon is seen now waxing, now waning according to the blocking or opening of channels. The circle of the sun is 27 times the size of the earth, the moon 18 times; the sun is the highest, and the circles of the fixed stars are lowest" (quoted in Kirk *et al.* 1983: 135).

Another remarkable feature of Anaximander's *cosmos* was its spatial symmetry. Because the four opposites were in perfect symmetry with one another, he reasoned that the *cosmos* was similarly symmetrical.[126] The earth remained stationary in the centre because it was equidistant from all points. There was no need for water to support the earth, as was believed for thousands of years. Here we have the introduction of the Principle of Sufficient Reason: the earth remains in position because it does not have sufficience reason to move one way or the other.[127] Symmetry and harmony went hand in hand because nothing could enter or leave; everything in space was contained. Although Anaximander did not know of the sphericity of the earth, philosopher Karl Popper (1902–1994) described his idea of the suspended earth in symmetrical space as: "One of the boldest, most revolutionary, and most portentous ideas in the whole of history of human thought. It made possible the theories of Aristarchus and Copernicus."[128] Although Popper's statement is exaggerated, Anaximander's chain of reasoning was nonetheless extraordinary.

Anaximander also mentioned innumerable worlds (or *cosmoi*), which came into existence at different times from the rotating *apeiron*.[129] Hippolytus (d. *c.* AD 235) quoted Anaximander as saying: "Besides this, motion is eternal and does not grow old, and it surrounds all the worlds."[130] Some believe the phrase "all the worlds" meant successive worlds appearing and disappearing in a series of natural cycles, as in older Hindu myths, while others believe the innumerable worlds coexisted with the present one. Nineteenth-century scholar Eduard Zeller (1814–1908) believed that Anaximander may have been referring not to separate worlds, but to the innumerable stars or heavenly bodies in the sky.

Anaximander: the first evolutionist

Living creatures came into being from moisture evaporated by the sun. Man was originally similar to another creature, that is, to a fish.   Hippolytus[131]

The first living creatures spontaneously emerged when the heat of the sun warmed the moist soil of the earth.[132] This idea of spontaneous generation dates back to the ancient Egyptians and survived up until the middle of the nineteenth century (see Ch. 9). Like his contemporary, Thales, Anaximander believed that all living things were created from water in the sea and on land, and arose from the interaction among opposites. And like rainwater, which circulates between earth and the clouds, so too life comes and goes from the four basic elements.[133] Anaximander saw nature as a self-regulating system of cycles.

Anaximander is thought to have reasoned further that human beings developed from lower animals via transmutation from fish.[134] If this is true, and the evidence is obscure, this places Anaximander among the first to propose an evolutionary theory and anticipate Ernst Haeckel (1834–1919) by some 2400 years. Haeckel proposed that the individual embryo developing from the fertilized egg into a human baby passes through successive stages resembling ancestral forms of the human species, leading to his famous "ontogeny recapitulates phylogeny".[135]

In summary Anaximander not only invented the physical *cosmos* in mathematical space without the need for intervention from the gods, but he saw nature as a balanced self-regulating system with human beings and other animals generated or evolved from lower forms. Anaximander appears to have started his intellectual journey with the natural world,[136] made it intelligible and then proceeded towards the highest principle, his "divine" *apeiron*.[137] Anaximander had a truly extraordinary prescient mind.

Anaximenes of Miletus (c.588–524 BC): air as the essence of all things

Anaximenes' first principle was air,[138] not Thales' water or Anaximander's *apeiron*. The idea was attractive because it shared with the *apeiron* the properties of "one" and "qualitatively boundless", but like Thales' water had the feature of a physical element of common experience.[139] In the reductionist tradition, Anaximenes reasoned that air, in its "most evenly" distributed state, was the atmosphere in which the earth, planets and heavenly bodies floated.[140] In its most "rarefied" state air became fire; in its "more condensed" state it became water; and in its "most condensed" state it became earth and rock. Thus, he had two intrinsic physical mechanisms to explain elements turning into others; rarefaction (thinning out) and condensation (compaction).[141]

Anaximenes' air was not just the physical element we breathe but was manifest in the "gods and things divine". Divine "air" was named *pneuma* (literally unseen "breath" or "spirit") and later in the fifth century was called the *aether* by Empedocles (*c*.495–435 BC) (see Table 4.3). Because of its eternal motion, the divine *pneuma* connected in some way to the human soul or *psyche* and to the "breathing" universe. In an extant fragment Anaximenes wrote: "Just as our *psyche* (or soul) which is air, holds us together and rules us … so do pneuma and air encompass the whole of the cosmos."[142]

This connection between the *pneuma* and human *psyche* and the universe was revolutionary. Air was not only the key to the well-being of animals and plants through soul but it now maintained the health and order of the *cosmos* and universe. This association led later philosophers Cicero (103–43 BC), Hippolytus and Diogenes (fl. AD 250) to equate the Anaximenes *divine air* with divine mind.[143]

Anaximenes' worldview

Anaximenes' *cosmos* was not a geometric spherical model; nor was there any trace of mathematics in his worldview. The heavenly bodies were circling above "like a hat round the head" to which the stars were fixed "like nails".[144] Everything moved above the earth, not around it – not under the earth – only to be obscured at times by the higher northern parts of the earth.[145] Underneath the hemispherical crystalline celestial vault were the flat sun, moon and planets,[146] all supported by compressed air.[147] The flat earth was also held up by "compressed" air, not the spatial symmetry of opposing opposites as Anaximander had proposed. Aristotle wrote, "Anaximenes and Anaxagoras and Democritus say that its [the earth's] flatness is responsible for it staying put: for it does not cut the air beneath but covers it like a lid, which is evidently what those bodies characterised by flatness do."[148] The fiery heavenly bodies were also supported by air and their movements caused by currents of condensed and opposing air.[149] In contrast to Anaximander, Anaximenes appears to have begun his cosmology by first *identifying* the physical and the divine in air then setting out to construct his *cosmos*. Anaximander went the other way, starting with the physical *cosmos* and working towards his *apeiron*. The net effect, however, was the same: the universe was not exclusively divine but possessed a physical intelligible *cosmos*. While Anaximenes' scheme was not as adventurous as Anaximander's, his approach still had a profound effect on later Greek philosophers, notably Heraclitus, Anaxagoras and Democritus.[150]

Xenophanes of Colophon (c.576–480 BC): abandonment of the Olympian gods

Xenophanes[151] was another polymath: a philosopher, a poet and a theologian.[152] Some regard him as the founder of natural theology, who began the great debate about faith and reason.[153] Of the extant fragments of his writings (about 100 lines), he is generally remembered most for his analysis of past religions and philosophical monotheism. Xenophanes was the first to accuse Homer and Hesiod of profane, irrational acts of anthropomorphic polytheism that effectively opened the door for his own views. We shall focus on his theology and not on his natural philosophy, which also showed elements of great innovation.[154]

The Olympian gods were a human creation

Xenophanes believed explicitly that traditional Greek Olympic religion was a social "creation" and not a divine "revelation". He denied the possibility of human knowledge through divine revelation, and thought that it was wrong for the Greeks to believe that their gods were created in their own image.[155] Xenophanes apparently came to the idea while travelling to different countries. He discovered that human beings had different gods tailored to their own physical appearances and beliefs. He wrote:

> The Ethiopians say that their gods are snub-nosed and black, the Thracians that theirs have blue eyes and red hair … But if cattle and horses and lions had hands or were able to draw or do the works that men can do, horses would draw the forms of their gods like horses, and cattle like cattle, and they would make their bodies (of their gods) such as they each had themselves.[156]

This statement was a complete denouncement of Homer and Hesiod's anthropomorphism. In Fragment 11, Xenophanes further states: "Both Homer and Hesiod have attributed to the gods all things that is shame and reproach among men: stealing, committing adultery, and deceiving each other."[157] Xenophanes was not only attacking Homer and Hesiod, however, but the very social fabric that had permeated Greek everyday life since most of the citizens embraced Olympian religion. Xenophanes' rejection of the local Greek gods offered an entirely new perspective on human ethics and morality. The focus shifted from the gods and their actions to mortal human beings themselves. Human beings had to depend on their own individual and collective efforts for social harmony, and not on worshipping the gods.[158]

One supreme god among lesser gods

Xenophanes advanced the idea of a "supreme" god as a cosmic entity.[159] Later Christian scholars misunderstood Xenophanes to mean one God, an idea they borrowed from Aristotle who believed Xenophanes was the first to teach the unity of the highest principle.[160] In a way Aristotle was right, but Xenophanes appears to be talking about a supreme god *among lesser gods*, not one God: "One god is the highest among the gods and men; in neither his form nor his thought is he like unto mortals."[161] Xenophanes may have associated his supreme god with the *cosmos*, but whether God was coextensive with the world or placed outside remains unclear.[162] Xenophanes' concept of a supreme god greatly influenced Plato (supreme craftsman) and Aristotle (unmoved prime mover) (see Ch. 5).

Xenophanes did, however, deny motion[163] to his supreme god, something Plato and Aristotle rejected. His supreme god was immovable, intelligible and capable of action at a distance through the act of thought:[164] "God sees as a whole, thinks as a whole, hears as a whole."[165] In other words, Xenophanes' supreme god (and lesser gods) did not meddle in daily human or natural affairs but was one who "agitates all things with the effortless thought of his mind".[166] This concept of divinity was of utmost importance in the development of philosophical religion in the classical period.

Heraclitus of Ephesus (533–475 BC): tapping into the fiery *logos*

Heraclitus was a singular thinker[167] with no apparent affiliations to any group.[168] He believed that philosophy was for everyone; every person had a moral duty to discover their true "inner self" or soul (*psyche*) because "The eyes and ears are bad witness if the soul is without understanding."[169] Heraclitus thought the external world could not provide truths, because it was in a constant state of change.[170] His famous quote was "You cannot step into the same river twice for new waters are ever flowing upon you"; a statement which has many parallels with the doctrine of Buddha in India.[171]

Once the "inner self" was found, a person could better himself in society.[172] Heraclitus called this "unseen truth" the *logos* of the soul.[173] However, the *logos* was more than a path of knowing because it possessed form, proportion and extension that permeated the entire universe, similar to Anaximenes' divine *pneuma*.[174] In addition, Heraclitus equated air with fire (its most rarefied state), and fire indirectly with the "inner self" of soul.[175] Thus the human soul was directly associated with Anaximenes' air, and indirectly with fire.

Why was fire the creative agent?

Fire appears to have been the imperishable basis of Heraclitus's universe, continuous with all its physical and divine manifestations. It was the cosmic power (perhaps, in more modern terms, energy), which provided the invisible harmony that unified Anaximander's opposites.[176] One famous story tells of Heraclitus warming himself by the fire in his kitchen and saying to his visitors standing at the door "Enter. Here, too, are the gods."[177] Why Heraclitus chose fire is not clear. Perhaps it was because fire is highly changeable, like the sense-phenomena he was trying to explain. Fire transformed physical objects into different states: wood into smoke and ashes; water into air and vapour; metals into liquids, and so on. Another reason is that fire represented a vitality of life and death, whether in a domestic hearth, an altar fire consuming a sacrifice, or a forest fire from which new life springs,[178] or perhaps from the heat of our own bodies (derived from what we now call metabolism). It is also noteworthy that the most visible cosmic form of fire is the sun, upon which all life depends.

Fire was more an essence or principle of the universe from which everything was composed, similar to Thales' water or Anaximenes' air,[179] yet quite different from Anaximander's *apeiron*. As discussed earlier, the physical world, for Anaximander, was not made of the *apeiron*, but was a product of it: Heraclitus's world was an eternal and ever-changing modification of fire. Presocratic scholar G. S. Kirk explains:

Many of the objects of our world, then, are not fire in the normal physical sense. They are fire which is being, or has been, extinguished; they are exchanged for fire; they are dead fire. Therefore they do not, presumably, share the *continuous* change of fire or flame itself. My argument is that Heraclitus regarded the world-order *as a whole* as a fire, and that this was the important thing for his theory of change. Parts of this cosmic bonfire are temporarily extinguished – mountains and rock, for example, for the most part. Yet not the whole of any of the major divisions of matter is "dead" – this would destroy both the measure and the "strife" on which the perpetuation of this measure depends (*Fragments* 80, 53); nor is it "dead" for ever, for the world is a place of change, a constant fire, and everything in it must eventually change too.[180]

The *logos*: toward a theoretical understanding of the *cosmos*

There is no single meaning of *logos*. The word means "what is said" or "an account of events" but also "is an account of why something is"; *logos* is often reason by way of significant description, explanation, and understanding of the world. *Logos* is *process*; a rational account of the world and human life as opposed to mere opinion or story-telling. It is something "shared by all": accessible to everyone, not a product of private fantasy.[181]

We can begin to understand Heraclitus's meaning of *logos* from his preoccupation with the way human beings think and form principles. *Logos,* he argued, was the human mind's way of forming generalities, starting from ideas and the sensory chaos and proceeding to a higher degree of universality or unity. *Logos* was order and reason, accessible to everyone if they studied philosophy. The *logos* led to a higher degree of truth because it demanded a more rigorous structure and use of logic than belief or opinion. In general, *logos* was the ability of the conscious "inner self" to explain the chaotic world using reason, brought about by tapping into the wider *logos* of the world.[182] Human thought was linked to reality via the inner and outer components of the *logos* (see Table 4.3).

For Heraclitus, when he first encountered the *logos* in himself, "he discovered it for a second time in the external world".[183] In other words, the living soul was in unity and inseparable from the cosmic principle of the universe. Presocratic scholar Charles Kahn believes this inseparable connection between the personal *logos* and the world through a limitless soul is the crux to understanding Heraclitus.[184] Opposites were not independent phenomena by themselves; they were part of an eternal cycle of nature, a unity, linked via the "deep *logos* of inner self" and the universe. Thus Heraclitus rejected the idea that the opposites – such as day and night, winter and summer, up and down, life and death, plenty and famine and war and peace – represented "true" reality.[185] The ever-changing fire, and its components making up the world, were a unity held together by a dynamic tension of contrarieties.[186]

This wise understanding was very much a part of the conscious human mind. Heraclitus viewed sleep as a halfway house to death; a state where the soul became separated from sense and lost contact with the soul-fire of the universe.[187] When a person slept, he or she entered a world of private fantasies and emotions. When they awoke, the balance was restored through the opening of the apertures of sense through which fire, rational thinking and consciousness returns. Heraclitus did not believe that the soul in sleep returned to its heavenly nature, as some later philosophers implied. The idea of truth "revealed" through dreams, emotions, oracles or waking visions played no part in Heraclitus' road to truth.

In short, *logos* was a universal principle in which "all things come to pass", with fire as its creative agent. Fire was synonymous with the world of change, and the fiery *logos* was the means of ordering and keeping the balance. Without the fiery *logos*, the world harmony, order and justice (the Egyptian *ma'at*) would collapse into total disarray. The *logos* was the cosmic means of steering world order, and making it intelligible (understandable) to humans. Human ignorance, Heraclitus argued, was the inability to understand this unity. The unity came from connecting human reason (personal fiery *logos*) with the intelligibility (universe fiery *logos*) and divine breath (*pneuma*).[188]

Kahn believes that the fiery *logos* in soul was a proxy for Anaximenes' divine air.[189] Heraclitus himself notes that fire was the most pure rarefied form of air. Human wisdom, as the power of rational thought, was gained through "breathing the *logos*" that connected the private to the public, and the personal to the universal. The rewards for each person who journeyed into the *logos* were the traditional virtues of the Greek *polis*; namely, self-control, moderation and lack of presumption. The pattern of human life and the pattern of cosmic order were one and the same.

The gods, nature and soul

Heraclitus, like Xenophanes, detested people worshipping images of themselves in their gods; and scorned the practice of blood sacrifice common among the Greek populace.[190] Sense-phenomena were not "direct" manifestations of the gods as abstracted by the ancient Near Eastern or Homeric mindsets. The gods, for Heraclitus, were connected to the human senses through the *logos* and were identified with the ever-living fire of the *cosmos* (intelligibility and divine air or *pneuma*). When Heraclitus referred to the gods at his kitchen hearth he was probably referring to this intelligent, purposive and controlling form of the cosmic fiery *logos*.[191]

By doing so, he set up a dualism between the divine (the ever-living fire of the *cosmos*) and the physical (fiery *logos* in physical sense-phenomena). This divine–physical dualism appears to have been linked via soul. Thus Heraclitus linked the divine and the physical manifestations of *logos* with soul, which permeated the universe.[192] In addition, unlike Homer, who ascribed no importance to the soul during life (i.e. the soul left the body at death and was the carrier of personal identity to Hades), Heraclitus believed that the soul was the carrier of personal identity and action during life.[193] The intelligent soul was responsible for the human power to articulate speech, and the *logos* was its vehicle. Heraclitus's theory of soul was therefore a theory of human nature, which in turn was linked to the *cosmos*.[194] Individual souls were fragments of the cosmic unity. The Pythagoreans too believed the human soul was a divine entity and separate from the physical body (see p. 117).

The *cosmos* as process

No god and no human being made this cosmos, but it always and is and will be an ever-living fire, getting kindled in measures and getting quenched in measures.

Clement of Alexandria[195]

In contrast to his fellow Ionians, Heraclitus rejected an origin of the world. He prescribed no rotating *apeiron*, cosmic seed, expanding "air" or god from which the world arose. Heraclitus held that the *cosmos,* and wider universe, had no beginning, a position supported by Aristotle. The *cosmos* had existed as a unity formed by "a harmony of conflicting opposites and balanced in perpetual tension, just like a string on a musical instrument".[196] Change was a dynamic motion, with fire and the *logos* as its currency of exchange. Heraclitus wrote "There is an exchange: all things for fire and fire for all things, like goods for gold and gold for goods."[197]

Meteorological phenomena were explained as physical transformations of fire, involving upward–downward cyclical movements. As the fire in the sun burns itself out, it is replenished by vapours from the sea: "transformations of fire are first of all sea; and half of the sea is earth, half whirlwind ... Earth is liquefied into sea, and retains its measure according to the same Law as it existed before it became earth".[198] Thus the world according to Heraclitus progressed upwards from earth to water to air to fire and back again in one dynamic. Heraclitus's scheme could incorporate Anaximander's opposites such as hot and cold, wet and dry, life and death, day and night. However, he thought of them as part of an eternal cycle of nature linked through the *logos*. Heraclitus's highly innovative scheme of a self-regulating perpetual cycle has some similarities to how we perceive the large and small matter–energy cycles today (see Ch. 9).

The Italian Schools: from mathematical numbers to "One Being"

Around 550 BC, the intellectual movement spread from the Ionian coast to mainland Europe, namely to southern Italy and Sicily (sometimes called "Greater Greece"). There were two main Italian groups or schools, the Pythagoreans (Pythagoras and his followers) and the Eleatics (Parmenides, Melissius and Zeno), although, strictly speaking, there was no Eleatic "School" in the sense of regular meetings, lectures and students.[199] The Pythagoreans were a religious brotherhood, much like freemasons. However, they employed mathematics to describe the world and believed in the transmigration of souls. The Eleatics took another direction and challenged past philosophers by arguing that change and motion were logically impossible, which set up an enormous problem for philosophers for many centuries. It meant that philosophy could not demystify the world. The earliest philosophers to tackle the relationships between matter, space and time were the fifth-century Empedocles and Anaxagoras, and Leucippus and Democritus of the Atomic School in Abdera.

Pythagoras (c.572–497 BC) and the Pythagorean tradition: mathematical construction of the universe

> The Pythagorean system that emerges from the totality of all our sources is a strange blend of religious dogma and mathematical speculation.   J. V. Luce[200]

The first we hear of Pythagoras is in the works of the Pythagorean Philolaus of Tarentum of the fifth century BC.[201] Pythagoras was a native of the Ionian island of

Samos and a contemporary of Anaximenes and Xenophanes. He was born around the same time as Nebuchadnezzar II sacked Jerusalem and is believed to have travelled extensively in Egypt and Mesopotamia, where he acquired vast knowledge.[202] In his early forties, Pythagoras migrated to Croton in southern Italy where he founded his famous school around 520 BC.[203] Plato has Socrates saying that Pythagoras was "especially loved as a leader of education in the private sphere".[204]

From his travels, Pythagoras became an extraordinary authority on moral and religious matters and reportedly educated his students in the noble pursuit of truth and self-improvement governed by these principles.[205] People varied in their reactions towards him, some finding him a charlatan and some a genius. Heraclitus called Pythagoras "the chief of swindlers" and Xenophanes mocked him, but Empedocles wrote that he "was a man ... who possessed the greatest wealth of intelligence".[206] His teachings and activities were surrounded in secrecy and included a long list of strange quasi-magical taboos and behaviours, ranging from not eating beans to never walking on roadways.[207] As a result of anti-social behaviours, the Pythagorean assembly of houses was burnt to the ground in the middle of the fourth century BC.[208]

From all reports, the Pythagoreans were attracted to mathematics. However, contrary to what is widely taught, there is no reliable evidence that Pythagoras proved anything remotely similar to Pythagoras's theorem or solved any other deep problem in mathematics, music or astronomy.[209] Hippasus (fl. *c.*470 BC) appears to have been responsible for founding the Pythagorean study of mathematics[210] and natural science.[211] Part of the problem in sorting out facts from fiction about Pythagoras is that he left no writings and we are wholly reliant on the authority of Philolaus, Plato, Aristotle and other later commentators Diogenes Läertius, Porphry and Iamblichus.[212] What follows is a blend of the traditional and more current scholarship on Pythagoras and the Pythagoreans, particularly the works of Philolaus.

Pythagorean cosmogony

> The Pythagorean cosmogony is obscure because of the fragmentary evidence. It seems that they viewed the *cosmos* forming in at least three stages. The first stage was its creation from a fiery unit-seed fueled by "breath". As more "breath" was drawn into the seed from the outermost reaches, the *cosmos* grew to its present size (there was no hint of the universe continually expanding as cosmologists believe today). "Breath" was not atmospheric air but divine "unlimited" air surrounding the world, analogous to Anaximenes' *pneuma.*   W. K. C. Guthrie[213]

The second stage of the Pythagorean cosmogony was associated with the appearance of physical things and numbers.[214] According to Aristotle, Pythagorean numbers were "the elements of all things",[215] including the arrangement of the heavens (see below). The number 1 ("unit-dot-point") was a divine creation from which light, the odd numbers and opposites arose.[216] The three-dimensional *cosmos* was described in progressive terms from a dot to a line to a plane (triangle or square) and on to the higher dimensional pyramid, cube and other bodies, such as a tetrahedron:[217]

$$1 = \text{point} \qquad 2 = \text{line} \qquad 3 = \text{surface} \qquad 4 = \text{solid}$$

with physical bodies then appearing from the geometrical solids. The "number" principles were the underlying construction of the different objects in the physical world.[218] The Pythagoreans apparently had no number zero.[219]

The third and last stage of Pythagorean cosmogony was the establishment of inner harmony and order, brought about by linking his theory of numbers to the ten opposites.[220] The ten principles of opposites arranged by Aristotle were:

Limit and unlimited	Resting and moving
Light and darkness	Straight and curved
Odd and even	Right and left
One and plurality	Good and bad
Male and female	Square and oblong

The Pythagoreans explained the inner harmony and working order of the *cosmos* from the ten opposites, each pair having a special creative function. Although mention was made of "resting and moving", unfortunately no explicit account of motion and change was given.

The Pythagorean worldview

> Most people, all, in fact, who regard the whole Heaven as finite – say it [Earth] lies at the centre. But the Italian philosophers known as the Pythagoreans take the contrary view. At the centre, they say, is fire, and the Earth is one of the stars, creating night and day by the circular motion about the centre. They further construct another Earth in opposition to ours to which they give the name counter-Earth. Aristotle[221]

According to Philolaus, the earth revolved around a central fire called the "Hestia".[222] The "central fire" should not be confused with the sun. Philolaus also appears to have been the first to propose that the earth was a *planet*, and *spherical* and thus abandon the millennial dogma of the earth shaped as a flat disk, log or a cylinder shape.[223] No one knows how he arrived at a perfect spherical shape. It may have emerged from his or others' observation that a ship's hull disappears before its mast as it sails out to sea, or from observing the earth's shadow crossing the moon during an eclipse.[224]

The Pythagorean universe was bounded by the "invisible" sphere of Olympus.[225] The "visible" sphere contained the fixed stars (also made of the divine air); the next sphere was the sphere of the five planets (Jupiter, Mars, Mercury, Venus and Saturn); followed by the spheres of the sun, the moon and the earth. The closest sphere to the central fire was called the counter-earth (Fig. 4.6). The sun was a "transparent" globe receiving its light and heat mostly from the central fire and from the outermost fixed stars.[226] As the number ten was perfection, so too there was a total of ten heavenly bodies within the sphere of Olympus: nine were visible and the tenth was the invisible counter-earth.[227]

Human beings lived on the side of the earth that always faced towards the outer sphere, which explains why counter-earth was invisible. The daily east–west movement of the sun and night were due to the earth revolving around the central fire in a perfect circle every 24 hours. Eclipses of the moon were caused by the moon's passage through

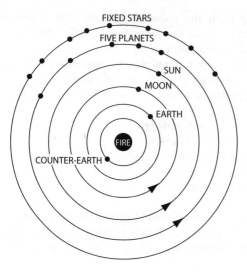

Figure 4.6 Schematic of Pythagorean cosmology according to Philolaus of Tarentum (*c*.430 BC). The universe is bounded by the sphere of Olympus, beyond which lies the unlimited (or indeterminate). At the centre of the universe is a fire, which is surrounded by ten revolving spheres.

the earth's shadow, but also occasionally by the shadow of the counter-earth, which was why there were more lunar than solar eclipses.[228] In accordance with astronomical observations, the moon revolved about the central fire every 29½ days, and around the sun every year. It was not until the middle of the fourth century BC that Heraclides of Pontus (*c*.350 BC) proposed that the apparent motion of the heavens was caused by daily rotation of the earth about its own axis.[229] A rotating earth meant there was no need for a counter-earth for explanation of astronomical phenomena. A rotating earth was not taken seriously until Aristarchus of Samos of the third century BC (Ch. 5) and Copernicus in the sixteenth century (Ch. 8).

Harmony of the spheres

Cosmic harmony and intelligibility have been implicit concepts in the Pythagorean cosmogony and cosmology. As mentioned, the harmony arose from numbers separating the heavenly bodies,[230] leading to his famous "harmony of the spheres". The "harmony of the spheres" refers to the heavenly bodies orbiting at different distances according to precise mathematical ratios with concordant notes.[231] Those bodies that revolved faster produced higher notes and the slower rotations produced lower notes. When combined, these notes made up the harmony. Wisdom was also linked to the harmony of the universe and both were the seed from which Greek philosophical religion developed.

The idea of "music" in nature was not unique to the Pythagoreans but has a long history in the East. In ancient China, the order of the seasons and the universe were matched to a system of musical sounds. In India, the sound *om* is the creative principle of the universe; and Vedic chants help maintain the cosmic stability and can influence the gods. In Babylonia, some of the gods were identified with musical instruments and/or with sounds produced by them.[232] The combination of number symbolism and music appears in many cultures and extends into Western culture in different ways from magic squares to numerology.

Transmigration of souls and immortality

The Pythagoreans were highly influenced by Orphic (and Dionysian) traditions. Orphic religion taught the doctrine of reincarnation and was adopted by the Pythagoreans, Empedocles and Plato.[233] Pythagoras may have learned of the doctrine from India or Egypt,[234] but it is unlikely to have been Egypt because transmigration was not part of the Egyptian worldview (Ch. 3). According to Xenophanes, the Pythagoreans believed that the soul was a separate spiritual entity that lived in the body for a limited time and moved on to another (transmigrated) after death. Apparently the soul wandered through the universe and was drawn into a living creature during the first breath at birth.[235] Xenophanes mockingly tells a story of Pythagoras witnessing a young dog being beaten by its owner. Pythagoras reportedly said "Stop, do not beat it; for it is the soul of a friend that I recognized when I heard it giving tongue."[236] Pythagoras's teachings on transmigration of souls became part of Neoplatonism, which was studied in the Middle Ages and during the European Renaissance.[237]

The Pythagoreans spoke of an intelligible universe "taking a breath from the surrounding void".[238] This breath was pure, everlasting, alive and intelligent. Although "breath" existed outside the world, there was mention that it penetrated the *cosmos* as well. The ensoulment of the universe was the basis of the Pythagorean belief in the unity of kinship of all forms of life and nature.[239] The souls of every living person, animal or plant were *portions* of the surrounding *pneuma* linked to the intelligibility of the *cosmos*. Again, Pythagoras's scheme shows many similarities with Anaximenes' living breathing universe.

The human soul possessed three quite separate elements: reason, intelligence and passion. Reason was the distinguishing feature, separating humans from the animals, while intelligence and passion were common to both. Singling out soul, divine reason and the intelligible order of the universe was an idea further developed by Plato and Aristotle (Ch. 5).

Parmenides of Elea (*c*.515–450 BC): impossibility of unity and plurality

The next major advance in philosophy emerged with Parmenides, who is often called the first metaphysician.[240] Although he wrote at some length on nature, this was completely overshadowed by his "way of truth".[241] Parmenides shocked the philosophical world when he totally denied the reality of change, motion and becoming. He did not deny that people saw a tree, witnessed the rising and setting of the sun, felt the wind on their faces or were made wet by the rain. But, Parmenides, following Heraclitus, insisted that human observations were not part of "true" reality. He told the reader that his own natural philosophy, and that of past natural philosophers, was false and "deceitful".[242]

Parmenides' reality was hidden in the absolute unity of the universe (or "One Being").[243] Nothing whatsoever in his universe "comes into or out of existence" (coming-to-be or ceasing-to-be). Everything we see, hear, smell, touch or taste was illusionary. How can fire change into water and into earth, and then from earth back again into water and fire? How can a thing be fire one minute and water the next? Parmenides' answer was that it cannot. The only truths he admitted were those based on strict logic. "What is, is; and what is not, is not." Only the "objects" of thought were real to Parmenides, which profoundly influenced Plato and his theory of ideas.

The "way of truth" as revealed to Parmenides by an unnamed goddess

In the prologue of *On Nature*, Parmenides tells how "the unshaken mind of well-rounded truth" was revealed to him by a goddess.[244] The revelation occurred while he was travelling by chariot to the "House of Night", where the paths of day and night meet.[245] The goddess told him of the "Law of One Being" and warned him against trusting the senses and "opinions of mortals".[246] According to Proclus (*c*. AD 410–85), the goddess said:

> Come now, and I will tell you (and you must accept my word away with you when you have heard it) the only ways of enquiry that are to be thought of: the one, that IT IS, and that it is impossible for IT NOT TO BE, is the path of persuasion (for she attends upon Truth); the other, that IT IS NOT, and that IT is needful that IT NOT BE: that I declare to you is an altogether indiscernible track: for you could not know what is NOT – that cannot be done – nor indicate it.[247]

After the goddess revealed the truth of "Being" (IT IS), the truth of "not-Being" (IT IS NOT), and the truth of "IT IS" and "IT IS NOT", the path was clear to Parmenides.[248] This amounts to what David Sedley called Parmenides' Law 1, which states: "There are no half-truths. No proposition is both true and false. No question can be coherently answered 'Yes and No'." Sedley continues: "This permits Parmenides to logically move to his total being or total not-being. To specify *what* a thing is, as mortals do, is implicitly also to specify what it is not, and this to fall foul of Law 1."[249] The prologue ends with the goddess stating: "Here I cease for you my trustworthy argument and thought about truth."[250]

"One Being" defined

Parmenides' truth appears to have been represented as a solid, unchanging, motionless, limited, indivisible, ageless, physical body, "like" a sphere equally balanced in every direction from centre to circumference and with a surface having no edge or centre. The "One Being" had no past, present or future. Nothing ever comes into being, therefore motion in time and space was logically impossible. Being simply "is" and what "is" cannot change. All natural phenomena exist as appearances and opinions only.

Parmenides believed that all natural philosophies were fatally flawed because their reasoning was logically inconsistent. On one level, they proposed a "unifying" principle, yet on another they spoke of space in which all things were contained. Parmenides argued that one cannot logically entertain both; you cannot propose that something "is" (unifying principle) and talk about something that "is not" (space) as part of "true" reality. To say something "is not" is to say nothing about the thing itself; for you cannot think of, and therefore enquire into, the non-existent.[251] Because space "is not", Parmenides denied its existence outright. He also denied the creation of the world; the world either exists or it doesn't. What "is" cannot change, hence the world of sense is illusionary. This is the crux of understanding Parmenides' philosophy. He rejected the Milesian philosophers' assumption that matter had an intrinsic principle of change.[252] We shall later discover how Empedocles, Anaxagoras, and Democritus solved the paradox; in short, they agreed with Parmenides that matter is itself "unchanging" (i.e. what "is"), but disagreed that it denied reality to nature.

Strengths and limitations of Parmenidean logic

The strength of Parmenidean logic was its logical consistency. The weakness was the way he had removed sense-experience from human reality. We all know that the tree growing in the front yard is "real" to our senses. It is not an illusion if you climb a tree or accidentally fall and break an arm. Parmenides made the mistake of asserting that human beings cannot know, or even think to know, "what is not" (e.g. space). Everything in Parmenides' "true" reality must be "it is". However, "If this were so", argued Russell, "Parmenides strictly could never assert anything either, and thus all discourse, all speech, all thought would be impossible ... Nothing survives [in the Parmenides world] except 'it is', an empty formula of identity."[253] Elaborating further, Russell wrote:

> Parmenides' reasoning is the first example in philosophy of an argument from thought and language at the world at large. It cannot, of course, be accepted as valid, but it is worthwhile to see what truth it contains ... The whole argument shows how easy it is to draw metaphysical conclusions from language, and how the only way to avoid fallacious arguments of this kind is to push the logical and psychological study of language further than has been done by most meta-physicians.[254]

In the end, Parmenides became a victim of his own rigorous logic, and had only one way out. His "true" reality completely obliterated the human world of sense. However, on a more positive note, his command of clear logic and strict definitions demonstrated to the philosophical world that, to talk about something, language must convey meaning and be logically consistent. Parmenides' language was logically consistent but not meaningful, at least for unravelling the mysteries of the world of sense.

Zeno of Elea (c.489–430 BC): paradoxes of space, time and motion

Zeno was a younger contemporary of Parmenides and became obsessed with trying to prove Parmenides' "One Being". According to fifth-century Neoplatonist Proclus, Zeno contrived some 40 arguments against plurality; that is, arguments to show that if more than one thing exists (what "is"), then paradoxes or contradictions follow.[255] He was deeply interested in seeking the relationship between the movement of an object and the immovable portion of space in which it moves. Two of Zeno's most famous arguments proving the impossibility of motion were the race between Achilles and the tortoise, and the paradox of the flying arrow.

Achilles and the tortoise

In a race, the tortoise is given, say, a 1000-m start over Achilles, who could run ten times faster. Zeno *logically* asserted that Achilles could *never overtake* the tortoise because when Achilles had travelled 1000 m, the tortoise would be 100 m in front. And by the time Achilles had covered the next 100 m, the tortoise would be 10 m in front; a process that would go on *ad infinitum*. The mistake Zeno made was assuming that the sum of the geometric progression with its infinite number of terms *must add to an infinite number*.[256] He assumed that the successive ten-fold decrements separating Achilles and the tortoise were 100 m, 10 m, 1 m, 0.1 m, 0.01 m, 0.001 m and so on add to infinity. This is wrong. The answer to this "converging sequence" is 111.1 metres. In other words, after Achilles had run 111.1 m he would be exactly even with the tortoise, and thereafter he would pass it and win the race.[257]

The flying arrow

The flying arrow is another of Zeno's proofs for the impossibility of motion. This time Zeno wanted to prove that a *moving object* is really "at rest" because, at any instant in time, the object always occupied a space equal to its own length. A flying arrow, he argued, cannot be in two places at the same time, or, in Parmenides' language, an arrow cannot be at a place that "it is not". The arrow in flight must be at rest at each point and what the human senses "perceive" is an illusion. Zeno's underlying assumption was that time, not distance, was infinitely divisible. Again, Zeno appealed to the maxim that the "whole" has more terms than "the part". His argument is logically correct if his initial assumption was correct. Since we know from experience that the conclusion is absurd, the starting-point must be rejected. Alternative explanations have to be sought to explain the apparent paradox.

Problems with Zeno's "way of knowing"

As with Parmenides, the major problem with Zeno's logic was that the human senses were not permitted into reality. By narrowing the conditions of the thought experiment, with watertight starting-points, Zeno could logically prove just about anything. However, if, as turned out to be the case, his starting-points were erroneous, alternative explanations must be sought to describe the phenomenon. If Zeno had permitted a sensible description of "the history" of Achilles or "the history" of the tortoise before, during and after the race, he would probably have reached a different conclusion. Similarly, if he had allowed human experience to describe the arrow before and after it had left the bow to a given end-point, a different story would probably have emerged. Motion would not have been denied to the arrow.

There is no question that the human senses can be illusionary; a stick in the water looks bent yet in reality it is straight. This is not grounds, however, to totally ignore the senses in a description of reality, as in Zeno's (and Parmenides') method. Although an argument may be logically valid, the conclusions reached may not describe reality. Nor should we always rely on our sense-impressions. To describe reality adequately we need reason and common-sense experience; our understanding of the world is possible only because we are participants, not merely spectators. Aristotle solved many of Zeno's problems by acknowledging that space and time were "potentially" divisible *ad infinitum*, but in the sensible world they were not. The complete solutions to Zeno's paradoxes had to wait for the mathematical development of limits of infinite sequences and new scientific concepts of analysing motion.[258]

Empedocles of Acragas (c.493–433 BC): ingenious reply to Parmenides' challenge

Parmenides' "One Being" sent shock waves into the heart of Greek philosophy. The first philosopher to reconcile Parmenides' being and becoming, permanence and change, unity and plurality, was the charismatic Empedocles.[259] He readily accepted the notion of "One Being", but not at the expense of human experience.[260] Empedocles agreed that "true reality" contained "unchanging" or permanent qualities, but denied that reality had unity and immobility. Empedocles' poem, *On Nature*, ingeniously solved the paradox between unity and plurality by giving each of the four physical elements the properties of the "One Being".[261] Water, air, fire and earth were all "unchanging", meaning that no element could be created or destroyed.

The question that now arises is if Empedocles denied the internal principle of change to his four elements, that is to matter, how was change explained? Empedocles explained that change and diversity arose from the interaction of the four elements *under the influence of Love (attraction) and Strife (repulsion)*. Hence, Empedocles introduced Love and Strife, later called external "moving cause" by Aristotle.[262] Empedocles called this combining process that gave rise to the world around us the "coming together", "scattering", "being born apart", "interchange of place" and "mixing".[263] Thus, he was the first philosopher to propose that the "nature of things" was not governed by "one" principle, but by "four" principles that combined and flowed under the influence of Love and Strife. This innovative idea greatly influenced Hippocrates, Plato and Aristotle.[264]

To explain how the four elements represented reality, Empedocles employed the analogy of a painter mixing four basic colours.[265] Nature was the painter who mixed the four colours under the influence of Strife, the cause of change.[266] Although the four colours had qualitative differences, they were able to "run through one another" to produce the world reality we experience.[267] Unlike Thales' water, Anaximenes' air, and Heraclitus's fire, Empedocles believed his "four elements" did not undergo transformations in themselves, but combined with one another in whole-number ratios to produce the infinite variety of compounds seen in nature. Empedocles agreed with Parmenides that nothing could come into and out of existence, and that the universe was full of eternal "stuff".[268] The "stuff" between nothing and being was Empedocles' four elements. His four elements were resolved in the concept of "becoming". Empedocles wrote:

All these [four elements] are equal and coeval [but each presides over its own office] … and each has its own character, and they prevail in turn as time comes around. And besides them, nothing further comes into being nor does anything pass away. How could it in fact be utterly destroyed, since nothing is empty of these? For only if they are continuously perishing would they no longer exist. And what could increase this all? Whence could it have come? No, there are just these, but running through one another they become different things at different times and yet ever and always are the same.[269]

The four elements were regarded as "entities forming temporary arrangements as their parts were bought into compounds of different shapes".[270] As they intermingled, they were responsible for the changes we observe.[271] The concurrence of multiplicity of the four eternal elements "running through one another" was Empedocles' answer to the Parmenidean paradox between unity and plurality.[272]

Love and Strife: external causes of the cycle of change

When the four eternal elements were completely separate, Strife occupied the space between; and when they mixed completely, Love cemented them. In the beginning, all the four elements mingled together in the form of one sphere.[273] During this early period of creation, there was no change, no motion and no physical phenomena because there was no "cause" to facilitate "coming into being". Only Love reigned supreme in the one sphere.

Diversity occurred only after Strife "entered" the sphere from the outer fringes. Strife (or Hate) was the "cause" necessary for the creation of the world and independent of the physical elements. The degree of change was determined by another factor called cosmic "justice", which prevented Love or Strife from dominating one another.[274] The process was cyclical not linear.

> And these [elements] never cease their continuous interchange, now through Love all coming together into one, now again each carried apart by the hatred of Strife [or Hate]. So, insofar as they have learned to grow one from many, and again as the one grows apart grow many, thus far do they come into being and have no stable life; but insofar as they never cease their continual interchange, thus far they exist always changeless in the cycle.[275]

Empedocles' world was an advanced stage of this cyclical process driven by the power of Love and Strife (attraction and repulsion), and sometimes called a "cosmic cycle".[276] His scheme defiantly contradicted Parmenides' scheme by claiming that unity and plurality were possible: a unity will continually form from plurality and vice versa.

Empedocles' concept of Love has some parallels with Hesiod's *Theogony*, in which Love was responsible for uniting heaven and earth before a long series of sexual procreations, which produced the world structure. Empedocles' Strife also parallels Hesiod's evil, the Titans, who were responsible for the unpredictable forces of adversity that tried to overpower the good in the world. Even in the Orphic (and Dionysiac) traditions, the Titans were conceived as powers of evil that were eventually overpowered by the more powerful Zeus and the Olympian gods.[277]

Cosmic cycle had no beginning or end

Empedocles' cosmic cycle dominated his philosophy. It appears that he thought the world arose out of chance and necessity, and not from a god's handiwork. As mentioned earlier, the very early universe was a uniform, boundless, motionless sphere with no change, no motion and no physical phenomena. The *cosmos* formed from some unspecified primordial mix as the eternal four elements began to intermingle when Strife entered the sphere. The *cosmos* formation followed a distinct order: air separated first, then fire and earth.[278] The air formed the arch of the heavens and the fire the sphere of stars beneath. The fourth element, water, was squeezed out as the earth compacted and formed the seas. Some water evaporated and produced the lower atmosphere. When Strife further penetrated the sphere, fire moved to the heavens, and the earth and water compacted further down. In the world's advanced stage of formation, Love was totally banished from the sphere, and so one cycle ended and another began. As Greek expert John Barnes notes: "The infinite alterations between sphere and world, world and sphere, marked the eternal and never changing history of the universe."[279]

Empedocles viewed the earth as stationary at the centre of two revolving hemispheres, which created night and day.[280] Each hemisphere moved by the "push of fire". The stars were fixed to the outermost periphery of the finite universe, and the planets moved freely in space beneath the canopy.[281] Evil filled the region between the earth and moon, a region that later became Aristotle's physical world (see Ch. 5). No mention was made of the annual rotation of the sun.

From cosmic cycle to life cycle

Empedocles believed that the pattern of the *cosmos* was mirrored in the life cycle on earth.[282] According to Aetius, Empedocles envisaged living forms "coming into being" in four stages. The first stage was the production of separate parts of life forms. The second stage was the coming together of these parts, such as arms and legs. The third change was the chance formation of forms including monsters, and the fourth and final stage was the reproductive success of these viable forms:

> Empedocles held that the first generations of animals and plants were not complete but consisted of separate limbs not joined together; the second, arising from the joining of these limbs, were like creatures in dreams; the third was the generation of the whole-natured forms; and the fourth arose no longer from the homoeomerous (things with like parts) such as earth or water, but by generation, in some cases as a result of the condensation of their nourishment, in others because feminine beauty excited the sexual urge; and the various species of animals were distinguished by the quality of the mixture in them.[283]

During the second and third stages, the parts combined at random, often producing monsters:

> Many creatures were born with faces and breasts on both sides, man-faced ox-progeny, while others again sprang forth as ox-headed offspring of man, creatures compounded partly of male, partly of the nature of female, and fitted with shadowy parts.[284]

Empedocles thought that the extraordinary diversity arose from some kind of evolution through a mechanism similar to survival of the fittest.[285] He also described human life history as progressing through stages from seminal chaos; to embryonic and juvenile development, with heightened perception and coordination; and then to maturity, after which the harmony began to decline and eventually led to death.

Mind, universe and immortal soul

In another poem, *Purifications*, Empedocles proposed an analogy between the human mind and the universe. Empedocles believed that "everything in the universe has thought" but was linked through the four elements: water, air, fire and earth.[286] Empedocles' supreme god was not an anthropomorphic projection in the Homeric sense:

> For he (god) is not furnished with a human head upon limbs, nor do two branches spring from his back; he has no feet, no nimble knees, no shaggy genitals; but he is Mind alone, holy and beyond description, darting through the whole cosmos with swift thoughts.[287]

Empedocles' supreme god was Mind, which permeated the universe. Mind was connected to the air breathed and the light seen: "the Law of all things is extended everywhere, through wide-ruling *aether* (divine Air) and the infinite light".[288] This again has strong parallels with Anaximenes' *pneuma* and Heraclitus's fiery *logos*, which permeated the cosmic soul and kept the universe in good health.[289] Both air and fire were connected to the inner human soul and the wider cosmic soul.[290]

Empedocles claimed, in contrast to the Eleatics, that the senses if properly used were roads to knowledge.[291] He explained sense-perception in purely physical terms.[292] Perception occurred from the ability of all things in the world to give off "effluences", which could be detected by the senses: "by earth we see earth, by water we see water, by air we see divine air, and by fire we see fire".[293] To perceive was to receive the "effluences" from the external four elements, which were recognized by the similar elements in the animal and human sense-organs.[294] Empedocles' theory of perception greatly influenced Plato and Aristotle.

In addition to proposing an analogy between the human mind and the universe, and how things were perceived, Empedocles also discussed the immortal soul and reincarnation. Influenced greatly by the Orphic–Pythagorean traditions, Empedocles viewed reincarnation as either a punishment or a reward. Those who had sinned (presumably caused by Strife), or who did not believe in the divine, were subjected to repeated incarnations in human, animal and plant forms:[295] "Happy is he who has acquired the riches of divine thoughts, but wretched the man in whose mind dwells an obscure opinion about the gods."[296] Thus, not all philosophers followed Xenophanes and removed the local gods from their worldviews. The way to reverse misery was to dedicate oneself to the service of Aphrodite (Olympian goddess of love) who kept Strife at bay.[297] All humans are fallen spirits and may return as human, animal and even plant flesh. Empedocles himself told us that he had been a bush, a bird, and a fish before he was clothed in human flesh.[298] Legend says that Empedocles died after leaping into the crater of Mount Etna in an effort to prove his immortality.[299]

Anaxagoras of Clazomenae (*c.*500–428 BC): neo-Ionian philosophy also defies Eleatic logic

> Like Empedocles, Anaxagoras accepted the Eleatic arguments to the effect that generation and destruction were impossible, but maintained that motion was nonetheless possible, and hence that change could take place in the world. Again, like Empedocles, he believed that our faculties, if properly used, would yield reliable information about the natural world. But in his conception of nature he differed fundamentally from Empedocles.
>
> J. Barnes[300]

Anaxagoras[301] rejected Empedocles' theory of four elements because he believed that it failed to explain the diversity in the world.[302] Instead, he smashed Empedocles' four elements (and Parmenides' "One Being") into an infinite number of eternal "germs" or "seeds" with all sorts of forms, colours and tastes, of which the four elements were the most complex. These seeds, like Empedocles' four elements, were Anaxagoras's answer to Parmenides' claim that Being itself was unchangeable. Anaxagoras, after

Parmenides and Empedocles, agreed that nothing can come from nothing; hence all the seeds and qualities always existed, and the *cosmos* was formed from them. And he agreed that you needed what Aristotle later called an external "moving cause". However, the ultimate "cause" of change in Anaxagoras's world was not some mythical Love and Strife but Mind itself. Mind, or *nous*, was a cosmic-ordering principle that initiated motion by a rotating action, and that later, after the *cosmos* formation, became the ordering and animating principle of natural phenomena (see Table 4.3).

Matter was infinitely divisible

Although Anaxagoras believed that Mind was a single principle (*archē*), he thought that: "there is a portion of everything in everything", and that: "The world is one world, and there is no gap between the things in it, no axe-cut separating hot from cold or cold from hot."[303] Anaxagoras seems to have followed Zeno's assumption that matter was infinitely divisible.[304] In the opening passage to his book, *Treatise on Nature*, Anaxagoras wrote:

> All things were together, infinite in respect of both number and smallness. For the small too was infinite. And while all things were together, none of them were plain (distinguishable) because of their smallness. For air and *aether* held all things in subjection, both of them being infinite; for these are the greatest ingredients in the mixture of all things, both in number and size.[305]

Anaxagoras was the first to connect the infinitely small to the infinitely large. In *Fragment 3*, he stated that "there is always a larger than the large, and it is numerically equal to the small".[306] Anaxagoras's concept of infinity anticipated the development of the theory of infinite sets some 2000 years later in the seventeenth century.

Every physical object has a *predominance* of qualities

If "there is a portion of everything in everything", the question arises of how a tree differs from a fish? How was an apple different from a leaf? Anaxagoras's answer was that every physical object (or part of an object) had a *predominance* of some "seeds" over others. Anaxagoras assumed that all these "quality" differences were due to differences in the properties of seeds.[307] Unfortunately, Anaxagoras is silent about how these "qualities" arose. Some scholars suggest that the seeds might have contained all the "opposites" of Ionian cosmology and a different blend of them may have given rise to different forms, colours, scents and flavours.[308]

Nous: first motion and cosmic organizing principle

- **First motion.** For Anaxagoras, the universe in the beginning was a motionless uniform mass of "seeds" (not unlike Parmenides' "One Being" or Empedocles' Love sphere).[309] The "first motion" came from the cosmic Mind,[310] which was eternal, infinite and self-moving.[311] As the mass rotated faster and faster, matter began to disperse according to the opposites: the heavier from the rarer; the darker from the lighter; the hotter from the colder; and the drier from the moist.[312] The heavier matter fell to the centre of the *cosmos* and formed the earth; and the hot, dry, and rarefied matter spread outwards to form the air, sky and the heavens. The sun, moon and stars peeled away from the earth. Nothing separated off completely, however, for there remained "a portion of everything in everything".

- **Cosmic ordering principle.** In Anaxagoras's cosmogony, the formation of physical *cosmos* was quite separate from the cosmic principle, *nous*. Otherwise *nous* could not have been "the finest of all things, and the purest, it has all knowledge about everything, and the greatest power".[313] Once the world structure had formed, *nous* took on a special role, permeated the universe and animated all living things. It was Anaxagoras's grand ordering principle. *Nous* represented a standard of goodness, justice and morality which every human being could tap into using reason. "All things which have life, both the greater and the less, are ruled by Mind (soul)."[314]

The concept of cosmic Mind was in the realm of pure thought, not in the physical body.[315] Anaxagoras's governing *nous* had striking parallels with *aspects* of Anaximander's *apeiron*, which "steered all things", Anaximenes' *pneuma*, which kept the universe in good health, and Heraclitus's fiery *logos*, which was wisdom of the highest order and connected a person's "inner self" and the cosmic *psyche*.[316] Just as animals undergo the process of birth and development, so too the universe was connected through *nous*.[317] Nowhere, however, did Anaxagoras refer to his *nous* as a god.[318] Presocratic scholar C. C. W. Taylor summarized Anaxagoras's views on the nature and the activity of *nous* as follows:[319]

Properties	Activities of cosmic Mind
• the finest and purest of all things	• first motion
• unlimited	• cosmic rotation
• self-directing	• controls everything that has a soul
• unchanging	• cosmic organizing principle

Physical explanation for the phases of the moon

By keeping *nous* separate from the physical, Anaxagoras started one of the greatest and unresolved debates about the relation of the mind to the body, the divine to the physical.[320] Anaxagoras was the first to give an accurate physical explanation of the phases of the moon and the nature of its light. The phases of the moon came from the different illumination by the sun, and moon eclipses occurred whenever the moon was screened by the earth.[321] The Babylonians were the first to compute eclipses accurately, but the Greeks were the first to explain them in physical terms.[322]

The sun, moon and stars were not gods

The earth was flat and remained suspended in the middle of the cosmos because of its large size and strong air movement.[323] Anaxagoras openly declared that the sun, moon and stars were not gods but fiery red-hot stones, which the rotation of the aether carried around with them. The moon likewise was made "of earth and had plains and craters in it", something Galileo confirmed in the early seventeenth century.[324] For these views, Anaxagoras was charged with impiety (wronging the gods) and fled Athens and returned to his home city Clazomenae on the Ionian coast.

The Atomic School: further reconciling the senses and Eleatic logic

> Whereas Anaxagoras made matter, like magnitude, infinitely divisible, the atomists
> maintained that it was composed of indivisible minima … The atomists regarded all
> substance as absolutely homogeneous and accounted for the apparent variety of
> phenomena by mere differences in shape, size, position and arrangement.
>
> G. S. Kirk *et al.*[325]

One spectacular outcome of Presocratic thought was atomism. The two architects of atomism were Leucippus and Democritus of the fifth century. They argued that what "is not", such as empty space, simply cannot be thought of, but at the same was just as real as the bodies that occupy the emptiness.[326] A tree was as real to the Atomists as empty space. Space was the place where atoms collide, unite, separate and change position, giving them their secondary qualities that we sense in the world. Atoms were: spatial entities and possessed their own inherent motion; indivisible units, infinite in number and all having the character of "One Being".[327]

Parmenides' paradox between unity and plurality was reconciled; unity was the atoms (what "is") and diversity was the way in which they interacted in space and time. Thus the Atomists, by way of reduction, argued that change arose from the rearrangement of eternally moving atoms, which themselves were intrisically "unchanging".[328] Matter was still denied an internal principle of change, as Parmenides' thesis of Being demanded, but change was logically possible and necessary.

Leucippus of Elea or Miletus (c.460 BC): father of atomism

Very little is known about Leucippus's life or philosophy. He was a contemporary of Empedocles and Anaxagoras and some suggest that he may have been a disciple of Parmenides or Zeno.[329] Tradition credits Leucippus with the famous statement about nature: "Nothing happens at random; everything happens out of reason and by necessity."[330] Aristotle wrote:

> Leucippus thought he had arguments which would assert what is consistent with
> sense-perception and not do away with coming into being or perishing or motion
> or the plurality of existents. He agrees with the appearances to this extent, but he
> concedes, to those who maintain the One, that there would be no motion
> without void, and says that the void is non-existent, and that no part of what is,
> is non-existent – for what is in the strict sense is wholly and full being. But such
> being, he says, is not one; there is an infinite number, and they are visible because
> of the smallness of the particles. They move in the void (and there is void), and
> when they come together they cause coming to be, and when they separate they
> cause perishing.[331]

Democritus of Abdera (c.460–c.370 BC): atoms and the void

Democritus is generally considered the principal architect of atomism, a theory that may have grown from a collaboration with Leucippus and what he learned in Egypt and perhaps even India. He thought atoms were not mathematical points but indivisible physical entities.[332] Atoms were eternal and unchangeable and, unlike

Empedocles' elements or Anaxagoras's "seeds", they possessed primary and secondary qualities.

Primary qualities were things such as size, shape, density, position and orientation. Some atoms were perfectly round, some had hooks, and some had grooves, eyes, bumps and humps. Thus the primary things were not Anaxagoras's observable stuffs and properties, nor Empedocles' observable four elements; nor were they the processes of mixing and separation. The primary qualities were physical individuals, which were unobservable and indivisible (*atomon* literally means uncuttable).[333] By contrast, the secondary qualities of atoms – taste, touch, colour and smell – enabled them to be perceived by the five senses.[334] Democritus wrote:

> By convention sweet is sweet, by convention bitter is bitter, by convention hot is hot, by convention cold is cold, by convention colour is colour. But in reality there are atoms and the void. That is, the objects of sense are supposed to be real and it is customary to regard them as such, but in truth they are not. Only the atoms and the void are real.[335]

All observable bodies were aggregates of basic individuals. Thus the "sensible" qualities *did not* belong to individual atoms but to the complex interplay between atoms, space and our senses. Anaxagoras described his "seeds" as infinite in number and varied in quality, but he never clarified how they became the things we sense.[336] All sense-objects in Democritus's worldview were a combination of atoms and space, which led to his separation of the appearance of a thing and the truth in reality that underpins it (see quote above).

Motion was explained by Democritus as an intrinsic property of atoms themselves, governed exclusively by mechanical causation principles (not some external agent like air, rotating *apeiron*, cosmic forces Love and Hate, *nous* or anything divine).[337] Their motion caused atoms to unite, combine and separate. Democritus, unlike Anaxagoras, was wholly silent on the cause of original motion (see below). Aristotle summarized Democritus's thought about atoms:

> As they [atoms] move they collide and become entangled in such a way as to cling in close contact to one another, but not so as to form one substance of them in reality of any kind whatever; for it is very simple-minded to suppose that two or more could ever become one. The reason he [Democritus] gives for atoms staying together for a while is intertwining and mutual hold of the primary bodies; for some of them are angular, some hooked, some concave, some convex, and indeed with countless other differences; so he thinks they cling to each other and stay together until such time as some stronger necessity comes from the surrounding (medium) and shakes and scatters them apart.[338]

Zeno had believed in infinite progression, but Democritus came to a different perspective about indivisibility of matter. A person can cut an apple in half, then that half in half, and so on. However, eventually he must reach something indivisible: hence the term atom.

Infinite worlds and the "necessity" of natural phenomena

In broad terms, Democritus (and Leucippus) viewed the universe as infinite, with innumerable worlds constructed of atoms and void. The Atomists' account of how the worlds formed in the beginning is full of obscurities, mainly from lack of texts. It appears that the first stage consisted of two distinct regions: concentrated atoms and empty space (no mention is made of a primordial chaos but presumably it was atoms and void). The second stage is the appearance of a vortex (origin not specified), which caused similar atoms to attract one another (not like Anaxagoras's particles coming together). The larger, heavier atoms congregated in the middle and formed the flat earth, and the smaller, lighter atoms were forced outwards. Some atoms became ignited from the high speed of rotation and formed the heavenly bodies.[339] Since there are infinite atoms and infinite void, Democritus (and Leucippus) postulated infinite worlds. Anaximander also proposed innumerable worlds, but these were formed from his unlimited *apeiron*.[340]

Democritus explained sense-phenomena in purely physical terms. Following Leucippus, nature operated by a kind of blind necessity, which contrasted the later purposiveness of Aristotle. Everything in the world could be explained by mechanistic necessity: every event had a cause, and causes necessitated their effects.[341] There are, therefore, no chance events in nature that simply happen. Every event has a prior cause, which required atomic interaction.

On explaining natural phenomena, Democritus agreed with Anaximenes that earthquakes arose from heavy rain filling cavities in the earth during drought periods. He also extended Thales and Anaxagoras's explanation that the annual Nile flood was not caused by a god, but began when water-laden clouds contacted the Ethiopian mountains.[342]

Soul, sensation and thought

> Leucippus, Democritus and Epicurus say that perception and thought arose from when images enter from the outside; neither occurs to anybody without an image impinging.
>
> Aetius[343]

Perhaps the best example of Democritus's application of his atomic theory was his account of perception and the objects of perception.[344] Perception was the result of the sensory activity of the non-rational soul, whereas thought came from the reflective activity of the rational soul.[345] The human soul consisted of spherical atoms spread throughout the body, and both the perceptive and thinking portions of the mind were a concentration of these atoms.[346] The soul atoms were extremely small and energetic, qualities he equated with fire.[347]

Thus human perception and thought involved the "primary" qualities of atoms (size, shape, density, orientation and position), which could escape the body, to be replenished by the process of breathing. Every physical body emits continuous streams, which we sense. When this flow of atoms between human perception and the objects of perception weakened, the person would go to sleep or become lethargic, and when there was no link, death was imminent. Death was an outflow of soul atoms from the body to the environment. If the soul was too hot or too cold, the mind wandered. The association of life and soul with heat led to the concept of the soul as "vital heat". Without exception, the soul was explained by Democritus in purely physical terms.[348] No mention was made of whether perception takes place by the interaction of opposites involving atoms.[349]

In Democritus's theory of sensation and thought, every act of human perception involved a physical contact between the external object being sensed (made of the secondary qualities of atoms) and the body's sense machinery. At one extreme, human thought comprised soul atoms, which could not be detected by the senses, and at the other extreme were the physical body atoms, which could be perceived.[350] Democritus (and presumably Leucippus) argued that thought and sense were manifestations of matter, and the task of theory was to bridge the gulf between appearance and reality.[351]

Democritus and religion

Democritus's idea of god(s) is not at all clear.[352] The gods were knowable to human beings mainly through dreams and explained as images (an idea extended by Aristotle). The gods inhabited the air and were made of soul atoms.[353] Sextus discussed Democritus's view of the gods:

> Democritus says that certain images come to men, some of which are beneficent and others maleficent (when he desired to meet with "propitious images"). They are large, indeed gigantic, and hard to destroy though not indestructible, and they show men the future in advance, by their appearance and by uttering sounds. Hence, the ancients, receiving a presentation of just these images, supposed that there is a god, though there is no everlasting god apart from them.[354]

Unlike many of his Presocratic predecessors, Democritus appears to have accepted the personal gods of Olympian religion and believed that there was a reason for believing in anthropomorphic beings. But like his philosophical colleagues, he rejected their involvement in natural phenomena.[355] The gods existed but they were indifferent to human affairs or ethical conduct.[356] He explained the popular Greek belief in anthropomorphic gods as a projection from dream images, which were a flow of atoms that impinge on the senses, and produce ideas of gods.

Democritus did not perceive the world as a living, breathing organism. There was no "divine mind, darting through the whole cosmos with swift thoughts"; nor was the world "a living creature with soul and reason".[357] The soul was mortal, and could not obtain eternal reward or punishment. In Democritus's world, soul (nor mind) was neither present in the beginning, nor did it play a role in ordering the world like Anaxagoras's *nous*.[358]

THE WESTERN MIND IN THE MAKING

> All philosophy is based on the postulate that the world must be an intelligible order, not a mere welter of sights and sounds flowing in upon the senses from moment to moment.
>
> F. M. Cornford[359]

Appreciating the difficulty of having only a few extant fragments written by the Presocratics themselves, and the appearance of a very complex secondary literature written many centuries later, six major features of the Presocratic intellectual legacy can be distilled:

- rejection of Homer and Hesiod's symbolism;
- invention of a single unified principle or *archē*;
- invention of a physical, intelligible *cosmos* (or *cosmoi*) with its own internal principles of order;
- introduction of the broad concept of causation to explain change as process;
- application of reasoned argument to distinguish truth from falsehood; and
- devising of a cosmic dualism by partially separating the physical and divine linked via soul (or *psyche*) and "breath".

Rejection of mythopoeic symbolism and the single unified principle or *archē*

The main function of Hesiod's *Theogony* was to link the existing Olympian pantheon to the great mystery of the origin of the universe.[360] The Presocratics denied the poet's claim to truth through myth, ritual and cult and introduced a radically new naturalistic approach. The Presocratics explained the origin, structure and maintenance of the world not by the actions of powerful creator-gods nor a series of divine births, but by manifestations of a single *archē* or unifying principle. Thales' single principle was water; Anaximander's was the *apeiron*; Anaximenes' was air; Heraclitus's was fire; the Pythagorean's was number; Parmenides' was "One Being"; Empedocles' was the four elements; Anaxagoras's was infinite "seeds"; and Leucippus and Democritus's was atoms and the void. In addition, despite broad concepts of internal or external causation to explain the process of change, the early Greek philosophers failed to advance a general theoretical framework to explore the deeper problem of causation as devised later by Aristotle (Ch. 5).

Nevertheless, the Presocratics tried hard to explain all sorts of change: astronomical change; day and night; meteorological change (summer and winter, cloud formation, wind, lightning, rain, earthquakes and the annual floods); life and death; evolutionary and geological change; and even the logical impossibility of change (and motion) itself. Each event or phenomenon was broken down into simpler conceptual parts, reassembled and explained using physical relations, not mythopoeic linkages to the divine. The world was no longer capricious and whimsical but a highly ordered, intelligible *cosmos* formed from the preexisting matter. A summary of the major doctrines of the Presocratics are in Table 4.4.

Invention of the physical object and physical *cosmos*

I believe that the first step in the setting of a "real external world" is the formation of the concept of bodily objects of various kinds. Out of the multitude of our sense

Table 4.4 Summary of the major contributions of the Greek Presocratics.

Philosopher	First principle	Main features of doctrine
Thales (c.624–550)	Water	• He broke away from tradition to look at the universe using philosophical reason. • He suggested that natural phenomena were linked by principle of water. • Water expands to produce air and contracts to produce earth. • The world is flat and floats in the sea like a cork (like Hesiod's cosmogony). • Earthquakes are caused by wave-tremors, not by Poseidon. • He explained the Nile flood in natural terms (not the Egyptian god Amon). • He linked the properties of a magnet to the idea of soul and motion.
Anaximander (c.610–546)	*Apeiron*	• There is one universe, which has been around for ever. • The universe is filled with *apeiron*, from which the present *cosmos* arose. • He suggested innumerable worlds or cosmoi. • He proposed the rotating *apeiron* as the principle of all things. • The *apeiron* gave rise to the opposites hot and cold, and wet and dry. • The physical universe and everything in it formed from those opposites. • The world is spherical with the flat circular earth lying motionless at its centre (because of symmetry). • The sun, moon and fixed stars arose from an expansion of vapour, which formed invisible concentric rings with holes. • The four seasons were interchanges between the opposites. • He explained thunder and lightning in physical terms. • He was among the first to propose an evolutionary theory for human beings and animals. • He rejected myths involving the gods as explanation. • In some contexts *apeiron* is physical and in others divine.
Anaximenes (c.588–524)	Air	• The physical universe arose from different degrees of rarefaction and condensation of air, which is always in motion. • Air in its most rarefied state becomes fire and in its most condensed state reduces to water; when even more condensed it becomes earth and rock. • Air (or *pneuma*) was the key to the well-being of all animals and plants and maintained the health of the universe itself. • The universe is a living organism continuous with *pneuma* and the human soul or *psyche* (or mind). • The earth is flat, like a table, held up in the middle of the universe by "compressed" air with a solid crystalline celestial vault revolving around it. • Air is not just a material or physical element, but also immaterial and divine.
Xenophanes (c.570–480)	God among lesser gods	• A theologian, he was among the first to consider Olympian religion a social "creation" and not divine "revelation". • Human beings created gods in their own image. • The heavenly bodies are not gods but burning masses of vapour. • There is one supreme god among other lesser gods, who "agitates all things with the effortless thought of his mind". • There is no possibility of knowledge by divine revelation.
Heraclitus (c.533–475)	Fire/*logos*	• None of his fellow Ionians adequately explained the basis of human sense: "The eyes and ears are bad witness if the soul is without understanding". • If change is a condition of the universe, so must be the principle behind it. • Reality has the element fire as its imperishable fundamental principle. • Fire is continuous with all physical and divine phenomena and connects with the *psyche* (Mind) through the *logos*. • *Logos* is the wisdom of philosophy and begins with ideas and observations from sense, proceeding to a higher degree of universality using reason. • Fire is connected to *logos* by unifying opposites and balanced in perpetual tension. • He had no cosmogony in the conventional sense but implied that the universe has always been in existence or uncreated. • The pattern of human life and the pattern of cosmic order are the same and are linked to the *logos*.

Philosopher	First principle	Main features of doctrine
Pythagoras (c.572–497)	Number	• Pythagoreans used the theory of numbers to describe the inner harmony and order of the universe. • He grouped numbers in physical units separated in space by divine air (*aether*). • The earth is not at the centre of the universe but is one of ten heavenly bodies revolving about a central fire. • Each heavenly body moves at a speed according to number and produces sound depending on its distance from the centre fire: "music of spheres". • Pythagoreans believed the ultimate reality is divine and not physical.
Parmenides (c.515–450)	One Being	• Parmenides' philosophy was revealed to him by a goddess. • He proposed the ultimate reality as Being. • Being is physical, motionless, changeless, limited, indivisible, ageless and sphere-like. It has no past, present or future; Being simply "is". Nothing can come into Being. • What "is" cannot change: hence natural phenomena as perceived by our senses are illusionary. • Motion is denied because it is a form of becoming, and all becoming is excluded from Being – even empty space and time are not real. • He made a sharp distinction between "the way of truth" through reason and "the way of seeming" through through the senses. • Nothing exists but thought.
Zeno (c.490–430)	One Being	• He produced some 40 arguments to prove that change, motion and diversity are all contradictory. • His arguments attacked the Pythagorean idea of the unit and the Presocratic notion of space, time and motion. • He argued the case against the infinite divisibility of space and time.
Empedocles (c.495–435)	Water, Air, Fire, Earth	• He gave the four physical elements (water, air, fire and earth) the properties of Being and motion by adding two cosmic forces: Love and Strife. • His four elements do not undergo transformation themselves (they are eternal and unchanging, after Parmenides), but by combining with each other. • Everything is in oscillation (or cycle). • The universe containing one world began in the early part of the cycle as a sphere with Love inside and Strife outside. • As Strife re-enters, the four elements mix and blend to create the universe. • His theory of life also involves the cycle caused by the Love–Hate exchange. • He talks about nature using only physical explanations but implies that the universe is divine in its entirety.
Anaxagoras (c.500–420)	Germs or Seeds	• He argued that there must be more than four elements because of the diversity detected by our senses. • He proposed an infinite number of "germs" or "seeds" having all sorts of forms, colours and tastes, of which the most complex were Empedocles' elements. • His ultimate cause was *nous* (or mind-intelligence). • *Nous* was a world-ordering principle that kick-started cosmic motion by rotation and was the ordering principle of all cosmic phenomena. • He smashed Parmenides' One Being and Empedocles' four elements into infinitely divisible pieces. • He believed that the sun was not a god but a red-hot body from which the moon obtained its light, and was charged with impiety for this belief (c.450 BC).
Democritus (c.460–420)	Atoms and Void	• His answer to Parmenides' One Being was an infinite number of atoms all having the character of One Being and interacting in the void or space. • The big difference between atoms and Anaxagoras's "seeds" is the distinction between primary and secondary qualities. • Primary qualities are size, shape, density and position not detected by sense. • Secondary or "sensible" qualities are those perceived by our senses, such as colour, smell, tastes and touches. • Secondary qualities do not belong to atoms but to the interplay between atoms and our senses. • He distinguished mind-atoms from body-atoms; both processes are exclusively physical. • Atomists believed in innumerable coexisting worlds.

experiences we take, mentally and arbitrarily, certain repeatedly occurring complexes of sense impression ... and we attribute them a meaning – the meaning of the bodily object. Albert Einstein[361]

The Presocratics were the first to invent the physical object, construct a physical *cosmos* and attribute meaning to it by ascribing *internal* principles of order. Depending upon the philosopher, each physical object was a different manifestation of water, air, fire, number, the four elements, seeds or atoms and the void. The major difference from past mythopoeic explanations was that physical objects acted upon one another according to physical transformations involving interactions of opposites, motion of fire or atoms, Love and Strife or Mind. This new form of causal reasoning involving physical objects, transformations and relations was largely devoid of magical or animated powers, spirits and gods.

While the Presocratic period marked a turning point in Western thought, a word of caution is necessary. Abstracting sensible things as relations among physical objects, while truly remarkable, does not necessarily translate to heightened inventiveness in all areas of culture. The earlier Sumerians and Egyptians did not introduce philosophical reason like the Greeks, but they invented writing, mathematics, time-keeping, monumental architecture, astronomy, medicine, metallurgy and a system of commensurate measures with standards. Greek philosophical reasoning may lead to discovery, but discovery is not conditional on philosophical reasoning. The Presocratic philosophers used their intuition and creativity in different ways than past thinkers. The philosophers were not as interested in finding better practical ways of "doing" things, but in better ways of "explaining" things.

Knowledge and truth: from divine norms to reason and refutation

What was more obvious, if not more important, the Milesians had succeeded in naturalising man in the *cosmos* but had done it so thoroughly as to reduce him to a physical object on the same level as all other physical objects. H. F. Cherniss[362]

The Presocratic way of explaining things meant that knowledge and truth were no longer attached to divine norms, but were the product of human exploration and thought. For most Presocratics, human beings had to depend on their own individual and collective efforts for their knowledge and social harmony, rather than interacting with various gods. Xenophanes gave the following captivating two-line account: "Yet the gods have not revealed all things to men from the beginning, but by seeking men find out better in time."[363] Xenophanes was suggesting that human investigation was a part of progress and rewarded in time, and involved studying, reasoning and argument. Knowledge and truth were no longer divine norms, but were part of a new reasoning process.

The introduction of Greek reasoning and argument into Western thought had another major consequence on truth. Since knowledge was no longer divinely sanctioned, absolute or certain, it became provisional or conjectural.[364] Thus the price Western thought has paid (and continues to pay) for introducing philosophical reason into its knowledge structure is that one might be wrong. Xenophanes seemed fully aware of this feature of reasoned knowledge when applied to the natural or divine realms.[365] Xenophanes wrote: "But as for certain truth, no man has known it, nor will he know it. And even if by chance he were to utter the final truth, he would himself not know it, for all is but a woven web of guesses."[366]

Heraclitus also expressed similar sentiments by contrasting reasoned knowledge with the absolute divine when he wrote: "It is not in the nature of character of man to possess true knowledge, though it is in the divine nature."[367] Democritus, too, reportedly said: "It will be obvious that it is impossible to understand how in reality each thing is … in fact, nothing do we know from having seen it; for the truth is hidden in the deep."[368] He may have arrived at this view from his contention that the only real things were atoms and void, and that all secondary qualities perceived by the humans senses are illusionary.[369] Truth, therefore, is to be discovered behind the appearances, behind the world of sensible phenomena. Protagoras of Abdera (c.490–420 BC) stated the possibility of knowledge in a different way; he believed that every person's sense-perceptions were true, but only true to the owner.[370] For Protagoras, something was "objectively" true if truth was not wholly dependent on the fact that one believes it to be true. Higher standards of criticism must occur before reliable knowledge is attained.[371]

In conclusion, alongside inventing the physical object and the physical *cosmos*, another momentous, and often overlooked, legacy of the Presocratics was providing the West with the provisional basis of our knowledge (introducing the possibility of error), and some of the philosophical methods for higher standards of criticism of that knowledge (reducing the possibility of error). Popper called this higher standard "critical rationalism" or "critical search for error".[372] Popper believed that the Presocratic distinction between the provisional and absolute foreshadowed the ethical rationalism of Socrates, and paved the way for Plato and Aristotle.[373] In contrast, the ancient Near Eastern "corporate-mind", with its truths sanctioned and framed by an exclusively divine worldview, could not have achieved anything remotely similar to the early Greek philosophers.

Where did the hundreds of gods go?

> They (the Presocratics) make the world a *cosmos* by keeping what was already there in the form of *physis* and cleaning out everything else … the demolition of the supernatural is accomplished without a single word about the victim (the gods).
>
> Gregory Vlastos[374]

Although most Presocratic philosophers were not explicit about what happened to the gods, they did introduce a reformed conception of divinity. For the most part, the concept of divinity shifted from the older mythopoeic "Office of Everyday Affairs" to the "Office of Cosmic Affairs". Thales' soul-magnetism, Anaximander's *apeiron*, Anaximenes' *pneuma*, Heraclitus's fiery *logos* and *psyche*, Pythagorean soul and Axaxagoras's *nous* were all part of the universe's grand divinity and cosmic governance. Divinity ascribed to these principles appeared in the metaphors of power-controlling, unbounded, unlimited, directing and steering.[375] The probable reason why the early philosophers were not explicit about the fate of the traditional gods was because Olympian polytheism was cherished by the Greek people,[376] and to outwardly mock them would have been foolish.

In the Presocratic world, human beings remained linked to the divine, not through everyday phenomena involving many gods, as in past millennia, but through mind and philosophical reason. Religion changed from a local phenomenon to a cosmic, philosophical one. On the topic of Anaximander's *apeiron*, and presumably most other unifying principles, Cherniss wrote:

> If this [*apeiron*] is to be considered in relation to theology, it must be admitted to be a complete rejection of all that was traditional in Greek religion. It is the

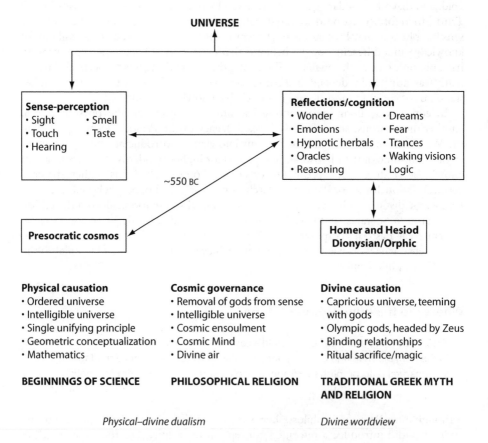

Figure 4.7 Diagram showing the broad mindset of most Presocratic philosophers. The Presocratics rejected myth and divine causation as explanations of sense-phenomena. The universe creation, structure and change were explained by physical causes, relationships and transformations. A new concept of divinity emerged, reducing the numbers of gods, redefining their roles, and shifting them from the "Office of Everyday Affairs" to the "Office of Cosmic Affairs". Human beings were still linked to the divine but more through mind and reason, not sense. Mind and reason permeated the intelligible universe. Most of the Greek populace, however, held on to their myth-based Olympian religious traditions.

denial that natural order can be suspended by any supernatural being or force, the denial in fact that any supernatural being can exist, and the assertion that, if the divine means anything at all, it can mean only the system of nature ordered according to infrangible law.[377]

In the Presocratic world, cosmic governance, order and intelligibility were manifested through immanent natural principles or laws.[378] The link between the physical and the divine was largely through soul (or *psyche*) and "breath". As long as there was "breath" there was "life"; and as long as there was "life" there was the "divine"; and as long as there was the "divine" there was mind and a healthy, ordered, intelligible, "ensouled" *cosmos*. The new concept of divinity meant that the gods were no longer aware of human beings' existence, let alone concerned about their fate. A broad schematic of the dualistic universe and the popular Greek Olympic mindset is presented in Figure 4.7.

Our constitution is called a democracy because it is in the hands of...
the many ... our laws secure equal justice for all in their private
disputes ... I say that Athens is the school of Hellas, and that her
citizens yield to none, man for man, in independence of spirit, many-
sidedness of attainment, and in body and mind.

Pericles of Athens (461–c.426 BC)[1]

CHAPTER 5

Classical philosophy:
different roads to truth

INTRODUCTION: FROM NATURE TO "KNOW THYSELF"

What logic seeks to clarify is the problem of the knowledge of reality; and this cannot
be solved in any other way than by analysing and tracing to their original conditions
the ideas of the human mind which form the basic material for all empirical
knowledge.

Ernst Cassirer[2]

As the grand river-valley civilizations of Mesopotamia and Egypt slowly declined under
Persian attacks and domination, so too the quiet intellectual revolution in Greek Ionia
ground to a halt. The new rising stars were the classical philosophers, who assured the
Greeks their place in history as the founders of Western philosophy. Fifth-century BC
Athens became the intellectual centre of Greece, where the primary focus in philosophy
shifted from the study of nature to the study of human beings themselves.[3] According
to Plato, it was Socrates who single-handedly turned philosophy around from the
observed to the observer.

With a penetrating lucidity and rigour, Socrates and his student Plato taught that
the "object" of thought was more real than the physical "object" of sense: the "idea"
of a tree in the mind was more real than the tree perceived by the senses. Whatever
really *is*, Socrates and Plato believed, must be eternal and changeless and the
philosopher's job was to discover this true, changeless being. Plato's world began with
his world of eternal Ideas on loan to us from the eternal soul. Where ordinary persons
were content to observe instances of truth, justice, virtue or goodness, Socrates, Plato
and the classical philosophers sought to know more of the origin and essence of the
truth behind these qualities. Correct thinking, Socrates argued, translated to correct
actions: not just *feeling* good but *doing* good.

Natural philosophy was not, however, totally abandoned. Aristotle saw the world
very differently from Socrates and Plato. Aristotle's reality did not begin with something
intangible and borrowed from the "outside", but with the physical things we sense in
the world. The tree was very real to Aristotle and a highly valued part of his common-

sense reality. Plato and Aristotle's opposing views on reality also impacted on the way they viewed myth and religion. Plato's supreme god was a craftsman, who created the universe from pre-existing matter, whereas Aristotle's god was the product of a long chain of reasoning required for first motion in a universe that was eternal. Plato's universe was a theological construction, whereas Aristotle's was more of a scientific one. Importantly, as in Presocratic times, most Greek people opted for the older Homeric–Dionysian polytheistic traditions. The philosophical world then, as now, was not universally accepted but largely restricted to academic circles.

In this chapter we shall explore the different ways Socrates, Plato and Aristotle sought truth, and the parallel developments going on in Hippocratic medicine around the same time (*c*.450–350 BC). Indeed, recent scholarship suggests that the origin of the debate between the rationalists (preference for reason over sense-experience) and empiricists (preference for sense-experience over reason) arose not from the classical philosophers, but from the medical doctors deciding between the spiritual and physical origins of disease and treatment. Lastly, we will consider another important turning point in Western history, which was the shift of science from Athens to Alexandria beginning around 330 BC, and known as the Hellenistic period. The classical and Hellenistic periods were extremely fertile in the sense that philosophers and scientists were always reinterpreting, reinventing and challenging themselves in their search for the truth.

SOCRATES TO ARISTOTLE

Socrates (*c*.469–399 BC): "Wisdom is knowing that we don't know"

> Socrates' discovery was that the true self is not the body but the soul. And by the soul he meant the seat of that faculty of insight which can know good from evil and infallibly choose the good. Self-knowledge implies the recognition of this true self.
>
> F. M. Cornford[4]

An eccentric "ugly little man" who cared little for appearance

The life and teachings of Socrates come to us mainly via Plato, Xenophon and Aristotle.[5] Socrates was born in Athens, and is often described as a short, thickset, "ugly little man" with a large mouth, piercing eyes, thick lips and a broad up-turned nose. Over the years, apparently, his physical appearance deteriorated and he adopted a peculiar gait, walking like a duck, and the annoying habit of rolling his eyes.[6] His clothes were old and shabby and he walked around barefoot, often lapsing into concentrated thought for hours. By all accounts, Socrates was an eccentric who cared little for his external appearance. Hidden behind this non-flattering description, however, was a man of giant intellect, who never ceased searching for truth. Surprisingly, Socrates wrote nothing.

Socrates rejected natural philosophy

> The unexamined life is not worth living.   Attributed to Socrates[7]

Socrates maintained that the natural philosophers[8] failed to find any grand scheme linking world order, harmony and purposefulness to the state, the city and the people.[9] There were no moral, ethical or political guidelines to determine who was right or wrong in daily living. He felt mathematics and geometry were better suited for buying, selling, building and agriculture.[10]

Socrates turned, instead, to the practical aspects of wisdom, arguing that there are absolute, cross-cultural standards of right and wrong, good and bad. His daily interviews or teachings were conducted in public marketplaces and multi-purpose gymnasiums. He was interested not in long, drawn-out speeches on a soapbox or treatises, but in conversations with the Athenian people.[11] Socrates' goal was to stimulate people to find their "inner self" through knowledge and work for the good of society, a goal similar to that of Heraclitus and Buddha in the previous century. Socrates particularly enjoyed targeting those high citizens who thought they were superior to the working class. In his *Apology* (from *apologia*, a formal statement of justification or defence), Plato puts the following words into Socrates' mouth:

> I shall never give up philosophising. I shall continue to give a clear exhortation to everyone I meet, using my customary language: "My good Sir, you are an Athenian, a citizen of the city which is the greatest and most noted for its wisdom and power. Are you then not ashamed to be worrying about your money and how to increase it, and about your reputation and your honour, instead of caring and worrying about the knowledge of good and truth and how to improve your soul?" And if anyone retorts that he does not care, I shall not let him off at once and go away, but I shall question him, and examine him, and refute him.[12]

Dislike for the Sophists

Socrates particularly disliked a group of public teachers, writers and lecturers known as Sophists.[13] Although they claimed to help the Greek people become more confident and successful, the Sophists charged exorbitant fees and taught how to argue only to win.[14] They were not seeking truth, as a philosopher would seek truth, but sought to win arguments using rhetoric as an alternative vision of literary discourse.[15] Socrates abhorred rhetoric and mind-trickery, and deemed all Sophists charlatans, who took advantage of people seeking guidance. The situation was made worse at a time of escalating social unrest in war-torn Athens.[16] Some of the more notable Sophists were Protagoras (*c.*490–*c.*420 BC), Gorgias (*c.*483–*c.*376 BC), Prodicus (fl. *c.*440 BC) and Hippias (*c.*485–*c.*415 BC).

In his *Republic*, Plato tells of a conversation between Socrates and Glaucon that clearly distinguishes a philosopher (or lover of wisdom) from a Sophist (lover of opinion):

> The philosopher, says Socrates, is a lover of learning, undertaking any study, always eager to learn more. But then, replies Glaucon, are we not to call lovers of spectacles (*philotheamenes*) philosophers, since they too delight in learning new things, scurrying from one Dionysian festival to another, never getting enough. The answer is obvious, but how is one to justify it? Socrates' solution is to show that

only philosophers are lovers of wisdom, since only they pursue knowledge (*epistēmē*) while lovers of spectacles in fact love only opinion (*doxa*).[17]

Socrates referred to what is now known as the "Socratic method" as *elenchus*, which eventually gave rise to *dialectic*: the idea that truth needs to be approached by altering one's position through questionings and exposures to contrary ideas. He challenged people to face their own ignorance and at the same time encouraged them to join with him in a genuine search for truth.

Wisdom and virtue

Socrates, then, the elder, thought the knowledge of virtue to be the end, and used to inquire what is justice, what is bravery, and each of the parts of virtue; and his conduct was reasonable, for he thought all the virtues to be kinds of knowledge, so that to know justice and to be just came simultaneously; for the moment we have learned geometry or architecture we are architects and geometers. Therefore he inquired what virtue is, not how or from what it arises.

Aristotle[18]

Socrates believed that once we recognize what is truly good, we shall act in accord with that knowledge, hence his claim that "the virtues are a kind of knowledge".[19] Socrates' wisdom was therefore a moral truth that led to virtue, goodness, moderation, courage and honesty. Virtue, in broad terms, was success and harmony in both personal and societal life within the State.[20] The first step towards attaining enlightenment was to define clearly one's terms and concepts. If you want to be a good shoemaker, Socrates argued, you must know what a shoe is and its purpose.[21] You must understand the concept of a heel, a sole, and have some measure of size.

To this end, every person must be able to discern between good and evil; honesty and dishonesty; tolerance and intolerance; generosity and greed; loyalty and disloyalty; indulgence and overindulgence; and order and disorder. After learning these virtues, Socrates believed, people could tap into their "inner self" (immortal soul[22] or *psyche*) and solve problems using reasoned argument as their final arbiter of truth.[23] According to Socrates, much of the social unrest and dislocation that swept fifth-century BC Greece was in part due to the lack of clear definitions.[24] For example, he believed disagreements occurred because people defined virtue and good differently.[25] However, there were problems: if virtue is a single defined entity, who was going to teach it to the Greeks? In particular, who was going to teach virtue to the Athenians and Spartans, who rarely agreed on anything and were constantly at war? Socrates never appears to have addressed this question.

Views on popular Olympian religion

Socrates had a deep mystical side and believed that he was guided by a *daemon*: a friendly spirit emanating from the depths of his soul, and intermediate between himself and the gods.[26] Indeed, he partly attributed his abandonment of natural philosophy to a conversation he had with his personal *daemon* in which he learnt that the practice was against the wishes of the gods.[27] He also believed in life after death, following the Orphic and Pythagorean traditions; he held that a person who had lived a good life, that is, who had "cultivated their Soul", warranted a more favourable position in an afterlife reincarnation than a person who had led a corrupt life.

Socrates' religious beliefs must not be confused with Olympian religion. He rejected popular Greek religion but did not publicly mock it. To do so would have been unlawful and foolish and would have served no purpose.[28] As a moral philosopher, Socrates believed that the gods must meet the same ethical standards of virtue and goodness that he asked of human beings.[29] Vlastos summarized Socrates' position on the supernatural:

> He (Socrates) subscribes unquestionably to the age-old view that side by side with the physical world accessible to our senses, there exists another, populated by mysterious beings, personal like ourselves, but, unlike ourselves, having the power to invade at will the causal order to which our own actions are confined …
> How they act upon us we cannot hope to understand. But the fact is they do and their communications to us through dreams and oracles is one of the inscrutable ways in which they display their power over us.[30]

The tragic death of Socrates

Over the years, the State increasingly resented Socrates especially because of his influence on the youth. When Socrates was 70, he was charged on three counts of denying the existence of the gods of the State, worshipping strange gods in their place and corrupting the Athenian youth by non-conformist attitudes. When Socrates was asked what he was accused of, he replied, "They say I am a god-maker; for making new gods and disbelieving in the old ones [Meletus] has brought this indictment against me."[31] In 399 BC a jury of 500 Athenians condemned Socrates to death. He was asked to drink hemlock, an alkaloid poison that after a brief stimulatory effect is followed by severe depression of the nervous system, paralysis and death. It was favoured by the Athenians and held to be a "humane" method of execution.

Although Socrates was given ample opportunity to escape during his 30-day incarceration, on moral grounds he chose not to do so.[32] He felt that it was his duty to respect the due process of the law in the city that had nurtured him. Plato presented the famous death scene in the *Phaedo* (114 E-118) and *Crito*, and it has been the source of many paintings, narrations and re-enactments. Socrates' symbolism was feared by those who thought themselves wise, and revered by the less able citizens of Athens, who held him in the highest esteem.

Plato (427–347 BC): the authority of the mind

> The whole *Republic* is an attempt to interpret human nature psychologically. The postulate upon which its method rests is that all the institutions of society, class organisation, law, religion, art and so on, are ultimate products of the human soul, an inner principle of life which works itself out in these outward shapes. R. L. Nettleship[33]

The establishment of the Academy

Plato was born into a family of great wealth and political influence. In his youth, he was an eyewitness to the brutal Peloponnesian wars, in which Socrates is said to have fought a courageous battle.[34] From the ages of 20 to 28, he studied in Athens under Socrates but left angrily after his beloved teacher drank the fatal hemlock. From Megara, Plato travelled extensively to other parts of Greece, Sicily and Italy, where he is believed to have studied under the Pythagorean Philolaus in the early 380s BC, and later under the prophets of Egypt.[35]

He returned to Athens in his early forties (around 387 BC) and soon thereafter founded his famous Academy.[36] Unlike Socrates, who frequented public places, Plato believed in a separate institution for higher learning. Plato modelled his curriculum on the Pythagorean schools[37] and his main goal was to train young men (and some women) to enter politics.[38] With proper training, he believed the next generation of "philosopher kings" could pass on their wisdom to the community. Certainly, Plato's "ideal state" was not a democracy, but an authoritarian state. It was a state where people were *without* political rights; ideas were censored; all poets and Sophists were *banished*, and all music outside the martial/nationalist type was *prohibited*.[39]

Plato considered that most Ionian philosophers were extreme heretics and he would have had them re-educated, jailed or condemned to death. In Book 10 of his *Laws*, Plato drafted a statute for all intellectual non-conformists that, according to Vlastos, "is without parallel in any surviving code of ancient Greece".[40] Even the mildest penalties would have led to five years' solitary confinement, followed by execution if the sinner had not reformed. Plato is also said to have urged the burning of Democritus's books because they were against his own teachings. Some experts believe that Plato's "ideal state", however, should not be taken literally. Plato's main purpose was not to tell of a philosopher's utopia, but "to urge the validity of certain principles: in particular, that politics is a vain business unless it is subordinated to an understanding of the good for man".[41]

Plato's lifelong goal was undeniably to achieve human good, perfection and wholeness through education.[42] In order to achieve this, he had to construct a theory of knowing with clear definitions and standards, from which ethical judgements could be made. He was particularly interested in solving the Presocratic problem of the difference between "true" objects of knowledge (or *epistēmē*) and belief or opinion (*doxa*). How were truth and belief linked to the "sensible" world? How do people discover truth and know when they have found it? What is the relationship between the eternal and immutable, on one hand, and change or what "flows", on the other, in both nature and society?

Plato tackled these difficult questions in different ways throughout his life. Over a period of five decades and some 34 separate works he wrote an extraordinary five million words. Plato's most highly celebrated doctrine was his theory of Ideas (or Forms) and absolute reality. He also formulated a theory of sense-phenomena in space and time; a doctrine of soul and its migrations; and a doctrine of ethics. Plato wrote in prose dialogue, often using real-life characters, a method possibly adopted to avoid the same fate as Socrates. Dialogue had the advantage of making attribution of contentional opinions difficult compared to a direct authorial voice.[43]

Plato's Ideas behind appearances

Nothing is more characteristic of Plato than his lifelong conviction that it is the imperative duty of the philosopher, whose highest personal happiness would be

> found in the life of serene contemplation of truth, to make the supreme sacrifice of devoting the best of his manhood to the service of his fellows as a statesman and legislator.
>
> A. E. Taylor[44]

Plato began his road to truth by assuming that "true" knowledge was eternal, unchanging, super-sensory and good.[45] He agreed with most Presocratics that hidden behind the world of appearances there must be something that never changes. However, unlike Empedocles' four elements or Democritus's atoms that never change, Plato believed that everything in the physical world erodes with time and there must be another answer. In an attempt to resolve the problem, Plato constructed two worlds: a world of eternal "being" in the mind and a world of "becoming" in the sensible world; a dualism reconciling Parmenides' "One Being" and Heraclitus's "Many" (Ch. 4). After long training in dialectics (a method of reason and logic used to demonstrate truth) and mathematics (whose language is absolute), Plato formulated what he believed was the answer. The eternal and immutable truth was not a Presocratic "*archē*" or "first principle", but was contained in Plato's famous theory of Ideas.[46]

Ideas (or Forms) had little or nothing in common with how the word is used today: "any object of the mind existing in thought; a notion, or mental impression; a formulated thought or opinion".[47] Plato's Ideas existed *independent* of whether we think of them or not. They were eternal and unchanging; *not* objects of thoughts or abstractions, but a permanent part of the spiritual world on loan while we are alive.[48] Plato believed that all trees were fashioned from an eternal and unchanging mould of a tree. When we see a tree, it stirs the intellect and recollects the eternal Idea of a tree in a special part of the mind. If the tree in your front garden were removed, the Idea of a tree in your mind would still remain. In Plato's world, the Idea tree came first, followed by the creation of all the sensory world of trees as copies: the Idea chicken came before the chicken and the egg. The same holds for every physical object in the world – a rock, a blade of grass, a dog, a fish, a mountain – and indeed it holds for the entire world itself.

For Plato, the world was created as an inferior or crude copy from a blueprint of a perfect world. If there were no Ideas, there would be no world "as we know it". His "true" reality was therefore something we cannot see, hear, smell, taste or touch. In addition, Plato also applied his theory of Ideas to knowledge. He, like the Presocratics, taught that human beings cannot attain the truth from a world that is constantly changing (or flows). We must seek truth in the eternal and unchanging world of Ideas using philosophical reasoning and mathematics. The Ideas, including good and justice, must be sought in a place where all thinking passes from absolute to absolute. For Plato, that place was the immortal soul in the mind, the realm of human reason: "it was the place which imparts truth to the known and the power of knowing to the knower".[49]

Plato's allegory of "the cave"

Plato's theory of Ideas is further illustrated in his allegory of the cave.[50] The story depicts the path of human enlightenment from the world of sense to the world of intellect. Plato asks the reader to picture a dark underground cave connected to a long steep passage that eventually opens to the external sunlit world. At the bottom of the cave are prisoners who have been sitting in the dark since childhood. They are chained, facing the end wall, unable to turn their heads. Higher up the cave, behind the prisoners, is a fire, and between the fire and the prisoners is a screen. Between the screen and the fire are people performing everyday activities, whom the prisoners see as shadows cast on the end wall. Plato intercedes at this point and tells the reader that the prisoners are like us, untrained in the theory of Ideas, with a reality wholly in the shadows or appearances. The prisoners can talk to each other and propose explanations for what they observe, but they know nothing about the "true" causes. In order to gain enlightenment, a prisoner is released from the shackles and forced to turn around and move up the cave. The prisoner realizes that his thinking about reality has been confused. He continues upwards and out of the cave into the sunlit world.[51] The sun was symbolic of Plato's Idea of good; the visible world was the intelligible world, light was his truth; and sight was knowledge.

According to Plato, the allegory stood for the upward journey of the soul from the world of sense (shadows) to the world of intellect (Ideas). It was Plato's invitation to enlightenment via thought, not through the senses. Knowledge from the senses was provisional because it comprised imperfect copies of "true" reality. The tree we sense is an imperfect copy of the Idea of a tree in the immortal part of the human soul borrowed from the eternal soul at birth. The path to enlightenment was taken by moving from the physical world to the world of Ideas.

Hierarchy of knowing as states of mind

Truth for Plato, however, was not a simple case of black and white, as it was for Parmenides, who denied any kind of knowledge from the senses. Plato permitted degrees of truth, with "true" knowledge at the top, belief (or opinion) in the middle and ignorance at the bottom (Fig. 5.1). The "objects" of sense, also termed "particulars", played an important role in Plato's theory of knowledge because they also shared in the Ideas of the mind.[52] However, opinions or beliefs were inferior because they required persuasive argument (they could not justify themselves as Plato's eternal Ideas).[53] And even if opinion turned out to be correct, the knowledge gained was inferior in comparison with the clarity of Ideas.

For Plato, the physical world was made "real" by the process of recollecting, reminiscing or matching the eternal Ideas to external appearances.[54] In the Socratic

True knowledge	Belief (opinion)	Ignorance
• What is • Absolute, unwavering	• What is and is not • Can be believed	• What is not • Cannot be believed
Clearest of all *(Super-sensory)*	*Intermediate* *(Sensory)*	*Most obscure*

Figure 5.1 Plato's scale of knowing. At one end are the absolutes, "those absolute, unwavering things that purely are", and at the other end are those things than can never be known or believed (objects solely of ignorance). In between these two extremes is "belief or opinion", which comprises both "what is" and "what is not".

style, what we truly *know* must be "true" by definition. What we *believe* must be provisional because it may be proved wrong.[55] Out of this intellectual framework, Plato constructed his two worlds: his eternal Ideas in the mind and changing belief (or opinion) in sense.[56]

How can "true" knowledge be attained?

In Plato's scale of knowing, how did his eternal Ideas relate to the things in everyday life? How was the appearance of a tree related to the eternal Idea of a tree, or how was good in the world related to the eternal good in the mind? To use the cave analogy, how were the shadows on the end wall related to the sun (good), sight (knowledge) and light (truth)? Plato's answer was through the study of philosophy using dialectics and mathematics. As mentioned, dialectics was a method of using thought alone to demonstrate the truth. Dialectics was the "art" of critical argument that operated independently of the "objects" of sense.[57]

However, critical argument was not enough. Secondary to attaining "true" knowledge was employing, wherever possible, the power of mathematics. It was essential to Plato's philosophy because of the purity of number, which never changes: the circle is divided into exactly 60 equal parts.[58] Mathematics was preparatory to dialectics because, like dialectics, it was a product of the immortal soul (not the senses). Mathematics and dialectics were a means of linking sense and reason via the immortal soul.[59]

Immortal soul as the source of knowledge

Immortal and rational soul in the brain is distinct from mortal soul, located in the thorax, which is filled with passions and dominated irrational sensations, and which is further divided by the midriff to form still another soul that is concerned with the wants of the body. Even animals were granted an inferior soul. Living man was a part of a living universe and shared its harmony.   G. L. Finney[60]

Plato divided the human mind into two parts: the rational and irrational. The rational part was the intellect (or reason) and the irrational contained the will and sense-perceptions (Fig. 5.2). The rational and irrational were connected by the inner soul (or *psyche*). Just as a city operated with hierarchical functions, so did the human soul.[61]

The human soul comprised three major parts: intellectual, appetitive and spirited parts. The intellect in the brain was the superior part of soul, which provided human beings with the ability to reason; its task was to guide the inferior parts of the body "wisely".[62] The appetitive soul function, in the liver, was the desire to learn from everyday experience, as well as to coordinate other bodily functions. The spirited soul, in the heart, was the eternal soul, which connected the intellect and appetitive soul. The spirited soul also provided human beings with qualities such as self-respect, self-control and the desire for glory. In another of Plato's famous myths, he likened the soul's movements between the mind and senses to "winged horses and their charioteer".[63]

As well as being a life-principle that animated bodies, the soul was also responsible for the first motion or psychic movement.[64] Plato regarded the soul as the *initiator* of movement in the celestial bodies,[65] an idea extended by Aristotle.[66] In the *Laws*, Plato

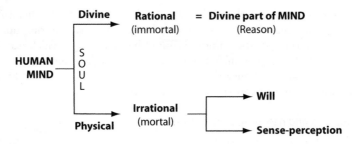

Figure 5.2 Plato's conception of the construction of the human mind. The rational part of mind or reason was divine and immortal, whereas the irrational parts of mind were not. The physical and divine faculties were connected via the immortal soul, which, in turn, was connected to the world-soul through reason. This metaphysical scheme of Plato's was his partial solution to Parmenides' problem of "being" and "becoming".

states that soul is "that movement which is capable of moving itself by itself".[67] Plato's first movement was different from Anaxagoras's, who believed that Mind or *nous* (universal reason) not soul (*psyche*), was the cause of first motion.

Plato's cosmogony and cosmology

> Plato describes the world as being created by a craftsman, *demiourgos*, the word for creator god which was to have a long history … This god has in view an eternal model for this creation.
>
> W. Burkert[68]

Plato's supreme god created the world

Plato's world was fashioned from pre-existing matter by his supreme god. It was not a creation "out of nothing" (*ex nihilo*), as in the Judeo-Christian-Islamic cosmogony. Plato's god was a craftsman, the ultimate philosopher-king: "a mathematician, and engineer, and above all, an artist",[69] who was co-eternal with matter.[70] He was eternal, uncreated, creative reason, who fashioned the visible world from the conflicting four elements of chaos modelled on his eternal Idea of good and perfection. The single *archē* of the Presocratics, as mentioned earlier, did not appeal to Plato.

After the body of the universe was constructed, Plato's god gave it life through ensoulment, after which the visible *cosmos* became a living, breathing organism: "a living creature with soul in body and reason in soul".[71] The next stage was to create the everlasting heavenly souls of the gods with their spherical bodies of fire.[72] These so-called star-gods were visible in the heavens and provided human beings with a means to measure time.[73] Time measurement by number was therefore born with the creation of the star-gods and first motion.[74]

The creation of human beings

Since everything fashioned by Plato's craftsman was immortal, he could not create the mortal components of the world and so assigned that job to the star-gods. In addition to creating the heavenly bodies, the star-gods created all the physical bodies of human beings and animals from the elements of the earth according to the divine laws that governed their own behaviour.[75] After human beings were created, the supreme god took charge again to create the immortal soul of human beings, which was linked to the world soul.[76] To help human beings reach their full potential, the star-gods created friendly *daemons* (or angels), who, from time to time, descended to earth "to direct us upward from Earth to kinship with Heaven".[77]

The supreme god and nature, reason and sense

> The kernel of Plato's ethics is the doctrine that man's reason is divine and that his business is to become like the divine by reproducing in his own nature the beauty and harmony revealed in the cosmos, which itself is god, a living creature with a soul in body and reason in soul.
>
> F. M. Cornford[78]

Once fitted with a soul, human beings could contemplate the order, beauty and good in the world and the mind of God. According to Plato, every person's soul at one time lived outside the physical body[79] in the realm of Ideas. At birth, the soul migrates into a physical body and moves about between the eternal Ideas and ever-changing illusionary senses.[80] It encounters many hostile disturbances until the immortal portion takes charge and provides order and harmony to the body.[81] After death, the immortal soul is freed from the physical body and returns to the super-sensory world of Ideas because it has a "longing to return to its true origin".

With proper education, the mind of human beings can become enlightened by stirring the soul through recollection of objects and events and surveying them in the world of Ideas, which is ultimately linked to the mind of God (Fig. 5.3). *God's superior mind and cosmic ensoulment endows each physical object with an intrinsic property that*

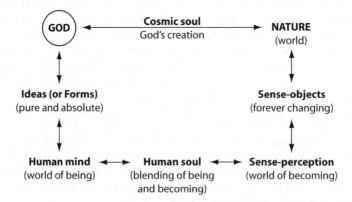

Figure 5.3 In Plato's world, the supreme god not only creates the world but ensouls it, making a living, breathing *cosmos*. Soul is the kind of super-stuff that contains no physical matter or properties other than life, mind and self-movement. Nature, in Plato's universe, is the objects perceived by the five senses, which are copies of the originals and created by God. By dividing the human soul into three parts (intellectual, appetitive and spirited) Plato cleverly linked the human mind to the mind of God.

determines its behaviour according to immutable laws.[82] For Plato, natural order and "cosmic" ensoulment are one and the same thing. These immutable laws were built into the universe according to "true" harmonious proportions, which could be studied by mathematics.[83] Mathematics thus provided Plato with a window into the mind of God.

An important point of emphasis is that Plato's supreme god is separate from the Ideas because nature was created as a "copy" of the eternal blueprint.[84] If God were *identical* to the Ideas, the world would be unchanging and perfect. In addition, the soul itself was separate from the Ideas because it had the characteristics of being alive and intelligent, whereas Ideas were "objects" of rational thought.[85]

Two cosmic causes: Reason and Necessity

Plato held that knowledge of the observable world had in itself no value, and that empirical investigation could not lead to any real truth. Nonetheless, if only to round off his metaphysical theory, he gave an account of the general nature of the sense-perceptible world, which appears in his *Timaeus*. It is put forward as being only a "plausible story" – which means that Plato was willing to revise it in the face of new evidence, but that he was uncertain how best to fit the observable world into his metaphysical scheme.

E. Hussey[86]

Plato depicted the physical world as the product of two causes; supreme god (or Reason) and "Necessity".[87] Reason overruled Necessity to bring about the construction of the sensible world. Necessity was an "impersonal" property of the world (sometimes called "the wandering cause") that came from the eternal matter in the chaotic state, from which the world was fashioned.[88] It came about because the world was always in the process of "becoming" (*genesis*); the things we sense in the visible world were only a copy of "true" reality.[89] Necessity, as "the wandering cause", had never been completely controlled by God (or Reason) and was associated with disorder in the world.[90] It seems that Plato's Necessity has some parallels with the negative forces that lived in the ancient Mesopotamian primeval waters or Egyptian Nun and which ventured out and tormented humanity; or the evil forces in the underworld who were kept at bay by the high priests or god-king pharaoh (see Chs 2 and 3).

In a more profound way, Plato's concepts of Reason and Necessity may have been his terminology for good and evil.[91] Good was the work of his supreme god and evil was the unpredictable forces of adversity. Evil was something fashioned from eternal matter that Plato's god did not get quite right. However, there is much controversy about whether Necessity was evil. Greek scholar A. E. Taylor argues that Necessity was not Plato's evil, but represents the change we see around us.[92]

World structure

Plato viewed the cosmos as a single,[93] perfectly spherical and geocentric world.[94] Earth was at the centre and the celestial bodies moved in perfect concentric circles. The moon orbited Earth, followed by the sun, the five planets (Mercury, Venus, Mars, Jupiter, Saturn) and then the fixed stars in the outermost circle (i.e. all the heavenly bodies except for the planets, sun, moon and comets) (Fig. 5.4), a scheme that seems

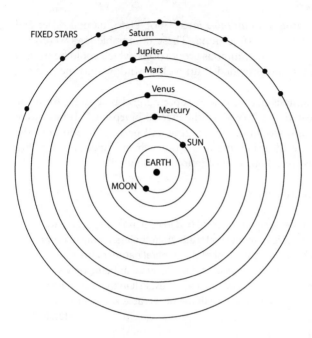

Figure 5.4 Scheme of Plato's cosmology (after *Eudoxus*). The spherical Earth and its four elements (water, air, fire and earth) are at the centre, bounded by the sphere of fixed stars in the outermost circle, with the moon and the sun and five planets inside.

very similar to that of the Pythagoreans (see Ch. 4). Plato believed that the cosmic distances separating the spheres (as indeed the structure of the soul) were governed by two geometrical progressions 1, 2, 4, 8, and 1, 3, 9, 27, which were related to the ratios of intervals in music.[95] According to Sir W. David Ross, later in life Plato replaced his eternal Ideas with numbers.[96] Plato, like Pythagoras, believed numbers were not human inventions, but actually existed and were divine.[97]

However, unlike the Pythagoreans, Plato did not believe that the planets produced harmony in the sense of "musical spheres". Circular motion in Plato's universe, as discussed above, was an intrinsic self-property of the divine soul from the star-gods.[98] The moon appears to be an exception. Its motion appears to be ascribed to mechanical processes transmitted from the outer divine sphere.[99] Plato's idea of outer shells (above the moon) and inner shell (sublunary) of the world operating separately, but still influenced by the divine, was an idea extended by Aristotle. Plato viewed gravity as the tendency of like bodies to cluster.[100]

Composition of the universe

> Plato's conviction that mathematical structures were at the heart of physics was based not at all on empirical investigations, but on his profound respect for the beauty, clarity, timelessness and generality of mathematical truth.   E. Hussey[101]

Another feature of Plato's cosmology was his account of the structure of the primary elements: water, air, fire and earth.[102] Water was for those inhabiting water; fire was the stuff of the celestial bodies (with the souls); air was for winged animals; and earth was for

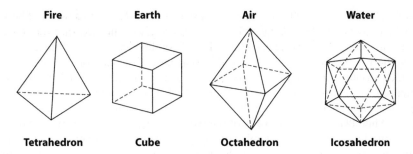

Fire	Earth	Air	Water
Tetrahedron	Cube	Octahedron	Icosahedron

Figure 5.5 Plato's conception of matter. Plato was highly influenced by the Pythagoreans and described the four elements in precise, geometrical forms. Friedrich Solmsen wrote: "For Plato matter is and remains in the full sense of the word something unthinkable"; it was something one could not "separate in thought". Plato talked about matter "in which" things arise whereas his student Aristotle talked about matter "out of which" things come into being (or are made) (Solmsen 1960: 43, 122).

those living on dry land.[103] Thus, Plato accepted Empedocles' four physical elements, but strongly rejected atomism.[104] Plato described the four elements in geometrical forms.[105] In other words, as Plato's god fashioned pre-existing "chaotic" matter into the *cosmos*, he did so by imposing on it regular stereometric forms giving rise to water, air, fire and earth.[106] Water was a 20-sided structure called an icosahedron; fire was depicted as a four-sided tetrahedron; air an eight-sided octahedron; and earth a six-sided cube (Fig. 5.5). There was a fifth shape, the dodecahedron (12-sided), but this was exclusively reserved for use by the creator for the entire world: "God used it for the whole."[107]

Plato used these basic geometrical forms to describe the structure of the world and explain change. Further, each element could be broken down into two-dimensional figures: weightless, non-material right-angled triangles.[108] This feature afforded Plato a mathematical means to help explain how one of the four elements may change or be built into another. Hussey has called this scheme "Plato's microstructure of matter".[109] Because fire had sharp particle points it could penetrate all other bodies, whereas water had smoother particles and flowed. When air condensed to water, it was due to a greater amount of air matter in a given space, not an internal alteration in physical structure.[110] Apart from this, Plato gives *no* account of physical transformations or constructions between states of matter, unlike the earlier Presocratics.

Timaeus: cosmology as myth

Plato's attempt to geometrize nature from the primordial "pre-existing" matter is found in his famous *Timaeus*. The dialogue portrays Plato's profound fascination with world order, which he associated with the mind of his supreme god. Vlastos believed that Plato's mathematical approach forged the way for contemporary and later Greek mathematicians – such as Eudoxus of Cnidos (*c.*408–355 BC), Apollonius of Perga (*c.*245–190 BC), Hipparchus and Ptolemy – to study the motions of the stars and planets.[111] Eudoxus, one of the foremost mathematicians of the day, moved his school from Cyzicus to Athens to join in cooperation with the Academy.

In contrast to many extant Presocratic writings, the *Timaeus* creation is steeped in mythopoeic symbolism involving a logical series of divine creations. Even Plato himself referred to it as a "likely" story because he was dealing with a world of becoming where no "true" knowledge existed.[112] Vlastos also conceded that the *Timaeus* was a "fairy tale",[113] as did Plato scholar I. A. Crombie, who wrote, "the purpose of giving the account being to give the reader some idea of the kind of account the truth of which would justify the claim that the world is rationally ordered, to put some content into the notion of rational order".[114] Having said this, it should be emphasized that there is no doubt Plato clearly knew the difference between myth and reason. While Plato employed many of the older mythical linkages we saw in Homeric Greece and in ancient Mesopotamia and Egypt to explain the creation of order from chaos, and being from non-being, he used reasoned arguments to justify them without committing himself to "absolute" truth. In fact, Plato's mythical cosmology seems to be the necessary outcome of the dualism he set himself between eternal Ideas in the mind and changing belief (or opinion) in the world of the senses.

Plato's spirituality

> It seems difficult to believe that Plato really wanted us to pray to the stars or to his immutable and impassible Creative Mind; and yet it seems certain that he wanted us to pray. It rather looks as if neither his intellect nor his imagination knew what the other was doing.   I. M. Crombie[115]

While Plato believed in a supreme god and gods, he never held traditional Olympian religious beliefs.[116] He was particularly against portraying the gods as moral and sometimes immoral divine beings who indulged in emotional excesses in the image of human beings.[117] In the latter part of his life, Plato bluntly denied all Greek anthropomorphic religions.[118] The following is the shorthand version of Plato's views:

> A man may give what account he pleases of Zeus and Hera and the rest of the traditional pantheon. But we must insist on the superior dignity of the visible gods, the heavenly bodies. The neglect of the Greeks to pay proper honour to the heavenly bodies, the gods whom we all actually see, is inexcusable. They [the gods] should be honoured not merely by feasts on the calendar, but by setting ourselves to get a scientific knowledge of their motions and periods. Every true Greek should recognise the duty of prosecuting astronomy in a scientific spirit and cast off the superstitious fear of prying into the Divine. God knows our ignorance and desires to teach us. The study we require to bring us to true piety, which is chief of the virtues, is astronomy, knowledge of the true orbits and periods of the heavenly bodies. But it must be pursued in the spirit of pure science, not that of Hesiod's farmer calendar. Without this scientific knowledge, a city will never be governed with true statesmanship, and human life will never be truly happy.[119]

Plato's philosophical religion was a celebration of the triumph of order, good and virtue over chaos and Necessity (his "wandering cause").[120] This is *logos*: living in mental harmony with the universe. But it is also wisdom, the philosophical study that teaches harmony and the right ordering of mind and body. *Logos* for Plato was "excellence of the whole".[121] Indeed, the main reason why Plato believed that human beings should embrace a supreme god was that it provided the best explanation for "good" and the order, harmony and perfection in the world. It was Plato's unwavering "faith" in divine order and harmony that led to his theory of Ideas, which we all have access to via our inner soul (or *psyche*). Plato died around 347 BC and was buried in the grounds of the Academy.

Aristotle (384–322 BC): from sense to intellect

In any attempt to understand the mind of Aristotle, perhaps the most important thing of all to remember is that he was an Ionian.   W. D. Ross[122]

Life and the Lyceum

Aristotle was born in Stagira in eastern Macedonia. His father was a physician and possibly influenced Aristotle's later interest in biology.[123] At the age of 17, he visited Athens and joined Plato's celebrated Academy, where he remained for some 20 years.[124] After Plato's death, Aristotle, now 37, left Athens[125] to travel and pursue his love of philosophy and biology. During his travels, he tutored the 14-year-old heir to the Macedonian throne, Alexander, later to become Alexander the Great.

In his late forties (around 336 BC), Aristotle returned to Athens (now under Macedonian rule) and opened his own school, the Lyceum,[126] which was located outside the city in a grove sacred to Apollo and the Muses (the Greek goddesses of wisdom). Members of the Lyceum became known as "peripatetic philosophers" because they were often seen in deep discussion while walking around the colonnaded courtyard or *peripatos* (from Greek *peri* meaning "around" and *patein* meaning "to walk").[127] In contrast to Plato's Academy, which showed little interest in natural philosophy, Aristotle's school grew to become more like a modern research institute with large systematic collections of zoological specimens, maps, library books and manuscripts.

About 38 of the 200 or so books Aristotle wrote exist today.[128] Each book began with a historical introduction criticizing his predecessors, followed by the presentation of his own ideas, arguments and solutions.[129] One of the most characteristic aspects of Aristotle's style was his ceaseless questioning: Why is the universe the way it is? Why do objects of sense appear in the form they do? Why don't things fall upwards?

Aristotle's long association with Macedonian royalty eventually backfired because, following the death of Alexander, the Athenians charged him with impiety. Rather than let the Athenians "sin twice against philosophy" (obviously referring to Socrates' death 76 years earlier),[130] Aristotle fled Athens in the spring of 323 BC. He spent the remainder of his life in his mother's family town of Chalcis (in Euboea), where he died of stomach disease at the age of 62.[131] His last will and testament shows him making charitable provision for his dependants and also awarding his slaves their freedom.

Aristotle's criticism of Plato

Aristotle shared Plato's passion for truth, but sought it by a very different path. Aristotle reportedly said, "Plato is dear to me, but dearer still is truth".[132] Although he accepted that the universals were the key to true knowledge, he rejected Plato's supreme god as a starting point. Some of the major issues of contention between the two were:

- **The theory of Ideas.** To Aristotle, all knowledge began with sense, not with the Ideas in the mind. Individual objects were real to Aristotle because they possessed matter and form, potentiality and actuality. Matter always existed in conjunction with some form. He had no need for Plato's higher reality in thought preceding the creation of the sensible world. There were no eternal innate Ideas. In effect, instead of separating the ever-changing sense-objects from the unchanging Ideas, Aristotle combined them, something that Plato said could not be done.
- **Number and mathematics.** Unlike Plato and the earlier Pythagoreans, Aristotle believed that numbers and mathematics were not actual realities in themselves, but abstractions of the human mind to serve scientific enquiry. Aristotle's distinction between sense-objects and our mental picture of them served as the foundation of his logical method.
- **Cosmogony and cosmology.** Unlike Plato, who resorted to a supreme god to fashion the universe from primordial matter, Aristotle believed that the universe was without a beginning or an end. The world was co-eternal with God. Aristotle abandoned the doctrine of cosmic-soul, and divided the cosmos into a physical region below the moon and a divine region above. Motion was up-and-down in the sublunary region, and eternally circular in the divine region. Aristotle conceived the world as a goal-directed hierarchy, where every object (including the universe itself) had its own function, purpose and end, which was "good". He referred to a specific kind of "internal" purpose in natural things as a final cause. The world was a purposeful place, and the purposes were inherent in the natural objects themselves. Aristotle rejected the Presocratic notion of a living, breathing *cosmos*.

All knowledge began with sense

The objects of thought are in the sensible forms ... hence, no one can learn or understand anything in the absence of sense.   Aristotle[133]

Aristotle's exploration of why the universe was the way it was began with the assumption that knowledge of sense-objects (or particulars) precedes knowledge of the universal. Nowhere did Aristotle and Plato differ more decisively. Aristotle regarded the information received by the senses as the source of all knowledge. He began with the sense-objects and went to the universals *using* mind.[134]

Plato's Ideas were no longer super-sensory, eternal and unchanging but simply the intelligent product of human beings "abstracting" the world around them. Ideas were not separate but were contained in the sense-objects, from which definitions and meanings were derived as part of language. Words were signs of "passions" or "conceptions" of the soul,[135] used to describe things and explain things. Aristotle regarded the tree as real; it was not a copy derived, contrived or separated from anything else. A tree was a physical object classified, identified and agreed upon as a tree by human beings after experiencing many trees. The general concept of "tree" was an object of the mind, not a copy of some mysterious, intangible eternal Idea. Aristotle's mind universals did not exist apart from the individual things we sense, but were *contained in them*. Our senses perceive a tree but our intellect "sees" a tree, which has already been mentally classified over the years, as part of human knowledge. Aristotle used the term "tree" as a perceptual representation of a sensible object, much as we do today.

From sense to intellect

Aristotle's own opinion is that all form is correlative to another element, which he terms matter; it is often *abstracted* from matter and this process is essential to science; but unmixed "form" is inconceivable and can have no place in the nature of things.

D. J. Allen[136]

Aristotle proceeded to explain the world by first breaking a sense-object such as a tree into two components: matter and form. *Matter* was the stuff from out of which a tree was made, and *form* was its organization, that is, roots, trunk, branches, bark and leaves. Form was the knowable part of sense-perception; it was the *end product* of change toward some prescribed goal or purpose. The form of a tree gave rise to the mind's concept of a tree as part of language that could be understood by the intellect.[137] Aristotle believed that every physical object has a purpose,[138] which helped him distinguish one tree from the next or indeed a tree from a table. All were made of wood, but their form was different and served different purposes in the overall design. Form was not something transcendent, eternal and separate like Plato's concept of soul. Form was a principle of structure that served a teleological "internal" purpose in natural objects or final cause (see below).[139] When the tree dies so does its form; the only thing that remains is matter.

In Aristotle's world, *form* bridged the particular to the universal: the senses to the perceptual representations in intellect (see Fig. 5.6). Form was made possible by a special activity called "substance", which drew matter into unity with its form to become the object. In his *Metaphysics*, Aristotle pointed out that the substance of an object (or its essence) was more than matter by itself;[140] a dead tree decomposes to matter, but it is no longer a tree. The essence of an object is what makes something what it is. It gives something an inner identity or property, which remains the same despite different forms.[141] Substance is essential for actual existence, but insufficient by itself without form and matter.[142] Aristotle's notion of substance (or essence), which existed independent of the object and was basic and irreducible, provided early Christian theologians with the linguistic tools to describe the relation between the divine and human in Christ (see "The mystery of the Holy Trinity", Ch. 6).

With few exceptions, matter and form were inseparable in Aristotle's world (Fig. 5.6). In addition to the decay of an object, where only matter existed, at the other end of the scale was Aristotle's god, which was pure form.[143] A summary of Aristotle's world and how he sought meaning about its presence and purpose is found in Figure 5.6.

The problem of change

The starting point [of Aristotelian philosophy] is located in the things of the sensible universe; the procedure is the explanation of these things through their causes; the

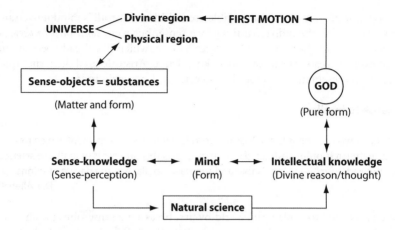

Figure 5.6 Aristotle's theory of knowledge. All knowledge was derived from sense. To Aristotle, Plato's Ideas (or Forms) were not separate from sense-objects but contained in them, and connected through form, which permeated both sense and mind. Aristotle believed the first motion in the physical universe was derived from God, who, in contrast to Plato's God, did not create the world because the world was eternal. Clear definitions were essential to language on one hand and knowing on the other.

goal is the ultimate causes that provide the final and fully satisfactory answer to the problems about which men wonder. In a word philosophy seeks the causes that explain the things of the sensible universe.   J. Owens[144]

We have presented a broad picture of Aristotle's role of the senses and reality, but how did he tackle the formidable problem of change? Like his description of a physical object, Aristotle explained natural order and change in purely physical terms, involving "matter" and "form". Change involved "four causes", potentiality and actuality. The four causes[145] were:

- a material cause (what the thing is made of, and the basis of any and every change);
- a formal cause (basic structure imposed on something or a "plan" among opposites[146] that gave rise to change independent of its material composition);
- a moving or efficient cause (or agent of an action); and
- a purposeful or final cause or teleology (the purpose for which the action is undertaken).[147]

The final cause was not the last, or ultimate end, but the result of doing something. For instance, it rains because animals and plants need water for life. Aristotle believed that each "effect" was the result of these four causes acting simultaneously.

Aristotle's four causes helped him to explain the substance of a tree, its form, what external or internal agency produced it, and its final purpose.[148] The next problem he tackled was how to explain the act of change itself: why do trees grow, decay, shed certain qualities and gain others? To this end, Aristotle invented the concepts of "potentiality" (sometimes called powers) and "actuality". Aristotle's matter and form defined the apple as round and red but the apple also has the "potentiality" to change colour on ripening. Potentiality was the capacity of an object to pass from one state to another (within limits). The ripening apple turns from green to red, but never from green to bright pink. This "natural" change arose from a previous "intrinsic" potency that Aristotle called "actuality".[149] Aristotle's four causes presuppose change, and potentiality and actuality helped to explain the process:[150] when you are asleep, you are potentially awake; water is potentially steam or ice; a seed is potentially a tree. The final cause is the "actualization" of form to become a tree as part of the "necessity" of nature.[151]

To sum up a complex scheme, matter to Aristotle was the basis of all being, which possessed the potential of becoming form and the actuality of changing. Change was neither potentiality nor actuality, but *the transition that occurred between the two states*. Aristotle's distinction between actuality and potency meant that change was a continuous process instead of some catastrophic recreation of new states. Aristotle believed that he had solved single-handedly Parmenides' problem of "being" and "becoming". Parmenides had denied the reality of change altogether and Plato had asserted that change had occurred, but it was not part of his "true" reality. He also made a clear break from Pythagorean number and the ten principles of opposites, Heraclitus's fire, Empedocles' Love and Strife, Anaxagoras's Mind, and the Atomists' "eternal motion". Aristotle believed all had erred because "being" had the *potential* to change.[152] Change occurred as *potential* being became *actual* being. Parmenides' logical absolutism had no place in Aristotle's world; otherwise a seed would never become a tree. In Aristotle's world, Plato's Ideas were pure actuality because they were super-sensory, unchanging and eternal.

Syllogism and logical method

Aristotle explained change in his formal set of logical proofs. Notwithstanding the advances made by Zeno, Aristotle is regarded as the first philosopher systematically to treat formal logic as the art of inference-building using reasoned argument.[153] Logic, as a theoretical study of argument, was Aristotle's tool to link language structure to the processes of thought, and tease truth from falsehood in statements. Aristotle considered logic to be not separate from the sciences but an essential component of *all* intellectual endeavours.[154]

Syllogism

Aristotle's method of drawing inferences was "syllogistic" and can be found in his *Organon* (or "instrument").[155] Syllogism is a logical analysis of a formal argument that consists of a major premise, a minor premise and the conclusion. For example:

Major premise:	Human beings (A) are fallible (B).
Minor premise:	Lawyers (C) are human beings (A).
Conclusion:	Therefore, lawyers (C) are fallible (B).

One of the great strengths of syllogistic argument is that if the first two premises are valid, so is the conclusion. Symbols can also be substituted for words and form mathematical proofs. In its simplest form: $A = B$, $C = A$ therefore $C = B$.

The syllogistic argument does, however, raise questions about one's starting-points. If the starting premise, "Human beings are fallible", is false, then the conclusion will also be false. In other words, a logical proof may not lead to the truth. Aristotle realized the problem and emphasized the importance of "right thinking" in forming the right premises. Early in his life, Aristotle claimed his starting-points were independent of what might be thought.[156] However, in later writings he qualified this by admitting that the premises need not be absolute but sufficiently valid.[157]

Aristotle classified at least three types of syllogism: scientific, metaphysical and Sophistic.[158] Scientific syllogisms were based on experience, observation and demonstration of individual facts, including mathematical syllogisms. Metaphysical or ethical syllogisms were those based on principles derived from opinion or rational thought but not experience. Sophistic syllogisms were those used by the Sophists, who advocated winning an argument at any cost, irrespective of the truth.

Deduction and induction

Aristotle recognized two basic types of inference drawing: deductive and inductive logic. All *teaching* proceeded via deduction and induction; all *convictions* arose from deduction or induction; and all *scientific* arguments were classified as deductive or inductive.[159] Deductive inference was the logical process leading to the conclusion. Aristotle defined deduction as: "A deduction is an argument in which, certain things being supposed, something else different from the things supposed follows of necessity because of their being so."[160]

Inductive inferences were in the starting-points. Induction argues a general truth or a claim extended from particular observations to universals: "human beings are fallible". If I throw a ball in the air, it will go up and fall to the ground. This premise can be tested many times and the same result will be obtained. However, a different result would occur if the experiment were performed in zero gravity. Inductive inferences require not only "right thinking" but some form of validation. Aristotle used three criteria to obtain these inductive premises or "true" facts: by observations or inference from observations; by seeking a common property that is verifiable; and by seeking scientific relations of form to matter via demonstration.

Science through demonstrative knowledge

Aristotle defined natural science as a theoretical and practical discipline derived from the *necessary conclusions* from the *necessary premises (or axioms)*.[161] The inductive premises were "true, primary, immediate, more intelligible than, prior to and explanatory of the conclusion".[162] To know anything in a scientific way was to know it in its causes. This required laying out an argument usually through demonstration, defined as "a deduction that makes us know", which sometimes employed mathematics.[163]

A famous example is how Aristotle deduced that a heavy object would fall at a faster rate than a lighter one. First he assumed that natural motion was an intrinsic property of a body in the absence of any external force (i.e. it is natural for a stone to fall downwards). He then reasoned the heavier weight would hit the ground first because of "its" greater pull towards the earth.[164] The starting premise focused strictly on the properties of the gravitating body (using his four causes, potentiality and actuality), and not on the place in space where the body was located. Aristotle's logic was sound, but if the experiment was carried out, he would have found that the heavy and light ball fall at the same rate (see Ch. 8 for a more detailed explanation). And based on this observation, Aristotle's starting premises (inductive principles) would have required modification.

Aristotle's scientific approach was revolutionary, despite the limitations. Indeed, he is among the first to distinguish between learning and understanding.[165] *Knowing* that something is "true" and *understanding* why it is "true" are very different. The type of knowledge Aristotle generated, using observational and categorical[166] demonstrations, is called *epistēmē*.[167] Another example of Aristotle's *epistēmē* was his cosmology.

Aristotle's cosmogony and cosmology

Aristotle's universe comprises a single *cosmos* of finite extent, outside which is nothing having spatial extension, not even a void. A satisfying construction, but radically at variance with the main Ionian cosmological tradition, to which in details Aristotle owed so much.
E. Hussey[168]

Cosmogony
Aristotle did not have a cosmogony, or a creator-god. The universe had no beginning or end because change was a continuous process and time was eternal. Aristotle defined time as a measure of motion with respect to a "before" and an "after".[169] Every moment of time was the end of the past and the beginning of the future; time was eternal.[170] Aristotle further deduced that motion must be eternal because if there is no time, there is no motion (see later). In contrast, time in Plato's visible world began with the creation.

Cosmology
Aristotelian cosmology was a complex blend of past myths and reason. His universe was finite and spherical with a stationary, spherical[171] Earth in the middle. Aristotle believed in only one world, which explains why the terms *cosmos* and universe were used interchangeably.[172] Aristotle was strongly influenced by Plato's colleague Eudoxus, who was among the first to develop the theory of mathematical concentric spheres (some say in response to a challenge from Plato's fascination with order).[173] However, mathematics was not Aristotle's master, but a servant to augment his physical construction.

Aristotle gave Plato's geometrical universe (depicted in Fig. 5.4) a physical–mechanical facelift with special emphasis on two clearly defined regions. The first was the sublunary physical–mechanical region, which was ruled by nature, and the second was the celestial or divine region, where God reigned supreme using his thought, desire and love. The sublunary world was always in the process of change. The two distinct regions seem to have been Aristotle's attempt to clarify the partial separation of the physical and the divine of the earlier Presocratics.

- **The sublunary region.** The sublunary world was the "physical" region where matter and form were inseparable and where phenomena could be studied by natural science. Aristotle wrote very little about the lunar boundary between the physical and divine. The Earth was associated with four terrestrial spheres, one for elemental earth followed by the spheres of water, air and fire.[174] The Earth arose from the natural tendency of the heavy elements to move towards the centre.[175] Sublunary "natural" movements were either up (associated with the lighter fire and air) or down (heavier water and earth) in a straight line.[176]

Any departures from free fall or free ascent were due to external forces or special agencies. Aristotle explained the movement of living things from "within" via the soul (or *psyche*). Non-living things (inanimate objects) depended on nature itself for movement, for example, a rock slide.[177] In Aristotle's physical world, movement did not lead to any permanent change, only transitory changes as "potential" states became "actual" states. Natural order was different as it was unchanging and eternal.

- **Celestial region.** The celestial region was the outer "divine" region from the moon to the outermost circle containing the heaven of fixed stars. Unlike in the sublunary region, none of the four traditional elements (water, air, fire, and earth) were present. The only element in the celestial region was the fifth element, Empedoclean *aether* (see Table 4.3). *Aether* was pure form, had no weight and was unchanging; it contained no "opposites" and had the property of perfectly circular motion of constant speed. All celestial motions were composed of the *aether* and could not change direction, even in the presence of an external force.[178] According to Aristotle, the *aether* permeated the lower sublunary sphere as part of the human mind, and was responsible for human reason (see later).[179] By contrast, Plato did not admit the *aether* either into his cosmogony or cosmology.[180]

    However, if the *aether* produced unchanging, perfectly circular motion, then why do the motions of the planets[181] appear to change erratically in the night sky? Aristotle adopted Eudoxus's explanation to "save the appearances" by describing planetary behaviour as a product of superimposed uniform circular motions.[182] Each planet's movement was derived from the outermost heavenly sphere, and each revolved around a different axis at a different *uniform* speed.[183] Aristotle deduced that the heavens comprised at least 55 such concentric spheres[184] made of the *aether*.

Conception of matter

Aristotle rejected any kind of atomism; whether it be the atoms of Democritus, the "seeds" of Anaxagoras or the two-dimensional weightless, non-material right-angled triangles of Plato. Matter did not require Plato's mathematical determinism or his Mind of God. Rather, Aristotle argued that all physical phenomena could be accounted for by Empedocles' four elements, and his own doctrine of four causes and potentialities and actualities.[185]

The four earthly elements – earth, water, air and fire – had their own natural place determined by their weight. As mentioned, earth was the heaviest and "wanted" to be at the centre of the universe and water was above the earth, with air above water, and then fire. For Aristotle, this made intuitive sense since solid ("earthy") bodies sink in water; air bubbles rise to the surface; and flames leap upwards during burning. Despite wood being a solid body, it could float because it contained both earth and fire; the fire was released on burning. The further a body was from the earth, the more perfect it became. The moon was the least perfect, evidenced by its uneven "appearance", while the outermost "fixed" stars composed of the *aether* were the most perfect of all.

Aristotle's primary elements, fire, water, air and earth, were also resolved into opposite qualities hot-moist, or cold-dry.[186] These four basic qualities did not refer to sensations, as they do today, but rather to qualities deemed truly to exist in the ontology of nature. In Aristotle's scheme, objects obtained their form-like properties from the opposites that enabled change from one element into another (Fig. 5.7).

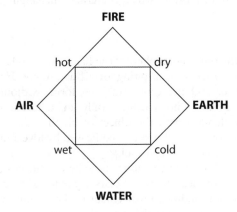

Figure 5.7 Aristotle's scheme of the four elements and pairs of four quantities. Aristotle dismissed the atomic theory of Democritus in favour of the four elements of Empedocles. Matter in the sublunar region of the universe was composed of the four elements. Aristotle rejected any kind of microstructure of matter. He believed all phenomena and objects could be accounted for by potentiality, which could not be reducible.

Postulates of God's existence

> Though Aristotle denies that either universals or mathematical objects are substances (complex of form and matter), he holds that there are non-sensible substances. There is in the first place god, the unmoved mover of the universe, and in the second place the intelligences which, moved by god, move the planetary spheres. And thirdly, he indicates that the human reason (or the "active" element in it) is, on the death of an individual, capable of existing apart from the body.   W. D. Ross[187]

Aristotle's god served two major functions: he was the source of first motion in the outermost celestial sphere; and he was pure form and actuality thus completing Aristotle's matter–form–potentiality–actuality scheme. Unlike Plato, Aristotle did not describe his cosmology as beginning with God's creation. In contrast, his cosmology began with the objects of the physical world and then, through the process of logical reasoning, came to the idea of God as the first mover giving rise to motion.[188] Aristotle was seeking the source of eternal motion.

Aristotle's five ways

Aristotle's justification of God is called the cosmological argument (meaning he started with a fact(s) about the world and proceeded to its cause). He listed five proofs for God's existence:[189]

- There exists an eternal circular motion in the outermost sphere of the cosmos that requires explanation.
- Everything that is moved is moved by something else.
- This something else is itself either moving or not moving. If it is in motion, then it is either self-moved or moved by another.
- Everything moved by another must *ultimately* be in motion solely due to a self-moved thing. And the whole series of self-movers *must* be in motion solely due to an unmoved mover.
- Therefore, there is an *unmoved* cause of motion, which is eternal, unchanging, and this is God.

Aristotle's prime mover

Aristotle's god was the prime mover of the outermost sphere ("the first heaven"). He caused the daily rotation of the stars around Earth by inspiring love[190] and desire. He was pure Mind (*nous*), perfect and alive: 100 per cent actualized form, without potentiality.[191] Since God was pure Mind, who engaged only in theoretical contemplation, his act of thinking was identical with the object of his thought.[192] Unfortunately, Aristotle was silent about how his god first moved heaven by love and desire but the implication was that "the first heaven" had soul.[193]

In addition to moving "the first heaven", God acted within the spheres. But how, and how far, he penetrated the sphere is not clear. Some scholars argue for a *direct* teleological causality,[194] but others for a more indirect involvement in the sublunary motions.[195] Again, Aristotle gave no unified statement about God's influence in the different regions of the universe.

The unity of human soul, mind and body

Aristotle defined soul or *psyche* as "the first entelechy (activity) of a natural body which potentially possesses life and is equipped with organs".[196] Soul was the life principle, or animator, and was responsible for the workings of the individual capacities of faculties in the body. In contrast to Plato, Aristotle did not believe that the human soul was immortal and separate, but rather saw it as part of a unity of faculties (*dynameis*) with Mind (or reason) alone connected to the divine (see later).[197] For Aristotle, soul was related to body as form was related to matter. In addition to the faculties of the mind (psychic faculties), others included nutrition, perception, imagination, growth, reproduction, locomotion and desire.[198]

All livings things have souls. The different faculties arose from "taking into themselves what was external to them".[199] The souls of plants (vegetative soul) were responsible for nutrition, growth and reproduction. The souls of animals (animal soul) were responsible for these faculties, and for locomotion, sense-perception, desire and imagination.

The human soul had all these faculties and reason,[200] which was pure form and the faculty that gave human beings their unique position in the animal kingdom.[201] The human soul was the perfection of the human being and gave rise to the concept of "self". Non-living things have no souls and no activity outside movement from some external source (e.g. a falling rock). Aristotle thus denied Plato's transmigration of souls and resurrection of the dead.

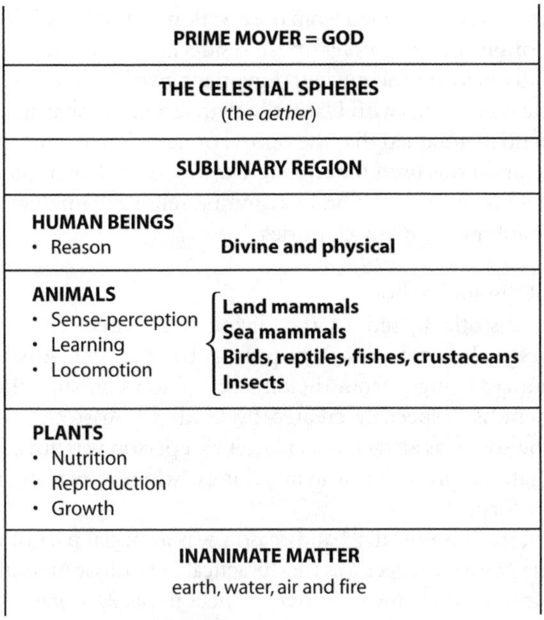

PRIME MOVER = GOD	
THE CELESTIAL SPHERES (the *aether*)	
SUBLUNARY REGION	
HUMAN BEINGS • Reason	**Divine and physical**
ANIMALS • Sense-perception • Learning • Locomotion	{ **Land mammals** **Sea mammals** **Birds, reptiles, fishes, crustaceans** **Insects**
PLANTS • Nutrition • Reproduction • Growth	
INANIMATE MATTER earth, water, air and fire	

Figure 5.8 Aristotle's classification of soul was useful in helping construct his scale of life (*scala naturae*). God was the highest with perpetual reasoning; next were human beings, followed by animals and plants; and at the bottom the lifeless four elements (earth, water, air and fire). The diagram is a modification of "The Ladder of Nature" in Farrington (1965: 83).

The Aristotelian world was one of ascendancy striving for perfection; the most primitive strove to become the most advanced. Aristotle believed that nature passed from inanimate objects through plants to animals in an unbroken sequence, which led to his *Scala naturae* ("scale of life" or "ladder of nature"). Everything in the natural world aimed to reach the final perfection: God (Fig. 5.8). The scale of life was Aristotle's attempt to explain the diversity and grand scheme of physical matter becoming form with different faculties of soul. Modern science knows that the form-giving principle of life is not soul, but genetic information passed to offspring through reproduction and in the kinds of genes turned "on" and "off" during different stages of embryonic development (see Ch. 10).

Aristotle's scale of life should not be seen, however, as an early description of higher organisms evolving from lower ones. Aristotle was fiercely opposed to the proto-evolutionary theories of Anaximander or Empedocles. Natural species and order were fixed, unchanging and eternal.[202] Aristotle taught that some animals spontaneously generated from dead matter while others originated from spawn from parents, and parents from grandparents, and so on down the line; the chicken always comes before the egg.[203] This view was wholly consistent with Aristotle's concept of time and the universe as eternal, having no beginning or end.

Common sense and the heart

Aristotle drew no sharp dividing line between mental activities and bodily functions, with the exception of reason (*nous*).[204] He believed that the faculty of common sense, self-awareness or consciousness was seated in the heart,[205] and he appears to have formed this conclusion after examining a developing chicken embryo, where he observed the first signs of life from the pulsating heart. He concluded from observation and syllogistic logic that the seat of the soul and origin of the nerves must reside in the heart, not in the brain.[206] The same belief was held by the ancient Egyptians two thousand years earlier.[207] On this point, Aristotle was at odds with Plato, the Pythagoreans, Anaxagoras, Hippocrates and many others, who maintained that the central organ of intelligence was the brain. Aristotle believed the brain was used for cooling the blood.[208] The immense popularity of Aristotle meant that his views on the brain, common sense and intelligence held back advances in brain physiology for many centuries.

Reason (*nous*) was immortal, not the soul or body

The one human faculty that Aristotle linked to the divine was reason (*nous*).[209] Whereas animals and plants passed their faculties from parents to offspring, Aristotle believed that reason came to human beings "from the outside". Later Christian theologians interpreted this statement as "especially created by God".[210] Aristotle never said this, but he did state that the soul was attracted to matter as a person was attracted to a lover.[211] Soul was an immaterial principle of living things, whereas reason (the highest power of soul) was pure form.[212]

Reason, not the soul (*psyche*), was immortal,[213] and reason was a special part of the intellect. At a most basic level, the *passive* intellect was the "practical" reason of Aristotle's *Ethics*, and at the highest level it was the divine or *active* intellect in his *Metaphysics*.[214] Reason provided the link, therefore, between human beings and God through thinking (or "thinking about thought").[215] *The "active" as opposed to the "passive" intellect was one and the same for all human beings,*[216] an idea that was later developed by Islamic philosopher Averroes (Ch. 7). Aristotle believed that as sensory information was processed and passed from the physical to pure thought, matter left and became pure form and "mysteriously" became divine.[217] His path to God was a series of logically reasoned steps leading to a final cause.[218] He argued that Plato's soul could not survive outside the physical body.[219] "How could my temper, my skills or my character survive me?", he asked.[220]

Aristotle on natural science, religion and myth

> The fundamental assumption in the Aristotelian conception of nature is that natural phenomena, that is, those arising from neither art nor chance, are intelligible; there is a regularity, a determined rationality about these phenomena which can be grasped. This must be the basic assumption of all science, for without it science itself is impossible.
>
> J. A. Weisheipl[221]

The sciences

Aristotle divided the sciences into three main branches: theoretical, practical and productive. The practical sciences improved human conduct (ethics, politics and economics). The theoretical sciences had three divisions: "first philosophy", including "theology" and later called metaphysics;[222] mathematics; and physics or natural sciences (Fig. 5.9). Each classification had its own assumptions about the sorts of truths they could generate, a feature that contrasted with Plato's approach of trying to derive all principles from some common, supernatural transcendent origin.[223]

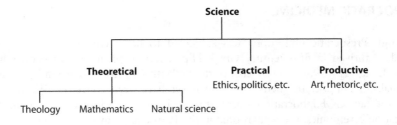

Figure 5.9 Aristotle's classification of the sciences.

Natural science was mostly the study of form in relation to matter. Aristotle recognized mathematics as an abstraction, from points and lines and numbers, and as a tool to help describe actual physical bodies.[224] Mathematical abstraction could be used to contemplate things divine (unchanging, eternal and non-physical) as well as things physical. Aristotle's use of mathematics is a fertile area of current investigation.

Theology was the study of pure form or of Aristotle's prime mover. The theological domain lay in the celestial region between the moon and the outermost sphere, and his natural philosophy lay within the sublunary region (with the exception of astronomy).

Religion and myth

Aristotle's god was "thought or contemplation *per se* and could not love the world, or mingle with the people".[225] Thus, Aristotle rejected the traditional Olympian religion with local anthropomorphic gods meddling in human affairs, and the religions of ancient Mesopotamia and Egypt. He separated his philosophy from past myths, as illustrated in the way he formulated his theory of causation in the natural world. Aristotle expressed his views on past religious practices in his *Metaphysics*:

> Our remote ancestors have handed down remnants to posterity in the form of myths, to the effect that the heavenly bodies are gods and that the divine encompasses the whole of nature. But the rest has been added by way of myth to persuade the vulgar and for the use of the laws and of expediency. For they say that the gods are anthropomorphic and like some of the other animals – and other things which follow from and are similar to this. But if you distinguish among what they say and accept only the first part – that they thought the primary substances to be gods – then you would think they were divinely inspired.[226]

Clearly Aristotle was attacking the manner in which people of tradition came to the idea of gods in the image of themselves; not through reason as he prescribed but through unsubstantiated myth. For most of his life, Aristotle abhorred Plato's allegorical use of myth as an educational tool to convey the difficult aspects of his theories. Aristotle believed that if a crisp statement could not explain something it was best left alone. However, the following sentence, written by Aristotle shortly before his death, implies that he may have been in two minds about his position, although admittedly we are left somewhat hanging on its full meaning: "The more lonely and alone I am the more I have come to love myths."[227]

HIPPOCRATIC MEDICINE

Although Presocratic philosophy was subjected to harsh criticism in the classical period, it thrived in fifth-century Greek Hippocratic medicine.[228] Classical scholar James Longrigg (1934–) even claims that: "Without this background of Ionian Rationalism, Hippocratic medicine could never have been conceived."[229] In many ways, the famous Hippocratic oath,[230] still used today in various forms at medical graduation ceremonies, is deeply rooted in the Presocratic way of thinking.

Homeric medicine and the gods

> It goes without saying that in Greece … there was a time when diseases were
> thought to be sent by the gods.   L. Edelstein[231]

The earliest textual evidence of Greek medicine is found in Homer and Hesiod's epic poetry.[232] Therein lies a wealth of information on attitudes towards injury and disease; the views are not very different from the beliefs of the people in ancient Mesopotamia and Egypt. One famous story in Homer's *Iliad* describes a plague that fell upon the Greek army under the command of King Agamemnon during the Trojan War. The plague was of supernatural origin sent by the Greek god Apollo for King Agamemnon's harsh treatment of Apollo's priest, Chryse.[233] For nine days, Apollo sent arrows into Agamemnon's camp and caused a plague, which killed many warriors.[234] Agamemnon finally submitted by returning Chryse's daughter Chryseis to her father to appease the angry god.

The arrows of Apollo appear elsewhere in Greek mythology and were directly associated with the cause of sudden illnesses, death and diseases.[235] As well as inflicting disease, the gods could also cure. Apollo's son, Asclepius, was one such "god of healing" and was worshipped in temples for many centuries. He became so famous that, from the fifth century BC, the popular word for physician or group of physicians was "Asclepiad", or "sons of Asclepius".[236] Interestingly, Apollo also became the god of healing in Roman mythology, apparently reaching Rome from the Greek settlements in Italy, and by way of the Etruscans. A temple was built in his honour in Rome after the plague of 433 BC.

Hesiod also wrote that diseases "come of themselves … come upon men continually by day and by night, bringing mischief to mortals silently; for wise Zeus took away speech from them. So there is no way to escape the will of Zeus."[237] During this period, magic (mostly in the form of incantations) was also employed in conjunction with supernatural interventions in the healing of wounds.[238]

The Hippocratic Corpus

> For where there is love of man, there is also love of the Art.
> Epitaph, Hippocrates of Cos

The Hippocratic Corpus is the first "rational" or empirical-based medicine of Greece. One of the first stories questioning the gods' involvement in human disease was reported by the fifth-century BC Greek historian Thucydides in his account of the Great Plague of Athens (430–427 BC).[239] Thucydides reported that both believers and non-believers died, and some survivors began to doubt the benefit of worship in protecting human beings from sickness.[240] Thucydides wrote: "Those who saw all perishing alike, thought that the worship or neglect of the gods made no difference."[241] Most survivors of the Great Plague responded in the true Olympian tradition: they did not reject the gods, but sought more powerful ones. Nonetheless, doubt began to filter into the minds of a few[242] about the social relevance of religion and the divine and physical causation of disease.[243]

Shortly after the Great Plague, around 420 BC, the writing of the Hippocratic Corpus commenced. The collection of some 60 books was completed in about 70 years and assembled into a corpus at the famous library of Alexandria in Egypt around 280 BC, under the supervision of Ptolemy I.[244] The Hippocratic collection appears to have been the first Greek documentary evidence of the removal of magic and supernatural causation of disease. The books dealt with internal diseases, surgery and gynaecology and offered reasoned empirical-based theories, clinical observations, causes and classifications.

An unresolved issue is whether Hippocrates had anything to do with the famous corpus.[245] Hippocrates was a contemporary of Socrates, Empedocles, Anaxagoras, Democritus, Pericles and Thucydides. He had a reputation in medicine based on his understanding of natural philosophy, anatomy and physiology.[246] He is believed to have been the son of an Asclepiad lay-healer, who was a member (or founder) of a movement around 600 BC on the Greek island of Cos in Asia Minor. Hippocrates' younger contemporary Plato called him "the Asclepiad of Cos" who taught students for fees,[247] and Aristotle also noted that he was a giant intellect.[248] Beyond these few scattered remarks, very little is known of Hippocrates' life and medical career.

The philosopher-physicians of the fifth and fourth centuries BC

The naturalism of pre-Socratic philosophers and of Hippocratic physicians had originated in a pagan society that demanded respect for the gods but left much freedom for speculation about the divine.   O. Temkin[249]

One of the most remarkable works in the Hippocratic Corpus is the manuscript *On the Sacred Disease* (c.410 BC) on epilepsy. The work illustrates the physical nature of disease and its author (presumed to be Hippocrates (c.460–c.377 BC)) clearly states that epilepsy is not caused by the "wrath of a god" or any other supernatural powers.[250] The "sacred disease" was a natural disease linked to a flooding of the brain with phlegm, especially prevalent when the winds blew from the south.[251] The relevant passage reads as follows:

And they who first referred this disease [epilepsy] to the gods, appear to me to have been just such persons as the conjurers, purificators, mountebanks and charlatans now are, who give themselves out as being excessively religious and as knowing more than other people ... Neither, in truth, do I count it a worthy opinion to hold that the body of man is polluted by God, the most impure by the most holy; for were it defiled or did it suffer from any other thing, it would be likely to be purified and sanctified rather than polluted by God ... But this disease seems to me to be nowhere more divine than others; but it has as its nature such as other diseases have, and a cause whence it originates, and its nature and cause are divine only just as much as all others are, and it is curable no less than others, unless when from length of time it is confirmed, and has become stronger than the remedies applied. Its origin is hereditary, like that of other diseases.[252]

The philosopher-physicians placed greater emphasis on experience, observation, causes and reason than on myth and religion.[253] Just as the Presocratics removed the local gods from natural phenomena, the philosopher-physicians removed the local gods from disease and sickness.[254] The Hippocratic Corpus was the end result of a closer relationship between natural science, causal relations and human health.[255] The corpus included definitions and standards of ethical practice designed to treat the patient and advance the profession as an independent field of enquiry. The importance attached to sense and reason can be illustrated in the following Hippocratic *Precepts*. These are remarkably similar precepts to those of modern medicine:

In medicine one must pay attention not to plausible theorising but experience and reason together – I agree that theorising is to be approved, provided that it is based on facts, and systematically makes its deductions from what is observed. But conclusions drawn by the unaided reason can hardly be serviceable; only those drawn from observed fact.[256]

Notwithstanding the greater reliance on empirical-based medicine, the separation between the supernatural and natural worlds was not always clear. Some physicians still sought help from the Greek god Asclepius in treating patients. It was common practice for a patient to solicit the help of one god for a particular disease and consult a physician for another.[257] Even the Hippocratic Oath begins with an invocation to Asclepius, his father Apollo, and two daughter goddesses (Hygeia and Panacea, from which come our words hygiene ("health") and panacea ("universal remedy")).[258] The great contribution of the philosopher-physician to Western medicine was the beginning of a pluralistic debate, with a greater openness about advancing the understanding of disease and its causes. Greek medical scholar, Vivian Nutton wrote:

Two features are often taken to mark the Greek approach to understanding disease – a willingness to indulge in speculation, and a reluctance to invoke the gods as the cause of individual disease. This reluctance should not be misunderstood. Throughout Antiquity there existed alongside healers (*iatroi*) others who offered a religious explanation and a religious cure for illness – diviners, exorcists, and various types of priests.[259]

The Hippocratic doctrine of nature as the healer of disease

The novelty of Hippocratic medicine was that human beings were subject to the same physical constraints as the wider living, breathing *cosmos*. The "natural" workings of the human body were a microcosm of the "natural" workings of the world. Empedocles taught that world order was a product of immanent law, just as the living body was a product of its constituent parts. Medical doctors had to work with nature, not against it. The restoration of the body's balance or harmony was essential to restore health, and this concept has many parallels with Greek philosophical concepts of order and change in the universe. A statement often attributed to Hippocrates is: "Every disease has its own nature and arises from external causes; from cold, from the sun, or from changing winds."[260]

Symptoms were thought to arise from an imbalance or disharmony of fluids (or *chymoi*) known as humours,[261] which were the immediate causes of disease. The four main humours were phlegm, bile, blood and black bile. Winter colds were ascribed to phlegm and vomiting to bile; life and well-being were linked to blood. Nature removed excesses from the body through such means as nose bleeds or menstruation. This idea that excess blood was bad led to the later medieval concept of blood-letting as a form of treatment. Another consideration was water balance; in some cases, sickness was treated by drinking water and producing copious urine. In Hippocratic medicine, the four main humours were only part of the cause of disease; lifestyle, exposure to cold and other climatic changes were also involved.[262] Heredity appears to have been another important influence. Disease in general was linked to the four seasons; to the four ages of human beings (child, youth, adult, elderly) and later to Empedocles' four elements adopted by Aristotle (see Fig. 5.10).

The Hippocratic scheme of relating nature and humours is usually attributed to Alcmaeon[263] (*c*.500 BC) and the Pythagorean tradition.[264] The relationship between nature, natural philosophy, causation and human health changed the course of Western medicine. Four major medical sects appeared around 100 BC: the Rationalists (for whom reason eclipsed observation); the Empiricists (who relied on experience); the Methodists (who rejected the four humours); and the Pneumatists (who reverted to the Pythagorean

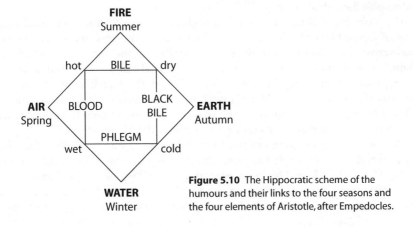

Figure 5.10 The Hippocratic scheme of the humours and their links to the four seasons and the four elements of Aristotle, after Empedocles.

four humours). It is also possible that Aristotle borrowed from the philosopher-physician's more theoretical approach to causal considerations.[265] Hippocratic "naturalism" was eventually accepted by the Christian Church during the first millennium AD with the stipulation that nature and physical phenomena were acknowledged as God's work, not given over to some fictitious divine character.[266]

FROM ATHENS TO ALEXANDRIA (c.322–30 BC)

The systems that survived and flourished (in Hellenistic times) were those which could offer a single ethical goal towards which all other permitted areas of enquiry might be geared – a goal which sought to encapsulate man's correct stance in relation to the world ... It has always been tempting to see this last development as a deliberate response to a cry for help – an attempt to restore moral purpose to life in an age when dynastic rule had stifled the old type of participatory city-state and was depriving the Greek citizen of a role in the politics of his own city.   D. Sedley[267]

The classical period came to end around 338 BC. A distinct, new Greek culture emerged not in Greece, but in Egypt. The shift from Athens to Alexandria[268] occurred during the reign of Alexander the Great, and marked the beginning of the Hellenistic period.[269] Alexander's dream was to blend classic Hellenic culture with the older Oriental and Near Eastern cultures.[270] Alexander's early death prevented him from seeing his dream come true, and the region's development was left up to his generals: Ptolemy I Soter (c.365–c.283 BC), ruler of Egypt; Seleucus and Lysimachus, rulers of Syria and the East; and Antigonus and Cassander, rulers of Macedon.[271] The Alexandrian period lasted three centuries and ended with the death of Cleopatra VII on 12 August 30 BC.

The city of Alexandria developed so rapidly that, two years after Aristotle's death, it had replaced Memphis as the capital of Egypt. By 300 BC, it had eclipsed Athens as a centre for learning and made Greek the official language in the country. Alexandria's success was largely due to the royal patronage offered by Ptolemy to attract mathematicians, astronomers, artists, poets and physicians from all over Europe and parts of Asia.[272] With this encouragement, the arts and sciences, including medicine but not philosophy, flourished in Egypt.[273]

The blending of Greek and Egyptian traditions was not without problems. As the gods of Egypt blended with the gods of Greece,[274] foreign cults, superstitions and magic arose (including the introduction of astrology in the first century BC).[275] In an attempt to unify the two cultures, Ptolemy introduced a new god named Sarapis, who was a hybrid of the Egyptian Osiris and Apis and the Greek Zeus, Asclepius and Dionysis.[276] These new hybrid gods were never accepted by the priests, who often referred to the foreign invaders as the "Ionian dogs" and in their hieroglyphic scripts told stories of them that often contained scurrilous double meanings.[277]

One of the great outcomes of the reign of Ptolemy I was the famous Alexandrian museum and library. Founded in about 290 BC, the museum was originally dedicated to the Muses (Greek goddesses of wisdom), hence "Shrine of the Muses".[278] The museum complex was modelled on Aristotle's Lyceum and carried out scientific research in the same way as a modern university.[279] During the reign of Ptolemy II,

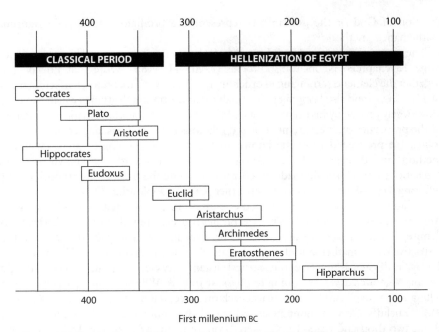

Figure 5.11 The significant philosophers and scientists of the classical and Hellenistic periods.

about 100 full-time professional scholars were working at the museum.[280] The library housed around 700 000 "books", making it the largest in the world. Travellers were required to surrender their books on arrival; they were copied by the library staff, and the copies (not the originals) were returned to the owners. For 300 years, the Alexandrian museum and library were the centres of Greek science, literature and art until they were destroyed by Julius Caesar's army in 47 BC.

Many great scholars visited the museum and their contributions to Western thought were immense. The six case histories considered below are: Euclid, Aristarchus, Eratosthenes, Archimedes, Hipparchus and Ptolemy (post-Hellenistic). Their timelines in relation to the classical Greek philosophers are outlined in Figure 5.11.

Euclid (c.330–275 BC):"There is no royal road to geometry"

> He used all the various forms of deductive arguments, some getting their plausibility from the first principles, some starting from demonstrations, but all irrefutable and accurate and in harmony with science.
>
> Proclus[281]

Very little is known about Euclid's life. The best information suggests that he was born to Greek parents and educated in Athens, and was highly influenced by the works of Plato and Eudoxus. He is believed to have visited Alexandria around 300 BC, where he taught mathematics at the museum.[282] His famous book, *Elements*, was regarded as a perfect work of almost divine authority (although Euclid makes no mention of God or the gods).[283] It represented a prodigious advance in rigorous mathematical method.[284]

The remarkable aspect of his *Elements* was the way Euclid organized his material into some 13 chapters. Neoplatonist Proclus (*c.* AD 410–485) wrote that Euclid "put together the elements, arranging in order many of Eudoxus's theorems, perfecting many of *Theaetetus*'s and also bringing to irrefutable demonstration the things which had been only loosely proven by his predecessors".[285] Euclid's work was a systematic presentation of the properties of, measurement of and relations between lines, angles, surfaces and solids. He proceeded from the known to the unknown via logical steps (synthetic method) and then posited the unknown and worked towards the known using his "analytic" method. Euclid made no effort to illustrate the truth of his propositions by referring to sense-experience or to any other practical application.[286]

Euclid's definitions, axioms and theorems were all accepted as "true", as were Aristotle's axiomatic methods. This was *Elements'* great strength, but later also led to its demise. Euclid's geometry dealt with a flat, two-dimensional space that became too restrictive to the mathematically curious. Euclidean space was only "one" kind of space. Today, in Einstein's universe, the shortest distant between two points is not a straight line but a gentle curve. According to physicist John A. Wheeler, "Space acts on matter telling it to move" and "matter reacts back on space, telling it how to curve" (see Ch. 9).[287] Euclid's *Elements* nonetheless remained the "gold standard" in geometry for about two thousand years. Copies were brought to the West by the Arabs and it was translated into Latin some time in the twelfth century.[288]

Archimedes (*c.*287–212 BC): the closest thing in antiquity to a modern-day scientist

Give me a place to stand on and I will move the Earth.

Statement attributed to Archimedes[289]

Archimedes was the closest person in antiquity to a modern-day scientist. He was not only a great mathematician but also a great physicist, astronomer and engineer.[290] He often visited Alexandria's museum, where he studied with Euclid's successors and made close friends with Eratosthenes,[291] but he always returned to his hometown, Syracuse, in Sicily. Syracuse was where Archimedes composed his major works, and where he died a most unfortunate death at the hands of a Roman soldier.[292]

Archimedes' contributions to science were immense and included masterpiece works in mathematics, astronomy, hydrostatics, mechanics and mechanical inventions.[293] In a rare passage describing his thought processes – found only recently in 1906 – he provides an inkling of how he used mechanics to advance his mathematics.[294] This insight into the workings of Archimedes' mind appeared in his introductory remarks in his famous *On the Method*, addressed to his friend Eratosthenes:

I thought fit to write out for you and explain in detail in the same book the peculiarity of a certain method, by which it will be possible for you to get a start to enable you to investigate some problems in mathematics by means of mechanics. This procedure is, I am persuaded, no less useful even for the proof of theorems themselves, for certain things first became clear to me by a mechanical method, although they had to be demonstrated by geometry afterwards because their investigation by the said method did not furnish an actual demonstration.[295]

Some of his mathematical discoveries included general methods for finding the areas of an assortment of plane figures and volumes bounded by curved surfaces. He applied these methods to calculating the area of a circle, sphere, cone, paraboloid, hyperboloid and spheroid. He also gave a method for calculating pi (π). He found that the value lay between $3\frac{1}{7}$ (or 3.143) and $3\frac{10}{71}$ (or 3.141). The modern value of π to three decimal places is is 3.142.

Archimedes invented a special notation capable of handling big numbers, such as those used in modern-day cosmology. He made an extraordinary calculation that there were not more than 10^{63} (1 followed by 63 zeros) grains of sand that would fill the universe.[296] Compare this with 1930s' physicist Arthur Eddington's (1882–1944) calculation[297] of the number of protons in the visible universe as 10^{80}, or modern cosmologists' calculation of the temperature of the so-called singularity at the time of the Big Bang as in excess of 10^{32} K (Ch. 9).

Archimedes invented integral calculus and anticipated the differential calculus later discovered independently by Newton and Leibniz in the seventeenth century.[298] He also used integral calculus to calculate the area of a circle, by dividing a circle into very thin parallel strips of the same width. The areas of the small pieces that lay outside the circle were so small that they were of no consequence, and the area of the circle was found by adding up all the long, thin areas. Greater accuracy was attained by making the strips thinner and thinner and taking the limit of the sum, using a process called "integration".[299] This method of summations is part of what we now call "integral calculus".

Archimedes' more celebrated discoveries were his technological inventions, although he himself did not hold them in high esteem. One invention was the water screw, which is still in use around the world today to raise water or grain from the ground to a higher storage area. Others inventions included war machines used against the Roman army[300] and the lever (leading to his famous saying "Give me a place to stand on and I will move the Earth"). The other was his determination of the proportions of gold and silver in a crown made for Hieron II, King of Syracuse. The king asked Archimedes to check if the crown was made of pure gold. Although most science historians believe that the account reported by Vitruvius (first century BC) is apocryphal, it is worth telling to illustrate what has become known as Archimedes' law of fluid displacement, or Archimedes' Principle.

While Archimedes was turning the problem over, he chanced to come to the place of bathing, and there, as he was sitting in the tub, he noticed that the amount of water which flowed over by the tub was equal to the amount by which his body was immersed. This indicated to him a method of solving the problem, and he did not delay, but in his joy leapt out of the tub, and, rushing naked towards his home, he cried out in a loud voice that he had found what he sought, for as he ran he repeatedly shouted Eureka, Eureka.[301]

Archimedes further reasoned that if the amount of water displaced by the crown was equal to the same displaced by an equal weight of pure gold; the crown was correctly made. If, on the other hand, a different amount of water was displaced, the crown was fraudulently manufactured, based on the different densities of pure metals. As the story goes, Archimedes concluded *on the basis of his measurements* that the king's crown had been alloyed with silver. His famous principle, with various refinements, was used to test the purity of precious metals for centuries.[302]

Aristarchus of Samos (c.310–230 BC): the Earth revolves around the sun

> Now you are aware that "universe" is the name given by most astronomers to the sphere the centre of which is the centre of the earth, and the radius of which is equal to the straight line between the centre of the sun and the centre of the earth; this you have seen in the treatises written by astronomers. But Aristarchus of Samos brought out a book consisting of certain hypotheses, in which the premises lead to the conclusion that the universe is many times greater than now so called. His hypotheses are that the fixed stars and the sun remain motionless (unmoved), that the earth revolves around the sun in the circumference of a circle, the sun lying in the middle of the orbit.
>
> Archimedes[303]

Aristarchus was a pupil of Strato of Lampsacus (third century BC), head of Aristotle's Lyceum in 288 BC.[304] After studying in Greece he visited Alexandria's museum, where he worked as a mathematician and astronomer.[305] Aristarchus rejected Aristotle's notion of a stationary spherical Earth in the centre of a finite universe. He further rejected the idea that the Earth was surrounded by concentric spheres bounded by a uniformly revolving sphere of fixed stars (i.e. all the heavenly bodies except for the planets, sun, moon and comets). Rather, he proposed that the sun was in the centre and the Earth revolved around it once a year (as we believe today).[306]

Aristarchus further asserted that the "fixed" stars, previously set in motion by Aristotle's God, did not move because they were positioned further away than anyone had previously thought. Having the Earth revolve around the sun meant that it was the Earth's motion itself that gave the "appearance" of the outermost sphere of "fixed" stars moving. Indeed, there was no further need for the outermost sphere because the stars were scattered through space at variable distances from Earth. The Earth was just another planetary sphere moving among the starry heavens. Using Aristarchus's new ideas, Seleucus (*c.*150 BC), explained the natural phenomenon of tides correctly as the moon's resistance to the rotation of the Earth.[307] Unfortunately, science historians know little about how Aristarchus came to his revolutionary views.

Aristarchus's *heliocentric* view was considered heretical because it conflicted with the teachings of Aristotle and with the religious convictions of the Jewish and other Eastern traditions of the Hellenistic population. The most vicious attack came from contemporary Stoic, Cleanthes (*c.*331–232 BC), who moved for his prosecution before a Panhellenic court on the charge of impiety. Plutarch (*c.* AD 50–120) made the following reference to Cleanthes' charge against Aristarchus in his *De facie in orbe lunae*:

Only do not my good fellow, enter an action against me for impiety in the style of Cleanthes, who thought it was the duty of Greeks to indict Aristarchus of Samos on the charge of impiety for putting in motion the Hearth of the Universe, this being the effect of his attempt to save the phenomena by supposing the Heaven to remain at rest, and the earth to revolve in an oblique circle, while it rotates, at the same time, about its axis.[308]

The only surviving work of Aristarchus is a short treatise entitled *On the Magnitudes and Distances of the Sun and Moon*. He was among the first to calculate the sizes and distances of the sun and moon from the Earth from pure mathematical deduction. Following Euclid's *Elements*, Aristarchus began his treatise with six "hypotheses", followed by 18 propositions. He observed that when the moon was half full, the angles between the lines of sight to the sun and the moon was less than a right angle by $\frac{1}{30}$ of a quadrant or 3° ($\frac{1}{30} \times 90° = 3°$). Using geometry he calculated that the ratio of the distance between the Earth and the moon to the distance between the Earth and the sun was between $\frac{1}{18}$ and $\frac{1}{20}$ (see Fig. 5.12). This value is half Exodus's estimate of $\frac{1}{9}$.[309]

Aristarchus measured the angle BAC at 87° but the actual value today is 89°50', which means that Aristarchus's ratio of distances was about twentyfold too low (the distance ratio of AC:AB is 400:1 not 19:1).[310] While there was inaccuracy in Aristarchus's observational data, there was nothing wrong with his methods.[311] Using these methods Aristarchus pioneered the basis of modern day astronomy.

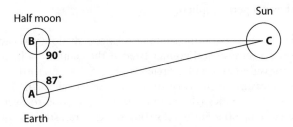

Half moon

Sun

B

90°

87°

A

C

Earth

Figure 5.12 Aristarchus found that when the moon was exactly half full, the angle ABC must be 90°. He then measured BAC, which was the angle between the lines of sight to the sun and the moon and found it to be 87°, that is, less than a right angle by $\frac{1}{30}$ of a quadrant. From this angle the ratio of the moon's distance from Earth to the moon's distance to the sun can be calculated. He found the ratio of AB to BC was $\frac{1}{19}$. We now know it to be about $\frac{1}{400}$.

Eratosthenes of Cyrene (c.276–195 BC): a "mathematician among geographers"

Eratosthenes was born in Cyrene, Egypt (now Shahhat in Libya), but spent most of his working life in Alexandria, where he was in charge of the library at the museum.[312] He was extremely well educated and had a broad knowledge of astronomy, mathematics, geography, poetry, philosophy, grammar and history. He was also the first Greek writer to undertake a serious study of the system of dating by Olympiads.[313]

Eratosthenes was also a good friend of Archimedes. One of Eratosthenes' great contributions to geography was to divide the world into zones and specify the position of a place by its latitude and longitude (as well as he could). For the grids, he used a parallel running from Gibraltar to the west through the Mediterranean Sea and to the Himalayas in the east, with the dividing lines of the inhabited world intersecting at Rhodes, a centre of Greek navigation.[314] Eratosthenes is most famous for his calculation of the circumference of the Earth. The account can be found in Cleomedes' *De motu cirulari*.[315] The calculation used the following observations and assumptions:

- The linear distance between Alexandria and Syene was 5000 stades (a stade was between 0.15 km and 0.2 km; see below).
- Alexandria and Syene were situated on a north–south line or, as Cleomedes expressed it, "under the same meridian circle".
- Syene was located at the extremity of the summer tropical zone (on the tropic of Cancer), a fact reportedly confirmed by Pliny, Arrian and others. At midday of the longest day in summer (summer solstice), the sun was directly overhead Syene and no shadow was cast there on the vertical time-measuring device known as a "gnomon". Instead the sun's rays at Syene were reflected from the very bottom of the deepest wells.
- The sun's rays hitting the Earth were parallel because of the enormous distance of the Earth from the sun. That is, the Earth could be considered to be a point with respect to the sun.
- The Earth was a perfect sphere.

In Alexandria, at midday on the summer solstice a shadow was cast by a gnomon; Eratosthenes used a thin vertical pointer fixed at the centre of a hemispherical bowl. The angle was measured as 1⁄50 of a circle (see Fig. 5.13). Eratosthenes deduced that this angle was a measure of the curvature of the spherical Earth. Therefore 1⁄50 of a circle is equal to 5000 stades (the distance from Alexandria to Syene), and the full circle must therefore be 50 × 5000 = 250 000 stades. Eratosthenes added 2000 stades to make the circumference (252 000 stades) divisible by 60. Apparently this was for arithmetical convenience as it was common practice in Greek astronomy to divide the circle into 60 equal parts, but not 360 parts (the degree was not introduced until Hipparchus, see below). From the Earth's circumference, the radius was calculated to be slightly over 40 000 stades.[316]

Our difficulty today is in working out what a stade meant in ancient times compared to linear measurements today. If one stade equals 0.185 km, then 252 000 stades is equivalent to 46 620 km, which compares well with today's equatorial circumference measurement of 40 075 km.[317] If, as some suggest, a stade was 0.158 km, then Eratosthenes' value is within 1 per cent of the modern estimate, demonstrating the impressive accuracy of his methods.[318]

What is more, Eratosthenes' method was carried out without the use of a telescope or any other precision instrument and his circumference was a considerable improvement over Aristotle's 400 000 stadia (presumably from Eudoxus or Callippus), and Archimedes' value of 300 000 stadia. Where his method fell short was not with errors of measurement, like Aristarchus, but with the small errors in his assumptions. Syene was

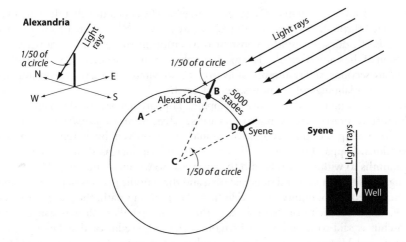

Figure 5.13 Depiction of Eratosthenes' estimation of the circumference of the Earth in the third century BC. He found that the angle of the shadow cast by the midday sun at the summer solstice was 1/50 of a circle. From simple geometry, the angle ABC was the same as BCA and therefore knowing that *BD* = 5000 stades, he calculated the circumference of the Earth to be 250 000 stades. Later he added 2000 stades to make the circumference divisible by 60.

not directly on the same north–south meridian as Alexandria (lying some 3° to the west) and the distance between the two was 4530 not 5000 stades.[319] This is a good example of science in action. There was nothing wrong with Eratosthenes' method, only with his starting-points or assumptions. As more information was gained, the value of the Earth's circumference became more accurate.

Hipparchus of Nicaea (*c.*190–120 BC): Babylonian measurement enriches Greek astronomy

Hipparchus was without doubt one of the greatest *observational* astronomers in antiquity. He was born in Nicaea in Bithynia (now in Turkey) but spent most of his life on Rhodes, a Greek island in the Aegean Sea. His scientific work comes down to us in Ptolemy's *Almagest*. Foremost among his accomplishments was that he established Hellenistic astronomy as an exact science: he "developed mathematical methods enabling one to use geometrical models for practical prediction and to assign numerical parameters to the models". In addition, he taught astronomy as an evolving science that could only be advanced through the open-mindedness and willingness of astronomers to abandon traditional views when they did not fit the observational data.[320]

Hipparchus is also credited with introducing to Greek astronomy the Babylonian invention of dividing the circumference of a circle into 360 degrees of 60 minutes.[321] He constructed several instruments, and measured and recorded the positions of some 850 stars. Hipparchus compared his star list with the maps of Eudoxus and Aristarchus, and of the earlier Babylonians and Egyptians. Instead of finding one or two discrepancies on positions he found a "systematic" change, from which he concluded that the Earth's axis had changed through an angle of about 45 " of arc per year.[322] The remarkable discovery that the Earth does not hold a constant orientation in space is now known as "the precession of the equinoxes".[323] The modern value for the movement of the Earth's axis is 50.27 arc seconds, and results primarily from the gravitational tug of the sun and moon on the equatorial bulge of the non-spherical Earth.

What Eratosthenes did for Earth mapping, Hipparchus did for sky mapping, but much more accurately. He even wrote a treatise, *Against the Geography of Eratosthenes*, where he anticipated that geography would be improved by better astronomical observations. Hipparchus's new and improved star map increased the accuracy of the lunar months to within seconds, and the solar year to within six minutes. He recorded the lengths of the tropical and sidereal years, and the synodic periods of the five planets. He determined the obliquity of the ecliptic and the moon's path, the place of the sun's apogee, the eccentricity of its orbit, and the moon's parallax, all with fair accuracy. Hipparchus is said to have invented trigonometry but credit for that belongs to the Egyptians and Mesopotamians.[324] In the eighteenth century, Edmond Halley (1656–1742) used Hipparchus's measurements to catalogue the motions and positions of the stars and planetary bodies.

Ptolemy of Alexandria (c. AD 100–168): matching theory with observation

Any attempt to reconstruct the origin of Hellenistic mathematics and astronomy must face the fact that Euclid's "elements" and Ptolemy's "Almagest" reduced all their predecessors to objects of mere historical interest with little chance of survival.

O. Neugebauer[325]

After Hipparchus's death, astronomy advanced little. The subject had to wait until the arrival of Ptolemy (Claudius Ptolemaeus) of the early Roman-Christian era. The name "Claudius" suggests that he held Roman citizenship, and "Ptolemy" that he was of Greek descent and lived in Egypt. He must not to be confused with the ruling Ptolemies of Egypt, but he was a native of Egypt.[326] Ptolemy was the last of the great Greek astronomers of the Alexandrian school in the post-Hellenistic period.

Ptolemy's greatest legacy was his *Almagest*,[327] which contained predictive mathematical models for the moon, sun and planets in 13 books.[328] He relied heavily on the works of Aristotle, Apollonius (fl. 200 BC) and Hipparchus. Ptolemy argued that Earth was at rest in the centre of the universe, and that all the planets and stars revolved around Earth in *circular* orbits at *uniform* velocities.[329] The fixed stars move together as a sphere.[330]

In the preface Ptolemy explained the importance of astronomy as an abstract science. He wrote that astronomy had considerable influence on human life by revealing the order of the creation. The first two books contain definitions and general elementary theorems. His treatment of trigonometry and his table of natural sines are particularly noteworthy. He proved that Earth is spherical and that gravity everywhere is directed towards the centre of Earth. In other chapters he gave the basis of time-keeping at different places on Earth and discussed the methods used to determine the motion of the sun and the length of the year. He extended the work of Hipparchus and replaced old theories with new ones.

In his seventh and eighth chapters he tabulated the locations of 1022 stars, described the Milky Way, and provided a method for constructing celestial globes. The remainder of the book was devoted to planetary theory, his most important contribution to astronomy. Ptolemy replaced Eudoxus's and Callippus's moving spheres with a system of moving circles (cycles, epicycles and eccentrics) and equants, which gave a better match between theory and observation (presumably after Apollonius and Hipparchus) (see Ch. 8). Ptolemy's Earth was not *exactly* at the centre of the circular orbits, which led him to his idea of "eccentric" motion to explain the brightness of the planets throughout the year and why the sun appears larger at midday in winter than summer.

Ptolemy spent much time on the motion of the planets, leading to his "theory of planetary motions". His attention to detail and use of mathematics were flawless. The mean motion of the planets was determined with small errors. Eclipses of the moon were determined with errors not exceeding 1½ hours in 1700 years.[331]

Ptolemy's cosmological *geocentric* system was very complex and required 70 simultaneous motions for seven celestial bodies. Although there was no accurate way to determine a planet's distance from Earth, he placed Mars, Jupiter and Saturn at increasing distances from the sun, and Venus and Mercury between the sun and the moon.[332] Ptolemy believed that one could not distinguish between the order held by the Greek astronomers (Earth, Moon, Sun, Venus, Mercury, Mars, Jupiter and Saturn) and the newer order from Babylonia (Earth, Moon, Mercury, Venus, Sun, Mars, Jupiter and Saturn).[333] With new techniques, Ptolemy favoured the Babylonian version first introduced to the West by Diogenes of Babylon (fl. 160 BC).[334]

Following Plato and Aristotle, Ptolemy distinguished the discipline of mathematical astronomy from theology. He did concede that astronomy was "the best science to help theology along its way, since it is the only one which can make a good guess at [the nature of] that activity which is unmoved and separated".[335] Ptolemy also appears to have adopted parts of Greek Olympian religion with Zeus as head of the pantheon: "When I trace at my pleasure the windings to and fro of the heavenly bodies, I no longer touch the earth with my feet: I stand in the presence of Zeus himself and take my fill of ambrosia, food of the gods."[336] To sum up, Ptolemy's success arose from matching observation, theory and measurement using the best instruments of the times. After the collapse of the Roman Empire, the Arabs preserved Ptolemy's works. The *Almagest* remained the standard textbook on the subject throughout the Middle Ages until the seventeenth century.

FROM NATURE TO THE NATURE OF KNOWING

O my friends, how can there be the least shadow of wisdom where there is no harmony? There is none; but the noblest and greatest of harmonies may be truly said to be the greatest wisdom; and of this he is a partaker who lives according to reason; whereas he who is devoid of reason is the destroyer of his house and is utterly ignorant of political wisdom.

Plato[337]

Different authorities of mind and sense

The Greek search for wisdom, as opposed to belief or opinion, was a major preoccupation of the classical and Hellenistic philosophers. For Socrates and Plato, truth was something we could not see, hear, smell, taste or touch. Truth belonged to the good, the true and the beautiful. To "know" meant human beings had to forfeit the pleasures of sense-phenomena and enter Plato's world of Ideas. Plato's world of Ideas was his answer to Heraclitus's illusionary senses, Parmenides' One Being and the Pythagorean concept of soul.

Plato's Ideas were attainable with proper training, through dialectics and mathematics. Ideas were eternal, super-sensory, absolute and unchanging. They existed in the mind as a "blueprint" from which the "visible" universe was created by God as a "copy". Ideas existed in reality, but not in the "changeable" objects of sense. Mind and sense were not totally separated, but connected through the immortal soul. The immortal soul was the source of knowledge that enabled a person to connect the eternal Ideas with everyday sense. Plato's hierarchy of knowledge had truth at one end, ignorance at the other and belief or opinion in the middle.

Aristotle rejected Plato's assertion that true knowledge relied on the immortal soul. Rather, Aristotle viewed the soul as a unity of faculties with only reason (*nous*) having connections to the divine. In addition, Aristotle rejected Plato's use of myth to explain difficult concepts. In one myth, Plato likened the voyage of the soul before birth to the passage of a winged chariot and horses past the stars to the vault of the heavens, where it contemplated the divine and eternal Ideas. Aristotle understood that Plato's use of myth was as a literary tool to bridge the literal and metaphysical, and that they were not truths in themselves, but analogies of truth. He opted for a more pragmatic use of language to describe difficult things.

Aristotle preferred to discover truth from the hard facts. His methodology recognized the *essential* dependence on sense-experience and the *essential* superiority of knowledge through universals: the properties or relations logically derived from a number of particulars. Aristotle's starting-point was sense, and from there he proceeded to the universals invented in Mind (from particulars to universals). Universals did not exist apart from the individual things we experience, as Plato taught, but were contained within them. Our senses perceive a tree but our intellect "invents" the tree as part of the grander conceptual scheme of things that make up our reality, and that society has agreed upon.

Aristotle proceeded from the senses to construct his physical world where everything (living and not living) was striving for a purpose. Unlike Plato, he clearly separated objects, qualities and quantities, but still accepted an ontological dependence between them.[338] Aristotle believed that Plato had blurred this distinction. "True" knowledge, for Plato, as mentioned, was transcendent, eternal, super-sensory and unchanging and existed beyond space and time, whereas Aristotle's "truth" was part of a mind abstraction derived from the world in which we live. Aristotle argued that in the human mind, thought and the object of thought were identical, whereas Plato (and Socrates) believed them to be separate and distinguishable.

Origins of the empiricist and rationalist debate

The terms "empiricist" and "rationalist" go back to antiquity. They have their origin in a particular debate among ancient doctors concerning the nature and origin of medical knowledge, indeed the nature and origin of technical or expert knowledge quite generally.

M. Frede[339]

As Plato and Aristotle were parrying back and forth about what constituted "true" wisdom in knowledge, a parallel debate was going on in Hippocratic medicine. The debate was between the doctors trying to establish the role of sense-data (in Greek *empeiria*) and reason (*logos* in Greek; *ratio* in Latin) in diagnoses and treatments of disease. From this debate, Frede argues, the terms "empiricist" and "rationalist" had their origins.[340] The medical empiricists (also called "memorists") argued that reason alone was insufficient in diagnosis because it led to an endless number of opinions and disputes. What made a good doctor, they argued, was the use of a "complex kind of experience" (*a posteriori*) relying more on observations to determine a diagnosis and treatment.[341]

The rationalists, on the other side, argued that "experience" alone does not amount to sound practical medical knowledge. Technical and practical medical knowledge could only be obtained after reasoning from "innate ideas", which included insight, understanding, inference and proof.[342] An important part of the debate among the empiricists and rationalists appears to be whether or not to incorporate the Presocratic concept of *physis* into the physical diagnosis and treatment, and whether or not the order and harmony in the *cosmos* could be reduced to the study of order and harmony of the workings of the human body. In addition, recent scholarship indicates that it was Hippocratic doctors who pioneered much of the rigorous thinking about causes, and not the early or classical Greek philosophers.[343] The debate among the doctors marked the beginning of evidence-based medicine in the West.

Aristotelian science as a road to truth

The birth of philosophy in Europe … consisted in the abandonment, at the level of conscious thought, of mythological solutions to problems concerning the origin and nature of the universe and the processes that go within it. For religious faith there is substituted the faith that was and remains the basis of scientific thought with all its triumphs and all its limitations: that is the faith that the visible world conceals a rational and intelligible order, that the causes of the natural world are to be sought within its boundaries, and that autonomous human reason is our sole and sufficient instrument for the search.

W. K. C. Guthrie[344]

Plato and Aristotle's differences in philosophy were no more evident than in their attitudes towards natural science. For Plato, the best natural science could do was to provide belief and opinion; which is partly why he viewed the *Timaeus* as a "likely" story. Natural science was provisional because certainty resided not in nature, but in the eternal Ideas. For Aristotle, however, science was derived from the senses and could lead to "true" knowledge.[345]

On closer examination, Plato was partly right in arguing that Aristotle's scientific statements were not absolute but more provisional in character. From a modern perspective, we would say that Aristotle's methodology lacked rigorous mathematical analysis;[346] failed to recognize the connectivity among concepts;[347] and generally lacked predictability.[348] Aristotle's authority rested on intuitive, self-evident concepts supplemented with axiomatic geometry, which today would belong more to metaphysics than natural science. The strengths and limitations of Aristotelian science will also be discussed in greater detail in Chapter 8, after we have considered the scientific revolution of the seventeenth century. In a nutshell, when Aristotle started with an absolute premise followed by a series of deductions it only makes what is already known more explicit; it does not necessarily lead to innovation and discovery.[349] There can be nothing to test in a statement that is true by definition. Historian of science, Marshall Clagett, summed up the state of science in ancient Greece:

> Greek science falls short in the maturity and the universality of its use of mathematical-experimental techniques. There is no question that a mathematical-experimental science existed in nascent form, at least in optics, in statics, and in applied mechanics; that a mathematical-observational science was present in astronomy; and that an experimental science existed in zoology and physiology. But the techniques of these sciences were not yet commonly considered as the necessary methods in all fields of natural investigation. Before mathematical and experimental techniques had become the *common* property of Greek science, that science began to level off.[350]

Philosophical religion and monotheism

> It was Plato who devised many of the elements of what would become Hellenic monotheism. Paramount to his theology is a teleological religious outlook: that divinity is always good and that the *cosmos* has within it a pattern of excellence ... [Plato's] cosmic deity is evident in his *Laws* (10) with its deep reverence for the heavenly bodies and its recognition of the one or many good and divine souls which direct the universe, as well as in his *Timaeus* (27C–53C), where the world soul is an immortal force of intelligent life which permeates the *cosmos*.   J. P. Kenny[351]

In Chapter 4, we saw that a product of Presocratic philosophical religion was mathematical astronomy, and God emerged largely as a governor likened to cosmic Mind. Plato's cosmic god was different; he was a creator who shared some parallels with the ancient Egyptian memphite god, Ptah. In Chapter 3 we briefly discussed that Ptah was the god of artists, sculptors and craftsmen, who created the world by divine thought.[352] Whether ancient Egyptian cosmogony influenced Plato's thinking, no one knows.[353] Aristotle's supreme god was different again; he was an unmoved, prime mover arrived at after a long chain of reasoning.[354] Aristotle's *cosmos* was a purpose-driven hierarchy with inanimate matter at one end, and his supreme god at the other. Every individual physical object in

Aristotle's world had its own function, purpose and end, which was good. Werner Jaeger described Aristotle's cosmology as "the first great attempt to render the problem of God amenable to scientific treatment, by basing dialectically cogent inferences on a consistent interpretation of nature".[355] By contrast, Plato's divinely created world was a theological construction, not a scientific one. Notwithstanding the different conceptions of God among the philosophers, they were fundamentally different from those Olympian gods worshipped by the Greek populace. The gods of the Greek philosophers did not live close by and cared little for human beings. As mentioned in Chapter 4, the general concept of God in philosophical religion shifted from the older mythopoeic "Office of Everyday Affairs" to the "Office of Cosmic Affairs".

Despite Plato and Aristotle having much sharper concepts of divinity than the Presocratics, Greek philosophical religion never became monotheistic. In Plato's world, a craftsman was mentioned among the lesser "star" gods, and in Aristotle's world,[356] a prime mover was present among lesser "star" gods.[357] The closest Greek philosophy came to monotheism was Stoicism in the first century BC. Originating earlier with Zeno of Citium (344–262 BC), the Stoics[358] taught that a single "divine *logos*" or "divine reason" governed the universe.[359] The Stoic god was not one god among lesser gods, but one unitary entity from which *everything*[360] in the world gained its divinity.[361] The Stoics called this "active" principle either God, *logos*, cause or *pneuma*, as opposed to "passive" formless "matter".[362] This "active" principle was a divine creative or generative force equated with divine wisdom, an idea that powerfully influenced the development of early Christian theology. In Chapter 6, we shall examine this relationship and continue to explore the profound legacy of Plato and Aristotle in shaping early Christian thought, and the wider debt owed to Greek philosophy in developing Christian doctrine and preparing defences against pagan censure.

There is but one river of truth.   St Clement of Alexandria[1]

CHAPTER 6

Early Christianity: the historical road to one God

The rise of Judeo-Christianity in the Greco-Roman world

Compared with other religions of its time and place, [Christianity] was far more successful in organising its beliefs into a coherent system. In doing so it borrowed largely from philosophy, especially from Platonism … Philosophy helped to mould its beliefs about God and the world, and taught it to uphold them in argument.   C. Stead[2]

With the repeated invasions of western Europe, the Greek Empire finally fell to the Romans in 146 BC. Over the next hundred years, Rome controlled much of Greece, Asia Minor and northern Egypt, and by 31 BC the Roman Empire was born. Rome was never a democracy as we understand the term, but a society firmly divided by class. Of the estimated 60 million people in the empire, about 2 per cent were wealthy, 8 per cent were middle class and the vast majority, the remaining 90 per cent, were poor and lived in rural areas.[3] Only the wealthy could afford to send their children to school. Girls usually left school at the age of 12, and married soon thereafter, while boys continued their education and aimed for the best occupations in the civil service and military.[4] Most of the populace could neither read nor write; only a handful of books were written, by the most learned scholars.

For much of the Roman Empire's history, the emperors sought to emulate the past by promoting the Roman way of life and traditions. However, the ruling classes always acknowledged a debt to the Greeks. Out of the wonders of Greek life they squeezed everything that was practical: philosophy, literature, education, mathematics, art, agriculture and engineering.[5] In contrast, natural science was not highly valued because the aristocracy and upper classes considered it a leisurely activity that generated only inferior knowledge. Despite efforts from the Latin popularizers and encylopedists such as Lucretius (d. 55 BC), Cicero (106–43 BC), Varro (116–27 BC), Pliny the Elder (*c.* AD 23–79), Aulus Cornelius Celsus (fl. AD 25), Seneca (*c.*4 BC–*c.* AD 65) and Galen (*c.* AD 130–*c.*201),[6] the study of nature entered a state of dormancy.[7] Because of its close connection with natural philosophy, little progress was made in medicine, too, apart from practical improvements to public health and sanitation.

The Roman Empire became so vast that it extended from the Atlantic Ocean in the west to Persia in the east, and from Britain in the north to regions south of the Mediterranean Sea. Eventually the empire was split administratively into two (AD 285), with Latin the official language in the west and Greek in the east.[8] Religion, too, was equally diverse, comprising a complex mixture of rituals, taboos and superstitions. The older practices were gradually displaced by the more fashionable cults of Isis, Mithras, Cybele and Sol Invictus (the unconquered sun).[9] Because the Romans possessed a pragmatic attitude to religion, the cults existed side by side for many generations without conflict.[10] Unlike in Israel, religious faith to the Romans was less a spiritual experience involving revelation than a contractual relationship between human beings and the supernatural.

Despite a healthy religious pluralism, it was Christianity that eventually emerged triumphant. By AD 313, under the reign of Christian convert Emperor Constantine (*c.* AD 274–337),[11] Christianity was an accepted religion in the Roman Empire and from AD 380 it was the official religion of the entire empire.[12] The history of the Roman Empire now became the history of the Church. The rise of Christianity was not born out of a human quest to discover an ultimate principle (*archē*) or from pondering over the nature of the mind; it arose from the abstraction of history as a moral and ethical order, beginning with Abraham and a number of historical events and revelations involving God, Moses, the prophets and sacred texts.

This chapter explores the development of early Christianity, and how the cult grew from worshipping a deeply mythologized tribal god of storms, war and agriculture to the God of the Hebrews, and later Christians. Christian theology did not develop in a vacuum, however, but relied heavily on borrowings from Greek philosophy and Jewish thought. The debt to the Greeks was so profound that the Hellenistic Jewish philosopher Philo (*c.*20 BC–AD 50), and many later Christian scholars, believed that Plato, and others, had access to and covertly plagiarized the early Hebrew sacred writings. Plato (and Platonism) was particularly singled out because he spoke of origins of the world and eternal divine Ideas (or Forms), which were more easily harmonized with the Christian tradition than was Aristotle's eternal cosmos. We shall examine this debt to Greek philosophy in the writings of St Justin the Martyr, Clement of Alexandria, Origen and Tertullian, and in the patristic writings of Latin Church fathers St Jerome, St Ambrose and St Augustine. Importantly, Christian theology extended far beyond Greek philosophy and profoundly influenced Western thinking for nearly 2000 years.

WHEN ISRAEL WAS A CHILD

From the earliest gospel records contained in the New Testament, the teaching of Jesus, with its forthright warnings and promises, furthered the prophetic tradition embodied in the Old Testament, the basic sacred writings of the Jewish people.

T. A. Burkill[13]

Yahweh and Abraham

The story of how Christianity arose from a small Hebrew cult to a world religion is truly remarkable. According to Hebrew legend,[14] the Eastern god Yahweh appeared to polytheist Abraham in his native Mesopotamia (first in Ur and later in Haran) and instructed him to stop idol worship and instead travel to the Promised Land.[15] "Behold," God said to Abraham, "my covenant is with you, and you shall be the father of a multitude of nations … And I will establish my covenant between me and you and your descendants after you throughout their generations."[16] Abraham's conversion around 1800 BC marked the beginning of Hebrew history.[17]

Yahweh and Moses

After Abraham's conversion there was a wave of westward migrations from ancient Mesopotamia to Palestine[18] or biblical Canaan. Canaan was located at the western end of the "Fertile Crescent", known as the land "flowing with milk and honey" (see Fig. 2.2).[19] Between 1300 and 1200 BC, God appeared again to the Hebrews, to Moses through an angel from a burning bush.[20] The religious significance of a burning bush is unclear, but many of God's appearances were associated with a flame and/or light, lightning, volcanoes and purity.[21] These different symbols in the Old Testament have many parallels in ancient Sumer, Babylonia, Egypt and ancient Greece. In Chapter 4, the Presocratic philosopher Heraclitus reportedly said to visitors standing outside his door, "Enter. Here, too, are the gods", referring to the fire in his kitchen hearth.[22] Fire–light symbolism became a dominant theme for pre-Christian and early Christian philosophers and was used to develop concepts of divine illumination and the cleansing power of God.[23]

From the burning bush, God commissioned Moses to rescue his "Sons of Israel" from Egyptian bondage[24] and return them from the harsh Sinai Desert to their Promised Land.[25] During the 40-year journey (about 320 km, or about 8 km per year[26]), Moses was further instructed by God to go to Mount Sinai (biblical Mount Horeb), where a new covenant on two tablets of stone was to be revealed to him.[27] The Sinai or Mosaic Covenant comprised a set of over 600 written religious and moral laws, including the famous Ten Commandments, for Moses to take to the people of Israel.[28] These laws[29] bound the Hebrews to a religious, family and community life.[30] Mosaism remained generally intact from the time of Moses to the time of Jesus, and is still intact in Judaism.

Yahweh's historicity: from a tribal god of storms and a desert god of war

When Moses asked God about his identity, Yahweh is represented as saying "I AM WHO I AM and tell this to the people of Israel, I AM has sent you."[31] The name Yahweh is also translated as "He causes to be (or creates) what comes into existence", and comes presumably from the Hebrew root *hayah*, meaning "to be".[32] In ancient Hebrew, the name appeared as four consonants, YHWH, because it was too sacred to pronounce. All knowledge of the vowel sounds has been lost. In the earliest English translations of the Old Testament, the vowels were assumed to have come from Adonai (meaning Lord), which is the verbal parallel to Yahweh (traditionally rendered Jehovah in English). Most Old Testament scholars believe that Yahweh is a more accurate translation.[33] During the third century AD the Jewish people refrained from using the name "Yahweh" in fear of violating one of the ten commandments: "Thou shalt not take the name of the LORD thy God in vain",[34] and used Adonai instead.[35]

Unfortunately, much of the cult of Yahweh belongs in myth and legend. The major difference between Yahweh and the older gods of ancient Sumer, Babylonia and Egypt (with the possible exception of Akhenaten's sun god, the Aten) was that he became established as the sole omnipotent creator-god of the universe and of humankind. However, before Yahweh became the sole creator-god of the prophets, he was depicted as a powerful tribal god of storms (similar to the Greek Olympian Zeus) and was also the thunderous god of the desert.[36] His voice was thunder and His arrow was lightning, but above all He was a jealous "god of war".[37] The jealous warlike character of Yahweh was essential to establish domination over his rivals. His early worship centred on ritual and bloody sacrifice of animals, whose flesh was cooked and consumed in a feast, and whose carcasses were burned.[38]

Yahweh eventually became an agricultural god to meet the needs of the Israelite tribes in Canaan.[39] He lived in heaven and frequented the "high places" of earth. To affirm his position as the one and only God, Yahweh said to Moses: "I am the Lord your God, who bought you out of the land of Egypt, out of the house of bondage. You shall have no other gods before me."[40] This implies that by around 1200 BC, the Israelites were not yet a community of monotheists in the strict sense. They may have worshipped Yahweh but they did not deny the existence of other gods. The Mosaic Covenant appears designed, in part, to abolish any remnant of historical polytheism. By around 1000 BC (the time of David), Yahweh was no longer restricted to war, the desert, agriculture, the sun, the moon or any single phenomenon but appears to have become a god of love, justice and mercy, who was at one with world unity.[41]

The prophets (c.750–550 BC)

The prophets were men chosen by Yahweh to promote the original purity of faith among the Israelites. Together with the high priests, the prophet's job was to purge Hebrew religion of its corrupting rituals, worship of idols and polytheism. Yahweh was seen as a god of justice and mercy but those who defied His sovereign "will" were subject to severe punishment. The prophets viewed the eighth century BC conquest of Israel by the Assyrian King Sargon II, and the Babylonian Exile[42] in the sixth century BC, as God's punishment against Israel for its continuing acts of apostasy. Loyality brought unity and victory and it was only after the exile that the Israeli attitude shifted from victim to aggressor.[43] The four major tasks the prophets accomplished were:

- **Reestablishment of the Mosaic Covenant as law:** The prophets reestablished the Mosaic Covenant with Yahweh as the sole God of Israel. Jeremiah taught that every person could achieve a lasting communion with God. In addition, Ezekiel emphasized divine retribution.[44] In Deuteronomy 30:15–20, the people of Israel were given choices between life and good and death and evil. The reward and punishment rested with "personal" choice, which was to be finally judged by God.[45] The older corporate self and solidarity, as in Sumer, shifted to a more personal binding interaction with God: "I will put my law within them, and I will write it

189

upon their hearts."[46] Unlike most other religions, the reforming prophets made Yahweh the one god of history, or, more precisely, the one god *in* history. He emerged from the "historical" experience of the ancient Hebrews during their "flight, Exodus and establishment of a new Promised Land".[47] Contemporary Bible scholars argue, however, that only a small minority of pre-exilic Israelites were developing monotheistic ideas.[48] Monotheism came later in the Babylonian Exile (586–539 BC), when later Old Testament traditions became more prescriptive.[49]

- **Yahweh as universal creator and Lord of the Universe:** The prophets established Yahweh as the universal creator[50] and one Lord of the Universe.[51] Before this, he was seen as saviour, bound to Israel through Noah, Abraham and Moses. The great composite work from Genesis through to 2 Kings includes a panoramic view of the creation of the world; the lost paradise and the origin of suffering and death; the Flood and the final dispersal of nations. As discussed in Chapter 2, some of these myths have striking Mesopotamian parallels dating back to 3000 BC. What appears unique to Judaic monotheism, however, was that Yahweh not only created the chaos "out of nothing" but He was believed to have existed independently of His creation.[52] This was very different from most of the cosmogonies in ancient Mesopotamia, Egypt and Greece. The primordial substance had been around for ever until it was fashioned by the creator-gods into the orderly and regular features of the visible world. Even Plato talked about his craftsman giving form to the "eternal and uncreated" matter.

  Yahweh also became a universal god of human beings and nations: "I will give you as a light to the nations, that my salvation may reach to the end of the Earth."[53] Before Isaiah, the Jews seldom thought of Yahweh as the god of all nations. One story has Yahweh dividing the heavenly bodies into several nations and leaving Israel for himself.[54] Another version has Yahweh choosing and revealing himself to Israel so that the Jews as a people could enlighten the rest of the world.[55]

- **Yahweh as good and just:** The prophets established Yahweh as a righteous god who was good and just. Human beings were created in God's image as companions,[56] not as slaves. Evil in the world arose from the wrongdoings of humanity itself: "He has showed you, O man, what is good; and what does the Lord require of you, but to do justice, and to love kindness, and to walk humbly with your God?"[57]

  In the prophetic age there was no conception of heaven and hell. According to Old Testament scholar W. F. Albright, the dualistic conception of God and Satan (good and evil) is not found until the late second century BC in the Testaments of the Twelve Patriarchs.[58] Nor was Judaism a salvation religion at this time.[59] Belief in the immortality of the soul (or retribution after death) and final judgement came late in Hebrew history around the first or second century BC, about the time when Judaism accepted resurrection of the dead.

- **The birth of an ethical religion:** The prophets established Judaism as an ethical religion with absolute values that condition human behaviour.[60] Their Yahweh cared little for anthropomorphic polytheistic worship, ritual, sacrifice or idolatry. The people of Israel were forbidden to make any image of Yahweh, living beings, flesh, fish or fowl because it was feared that they might worship the image, not Yahweh himself.[61] In the prophetic age the nature of God is represented as part of the visible world, like the sun, moon or heavenly bodies.[62] All Yahweh asked for was "to do justice, and to love kindness, and to walk humbly with your God".[63] There was also the promise in the Old Testament[64] that Israel would rise once again to a new "Golden Age" with the coming of the Messiah.[65]

The Old Testament: scriptural access to the divine

After the Babylonian Exile, the high Priests of Israel set about assembling and codifying God's revelations[66] to the people of Israel. The monumental task took over a hundred years, and was not completed until around 400 BC. The first five books of Moses were called the Pentateuch (from the Greek for "five rolls") or Torah (a Hebrew word meaning "the Law"), which later became known as the Old Testament. To these were added The Prophetic Books (Jewish history and ethics) and The Writings (proverbs, psalms and moralistic narratives).[67]

The Pentateuch or Torah was translated into a number of languages for Jews living outside Palestine. The Greek translation, or *Septuagint* (the "work of the seventy"), was completed in Alexandria around 250 BC under the sponsorship of King Ptolemy Philadelphus of Egypt.[68] According to legend, some 70 translators were involved and the work took 70 days to complete, with each scholar miraculously coming up with an identical version.[69] Philo of Alexandria believed that the Greek translation was divinely inspired by God. From that time on, many of the Greek writers in Alexandria (e.g. Hecataeus of Abdera, Megasthenes and Clearchus of Soli) recognized the Jewish people as a "philosophical race".[70] The Greek philosophers conceded that the Jews had held the idea of a "oneness of the divine principle of the world" *long before* it emerged in ancient Greece.[71]

Hebrew history and Judaism in perspective

> The tenacious survival of the Jewish people, its original culture intact and its spiritual integrity uncompromised, is a story unique in history. It was made possible by a unique religion … It was Judaism, not any racial features, that gave the Jews their separate identity and it is Judaism that has kept them a separate people until today.
>
> A. Schalit[72]

The ancient Israelites made three outstanding contributions to Western thought: (i) the Mosaic Covenant, (ii) an ethical religion *for all humanity* and (iii) biblical scripture.[73] Fundamental to Judaism was the belief that God revealed his "oneness" to the Jews through history, revelation and prophecy. The principal Mosaic doctrines included the belief that Yahweh was the Creator (the world was not eternal); that he loved his creation; and that he was the eternal saviour.[74] God was lord of the universe and acted in and controlled history.[75] The Mosaic worldview was indeed, therefore, a grand expression of God's goodness.[76]

The intellectual depth of the Mosaic worldview is truly remarkable given that the Hebrews and Jews rarely ruled their own nation; had little or no success in war, were exiled for nearly 50 years in a foreign land, and on return to the Promised Land were ruled in succession by the Persians, Greeks and Romans. It is extraordinary how, after more than a thousand years of invasions, intrusions and political disruptions, a people held on to the belief that they were God's "chosen people". Implicit in the belief was always the hope that something better was just around the corner; that "something better", at least for one sect within Judaism, was Christianity.

CHRISTIANITY: ITS DOCTRINE, EXPANSION AND SIGNIFICANCE

> Faith that Jesus was God's anointed prophet and king [Messiah] was basic to self-definition for the first church … To the earliest Christian communities Jesus was not the founder or originator of the community of God's people, but the climax of an already long story of a divine education of humanity through the special illumination given to the prophets of Israel.   H. Chadwick[77]

Christianity began as an event in history at a time of great social unrest, particularly in Palestine. Palestine feared foreign domination by Roman rule and resented the cultural pressure to conform to Greco-Roman civilization.[78] The new movement arose out of the life, preaching and death of Jesus of Nazareth. Christianity was not a new religion but developed from a small "Christianoi" sect that broke away from Judaism.[79] The sect was concentrated in Antioch, a Hellenized city located in northern Palestine in Syria (now part of Turkey), and believed that Jesus was the confirmation of God's promise to Israel, and that they were the people of the new convenant foreshadowed in Jeremiah 31:31–2:

> Behold, the days are coming, says the Lord, when I will make a new covenant with the house of Israel and the house of Judah, not like the covenant which I made with the fathers when I took them by the hand to bring them out of the land of Egypt, my covenant which they broke, though I was their husband, says the Lord.

Jesus, a Jew, had a mainly Jewish following, but gradually his teachings attracted people of different faiths and became the focus of a new, independent religion. According to Acts, the sect ceased to be an internal Jewish movement with St Peter.[80] The word "Christianity" had its origins in the late first century AD when Bishop Ignatius of Antioch (fl. AD 90) contrasted the sect's beliefs with traditional Judaism.[81] Members of the sect were called "Christians",[82] and acknowledged Jesus as their Messiah[83] and Christ,[84] a belief firmly rejected by orthodox Jews and later Muslims. Jesus reportedly began with about 100 devotees and by his death the number increased to over 3000.[85] His following was limited at first to the Roman Palestinian provinces of Judea and Galilee.[86] Today there are over two billion Christians (about 35 per cent of the world's population) according to *World Christian Trends*.[87]

Jesus of Nazareth (c.5 BC–AD 33)

Jesus wrote nothing, and no one wrote about him in his lifetime. The earliest sources on his life and mission are found in the letters of St Paul (*c.* AD 55) and the Acts of the

Apostles (*c.* AD 60).[88] The first historical account came later in the four gospels of the New Testament.[89] The Gospel according to Mark is probably the earliest (before AD 70) and most historical; Matthew and Luke wrote between AD 70 and AD 90, and John around AD 90–120.[90] At this stage there was no Bible as we know it, but an authorized collection of *graphia* ("writings"), comprising the sacred books of the Jewish people and selected writings of the Christian community in Greek.[91]

There is much controversy surrounding the accuracy of the Christian corpus since it was written and compiled decades after Jesus's life.[92] By all accounts, Jesus appears to have been a compassionate person who fully accepted the Jewish scriptures and Mosaic law. Most Christians believe that he was the Son of God and existed with God before time, and that he only became human (incarnated from the divine) when Mary gave birth to him through the power of the Holy Spirit, although conflicting stories do exist.[93] The main purpose of Jesus's physical incarnation was to reconcile humanity with God.

Jesus as the revealer of God's love and goodness

Jesus was not a philosopher, a critic or a theologian. Nor was he concerned with formal logic, abstract theories or proofs about God's existence. Rather, his overall message can be summarized in the answer he gave to a scribe who asked "Which commandment is the first of all?": "The Lord our God, the Lord is one; and you shall love the Lord your God with all your heart, and with all your soul, and with all your mind, and with all your strength. The second is this: 'You should love your neighbour as yourself.' There is no other commandment greater than these."[94]

Jesus's teachings stressed the ancient Hebrew commandments to love God and one's neighbour. Moreover, Jesus taught that everyone could become one of God's children by following the same rules of morality. Everyone could achieve harmony and could be delivered from sin and attain salvation by understanding the will of God.[95] There was no moral aristocracy, no elite dividing society. God's "will" was expressed in forgiveness, mercy, righteousness and truth appropriated through faith.

By having faith, Jesus did not mean that one should adopt a particular theology or some complex theory about the nature of things, but rather should build an inner attitude of surrender and openness to God.[96] Faith in God via the teachings of the gospels could lead a person to immortality, pardon and freedom from harmful demons. Jesus further presented God as a merciful and loving father in Heaven, whose kingdom would shortly come to an end. As in Judaism, Christians served God by practising love and kindness and through personal worship and prayer.

Jesus's view of human beings and sin

Importantly, Jesus does not appear to have viewed the physical body as corrupt, only the human spirit. He taught that suffering indicated an unhappy and disorientated soul ready to receive divine grace with the right guidance.[97] He saw communion with a merciful God as a part of human experience, *available to everyone irrespective of social background*.

However, not all Jews agreed with Jesus's view of the human condition. Among his severest critics were the Pharisees,[98] many of whom believed that the poor and suffering found themselves in their predicaments because of some violation of the natural or moral law (or sin).[99] They were offended by what they saw as Jesus's flagrant disrespect for their historical interpretation of the Torah and its unwritten laws,[100] and most detested what they saw as Jesus's self-imposed grandeur in not consulting with leaders of the Jewish brethren. For the Pharisee Jew of the synagogue,[101] all authority was derived from the divine "will" of God,[102] not Jesus.[103] Following the destruction of Jerusalem[104] in AD 70, the Pharisee movement grew to become Rabbinical Judaism, which still survives today in many parts of the world.

Sacrificial death, resurrection and ascension

Many miracles were reported to have taken place in Jesus's lifetime, and many rituals were started then.[105] Jesus's greatest miracle was his resurrection three days after his crucifixion.[106] After spending a short time with his disciples, Jesus "ascended" into Heaven with the promise to send the Holy Spirit to guide and enlighten the Church, and to return one day to judge "all souls". Jesus would punish the wicked, receive the righteous into the Kingdom of God and "restore the kingdom of Israel".[107] Jesus's death was seen as God's way of breaking the power of sin and evil in the world. And his rising symbolized the triumph of life over death, good over evil, and opportunity for eternal life. Today, one belief in the afterlife common to most Christians (and Jews, and later Muslims) is that the human soul is non-physical and immortal, which leaves the body after death and resides in a place of happiness with God (heaven) or a place of torment (hell). The Bible (and the Koran) teaches that God's judgement determines if your soul goes to heaven or hell.

People could be initiated into Christianity in a number of ways: the sacrament of baptism, the forgiveness of sins and the Eucharist (Lord's Supper). However, the most important way was by joining the Christian community: the church that celebrated the festivals of Easter and Christmas. Thus Christianity developed into a personal religion involving personal salvation through the person of Jesus. This was quite different from the philosophical principles we saw in ancient Greece and the polytheistic practices we saw in the mythical world of the Sumerians and Egyptians.

St Paul (died c. AD 65): the establishment of the early church

> For as many of you as were baptised into Christ have put on Christ. There is neither Jew nor Greek, there is neither slave nor free, there is neither male nor female; for you are all one in Christ Jesus.
>
> Galatians 3:27–8

The future of Christianity lay in the evangelical missionaries. The best known were the missionaries of Paul, who, following his conversion,[108] brought the "good news" to the Gentiles (or non-Jewish peoples).[109] This led to the establishment of churches throughout Asia Minor and Europe.[110] Paul believed that the successful spread of Christianity lay in the teaching of historical facts and a non-literal interpretation of the Scriptures.[111] Christian truth was not a matter of reasoning, but of transcending faith. Faith was a gift given to all human beings by God. St Paul holds a special place in Christian history for his missionary work, and became known as the Apostle to the Gentiles.[112] He was instrumental in transforming Christianity from a small predominantly Jewish cult into a universal world religion.

St Paul's interpretation of human beings and sin

Because of St Paul's celebrity, some scholars regard his 13 letters as a primary authority for Jesus's teachings;[113] others, however, have not been so gracious. Despite St Paul's intent to promote God through Jesus, he was never an eyewitness to Jesus's teachings. Paul taught the people and the Church to worship Jesus, whereas Jesus taught his disciples to worship God.[114] St Paul also taught that the flesh (the physical body) was corrupt. This is something Jesus never taught, at least not according to the Gospels. These apparent contradictions (and many others) set the scene for future controversy and distortion of what Jesus actually said. One area St Paul was careful to avoid was the relationship between God and Jesus. Although he frequently referred to Jesus as the "Son of God", it was a term he did not clarify.

In the end, the core of St Paul's gospel revolved around the significance of Jesus's death and resurrection. Human beings inherited deep moral corruption after the Fall of Adam (original sin), and a symbol of repentance was baptism, in which every person was ritually identified with Jesus in his death.[115] For St Paul, "It is not I who live, but Christ who lives in me."[116] Jesus's death was a gateway to a new life of glory and liberation from bondage. Salvation was not something that occurred after death but could take place during life. St Paul's discussion on salvation brought to the fore the doctrine of divine "predestination" and human "free will", which had a powerful influence on Catholicism.

St Paul disappears from history[117] around AD 65, leaving behind his controversial letters and a bountiful legend.

Christianity and the rule of faith

> Faith intervenes not to abolish reason's autonomy nor to reduce its scope of action,
> but solely to bring the human being to understand that in these events it is the God
> of Israel who acts. Thus the world and the events in history cannot be understood
> in depth without professing faith in the God who is at work in them.
>
> Pope John Paul II[118]

The Christian dimension of faith is enormously complex. The difference between Christianity and Greek philosophy is that knowledge-seeking in Christianity was always framed by the foundational tenets of faith. Knowledge-seeking in Greek philosophy began with a set of premises from which a conclusion was formulated by logical inference. The axioms or starting-points were always open to debate, even though the philosophers who proposed them defended them vigorously. Faith in Greek philosophy never commanded the same authority it did in Christian theology. Aristotle used the word faith (*pistis*) as a designation of "undemonstrated" *immediate* knowledge ("firm assurance") and as demonstrated *derivative* knowledge ("that which gives firm assurance").[119] Faith signified intellectual ascent based on "unspecified" grounds and contrasted with "true" knowledge.[120] Christian faith and certainty, on the other hand, were used synonomously. Faith provided a key to a very different kind of super-sensory experience, one beyond ordinary human reason, but *never* irrational. In Hebrews 11:1 faith is most evocatively defined as "the assurance of things hoped for, the conviction of things not seen". The passage continues: "For by [faith] the men of old received divine approval ... By faith we understand the world was created by the word of God ... By faith Abel offered to God a more acceptable sacrifice than Cain ... By faith Abraham sojourned in the land of promise ... By faith Moses left Egypt."[121] Within the tradition of the Church, faith was a belief that could be trusted. St Clement of Alexandria argued that there were two kinds of faith. First, there was "faith in God" through "obedience to the commandments", which was consistent with Hebrews 11:2–27. The second kind of faith was a demonstration that "produces scientific faith which becomes knowledge".[122] Knowledge in turn "is a sure and strong demonstration of what is received by faith".[123] So here we have the beginnings of the concepts of "simple" faith in God that stands alone, and a "rationalized" faith illuminated by subordinated reason.

St Clement was instrumental in drawing together Greek and Christian traditions with a particular emphasis on trust, which was used in the Christian defence against pagan[124] (Platonic) criticism. He, and most of the early Church fathers, adopted St Paul's view that faith was a special kind of wisdom that human beings received from God: a secret and hidden wisdom decreed before the ages for their glorification.[125] The subordination of human reason came from the framing belief that the wisdom of the Scriptures is God's word as part of revelation. The wisdom of philosophy, on the other hand, was a *product of human reason*, not faith.[126] Within this frame, Greek philosophy helped many early theologians sharpen their definitions of faith. In the end, however, most theologians agreed that faith *by itself* was an "inferior form" of human knowing but Christian faith was "authoritative" because its source was "divine revelation".[127]

Before we go further in examining the relation between faith and reason, and discussing truth in Christian theology, we must return to Alexandria in Egypt around the time of Jesus, before St Paul, and consider the work of Philo Judaeus (Philo of Alexandria). Philo was instrumental to the development of Christian theology because he was the first to blend systematically Hebrew monotheism with Greek philosophy. Ironically, however, Philo knew little or nothing about Jesus or Christianity.[128]

Philo Judaeus (c.20 BC–AD 50): the first "Christian" philosopher

> The history of Christian philosophy begins not with a Christian, but with a Jew, Philo of Alexandria, elder contemporary of St. Paul ... Philo's statements about the Logos were to have a notable future when adopted to the uses of Christian doctrine ... We may see some symbolic recognition of the Christian debt to Philo in the legend quoted by Eusebius that when Philo went on his visit to Rome, he met St. Peter.
>
> H. Chadwick[129]

Philo Judaeus was the beneficiary to at least three different cultural traditions: the "Jew" in Philo believed that the Mosaic law was infallible and directly revealed by God; the "Greek" in Philo viewed the wisdom of Greek philosophy as a product of human reason; and the "Hellenized Jew" in him held that reason was subservient to faith.[130] Philo believed that Plato, and the other Greek philosophers, had obtained their wisdom from reading the Hebrew scriptures.[131]

Philo stands as one of the founding "fathers" of Hellenized Christianity in its eastern (Greek) and western (Latin) forms.[132] He fortuitously anticipated Christian theology and opened the way for St Clement of Alexandria, Origen, St Dionysius of

Alexandria and St Ambrose to formulate the Church's position on some complex issues. Philo also influenced the later philosophy of Plotinus, Augustine and the Christian, Islamic and Jewish scholars of the Middle Ages. Ironically, Christian philosophy began not with a Christian but a Jew.[133]

Plato's Ideas (or Forms) as "thoughts" of God

Philo cleverly united Old Testament faith with the religious side of Platonism[134] by interpreting Plato's Ideas as the "thoughts" of God.[135] Philo did not interpret the Scriptures literally, as did many of his Jewish contemporaries, but allegorically, using metaphor and analogy. For example, he believed that Plato's *Timaeus* cosmology could easily be reconciled with the story of Genesis. Before the creation, God had to create all the non-physical Ideas from which all the ensuing cosmological events were derived.[136] Philo rejected Aristotle's eternal "uncreated" universe. The creation, order and rationality of the universe were from God's own reason or *logos*. The *logos*, in Platonic terms, was the "idea of all ideas".[137]

First principles: God and the "divine *logos*"

> The "Logos" is the highest mediator between God and the world, the first born son of God, the archangel who is the vehicle of all revelation, and the high priest who stands before God on behalf of the world. Through him the world was created, and so he is identified with the creative Word of God in Genesis. Here again we see the philosopher is unable to escape from the difficulty that the "Logos" is at once the immanent Reason of God, and yet also an hypostasis standing between God and the world.
>
> E. Churer & C. Bigg[138]

Philo borrowed the concept of "divine *logos*" from Platonism and Stoicism (a unified logical, physical, moral philosophy; see Ch. 5). Heraclitus was the first to use the term "*logos*" when he described it as the imperishable basis of the universe, continuous with all its physical and divine manifestations held together in tension by opposing forces (see Ch. 4). Philo's *logos* had two stages of existence: it existed within God and was sometimes identified with him;[139] and it was a "real being" that came into existence from the act of God's creation.[140] The powers emanating from God were not only in his thoughts but

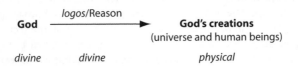

Figure 6.1 Philo of Alexandria combined Stoic and Platonic traditions and argued for the "divine *logos*" as an intermediary being between God and the creation of the universe. The "divine *logos*" was a messenger of sorts that not only created the world but actively permeated minds so that human beings could understand the world. The "divine *logos*" ensured that God was separate from his creation. This clever distinction led the later Latin Church fathers to borrow from Philo and equate the "divine *logos*" with the historical Jesus, not God. In contrast to Plato, Philo did not believe the universe possessed "a soul" linking the physical to the divine.

also in the active ruling principle of nature, as the Stoics had envisaged.[141] The beauty of the "divine *logos*" was that it provided Philo with a way to solve the paradox between God's transcendence and immanence, the divine and the physical (Fig. 6.1).

Philo's "divine *logos*" was also equivalent to the wisdom of the Old Testament and other Rabbinic traditions: "By the word of the Lord the heavens were made, and all their host by the breath of his mouth."[142] "Divine *logos*" was God's wisdom or law, but at the same time quite distinct from God.[143] Equating the "mind of God" with "world reason" meant that God was synonymous with harmony, justice and good: another Greek idea.

The human condition and evil

Another aspect of Philo's "divine *logos*" was its relation with the different authorities of mind and sense. The *logos* actively permeated the world of intellect, not the senses.[144] The intellect enabled human beings to understand God and his creations through the "divine *logos*". Philo wrote: "If I see or feel a tree, I am in the sensible world. If out of seeing or feeling many trees I move on to fashion the idea about what trees are, I have moved into the world of concepts, into the intelligible world. I make this move by utilising my reason."[145] One can immediately see Plato's profound influence on Philo's thinking. The "divine *logos*" never descended into the sensible world;[146] only the "powers" or "forces" emanating from it entered the world.[147]

The *logos* entered the human intellect as the "higher" soul and was imprisoned in the body for as long as there was life.[148] The "lower" soul, on the other hand, was in contact with the senses and matter, and was the source of sin and evil. The human body imprisoned the soul, which sought to rise again to God. Philo also believed that the soul's ultimate goal was to escape the physical and, after many trials, return to its origin in God. Immortality of souls seems to be a necessary consequence of Philo's thinking, but he makes little mention of it.[149] Importantly for Philo, the goal of religion was to rise above the physical (corporeality) and to receive the vision of God through the "divine *logos*" using the intellect.[150]

How did evil creep into the world?

Philo argued that evil (or imperfections in the world) was not a manifestation of God's righteous powers but arose from the properties of physical matter. Physical objects were made of matter, which stood in opposition to God and forever thwarted his plan and purpose for the "divine *logos*". Since the world comprised ever-changing transformations of matter, evil will be manifest. This view differs from that of Jesus, who, as mentioned earlier, did not view the physical body as corrupt, but only the human spirit. Philo also held that final redemption occurred by leading a moral life of intellectual communion with God. Understanding God's word in the ethical teachings of the Old Testament guaranteed salvation. Scientific pursuits and logical thinking alone were incapable of reaching a final truth; they were preparatory to reaching out to God.

Church apologists and theologians: in defence of the faith

> The history of Christian doctrine is the record of a series of attempts made in successive periods to embody the contents of the Gospel in clear and self-consistent propositions.
>
> S. Sandmel[151]

The second and third centuries mark the growth of Catholic Christianity, defined by the combination of bishop, creed and scriptural canon.[152] It was an era of great uncertainty, when Christians found themselves under attack from every corner of Roman society: government, Greek philosophers, literary scholars, orators and historians. In response to these attacks, a number of converts came to the defence of Christianity. One group of writers, who became known as the Christian apologists, were well trained in philosophy and heavily influenced by Philo. The word "apologist" comes from the Greek *apologia*, meaning "to explain".

The apologists and early Church leaders believed it was their job to take the gospel to the ends of the earth[153] and to defend it against attacks. The apologists set forth on the Herculean task of presenting reasoned expositions and defences of Christianity to non-Christians, including Celsus,[154] Porphyry and Julien, and later to breakaway groups including the Gnostics[155] and Marcionists.[156] Some of the non-Christian religions targeted were Judaism, Mithraism (of Persian origin), Manichaeism, the Hellenistic mystery religions (e.g. Zoroastrianism) and the older traditional Roman cults of Jupiter and Liber Pater.[157] The apologists' plight was exceedingly dangerous because of the continual threat of persecution by the Romans.

The apologists' strength in promoting and defending the faith was their consistent use of allegory and metaphor to buttress their arguments against alternative explanations.[158] They also adopted a branch of Greek questioning known as "scepticism" to challenge aspects of classical Greek thought in favour of Christianity. Most apologists agreed that Plato's *Timaeus* creation was a partial revelation but believed it fell short of affirming God's transcendence and immanence. While generally agreeing with Philo's doctrine of the "divine *logos*", the apologists preferred to think of *logos* as God's "essence", not his creation.[159] This was highly significant because it meant that the "divine *logos*" was not separate from God but, indirectly, a part of him and associated with Jesus. We shall now consider some of the prominent apologists and their views and show how they helped to Hellenize[160] Christian theology and eventually win the battle over paganism.[161]

Justin the Martyr (*c.*100–*c.*165): philosophy in the service of faith

> Justin vigorously rejected pagan myth and cult as gross superstition infected by evil, but gave the most positive welcome possible to the classical philosophical tradition. The transcendent God of Plato, beyond mortal comprehension, is the God of the Bible. Socrates rightly perceived how corrupt the old religion was, and in consequence was hounded to death by the Athenians – a model of integrity for Christian martyrs.
>
> H. Chadwick[162]

The first Christian apologist was St Justin the Martyr, a Greek Samarian and contemporary of Pliny, Plutarch, Celsus, Aelius and Galen. Three of his works survive: two *Apologies* (the first addressed to Emperor Antoninus Pius *c.*151) and a supplement (*c.*160; issued in Rome at the time of persecution) and his *Dialogue with Trypho* (*c.*155).[163] The first *Apology* (and supplement) was a defence against Gnostic heresies and vulgar slanderers, whereas the *Dialogue* was a debate to persuade a Jew to the truth of Christianity.[164]

The life-changing event that eventually led to Justin's conversion occurred in Ephesus, where he was studying philosophy. He met an old man on the seashore at the mouth of the Kaystros, who discussed his objections to the Platonic doctrine of the immortal soul as a path to God. The old man also spoke of the Old Testament prophets who foretold the coming of Jesus.[165] Justin was captivated with the old man's stories and, after further enquiry into the credibility of the Christian religion, eventually converted around AD 130, when he was about 35 years old. St Justin's conversion was not something he entered into lightly, as he explains in this treatise *Apologies*: "hearing the accusations made against the Christians and seeing them intrepid in the face of death and of all that men fear, I said to myself that it was impossible that they should be living in evil and in the love of pleasure".[166] For Justin, Christianity was the best path to God, combining truth with moral reform in the Roman Empire.

Justin, however, did not abandon philosophy altogether. He agreed with Philo that Plato's Ideas were God's thoughts; that the "divine *logos*" bridged the physical and divine; and that most Greek philosophers had knowledge of Old Testament Scriptures. Justin also acknowledged Plato's definitions of God as immutable, incorporeal and transcendent. Indeed, Justin believed that Plato's God was the God of the Christians. However, he rejected Plato's transmigration of the soul and his polytheism. He believed that the Greek philosophers discovered so many truths about God because of their study of the symbolic language of the Old Testament, and from the inward workings of the *logos*, the wisdom of God, which was associated with the highest goodness and intelligence.[167]

All rational beings shared the "divine *logos*". Human beings' faculty for reason was a gift from God and the providential instrument for seeking truth. Justin's cheerful optimism in "reasoned" faith led him to explain paganism as arising from the intervening "malevolent spirits" from the older polytheistic religions.[168] He argued that the biggest enemies to Christianity were ignorance and prejudice. Justin was executed for his Christian beliefs around AD 165, by the Roman Emperor Marcus Aurelius (161–180). In later centuries, Justin was celebrated as a Christian martyr of the second century.

St Clement of Alexandria (*c*.150–*c*.215): philosophy as a preparation for revealed theology

> But the teaching, which is according to the Saviour, is complete in itself and without defect, being "the power and wisdom of God"; and the Hellenic philosophy does not, by its approach, make the truth more powerful; but rendering powerless the assault of sophistry against it, and frustrating the treacherous plots laid against the truth.
>
> Clement of Alexandria[169]

Justin's work was complemented by another wandering scholar, Clement of Alexandria. Clement was a quiet, enigmatic Gentile convert, and, like Justin, he valued logic as a philosophical tool of systematic theology. Clement was influenced by an extraordinary number of Christian teachers from around the empire.[170]

Clement saw no conflict between faith and reason, but considered them mutually necessary. Philosophy fortified faith, and revelation required trust in God.[171] In his famous book *Stromata* (II 7f), Clement viewed faith as analogous to a working hypothesis that was verified later through moral experience or by assenting to the authority of divine love.[172] Philosophy as a tool was also used to refute heresy, defend the faith and explain the Creation,[173] and to expound central matters of the Christian doctrine.[174]

Clement wanted to show that a Christian could be educated and intelligent without abandoning the apostolic rule of faith in the New Testament.[175] And it was the role of Greek philosophy to help prepare the way for Christian faith by recognizing the unity of divine Being. Clement believed that God had implanted the "seeds" of rationality, which allowed the Greeks to glean and understand the ancient Hebrew scriptures. In other words, philosophy was God-given and ranked "among the good things of Providence".[176]

Clement believed everyone was in need of divine education, which could only be achieved by accepting God's will through the universally operative "divine *logos*".[177] Clement's "divine *logos*" was the Holy Spirit, not Philo's *logos*. Clement took issue with St Paul's concept of original sin: that humanity inherited deep moral corruption after the Fall of Adam. Each soul, he argued, came into human life perfect, and Adam suffered only from his personal abuse of free will: an argument later taken up by Pelagius against Augustine. For Clement, God does not change his "will" by the incarnation; he wills a change in humanity.[178]

Origen (c.184–c.254): "Human wisdom is a means of education of the soul and divine wisdom being the ultimate end"

> … but when the Logos of God says that "No man has known the Father except the Son, and the man to whom the Son may reveal him", he indicates that God is known by a certain divine grace, which does not come about in the soul without God's action, but with a sort of inspiration. Moreover, it is probable that the knowledge of God is beyond the capacity of human nature (that is why there are such great errors about God among men). Origen[179]

Clement's contemporary and outspoken Alexandrian successor was the Greek scholar Origen.[180] Origen was a prolific writer, deeply influenced by Clement's allegorical defence of Christianity.[181] Origen's most famous works included *On First Principles* (*c.*225), *Against Celsus* (*c.*248) and many biblical commentaries. *On First Principles* gave Christianity a philosophical framework and argued for harmony between Church and empire.

Origen agreed with Clement that rigorous academic training was necessary for spiritual enlightenment and moral reform. Faith must be supplemented with reason and it was the duty of the theologian to clarify the first principles underpinning the articles of faith using reason.[182] Origen's aim was to set down "a connected series of truths agreeable to reason" to clarify the Scriptures.[183] Again, after Philo, an enormous amount of time and energy was invested by these early theologians to fit God's revealed religion into a philosophical framework based on Platonism.

Like Philo and Clement, Origen favoured an allegorical approach rather than a literal interpretation of the Scriptures. He insisted, like Clement, that the Fall was not something inevitable to human nature but arose from Adam's misuse of free will. Nor was the virgin birth of Jesus to be taken literally, but as an analogy of the birth of the "divine *logos*" in the soul.[184] Origen believed that the Bible was not meant to be concerned with matters of history but with the revealed word of God. He also questioned the authority of the Septuagint (the Greek translation of the Old Testament), which angered many later theologians. In addition, he believed that the Jews had altered the sacred texts of the Scriptures when it suited them, and he learned Hebrew so that he could argue his case in defence of Christianity. To this end, Origen produced a complex edition of the Old Testament in which the Hebrew, the Hebrew transliterated into Greek and four Greek versions were presented side by side.

For Origen the Scriptures had three levels of reality: a "literal" historical sense, a "moral" (or psychic) meaning and a "spiritual" interpretation.[185] This three-pronged approach to understanding the Scriptures reflected the Platonic analogy of human beings as tripartite: consisting of a body, soul (*psyche*) and spirit.[186] Meaning was brought about from a union between body and soul, soul and spirit, and ideas and reality. Knowledge, in all its forms, possessed objective meaning because it grasped the objective reality and order created by God.[187]

For Origen, sense-perception led to true knowledge when the perception of the present was seen as relating simultaneously to the revelation of the Scriptures and contained in the *logos*.[188] Origen further believed that God's revelation could be understood by studying nature, but this idea was not seriously taken up until the Islamic philosophers, followed by Aquinas, Grosseteste, Bacon and Ockham in the later Middle Ages.[189] In contrast to Philo, Origen (and Clement) did not believe that the universe was created by God "out of nothing".[190] Rather, Origen made the bold suggestion that before creating the world, God may have created others, forming multi-worlds. It is not clear, however, whether he agreed with Clement that "God was God before becoming a Creator" or whether he thought the world was necessary to the existence of God.[191]

Origen's most controversial belief was his doctrine of pre-existent souls. "Before all ages", he wrote, "minds were all pure, both demons and souls and angels, offering service to God and keeping his commandments."[192] At the original creation, all souls (spirits) were created equal and everyone failed the test except "one". The "one" eventually gave rise to the *logos* and became the human soul of Jesus. No higher function bestowed free will. Of all the other fallen souls, some fell a short distance and became angels, while others fell a long way and became devils. Most fallen souls became human beings, whom Origen regarded as striving to become better.[193]

Origen's mythical "hierarchy of being" was, in part, his apologetic defence against the Gnostic charge of God's injustice and arbitrariness. He argued that even the most wayward sinner would eventually attain salvation. Origen further taught that the human soul might require many cycles before being cleansed.[194] This highly controversial doctrine of cyclical time, linking the transmigratory soul and God, implied that the devil himself could be saved: a view that particularly shocked St Jerome. Origen was condemned and fled to Palestine, where he was exiled for the remainder of his life. His views were condemned again in AD 400, and at the second council of Constantinople in AD 553.

Tertullian (*c.*155–*c.*220): what has Jerusalem to do with Athens?

> Tertullian's apologetic style is one of invective and denunciation. He aims at the complete demolition of his opponent, not his persuasion. Reveling in flamboyant rhetorical excess, his weapon of choice is the bludgeon not the scalpel.   M. L. Colish[195]

Not every apologist shared Clement's or Origen's enthusiasm for Greek philosophy. One who did not was the North African convert Tertullian, who was the first Latin apologist and Latin Christian writer to use arguments against breakaway Christian and non-Christian religious groups. Unlike those of his predecessors, Tertullian's arguments were based more on faith than on philosophical reason.[196] Indeed, he was adamant in arguing that philosophical reason had no supportive status in theology, although in the same breath he appears to have accepted many of the Stoics' ideas.[197] The superiority of faith over reason was found in its supra-rational property. Important to Tertullian were a consensus of the bishops and the doctrinal authority of the Church. His outspoken contempt for philosophy can be read from the following excerpt of his famous *The Prescription against Heretics:*

> From philosophy come those fables and endless genealogies and fruitless questionings, those "words that creep like as doth a canker." To hold us back from such things, the Apostle testifies expressly in his letter to the Colossians that we should beware of philosophy. "Take heed lest any man circumvent you through philosophy or vain deceit, after the tradition of men", against the providence of the Holy Ghost. He had been at Athens where he had come to grips with the human wisdom that attacks and perverts truth, being itself divided up into its own swarm of heresies by the variety of its mutually antagonistic sects. What has Jerusalem to do with Athens, the Church with the Academy, the Christian with the heretic? …
> I have no use for a Stoic or a Platonic or a dialectic Christianity. After Jesus Christ we have no need of speculation, after the Gospel no need of research. When we come to believe, we have no desire to believe anything else; for we begin by believing that there is nothing else which we have to believe.[198]

For Tertullian, therefore, Greek philosophy was of no interest or had no application to Christian orthodoxy. Tertullian's anti-Greek sentiments and views of orthodoxy[199] foreshadowed many later developments of the ecumenical councils towards institutional episcopal consensus. In the fifth century AD, Vincent of Lerins recast Tertullian's norms of orthodoxy under the general formula that a doctrine is true if held "always, everywhere, by everyone".[200]

CLASSICAL PAGAN PHILOSOPHY: NEOPLATONISM AND ITS IMPORTANCE TO CHRISTIAN THEOLOGY

The development of Christian theology did not rely solely on Christians. The chief non-Christian philosopher to have a profound influence on Christian thought in late antiquity was Plotinus of Alexandria. He is known as the founder of Neoplatonism and was an older contemporary of Clement, Origen and Tertullian. Neoplatonism grew from a synthesis of the major currents of Greek philosophy (Platonism, Pythagoreanism, Aristotelianism and Stoicism) infused with an oriental and mystical spirit (Egyptian, Phoenician and other Near Eastern religious and ethical elements). The philosophy, as we shall see, generally identified creation with emanation from a source: a continual process of generation, with no beginning or end. This was totally counter to the Judeo-Christian idea of God creating the world out of nothing at the beginning of time. Nevertheless, parts of Neoplatonism, as a doctrine, were adopted by Christian scholars and theologians to help interpret the Scriptures, and were later enthusiastically embraced by the religion of Islam itself.

Plotinus of Alexandria (c.205–270): the philosophical road to "the One"

> For the Intellectual principle is the earliest form of Life: it is the activity presiding over the out-flowing of the universal Order, that is, of the first moment not that of the continuous process. For the Universe is not a Principle and Source; it springs from a source, and that source cannot be the All or anything belonging to the All since it is to generate the All.
>
> Plotinus[201]

Plotinus was not a Christian but a pagan philosopher of the Greco-Roman world.[202] For him, philosophy rather than religion or science was the road to truth. According to his student Porphyry (c.232–305), Plotinus became so immersed in the higher world of the intellect that he "seemed ashamed of being in a body".[203] Plotinus lived an ascetic life, surviving on a few hours of sleep, minimal food and reportedly no baths. He dreamed of founding an ideal "Platonic city" (Platonopolis) in Campania, a favourite resort of distinguished Romans.[204]

God was not discounted altogether, however, because the universe emanated and obtained its order and beauty from "the One" or "the Good".[205] Plotinus's philosophy was a "lifting up the heart and mind to God",[206] in which revelation, prayer, religious rites, sacrifice or idolatry did not belong. It was the vehicle of the soul's return to its intelligible roots.

What Plato took from Parmenides, Plotinus took from Plato
Plotinus's system should be seen as standing in the Greek philosophical tradition. For Parmenides, true reality was "One Being", a principle revealed to him by a goddess (see Ch. 4). Plato adopted a similar principle in his supreme god but proposed a theory of knowledge that described degrees of truth oscillating between "true" universals in mind and "likely" particulars in sense. Plotinus similarly asserted that "the One" was the highest creative principle and that all reality emanated from this source; the further away from the source the less perfect or less good something became, and this helped explain how evil entered the world.

Plato's Ideas were not only objects but living thinking subjects as part of the intellect in contemplation of "the One"
Unlike Plato (and Socrates), who held that "thought" and the "object of thought" were separate, Plotinus sided partly with Aristotle and placed both thought and object

on an equal footing. This is central to understanding Plotinus. In knowing the Ideas, the mind knows itself, *but the Ideas were not their source* because thought and objects were indistinguishable in the mind.[207] The source, Plotinus reasoned, must come from the outside: from his "One", who was beyond knowing.

Cleverly, however, Plotinus retained Plato's eternal Ideas and incorporated them into his own theory of emanation. Because the universal emanated from God, it was more real than the physical, but not eternal, as Plato had held. By locating the world of Ideas within the divine mind or intellect, Plotinus felt that he had solved the age-old Greek mind–sense dualism: he had connected the transcendent "One" with the physical world without losing relations between them. He had "intellectualized" the Platonic concept of eternal truth.[208]

"True" reality divided into three divine substances

Plotinus's true reality existed beyond the physical realm and was divided into three hierarchical *hypostases* or divine substances.[209] First was the transcendent "One", second was the divine mind, and third was the soul (with a divine and physical component).[210] In contrast to the Christian God's creation "out of nothing", Plotinus's world had no beginning or end because it emanated from "the One" via thought and soul.[211] Notably, Origen, who had the same teacher as Plotinus, also put forward a theory of the trinity involving three *hypostases*.[212]

Plotinus's trinity

- **The transcendent "One".** A concept often equated with God and beyond the reach of human words or thought. God contains all things but is contained by nothing. He is transcendent and the unknowable object of worship and love. God is not the intellect or mind but the *source* of the universal intellect (divine mind). God was the highest principle of reality, "the wise", "the good", "the first", "the absolute" and "the infinite". The subordinate realities should not be viewed as flowing out automatically from the source in an unconscious manner.[213] The creation by "the One" was eternal (with no beginning or end), without care or choice for what was created.[214] God's creations were not from some pre-existing matter co-eternal with God (Plato); nor was his world in its completeness co-eternal with God (Aristotle). Plotinus saw the creation as being eternally created or emanated from the essence of God. Creation *ex nihilo* was the temporal generation of the world from God's essence.[215]
- **The divine mind or intellect, spirit or *nous*.** The second highest principle of reality was the emanation of divine mind or the intellectual principle that determined the realm of being or consciousness. Mind was the place where thought and the object of thought were indistinguishable. From "the One" derives the potential for coming-into-being. Intelligence was the eternal or timeless repository of Ideas (Forms) in the mind of God (also conceived as the realm of number). Mind, as the "first being" was less than unity. Human beings can connect to "the One" via love.
- **The soul or *psyche*.** The soul is the third principle of reality and an emanation of the divine mind or the intellectual principle. The soul is what formed, governed and animated the physical world (the nature principle). The soul operated at two levels:

the highest was a divine component linked to God, and the other was a physical component linked to nature. The higher soul component contemplates mind and the lower part represents the principle of the order of the universe. The soul is the cause of all movement and rules the physical world "from above". The lower soul reproduces the Ideas or Forms contained in the thought of the mind. The physical world was formed as a bridge between the world-soul and pure matter (much as each individual soul unites with each body to make up a living being). Human beings properly belong to this reality. The soul was an intermediary between our thoughts and the physical. The further away from "the One", the less perfect and good something was. Matter was indeterminate, without soul, life or body; it was the furthest away from "the One" and the source of human sin and evil.

The human condition

Plotinus viewed human beings as living souls in a body. The soul, as the originative principle of movement and life, bridged the intellectual and the sensible worlds (not the *logos*, as Philo had asserted[216]).[217] Just as the universe had a higher "ruling" and a lower "physical" soul (nature), so did human beings. The higher soul was the eternal self, immortal, divine and capable of transmigration.[218] The lower soul was part of everyday experience, that perceived order and change around us.[219] The lower soul underwent a series of successive reincarnations and punishments in the underworld.[220]

Human sin and evil were explained by the lower soul's contact with matter.[221] Physical matter was the lowest kind of material, indeed was almost non-being: a position quite different from those of Aristotle and Plato.[222] Matter was the outer emanation of the soul's descent from God. God remained absolutely perfect but what emanated from him through the zones of reason and soul to matter introduced the imperfections. One of philosophy's major tasks was to help order the lower self and free human beings from bodily things that weigh them down in life. Plotinus believed that only human asceticism could strike the correct balance in "lifting up the heart and mind to God".[223] At death, the soul disentangles itself from matter and returns to the cosmic "One".

CHRISTIANITY AS THE SOLE RELIGION OF THE ROMAN EMPIRE

The Latin Church fathers and Roman Catholic thought

> It is our pleasure that all nations which are governed by our Clemency and Moderation should steadfastly adhere to the religion which was taught by St. Peter to the Romans, which faithful tradition has preserved, which is now professed by the Pontiff Damasus and by Peter, Bishop of Alexandria. We authorise the followers of this doctrine to assume the title of Catholic Christians, and we brand all others with the infamouse name of heretics. They must expect to suffer the severe penalities which our Authority, guided by the heavenly Wisdom, shall think proper to inflict upon them.
>
> Theodosius[224]

The next instalment takes us to the Latin Church fathers (or doctors) of the fourth and fifth centuries. The fourth century was revolutionary for the Church, particularly after Emperor Constantine moved the capital of the Roman Empire from Rome to Constantinople[225] (considered to be the "Second Rome") in AD 330.[226] What began with violent persecutions of Christians under Emperor Diocletian[227] ended in 381 with Emperor Theodosius decreeing Christianity the sole religion of the Roman Empire. By 392, Christianity was the state religion; Jewish temples were ordered to close and the worship of multiple gods was high treason.[228] Paganism had almost vanished. The period was the golden age of patristic literature, creeds and definitions, and saw the building of the Vatican and Lateran basilicas at Rome.

The Christian message was clear and powerful: a united faith in the Old and New Testaments and belief in the Catholic Church was the way to God and salvation. Science and "speculative" philosophy remained suppressed, with most Church leaders considering them to be irrelevant, meddlesome and impertinent. In 398, the fourth Council of Carthage banned all secular books except those used by bishops for pious ends.[229] Although philosophy did witness a brief resurgence in the middle of the fourth century, with Marius Victorinus's translations of works by Plato, Aristotle and Porphyry,[230] they were not widely read.[231] The Byzantine Emperor Justinian finally closed Plato's Academy, the last bastion of Greek paganism, in 529, and in the same year the Benedictine order was founded and monasteries controlled all education and scholarship.[232]

The widespread conversion to Catholicism was not without its problems. A number of heretical movements appeared; the most influential were Christian Pelagianism,[233] Donatism,[234] Manichaeism and Pricillianism.[235] Ironically, these anti-Catholic groups contributed greatly to the Church's rise to power; it provided an opportunity for the Church to develop and expound its own theology using the most highly educated converts, who were attracted to monastic life. And it played a significant role in the rise and quality of Western patristic literature, including apologetic, dogmatic and polemical treatises, poetry and letters, biblical translations, exegesis, sermons and Church history.[236]

The four Latin Church fathers largely responsible for the establishment and proclamation of Catholic orthodoxy were St Ambrose, St Jerome, St Augustine and St Gregory I (the Great).[237] All played key roles in different periods and shaped much of Christian thought for the next 800 years. Ambrose was renowned for developing a strong relationship between Church and State; Jerome was responsible for introducing the Latin Bible, and was a defender of monasticism; Augustine was famous for his scholarship in laying down a broad Catholic theology; and the later Gregory I (c.540–604) was notable for his practical efforts in institutionalizing Catholicism after the collapse of the Western Empire. Before meeting Ambrose, Jerome and Augustine, we shall set the stage by introducing one of the most significant theological debates of the period that helped to define the early Catholic Church.

The mystery of the Holy Trinity

The idea of God in the Gospels is no longer restricted to the lofty, but rarefied ethical monotheism of Deutero-Isaiah. A nearly complete cycle separated the beginnings of Israel from the beginnings of Christianity, and the anthropomorphic concept of God in early Israel returned at the end of this cycle to the center of our field of vision – but

the human forms and emotions of Yahweh had become spiritualised in the process
... There is still one God as in Israel, but the acute danger of polytheism is over and He
appears in three complementary hypostases. In one hypostasis He has drawn closer
to man ... In another He is one eternal Creator and Lord of the universe (as He was to
Deutero-Isaiah) ... [And third] He was the Holy Spirit, alternatively conceived as the
Divine Wisdom.   F. Albright[238]

Historical background

The development of the notion of Trinity can be traced back to Philo, who equated
God's creative "word" with the Greek "divine *logos*" (divine reason or divine word).
Philo had borrowed the idea from the Greeks and believed he had solved the paradox
of God's transcendence and immanence. God's "thoughts" were part of the "divine
logos", from which the physical world was created.[239] Philo's clever distinction led
many apologists to equate the "divine *logos*" with Jesus, who was envisaged as the
mediator between the physical and the divine, *for which God was ultimately responsible*,
but could not be directly involved.[240] The "divine *logos*" was no longer God's
creation, as Philo had proposed, but was his "essence".[241] A critical question
remained: how was the divinity of God linked to the physicality of Jesus?

In the New Testament, Matthew 28:19 reports Jesus as exhorting the disciples to
perform baptisms "in the name of the Father and of the Son and Holy Spirit" and St
Paul uses similar words in 2 Corinthians 13:14. But these statements are a long way
from the Trinitarian concept developed by the Catholic Church. Ostensibly, the
person who tackled the problem head-on was Clement of Rome (*c*.30–*c*.101). In a
letter to the Corinthian Church, Clement wrote: "Have we not one God and one
Christ and one Spirit of grace, the Spirit that has been poured out of us."[242] The Holy
Spirit was directly related to the practical experience of Christian life within the
Church in terms of "grace, "power", "illumination" and "prophetic" gifts.[243] A
similar passage in Clement's letter states: "For God lives, and Jesus Christ lives, and
the Holy Spirit and the faith and hope of the elect."[244]

Clement's elder contemporary, St Ignatius (fl. AD 115) also used the Trinitarian
language when he wrote "by faith and by love, in the Son and Father and in the
Spirit".[245] More important was Ignatius's direct ascription of deity to Jesus as the Son
and Word of God: "The one God manifested himself through Jesus Christ his Son
who in his Word that proceeded from silence."[246]

The confusion of ecclesiatical relations reached its climax with the Libyan
theologian Arius (*c*.250–336)[247] when he and his followers appealed to Colossians
1:15–16: "He [Jesus] is the image of the invisible God, the first-born of all creation,
in heaven and on earth, visible and invisible, whether thrones or dominions or
principalities or authorities – all things were created through him and for him." For
Arius, Jesus was metaphysically and morally inferior to God the Father and belonged
to the created order. The Arians concluded that Jesus was not fully God, but neither
was he fully human. Arianism angered many contemporary bishops because if
hypostasis, the Greek equivalent of substance, was synonymous with essence, then to
speak of "three hypostases" verged on three separate Gods.

The Council of Nicaea of AD 325 and the Nicene Creed

The Council of Nicaea was a turning point in Catholic history. Newly converted Constantine (converted around 317), who believed that he was "divinely" selected to ensure the Church's unity in the Roman Empire, summoned a gathering of bishops in Nicaea (now Iznik in western Turkey) on 20 May 325 to rule on the Holy Trinity.[248]

The Council was attended by about 220 of the 1800 bishops in the Roman Empire (although some reports say that 318 bishops attended), and only a handful of these came from the Western Empire.[249] To the delight of the emperor, there was nearly unanimous agreement[250] that Jesus was "of one substance" (*homoousios*) with the Father, created from his Word. Jesus was declared the incarnate Son of God (spirit in body). That Jesus and God were "the same" became an article of faith. But what about God's other creations in the natural world? In Alexandria, St Athanasius (*c*.296–373) proposed adding a third member: the Holy Spirit.

The Holy Trinity now symbolized God revealing himself in "three persons" of the same substance (*homoousion*) in different forms:[251] (i) the Creator, Lord of Salvation, Father and Judge, who revealed himself to Christians in the Old Testament; (ii) the Lord, who in Jesus Christ lived among humans and revealed God's love and purpose to humanity; and (iii) the Holy Spirit, which was God's guide or power to instruct the world. In this new system, there was no subordination of divine realities, only three modes of self-disclosure of God's substance or essence (*ousia*). The official minutes of Nicaea have not survived, but the exuberance in Emperor Constantine's proclamation has:

> Beloved brethren, hail. We have received from divine Providence the blessing of being freed from all error, and united in the acknowledgement of one and the same faith. The devil will no longer have power over us ... Wherefore we all worship the one true God and believe that he is. But in order that this might be done, by divine will I assembled at the city of Nicaea most of the bishops; with whom I also, who am but one of you, and rejoice exceedingly in being your fellow-servant, undertook the investigation of the truth.[252]

The Holy Trinity was very different from Plotinus's triad. The cosmic soul of the Platonists and Neoplatonists was rejected outright by Christians. For them, "soul" was not coequal with the Holy Spirit, nor was the "divine *logos*" of Philo an *intermediate* between God and the physical world.[253] Indeed, the Council sharply repudiated the older *logos* theology of Philo, Arius, Tertullian, Origen and Eusebius (*c*.260–340), who believed that Father and Son were of "separate" substances of different divinities.[254] However, at the same time, the Holy Trinity was a culmination of many centuries of patristic borrowing, debate and reworking of parts of Hellenized Platonism, Stoicism and Judaism to fit Christian theology.

St Ambrose (*c*.339–397): authority in the Scriptures and the Church

> The knowledge of God cannot be compassed by human wisdom. It is through their reliance on philosophy that pagans fall into error. "He who follows the corruptible

things of the world and imagines that from them he can comprehend the truth of the Divine Nature, is certainly fooled by the subtlety of deceitful disputation."

F. H. Dudden, quoting Ambrose[255]

St Ambrose was a bishop of and statesman in Milan, an Italian city that had replaced Rome as the capital city of the Roman Empire at the end of the fourth century. Ambrose's office was guided by practical concerns and grew to become one of the most influential in the Latin Western Empire. His writings fall under four main headings: biblical exegesis, dogmatic works, liturgical poetry and ethical treatises.[256] Drawing on the work of Philo and Origen, he introduced into Latin exegesis the idea that the Bible contained four levels of meaning: literal or historical, moral, allegorical and anagogic.[257] Meaning was sought in the Scriptures and accepted by faith: "By faith we come to knowledge."[258]

Ambrose's firm belief was that the texts of the Scriptures were communicated to the sacred Hebrew writers as utterances of the Holy Spirit. He consistently devalued reason in relation to divine things: "it was not by dialectic that it pleased God to save his people; for the kingdom of God consists in simplicity in faith, not in wordy contention".[259] Ambrose had a profound suspicion of philosophy, and often warned people against it. He believed that, in addition to scriptural authority, religious truth was found in the Church's orthodox Trinitarian and Christological traditions. He denounced paganism, Gnosticism and the Arian movement and employed platonic arguments to strengthen the position of the Orthodox Church.

Unlike Jerome and the later Augustine, Ambrose did not try to be original, but was practical, and used his great skills as a statesman and polemicist.[260] He, more than most, removed the last vestiges of paganism. He was not interested in developing new formal proof of the existence of God, for he believed that human beings can no more doubt his existence "than a blind man can doubt the existence of the sun, which he cannot behold, but whose heat he feels".[261] He taught the public that God was the creator: one, simple, immutable, infinite and eternal.

Perhaps Ambrose's most original contribution was to assert the need for the separation of Church and State.[262] As the Church grew in power, the Roman Imperial court grew weaker and Ambrose, the friend and advisor of emperors, took full advantage of the situation. Ambrose's power became so great that in AD 390 he excommunicated Emperor Theodosius I for indiscriminately massacring thousands of civilians in the city of Thessalonica in retribution for the actions of a rebellious few.[263] Realizing the greater power of God and the Church, the emperor humbled himself and accepted public penance for his crime.[264] The emperor's public repentance set a precedent for the Church–State relationship for many centuries to come.

St Jerome (c.331–420): translator of the first Latin Bible

For most of his adult life Jerome had been the focus of bitter controversy, as passionately detested in some circles as loved and admired in others. By the time he died the suspicion and hostility he aroused had begun to die down, and for the next thousand years and more a crescendo of adulation was to surround him.

J. N. D. Kelly[265]

Jerome was more of a prolific "private" scholar than Ambrose, and lacked his self-confidence and civic responsibility.[266] After being educated in Rome, he left for the East (around 372) where he lived an ascetic, troubled life.[267] Jerome was eventually ordained presbyter at Antioch. Soon afterwards (377) he returned to Rome and began to translate Origen's writings and many other works. Jerome's reputation was soon recognized by Pope Damasus I (305–384), who commissioned him to translate into Latin the Book of Psalms, and later the entire Bible.

Jerome was ideally suited for Bible translation because he was trilingual in Latin, Greek and Hebrew. Around 390, he embarked on an entirely new Latin translation of the Old Testament from Hebrew.[268] This was to become Jerome's greatest literary achievement, and it eventually led to the displacement of the Septuagint in the West. The translation elicited sharp correspondence with St Augustine, who had wanted Jerome to translate the contemporary Greek version with Origen's corrections.[269] Jerome refused, and his works became the standard Latin Bible in the ninth century (called the "Vulgate" in the 1530s).

Like many early Church theologians, Jerome believed that the Bible required allegorical, not literal, interpetation. Although Jerome was not an original thinker in theology, he was a man of letters and employed Greek philosophy to serve Christianity. Philosophy was useful as long as it was subordinate to Christian faith.[270] During his early life, Jerome denounced pagan learning, but apparently tempered his dislike over the years as long as pagan literature was in the service of faith. His other contribution was as a zealous defender of the monastic life.[271] As a result of his unpopular sarcasm and invective qualities, however, Jerome was forced to flee Rome to Bethlehem, where he lived the remainder of his complex life.

St Augustine of Hippo[272] (354–430): the greatest philosopher of Christian antiquity

It is loving faith which *prepares* the mind for reason.   Augustine[273]

Without doubt, Augustine was the greatest Church Father and scholar of Christian antiquity. He thought of himself not as a philosopher, but as a theologian. William James called him "the first modern man".[274] No Christian scholar in the West, apart from St Paul, was more influential in spreading the word of God. Augustine's doctrines include: a theory of knowledge (truth); the doctrine of soul, which linked sense to the intellect and spirituality; the nature of God; the Creation; a theory of time; and the doctrine of original sin. Augustine was a master of prose and the author of a staggering 105 books.[275]

Early life: restless wanderings
Augustine was born in North Africa[276] about 12 years after Jerome and 15 years after Ambrose. His father was a pagan for most of his life, but his mother was a devout Christian. Before converting, Augustine ventured down a number of roads, ranging from astrology to Manichaeism: a dualistic occult theosophy that rejected the Old Testament's one creator and saw matter as evil and spirit as good, with each having their own god fighting for dominance.[277]

211

Early in his adult life, Augustine became fascinated with Greek philosophy, and accepted Cicero's claim that philosophy was a means to happiness.[278] He became interested in the Greek works on logic and valid inference, and in Stoic ethics. The philosopher he most admired (and later criticized) was Plato. The "true" universals in mind were more real to Augustine than the particulars in sense. Augustine rejected the Greek "scientific" attempt to explain reality in physical terms: "Let Thales depart with his water, Anaximenes with his air, the Stoics with their fire, Epicurus with his atoms", Augustine wrote in his *City of God*.[279]

Augustine and Neoplatonism

Augustine had interpreted Plato and Neoplatonism as arguing that the physical world was a mere shadow of a greater reality that was linked to the mind of God. Augustine's conversion to Neoplatonism occurred almost simultaneously with his conversion to Christanity at the age of 32.[280] The God of the Christians seemed to him very close to the God of the Neoplatonists, but with some major corrections. While Augustine was fascinated with Plotinus and Porphyry he rejected the "emanation" theory.[281] In addition, Neoplatonism explained evil by placing it in the realm of non-being *in the absence of God*, which Augustine did not find in either Stoicism or Manichaeism.[282] He believed that evil came from human disobedience: a falling away from God's work. Overall, Augustine found the harmonization between many parts of Neoplatonism and the Bible profoundly rewarding as a path to God.

Augustine's world began with God as "first cause" and proceeded to the three manifestations in the Holy Trinity.[283] Truth and certainty were direct outcomes of the nature of the Trinity.[284] Working on the analogy of the resurrected Christ, Augustine also believed in the resurrection of the physical body. Like the Jews and Christians, he believed that history was a linear process with a beginning and an end. The Creation was a free and deliberate act of God, and everything in the universe was God's creation. Augustine's writings on these subjects were to deny the dualistic heresies of the Manichaeans (to which he once belonged), the Donatists (who believed the Catholic Church was infected with mortal sin) and the Pelagians (who taught that sin was not inherited).

The path to God was through the soul

> It is God and my soul I want to know. Nothing else? No; nothing whatever.
>
> Augustine[285]

Augustine wrote these famous words in 386–7 to confirm his commitment to God. He viewed the soul as occupying the bridge between the higher realities we think, and the physical things we sense. Knowing an object as a tree is separate from knowing the tree itself. All knowledge was the work of the soul and was inseparable from reason. Soul was defined as the non-physical "substance endowed with reason and fitted to the body".[286] All human beings were thinking souls. This was quite different from Plotinus, who taught that the soul emanated from Mind. For Augustine, all human souls were "created" by God at conception, rather than emanating in some hierarchical fashion, as Plotinus had it.[287]

Through faith and mental training, the soul provided the path to God. To get there, one must separate the mind from everything physical. However, there were limits. God could never be "fully" known, only experienced. He was beyond knowing because of the limitations of finite human minds to understand the infinite and the eternal. Nor could human beings know the exact nature of "soul" or how God created it.[288] Augustine viewed Christianity as the inward purification of the soul through Jesus Christ and the word of God. By knowing Jesus, everyone could discover the eternal wisdom of God.[289]

Faith, reason and absolute truth

Understanding is the reward of faith. Seek therefore that you understand in order that you may believe, but believe in order that you may understand.　　Augustine[290]

Augustine viewed Christian faith as authoritative because of divine revelation. Christian faith demanded the act of will separating it from the older Greek *pistis*. Without faith, reason was powerless. Philosophical reason was always the mistress to the Scriptures and the Catholic tradition. Not only was Christian faith a gift from God, as St Paul taught, but it was inseparable from trust and goodness.[291] Faith was what distinguished the truth from belief. One of Augustine's favourite sayings from the Old Latin Bible was "Believe in order that you may understand",[292] which led thirteenth-century Aquinas to write: "Whenever Augustine, who was imbued with the doctrines of the Platonists, found in their writings anything consistent with the faith, he adopted it: and whatever he found contrary to the faith he amended."[293]

Augustine distinguished "truth" from "what is true" (e.g. a physical object) by arguing that the former cannot perish, whereas true things can.[294] Understanding truth in the Bible required training; its complex linguistic structure was God's way of challenging those seeking him out.[295] He claimed the inconsistencies provided its readers with facets of truth waiting further discovery. The role of religion was to engage the mind in seeking deeper and deeper truths, and ultimately to an inner illumination from God.[296] Mind could only be known by mind, which is why prayer was so important.[297]

Music and mathematical truths

Like the Pythagoreans and Plato, Augustine was fascinated with music and wrote six books on the subject.[298] Music assisted in bringing out meaning where words failed. Augustine was amazed how the mind could recall music without actually hearing the sounds, which he further used to support the notion of the soul's "transcendent" nature.[299] In his sixth book, *On Music*, Augustine claimed that mathematical principles were the basis of God's creation and underlay its order, harmony and beauty. Notwithstanding Augustine's expressed dislike for natural philosophy, it was his deep conviction about mathematics and order that provided part of the impetus for the development of modern science some one thousand years later. To Augustine, God was not nature but the unifying force behind nature. So for him, some knowledge of nature was important to understand the revealed word of the Bible, and the study of Greek philosophy was entirely appropriate for this purpose. Augustine anticipated the late medieval philosopher-theologians in realizing that when human beings endeavour to understand nature, they are experiencing God.[300]

Proof of God's existence

> All agree that God is what they place above all other things.   Augustine[301]

Augustine's proof of God's existence began with conscious judgements on truth and on the belief that there was something higher than reason.[302] To know anything truthful, good or beautiful, Augustine argued, we must first have a standard. This standard must be an absolute, eternal truth that exists and is superior to our minds. After establishing the reality of an eternal truth in his *De Libero Arbitrio 2*, Augustine logically progressed from world order and proceeded to God.[303] In the end, Augustine's proof was an extension of the Neoplatonist argument for the reality of universals. The universals were eternal, absolute truths of a transcendent moral type equated with concepts such as good and justice, or the mathematical truths that describe the universe and are equated with the "thoughts in the Mind of God". The inference was that "God's thoughts exist, therefore God exists".[304] Anyone denying God must first deny certainty in knowledge and virtue.

Augustine's proof contained elements of faith, revelation and solid philosophical argument. A major difference between Augustine's argument and the older Greek thinking was that, for Augustine, God cared for His creations; He was not only good for human beings *but was good to them*.[305] God's love for and separation from his creations were Christianity's great successes over Neoplatonism and Stoicism.

The meaning of time: what was God doing before He created the world?

> On the other hand, if before Heaven and Earth there was no time, what is meant by the question "What were You (God) doing *then*?" If there was not any time. There was not any "then".   Augustine[306]

Augustine's God was timeless and transcendent; he stood eternally outside the flow of time. To the famous question "What *is* time?", Augustine answered "If no one asks of me, I know; if I want to explain it to a questioner, I do not know."[307] On further asking "What was God doing before He made Heaven and Earth?", Augustine light-heartedly answered, "(God) was getting Hell ready for people who pry too deep".[308] Augustine knew this was a nonsense question because the words "before the creation" have no meaning if time was co-created with Heaven and Earth. Using similar logic, God did not create the universe sooner because there was no "sooner". Augustine was quite happy to accept that time and matter were created "out of nothing", as an act of faith supported by reason.[309] The creation did not proceed from the "substance" of God, as in Plotinus's emanation theory; it was the "act" of an instant, marking the beginning of time.

God and world redemption

Just as ancient Near Eastern and Greek cultures believed world harmony was maintained by divine action, Christian thought introduced God's grace. Grace was the free act of a merciful God to alter the course of events for some greater good.[310] The loss of life from a plague, an earthquake, lack of food, cyclone or a tidal wave was really "good" if viewed from the vantage point of God's overall plan.[311] Such events were God's warning to human beings to repent before it was too late. God's grace was the ultimate source of good perfecting nature.[312]

Augustine's God was separated not only from His creations but also from the rule of grace.[313] Grace accounted for the unexplained changes in the normal running of the world. Augustine viewed the unexplained changes as lying not outside the natural laws but within God's rule of grace.[314] Nature was not, therefore, self-regulating, as twenty-first-century science posits.

God and human redemption: the doctrine of "original sin"

> Sin loomed large in the Christian view of the world. Adam's legacy to his descendents was the original sin and that in itself made them worthy of damnation.   J. H. Lynch[315]

The rule of grace also extended to human beings. Augustine believed that all human beings were bound to the sin of Adam.[316] Sin was that special form of evil connected to the misuse of free will.[317] Free will was the basis of moral conduct in deciding right from wrong. As soon as Adam and Eve had committed the original sin by taking the first bite of the apple, every human being thereafter inherited their moral disease. The chance for human immortality[318] was lost for ever. Before Augustine found Christianity, he described himself as "crooked and sordid, bespotted, and ulcerous".[319] Human beings can only become loving, good and ethically free through God's grace. Salvation was also a gift of grace that came from the soul after death as one ascended towards pure reason and God.

Unfortunately, Augustine never discloses who were to be saved. Apparently, the lucky ones discovered their destiny at death, and the rest of humanity was damned to hell.[320] There was nothing anyone could do about their fate, no matter how well they lived. Augustine's interpretations of the original sin and predestination were highly controversial. His most outspoken critic was the Irish monk Pelagius (c.354–c.418), who taught that human salvation *could be* attained through a person's good deeds in life. Otherwise, Pelagius argued, Jesus's crucifixion was without purpose. Immortality was a matter of personal choice, not of predestination. Adam's fault lay in his example, but this did not infect the entire human race;[321] people could escape by free choice. Augustine partly agreed with Pelagius that humanity had free choice not to sin, but he steadfastly believed that each individual forfeited all rights *after* the fall of Adam. In Augustine's world, everyone was born free and guiltless but suffered from moral sin.[322]

However, Augustine maintained that human beings had elements of dignity and greatness evidenced by their inventions and discoveries in agriculture, arts and exploration (*City of God*[323]). Through ascetic restraint, and by seeking wisdom, the soul can ascend to its true fulfilment, which Augustine called "the enjoyment of God".[324] Importantly, he made a clear distinction between the creation of human beings and the Fall; the Fall was only concerned with the rise of humanity, not its origins. To argue otherwise, Augustine would have directly challenged the entire significance of Genesis 1:31.

Human beings as the source of evil

For Augustine, evil was sin and suffering and was the result of human beings making free choices in the absence of good. God was not the creator of evil, nor did evil come from matter, as Plotinus had taught. Augustine preferred to think of evil as the soul's "weakness", which, when left unchecked, was capable of sinking to "pride, envy and carnal things" as Augustine had experienced before his conversion.[325] The soul's predisposition to sin arose because it was created "out of nothing" and lacked perfection. Human beings thus possessed an inherent tendency to slip back into nothingness, as did the world order.[326]

Evil in the world arose from a lack of willingness to fulfil God's will and accept God's help. Evil in the world, in a metaphysical sense, arose now and again from the loss of cosmic order and harmony. Although world order was an expression of God's creation and his rationality, it was not perfect because only God was perfection. The world's own determinate inclinations were responsible for the disorder or descent to non-being. This lack of perfection is very different from the moral evil discussed above for human beings, which was an action against God's will. Augustine's metaphysical evil and the idea of being (order) and non-being (disorder) have parallels in Plato's concept of divine mind and necessity as a possible literary abstraction of good and evil, respectively. Divine mind was Plato's supreme god and was equated with good, whereas necessity was an "impersonal" disordered property of the world (sometimes called "the wandering cause").

The Church as the seat of religious authority

Augustine regarded all civil authorities as serving God's providence, and effective only as far as each leader acted justly. Like Ambrose, Augustine maintained that the Church was the seat of religious authority, and the sole dispenser of the divine grace that guaranteed human and world salvation. The Church was the place, through the sacraments and the liturgy, where Christians united with God; where the major Christian beliefs were re-enacted or even recreated for individuals and groups.[327] It was the place to absolve post-baptisimal sins through acts of repentance, confession and self-sacrifice, although before AD 400 baptism was commonly deferred until near the end of life because of the formidable nature of the penances.[328] What made the Church holy, therefore, was not so much its character, but its purpose. Augustine's conception of the Church paved the way for the medieval papacy to become an absolute power for the next 600 years.

THE SHAPING OF EARLY CHRISTIAN THOUGHT: THE DEBT OWED TO THE GREEKS

It is crude, but not wholly inaccurate, to say that the classical period provided the tools of reason which were applied to faith, and have been ever since ... This is because the writings which formed the revelation of the Jews, together with those writings which, added to the Old Testament, formed the revelation for Christians, are not argumentative in the philosophical sense. P. Helm[329]

As we close the doors on Western antiquity, one feature that stands out in the development of early Christian thought is the profound debt it owed to Greek philosophy. As Christianity became more popular in the West, Western philosophy took on a greater religious role. Through its logic, reason, dialectic and allegory, Greek philosophical argument helped to define doctrine and systematize Christian theology, and prepare defences against pagan censure. However, as we have shown, not all scholars were in agreement about how much Greek philosophy was necessary to help defend the faith.

Christianity's response to Greek philosophy

Paul Helm has proposed that there were at least three broad Christian responses to Greek philosophy.[330] The first was the "supplanting" strategy, whereby Neoplatonism was extended and adapted to accommodate the Christian God and his creations. It appeared in some of the writings of Justin the Martyr and Augustine, where the Christian God had striking similarities to Plato's supreme god. Both the Old Testament Genesis and Plato's *Timaeus* taught of a world created by God and dependent on Him. Using this approach, Christianity fulfilled and superseded the wisdom of the Greeks.

The second response to Greek philosophy was more radical and Helm calls it the "confrontational" strategy.[331] It is best illustrated in the views of Tertullian, who viewed Greek philosophy as the "mother of heresy": "What has Jerusalem to do with Athens" or "the Academy with the Church?"[332] Using clever sophistry, Tertullian wrote scornfully about the ability of philosophers to discern truth from falsehood. He believed that Christians should eschew the devil of paganism and demanded a total separation of philosophy and theology. He also objected to orthodox Christians attending public shows, serving in the army and civil service and even going to school.[333] Faith to Tertullian meant exclusive devotion to God.

The third response to Greek philosophy, and by far the most common, was the "fortifying" strategy, where Neoplatonism was used to help build and buttress Christian theology. Many ideas and concepts, such as the "*logos*", "substance", "being", "non-being", "elements" and "essence", were borrowed from the Greeks to help formulate, promote and defend Judeo-Christianity. The "fortifying" strategy began with Philo of Alexandria. Over the next four centuries, the writings of the apologists Clement of Alexandria and Origen and the Latin Church fathers Ambrose and Augustine contained many further developments and interconnections between Neoplatonism and Christianity.

Faith and reason

Despite the widespread belief among the Christian scholars that some early Greek philosophers covertly plagiarized the sacred Hebrew documents, there were fundamental differences between the two modes of thinking. In general, Christian philosophy's self-imposed boundaries were narrower than those of Greek philosophy. Although the Christian apologists and the Latin Church fathers used the Greek power of logic, dialectic reasoning and allegory with equal effectiveness, their arguments always reached a conclusion predetermined by their faith. That is, Christian scholars framed their reality around their historical road to God, revelation, prophecy and divine creation, as prescribed in their sacred texts.

The earlier Greek philosophers, in contrast, began their search by seeking wisdom in knowledge or *epistēmē*, and journeyed down whichever path they were steered to by logic and reason. These different roads to God admitted many more starting-points, from which the Greek philosophers built different realities and truths. The Western philosophical tradition was always reinterpreting, reinventing and challenging the starting-points and boundaries.[334] Plato, Aristotle and most of the Presocratics serve as good examples. Unlike Christianity, the first principles of Greek philosophy were always open to doubt, which led to a myriad of worldviews and perceptions of a supreme god. In early Christian doctrine, faith set the boundaries, not reason. Reason was the servant to faith, never its master.

Most theologians, however, did accept Plato's concept of God's transcendence, but rejected his doctrine of transmigration of souls. Most accepted the Stoics' ethical good but rejected their pantheistic, materialistic and deterministic worldview. Most agreed with Aristotle's "first cause" but not his eternal world, or sublunary sphere of natural causes without divine providence. The world and matter had not been around for ever, but were created by God, who controlled world events through his "essence" or his "will". By the end of the Greco-Roman period, the Greek God of reason (without a "will") was of little significance in the West; nor were the older mystery gods of the polytheistic religions in the Near East and West. What had been part of human religious experience for centuries, if not millennia, was regarded by Christians and the Church as gross superstition. Christianity had superseded myth as the bona fide way of ordering and harmonizing the Western experience.

Greek *paideia* and the rise in Christianity in the West

As mentioned earlier in the chapter, Christianity did not attract mass conversions overnight; rather its teachings slowly percolated through a highly structured Roman social matrix known in Greek as *paideia*.[335] *Paideia* was an advanced learning culture that operated in an education system within the Roman upper classes and was associated with the humanistic ideals of courtesy, virtue and self-control. As cultural historian Peter Brown (b. 1935) wrote, *paideia* was "the exquisite condensation of hard-won skills of social living – the one, reliable code that governed the behaviour of the powerful".[336] And it was within these ranks that the growing interest in Christianity was fostered, particularly as Roman leaders began to rely more heavily on Church leaders for advice on social and religious matters. Indeed, it was the *paideia* culture that eventually led to the conversion of emperors Constantine in the early fourth century, and later Theodosius I. These conversions set the stage for further intellectualization, popularization and institutionalization of Christianity in the West.

To conclude a complex story, the relationship between Greek philosophy and early Christianity was indeed a profoundly rich and rewarding one. Philosophical speculation and an individual's mastery of argument, allegory and rhetoric were not obstacles to the rise of Christianity, but vehicles for the development of a systematic theology. The marriage was, in part, born out of a process of harmonizing the biblical evidence to form a coherent worldview in a moral framework. However, within theology's highly prescribed framework, doctrinal "interpretation" suffered exactly the same epistemological problems as those that confronted earlier Greek philosophy in separating truth from falsehood. The difference was that the final arbiter of truth in theology was the authority of the early Church, and any hints of dissent were seen as arising from either heretics or pagan philosophers.

Power tends to corrupt and absolute power corrupts absolutely.
Lord Acton (1834–1902)[1]

CHAPTER 7
Medieval Christendom: faith and reason

THE MIDDLE AGES: HEIR TO THREE CULTURES

A common thread underlay all the activity of medieval society: the importance of
Christian beliefs and Church doctrine. The entire period can be characterised as one
with a unifying and forceful set of Christian ideas about moral and intellectual conduct
which were considered to be the foundation of all human activity.   B. B. Price[2]

Following the decline of the Roman Empire, western Europe entered a period we now
call the Middle Ages,[3] a period that extends roughly from the sacking of Rome to the
Italian Renaissance (Ch. 8). The idea of the Middle Ages developed gradually in the
fourteenth century from Petrarch and the Italian humanist's attack on the Augustinian
view of history, which had dominated Western thought for nearly 1000 years.[4] The
Middle Ages was the heir to three distinct cultures: European Christendom in the West
and Byzantium,[5] and Arabic Islam[6] in the East. It was from the multifaceted exchange
between these highly heterogeneous cultures that eventually gave birth to modern
Western civilization.[7] The long period is normally divided into the early Middle Ages
(*c*.500–*c*.1050) and the high Middle Ages (*c*.1050–*c*.1450).

- **The early Middle Ages.** The early Middle Ages or "Dark Ages"[8] were
characterized by barbarian conquests, political anarchy, severe economic dislocation, invasion, incursion, diffusion, East–West conflicts and transcontinental
migration. Against all odds, the Church began rebuilding Europe and the popes,
bishops, priests and monks quickly gained respect from the barbarian warlords
and their armies.[9] Indeed, the strategic alliances formed between the Catholic
Church and the warlords were the threads that held western Europe together.[10]
One remarkable peace settlement in the sixth century was between St Gregory
the Great and the aggressive Lombards.[11] In the late sixth century, Gregory, now
pope, also allied the papacy to Benedictine monasticism,[12] and proclaimed God
and the Church the sole mediators of saving grace.[13] The question in the

monasteries changed from "What is a Christian?" to "How should a Christian live and behave?"

The monasteries also became the main centres of political and philosophical thought as well as centres of agriculture, arts and crafts and teaching institutions. Since books of learning were scarce, many were copied from Neoplatonic distortions of the Greek classical literature, particularly of Aristotle.[14] Most of these mistranslations were not recognized until the twelfth and thirteenth centuries, when the original works by Aristotle (and others) were rediscovered in western Europe.[15]

- **The high Middle Ages.** The high Middle Ages were less tumultuous but nonetheless spirited. Beginning around 1050, town life, trade and commerce began to develop in western Europe as the Roman papacy became more secular.[16] At different times during the eleventh and twelfth centuries, the Church joined forces with a number of European armies to reclaim Spain and the Holy Land from the Arabs.[17] The Crusades, as they became known, partly unified western Europe, and were associated with increased trade and learning between the East and West.[18] Educational reform witnessed the rise of the first universities and their expansion of learning beyond theology into natural philosophy (a prelude to natural science) and into the broader fields of medicine, politics and architecture.[19]

One is left with a feeling that by the end of the Middle Ages there was a new western Europe with extraordinary political and intellectual vigour. As a result of townspeople searching for new political and intellectual freedoms, the Church became more decentralized and responded by becoming more authoritarian and dogmatic. The Church's response to changing times met strong resistance and some of its most outspoken critics were its own younger theologians.

This chapter discusses the new learning and scholarship that swept over western Europe. As with the rise of early Christianity, medieval Europe owed a profound intellectual debt to Greek philosophy in all its varied forms: first Neoplatonic and then Aristotelian influence. Neoplatonism was already present in the writings of the early Latin Church fathers and continued in Boethius and Eriugena, Islamicized by Al-Kindi and Al-Farabi, Avicenna and Averroes (and many others), and developed in the later writings of Peter Abelard and Anselm of Canterbury. After the thirteenth-century rediscovery of Aristotle's original corpus, the writings of the theologians took a major turn, exemplified in the works of Aquinas, Grosseteste, Bacon and Ockham. It was within this academic culture that the new attitude towards the world of sense and natural science developed. Of lasting importance, natural science was viewed no longer as inferior to natural theology, but as complementary to it.[20] The attitude towards natural science began to shift in the twelfth and thirteenth centuries as many theologians taught that God had conferred on nature the power and ability to cause things, and these harmonious, lawful, well-ordered causes could be investigated without conflict with the Scriptures.

CHRISTIAN NEOPLATONISM: "A CANDLE IN THE DARK"

Scholars of the early Middle Ages had no direct contact with the sources which could have transmitted to them the fundamental questions, arguments and theories of ancient philosophy. Their direct reading of Plato was limited to an incomplete translation of one dialogue, the *Timaeus*; Aristotle's philosophical works – as opposed to his logic – began to become known only in the mid-twelfth century.   J. Marenbon[21]

Neoplatonic philosophy in late antiquity, defined as a synthesis of the major currents in Greek philosophy and oriental religious and mystical spirit, continued to have a profound influence in the Middle Ages. Its immense explanatory power fit rather neatly into religion and assisted scholars with some of the deep theological mysteries, ranging from the gradations of reality, the soul, angels, the Fall and the Incarnation to the absolute good and truth in God. The Greek concept of *logos* continued to be a key means to connect the world of sense to the human soul and thus to God. Two extraordinary scholars who kept the Neoplatonic flame alive were Boethius and John Scotus Eriugena of Ireland. Other influential thinkers were Claudianus Mamertus (d. *c.*473) (a Gallo-Roman theologian strongly influenced by Augustine), St Gregory the Great (the fourth Latin Church father), Cassiodorus (*c.*490–*c.*580) (Boethius's immediate successor), St Isidore of Seville (*c.*560–636), St Bede the Venerable (*c.*672–735) and Alcuin of York (*c.*735–804) (appointed Abbot of St Martin's at Tours by Charlemagne, where he formed a model monastic school).[22]

Boethius (c.480–c.525): in the classical tradition

The execution of Boethius marks the close of an era for the historian of philosophy in a way far more absolute than it could do for the investigator of political or more broadly cultural events.   J. Marenbon[23]

Boethius was born into Roman aristocracy shortly after 480. He was a Christian–Stoic–Platonic scholar who wanted to revitalize the old Roman secular and Christian cultures.[24] There is some doubt whether he was a Christian, but there is no doubt about his passion for philosophy and theology.[25] Boethius read and wrote commentaries on Greek logic, arithmetic, science, medicine, music and theology. The classic works of great interest to him were those of Plato and Aristotle, perhaps Archimedes' "mechanics", Euclid's "geometry", Ptolemy's "astronomy" and Galen's "biology and medicine", as well as numerous other medical texts and astrological books.[26] Boethius' original intent was to harmonize Plato's *Dialogues* with the works of Aristotle but, unfortunately, he failed to complete the task. He did, however, translate into Latin the texts on Aristotelian logic – *Categories* and the entire *Organon* – and these translations were used in the Middle Ages.

Boethius identified three areas of philosophy – *speculative* (the nature of things); *moral* (the "honourableness" of life); and *rational* (logic) – which all became part of the liberal education known as the trivium (three ways of knowledge[27]) in the Latin West.[28] Unlike Jerome, Augustine and Gregory the Great, who treated all education as direct instruments of Christianity, Boethius made no such claim. He broadened education by teaching the importance of judging the validity of an inference, emphasized mathematics (arithmetic, geometry, astronomy and music formed his quadrivium[29]) and taught that reason and revelation were related, but very different, ways of understanding the mystery of God.[30]

In recognition of Boethius's contribution to liberal education, King Theodoric appointed him Master of the Offices in his court in 522.[31] Unfortunately, not long after joining the court, he was found guilty of treason, a charge that he vigorously denied. Apparently, Boethius found himself embroiled in a scandal while assisting Senator Albinus, who was accused of conducting a treasonable correspondence with the eastern Emperor Justin I.[32] While in prison before his execution (c.525), Boethius wrote his lasting masterpiece *De Consolatione Philosophie* (*The Consolation of Philosophy*). In this great work of prose and verse, he paralleled his own wretched suffering in jail to the general suffering of humanity, remembering those days when he was free to contemplate the sun, moon and stars, and to understand their movements by the use of numbers.[33]

The Consolation of Philosophy also questioned God's providence and the Church's interpretations of the Scriptures. If God was the ultimate good, why does evil exist in the world? And why is virtue often punished and vice rewarded? Boethius showed by philosophical reasoning that God's providence was righteous, and that fortune, riches and fame were transient. His reasoning argued for a divine framework where God remains a foreknowing spectator of all world events, and grants rewards to the good and punishment to the wicked.[34] Boethius's work was the most widely circulated corpus of all early medieval writings. The original Latin version of *The Consolation of Philosophy* was translated numerous times during the Middle Ages into German, French, Italian, Spanish and Greek and later into English by King Alfred, Geoffrey Chaucer and Queen Elizabeth I.[35]

Charlemagne (742–814): the Carolingian Renaissance of the eighth century

It was not until the eighth and ninth centuries that greater calm returned to western Europe with the rise of Charlemagne, King of the Franks (768–814) and Emperor of the West (800–814).[36] Charlemagne rose to power through his military success and the Christianizing of the Saxon tribes of northern Germany and warring Lombards[37] of northern Italy.[38] His kingdom grew rapidly to the size of the old Roman Empire, and included France, Belgium, eastern Netherlands, Switzerland, much of Germany, Denmark, northern Italy and portions of northern Spain.

Charlemagne was quick to realize that social progress required educational and Church reform, and to this end he released a royal edict in 789 that instituted a programme to increase the moral and intellectual qualifications of the bishops.[39] The subsequent Carolingian Renaissance extended into all levels of society and also shifted the main centres of learning from the British Isles to the European continent. Recent scholarship indicates the movement produced far wider literacy than previously thought.[40] In a famous capitulary, Charlemagne passed a statute that "in every bishop's see, and in every monastery, instructions shall be given in the psalms, musical notation, chant, the computations of years and seasons, and in grammar".[41]

Charlemagne invited a number of expert scholars to help with his educational reform. Around 781, English scholar Alcuin of York (c.735–804) and his three assistants from Parma, in northern Italy, visited the monastic schools of Frankland. Alcuin was a theologian, teacher and reformer of education, not a philosopher.[42] He prepared textbooks and pedagogic dialogues on grammar, rhetoric, logic and parts of the Scriptures. He also wrote theological works summarizing Augustine's *De Trinitate* and was well read in Boethius. The Carolingian reform produced a generation of scholar-poets, historians, textual commentators, theologians and philosophers whose collective achievements began to rival those of late antiquity.[43] Renewed interest in Neoplatonic philosophy also came through the study of logic and theology.

The Church enthusiastically supported the reform to bring education and Christianity to everyone in the Carolingian Empire. Despite Charlemagne's Herculean efforts, western European society, however, remained fragile. Not long after his death the West slipped back into the hands of regional aristocracies after a series of invasions and migrations by the Norsemen (Vikings), the Muslims (mostly Arabs) and, later, the Magyars from the East.[44] Despite the calming efforts of men like Alfred the Great (849–899), western Europe as a whole did not recover for many centuries. The following excerpt from a medieval chronical of 884 gives a chilling account of society on the northern coast of Frankland:

> The Northmen [Danes and Norwegians] ceased not to take Christian people captive [but to] kill them, and to destroy churches and houses and burn villages. Through all the streets lay bodies of the clergy, of laymen, nobles, and others, of women, children, and suckling babies. There was not road or place where the dead did not lie, and all who saw Christian people slaughtered were filled with sorrow and despair.[45]

Two survivors: the Church and feudalism

The two survivors of the Carolingian Empire were the Church and feudalism. Feudal states[46] developed in the West Frankish monarchy in the middle of the ninth century.[47] Feudalism was western Europe's attempt to maintain social solidarity and was based on vassalage: the obligation of a lesser lord to a more powerful king or overlord in return for the right to a "fief", generally a property known as a feudal estate.[48] The feudal estate was a communal association, passed down from generation to generation and built upon the mutual loyalties between the overlord and lesser lords. The king was at the top, then lords, lesser lords and knights, followed by the peasants. In contrast to the concept of Greek citizenship to the State, feudalism emphasized personal allegiance to one's immediate landlord.[49]

Feudalism also influenced the Church; its leaders became powerful prince bishops who held secular as well as religious power and to whom lower clergy were bound.[50] The clergy were usually the sons of noblemen and were familiar with a long military heritage.

Eriugena of Ireland (c.810–c.877): "Nature is synonymous with reality and also with God"

Ironically, when the Carolingian Empire was on the verge of collapse, the Carolingian intellectual advancement in Europe was at its height.[51] Before Charlemagne,

Neoplatonism had almost vanished in the West. One shining light and a product of Charlemagne's revival programme was John Scotus[52] Eriugena. Eriugena was a philosopher and a theologian who presented a fresh blend of Greek metaphysics within the orthodox Christian position, and was arguably one of the most important thinkers in the Christian world between Augustine and Anselm.[53] He was commissioned by the court of Charlemagne's grandson, Charles I "the Bald" (823–77) to translate past Neoplatonic Greek patristic authors such as pseudo-Dionysius (480–510) and Christian writers Gregory of Nyssa (331–395) and Maximus the Confessor (c.580–622).[54]

Drawing on these literary sources and others, Eriugena developed his own theological system, which he described in his *Periphyseon* (*On the Division of Nature*).[55] He viewed reality as a cosmic process where all beings proceed from God and return to him. Three main features of his literary style were: his somewhat dismissive attitude towards history because he wished to free himself from the world of time and change; his allegorical use of the Scriptures; and his love of logic.[56] In this way, Eriugena tackled the genuine problems in philosophy rather than expounding Christian texts or dogma.

Eriugena believed the world was created in two stages: the intelligible world followed by the creation of the sensible world (the one around us).[57] "Nature" was a divine progression embracing every object of thought and sense.[58] Eriugena divided nature into four classes: (i) eternal God the creator; (ii) Ideas or archetypes that subsist in God (intelligible); (iii) the physical world (sense); and (iv) God, the End and Purpose of all things (final cause).[59] God's essence was therefore in all things: the beginning, the middle and the end. The bridge between "the one" and "the many" was the "divine *logos*" (reason).[60] In his *Periphyseon*, Eriugena wrote the following on this close parallelism between human and the divine:

> For just as God is both beyond all things and in all things – for He Who only truly is, is the essence of all things, and while He is whole in all things He does not cease to be whole beyond all things, whole in the world, whole around the world, whole in the sensible creature, whole in the intelligible creature, whole creating the universe, whole created in the universe, whole in the whole of the universe and whole in its parts, since He is both the whole and the part, just as He is neither the whole nor the part – in the same way human nature in its own world (in its own subsistence) in its own universe and in its invisible and visible parts is whole in itself, and whole in its whole, and whole in its parts, and its parts are whole in themselves and whole in the whole.[61]

Eriugena's all embracing concept of nature had a strong Neoplatonic pantheistic bias, without violating his strong Christian faith, at least in his mind. His attempt to understand the universe was bound within his metaphysical and theological frame of divine progression, which began and ended with God.[62] When Eriugena talked about God's creation "out of nothing", he equated nothing with God himself in the sense that he transcends all knowledge. In his other works Eriugena presented long, reasoned arguments why St Augustine's concept of original sin was not traceable to Adam and Eve. Eriugena appears to have sided with Pelagius, who argued that sin had its source in human beings making wrong "choices". Human salvation could be achieved by leading a good life, doing good deeds and loving God. Eriugena believed that the stories in the Bible must be taken not literally but allegorically. Although Eriugena was deeply Christian and viewed reason and revelation as two sources of truth, reason for him appeared to override orthodoxy when the two areas conflicted. He believed that philosophy could uncover the true meaning of faith. This was quite different from the epistemology of the apologists and early Church fathers. True philosophy for Eriugena was true religion and true religion was philosophy. On the doctrine of predestination (i.e. that God had destined most human beings for damnation in hell), Eriugena reasoned that God cannot "will" misery and that hell does not really exist. These views were condemned by the councils of Valence in 855 and Langres in 859, who described them as *Pultes Scotorum* ("Scots porridge") and *urn diaboli* ("an invention of the devil") respectively. There is much debate about how Eurigena died; one story, dating from the twelfth century, records that his students stabbed him to death with their pens.[63]

THE ARABIC CORPUS ENTERS THE WEST

The Greek learning which Islam acquired from Christendom and which, later, Christendom received from Islam, was to a greater or lesser extent transformed by the medium through which it passed … The contribution of Greek learning, transmitted through Islam, to the development of Christian philosophy, is so great it cannot be quantified … In part, this is because Western Christian and Muslim intellectuals almost never got together … Language was not, however, the only barrier between Latin and Muslim scholars. Muslims showed a general disdain for the West. The attitude persisted into the twelfth and thirteenth centuries when, for the first time, Western scholars had attained an intellectual level at which dialogue would have been possible … During the eleventh to thirteenth centuries, Latin Christendom developed a profound respect for aspects of Arab learning.   J. Johns[64]

We have to momentarily leave the West to introduce the Arabs. The Arabs are vitally important to our story because they embraced ancient Greek literature and Neo-platonism and passed them on in various forms to the West. The Arab corpus not only had a profound influence on later Christian philosophy and theology but, as we shall see, inspired the rise of Western science in the high Middle Ages.[65] To place the Arab contribution in perspective we have to return to the early seventh century.

As the Latin West was in cultural turmoil, the world of Islam in the East was thriving. The Arabs were united by a powerful and charismatic leader, Mohammed[66] of Mecca (*c.*570–632).[67] According to Islamic history, Mohammed's life was transformed at around the age of 40 when he frequented a mountain cave for devotional purposes. One story has a voice saying, "Mohammed, you are God's messenger". The voice was later identified as the angel Gabriel – "I am Gabriel and you are God's messenger" – who then ordered him to recite from a heavenly tablet, which later became part of Chapter 96 (verses 1–5) of the Koran.[68] Over the next two decades, between 610 and 632, God's word was revealed to Mohammed and formed the basis of the Koran, the sacred book of Islam.

Mohammed believed that God had sent him to deliver the "good news" to the Arab world. He was warned against worshipping idols or graven images, as was Moses on Mount Sinai.[69] Those who lived by the Koran were rewarded in paradise and those who didn't were punished in hell. To the people of Islam, Mohammed was the last great prophet after Abraham, Moses and Jesus. The God of Islam, Allah, was the same God as that of the Hebrews and Christians, but Islamic theology was firmly monotheistic without the elaborate a posteriori Christian Trinity (see Ch. 1).

Muslim expansion and conquest society

Mohammed taught that every Muslim had a sacred mission to spread Islam to unbelievers. Only in special circumstances did he urge a *jihad*, or "holy war", against the unbelievers as a part of God's plan.[70] Over the next few centuries, the Muslim leaders conquered Arabia, swept north into Syria and Persia, Egypt and North Africa and eventually northern India.[71] The next prize in sight was western Europe. The Saracen army[72] (Arab, mostly Muslims) defeated the Latin Christians of Spain in 712. They reached the Pyrenees but were forced back by Charles Martel, known as the Hammer, and the Frankish Army in the famous Battle of Tours (732).

The Arab Empire in the ninth and tenth centuries had expanded to nearly twice the size of the old Roman Empire.[73] The booty was not only land or material wealth but something more precious: knowledge. From the invasion of Mesopotamia (639–646) and Egypt (640–642) the Arabs learned about agriculture; from Syria (635–638) and Persia (633–651) they embraced Greek philosophy, science and medicine; and later from India (~1000) they learned about numbers, mathematics and astronomy.[74]

Arab scholarship and its debt to Neoplatonism

Arab philosophy was shaped by Neoplatonism, which was passed to them through Syria (Alexandrian) and southern Iran or Persia (Athenian).[75] The caliphs, Mohammed's non-prophet successors, collected and preserved every piece of advanced learning of antiquity they could get their hands on.[76] Unfortunately, many of the Greek philosophical texts turned out to be thirdhand translations.[77] For example, the famous *Theology of Aristotle* had nothing to do with Aristotle but was mostly a translation of Plotinus's *Enneads* 4–6, and Aristotle's *Liber de Causis* (*Book of Causes*) had its basis in the *Elements of Theology* by Proclus of the fifth century.[78]

Mistakenly, but quite understandably, the Arabs believed that Aristotle and Plato were in agreement on many fundamental philosophical issues.[79] This partly explains why aspects of Arab philosophy contained a complex mosaic of Aristotelianism, Neoplatonism and Platonism. Despite the literary obscurities, most Arab scholars appear to have been aware of the true Aristotle, particularly after Al-Farabi's work in the tenth century.[80] By the eleventh century, at least 80 Greek authors had been translated on a wide variety of subjects including astrology, astronomy, alchemy, magic, mathematics, geography and medicine.[81] It is important to stress, however, that Islamic philosophy did not grow on the back of Greek philosophy; it grew from the application of Greek thought as a methodology to Islamic subject matter and cultural pursuits.[82]

Islamic theology and philosophy as separate endeavours

In contrast to the Latin West, there was a clear demarcation between the Arab theologians and philosophers.[83] Many Arabic philosophers were independent as a group and did not take orthodox theology as their starting-point.[84] They preferred to follow the older Greek method "of research independent of dogma".[85] Thus the pursuit of Arabic philosophy was mostly a private affair and, not surprisingly, its clearer separation from Islamic theology (*kalam*) led to deep tensions among Arab theologians and philosophers (*falsafa*).[86]

By far the most outspoken and revered theologian was Al-Ghazali (1058–1111), who, in his *The Incoherence of the Philosophers*, strongly attacked the arguments of the philosophers by showing first how their own arguments did not hold up to the criteria of validity that philosophy itself advocated – the test of reason – and, secondly, that the conclusions they formed violated the fundamental principles of Islam.[87] He particularly singled out Al-Farabi and Avicenna. While conceding that they did not set themselves against Islam, Al-Ghazali believed they had denied the body's resurrection, had a defective view of God's providence and proposed a world *without a creation*.[88] If the world was co-eternal with God then his absolute transcendency and creative role were diminished. Al-Ghazali summed up his attack by claiming that the philosophers were forgetful of the higher degree of certainty in the faith articles of Islam.[89]

While Al-Ghazali raised important issues, not all Islamic philosophy could be as easily stereotyped as he had envisaged. For our discussion, we shall concentrate largely on those Arab philosophers who exerted the most influence on the revival of learning in the West. Two groups of Arab philosophers emerged: an eastern group, who flourished in Baghdad from the ninth to the twelfth centuries; and a western group in Spain from about the tenth to the twelfth centuries. After this time, interest in the so-called peripatetic tradition of Greek philosophy declined in the Islamic world but thrived in the Latin West.[90]

Al-Kindi of Bagdhad (*c*.801–873): revelation superior to philosophy

> Al-Kindi appears to be convinced that revelation and human reason ultimately come to the same conclusions although they follow different paths; he is prepared to subordinate philosophy to Scripture, and does not proclaim the absolute authority of philosophy as Al-Farabi does.   R. Walzer[91]

Al-Kindi is often called the first Islamic "philosopher of the Arabs", and he was responsible for establishing Neoplatonized Aristotelianism as a new discipline of learning.[92] Unlike Boethius and Eriugena, Al-Kindi knew little or no Greek. His overall goal was to defend the Koran against rival beliefs by maintaining that no conflict existed between faith and reason. In theology, Al-Kindi was interested in divine simplicity, unity and justice, the character of the divine agency, the creation, revelation, miracles and resurrection of the body.[93] In short, Al-Kindi, like the Islamic philosophers who followed him, *sought to harmonize a rational philosophical system with the teachings of Islam.*

Where conflicts arose, Al-Kindi followed orthodox Islam and acknowledged the superiority of the sacred writings and inspired prophecy of Mohammed.[94] Philosophy was always subordinate to "revealed" natural theology. Al-Kindi supported the cosmological argument for God's existence and the traditional idea that the universe was created "out of nothing" (including time).[95] Most of his philosophic successors, including Al-Farabi, Avicenna and Averroes, departed from this line and preferred Aristotle's explanation of an eternal universe and eternal matter.[96]

Another important aspect of Al-Kindi's philosophy was his attempt to explain the mind's ability to formulate ideas and seek the cause of things to better understand the world. "We do not find the truth we are seeking," he wrote, "without finding a cause."[97] To explain mind and formulate a theory of knowledge, Al-Kindi borrowed heavily from the Neoplatonic interpretation of Aristotle's "active" intellect.[98] The one thing Aristotle granted transcendence to was the intellect (*nous*), not Plato's eternal Ideas and soul. Aristotle separated the intellect into the "active" (outside the soul) and the "passive" (within the soul).[99] "Just as things can exist [in the mind] separate from matter", Aristotle wrote, "so what belongs to the intellect is separable."[100] The "active" intellect provided human beings with a *special kind of reason connected to the divine*, which separated them from other living creatures. As information was passed from the physical world to the abstract world – from the passive to the active intellect – matter and thought became pure form and divine.[101] For Aristotle, the soul was an integral part of a person as its form. And once the individual dies, the soul dies but not the "active" intellect, which lives for ever (Ch. 5).

Al-Kindi, like most Muslim philosophers, believed that the soul comprised non-rational and rational parts.[102] The non-rational part was divided into animal (and plant) souls, and managed the body. The rational part was divided into the practical and theoretical intellects (Fig. 7.1). The practical intellect concerned itself with

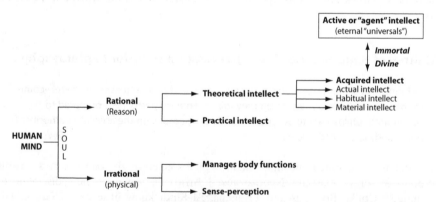

Figure 7.1 Soul in Islamic philosophy. Ordinary people can know something of the physical and spiritual worlds but the latter are limited to the images and allegories of religion. Philosophers are distinguished from everyone else in attaining much higher levels of knowledge. They have access to the universal premises from the acquired intellect's interaction with the external "active" or "agent" intellect "from outside" (Inati 1998a: 103). The application of the dialectic and logic using these universal premises leads to universal truths, which underpin "true" reality. The universals, as opposed to the sensible particulars, were the eternal Ideas that existed independently of things.

proper management of both the body and theoretical intellect (i.e. understanding the particulars); it was the rational soul *with its face downward*. The theoretical intellect, on the other hand, was responsible for true knowledge and could act by rational choice to grasp the eternal universals in their purest form; it was the rational soul *with its face upward*.[103] The universals, as opposed to the particulars, were the eternal Ideas that existed independently of things. Note here the blend of Platonic, Neoplatonic and Aristotelian dimensions in Al-Kindi's epistemology.

The theoretical intellect was itself divided into material, habitual, actual and acquired intellects, with the latter existing as the highest human state and the point of contact with the divine (Fig. 7.1). Al-Kindi agreed that the "active" intellect was an agent "from the outside" that activated the theoretical (acquired) intellect to form true knowledge. He did not, however, identify the "active" intellect with God, but with the lowest intelligence of the divine world, which he called the "first intellect".[104] Al-Kindi believed in the immortality of the individual soul and in the resurrection of the body.[105] The latter he acknowledged as an article of faith not reason.

Al-Farabi of Baghdad (*c.*875–950): revelation inferior to philosophy

Now truth – properly known to philosophers only – is reproduced for each nation and for the people of each city by those symbols which are most apt to be understood by them; but what is most apt to be understood is, in general, not the same among all nations; most, or a least part, of it varies. Hence the truth is expressed for each nation in symbols which are not the same as those used by any other nation. Thus is is possible that several excellent nations and several excellent cities exist whose religions are unlike – although they all have as their goal one and the same felicity and one and the same purpose.
Al-Farabi[106]

Al-Kindi was soon eclipsed by Al-Farabi, who was hailed by the Arabs as the "second teacher" (Aristotle himself being the "first").[107] Al-Farabi was also the "founder of Arab Neoplatonism".[108] He argued, as did Plotinus and the Neoplatonists, that philosophy was superior to religion. Truth was sought through strict philosophic demonstration and intuition (or insight), not from history, religion, revelation or prophecy.[109] By proposing this, he angered orthodox theologians like Al-Ghazali yet set much of the agenda between philosophical reason and faith for the next four centuries. Importantly, Al-Farabi did not intend to pit rational philosophy against the teachings of Islam, only to clarify the different roles of reason and faith in one's religious beliefs.

For Al-Farabi, *there was only one true philosophy, but many different religions suited to different people.* Philosophical truth was the same for everyone, but symbolic "revelatory" truths varied from place to place.[110] Al-Farabi believed that he had solved the deep problem of religious pluralism; the "first cause" of the Greeks was the same as the God of the Jews, Christians and Muslims. Earlier civilizations had called the "first cause" Zeus, the sun god Re, and so on down through time.[111] Al-Farabi's historical view had a similar precedent in Herodotus's canon of equivalence of gods, and was again adopted by Isaac Newton in the seventeenth century. Newton held that all the ancient people worshipped the same universal god under different manifestations and names in honour of their specific cultures and heritages (see Ch. 8).[112]

On human knowing, Al-Farabi distinguished three major parts of the theoretical intellect (slightly different from Al-Kindi): (i) material or potential intellect; (ii) actual intellect, which is activated by first principles; and (iii) acquired or educated intellect, which makes a person "divine". As with Al-Kindi, human beings did not actualize the universals themselves but required an external principle. The external "active" intellect was named by Al-Farabi "agent intellect" or "the giver of forms".[113] This was an important recurring theme in Islamic philosophical theology. Al-Farabi, like Al-Kindi and most Muslim philosophers, held that the world around us was necessary for true knowledge and that the universal Ideas were transmitted to us via the "agent" intellect that already contained them (Fig. 7.1). To reiterate, universal Ideas were eternal and existed *before* things, *in* things and *after* things. Human scholarship and imagination prepared the theoretical intellect to receive the universals from the "agent intellect". Once again we can see here the strong influence Plato and Aristotle had on Al-Farabi's thinking.

Al-Farabi also believed that the "agent" intellect was partly responsible for the symbolic truth in Islamic revelation and equated with the Koran's "faithful spirit" and "spirit of holiness" as portrayed by Gabriel to Mohammed.[114] Once first principles were received from the "agent" intellect, human beings could proceed towards true knowledge and happiness, and God, which could also be manifest in dreams. Al-Farabi's "hierarchy of being" placed God at the top, above a total of ten intellects, which emanated from him.[115] The tenth intellect was the "agent" intellect, which bridged the heavenly and physical worlds and from where the universal Ideas emanated to human beings and actualized the potentiality of knowledge.

On the question of the immortality of the soul, most Muslim philosophers believed that the non-rational part came into existence at birth and perished when the body died. The individual rational soul was different. Al-Farabi, Al-Kindi and Avicenna, but not Averroes, generally believed that all *individual* rational souls were immaterial, indestructible and immortal. For Al-Farabi, the basis for immortality of the rational soul was its ability to know the eternal aspects of the universe.[116]

Al-Farabi departed from Al-Kindi and orthodox Islam by holding that the world was not created "out of nothing". He believed, after Plotinus, that the world was part of the unwilled Neoplatonic emanation from the "first cause".[117] Al-Farabi understood the concept "out of nothing" as a symbolic description of a metaphysical process that was beyond human understanding.[118] The world was seen as eternally generated from the essence of God, who indirectly was responsible for everything through his emanation.

Avicenna of Persia (980–1037): towards a middle ground

[Avicenna] shows a deeper sympathy for mysticism than Al-Farabi and tries to explain it in philosophical terms. He also assesses the relation between Islam and philosophy in a way which reminds us of the Neoplatonic attitude to Greek religion: he neither subordinated philosophy to revelation – as did Al-Kindi – nor did he, like Al-Farabi, give the second place to Islam by upholding the primacy of reason.   R. Walzer[119]

Avicenna (Ibn Sina) was perhaps by far the most innovative Eastern philosopher to build on the Aristotelian–Neoplatonic foundations of Al-Farabi.[120] His autobiography tells that he reportedly read Aristotle's *Metaphysics* 40 times but it was not until he read Al-Farabi's assessment of it that understanding finally came to him.[121] He was also a distinguished physician,[122] a natural philosopher[123] and a scholar-in-residence at many Islamic courts. In metaphysics, he effectively bridged the rival tendencies between Aristotelian–Neoplatonic traditions and the creationist monotheism of Islamic theology.[124] One of his greatest achievements was the employment of syllogistic logic to preserve Aristotelian naturalism alongside the scriptural idea of the contingency of the world. Interpreting Islam in Aristotelian and Plotinian terms was the highest ideal anyone could accomplish in life.

For Avicenna, philosophy and religion commanded equal status *provided that religion was interpreted in philosophical terms.*[125] He denied, for example, the orthodox Islamic position that God created the world "out of nothing". Like Al-Farabi, he believed in the eternity of the world and of matter.[126] Belief in an eternal world should not be mistaken for pantheism. In Aristotelian terms, matter existed as pure potentiality and was quite independent of God (who was pure actuality).[127] God was the "first cause" and the source of all light, the highest intellect and the highest love, but he did not exist in all things.[128] He was responsible "indirectly" for everything through his successive emanations, which Avicenna believed did not violate the teachings of Islam.

Avicenna's main proof for God's existence appears to have developed from Al-Farabi's concepts of being, necessity and possibility (chance or contingency). God was an absolute "necessary being" and everything else existed according to a causal "emanative" plan.[129] Causality was added to the proof only after a long discussion about the intelligibility of the necessary and possible being.[130] The difference, therefore, between the possible and existent was that a "cause" is required for something to exist.[131] In broad outline, Avicenna's world was contingent in itself but necessitated through its causes, which extended all the way back to the highest cause of causes, and that was God.[132]

Avicenna added one more feature built on Aristotle's distinction between the nature of a thing and its existence.[133] That was that the world was composed of essences (or natures), which linked all the individual things we sense to the universal things we think.[134] Essence was the "nature" of a thing, and existence was the "being" of the thing. When you were born, your essence became conjoined with your existence. Avicenna's essence–existence and cause hypothesis was applied to everything except God, because God's essence was his existence. This sharp contrast of necessary and contingent existence, and the series of causes leading to God, greatly influenced Aquinas and Duns Scotus in the Latin West.[135]

The question remains: how was the world and its order emanated from God? According to Avicenna, God's first act was awareness of his own existence (the first intelligence conceived the necessity of its own existence) followed by other intelligences, for example, a celestial soul and body, which engaged in their own cognitive acts of diminished power, which eventually led to the world we sense. The final act in God's hierarchy was his tenth intelligence or "agent" intellect. Following Al-Farabi, the "agent" intellect not only produced the sublunary world but governed change and illuminated the human mind. The "agent" intellect was the principle that allowed the theoretical intellect to progress from potentiality to actuality. And the trained person must continually revisit the external "agent" intellect to refresh their knowledge because the soul lacked the ability to retain eternal Ideas itself.[136] Avicenna believed in the immortality of individual souls and that each soul survived according to the degree of perfection attained during its time in a body.[137] This was, for Avicenna, the real meaning of Islamic belief in resurrection. The body was not resurrected, only the soul.

Averroes of Cordova (1126–1198): three roads to one truth

Averroes' cosmology reveals a different perspective from that of Avicenna, whose emanation theory he criticised. Instead of viewing the universe as a series of emanations, Averroes sought to explain it in terms of the doctrines expounded chiefly in Aristotle's "Physics and Metaphysics", in terms of matter and form, potentiality and actuality and motion.

M. Haren[138]

Averroes (Ibn Rushd) was among the last of the great peripatetic Islamic thinkers who appeared about 300 years after Al-Kindi had formed the first bridge between Greek and Islamic philosophy in the East. He was not nearly as influential in the Islamic world as he was in medieval Europe.[139] A product of twelfth-century Islamic Spain, Averroes attempted a fresh account of integrating Aristotelian philosophy with Islamic thought. In the West, he became known as "the Commentator", an unfortunate label because it undervalued his important contributions to the understanding of the "true" Aristotle. Part of the problem was that Averroes's ideas were not easily reconcilable with Christian doctrine, which forced many Latin scholastics to rethink the relationship between philosophical reason and the teachings of faith. "Averroism", as it became known in the nineteenth and twentieth centuries, was a term used to broadly describe the influence of Averroes on Western thought.

Faith and reason

In an effort to reconcile philosophy and religion, Averroes cleverly adopted Aristotle's *Rhetoric* and showed how one could understand the Koran using three different proofs:[140] (i) the "revelatory" proof of God through persuasive symbolic language via revelation and faith, accepted by the uneducated masses; (ii) "theological" proofs, having premises that were provisional, not certain, and formed by using "purely" dialectic arguments of theologians, which combined reason and faith; and (iii) "philosophical" proof, the most rigorous, from demonstration using reason.[141] The third proof comprised scientific truths verifiable from logical deduction and the method of the philosophers. Averroes's three roads (revelation, theology and philosophy) all led to the same truth but were expressed differently according to the different method of attainment.[142]

Averroes saw no disharmony between faith and reason. Where disagreements arose in the analysis of the Koran, logical analysis showed them to be apparent, and they could be solved by interpreting the Koran allegorically.[143] Averroes knew that his position on seeking truth and the power of philosophy would anger most Arab theologians, and his book *The Incoherence of the Incoherence* was a direct rebuttal of theologian Al-Gazzali's book, which claimed among other things the certainty of revelatory truths beyond reason.[144]

The doctrine of double truth

Most Latin medieval scholars appeared to have misinterpreted Averroes's position on faith and reason by ascribing to him the doctrine of "double truth". This doctrine held that a proposition can be true in philosophy but false in religion, and vice versa.[145] That the world is eternal was true in philosophy but not in the Koran (or the Bible). This interpretation by Western scholars appears to be a total misrepresentation of Averroes. As mentioned above, he maintained that there were different roads to the same truth. To Averroes, the orthodox position that the universe had a beginning at time zero was only one of a whole range of possibilities based on religious symbolism and theological argument. Using reason, many different answers could be obtained and be wholly consistent with revelation and theology.[146] Both could offer equally valid views of the same truth.

God and the eternal world

Averroes, like Avicenna, was deeply interested in how things in the world achieved their existence. Everything was striving to become, which led him to conclude that all things "possible" must have an unmoved mover. His argument for the existence of God began with God as the first and final cause followed by a posteriori argument based on the requirement of causes for all physical phenomena. Averroes rejected the Plotinic emanationist models of Al-Farabi and Avicenna, and the subordinate intelligences in uniting matter and form.[147] God must be kept quite separate from contingent and accidental physical phenomena, although his essence is not totally unconnected with such phenomena. In Averroes's model, God's essence was part of the organization of the universe through its natural laws, an idea that was hugely influential in the West and stimulated interest in natural philosophy.

Averroes's cosmological argument for God's existence was as follows:

1. There are contingent things.
2. Contingent things always have causes.
3. If all such causes are contingent, they must have further causes and so on *ad infinitum*.
4. Therefore there must be a necessary cause.
5. If a necessary cause has a cause, then it too must have a cause and so on *ad infinitum*.
6. Therefore there must be an "uncaused" necessary cause, which is God.

A general point worth mentioning is that most "proofs" by the Islamic philosophers (as well as most medieval Christian and Jewish philosophers) were not designed to reinforce God's existence *per se* because his existence did not need to be proved. The "proofs" were more of a literary device for philosophical discourse showing a philosopher's skill in harmonizing philosophy with theology. A philosopher used the aspects of the dialectic and logical method that he believed were the most powerful to buttress his assertions about other issues in philosophy and theology. The same use of literary form was masterfully employed by Anselm and Aquinas, although Aquinas was convinced that human reason could prove that God exists (see later).

Denial of the eternal existence of individual souls

Averroes, like most Islamic philosophers, sought the relationship between seeking meaning about the world and a philosophy of the human mind, including immortality of the soul and the afterlife. Like most, he asserted that the acquired intellect (part of the theoretical intellect) was the highest "human" state of knowing and the point of contact between human beings and the divine (see Fig. 7.1). As mentioned earlier, the one thing that separated human beings from animals was their ability to reason, and divine contact was assured through the sublunary "agent" intellect from which human beings acquired higher knowledge and could experience the power of God. This knowledge was accessible to the ordinary person in metaphors, images and allegories of religion, but deeper meaning required the superior training of the metaphysician. In Averroes's case, enlightenment came through understanding revelation, theology and philosophy.

Averroes's attempt to understand the workings of the human mind led to a major departure from most of his Islamic colleagues. Whereas Al-Kindi, Al-Farabi and Avicenna believed that the "agent" or "active" intellect was separate from the material intellect, Averroes argued the opposite. Averroes believed that the material intellect was not material (or physical) at all. When the "active" intellect became embodied in human beings at birth, it was the material intellect. Averroes believed that the material intellect operates through its own act of understanding "material" forms and then progresses to the more abstract, immaterial, eternal and "intelligible" forms. They are one and the same, which is why he argued that the material intellect must be numerically "one" for all human beings. The "one" means that the theoretical intellect encompassing the material, habitual, actual and acquired intellects (see Fig 7.1) was immaterial, eternal and common to all human beings.[148] This view had major repercussions as it denied the eternal existence of individual souls. Life after death was generally thought to occur when the *individual* rational soul was released after death. However, Averroes reduced the concept of innumerable *individual* souls to "one" and common to all human beings. In Averroes's model, if anything was to survive death it must be the species, not the individual. In addition to denying the eternal existence of individual's souls, he believed that personal immortality could not be understood by the philosopher or philosophy.[149] Philosopher Oliver Leaman (b. 1950) wrote the following on Averroes's controversial view:

> For the philosopher, this should not be understood ... as the individual survival of a person after his or her death in an environment rather like the environment of the world of generation and corruption. Once our body perishes, there is no sense in thinking of the continuing existence of the individual soul, since the soul is just the form of the material body, and once the latter disintegrates, there is no longer any matter to be informed by the soul.[150]

Averroes believed that people are combinations of soul and body, and in the absence of a body the meaning of a person disappears. For his controversial views on the mind, body and afterlife, Averroes was accused of cultivating the philosophy of the ancients at the expense of true Islamic faith and was exiled to a place near Cordova, and then to Morocco. Arab leaders in the East and West ordered the burning of many of his books on logic and metaphysics, and the Church in the Latin West vigorously condemned his doctrines of immortality, world eternity and double truth. Despite this rather harsh response, two important legacies of Averroes remain: first, his view that the human soul and intellect did not involve an immediate transcendent agent, thus rejecting past Neoplatonic "emanation" theories; and secondly his view that religions were not absolute but evolving traditions, profoundly shaped by epistemological influences from other traditions.[151]

Jewish scholars within Islam

> If philosophy was capable of coexistence with the Koran, why should it not also be capable of harmonising with the Old Testament and the Law? As the Jews were not outcasts from Islamic society but, to a large extent, members of it, it was only natural that intellectual trends in Islam should make their influence felt in Jewish circles.
>
> F. C. Copleston[152]

Islamic thought also influenced Jewish scholarship, which was transmitted later to the Latin West. Judaism, in its rabbinic form, did not disappear after the destruction of Jerusalem in AD 70 because many Jews fled to Rome, France, Spain, Asia Minor and the Byzantine Empire.[153] For centuries, Jewish religion survived and indeed flourished in small, isolated pockets in these areas.[154] Jewish scholarship received a further injection during the Arab conquest of Spain and Sicily.[155] The exchange was facilitated when the Arabs provided Jewish scholars with translations and commentaries on Greek Neoplatonic philosophy. Some Jewish philosophical treatises were written in Arabic, reinforcing the close relationship between the two cultures.[156] We shall now consider two of the most highly respected Jewish philosophers from Spain – Avicebron and Moses Maimonides – to illustrate the Judeo-Arabic symbiosis.

In the eleventh century, Avicebron (Ibn Gabirol) (c.1021–1058/70) was deeply influenced by the Neoplatonic conception of reality and by the Aristotelian concepts of matter and intellect.[157] He proposed three grand divisions of the universe: (i) God, (ii) his will and (iii) the universal being composed of matter and form.[158] The act of free will appeared between God and the Creation, thus avoiding the apparent pantheistic emanation theory held by many of the Islamic philosophers. Avicebron wanted a clearer separation between God and his creations. God was "the ineffable One" *who issued his "will" to create and produce "form" and matter (as potentiality)*. Matter was separate from the actuality in God. Since everything came from God's will, human beings were no longer reliant on the external "agent" intellect. Knowledge of the world (matter and form) did not furnish certain truths; rather it was a road to better understand God and his creations.[159] Avicebron believed that the scientific unravelling of a mystery could illuminate the hidden sense found in the allegorical exegeses on Genesis 2:8 and Genesis 28:12.[160] Contrast this attitude with the majority of theologians in the early medieval Latin West who failed to appreciate the intrinsic power of natural science to unlock God's secrets.

Moses Maimonides of Cordova (*c.*1135–1204) lived in the twelfth century and was a contemporary of Averroes. Maimonides was not only a philosopher but a theologian, legal codifier and jurist. As a product of the times, Maimonides was greatly influenced by Islamic Neoplatonic and Aristotelian thinking.[161] He was mainly concerned with bridging philosophy and religion. Where deadlocks arose, the theologian in Maimonides sided with revelation and Torah scripture and traditions.[162] Thus he rejected the Islamic eternity of the universe and the belief that matter was coeternal with God.[163]

Using persuasive arguments, Maimonides held that the Islamic eternalist's world was wrong. And if God was causally connected to constant emanations in the world, he must be a constant creator.[164] He concluded that aspects of Islamic natural philosophy were not only unintelligible but irrational, as theologian Al-Ghazali had presupposed. Indeed, Maimonides posits that Aristotle could not have argued for the eternity of the world, because this was not something for which evidence could have existed.[165] Maimonides supported his monotheistic views by proposing a series of 26 proofs of God, beginning with the cause of motion and ascending to the prime mover or God.[166] God was pure perfection and absolute simplicity. When God is associated with a variety of phenomena, we are not referring to God, but to the multiplicity of God's *effects*.

Maimonides acknowledged that philosophy could not prove all the faith-claims of Judaism but equally he argued it could not disprove them either.[167] In case of doubt, he appealed to common sense and to Scripture.[168] Some of Maimonides' views were plagued by controversy. For example, he appears to have adhered to Aristotle's argument (and Averroism) and rejected the theory of personal immortality – the soul was not a separate entity from the body; it was only reason that was immortal and the direct human link with the divine.[169] In his early twenties, around 1148, he was forced into exile to Egypt by the new Almohad rulers (an anti-Jewish Muslim sect) of Spain.[170] Most Jewish scholars considered his Jewish Averroism heretical and eventually persuaded Christian authorities to argue against him. Aquinas, however, highly valued some of Maimonides' brilliantly well thought out arguments and used them to harmonize Aristotle's philosophy and the Christian scriptures.[171]

The legacy of Islamic–Jewish philosophy: reason, revelation and reality

Many Western commentators on Islamic philosophy take the conflict between reason and revelation as its central issue. This is often symbolised as the struggle between Athens and Jerusalem, or between philosophy and religion. While this is far too crude to be an accurate description, it does raise an important issue which has been discussed ever since Islamic philosophy began and which is still a live issue today in the Islamic world. If revelation tells believers everything they need to know, why bother to explore the same topics with reason?   O. Leaman[172]

A fascinating aspect of the Muslim–Spanish phase of Islamic philosophy, and later Jewish philosophy, was how the different philosophers embraced and styled Neoplatonism(s) to suit their respective "books of religion". Just as in early Christian theology, the traditions of Islamic and Jewish philosophy were framed by their own inner dynamic, purpose and historical meaning. The ordinary person could know something about the sensible and spiritual worlds, but the philosophers and theologians could attain much higher levels of knowledge to underpin the whole of reality.

In marked contrast to early Christian theology, Islam encouraged the study of the world; the Koran repeatedly invites Muslims to gain knowledge and investigate systematically natural phenomena as a means for getting close to God.[173] Treatise after treatise appeared with logical and literary methods designed to explore God's world and explain how human reason, revelation and faith could be integrated in pursuit of truth. Part of the answer to Oliver Leaman's question on why reason and revelation were both needed in Islamic thought (raised in the quote introducing this section) comes from the Koran itself, which stresses the importance of rational enquiry for the evidence for Islam. Reason was essential to discover the deeper revealed truths in the Koran.

In all cases, the use of reason in Islamic philosophy, despite the diversity of outcomes, was always bounded by God's ultimate and absolute unity, providence, will and wisdom. God provided all human beings with some rational ability to understand the world, and it was up to the individual how they chose to use it for greater knowledge. Perennial questions among the philosophers and theologians included arguments for the existence of God, how the world was created, the nature of being, and the place of human beings in the wider world and mind of God. We saw similar questions in ancient Greek philosophy but the boundaries framing the enquiries were very different. Plato's supreme god was a creator, the god of artists, sculptors and craftsmen and, together with the help of many lesser gods, created and organized the world; Aristotle's god was a prime mover, himself unmoved, and was only arrived at after a long chain of reasoning. The starting-point and end-point for medieval Islamic, Jewish and Christian philosophies was a reality framed by faith in a historical God, revelation and prophecy. Human beings cannot know God directly, but can reason to knowledge of him by moving from created/emanative effects to awareness of him as their uncreated "necessary" cause.

What follows is an account of the impact of Eastern scholarship on the West and specifically how its extensive corpus influenced the development of Latin scholasticism. Greek philosophy, after being translated, nurtured and developed by its Arab custodians since the time of Boethius, had come full circle. By the end of the twelfth century, its transmission to parts of western Europe stimulated a genuine intellectual revolution.[174] During this time Latin Christendom developed a profound respect for aspects of Arab scholarship, which contrasted strongly with Muslim contempt for the Latin West.[175]

EDUCATIONAL REVIVAL IN THE LATIN WEST

> One of the curious things about the Middle Ages is that they were original and
> creative without knowing it.   Bertrand Russell[176]

The rise of scholasticism and the universities

In the eleventh and twelfth centuries, the Catholic Church strived for greater unification and harmony in part as a result of: a succession of military Crusades against its Muslim enemies;[177] the slow demise of feudalism;[178] and the accompanying rise of a new enterprising "middle" class of townspeople in its place. The new citizenry and enterprising spirit led to increased exchanges between the East and West, greater commerce and industry and a new yearning for discovery and exploration.[179] The changes were so profound that from the turn of the millennium to AD 1300 the population of western Europe more than doubled from about 24 million to 55 million.

Educational revival was a key development in the reform programme. Latin scholasticism[180] began in the eleventh century within the cathedral schools and was originally identified with the methods used by civil and canon lawyers to reconcile seemingly contradictory statements.[181] From the law schools – notably at Bologna – the method was then transferred into theology and philosophy by a series of masters, who included French scholars Peter Abelard (1079–1142) and Peter Lombard (1095–1160). Scholasticism was both a method and a system that arose largely from the Church's attempt to rationalize its theology: to use the dialectic or reasoned arguments to disclose truth and gain greater knowledge of God.

By the twelfth century, the cathedral schools and to a lesser extent the monastery schools (devoted totally to teaching of a monastic life), grew in size to form the first European universities.[182] Some of the oldest universities were Bologna (c.1150), Paris (c.1200) (the most famous theological school of the Latin West in the high Middle Ages), Oxford (c.1220), Padua (c.1220) and Cambridge (c.1225). In the second half of the twelfth century, the Islamic, Jewish and Greek corpus began to be transmitted into western Europe.[183] Before this time, the West had only a few texts of ancient Greek philosophy: those of Aristotle's "old" logical treatises (*Categories* and *De interpretatione*), some of Porphyry's and Boethius's writings and a small part of Plato's *Timaeus*. The new literary finds – which included the remainder of Aristotle's "new" logical works (*Prior* and *Posterior Analytics*), most of his natural philosophy (*Physics* and *On the Soul*) and his *Metaphysics* and *Ethics* – were not fully absorbed until the late-thirteenth century, which capped off a period often referred to as the "Age of Translation".[184]

The emerging university culture was nothing short of what medieval historian David Knowles called a "philosophical revolution".[185] Young Latin scholars or masters, armed with new exciting literature and a deep respect for ancient learning and the early Christian patristic scholars (e.g. Augustine), began to challenge orthodox interpretations on the workings of the mind, nature and God's participation. Formal commentary on standard texts was popular both as a pedagogical tool and as a literary form, and their disputations were mostly dialectic. A typical disputation identified a master: raising a precise philosophical or theological question; providing two sets of preliminary arguments, one for and the other against; presenting and defending his own resolution to the question; and summarizing the range of preliminary answers and his concluding stated view.[186] Thus medieval philosophy and theology were products of the thirteenth-century university environment. The degrees offered were the Bachelor and Master of Arts and, for those who wanted to go beyond the arts curriculum, the degree of Master of Theology was offered.

Educational reform will be illustrated here by the works of two scholastics who commanded great respect in the Latin West: St Anselm and St Thomas Aquinas. The comparison is interesting because Anselm had little or no knowledge of the "new" Aristotle or the Arab–Jewish corpus, whereas in the following century Aquinas immersed himself tenaciously in the freshly translated literature. As a result, Anselm adopted the older patristic tradition under the influence of Augustine's Christian Platonism and the "old" Aristotle (Boethius's Latin translations). In contrast, Aquinas generated a newly styled Christian worldview that challenged Church orthodoxy. Of importance, Aquinas, like other medieval scholastics, had almost no direct access to Plato's works; it was only through Augustine and pseudo-Dionysius that Platonism was transmitted.

St Anselm (1033–1109): faith seeking understanding

> For I do not seek to understand so that I may believe, but I believe so that I may understand ... The Christian ought to advance to knowledge through faith, not to come to faith through knowledge ... The proper order demands that we believe the deep things of Christian faith before we presume to reason about them.   Anselm[187]

St Anselm was appointed Archbishop of Canterbury in 1093. His talents in logic and rational argument to discover truth (dialectic) were so impressive that he is often considered the father of scholasticism. As the above quote illustrates, Anselm described himself as someone with faith seeking understanding, and this was prefaced by: "I long to understand in some degree thy truth, which my heart believes and loves."[188] These telling words reflect the deep passions of a man who was always reaching out towards God, from whom he felt himself separated by sin.[189] His spiritual writings consist of 11 treatises or dialogues, 3 meditations and 19 prayers.[190]

Anselm's benchmark in theology and philosophy was his strong conviction that faith could be studied using logic and reason.[191] His originality came not from challenging Church dogma, but in finding new ways to buttress and clarify the truths of faith.[192] Anselm's worldview was constructed from the starting-point of believer and proceeded to God from the "necessary reasons" as part of faith.[193] Logical necessity and clear thinking were his ways of accepting the Church's greatest mysteries: the Holy Trinity and the Incarnation.[194] In the end, he conceded that the internal relations between the persons of the Holy Trinity lay beyond reason's reach and rested with faith.[195] To Anselm, faith and reason were not antagonistic but in harmony. If misunderstandings occurred, a good Christian must bow in reverence to Scripture and Church doctrine. To do otherwise, Anselm believed, was intellectual laziness. No matter how irrefutable our reasoning may appear, if it is in conflict with Scripture it must be let go because Scripture leaves no room for error.[196] Anselm wrote: "if Scripture clearly contradicts what we think to be the case, even if, to us, our reasoning seems irrefragable, it should not be thought to contain any truth".[197]

Anselm's most famous philosophical work is certainly his *Proslogion* (*Of the Soul to God*) (1078). A notable aspect of his thinking was the way he interspersed speculative philosophy with prayer, and rational reflection with monastic meditation. He is famous for formulating what Immanuel Kant (1724–1804) later called the "onto-logical proof" for the existence of God. Although Anselm knew that the "essence" of God was unknowable, he believed that an "understanding" of his existence was not. The ontological argument was rejected by Aquinas, Hume and Kant, while Bruno of

Table 7.1 Anselm's proof of God's existence

- God is defined as a supreme absolute perfect being and having the highest of thought. He is simple, without beginning or end, omnipresent, unrestricted in place and time and immutable.
- Even the fool has an idea in his mind of such a being greater 'that-than-which-no other-being can-be-thought' to exist (see discussion below).
- Such a being must really exist, for the very idea of a being implies existence, otherwise there would not be an idea of a being greater than which no other being exists.
- Therefore God does not only exist in the mind of man but also has a real existence outside mind.

Segni, William of Auxerre, William of Auvergne, Alexander of Hales, Bonaventure, Descartes, Spinoza and Leibniz accepted it.[198] The proof appeared in *Proslogion* Chapters 2 and 3,[199] and is summarized in Table 7.1.

Anselm's "proof" is often represented as a Neoplatonic celebration of the relation between an abstract definition or concept, thinking about it, and its actual existence. That is:

God is defined as absolute and having the highest thought	$\rightarrow$	We all believe that something greater exists	$\rightarrow$	Therefore, God exists in our minds and everywhere

Anselm does not appear to be trying to bridge between "idea" and "existence", as many medieval successors and modern philosophers believed. His goal was a personal communion with God. The "proof" was more a statement of true faith that had developed after deep personal reflection than a freestanding proof of God's existence.[200]

The "proof" was a reflection on the inner nature of God derived from the logical implications of his divine attributes: perfection, eternity, omnipresence and immutability. Anselm defined God as "that-than-which-nothing-greater-can-be-thought".[201] He claimed that even someone who denied God's existence could understand this concept. Anselm told his reader that the "greater" truths exist in the mind and reality, not just the mind itself. Any concept, for example, a unicorn, could exist in the mind, but if a concept could exist in the mind and in reality, then that which exists in reality is greater. If God is "that-than-which-nothing-greater-can-be-thought" then He must exist in reality as the most perfect, eternal, omnipresent and immutable being. Significantly, Anselm makes no mention of God's creations in his proof, his threefoldness in the Trinity or whether the universe had a beginning in time.[202] He appears more concerned with the being of God, and not so much with proofs or explanations of the natural world.

Criticisms of Anselm's proof

Assuming for the moment that Anselm's argument was a proof of God's existence, it would appeal to anyone who supports the Christian Platonic position that the "idea" of a tree is more real than the tree itself. The universals have super-sensory realities independent of the particular objects we sense. French Benedictine monk Gaunilo (d. 1081), Anselm's contemporary, criticized the *Proslogion* for equating the *idea* of a perfect being with its *existence*. In *In Defense of the Fool*, Gaunilo argued that the *idea* of a perfect island does not necessarily imply that the place actually exists.[203] Thinking about a tree growing in your front garden does not automatically mean that the tree exists. An *idea* is not a demonstration of *existence*. Anselm's defence to Gaunilo was threefold: (i) the purpose of *Proslogion* was faith seeking understanding and his starting-point was God, not some *idea* or physical character; (ii) the sequence moves from being in mind to being in both mind and reality; (iii) islands, however perfect, are not analogous to God as a necessary being – perfect islands are contingent.[204]

Another critic was Roscellinus of Compiegne (*c*.1050–1125). Roscellinus rejected Anselm's argument by contending that truth could only be reached through demonstration and reason.[205] As a secular master of the liberal arts (and one of Abelard's teachers), Roscellinus argued more along the lines of Aristotle. Individual things in the world were real, not the universals or general concepts in mind; a position today known as "nominalism". Roscellinus held that the general concepts are nothing more than *flatus vocis*: vocal sounds standing for imaginary names or verbal expressions.

Anselm's argument was reformulated in the seventeenth century by Descartes, Leibniz and Spinoza, successively, and in symbolic form by mathematician Kurt Gödel in the twentieth century.[206] Aquinas rejected the proof because it contained no elements of human experience. In the eighteenth century, Kant agreed but went much further. He argued that the ontological argument conflated two very separate categories of human thought: pure reason and experience. Kant felt that any proof of argument sustained by logic, reason and definitions was empty without experience. *Existence*, he argued, was not a quality or attribute like perfection or goodness. It was impossible to proceed from the *idea* of a thing to its *existence*.[207]

Anselm on natural theology

In Anselm's world there was little or no room for studying the physical relations as independent objects of human thought. The physical world existed only as an inferior reflected reality of divine origin, a Christian Platonic view wholly consistent with earlier patristic traditions. One scholastic who contributed to a new perspective on the importance of sense experience and physical reality was theologian/philosopher Thomas Aquinas.

St Thomas Aquinas (1225–1274): faith and reason as two ways

> It may almost be said of [Aquinas] that he achieves fusion of the academy [Plato] and Lyceum [Aristotle] that so many of his predecessors and contemporaries were attempting. He accomplishes this, however, not by synthesis, but by using the elements from Platonism mainly in the higher levels of metaphysics ... In this way he adds all that is true in Plato's idealism, other worldliness and spirit of love to the common sense, rationalistic empiricism of Aristotle.
>
> Knowles[208]

Aquinas[209] was one of the most outstanding scholastics and was highly influential in the later development of the Catholic tradition.[210] He differed from most of his thirteenth-century Christian colleagues by acknowledging the scope and depth of Greek, Islamic and Jewish scholarship, particularly the works of the "new" Aristotle, Avicenna and Maimonides. He applauded the Islamic and Jewish use of logical analysis and argumentation in philosophical theology and tackled similar themes.

Aquinas's crowning literary achievement was his famous *Summa Theologica* (*Synopsis of Theology*), where he attempted to reconcile Aristotelianism and Neoplatonism with Christian faith, something Boethius tried but never finished many centuries earlier.

Aquinas's major concern was to formulate and defend a "naturalistic" Aristotelian Christianity in opposition to the older Neoplatonism of Augustine and others. Aquinas was enamoured with the "original" Aristotle, who he often cited in support of a particular thesis he wanted to defend: *the rationality of the physical world as God's divine revelation*. Throughout his writings, Aquinas viewed philosophy as proceeding from the facts to God, and theology from God to the facts. Unlike Anselm, Aquinas adopted a more impersonal or neutral style of writing.[211]

Aquinas's solution to the faith–reason controversy

> The principles of Aquinas on the relations between faith and reason were solemnly proclaimed in the Vatican Council … First, reason alone is not sufficient to guide men; they need Revelation; we must carefully distinguish the truths known by reason from higher truths (mysteries) known by Revelation. Secondly, reason and Revelation, though distinct, are not opposed to each other. Thirdly, faith preserves reason from error; reason should do service in the cause of faith.   C. G. Herbermann *et al*.[212]

In true Aristotelian style, Aquinas held that human sensory experience was the starting-point of *all knowing*. From this starting-point he moved forwards to define the relationship between faith and reason, theology and philosophy. While acknowledging faith as our ultimate refuge, he insisted that faith and reason were not in conflict, since God would not have made a world that did not ultimately match up with revealed truth. In his *Summa Contra Gentiles* (I, nos. 4–6), Aquinas claimed that reason and faith led to different kinds of truths but there was a region of overlap where the same conclusions could be drawn from either direction (Fig. 7.2). A similar distinction was emphasized in the ninth century by Eriugena, who, as we discussed earlier, viewed reason and revelation as two sources of truth, and not in conflict.

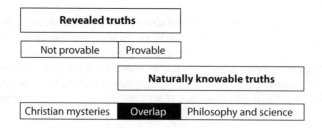

Figure 7.2 Broad schematic of Aquinas's views on the totality of human knowledge (modified from Tranoy 1964: 98). God was the author of all knowledge, revealed and natural. Natural theology is the overlap region between the "revealed truths" and "naturally knowable truths". The rest below comprises secular philosophy and natural science. When Aquinas uses terms like "proof" or "provable" he is not using theological premises or revelations as starting-points but sense-experience and the self-evident principles of philosophy (i.e. principle of contradiction).

Importantly, Aquinas's separation of faith and reason was not a dualism between the objects of mind and sense. The objects of knowledge were the same in theology (faith and grace) as in philosophy (reasoning). The difference was that sensory or natural knowledge, in contrast to faith, had no divine support and was influenced only by the known object itself. Theology dealt with propositions accepted on faith, whereas natural philosophy was a discipline to discover God's creations. Faith was not opposed to natural philosophy but worked alongside it, sharing the same objects of knowledge to reveal God's "truths". Aquinas taught that faith was a matter of will, which was influenced by God, and commanded acceptance and safeguarded reason from error. Because revelation and reason are both given to human beings by God, they can never be in conflict. Apparent conflict does not come from God but from wrong reasoning of human beings.[213]

Within this highly original theological framework, Aquinas (unlike Augustine) made room for two kinds of truths: "not provable" truths and "provable" truths, where reason subordinates faith (Fig. 7.2). "Not provable" truths were the Creation, the Trinity, the Incarnation and the Last Judgement. While Aquinas agreed that the eternal world of Aristotle and many Islamic philosophers could not be accepted or refuted from the senses or human reason, he believed that the claim could be refuted by revelation: the form of knowledge that trancends our sense and reasoning power. The "provable truths" in Aquinas's scheme were the existence of God (his "five ways") and the immortality of the human soul (salvation). The overlap of the divine and physical was the place where human understanding could be obtained by grace "from above" and by nature "from below". Knowledge "from above" was made possible by the grace of God, which Aquinas acknowledged was not self-evident; otherwise everyone would be a Christian.[214]

The remaining "naturally knowable truths" were the domains of philosophy and natural science. These truths start "from below" in the sensible world of experience, and move upwards towards God. In this way, Aquinas does not limit philosophy and natural science but rather makes explicit provisions for extending them to God. The separation of philosophy and natural science from the revealed truths highlights their different structures in the totality of human knowledge. Lastly, although Aquinas affirmed that natural truths were ultimately grounded in observation, the fact remains that he observed very little compared to many of the later theologians/philosophers, such as Grosseteste, Bacon and Ockham (see below).

Knowledge and soul

Knowledge is built from the self-reflexive capacity of human beings for recognizing the truth and seeing how it corresponds to reality.[215] Because of our physical nature, Aquinas believed that all knowledge begins with the senses, whereas God's knowledge was eternal, perfect and unchanging.[216] In his own words: "It is natural to a human being to attain what is intelligible through objects of sense, because our knowledge originates from sense."[217] Aquinas rejects Augustine's Neoplatonic view that human beings need divine illumination to attain true knowledge.[218] We were all born with a clean slate with no innate ideas. Our intellect possesses a "natural light" that is sufficient for the knowledge of truths.[219] Concepts are abstracted from sensible phenomena and we work up to the universals and cause–effect relationships.[220] Any physical object can be known as something sensible, and as something intelligible. Natural cognition (information processing) and knowledge involves both sense and intellect. In this respect, Aquinas's theory of knowledge has all the hallmarks of Aristotelian epistemology.[221]

But knowledge was only possible from sense if the soul had specific powers. The faculty of soul responsible for knowledge was the highest of five faculties of the body. In ascending order there was: the vegetative faculty (involved in food, drink, sex and growth); the sensible faculty (the five senses, plus the common sense that binds sensations together); the locomotor faculty (which permits movement); the appetitive faculty (which consists of our desire and will); and the intellectual faculty (passive and active, thought and reason). *The intellect, as human beings' greatest treasure, was an intrinsic part of body and soul responsible for abstracting a universal from a particular sensible image.*[222]

In agreement with Avicenna (after Al-Farabi), soul was the "form" of the body, and life after death was possible only because the "form" itself does not perish.[223] As philosopher Simon Blackburn asserts, "It is therefore not I who survive bodily death, but I may be resurrected if the same body becomes reanimated by the same form."[224] Aquinas's proposal that soul and body were essentially one flew in the face of the Neoplatonic ideas of Augustine and the other Church fathers, and angered many orthodox Fransciscan monks. To make things worse, Aquinas taught that the soul without the body would have no personality, because individuality comes from matter, not spirit.[225] For this reason, resurrection of the body is crucial to the idea of personal immortality. Aquinas rejected Averroes's idea that only an "impersonal" soul survives death. Likewise, he rejected Aristotle's "active intellect" coming "from the outside".[226] Aquinas identified Aristotle's "active" intellect or Islam's "agent" intellect with the Christian immortal soul as the "form" of the body, not something external.

God as pure *esse*
In order to distinguish between the nature of something and its existence, Aquinas borrowed heavily from Aristotle and Avicenna. Avicenna believed that the world was composed of essences (or natures), which linked the individual things we sense to the universal things we think. Essence was the "nature" of a thing and existence was the "being" of the thing. Aquinas adopted a similar scheme where "essence" was the composite of matter and form, not unlike the Greek *ousia*, or substance (see Ch. 5). In addition to clearly separating God from his creations and avoiding any suggestion of pantheistic emanation, he added a new term for bringing something into existence: the *esse*.[227] The *esse* was derived from the Latin verb meaning "to be" and from the noun "existence". It brought something into being or existence by combining with the *essence* of a substance.[228] Nothingness was defined as the state of the possibility of being something, but not actually being or existing.[229] Unlike many of the Arab philosophers, Aquinas denied the chance or contingency of existence. Everything was created by the purposive act of God through his word. There were no intermediary emanations in creation, as appeared in the system of Al-Farabi and Avicenna.

The *esse* and "essence" were Aquinas's attempt to distinguish his different categories of being, as well as explaining diversity in the world.[230] All things created by God had received the *esse* but they were not all absolutely perfect. The world of imperfections was God's physical revelation and the domain of natural theology. In Aristotelian terms, the imperfections were the potentialities not fully actualized. Aquinas argued that the deeper truth not known to Aristotle was that God makes himself known through his "revealed" and "naturally" knowable truths. It was only God's creative act that turned a possible essence into an actual being. Aquinas's God was pure *esse*.

Aquinas's five ways for proving the existence of God

Aquinas's cosmological method began from a particular physical object or phenomenon and proceeded to its cause or to God.[231] When he used the word "proof" he was generally referring to a particular datum of sense-experience. Aquinas's starting-points were self-evident philosophical first principles, not revelations. Aquinas considered each principle to be a distinctive and demonstrative "proof" of God's existence.[232] The first three were cosmological, the fourth Platonic and the fifth was from design or teleology (see Table 7.2).

Aquinas was well aware that his proofs were not original but were known to many contemporary theologians, as they were known to Aristotle, Al-Farabi, Avicenna and Maimonides.[233] The widespread appeal of the proofs was that every Christian could agree on the starting-points as they provided the greatest insights into the nature of God.[234]

Prime mover	=	First efficient cause	=	Necessary being	=	Supreme good and intelligent creator

Table 7.2 Aquinas's five ways for proving the existence of God (Kenny 1969; Davies 1993: 83–93).

Aquinas's five proofs ended in a first mover, a first efficient cause, a necessary being, a supreme good and a universal orderer (Kenny 1969).

1. **Argument from motion to a prime mover.** Aquinas's first proof starts off with the observation that something is always moving around us and is in the process of change: "It is certain and sensation tells us that something is being moved in this world. But everything which is moved is moved by another". Aquinas logically argued that this process cannot go on for ever "because in that case there would be no First Mover. Consequently, there would be nothing which moved another, for secondary movers do not move except as they are moved by a First Mover – Ergo, it is necessary to arrive at a first mover, which is moved by nothing, and this everybody understands to be God".

2. **Argument from cause-effect and impossibility of infinite regress.** Aquinas's second proof follows a similar line of argument as in Proof 1 but instead of motion it is the nature of "efficient causation". In the world of sense there is order of efficient causes but there cannot be an infinite series of efficient causes. There must be a "first efficient cause", which is God.

3. **Argument from possible or contingent beings to a necessary being.** Aquinas's third proof is stated in terms of the concepts of possibility, contingency (chance) and necessity as they apply to the physical objects around us. Aquinas argued that contingent things in the world are generated (come into being) and perishable (go out of being) like a tree. But because these things are transitory it is impossible for them to always exist. To Aquinas "all things cannot be merely possible things" otherwise at one time you would have had nothing. If this was true, nothing would be in existence, which is absurd. In this way he rejected contigency. There must be something non-transitory or "necessary", which in turn owes its existence to another "necessary" being and so on. The process must stop somewhere, similar to his "efficient causes". The series of "necessary" beings has its source in God.

4. **Argument from degrees of goodness to a supreme good.** Aquinas's fourth proof follows on from the third to include various degrees of perfection and goodness in the world of sense, which must come from a unique source of perfection and goodness that is God.

5. **Argument from order of the universe to a supreme and intelligent orderer.** Aquinas's final and fifth proof is framed from teleology and purposefulness in the world. Even lifeless things act in the same way as intelligent beings to obtain the best result. Their ends and purpose is achieved by design and directed by the intelligent God. God directs all natural things in the world.

The major difficulty with the ontological, cosmological and design arguments is that God's existence simply cannot be proved or disproved from reason alone. Today the belief in God may come from any number of sources: social influences, an inner illumination, divine revelation, family traditions, a near-death experience or personal tragedy. Any number of experiences can lead human beings to rise above logical proof and enter the transcendence of God's word. This does not mean that God does not exist, only that our thought and language processes cannot prove or disprove the belief. Faith is absolutely mandatory.

CHALLENGES TO CHURCH AUTHORITY: THE BEGINNING OF THE END

[Traditionalist theologians,] ignorant themselves of the forces of nature and wanting to have company in their ignorance, they don't want people to look into anything; they want us to believe like peasants and not ask the reason behind things ... But we say that the reason behind everything should be sought out ... If they learn that anyone is so inquiring, they shout out that he is a heretic, placing more reliance on their monkish garb than on their wisdom. William of Conches[235]

William of Conches's (*c*.1121) scathing criticism of dogmatic theologians (in the above quote) was echoed by many of the younger scholastics. As could have been predicted, any change to the orthodox Christian worldview met strong resistance. The works of Aquinas and Averroes were especially targeted by the Church for emphasizing too much reason and not enough faith. So too were the works of Aristotle. In 1210 a provincial synod prohibited the University of Paris from "reading" Aristotle's metaphysics and natural philosophy, and renewed the prohibition again in 1215. There was no such ban at the University of Naples, where Aquinas was a student, and it was not until 1255 that the University of Paris reversed its decision and officially approved the study of Aristotle's natural philosophy alongside his logical writings.[236]

After Aquinas's death, the orthodox Franciscans and secular masters of France and the theologians at Oxford requested wider bans on Aristotelianism and Aquinas himself. To this end, in 1277 Pope John XXI asked Bishop Tempier of Paris to investigate Aristotelianism being taught at the city's university. Tempier set up a commission of theologians and on 7 March 1277 condemned a collection of 219 propositions.[237] A few weeks later in Oxford, the Archbishop of Canterbury compiled a shorter list of propositions that directly targeted aspects of Aquinas's teachings.[238] The Condemnation of 1277 also targeted the art masters Siger of Brabant, Boethius of Dacia and other Latin Averroists who taught the "eternity of the world" and that the "intellect was one and the same for all human beings", which opposed the Christian teachings of individual immortality and personal moral responsibility.[239] The Church responded by introducing new civil laws, which led to the establishment of the Inquisition, where heresy was no longer a misdemeanour subject to spiritual correction, but a criminal offence punishable by death, including burning at the stake.[240] Both Siger and Boethius fled France for Italy in fear of their lives. In a courageous move after Aquinas's death, his fellow Dominicans rallied to his defence and officially accepted Thomism in 1278; Aquinas was canonized 44 years later (1323).

Although the Inquisition has captured much public interest, we must be careful not to dwell on the condemnations. The Inquistion was not an institution but one of many responses the Church sanctioned to tighten control in a changing social and intellectual climate.[241] In addition, the Church was under mounting internal pressure from the free-thinking masters, who wanted to explore wider epistemological and theological boundaries.[242] The masters, who taught in the cathedral schools of the twelfth century and the universities of the thirteenth, were the new force in the Church.

We shall now present the views of some of the more "heretical" thinkers. We shall begin with Abelard, who lived in the twelfth century, and move through to Aquinas's contemporaries Robert Grosseteste and Roger Bacon, and the later William of Ockham of the fourteenth century. These scholars were chosen for their revitalized interpretation of the Scriptures and more operational approach to natural philosophy as a means to knowing more about God.

Peter Abelard (1079–1142): Shall we fill Hell with non-believers?

Peter Abelard is a persecutor of the Catholic faith and an enemy of the cross of the Christ. Outwardly he is a monk but inwardly he is a heretic. His inexperienced auditors who are scarcely able to bear the first elements of faith, he introduces to the mystery of the Trinity, to the holy of holies, to the chamber of the Kin. With Arius [he] distinguishes grades and steps in the Trinity; with Pelagius he prefers will to grace; with Nestorius he divides Christ. Thus traversing almost all sacred subjects he boldly attacks them from end to end and disposes of each is a damnable manner.

St Bernard of Clairvaux[243]

Verbal cleverness, a readiness to challenge older doctrine and responsiveness to new trends were exemplified in the flamboyant scholastic Peter Abelard. One could not imagine a greater contrast than that between Abelard and his teacher, Anselm, who, as we discussed, retained the orthodox line of scriptural interpretation. Abelard sought to interpret the Scriptures using an unorthodox application of logic to discover truth.[244] "By doubting, we come to inquire and by inquiry we arrive at truth."[245] Abelard believed that the Holy Trinity was the "One, Mind and world soul" of the Neoplatonists.[246] He also believed that sin was a matter of evil "intent", not "action" of the perpetrator, which placed human choice and free will at the centre of human ethics. For Abelard, Christianity was the rehabilitation of the natural moral law of the ancient Greeks. The Church did not share these beliefs and condemned his teachings and writings twice, first in 1121 and again in 1140.

Abelard's less dogmatic approach to Christianity was also exemplified in his theory of knowing. He is often regarded as the founder of conceptualism, which was somewhere between nominalism (the idea that nothing is common to objects except the words applied to them – *flatus vocis*, or "breath of the voice") and realism (where the universals exist independent of our thought or reality).[247] Some of the questions Abelard tackled were:

- Do words refer to real entities?
- How do the particulars in sense relate to the universals in mind – the "problem of universals" of Plato and Aristotle (see Ch. 5)?
- What is the interaction between sense-experience and our cognitive powers to form concepts to understand the world?

Abelard did not believe that every particular thing was a copy of some Neoplatonic eternal Idea (realism), nor did his search begin with physical objects. Abelard began with language, and anticipated Aquinas by nearly a century. He argued that human beings do not predicate an object, but conceptualize an object using words, which convey meaning from which knowledge grows. A question that interested him was how a particular object related to the diversity of objects, i.e. how a particular tree related to the diversity of trees, and vice versa, as part of human knowing. Abelard's solution was that while true universal words "signify no one thing" (a position taken by the nominalists), it does not follow that universal words are "empty of meaning".[248] Abelard proposed a way out of this dilemma by claiming, after Aristotle, that the human mind had the power to form "abstractions". Abelard wrote: "The conceptions of universals are formed by abstraction, and we must indicate how we speak of them alone, naked and pure but not empty."[249]

The mind can form ideas about particulars and the parts of these particulars form a universal idea. A tree is one tree but its parts (e.g. roots, stem or leaves) that make the whole are common to all trees. The senses perceive a tree but our intellect abstracts a tree in relation to the grander scheme of things. Aristotle used the word "abstraction" in a narrower sense of separating the objects of mathematics from the objects of sense.[250] For Aristotle, the objects of mathematics were not actual realities but abstractions of the human mind to serve scientific enquiry (see Ch. 5). Using penetrating logic, Abelard extended Aristotle's application from mathematical symbolism to include intrinsic parts of actual realities. This realization had enormous consequences for the development of the scholasticism of the twelfth and thirteenth centuries, and later natural philosophy (a precursor to natural science), although during his life he restricted himself to logic and ethics.

Importantly, Abelard did not reject the Neoplatonic universals altogether. In the broad tradition of Philo, Abelard claimed that the universals existed first in God's intellect (Ideas of God = thoughts of God), second as common natures shared by individual substances in the sensible universe, and third as the general concepts formed in our human minds. However, unlike the Neoplatonists and some medieval Latin, Arab and Jewish realists, Abelard *did not believe that the "universal" has a distinct and separate object*. The universal was not an eternal entity in its own right. For Abelard, the abstracted concepts ground our universal knowledge of sensible things, a notion fortuitous to the development of natural philosophy with the emerging translations of Aristotle with Grosseteste.

Robert Grosseteste (*c.*1168–1253): a prophet of natural science

Among the first to understand and use the new theory of experimental science was Robert Grosseteste, who was the real founder of the tradition of scientific thought in medieval Oxford and, in some ways, of the modern English intellectual tradition. Grosseteste united in his own work the experimental and rational traditions of the twelfth century and he set forth a systematic theory of experimental science.

A. C. Crombie[251]

Another towering intellect with a readiness to challenge Church doctrine and orthodoxy was Robert Grosseteste. Grosseteste was a theologian, philosopher and Bishop of Lincoln (1235), who, unlike most medieval scholars, came from a peasant background.[252] He held, like Abelard, that the universals did not belong to the real world of existing things, nor did they exist alone, but rather corresponded to something in the external world of particulars. Grosseteste claimed that universals were a kind of mediator between a concept and a definition, since it was the mind that brought the two together by deciding to use the term in the first place. Grosseteste had little time for the Neoplatonists' eternal Ideas or the notion of Aristotle's "active" or Al-Farabi's "agent" intellect.

Grosseteste was pivotal in the thirteenth-century reintroduction of the original Greek philosophical and scientific writings in the West.[253] He detested past and contemporary theological efforts to massage Aristotle into Christian thinking: "Those trying to make Aristotle a Catholic are themselves heretics", he claimed.[254] Grosseteste, like Aquinas, held that there was a natural order of things in which God did not intervene directly but was indirectly responsible through natural laws. For his penetrating genius, Grosseteste is considered one of the framers of the modern scientific tradition in the West, an honour that is often bestowed on Roger Bacon.

Natural science and the search for causes

Grosseteste's approach to science was based on Aristotle's principle of uniformity and economy (nature operates in the best and shortest possible way).[255] Grosseteste agreed with Aristotle that there are four causes: the material and formal causes, the final cause and the efficient cause. Equally important was Aristotle's distinction between "the fact" (*quia*) and the "reason for the fact" (*propter quid*).[256] Physics by itself was *quia* ("of the fact") but with mathematics could become a science *propter quid* (providing knowledge "of the reasoned fact").[257] Thus mathematics provided a more penetrating representation of the facts by providing a knowledge of physical relations given by means of lines, angles and figures, not just observations.[258]

To understand the physical world, a person needs both to observe phenomena, and have a knowledge of mathematics to interpret the phenomena. All motion, Grosseteste believed, could be described in mathematical terms. This brilliant insight into mathematics as a language was truly innovative. Moreover, although mathematics was precise, Grosseteste knew only too well that the results from its application to science would be provisional because not all causes were fully knowable. Science would only provide probabilities about God's creations, not absolutes.[259]

"True" knowledge was faith in God, not belief in science. God was the direct cause of the world and everything in it, *but he was not the direct cause of effects; these were contained in the intrinsic properties of the physical objects interacting according to God's laws.*[260] This has all the hallmarks of the Islamic philosophical position we discussed earlier. Grosseteste searched for these secondary "cause–effect" relations by first breaking the complex natural phenomena into simpler parts or facts, and then reassembling them using deductions to explain the original phenomena of interest.[261] This reconstruction phase of Grosseteste's double method was called *composition*.[262]

Grosseteste's greatest contribution to the development of natural science was his explanation of the experiment.[263] Experiments could provide decisive and agreed-upon ways to determine which hypothesis was best. This is an area in which Greek science had few answers. He knew from the Aristotelian tradition that it was much easier to prove something false than prove something true. We saw a similar approach in Aquinas when he was trying to make the intelligible connection between God and the world. But Grosseteste went much further than either Aristotle or Aquinas by introducing to the demonstration "a test" or experiment (*experimentia*). *Experimentia* was a controlled procedure intended to verify or eliminate a scientific hypothesis.[264] Grosseteste demanded the rejection of all conclusions that were not logically compatible with the premises based on a priori demonstrations, new observations and original intuitions.[265]

Grosseteste may have arrived at the importance of "experiment" from Arabic science, perhaps from Avicenna, as transmitted through the works of Al-Ghazali and others.[266] Again, the contrasting difference was that Grosseteste (and Bacon after him) concentrated more on the applications of mathematical methodology and the conception of what constitutes a scientific explanation than the Arabs.[267] As Alistair Crombie points out, understanding the process of science (which still remains imperfectly understood today) is quite different from practising science.[268] However, there are many who would challenge this view about the contributions of Arab polymaths to Western science.[269] Recent scholarship shows that the Arabs placed great emphasis on systematic observation, experimentation and theory-building.[270] Given the profound impact of Islamic philosophy on Western thought, it is hard to believe that their practice of science went unnoticed. The closer truth may lie in Arab science being known to many Latin scholars but not widely acknowledged in the shadow of highly celebrated Aristotle.

With the advantage of hindsight in evaluating Grosseteste's methodology, the shortfall of his "experiment" was that it still relied too heavily on his own experience, or on a priori reports he had read or heard about, without critical "independent" analysis. Grosseteste's development of natural science using induction, mathematics and empirical laboratory experiment did not reach its full maturity until some 400 years later in the seventeenth century.

Faith and reason

> Since the truth of each thing is its conformity to its exemplar (ratio) in the eternal Word, it is clear that every created truth is perceived only in the light of the Highest Truth.
> S. P. Marrone[271]

In Grosseteste's world, faith and reason were not in conflict. Grosseteste had two notions of truth: simple and complex. Simple truth was something attached to the object of knowledge conforming to God's word in the Scriptures (e.g. as creator), whereas complex truth was a kind of quality of knowledge that could be, in part, tested by way of experiment.[272] Simple truths were the framework of God's being and creations, whereas complex truths were accessible to analysis and of two types: *intellectus* and *propter quid* (scientific truths). *Intellectus* were self-evident truths in Aristotelian language and accepted as "articles" of faith from which all other complex truths were derived. In contrast, scientific truths were not certain and required reason and demonstration to decide right from wrong.[273]

Later in his life, Grosseteste took the simple truths involving God out of the equation and focused more on *intellectus* and natural science. God was still implicated through his natural laws, but his earlier definition of simple truth implied that knowing the truth in some way involved knowing or seeing God in a literal sense.[274] By keeping simple and complex truths separate, Grosseteste prevented equating God's creations with God himself (pantheism). Light formed the basis of Grosseteste's theology and natural science. Briefly, he proposed that light (*lux*) and matter were the major instruments by which God created the universe.[275]

Roger Bacon (*c.*1214–1294): anticipation of mathematics and science

> For, during the twenty years in which I have laboured specifically in the study of wisdom, after disregarding the common way of thinking, I have put down more than two thousand pounds for secret books and various experiments, and languages and instruments and tables and other things; as well as searching out the friendships of the wise, and for instructing assistants in languages, in figures, in numbers, and tables and instruments and many other things. Roger Bacon[276]

Roger Bacon, like Grosseteste, regarded the study of languages as essential to the accurate translations of philosophy and theology, and became well versed in Latin, Greek, Hebrew, Arabic and Chaldean.[277] In his *Opus Majus* (*Greater Work*), written in 1268 for Pope Clement IV, Bacon sharply criticized[278] the translators of Aristotle's works.[279] Ten years later, around the time of the "Great Condemnation of 1277", Bacon himself was condemned by his own Franciscan order and imprisoned in Paris for "suspected novelties".[280] These "novelties" were probably theological in nature. In a moment of extreme frustration Bacon anticipated Luther by declaring: "the whole clergy is given up to pride, luxury, and avarice. Their quarrels, their contentions, and their vices are a scandal to laymen."[281]

Roger Bacon on truth and experimental science

> Since this experimental science is wholly unknown to the rank and file of students, I am therefore unable to convince people of its utility unless at the same time I disclose its excellence and its proper signification. Roger Bacon[282]

Bacon identified four main barriers to seeking truth: frail and unsuitable authority, long custom, uninformed popular opinion, and the knowing concealment of one's ignorance in a display of apparent wisdom.[283] Wisdom was a gift from God accessible to human beings through reason and validated by experience.[284] To help achieve the unity in wisdom, Bacon proposed educational reform in the languages, mathematics (astronomy and astrology), optics, *scientia experimentalis*, alchemy, metaphysics and moral philosophy, in that order.[285]

In order to validate knowledge, Bacon distinguished two kinds of experience: first, that obtained through the external senses aided by instruments and sharpened by mathematics, and second, experience from mystical inspiration through illumination from God.[286] After visiting Grosseteste at Oxford in his early thirties, Bacon became preoccupied with mathematics (arithmetic, geometry and astronomy), which he regarded as the foundation of all scientific enquiry. He said, "For the things of this world cannot be known without a knowledge of mathematics."[287]

For Bacon, science provided a means to know God's creations and therefore the creator himself. The *ultimate* utility of natural science was in the service of the Church.[288] Furthermore, he argued that experimental science provided a more trustworthy knowledge than philosophical argument. Like Grosseteste, Bacon foreshadowed experimental science as a new intellectual and technical force that could rediscover the past, prolong human life and discover new inventions.[289] The role of experimental science was threefold: first, to certify the conclusions of the theoretical science (including mathematics); second, to add new knowledge not discoverable by reason alone; and third, to study the secrets of nature beyond the scope of the other sciences.[290]

The major shortcoming of Bacon's "experimental science" was that he never really put what he taught into practice.[291] He did continue Grosseteste's work on optics in a laboratory setting and began a dissection of the eye to help understand the working of lenses. Bacon did not distinguish between observation and experiment outside the collective term "experience". In the end, despite his emphasis on the need for observation, and explanation of many interesting phenomena, his scientific attitude fell well short of modern science. As was common in the times, he often mixed astrology with astronomy, magic with mechanics and alchemy with chemistry.

William of Ockham (*c*.1285–1349): calling for the separation of theology and natural science

> The problem for the philosophers was at once epistemological and theological. The epistemological problem of defining what could be known about different subject-matters and with what degrees of certainty was subordinated to the theological principle that the entire created world was contingent upon the inscrutable omnipotence of the Creator. A. C. Crombie[292]

Ockham is the last figure we shall consider from the high Middle Ages. Like Bacon he was a Franciscan scholar of unbridled originality. Ockham held that there were three kinds of human knowledge: intuition, abstraction and faith. Knowledge and intuition required reason, whereas faith required revelation and grace.[293] Ockham believed that faith and reason were separate spheres of knowing.[294] Faith and reason were different commitments to truth. When contradictions arose, Christian faith was always the victor.[295] Philosophy could not prove the truths of religion, such as the existence of God or many other mysteries.[296] Nor did Ockham believe that human beings should import the conclusions of dogmatic theology into philosophy without an acute awareness of the deep unsolved mysteries.[297] Ockham's separation of faith and reason must not be seen as a double-truth, but a theory in which the truth can be explored within the limits of human knowledge.

Ockham's views on natural science

Ockham was fascinated with nature and the knowledge of physical objects and their relations.[298] Against the scholastics, Ockham argued that there was no "inherent" necessity determining anything in the universe: "I say that although God acts through the mediation of secondary causes", such "action is voluntary, not necessary".[299] God, for Ockham, could create "without causality" and quite contrary to the "necessary" way Aristotle or Islamic philosophers believed. *God was free to do whatever he wished to do.* Ockham still believed in cause and effect, however, as something we can observe and test empirically, but not in the same way as Aristotle (see below). He saw no contradiction if God, by his absolute power, produced an effect without its cause. Thus, for Ockham, cause and effect was not a necessary relationship.

Ockham's desire to separate theology from scientific truths may have influenced his decision to seek the simplest explanations of the physical world. His first step was to eliminate Aristotle's theory of causality. Ockham anticipated Galileo by some 300 years by rejecting all extraneous complicating metaphysical "distinctions", definitions and abstractions such as *esse*, essence, accident, contingency, existence, actuality and potentiality. He denied any common reality existing in things.[300] Reality, to Ockham, was restricted to individual "absolute things", which could only be substances and qualities. Ockham wrote: "Besides absolute things, namely substances and qualities, nothing is imaginable, neither actually or potentially."[301] Following Grosseteste and Bacon, Ockham argued that "the statements of science" provided only "provisional" descriptions of the world. Science was the discipline not of universals, but of concepts.

Ockham viewed natural science as a discipline established by inductive generalization from singular judgements evident by experience. His "ideal" of science was essentially Aristotelian, but he did not believe in any need to seek the "cause" of any motion (uniform or accelerated), since motion was not an entity requiring "an efficient cause".[302] Aristotle's definition of nature posited the ideas of change and motion as essential parts of the definition.[303] For Ockham, words like "motion", "quantity", "time" and "place" were abstract nouns that had no real reference to nature except to describe an individual substance, thing or its qualities.[304] Motion was not a thing distinct from the thing in motion. Andre Goddu clarifies Ockham's views on motion:

> To refer to a change and motion as distinct entities is to commit the mistake of taking a connotative term for an absolute term. "Motion" is a connotative term, and the misuse of that term illustrates the dangers of using abstract terms as a kind of shorthand for more complex expressions and events.[305]

Ockham rejected all explanations of motion requiring an "efficient" cause beyond simply the moving body itself. It was pointless, he argued, to use more entities than necessary to explain motion.[306] Time was another term that could not be viewed distinct from change and motion, as it is the number or measure of motion.[307]

For Ockham, "nature" was a connotative term that referred to the totality of sensible substances composed of matter and form whose principle of motion was contained in themselves. Nature, as God's creation, possessed an ordered component (regular and predictable such as the heavenly motions) and a disordered component always undergoing change; when water becomes lighter it evaporates, only to return again as rain. However, through repeated experience, statements about order and disorder can be formulated, but they are not statements about natures but about individual things created by God with the power to act by themselves. This is at the heart of understanding Ockham and the medieval natural philosophers and theologians.

The role of the universals in human knowing

Ockham took the nominalistic (anti-realist) approach to reality by arguing that universals had no real existence.[308] The "real" consisted of individuals like a tree, an apple or a man, not universals.[309] Universals have no existence whatsoever; they are mere names. However, Ockham could not abandon universals altogether, because to do so would have denied a universal knowledge of sensible things and natural science. Instead, he proposed that all natural knowledge began with particulars and that universals were concepts formed through a process forming generalized truths. In Ockham's world, there was no "problem of universals", as they were concepts or words and as such could signify only individual things.[310]

A universal of a sense-object was simply a tool used in natural science and quite distinct from universals in logic, which were objects of thought. This is why Ockham called the natural sciences the "real" sciences, and logic a "rational" science.[311] Ockham rejected the Neoplatonic universal Idea as having a permanent reality while the physical world was inferior. Only particulars exist. Universals have objective value as part of our thinking process via language.[312] The notion of the "active" or "agent" intellect had no place in Ockham's worldview because abstraction follows "naturally" from perception and intuition, and is not something supernatural entering "from the outside". Instead of viewing the universal as something independent in the mind, Ockham argued that it arose from the act of thinking itself.[313] *What we think about* are the individual particulars and the tools we use to think about them are the universals.

Ockham's razor as a principle of economy

Ockham's principle of explanation was one of "economy". The removal of all the unnecessary or superfluous facts from a problem became known as Ockham's razor. It is frequently expressed as "What can be accounted for by fewer assumptions is explained in vain by more": *Pluralites non est ponenda sine necessitate* ("Plurality is not to be posited without necessity").[314] Ockham wrote: "Nothing is to be assumed as evident, unless it is known *per se*, or is evident by experience, or is proved by the authority of Scripture";[315] and "What can happen through fewer [principles] happens in vain through more ... when a proposition is verified of things, more [things] are superfluous if fewer suffice."[316] Ockham was not the first to recognize the principle of parsimony. Indeed, Aristotle believed that "God and nature work not in vain ... It is vain to expend many means where a few are sufficient."[317] However, Ockham applied ontological reduction differently from Aristotle by claiming that "final causality" was unnecessary, and in its place favoured experiment, mathematics and argument.

Ockham's condemnation and his expulsion from the Church

Ockham's originality and independence upset his Dominican masters and his own Franciscan order; namely, the supporters of Duns Scotus and Aquinas.[318] In 1323, arch-Thomist John Lutterell pressed charges against Ockham at the papal court in Avignon. In the following year, the court, after long deliberation, recommended that no action be taken.[319] Meanwhile, a few years later Ockham became embroiled in another dispute in Avignon over the question of evangelical poverty. The debate was between Pope John XXII and the Minister General of the Franciscan Order, Michael of Cesena (*c*.1290–1342). Ockham supported Cesena, and in 1328 was served condemnation papers by the papacy for this association. Ockham (and Cesena) fled to Germany.

On fleeing to Germany, and realizing his vulnerability in a foreign country, Ockham is reported to have said to the German Emperor, Louis IV of Bavaria (*c*.1283–1347): "If you defend me with the sword, I will defend you with my pen."[320] The Pope learned of this and became so enraged that he excommunicated both Ockham and Cesena. In his Munich years, Ockham wrote a number of treatises directed against the Pope and his institution, highlighting the inconsistencies between the Church and State. Human freedom was found in choice, not authoritarian rule. To Ockham, the law of God was a law of liberty.

THE FOUNDATIONS OF NATURAL SCIENCE IN THE HIGH MIDDLE AGES

Contrary to prevailing opinion, the roots of modern science were planted in the ancient and medieval worlds long before the Scientific Revolution of the seventeenth century. Indeed, that revolution would have been inconceivable without the culminative antecendent efforts of three great civilizations: Greek, Islamic, and Latin.

E. Grant[321]

Western Europe entered the high Middle Ages around AD 1050 in the deep conviction that its nations were part of the greater state of Christendom with the papacy standing at the centre of political, intellectual and theological thought. By the end of the high Middle Ages (around 1450), the Church had become increasingly decentralized. The main factors responsible for bringing about change were: the rise of towns with new political independence and enterprising spirit; the influx of previously unknown literary sources; and the development of the medieval university with its more secular academic pursuits, including the rebirth of natural philosophy or natural science.

As a result of social and educational reform, the Western medieval mindset changed from believing that the intellectual powers of human beings were inadequate to control their destiny (full potential could only be realized through God's grace) to the belief that human beings could attain, through their own thought and efforts, some measure of truth and personal fulfilment. This new outlook can once again be traced back indirectly to the highly valued and profoundly rich legacy of the ancient Greeks, which had found its way into the writings of a number of scholars over the centuries. It was associated with the rediscovery of the treatises and texbooks of the Latin-speaking Platonists (mostly Plotinus and Boethius), the patristic writings of the Latin Church fathers (mostly St Augustine), the twelfth-century translations of the Arab and

Jewish corpus, and the rediscovery of Aristotle's original works in the thirteenth century.

The immense importance of the Arabs to the changing medieval mindset in the West cannot be overstated. However, as medieval scholar F. E. Peters once remarked, "There was no Arab Thales pondering the possibility of reducing all things to the principle of sand."[322] Peters's statement in no way detracts from centuries of Arab brilliance; it only highlights that most of their scholars were not searching for a "first principle" in the same way as the Greek philosophers. In general, Islamic, Jewish and Christian thought had its source firmly planted in faith in God with divine revelation as the principal means of acquiring "true" knowledge. Thus the starting-point was not Thales' water, Plato's eternal Ideas, Aristotle's sensible phenomena or Plotinus's "One", but God's transcendence, grace and immanence. The boundaries pre-set by Islamic, Jewish and Christian traditions were very different to those of the ancient Greeks.

Despite having different boundaries framing their thinking, the vast majority of medieval scholars employed parts of Greek philosophy to help interpret the Scriptures as well as expound epistemological and ontological theories about God and his creations. Philosophical reason was widely employed to elucidate, speculate about and defend the faith within a particular culture. If conflict arose between reason and faith, faith always reigned supreme. Thus the starting-point and end-point for philosophical enquiry was always a reality framed by the acceptance of truth in a historical God, revelation and prophecy. The medieval experience, whether Christian, Jewish or Islamic, was unreservedly framed by the underlying dictum "I believe in order to understand", and not the Greek philosophical "I understand in order to believe".

A notable legacy of the high Middle Ages was the rebirth of natural science.[323] What the Church had considered a futile exercise for over a 1000 years found renewed theoretical interest within the medieval university.[324] Instead of natural science being viewed as empty and inferior, it was now perceived as a path to the glorification of God and potentially of great service to humankind. Knowledge of God extended as far as his causality; and the active power of God extended not only to forms, but to matter, by which forms are individualized in physical objects, in an Aristotelian sense. The greater acceptance of natural science was not to confront articles of faith but to explore the deeper meaning of God's creations, something that Islam had recognized and adopted centuries earlier. The first hints of change in the West came in the twelfth century with Abelard's early call for healthy scepticism as an essential part of social and intellectual progress. Although Abelard did not directly advocate natural science, his scholastic programme opened the door for its approval in the later universities.

Heightened interest in natural science, with its renewed rethinking of the physical object, did not occur until the writings of Aquinas, Grosseteste, Bacon and Ockham and their respective students and successors. The underlying assumption was that God had conferred on nature (comprising physical objects) the power and ability to cause things via harmonious laws, which could be investigated by the human intellect. God was the creator of the world and everything in it, but he was not the direct cause of effects that occurred in the world; these effects were products of secondary causation and the domain of natural science. In many ways, the new concept of nature with its own operative laws, causes and powers preconditioned the West for the scientific revolution just around the corner.

The roads by which men arrive at their insights into celestial matters
seem to me almost as worthy of wonder as those matters in
themselves.   Johannes Kepler (1571–1630)[1]

CHAPTER 8

The triumphant rise of Western science: methodologies, mathematics and measurement

THE DAWN OF THE MODERN ERA: FROM REFORM TO THE RENAISSANCE

No man is more disgusted than I am with the ambition, the avarice, and the profligacy
of the priests, not only because each of these vices is hateful in itself, but because
each and all of them are most unbelievable in those who declare themselves to be
men in special relations with God.   F. Guicciardini[2]

In the four centuries between Aquinas's *Summa Theologiae* (1266) and Newton's *Principia* (1687), western Europe underwent further social change. The merchants, bankers, lawyers, tradesmen, artisans and teachers allied themselves more with the king than with the feudal lords and Roman Catholic Church.[3] The new social order believed that a strong state with centralized authority was the key to greater competition, financial success and personal freedoms. Nationalism empowered the people with greater intellectual freedoms and human rights.

By the sixteenth century, western Europe had changed so dramatically that cultural historians call the period a Renaissance (*or new birth*).[4] The transition began as a literary movement in fourteenth-century Italy[5] and is associated with the humanist[6] Petrarch's classical revival of Platonism (as a theological alternative to Aristotelianism), poetry, literature and letters. Petrarch felt the late medieval Latin translations were "barbaric, tediously pedantic, arid and incomprehensible".[7] Petrarch, however, did not idealize antiquity, but promoted its moral philosophy by embracing the arts and sciences.[8] The humanistic movement emphasized the dignity and worth of the individual and sought a new golden age of peace and prosperity.

Petrarch's vision for the West was nothing short of remarkable, and embellished in the artistic genius of Leonardo da Vinci, Raphael and Michelangelo. Another early influential humanist was Byzantine scholar Manuel Chrysoloras who, in 1396, introduced the study of Greek to Florence. His "rough" Latin translation of Plato's *Republic* in 1402 was instrumental in the revival of Platonism.[9] A further break in tradition came in the field of history, where people like Niccolo Machiavelli (1469–1527) reintroduced and revitalized the works of the great Roman historian Titus Livius (Livy) in the hope that Florence would imitate Rome in its accomplishments.

In the sixteenth and seventeenth centuries the cultural Renaissance movement spread from Italy to France, Germany, the Netherlands and England.[10] It was a revolution of great literary finds, innovative art, educational reform and new attitudes towards philosophy and morality, technology, exploration and scientific discovery.[11] Christianity itself divided into two religious camps: the Catholics and Protestants. The earliest Protestants – the Lutherans and Calvinists – rejected medieval Catholicism and wanted to see human beings more immediately responsible to God, and freer to experience his grace through faith. They saw faith as trust in, and commitment to, God and rejected the Catholic belief that human beings were in part brought back to God through their own merits and through the mediation of a highly prescribed sacramental and clerical system.[12]

The "official" date for the beginning of religious reform was 31 October 1517, when Martin Luther (1483–1546) nailed his 95 *theses* (*Disputation on the Power and Efficacy of Indulgences*) to the front door of the Wittenbery Castle Catholic Church.[13] Luther despised the Catholic Church's overindulgences and its "pay as you go" scheme for absolving sins. Thesis 35 read: "It is not in accordance with Christian doctrines to preach and teach that those who buy off souls, or purchase confessional licences, have no need to repent of their own sins." The Christian reformers sought to recover the lost golden age of primitive purity set forth in the Bible. The Catholic Church responded to the Protestant Reformation by consolidating its power under the popes of the Counter-Reformation.

Natural science also underwent enormous change during the Renaissance.[14] Science and technical innovation were not widespread phenomena but were practised by men who either possessed inherited wealth, made their living in another profession or retained patrons who would support them in their work.[15] Unlike a merchant's business, science and scientists had fewer opportunities for rapid financial returns. Nevertheless, it aroused increasing public interest, facilitated by the invention of Gutenberg's printing press (the first book was printed in 1456, and by 1473 there were some nine million copies of 35 000 titles on diverse topics in circulation).[16] The new scientific enterprise was more than a tool for understanding, it was a tool to change the world. Its rebirth can be directly traced back to what leading science historian Edward Grant calls "three crucial preconditions":[17] the twelfth-century translations of Greco-Arabic works into Latin; the formation of the medieval university; and the emergence of theologian natural philosophers (considered in Ch. 7).

In a little over 100 years some of the outstanding scientific achievements were:

- Leonardo da Vinci's investigations of anatomy and mechanics, analysis of bird flight and prototype designs for the parachute, submarine and helicopter;
- Copernicus's heliocentric theory (1543);
- Vesalius's book on human anatomy (1543);
- Brahe's astronomy (1572);
- Galileo's telescopic astronomy and mechanics (1590–1638);
- Gilbert's experiments on magnetism (1600);

- Kepler's laws of planetary motion (1609–1619);
- Harvey's discovery of the double circulation of the blood (lung and body) (~1628);
- Descartes's theory of coordinates (1637);
- Pascal's formulation of a theory of mathematical probabilities (1640s) and invention of the first digital calculator (1643);
- Torricelli's barometric pressure (1644);
- Guericke's air pump (1647);
- Malpighi's discovery that capillaries connect arteries and veins (1660);
- Boyle's gas laws (1662);
- Huygen's proposal of a wave theory of light (1670s);
- van Leeuwenhoek's pioneering microscopic research (1672–1723);
- Newton's theory of universal gravity (1687);
- Leibniz's theory of monads (1714); and
- Harrison's portable maritime clock (1750s) to measure accurately longitude meridians over long distances.

During the seventeenth century, treatise after treatise contained hypotheses, observations, models, mathematics, measurements and methods of proof presented in unprecedented detail. It was a period when new competing methodologies emerged and the medieval scientific legacy of Grosseteste and Ockham began to bear fruit. This chapter will explore some of these exciting developments by contrasting the "methodologies" of Francis Bacon and René Descartes, followed by a number of case histories from Copernicus to Newton. Such a streamlined approach in no way implies a linear, cumulative series of breakthroughs; rather, it highlights a number of turning points as part of a more complicated picture that historians of science are still trying to unravel. As in the late medieval period, we will show that there were no deep conflicts between religion and science for most natural philosophers. Most conflicts arose when new observations, theories and discoveries bumped into the traditional scriptural interpretations of the Catholic and Protestant churches. Amid the rich diversity of competing theories involving a complex mosaic of Aristotelianism, Neoplatonism, atomism, corpuscularism and geometrical philosophies, new knowledge was forged, worldviews were transformed and the very nature of proof and certainty came under the spotlight.

NEW-AGE SCIENTIFIC "METHODOLOGIES": BACON AND DESCARTES

> The logic which is received, though it to be very properly applied to civil business and to those arts which rest in discourse and opinion, is not nearly subtle enough to deal with nature; and in attempting to what it cannot master, has done more to establish and perpetuate error than to open the way to truth.
>
> Francis Bacon[18]

Strongly echoing the sentiments of Grosseteste, Roger Bacon and Ockham, in his famous *Novum Organum* (*New Instrument*), Francis Bacon (1561–1626) argued for the need for a new methodology to demystify the physical world.[19] What emerged was a new method of science that was not opposed to, but closely intertwined with, religious and political reform.[20] Bacon felt that his method was vastly superior to Aristotle's causes and pure scholastic deductive logic, and would improve the quality of life and provide human beings with a way to control nature as in no other period in history.[21]

Bacon further anticipated the rise of a scientific community with academies and societies to disseminate the new knowledge as public knowledge.[22] In this sense, he is truly modern, even though he discovered nothing himself except a hint of the possibilities of refrigeration through the occasional experiment involving stuffing a chicken with ice. Twentieth-century historian of science Alexandre Koyre (1892–1964) describes Bacon as "the announcer, the *buccinator* of modern science, but not one of its creators".[23] He was the consummate systematizer; he was not a practitioner or theoretician.[24]

Bacon's scientific methodology comprised four parts: (i) it involved the "reliable" testing of an idea, usually involving an experiment; (ii) the information was then classified in "tables of invention"; (iii) minor generalizations were formed via induction (from particulars to universals); (iv) the laws formulated were to be verifiable by predicting and testing again by way of experiment, although he never fully clarified this approach.[25] Some historians of science claim that Bacon's method preempted Karl Popper's "falsification" method, which states that the laws of nature or theories are not verifiable but falsifiable, but this is highly controversial.[26] The main problem with Bacon's "method" was its deficiency in emphasizing the importance of raw intuition and mathematical relations in the process of discovery.

Although Bacon clearly separated divine revelation from sensible knowledge, he nonetheless viewed the speculative and practical sciences as religious duties.[27] It would be a mistake, therefore, to think that he disparaged religion in favour of science (this did not begin until the eighteenth-century Enlightenment). Indeed, Bacon proclaimed that the "practical sciences" had a religious function, and he helped science achieve early public acceptance; the "speculative" sciences helped people understand God's creation, whereas the "practical" sciences helped lay the foundations for human beings to have some control over the world.[28] Bacon also had the overarching vision that science would help to restore God's Creation to its pristine condition before the Fall, when the human race sacrificed its dominion over nature.[29]

While Bacon aimed to construct a scientific methodology relying heavily on sense-experience, René Descartes (1596–1650) was at the other end of the ontological spectrum of discovery. Born 35 years after Bacon, Descartes wished "to demolish everything completely and start again right from the foundations".[30] He wanted to replace the science of the day with a genuine *scientia*, "true knowledge", where every assertion had its own proof from a strict philosophical method.[31] The rationalist in Descartes proclaimed a similar methodology to the "dialectic" in Plato's *Republic*.[32] Descartes began with "absolute" truths and deduced, by strict logic, new knowledge about nature.[33] Descartes's epistemology was constructed from "subjective" precision with reason and logic as his prized criteria of truth. He wrote: "we should busy ourselves with no object about which we cannot attain certitude equal to that of the demonstration of arithmetic and geometry".[34]

Descartes began by doubting everything except his own existence. He proceeded to deduce explanations, from the existence of God to the nature of the whole physical universe. In his highly acclaimed *Discourse on Method* (1637), "provisional" knowledge played no part in his logical, mathematical method. The scientist, he believed, should arrive at his "absolute" axioms of nature by hard thinking and reasoning, and should start with only a minimum of observations.[35] Each step was to be as clear and certain as a mathematical proof. Not surprisingly, Descartes found Bacon's methodology and Galileo's "new" science totally inferior, and likened them to building a house from the roof down.

Descartes's methodology began with his "first principles" and explained the world by logical deduction, whereas Bacon's methodology went the other way: from observations and testing to establish natural laws by way of induction.[36] His science was clearly based on philosophy, not common experience. In Descartes's mind, the need to experiment was an expression of the failure of the ideal.[37] However, in practice, Descartes's grasp of natural science improved as he relied less on deducing solutions from his "first principles" and more on experimentation. The best scholarship now recognizes that there is often a crucial gap between the methods actually employed by natural philosophers (including scientists today) and the formal descriptions of their methodology. Indeed, Descartes made many important scientific inroads in the areas of cosmology, astronomy, geometrical optics, meteorology, biology, anatomy, physiology and medicine.[38]

THE WORLD BEFORE COPERNICUS

Aristotle and Ptolemy shared a few basic concepts. They both believed that each of the seven planets was embedded in its own ethereal sphere and was carried around by it. They further assumed that the fixed stars were located on a single sphere that surrounded and encompassed all the planetary orbs. Finally, both agreed that each planetary sphere consisted of a plurality of subspheres that were needed to account for the resultant motion and position of the planet that was being carried around.

E. Grant[39]

Before the Renaissance, the Western "astronomical" worldview was a blend of the collective authorities of Aristotle, Ptolemy and the Catholic Church, with borrowings from Arab-Jewish scholarship.[40] The universe was a giant sphere *containing* a number of invisible ethereal spheres carrying the seven planets with the Earth immobile in the centre (Fig. 8.1). These crystalline (or transparent) spheres moved in perfect circles at uniform speeds, and in the opposite direction to the motion of the eighth sphere.[41] The eighth sphere contained the "fixed stars" (all the heavenly bodies except for the planets, sun, moon and comets) and rotated rapidly around the spherical, stationary Earth, which explained night and day, and the rising and setting of the stars.[42] God apparently lived in the ninth sphere beyond the fixed stars: "the abode of God and all the Elect".[43] The ninth sphere was associated with the biblical waters above the firmament (usually the eighth sphere). The tenth sphere was the "first movable sphere" because it was the first enclosed by the outermost, stationary, empyrean heaven (see Fig. 8.1).

The spheres were kept in eternal motion by God as prime (unmoved) mover or "first cause" and by secondary causes. The secondary causes were God's own creation: external and separate intelligences, namely angels.[44] Medieval natural philosophers

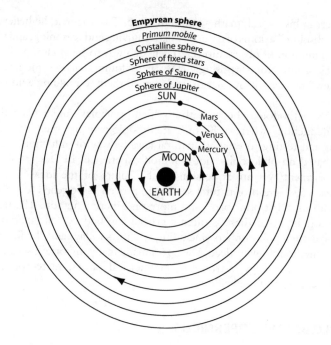

Figure 8.1 Typical representation of the geocentric pre-Copernican universe in the high Middle Ages and early Renaissance (modified after Grant 1996: 108). The westward diurnal motion of the sphere of fixed stars was opposite to the direction of the planetary spheres and the sun.

taught that eternal motion was accomplished by three non-physical faces: intellect, will and a finite motive force or "executive power".[45] The "executive power" carried out the commands of the intellect and will.

Unlike Robert Holkot (d. *c.*1349) and Thomas Bradwardine (*c.*1290–1349), who speculated about the possibility of other worlds,[46] most late medieval scholars believed that nothing at all existed beyond heaven: no matter, no space – nothing. Hell was a slippery concept and generally considered to be somewhere below the Earth.[47]

Ptolemy was unquestionably the principal authority on the observed motions of the moon, sun and planets. Using three mathematical constructions – the eccentric, epicycle and equant – he presented an ingenious model to describe the movements of the planets, which Aristotle's geocentric cosmology, with its perfect homocentric spheres, failed to adequately explain.[48] The eccentric construction positioned the Earth (E) slightly away from the centre of all planetary motions (C) (Fig. 8.2). Thus the centre was a point that could rotate around the Earth. This model was good for describing some non-uniform motion. Ptolemy found it necessary to introduce the epicycle-on-deferent model, which had a planet move uniformly around a small circle that itself moved uniformly around a larger circle ("carrying circle" or "deferent"), with the Earth at its centre (Fig. 8.2). By using this model, and choosing the appropriate speed of each planet, Ptolemy was able to explain the retrograde motion

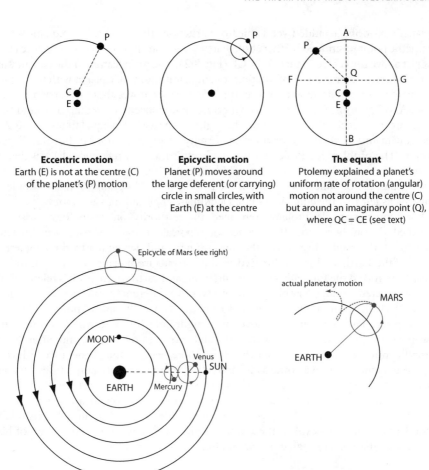

Eccentric motion
Earth (E) is not at the centre (C)
of the planet's (P) motion

Epicyclic motion
Planet (P) moves around
the large deferent (or carrying)
circle in small circles, with
Earth (E) at the centre

The equant
Ptolemy explained a planet's
uniform rate of rotation (angular)
motion not around the centre (C)
but around an imaginary point (Q),
where QC = CE (see text)

Figure 8.2 Ptolemy's mathematical construction of the world combined the eccentric, epicycle and equant models to match geometrical theory with the observed irregularities of motions of the planets. For each planet's carrying circle, there were three points: the fixed Earth (E); the fixed geometric centre of the circle (C); and the equant point (Q). The planet moved around its equant point with uniform rate of rotation (or angular speed). Ptolemy's complicated system, with minor modifications, explained the motion of the sun, moon and planets and remained popular in the West until it was superseded by the sun-centred Copernican system.

of the planets. Retrograde motion of a planet was its deviation and occasional reversal of direction relative to the "fixed stars". Normally the planets move in an eastwards direction viewed from Earth, but astronomers for thousands of years have recorded annual east to west movements before the planets resume their normal direction. By adjusting the size of the epicyle (and therefore speed), Ptolemy could account for this behaviour.

However, Ptolemy's eccentric and epicycle-on-deferent models still did not fully explain all observed planetary phenomena. To account for the apparent irregularities of a planet's motion, he added yet a third construction, the equant. The equant was a geometric point positioned neither at the Earth's position (E) nor geometric centre (C), but just above the centre so that QC = CE (Fig. 8.2). The main feature of the equant was that it ensured a uniform rate of rotation (or angular motion) of a planet with respect to its equant point, not its geometrical centre.[49] As a planet moves about its carrying circle (from A to F, F to B, B to G or G to A), greater linear speeds are required around the longer arcs so that equal angles (four right angles) are travelled in equal times (Fig. 8.2). The equant model therefore retained uniformity of *angular* motion, but not *linear* motion. The problem for Ptolemy from the Earth's frame of reference (E) was that it introduced a non-uniform motion or wobble into the "fixed" heavens and violated one of the oldest astronomical principles of the perfect circle.[50] Because of this "wobble", Copernicus felt that the equant was not a legitimate application to astronomy.[51]

For centuries, while Ptolemy remained the authority on cosmology, Aristotle remained the authority on the science of physical change.[52] Aristotelian change occurred in the region just below the moon sphere and descended to the geometric centre of the Earth, and was influenced by the currents from planetary motion, which moved and mixed the four elements fire, air, water and earth. In Aristotle's teleological or goal-directed world, every physical object was of a different "form" acting on prime matter,[53] which, if left unimpeded, would act under its own "primary" power to find its natural place. The four elements moved in straight lines (up or down) and sought to rest in their natural state; with earth and water moving downwards, and air and fire naturally moving upwards. The Earth was a sphere because the element earth had a natural tendency to move towards a centre in a symmetrical fashion In descending order from the moon, the natural places (or orbs) were fire, air, water and earth. A primary cause produced an effect by its "own" intrinsic power. If a body acted on another body, however, the explanation was different and required Aristotle's secondary causation to explain the effect. Secondary causation was composed of his four causes (material, formal, efficient and final) acting simultaneously.[54]

COPERNICUS AND THE NEW ASTRONOMY

> [Copernicus's] first sketch of a heliocentric planetary theory was worked out by about 1510. In a few sheets, Copernicus described the chief features of his Sun-centred system, and the connections of the planets' apparent motions to actual motion of the Earth.
>
> J. Evans[55]

Nicolas Copernicus (1473–1543) was born in Torun, Poland, on 19 February 1473. He was not a radical, as one might expect, but a quiet Polish Church official at the cathedral of Frauenberg (Frombork) with impeccable Catholic credentials.[56] After receiving a solid scholastic education at the University of Cracow (1491–94), and visiting universities throughout Renaissance Italy, Copernicus pursued astronomy, astrology and mathematics privately alongside his theological studies.[57]

After much deliberation, Copernicus was convinced that Ptolemy, and most astronomers, had erred on two counts: the sun did not orbit the Earth; and the heavens did not move in the sky at night.[58] To Copernicus, the Earth was moving, not the heavens; the Earth revolved around the sun once a year, producing the seasons, and rotated on its axis every 24 hours, generating night and day. The Earth's daily rotation also explained the roll of the stars eastwards to people gazing into the night sky. In true Ockham's razor style, there was no need to invoke a rotation of the "eighth sphere" containing the fixed stars.

Copernicus's idea was not new. About 1800 years earlier, as discussed in Chapter 5, the Greek Aristarchus of Samos had postulated a similar idea, but no one believed him. Ptolemy had dismissed the idea of a moving Earth as "utterly ridiculous",[59] because, not least, all bodies tended to fall to the centre of the Earth.[60] Ptolemy was able to demonstrate that no contrary observations had ever been obtained, and so therefore rejected a moving Earth. A moving Earth did receive some support in the fourteenth and fifteenth centuries from French scholastic Jean Buridan (*c*.1295–1358), astronomer Nicole Oresme (*c*.1320–1382) and mathematician Nicholas of Cusa (*c*.1401–1464), but none of them broke completely from the Ptolemaic or the Aristotelian tradition.[61] Accepting a rotating Earth would have meant completely revising Aristotle's physics and, not least, confronting the authority of the Church.

The main objection to a rotating Earth was that the rotation would be so violent that it would have broken up and scattered around the heavens. Everything, including human beings, would be thrown off by this violent centrifugal force, as if they were objects placed on a potter's wheel.[62] If the Earth were moving, then it should surely experience constantly high winds. It was further reasoned that stones dropped from high towers would not fall in straight lines to the centre of the Earth.

Copernicus's starting-points

In sum, Copernicus's theory of the superior planets contains a mixture of radical innovation and conservative practice. To launch the Earth into orbit was a bold move. The Sun-centred theory does have great explanatory advantages. And it does turn the whole solar system into a unified whole, as Copernicus himself stressed. But in the technical details of his planetary theory, Copernicus remained a part of the Ptolemaic tradition.   J. Evans[63]

A moving Earth

Copernicus clearly understood the arguments against a moving Earth. However, he turned the question around and asked why the outer celestial sphere did not fly apart in the Ptolemaic model. Since ancient times, most astronomers knew that for the outer sphere to rotate around a central stationary Earth, it must move at extraordinarily high speeds to complete one revolution every day. Copernicus recognized, as did Buridan before him, that the problem of a rotating Earth was one of relative motion. Using the modern-day analogy of Grand Prix racing, everyone knows who is moving as the cars speed past. If, however, you were in one of two racing cars speeding side by side, from your frame of reference the other car's speed, relative to yours, is zero. Likewise, the motion of the air produced by a rotating Earth would not be felt by a person standing on the Earth because a large part of the air in which the clouds are floating is moving at the same relative speed.[64]

Copernicus also clearly understood that if the Earth were moving and rotating, the motion of a falling body would be a function of both linear and circular motions. He wrote: "The motion of a falling or rising body in the framework of the universe is twofold, being in every case a compound of straight and circular."[65] For these reasons, Copernicus saw nothing wrong with a rotating Earth and he saw many more reasons for the idea of rotation. By assuming the daily rotation of the Earth about its axis, he explained the rising and setting of the fixed stars, of the sun, the moon and the planets.

The Earth was not at the centre of the universe

Having proposed plausible arguments against a stationary Earth, Copernicus turned to the question of the Earth's centrality. He acknowledged Ptolemy's argument that the Earth was at the centre of the universe – or *near the centre* – because of observed irregularities in the planetary movements. But he did not believe it. Instead, he put to one side the Aristotelian assumptions about heavy matter moving to the centre of the *cosmos* and cleverly reasoned that there may be other centres of gravity in the universe "to save the appearances" (a Greek expression for defending the reality of sense-experience). Copernicus wrote: "I am of the opinion that gravity is nothing but a certain natural tendency to draw together, which is implanted in parts by the divine providence of the Maker of all things, that may collect themselves into unity and completeness, being assembled into the form of a sphere."[66] Copernicus did not restrict his definition of gravity to concentrate all matter at one point to form the Earth, but as "the tendency of like bodies to cluster".[67] The strong implication was that gravity was a universal attribute of spherical bodies regardless of whether they were in the sublunary or celestial spheres.[68] In addition, Copernicus proposed that the Earth had a slight tilt[69] about its poles, relative to the sun's rays during a 12-month period.[70] This slight tilt (now known to be 23.5°) provided the explanation for the seasonal differences in day and night; that is, it explained the seasons and precession of the equinoxes (north–south motion of the sun over the year).[71]

The order of the planets

If Copernicus was correct about the Earth not being stationary and not in the centre of the universe, how did he envisage the order of the planets? In the sixteenth century there was unanimous agreement that the moon was nearest the Earth and Saturn was the most distant. But Mercury and Venus were problematic. Plato (via Eudoxus) had placed both planets above the sun, Ptolemy placed them below, and some Arab astronomers placed Venus above and Mercury below.[72] Copernicus explained the order as Sun–Mercury–Venus–Earth–Mars–Jupiter–Saturn (Fig. 8.3). By delegating the Earth to a planetary status, and having all the planets revolve around the sun, Copernicus simplified the analysis tremendously, ordering the planets according to their orbital periods. An orbital period was the time taken to complete one revolution, and the planetary distances could be estimated using a constant celestial yardstick of the Earth–sun radius.[73] The apparent retrograde motion of the planets (Mercury, Venus, Mars, Jupiter and Saturn) was a result of the relative speeds of the Earth and the planets as observed from the Earth with no need to invoke Ptolemy's epicycle and deferents. In Copernicus's system, the inner planets moved faster than outer ones, and they "lapped" them. From the frame of reference of a fast planet, the outer slower

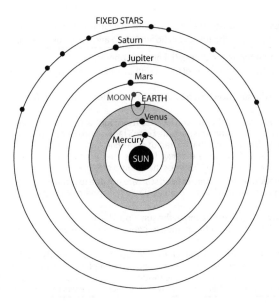

FIXED STARS
Saturn
Jupiter
Mars
MOON EARTH
Venus
Mercury
SUN

Figure 8.3 Copernicus's heliocentric cosmology. The sun is at the centre of the universe with the planets carried around by six major concentric spheres. This simplified representation omits the many epicycles Copernicus used in his system. The planets are bounded by the sphere of fixed stars in the outermost circle, which contains the Zodiac.

ones sometimes appear to stop and change direction. Copernicus was able to calibrate his heliocentric model by adjusting the size and speed of a planet's orbit.

In a nutshell, Copernicus abandoned geocentrism, removed Ptolemy's celestial spheres and geometical constructions, and had no further use for Aristotle's dualistic cosmology. The "fixed stars" were physical objects just like our sun, but located much further away. Copernicus's universe was spherical and finite, and at least 400 000 times larger in volume than Ptolemy's.[74] He did, however, retain Aristotle's notion of the sphere as the perfect shape in his account of gravity and the notion of final causes. Copernicus's astute reasoning provides an excellent example of how different starting-points in natural science (or any curiosity-driven endeavour) can lead to vastly different interpretations, yet remain true to the belief in God's rational plan.

De Revolutionibus Orbium Coelestium

What was unprecedented was the mathematical system that Copernicus built upon the earth's motion. With the possible exception of Aristarchus, Copernicus was the first to realize that the earth's motion might solve an existing astronomical problem or indeed a scientific problem of any sort. Copernicus' mathematics distinguishes him from his predecessors, and it was in part because of the mathematics that his work inaugurated a revolution as theirs had not.   T. S. Kuhn[75]

Table 8.1 Copernicus's seven postulates (1510), adapted from his *Commentariolus [Little Commentary]* found in Evans (1998: 415), with the full text in Rosen (1971) and Swerdlow (1973).

- There is not one single centre for all celestial orbs or spheres.
- The centre of the Earth is not the centre of the world, but only of the heavy bodies [gravity] and of the lunar orbit.
- All the orbs encircle the sun, which is so to speak, in the middle of them all, for the centre of the world is near the sun.
- The relation of the distances of the sun and Earth to the height of the firmament [the radius of the sphere of fixed stars] is less than the ratio between the Earth's radius and the distance from the Earth to the sun. [Copernicus's assumption here was that the radius of the Earth's circle about the sun was vanishingly small compared to the radius of the sphere of fixed stars. Copernicus's universe was much larger than the traditionally held view: at least 400 000 times the volume of Ptolemy's universe.]
- What appears as motions in the sphere of fixed stars are not due to it, but to the Earth. Therefore the Earth rotates in a daily motion around its fixed poles, while the sphere of fixed stars or last heaven remains stationary.
- What appears to us as motion in relation to the sun is not due to the sun itself, but to the Earth, which we are moving around just as any other planet. In consequence, the Earth is carried along with several motions.
- What shows itself in the planets as retrogradation [apparent backwards motion of Mars and Jupiter from east to west] and direct motions [normal motion of a planet from west to east] does not come from their own but from the Earth's part. The motion of the Earth alone is sufficient to explain a wealth of different phenomena in the heaven. [This was one of Copernicus's most significant insights.]

Copernicus's book *De Revolutionibus Orbium Coelestium* (*On the Revolutions of the Heavenly Spheres*) was published in 1543. Thirty years earlier he had sketched his theory in a short *Commentariolus* (*Little Commentary*) (1510), which contained seven postulates from which his world system was constructed (Table 8.1). The two-page commentary was circulated among his close friends, but not published.[76] Copernicus's approach to astronomy was largely mathematical. He used essentially the same data as Ptolemy, and modelled his treatise[77] on Ptolemy's *Almagest*.[78] Copernicus's book went through many editions (1566, 1617, 1854) with numerous and extensive alterations, insertions and cancellations.[79] Today over 500 copies survive.

The Catholic and Protestant response

> I should like your Holiness to know that I was induced to think of a method of computing the motions of the spheres by nothing else than the knowledge that mathematicians are inconsistent with their investigations ... Their computations are inexact and inconsistent with their hypotheses, their mathematical methods are clumsy, and they cannot make the universe a coherent whole.   Copernicus[80]

The Church's response to Copernicus's book was complicated by the Protestant Reformation and the Catholic Counter-Reformation. In 1545 Pope Paul III (1534–49) was trying desperately to restore dignity to the Church. The Pope's goal was to consolidate the people by restructuring the roles and activities of his cardinals, bishops and priests, who had corrupted the system for so long.[81] There were far more pressing concerns confronting the Catholic Church than discussing Copernicus's theory. Nevertheless, Copernicus's book had received support from Cardinal Schoenberg and Bishop Giese, who approved its dedicatory preface to Pope Paul III.[82] Its early acceptance appears to be related to Copernicus's position in the Church and the statement in the preface that his arguments were mathematical propositions, not firm statements about physical reality.

The early Protestant leaders were much more outspoken against Copernicus. In 1539, before the publication of *De Revolutionibus*, Martin Luther openly attacked Copernicus for daring to challenge the literal teachings of the Bible. Luther reportedly said:

> People gave ear to an upstart astrologer who strove to show that the Earth revolves, not the heavens or the firmament, the sun and the moon. Whoever wants to be clever must agree with nothing that others esteem. He must do something of his own. This is what that fellow does who wishes to turn astrology upside down. Even in those things that are thrown into disorder I believe the Holy Scriptures, for Joshua commanded the Sun to stand still, and not the Earth [see Joshua 10:12–13].[83]

Protestant reformer John Calvin (1509–1564) was equally scathing. Calvin[84] quoted from Psalm 93 and pointedly asked: "Who will venture to place the authority of Copernicus above the Holy Spirit?"[85] Protestant scholastic Melanchthon (1497–1560) was another who sharply criticized Copernicus and quoted from passages in Psalms (93:1, 104:5) and Ecclesiastes (1:5), stating that the Earth stood firm in its place, unmoved, with the sun moving above it; to which he added: "Fortified by these divine testimonies, we will cling to the truth."[86] However, he did place high value on the study of mathematics in studying natural phenomena.

In the next century, Copernicanism became more popular, and the Catholic Church responded by officially condemning the treatise on 5 March 1616; it remained on the Catholic Index of Prohibited Books (*Index Expurgatorius*) for some 200 years.[87] In spite of its condemnation, the book was still admired by most professional astronomers.[88] Most were interested in better mathematical tables for astrology, improvement of navigation (the problem of "longitudes"[89]) and, most importantly, reforming the solar–lunar calendar for the Christian year.[90] Ironically it was only after the book was banned that astronomers started to take the Copernician model more seriously, particularly after Galileo's development of telescopic astronomy in 1610 and, again later, when Newton transformed its broad cosmological structure into a new physics.[91]

The mystery preface

As mentioned above, one reason for the Catholic Church's initial acceptance of Copernicus's *De Revolutionibus* in 1543 was that its arguments were cast primarily as mathematical propositions and not physical reality. This view was reinforced in the preface to the book, which was titled "To the reader concerning the hypotheses of this work". The reader was warned not to take the heliocentric hypothesis of the Earth's motion literally, "lest he accept as the truth ideas conceived for another purpose, and depart from this study a greater fool than when he entered it".[92] Cardinal Robert Bellarmine would cite this preface some 70 years later, in a letter to one of Galileo's supporters, to illustrate the Catholic Church's view of the proper way to discuss Copernicanism.

However, a startling fact was to emerge. The preface was not written by Copernicus at all, but by a Lutheran pastor, Andreas Osiander (1498–1552). The discovery of the unauthorized preface was not made public until some 60 years later, when Kepler reported the events on the reverse of the title page of his *Astronomia Nova* (1609).[93] Apparently, during Copernicus's declining health he had asked his student Georg Joachim Rheticus (1514–1574) to organize the book's printing at Nuremberg.[94] In 1542, Rheticus had to leave Nuremberg for a teaching appointment and the job of publication was passed over to Andreas Osiander, who had some knowledge of astronomy.[95] The remarkable irony was that Copernicus wrote to Osiander three years before the publication about ways to ward off "calumnious attacks" from theologians who did not value mathematical truths.[96] About a year later (1 April 1541), Osiander replied:

> For my part, I have always felt about hypotheses that they are not articles of faith, but bases of calculation, so that even if they be false, it does not matter so long as they exactly represent the phenomena of the [celestial] motions … it would therefore seem an excellent thing for you to touch a little on this point in the Preface. For you would thus render more complacent the Aristotelians and theologians whose contradictions you fear.[97]

After agreeing to take over the publication from Rheticus, Osiander took full advantage of the occasion and wrote the "unauthorized" preface, where he appealed to traditional theology as the higher intellectual discipline, not astronomy.[98]

When Bishop Giese, Copernicus's ardent supporter, discovered what had happened, he became so outraged that he wrote a strong letter to Rheticus on "the abuse of confidence and the impiety" on behalf of the printer (or some depraved person who could not relinquish tradition).[99] Rheticus too was furious, so much so that he filed a legal action against Nuremberg's City Council ordering a republication without the preface.[100] Rightly, the legal suit failed because the printer, Johannes Petreius, was not liable because he printed what was handed to him. Supporters of Osiander came to Osiander's defence by claiming his action was well intended and designed to diffuse criticism from the Church.[101]

Copernicus received a copy of his book on the day of his death, 24 May 1543. It is not known if he read the preface, but almost certainly he would have taken exception to Osiander's assertion that mathematical astronomy lacks the power to reveal the truth. Scholars agree, however, that Copernicus thought of himself as reviving the best traditions of Greek astronomy and believed that his mathematical approach represented a physical truth or reality as part of God's creation.

TYCHO BRAHE AND GIORDANO BRUNO

[Tycho's cosmology] reconciled the combatants without compromising any essential issue; it took all that was scientifically sound from Copernicus, and for the rest clung to the common sense.   A. R. Hall[102]

The main problem with Copernicus's planetary system, apart from its radical departure from "saving the appearances", was that astronomy was not sufficiently advanced to decide which construction was right or wrong. A "direct" proof of Copernicus's system was not available until the nineteenth century, in the famous experiment using the Foucault pendulum.[103] In the meantime, one early critic of the Copernican and Ptolemaic systems was the great Danish astronomer, astrologer and alchemist Tycho Brahe (1546–1601). Tycho was a Lutheran and spent most of his life patiently observing and measuring celestial movements using larger and more accurate instruments (but still preceding the telescope). Tycho relegated Copernicus's and Ptolemy's models to mere hypotheses, and proposed his own, which he regarded as his intellectual property.

Tycho's worldview contained some elements of Islamic astronomy and was a compromise of sorts with all the planets moving around the sun, and the sun and moon *orbiting a stationary Earth*.[104] This model had the advantages of the Copernican system but required no parallax (apparent relative motion among the fixed stars).[105] Tycho correctly reasoned that if the Earth were moving then the stars would have to be enormous distances away. Because Tycho retained a geocentric system while still embracing the mathematical advantages of the Copernican model, his hypothesis received support from the Jesuits and survived well into the seventeenth century.[106]

Another variation of the Copernican theory came from renegade Dominican monk and pantheist Giordano Bruno (1548–1600). Bruno largely agreed with Copernicus, but after studying Lucretius's cosmological poetry and the metaphysical works of the Neoplatonists, he envisaged a centreless and infinite universe with innumerable worlds.[107] Bruno wrote:

> To a body of infinite size there can be ascribed neither centre nor boundary ... Just as we regard ourselves as at the centre of that [universally] equidistant circle, which is the great horizon and the limit of our own encircling ethereal region, so doubtless the inhabitants of the moon believe themselves at the centre [of the great horizon] that embraces this earth, the sun and the other stars ... Thus the earth is not in the centre of the universe; it is central only to our surrounding space ... There is a single vast immensity which we may freely call *Void*; in it are innumerable worlds like this on which we live and grow. This space we declare to be infinite.[108]

Bruno believed that his idea of an infinite, centreless universe was best because it reflected the infinity of God as divine creator. For his pantheistic views proclaiming the infinite procreativeness of God and his critique of the Church, Bruno was tried by the Inquisition in the 1590s. Bruno was burned at the stake on 16 February 1600 in Rome.[109]

JOHANNES KEPLER (1571–1630): A MATHEMATICIAN WHO SOUGHT A NEW CELESTIAL PHYSICS

But though Kepler was full of praise for the conception of the sun-centered planetary system, he was quite critical of the particular mathematical system that Copernicus had developed. Again and again Kepler's writings emphasized that Copernicus had never recognized his own riches and that after the first bold step, the transposition of the sun and the earth, he had stayed too close to Ptolemy in developing the details of his system.   T. S. Kuhn[110]

One of the most courageous people to think beyond the narrow limits of Catholic and Protestant Church dogmas was Johannes Kepler, a colleague of Tycho Brahe.[111] Some historians quip that Tycho's most important discovery was Kepler, who formed a bridge between Gilbert and Copernicus and Galileo and Newton. Kepler was a mathematical astronomer and a well-known astrologer. Predicting a person's future from the position of the stars (judicial astrology) or predicting the future position of stars themselves (natural astrology) was a *bona fide* occupation, and Kepler (and Tycho Brahe) used the art to support their astronomy financially.[112] Astronomy was generally seen as a theoretical underpinning of astrology.

Kepler's formative years

Kepler was born into a Lutheran family in Württemberg, South Germany on 27 December 1571. At the age of 18, he enrolled to prepare for the Lutheran ministry at the University of Tübingen.[113] In his own words, "I wanted to become a theologian; for a long time I was restless. Now however, observe how through my efforts, God is being celebrated in astronomy."[114] While at the University of Tübingen, Kepler's growing interest in astronomy was encouraged by his teacher, mathematician and astronomer Michael Maestlin, a converted Copernican. Kepler was immediately impressed with the elegance of the Copernican system and began studying astronomy and mathematics in his spare time.[115]

As Kepler became increasingly disenchanted with some of the Lutheran doctrines, he became increasingly enchanted with mathematical astronomy, and eventually moved to Graz, Styria (now Austria) where he was appointed professor of mathematics at a Lutheran seminary. The position involved teaching and also acting as district mathematician to help refine astrological calendars. After being embroiled in a number of religious and political tensions between Lutherans and Catholics, Kepler was forced to flee Graz but never lost his faith in God.[116] Kepler believed that astronomy granted an opportunity to know and praise God. Immersing himself in Renaissance Neoplatonic–Pythagoreanism, he viewed the universe as a physical machine with perfect mathematical harmonies. God was embodied in the observable world that could be described in geometric terms. Kepler regarded geometry as a gift to human beings from God. In a much-quoted passage, he wrote:

> While in theology it is authority that carries the most weight, in philosophy it is reason. Therefore, Lactantius is holy who denied that the earth is round, Augustine is holy who, though admitting the roundness, denied the Antipodes, and the Holy Office nowadays is holy which, though allowing the earth's smallness, denies its motion. To me, however, the truth is more holy still, and (with all due respect to the Doctors of the Church) I prove philosophically not only that the earth is round, not only that it is contemptibly small, but also that it is carried among the stars.[117]

In 1596, Kepler published his *Mysterium Cosmographicum* (*Cosmographic Secret*), where he presented his first public defence of Copernicanism. However, he believed that Copernicus had failed to achieve the ideal of Neoplatonic–Pythagorean geometric simplicity and set out to show the errors.[118] Kepler's model of the universe had the planetary spheres of Mercury, Venus, Earth, Mars, Saturn and Jupiter separated from one another by an octahedron, then an icosahedron, a dodecahedron, a tetrahedron and a cube.[119]

Mixed in with this geometrical mysticism and search for underlying harmonies, Kepler's goal was to understand how a planet's position moved along its entire orbit, not just at selected points. "Saving the appearances" were not sufficient grounds to establish truth because many mathematical constructions could achieve the same result, including Ptolemy's, Copernicus's and Brahe's different constructions. For Kepler, the geometric relations must be explained causally and be in perfect harmony. This was highly significant because causal investigations were the domain of natural philosophy, not astronomy. Astronomy was a mathematical endeavour that provided "hypotheses" with no claims to physical reality. Kepler's work was so original that in 1596 his early teacher Maestlin wrote the following to the rector of Tübingen university: "the theme and ideas [of Kepler's *Mysterium Cosmographicum*] are so new that they have not yet occurred to anyone else".[120]

Kepler sought a physical force to move a physical body

Kepler's astronomy was nothing less than a complete reformulation of this subject in terms of its aims, methods, and principles. Before Kepler the goal of astronomers had been purely cinematical, that is, to produce a kind of celestial geometry (based on circles on circles) that would yield planetary positions agreeing with observation.

I. B. Cohen[121]

Kepler was a truly gifted mathematician. After leaving the University of Graz in 1600, he was appointed assistant to Tycho Brahe at a planetary observatory near Prague.[122] They were a good team because Tycho lacked the mathematical skills to analyse his observational data and Kepler lacked the data to fit his mathematics. Before his death, Tycho apparently pleaded with Kepler to use the data to build the new universe on a Tycho system.[123] Although Kepler highly respected Tycho, it was clear that he was going to use the data to suit his own needs. Indeed, in a letter to Heydon in October 1605 Kepler admitted, "I confess that when Tycho died, I quickly took advantage of the absence, or lack of circumspection, of the heirs, by taking the observations under my care, or perhaps usurping them."[124] A short time later, he was invited to take over Brahe's position as the imperial mathematician to Holy Roman Emperor Rudolph II, which he held from 1601 to 1612.[125] Armed with Tycho's observational data, the period was the most fruitful in Kepler's life.

As a preliminary, Kepler, like Copernicus, viewed a planet as a physical object (he used the word "satellite") and rejected Aristotle's "prime mover" for "first motion".[126] He believed that the physical force responsible for the motion of the planets was magnetism, an idea he derived from the work of Gilbert. Kepler pictured the magnetic force emanating from the sun pulling the planets along in their orbits and obeying an inverse-square law in regard to distance. The magnetic force was quite separate from the animistic "soul" principle, which he believed was responsible for the 24-hour rotation of the Earth.[127] Kepler wrote about magnetic force and his thinking about physical causes in a 1605 letter to his friend and major patron Herwart von Hohenburg, Bavarian chancellor with an interest in astronomy:

> I am much occupied with the investigation of the physical causes. My aim in this is to show that the celestial machine is to be likened not to a divine organism but rather to a clockwork ... insofar as nearly all the manifold movements are carried out by means of a single, quite simple magnetic form, as in the case of a clockwork all motions [are caused] by simple weight. Moreover, I show how this physical conception is to be presented through calculation and geometry.[128]

Thus Kepler's search for geometrical structure went hand in hand with his search for physical causes; the two constituted his reality. The significance of Kepler's treatment of celestial bodies as "points", and using mathematics to describe these "points" in motion, was ingenious. And so was his deep conviction that simple relationships existed to describe celestial phenomena on a vast scale, and they could be discovered by human beings. By establishing mathematical relationships in the form of equations, physical concepts and constants, he achieved something that ancient Greek and medieval science generally lacked. Kepler's long obsession with describing a geometric, harmonious universe running like clockwork culminated in his three laws of motion.

Kepler's three laws of motion

> The physical principles he employed expressed the basic propositions of Aristotelian dynamics, and the 17th century replaced them with a wholly different set.
> Nevertheless, Kepler was the founder of modern celestial mechanics. He was the first to insist that the long-accepted crystalline structure of the heavens did not exist and that a new set of questions about celestial motions had to be formulated.
>
> R. S. Westfall[129]

One of Kepler's greatest ideas was his use of elliptical or "egg" shaped planetary orbits rather than circular ones. This reformulation of the Copernican model was a radical departure from orthodoxy; not even Copernicus or Galileo (see later) had considered the possibility of non-circular orbits. This single discovery using Tycho's observational data revolutionized astronomy. The ancient's view of the circle being perfect, unchangeable and divine was no longer tenable. In addition, Kepler smashed another ancient Greek view and showed that each planet travelled faster the closer it approached the sun, and slower when further away. It was this fundamental discovery that led him to change his mind about a "motive soul" to a mechanistic "physical" force.[130] The mystic in Kepler also set out to discover the celestial harmonies, not unlike the Pythagorean "music of spheres".

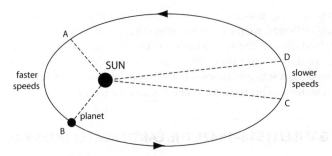

Figure 8.4 Kepler's first and second laws of motion state that the orbits of planets around the sun are not perfect circles but ellipses, and that each planet anywhere in its orbit carves out equal areas in equal times. For example, the time a planet takes to move from A to B *equals* the time it takes to move from C to D so that the area ABS is equal to area CDS. This relationship arises because planets gain orbital speed as they move closer to the sun and slow down as they move further away.

The unique aspect of Kepler's thinking was that he sought precise numerical relationships between orbit size and period and he wanted to relate the celestial sphere to the image of the Holy Trinity: *the sun with God the Father, the fixed stars with God the Son, and the intermediate with God the Holy Ghost.*[131] It was from this conception that Kepler published, in 1609, the physical relations between the time taken for a planet to complete one revolution (its period) and the axis of its orbital ellipse. Again, he believed that the magnetic forces emanating from the sun were responsible for his three laws. Kepler's three laws of planetary motion (Fig. 8.4) are:

1. **The law of elliptical paths:** The orbit of each planet is not circular but elliptical with the sun at one focus (not the mean position as Copernicus held).
2. **The law of equal areas:** A line drawn from the sun to a planet sweeps out equal areas of the ellipse in equal time. In other words, as a planet moves closer to the sun it moves faster and traces out a short fat triangle in the same time compared to a long thin triangle when it is moving slower further away.
3. **The law of harmony:** The ratio between the time for one revolution about the sun (the orbital period) to the mean radius of the orbit for any planet is constant (the square of the orbital time is related to the cube of the radius: $T^2 = kR^3$). The constant, k, linking the two, is the *same for all planets*. Copernicus had pointed out that a larger orbit had a longer revolution but Kepler provided a quantitative mathematical expression linking the concepts.

Kepler's first and second laws were published in his *New Astronomy Founded on Causes* (1609), and his third law, linking all motions in the solar system, was published ten years later in *Harmonice Mundi* (1619). On arriving at his third law, Kepler wrote, in a state of jubilation, "it overcame by storm the darkness of my mind with such full agreement between this idea and my labor of seventeen years on Brahe's observations that at first I believed I was dreaming".[132] Kepler's laws have been instrumental in describing planetary motion from the very large to the very small, including the motions around nuclei under the action of electrical forces. Notwithstanding Kepler's mathematical brilliance, we must keep in mind that his three laws only asserted that the planets revolved around the sun. Moreover, his three laws were not popular among astronomers in the seventeenth century until Newton incorporated them. From the observational data, it was still impossible to choose between the Copernican, Tychonic or Keplerian systems. This is where Galileo enters the picture.

GALILEO GALILEI (1564–1642): THE EARTH REALLY DOES MOVE!

> The scientist who, more than any other, was first and foremost in advancing the new art of experimental science was Galileo. Galileo's scientific program was certainly as revolutionary as Kepler's, and had a greater import in that it encompassed methods and results that could potentially affect all the sciences.
>
> I. B. Cohen[133]

Galileo Galilei was born in Pisa on 15 February 1564, the year of Shakespeare's birth and Michelangelo's death. He was an elder contemporary of Kepler and made fundamental contributions to the sciences of motion, astronomy, and the experimental method.[134] He was a natural philosopher, astronomer and mathematician and employed observation, experiment and measurement whenever he could.[135] There is a famous quote attributed to him that goes: "Measure what is measurable, and make measurable what is not so."

Galileo was a "diehard" Copernican, and he never accepted Kepler's theory of the planets moving in elliptical orbits, preferring traditional circular orbits. He also thought Kepler's idea about the planets generating music to be heard by the angels totally fanciful. Galileo also explicitly rejected Kepler's idea that the tides were caused by forces exerted by the moon, which ran counter to his own belief that the tides were caused by the Earth's rotation; Kepler was right. Having said this, Galileo and Kepler probably agreed more than they disagreed, particularly in unifying mathematics with the physical sciences and *not accepting an idea merely because it was the accepted "truth"*. Although they never met, they exchanged letters complimenting each other on their discoveries and openly discussed the different methodologies of science.[136]

Galileo's discoveries with the telescope

> Even his discoveries with the telescope, as interesting as they are in themselves – and it is hard to think of more surprising discoveries in the history of science – are of still greater interest for the conclusions that he drew from them, for nearly all of them could be turned to the criticism of Aristotle and the defense of Copernicus.
>
> N. M. Swerdlow[137]

Galileo turned his metre-long custom-built telescope[138] (20–30× power) to the skies from around 1610.[139] He observed that the moon was not perfectly smooth and spherical, as had been supposed for millennia, but had huge dark and light patches (mountains and craters) on its surface.[140] Galileo also observed the crescent-like shape of Venus and immediately saw parallels with it and the changing phases of the moon.

The key point was that Venus showed a crescent when large in appearance and looked like a full moon when smaller and therefore further away from the Earth. The observations implied that it was possible for Venus to be beyond the sun as seen from the Earth, consistent with the Copernican model.

Galileo also observed sun-spots and, by following individual spots around the sun, later used them to show that the sun rotated completely about its axis in 27 days.[141] He also observed the three rings of Saturn (which he mistakenly called "satellites") and the four satellites of Jupiter (at least 63 were known in 2004).[142] Galileo also identified the Milky Way as a long luminous cloud containing an aggregate of countless stars so dim that they were not visible to the naked eye. Everywhere Galileo looked, new vistas emerged "never seen from the creation of the world up to our own time".[143]

In Galileo's mind, Copernicus's sun-centred world was validated.[144] What Galileo failed to tell his audience was that these observations were also entirely compatible with Tycho Brahe's model with a stationary Earth. Most astronomers of the time, in fact, favoured the Tychonic system. Galileo's observations, and in particular his observations of the phases of Venus, certainly made the Copernican theory more probable. Moreover, Galileo agreed with Tycho and Bruno, and Holkot and Bradwardine before them, that the universe was much bigger than anyone had imagined. Up until that time most astronomers, including Kepler, believed that the universe was packed with matter, with little or no empty space.

In great haste, Galileo, at the age of 46, published many of his telescopic observations in *Sidereus Nuncius* (*Starry Messenger*) (1610). In that summer he resigned his chair at Padua to become court mathematician and philosopher to the Grand Duke of Tuscany, an appointment that enabled him to devote more time to research. In Florence Galileo continued his work on motion and on mechanics, and began to enter into disputes about Copernicanism. In 1611 Galileo wrote to Kepler expressing his dismay at astronomers' unwillingness to accept the scientific inferences of his telescopic observations:

I am very grateful that you have taken interest in my investigations ... and you have become the first and almost the only person who gives full credence to my contentions; nothing else could be really expected from a man with your keenness and frankness. But what will you say to the noted philosophers of our University who, despite repeated invitations, still refuse to take a look either at the moon or the telescope and so close their eyes to the light of truth? This type of people regard philosophy as a book like Aeneid or Odessey and believe that truth will be discovered, as they themselves assert, through the comparisons of texts rather than through the study of the world of nature. You would laugh if you could hear some of our most respectable university philosophers trying to argue the new planets out of existence by mere logical arguments as if these were magical charms.[145]

Galileo also told the story of an astronomer who (probably half-jokingly) refused to look through the telescope "because it would only confuse him".[146] Others labelled Galileo's celestial observations fraudulent. However, he rose above these attacks and continued his scientific investigations. In 1611 Galileo also went to Rome to show his discoveries to the Jesuits of the Roman College and, instead of mocking him, they congratulated him, as did Pope Paul V and several Cardinals.[147]

Defence of Copernicanism, 1613–1615

There are more things in Heaven and Earth, Horatio,
Than are dreamt of in your philosophy.   William Shakespeare[148]

Within a year of publishing *Sidereus Nuncius*, Galileo was a celebrity. Problems did not begin until he publically endorsed Copernicus's system in his *Letters on Sunspots* (1613), and again after 1632 when he published his famous *Dialogue Concerning the Two Chief Systems of the World: Ptolemaic and Copernican*.[149] The controversy began in December 1613 during a court breakfast when one of Galileo's opponents, Cosimo Boscaglia, persuaded the Grand Duchess Christina of Lorraine to ask Father Benedetto Castelli, Galileo's former student, to explain the significance of the new astronomy.[150] Some say it was Boscaglia's indirect way of discrediting Galileo without himself confronting him. Specifically, the question was asked about the apparent contradiction between the Copernican system and the Scriptures.[151] Father Castelli, reflecting later on the occasion, described his own response to the Grand Duchess as "behaving like a champion" in deflecting the line of attack.[152]

On hearing of the exchange, Galileo believed that his position had not received fair representation. To set the record straight, he sent a long letter to Father Castelli in which he outlined his views on the relationship between theology and science; that is, there should be no theological interference in purely scientific matters. While the Scriptures gave infallible guidance concerning the way of salvation, they should not be involved in disputes concerning physical interpretations or in teaching astronomy. What human beings discover using their senses and reason should be interpreted in the light of experimentally established facts.[153] In those cases, where the Scriptures pertained to matters of science, God's word must not be taken too literally. In Galileo's eyes there was no conflict between the two sources of truth. Some of his views on the relation between science and faith can be found in his *Letter to the Grand Duchess Christina* (1615):

> I think that in discussions of physical problems we ought to begin not from the authority of scriptural passages, but from sense-experiences and necessary demonstrations; for the Holy Bible and the phenomena of nature proceed alike from the divine Word, the former as the dictate of the Holy Ghost and the latter as the observant executrix of God's commands … For that reason it appears that nothing physical which sense-experience sets before our eyes, or which necessary demonstrations prove to us, ought to be called in question (much less condemned) upon the testimony of biblical passages which may have some different meaning beneath their words. For the Bible is not chained in every expression to conditions as strict as those which govern all physical effects; nor is God any less excellently revealed in Nature's actions than in the sacred statements of the Bible.
>
> … I would say here something that was heard from an ecclesiastic of the most eminent degree: "That the intention of the Holy Ghost is to teach us how one

goes to Heaven, not how Heaven goes" ... Hence, I should think it would be part of prudence not to permit anyone to usurp scriptural texts and force them in some way to maintain any physical conclusion to be true, when at some future time the senses and demonstrative or necessary reasons may show the contrary. Who indeed will set bounds to human ingenuity? Who will assert that everything in the universe capable of being perceived is already discovered and known? Let us rather confess quite truly that "those truths which we know are very few in comparison with those which we do not know".[154]

Unfortunately for Galileo, his letter ended up in the wrong hands. Eventually, inaccurate copies reached the Congregation of the Holy Office in Rome, which was the Church's arbiter on matters of faith and morality. On hearing this, Galileo asked if he could send the "correct" version via Monsignor Pero Dini, who could pass a copy on to Cardinal Robert Bellarmine (1542–1621), the Pope's theological adviser.

Galileo also became aware through Monsignor Dini that Cardinal Bellarmine did not believe that Copernicus's *De Revolutionibus* opposed the Church's teachings, if the appropriate amendments were inserted. Bellarmine argued that the reader must understand that the Copernican model was "a way to save the appearances, in a manner of those who have put forth epicycles, but do not really believe in them".[155] Bellarmine's argument shared many similarities with Osiander's claim in Copernicus's "unauthorized" preface, 70 years earlier, that mathematical astronomy makes no claim to truth about reality. The Copernican model must be understood as a hypothesis, not a definitive proof.

In an exchange of letters with Dini, Galileo countered Bellarmine's exegesis and unfortunately violated his own conviction that science and religion should be kept separate. Fortunately for Galileo, Dini did not pass the letter on to Bellarmine. About the same time, Galileo received some good and bad news from his friend Giovanni Ciampoli. The good news was that the Dominicans in Rome were not out to condemn him. The bad news was that Cardinal Barberini (who was later to become Pope Maffeo) cautioned him not to exceed beyond the boundaries of physics and mathematics, emphasizing again that Copernicanism was a hypothesis, not a truth of reality.[156] Thus the conflict between Galileo and the Catholic Church was strongly hinged upon authority deciding what constitutes reality and a scientific truth (or lack thereof).

The Inquisition: "Church authority rules"

Galileo's conflict with the Roman Catholic Church has long held a very special fascination. The prime reason for this, of course, is that the Galileo affair has come to be seen as the paradigm case of the troubled interaction between science and religion. Another reason is the sheer dramatic power of events involved, which continue to attract the attention of the scholar, the novelist and the playwright.

R. Blackwell[157]

Following instructions from Pope Paul V, Cardinal Bellarmine summoned Galileo for a private discussion on 26 February 1616. What transpired no one knows for sure, but the relations between the truths of science and religion began to sour.[158] A week later on 5

March, the Holy Office pronounced the Copernican theory heretical. A moving Earth and stationary sun were contradictory to numerous passages in the Scriptures. The Inquisition's public decree of 1616 announced that the Copernican hypothesis was "false and completely contrary to the divine Scriptures".[159] All recent books that supported the Copernican theory were banned, as were some more technical and non-theological works, such as Kepler's *Epitome of Copernican Astronomy*. Copernicus's book was not banned outright because of its relevance to Catholic Calendrical Reform, but it was "suspended until corrected".[160]

Many historians of science believe that the decree against Copernicanism was not a direct outcome of Galileo's growing celebrity, although it must have been a factor; rather, it was part of a wider response from the Catholic Church to the Reformation.[161] It was a belated response to Luther's doctrine of "private" interpretation of the Bible in favour of traditional biblical exegesis.[162] Interpreting the Bible was a task that had been reserved for approved theologians in the wake of the Council of Trent (1545–63), which had pronounced that if the early Church fathers had reached a consensus on how a verse of the Scriptures was to be interpreted, that consensus had to be respected. These interpretations, as discussed in Chapter 7, were a complex mix of literal, allegorical, symbolic and typological readings. It just so happened that Cardinal Bellarmine did pronounce that the verses referring to the Earth and sun should be taken literally.

Galileo was in trouble. Although he was not mentioned directly in the decree of 1616, he was explicitly told by Cardinal Bellarmine not to "hold, teach or defend" the Copernican theory "in any way whatever, either orally or in writing", and he apparently agreed to do so.[163] About seven years later tensions began to ease when Galileo's friend Cardinal Maffeo Barberini became the new Pope Urban VIII (1623). After several visits to Rome in 1624, Galileo was given permission to proceed with writing his *Dialogue Concerning the Two Chief Systems of the World* but with the clear proviso that Copernicanism was to be treated as a "hypothesis", and not a fact of reality.[164]

Nearly a decade later, in 1632, Galileo's *Dialogue* was published and immediately became popular. The book set out to demolish Aristotelian physics and Ptolemaic astronomy. It was written in the form of a four-day dialogue between friends Salviati, Sagredo and Simplicio. Salviati was the spokesperson for Galileo, Sagredo was a neutral intelligent layman and Simplicio was a spokesperson for Aristotelianism and Ptolemaic astronomy. The first three days of arguments described "saving the appearances", regardless of whether the Earth moved or not. The last day's argument was not to show that the Copernican system was possible, but that it represented reality. Salviati argued that tidal motion ("sloshing around") of the seas was caused by the Earth's twofold motion (rotation and revolution, which we now know was wrong). Salviati ended his argument by saying: "From this I forthwith conclude that, this being so, it would be excessive boldness for anyone to restrict the Divine power and wisdom to some particular fancy of his own." Galileo's subtle reference to the fanciful biases of authority beyond which they know little was blatantly obvious.

What followed was even more portentous, at least on face value. After Salviati concluded his statement, Galileo gave Simplicio the final word arguing that God in his omnipotence could have made a particular phenomenon like the tides in any number of ways and that it would be highly presumptuous for anyone to claim to know the ultimate mechanism underlying it. Galileo had used Pope Urban VIII's favourite argument in the mouth of the Aristotlian Simplicio, who had been constantly ridiculed by Salviati and Sagredo throughout the dialogue.[165] Galileo had, wittingly or unwittingly,[166] over-stepped the mark. Rumours began to spread, and in 1632 Pope Urban VIII convened a special commission to examine the book and make recommendations; the commission found that Galileo had not really treated the Copernican theory hypothetically and placed the book on the Index of Prohibited Books, where it remained until around 1824. The commission also recommended that the matter be examined by the Inquisition or Holy Office,[167] who summoned Galileo to Rome.

Galileo arrived in Rome in the spring of 1633 and after a number of interviews he was charged with violating the edict of 1616.[168] The charge against him was one of personal disobedience for "defending" the Copernican theory, not contradicting the Bible himself.[169] It was a matter of authority, not truth, although Galilean scholar Stillman Drake believes that hostility of contemporary philosophers towards Galileo would have played a deciding role.[170] On 22 June 1633, Galileo had to recant the belief that the sun was the centre of the world and that the Earth rotated and orbited the sun, and sign a document apology to the Catholic Church. The Church wrote a humiliating abjuration for him to recite on his knees. Afterwards, it was to be read to the public from the pulpits throughout Italy. The renunciation ended with these words:

> I swear that in the future I will never again say or assert, verbally or in writing, anything that might furnish occasion for a similar suspicion regarding me; but, should I know any heretic or person suspected of heresy, I will denounce him to this Holy Office or the Inquisitor or Ordinary of the Place where I may be.[171]

Galileo did read the renunciation, but then, in a final act of defiance against Church authority, he rose to his feet and is reported to have whispered *Eppur si muove*: "and yet it does move". These words are, however, of doubtful authenticity. At the age of 69, Galileo was placed under house arrest until his death in 1642.

An interesting footnote is that Descartes, on hearing of Galileo's ordeal, quickly postponed publishing his views on a moving Earth in *Le Monde* [*The World*].[172] In a letter, dated April 1634, Descartes wrote:

> Though I thought they were based on very certain and evident proofs [referring to the movement of the earth], I would not wish, for anything in the world, to maintain them against the authority of the Church. I desire to live in peace and to continue the life I have begun under the motto *to live well you must live unseen*.[173]

Le Monde was eventually published 14 years after his death in 1664.

Galileo the "physicist"

The new basis for Galileo's science of motion was careful measurement, through which he began to replace the ancient search for cases with the modern search for physical laws.

S. Drake[174]

Although Galileo's work on mechanics did not attract the same public notoriety as his telescopic astronomy, it was no less significant to the history of science. Like Archimedes and Hipparchus, Galileo was interested in the geometrical framework of different kinds of natural motion. The first motion involved an initial horizontal force, like an explosion of a gun, which could keep a body moving along a straight line at constant velocity. The second motion involved a force applied constantly to a body in a vertical direction, which could make the same body drop downwards *with constant acceleration* (i.e. where the velocity increases by a constant amount during each interval of time). And the third was a combination of the two, which would cause the body to follow a parabolic curve. In addition, lacking the idea of Newtonian gravitation, Galileo analysed circular motion and concluded (mistakenly) that because circular motion was natural and eternal, no force was required to act on the planets to keep them in motion. This preconception prevented him from formulating the correct principle of inertia.[175] Galileo, like Descartes, believed that the idea of a universal force of gravitation was an "occult" quality.

One of the most famous experiments attributed to Galileo is the dropping of two cannon balls of unequal weights from the top of the Leaning Tower of Pisa and seeing which hit the ground first. Although historians of science agree that the Leaning Tower was probably not the venue for Galileo's famous free fall experiment, his notebooks do mention that he dropped weights "from a tower".[176] Centuries before this, Aristotle had argued that a heavier ball would hit the ground first. Galileo demonstrated that they arrived at very similar times, implying that there was a uniform constant acceleration. The very slight difference, which he could not accurately measure, was correctly attributed to difference in air friction and the ability of the heavier ball to overcome this resistance.[177] Galileo deduced that if the experiment were performed in a vacuum, the cannon ball and a feather or a snowflake would hit the ground at *exactly* the same time. This direct experiment had to wait some 370 years, until astronaut David Scott demonstrated on the moon's surface that a feather and lead weight dropped from the same height hit the ground at identical times.

In 1604, knowing that he could not accurately measure the different times and distances of a body during free fall, Galileo devised an ingenious model to simplify the phenomenon. Instead of using a tower, he ran a "slow motion" experiment on an inclined plane (about 2 degrees).[178] "Diluting" the effect of gravity permitted him to control more carefully and simplify conditions, allowing him to measure times and distances, and therefore speeds in acceleration.[179] Galileo calibrated his system by letting a ball roll down the slope and marking its positions after a series of equal times using musical beats of about half a second, and other times using his own pulse.[180] These distances were measured in units of about one millimetre, after which he demonstrated that balls of different weights fell at the same rate.[181] In his own words, "A body is said to be uniformly accelerated when, starting from rest, it aquires equal increments of velocity during equal time intervals."[182]

In the process of testing the mathematical relations of uniformly accelerated motion in the real world, Galileo introduced a fundamental constant into physics: the acceleration of gravity. Today, the uniform acceleration of gravity is accepted as about $9.8 \, \mathrm{m \, s^{-1} \, s^{-1}}$. In addition, and vitally important to the development of science, Galileo described his experiments in enough detail in his *Two New Sciences* (1638) for other physicists of his time to repeat them and check his calculations and conclusions independently. In 1961, historian of science Thomas Settle decided to repeat Galileo's "slow motion" experiment and estimated the errors of his measurements to be within 1–2 per cent.[183] This access to repeatability constituted an important milestone in the birth of modern science. Although interest in error calculations began with Grosseteste, it did not come to the fore until Pierre Laplace (1749–1827) joined forces with Antoine Lavoisier (1743–1794) in the eighteenth century, when they raised the subject at the Paris Academy of Sciences in June 1783.[184] Apparently the first scientist to attempt a valid error calculation was Henry Cavendish, who estimated the error of his measurement of force of electrical attraction in 1771.

Galileo on science and religion

> By subordinating mechanical laws of nature to divine guidance, mathematical physics provided the key to knowledge of God. In the scientific early culture of early-modern Europe, Galileo becomes the forerunner of Descartes, Malebranche, and Newton rather than the follower of Lucretius, Epicurus, and Democritus.   P. Redondi[185]

Volumes have been written about Galileo's views on science and religion. Galileo viewed the universe as an ordered system created by God that could be studied by science and religion without conflict.[186] He viewed himself as a steward of God's revealed truth. To him, the job of the natural philosopher was to seek knowledge using intuition, observation and experiment.[187] And if propositions were rigorously demonstrated and seemingly in conflict with the Scriptures or Church teachings, some decisions had to be made.

Two aspects of Galileo's scientific philosophy stand out: first, sense-experience combined with experiment about the physical world was superior to philosophical and theological dogmas; and, secondly, and perhaps the most innovative, was the "worthlessness of authority in deciding any scientific question" without rigorous demonstration.[188] His faith in nature, and its laws, went side by side with his faith in God. It would be a mistake to think that Galileo was trying to convince the Church that it was wrong and the Copernican system was right.[189] Galileo never intended to pit natural science against faith. Further, Galileo was not challenging any of the moral teachings of the Church.

Among Galileo's most revealing views on scriptural exegesis is his *Letter to the Grand Duchess Christina* (1615). The letter was to affirm that there was no conflict between the new Copernican doctrine and the Bible, when properly understood.[190] Galileo wrote:

> I think in the first place that it is very pious to say and prudent to affirm that the Holy Bible can never speak untruth – whenever its true meaning is understood. But I believe nobody will deny that it is often very abstruse, and may say things which are quite different from what its bare words signify ... But I do not feel obliged to believe that the same God who has endowed us with senses, reason and intellect has intended to forgo their use and by some other means to give us knowledge which we can attain by them. He would not require us to deny sense and reason in physical matters which are set before our eyes and minds by direct experience or necessary demonstrations.[191]

Three themes were important to Galileo: first, understanding nature was one of the best guides in the interpretation of the Scriptures – Galileo believed that the Copernican system gave one a better understanding of the miracle of the long day of Joshua than did the Ptolemaic system; secondly, natural knowledge through sense-observation and rigorous demonstration[192] was provisional; and, thirdly, divine wisdom was beyond human understanding.[193] The authority of the Bible was limited to those truths that were inaccessible to natural knowledge. To Galileo, "the language of the Scripture was the language of men who were historically context-bound to their time and who had as their purpose the persuasion of others to accept the 'true' faith".[194] He firmly believed that the compilers of the Scriptures did not intend to teach us about the structure and motions of the heavens and stars, and deliberately refrained from doing so.[195] However, Galileo did not help his cause by repeating the wry remark he attributed to Cardinal Baronio: "The intention of the Holy Spirit is to teach us to go to Heaven, not how the heavens go."[196]

Galileo's struggle for intellectual freedom

Go Wond'rous creature, mount where Science guides.   Alexander Pope[197]

Although the Catholic Church turned its back on Galileo, Galileo never turned his back on God. Throughout his life he tried desperately to preserve the credibility of the Church. Before the Inquisition, he had submitted a programme to Catholic authorities about how to prevent conflict on matters of science. In a moment of frustration during the Inquisition, Galileo admitted that he had thought of burning all his works on science; but never his belief in God.[198] Galileo continued to respect theology and philosophy, but not when they entered the domain of science.[199]

Despite decades of personal persecution, Galileo blamed only a few wrong-thinking individuals.[200] The error of theologians in 1616 was a misapplication of law established by the early Church fathers, who had wisely separated science from religion. Galileo's enemies included highly conservative scholastics, most philosophers and those scientists who had publicly challenged him.[201] For most of his life, Galileo's friends included men of letters, artists, mathematicians, scientists, craftsmen and cardinals. He died with a clear conscience on 8 January 1642, and was buried next to his father, Vincenzo, and family in the Basilica of Santa Croce. On hearing of his death, Luke Holste of the household of Francesco Cardinal Barberini (the nephew of the Pope who did not sign Galileo's condemnation), wrote the following to a friend in Florence:

Today news has come of the loss of Signor Galilei, which touches not just Florence but the whole world, and our whole century which from this divine man has received more splendour than from almost all the other ordinary philosophers. Now, envy ceasing, the sublimity of that intellect will begin to be known which will serve all posterity as guide in the search for truth.[202]

SIR ISAAC NEWTON (1642–1727): THE GREATEST GENIUS THAT EVER EXISTED[203]

Nature and Nature's Laws were hid in the night,
God said,"Let Newton be," and all was light.

Alexander Pope[204]

Galileo and Kepler made extraordinary progress in discovering the laws and principles of motion. But it was left to Isaac Newton to infer and confer their universality through tireless reading, innovation, raw intuition and maintenance of his faith in God, whose omnipresence constituted space.[205] Newton gave the Western world a whole new perspective on reality, and a way of seeking scientific truth using mathematics and his "rules of reasoning" (see below). French mathematician Joseph Lagrange (1736–1813) may have been correct when he proclaimed Newton "the greatest genius that ever existed". Despite his genius, Newton was a highly complex person: a quiet, unsettled boy who grew to become a man of many ranging hatreds and dislikes in both science and religion. It is estimated that he wrote about 1 million words in scientific papers and about 2 million words in theological writings.

A quiet boy with low grades

Newton was born early on Christmas Day (25 December) in 1642. Like Kepler, he was born prematurely and often told the story of how at birth he could fit into a quart mug. Newton had a turbulent childhood, with his father dying before he was born and his mother leaving when he was 3 years old to live with an aging vicar in a nearby parish.[206] His mother returned some eight years later. Newton was a quiet solitary farm boy who lived his early years with his grandmother in Grantham. He showed no special gifts at school, was inattentive and ranked very low among his classmates.[207] Apparently, all this changed one day when a bully kicked him in his stomach on the way to school. Newton retaliated by challenging the bully to a fight after school and beat him quite badly. Newton's vivid recollection 70 years later suggested that he was deeply affected by the crisis and genuinely regretted beating the bully so relentlessly. Newton further recollected that he decided to beat the bully in scholastic endeavours as well.[208] As we shall see later, this spitefulness was to become a darker side of Newton's character, which he used against many of his opponents during his career.

The townspeople of Grantham also had vivid memories of Newton. He was remembered for "his strange inventions and extraordinary inclination for mechanical works".[209] Newton was a consummate tinkerer and built mousetraps, model windmills and mechanical carriages powered either by wind or "mouse" energy. He contrived many experiments for his classmates, including tying paper lanterns to the kite-tails and spooking the neighbourhood with mysterious night-flying objects.[210] Newton was particularly intrigued with the measurement of time and he built a water clock, which was fully operational and used in his home. He also built a sundial, known as Isaac's Dial, which was widely used by townspeople.

An explosion of mathematics and invention

In Cambridge, Newton [found] that a new world had been discovered. He discovered as well something still more important. The early adventures had only scouted its coasts. Vast continents remained to be explored.   R. S. Westfall[211]

In 1661 Newton entered Trinity College at the University of Cambridge, one of the most famous colleges in the university, which became his home for the next 35 years. He studied mathematics as it applied to astrology, and soon became most impressed with the eminent mathematician Isaac Barrow. Four years later, at the age of 23, he returned to his Lincolnshire home to avoid the plague. During these years, Newton made some of his most spectacular discoveries.[212] His genius seems to have not developed slowly, but exploded. By the end of 1666, he had invented differential and integral calculus or "fluxions" (independently of the German philosopher and mathematician Gottfried Leibniz). He invented the binomial theorem and various properties of the infinite series and method of iteration used today in computers. He proposed new scientific instruments such as a reflecting telescope, and invented the primary concept of mass as opposed to weight. He also developed the law of gravitation, with its dynamical parts, including a theory of the tides.[213] He invented a theory of light, and showed how a narrow beam of sunlight could be split into a spectrum of colours using a prism. Last, but not least, Newton constructed theories of matter, heat, alchemy and chronology.[214]

Added to these momentous discoveries was Newton's new methodology of science; he was not only an outstanding inventor and an outstanding theoretician, but also an outstanding experimentalist. Even Darwin and Einstein did not possess all these gifts. Newton wrote the following on his achievements:

And the same year I began to think of gravity extending to the orb of the Moon, and from Kepler's Rule [third law] I deduced that the forces which keep the Planets in their orbs must [be] reciprocally as the squares of their distances from the centres about which they revolve; and thereby compared the force requisite to keep the Moon in her orb with the force of gravity at the surface of the earth, and found them to answer pretty nearly. All this was in the two plague years of 1665 and 1666, for those days I was in the prime of my age for invention, and minded Mathematics and Philosophy more than at any time since.[215]

Newton wrote his most famous book, *Philosophiae Naturalis Principia Mathematica* (generally known as the *Principia*) in about 18 months, persuaded to do so by astronomer and mathematician Edmond Halley (*c*.1656–1742) of Halley's Comet fame, and it was published in 1687. After this time, Newton began to tire and apparently suffered a nervous breakdown a few years later in 1693. Notwithstanding the many honours Newton received after the publication of the *Principia*, he made no new important discoveries. Unlike Galileo who thrived in science in later life, Newton turned his attention to writing more about theology, a passion that began in the years before working on the *Principia*. Newton was knighted in 1705 and was president of the Royal Society of London from 1703 until his death in 1727 at the age of 85.

"Seeing further"

If I have seen further it is by standing on the shoulders of Giants.   Isaac Newton[216]

Notwithstanding the profound legacies of Bacon, Descartes, Boyle, Huygens, Kepler and Galileo, Newton advanced the method of science single-handedly using unparalleled intuition, mathematical analysis and vigour. When he had become famous, Newton was asked how he had discovered the law of universal gravitation and his answer was "by thinking on it continually".[217] And when asked about his place in history, Newton replied:

> I do not know what I may appear to the world, but, to myself, I seem to have been only like a boy playing on the seashore, and directing myself in now and then finding a smoother pebble or a prettier shell than ordinary, while the great ocean of truth lay all undiscovered before me.[218]

Newton's first research interests were in the field of light. Six years after formulating his theory of light (1672), Newton submitted a research paper on colours to the Royal Society, which had been founded by King Charles II in 1662 for the advancement of science. Within a week, Newton found himself embroiled in an attack from Royal Society member, chemist and physicist Robert Hooke (1635–1703). Angered by Newton's claim that light was indisputably a body, Hooke wrote a condescending letter suggesting that he himself had done the experiments and Newton had copied them.[219]

Newton became terribly embittered. He had spent over six years, with many sleepless nights, thinking and carrying out his experiments on light. Newton explained to Hooke, in an equally sharp letter, that he had not invented a hypothesis about colour and fitted it to his observations, but had worked in reverse from observations to theory.[220] After setting Hooke straight on how science should be practised, Newton added salt to the wound by touching on a subject on which Hooke considered himself to be the world expert: how to perfect optical instruments. Hooke resented Newton's upstart magisterial tone. And it was in a letter to Hooke (dated 5 Feb 1675) that Newton's famous statement appeared: "If I have seen further it is by standing on the shoulders of Giants."[221]

Most of us believe that Newton's remark was referring to the giants before him: Aristotle, Ptolemy, Copernicus, Kepler and Galileo. Not so, says British researcher John Faulkner, who argues that "on the shoulders of Giants" was Newton's deliberate attack on the rather stunted Hooke's self-imposed grandeur. After reading all the correspondence, Faulkner concluded that Newton's meaning (taking particular notice of the capital G in "Giant") was "*my* research owes nothing to anybody *except* the ancients, least of all to a little runt like you".[222] Some caution should be exercised with Faulkner's interpretation because the statement "standing on the shoulders of giants" was not peculiar to Newton but a *cliché* that dates back to John of Salisbury in the twelfth century.[223]

Newton's laws of motion

Newton built his universal mechanics on a small, rigorous logical structure. The eight definitions (and scholium) and the three laws of motion – the principle of inertia, the proportionality of force and mass and acceleration, and the equality of actions and reactions – and their corollaries are all stated in the first forty pages of the *Principia* (1687).   W. Hooper[224]

Newton eventually settled down and began to concentrate on his next momentous challenge: a universal theory of gravitation. He began with a set of "definitions", such as mass, force, momentum, absolute and relative space, time and motion.[225] Using them, he showed the linkage between Kepler's three laws and Galileo's observation that objects of different weight free fall with identical acceleration.[226] Newton compressed all that was known at the time on kinematics and dynamics into his "Axioms", or three laws of motion,[227] which became the foundation of classical mechanics. Nowhere in Newton's *Principia* can you find Aristotle's natural place, affinities, the four causes, actuality and potentiality, and so on. Instead, you find highly intuitive measurable concepts linking different kinds of motion to mutual attractions of physical bodies.

Newton applied his laws of motion to all kinds of motion, including free, resistive, straight, curved and wave motion, from large bodies to moving points or particles. He further showed, in Book II of the *Principia*, how Descartes's theory of celestial vortices, whirlpools of subtle matter, was mechanically impossible, and could not be reconciled with Kepler's laws. Descartes argued that the heliocentric universe was filled with celestial fluid (i.e. no vacuum), and that after God caused first motion, each star had a vortex, and the vast system of vortices kept the planets in circulation around the sun.[228] Descartes did not believe in invisible forces, powers, spirits or matter attractions. Apart from "mind", the world was made of physical matter with one real property: extension (size, shape and volume). In his theory, bodies fall towards the Earth because they are pushed downwards by extremely small particles that swirl around our planet, and these same particles in vast whirlpools keep the planets moving in perfect circles. Cartesian theory, while brilliant, turned out to be mistaken.

Four rules of reasoning

The essence of Newton's revolutionary science, as I see it, is to be found in what I have called the "Newtonian style".   I. B. Cohen[229]

Newton's laws of motion were the basis for calculating the gravitational force between the Earth and the moon, or any two masses in the universe. Newton's "Rules of Reasoning in Philosophy" appeared at the beginning of Book III (see Table 8.2). Newton wrote: "In the preceding Books I have laid down the principles of philosophy; principles not philosophical, but mathematical; such, to wit, as we may build our reasonings upon in philosophical inquiries … It remains that, from the same principles, I now demonstrate the frame of the System of the World."[230]

Table 8.2 Newton's four rules of reasoning (adapted from Newon 1848: 384).

Rule 1	We are to admit no more causes of natural things than such as are both true and sufficient to explain their appearances.
	Newton appears to be paraphrasing what Ockham wrote some 250 years earlier; don't introduce any more hypotheses than are sufficient and necessary for the explanation of the observed facts (see p. 254).
Rule 2	Therefore to the same natural effects we must, as far as possible, assign the same cause.
	Newton gave some examples, such as respiration having the same cause in man as in animals; that the light of our cooking fire has the same cause as of the sun; that the reflection of light in the earth has the same cause in the moon and in the planets.
Rule 3	The "properties" of bodies within reach of our experiments are to be assumed to be the same properties of all bodies outside our reach.
	Newton gives examples of extension, hardness, impenetrability, mobility, inertia, and the gravitational effect of the Earth on the moon and planets.
Rule 4	In natural science we are to look at the propositions obtained by induction from phenomena as approximately true or provisional until such a time as they may be corrected or are liable to exceptions.

The falling apple

Newton's law of gravitation states that the *attraction between any two bodies is proportional to their masses and inversely proportional to the square of the distance between them* (see Ch. 1). This attractive force is called "gravitation" and it is a property of matter.

The often-told story that Newton came to the notion of gravitation after witnessing the "fall of an apple" in his mother's garden is apocryphal.[231] It took him many years to formulate his theory of gravity. He envisaged that gravity was not only a property of attraction of the Earth, but a property of attraction of all bodies in the universe. The bigger the body, the stronger the attraction. This insight led Newton to propose that gravity acts over vast cosmic distances, and that as bodies become further apart their attraction becomes weaker. Galileo had estimated this force on the surface of the Earth, but Newton wanted to know what the force would be on the moon.

At first, Newton's "falling" moon–apple analogy agreed only approximately because he took the wrong radius of the Earth. It was not until 1685, some 20 years later, that he found his mistake while he was writing the *Principia*. The distance from the Earth's centre to the apple and to the moon was about 6440 km and 386 230 km, respectively. Therefore, on the basis of his inverse-square law, Newton reasoned that since the moon was 60 times further away from the centre of the Earth than the apple, the force of attraction (acceleration of free fall) would be $1/(60 \times 60) = 1/3600$ as great. In one giant leap, Newton successfully extended these laws to cosmic distances. Using his inverse-square law, he showed that when a planet is closest to the sun, the force is stronger than when it is further away; an idea entirely consistent with Kepler's second law. Newton assumed that the entire mass of the Earth and moon resided at their centres, which simplified his mathematical calculations enormously. Following Kepler, Newton considered each body a particle, which permitted him to extend his famous inverse-square law to the most remote regions of the universe.[232] Newton shied away from saying the force was a "property of matter" because this could have implied a materialism in which he probably did not believe in light of his theology (see below).[233]

Newton's concept of gravity

When Newton showed how his inverse-square law could be derived from Kepler's second and third laws, and then the first law deduced from this, the "laws" were back in business with new theoretical support, but, despite the use of distance-related forces, this was very different from that provided by Kepler.　　　　G. Molland[234]

Newton did not discover gravity. The concept of gravity dates back to Plato, and probably earlier.[235] Copernicus spoke of attraction and implied that each planet was a separate centre of gravitational phenomena, and bodies fell towards them in order to participate in the perfect shape of the sphere. Kepler viewed it as the tendency of bodies to attract one another, and the force that gave rise to the tides. However, he had difficulty equating it with Gilbert's force of magnetism. Newton combined Kepler's laws of motion with Christiaan Huygens's theory of centrifugal force (actually Newton used the centripetal force) and applied it to his famous "moon test".

In the early 1680s Newton began to master all his dynamical principles to solve the puzzle of the universality of gravitation. To his dismay, another person entertaining a theory of gravity was none other than Hooke. Through a rigidly polite exchange of letters, Hooke wanted to know the law of central force that could turn straight-line motion into a Keplerian ellipse.[236] In 1684 Halley visited Newton in Cambridge and asked him what path a planet would follow under the action of an inverse-square force. He told Newton that Hooke, Christopher Wren[237] and himself had failed to solve the problem. To Halley's amazement, Newton knew the answer: an ellipse. However, Newton couldn't find the pieces of paper containing his mathematical proof.[238] From this discussion, Halley persuaded Newton to write up his results in the *Principia*. The Keplerian heliostatic model was at last established as a scientific fact, and generally accepted throughout much of Protestant England and Europe.

Newton explained "how" gravity obeyed his inverse-square law, but on the question of "why" he wrote: "*Hypotheses non fingo* [I frame no hypotheses]".[239] Further, he believed that the ultimate "first cause" was not matter, but the lawful will of God. Newton believed that the world could not survive without the creator. Today, the gravitational force between the sun and the Earth, or any two celestial bodies, is thought to arise from the exchange of gravitons between the particles that make up the two bodies.[240] The graviton has no mass of its own, which is why it is long ranging. Classical physicists believe that gravitons collectively make up gravitational waves, which are very weak, and have not been detected with current technology.[241]

The Holy Trinity as a "monstrous fraud"[242]

So then the first religion was the most rational of all others till the nations corrupted it. For there is no way without revelation to come to (the) knowledge of a Deity but by (the) frame of nature.　　　　Isaac Newton[243]

Newton, like Copernicus, Kepler and Galileo, was highly religious and a product of the Reformation. He was a Christian who deplored authoritarian centralized Catholicism.

For someone who was always thinking about the problem, religion provided Newton with perhaps his most difficult challenge. To him, the physical universe with all its beauty and order was God's revelation, as was the Old Testament. However, he did not share with Kepler the ancient Pythagorean a priori assumption that the universe was built on mathematical harmonies unified by a cosmic soul. Newton's physical world embodied God's spirit, not God himself. In the General Scholium to the second edition of his *Principia* (1713), Newton wrote:

This most beautiful system of the sun, planets and comets, could only proceed from the counsel and dominion of an intelligent and powerful Being. And if the fixed stars are the centers of other like systems, these, being formed by the like wise counsel, must be all subject to the dominion of One; especially since the light of the fixed stars is of the same nature with the light of the sun, and from every system light passes into all the other systems: and lest the systems of the fixed stars should, by their gravity, fall on each other mutually, he hath placed those systems at immense distances one from another.

This Being governs all things, not as the soul of the world, but as Lord overall; and on account of his dominion he is wont to be called Lord God or Universal Ruler; for God is a relative word, and has respect to servants; and Deity is the dominion of God not over his own body, as those imagine who fancy God to be the soul of the world, but over servants ... And from his true dominion it follows that true God is a living, intelligent, and powerful Being; and, from his other perfections, that he is Supreme and most perfect. He is eternal and infinite, omnipotent and omniscient, that is, his duration reaches from eternity to eternity; his presence from infinity to infinity; he governs all things, knows all things that are or can be done. He is not eternity or infinity; but eternal and infinite ... He is utterly void of all body and bodily figure, and therefore can never be seen, nor heard, nor touched; nor ought he be worshipped under the representation of any corporeal thing. We know him only by his most wise and excellent contrivances of things, and final causes; we admire him for his perfections; but we reverence and adore him on account on account of his dominion.[244]

It is this reverential aspect of Newton's theology that gets lost in accounts that try to turn him into a deist. Newton's God seems to be a complex blend of an anthropomorphic Stoic God with Presocratic roots, and the Hebrew God of the Old Testament. His God was not unlike that described by the Hellenistic Jewish philosopher Philo Judaeus. As a supreme world "governor", God revealed himself in the simplicity, order and design of nature. For Newton, the best arguments for the existence of God were: the Creation; the setting in motion of the world in accordance with prescribed laws; its continual workings; its occasional reformation; occasional spiritual intrusions (e.g. comets and epidemics) and miracles.[245] Newton believed that all these features could be traced back to God as "first cause" and that he could demonstrate the dominion of God over the Creation. In this respect, arguments from the fulfilment of biblical prophecy were as important, perhaps more so, than arguments from natural philosophy, in that Newton saw the hand of providence in human history.[246] In the end, Newton's theology provided him with a grand scheme, of which natural science was a part. Natural science was "that part of theology which could be reduced to demonstrative form, the highest form of reasoning about God".[247]

In addition to writing about God in his *Principia*, Newton's religious convictions after about 1672 are also expressed in many private letters and notes.[248] From these letters and notes, it appears that Newton wanted to systematize the study of the Bible. He tells how his God was hidden away in the Scriptures "before" the pages had been corrupted by Christian writers of the third and fourth centuries. Newton did not believe in original sin or the Holy Trinity. In one of his scathing letters on the "Notable Corruptions of Scripture", Newton viewed the Holy Trinity as a "monstrous fraud" that had perverted the nature of Christianity for over 1000 years.[249] He traced the corruption back to the theologian St Athanasius, who rejected outright the older Arian notion that the Father and Son were of separate substances of "different" divinities.[250] Long before 1675, Newton had become an Arian by recognizing Christ as a divine mediator between God and human beings, but subordinate to the Father, who had created him.[251] God, Jesus and the Holy Spirit were not the Trinitarian "three persons" of the same substance in different forms. Newton's God was a designer God, and the Catholic dilution of deity lessened his supreme dominion and constituted idolatry.[252]

Later in the 1680s, before the publication of the *Principia*, Newton became even more radical and rejected any concept of divine revelation, apart from nature.[253] He read Father Richard Simon's erudite *Critical History of the Old Testament* (1678) and Spinoza's *Tractatus*, and agreed that the present texts of the Old and New Testament contained many distortions.[254] Newton did believe, however, that the prophetic texts of Daniel and Revelation were accurate and could be accepted.[255] Newton's next major theological undertaking was his own treatise *The Philosophical Origins of Gentile Theology* (or "*Origines*"), which was never completed.[256] Newton makes extensive use of the classical authors – including Virgil, Ovid, Macrobius, Pliny, Strabo, Lucian, Herodotus, Cicero, Plato, Homer, Plutarch, Seneca, Xenophon, Aeschylus and Tacitus – and some contemporary sources, to resurrect the "true" religion.

Newton began his radical *Origines* with Jewish and Hebrew history (from Noah to Abraham, Isaac, Jacob and Moses) and he told how the Hebrews had fallen into idolatry, as the Egyptians had done before them. Egypt was the original home of Gentile theology and where Noah settled after the Flood. Newton believed that Pythagoras had taken this "corrupted version" from Egypt and introduced it to the West.[257] Newton argued that all the ancient people worshipped the same basic god under different manifestations and names in honour of their specific cultures and heritages.[258] He wrote:

> It cannot be believed, however, that religion began with the doctrine of the transmigration of souls and the worship of stars and elements: for there was another religion more ancient than all of these, a religion in which a fire for offering sacrifices burned perpetually in the middle of a sacred place. For the Vestal cult was the most ancient of all.[259]

The prophets' job was to clear away these muddy waters and restore religion to its original state. Newton called this "true" religion the "Moral Law of all Nations", which had two basic commandments: the duty to love God, and the duty to love one's neighbour.[260] The "true" religion was the oldest in the world that united all nations. Despite the far-reaching scope of *Origines,* Newton treated most of the historical books of the Old Testament as containing no more validity than the writings of the ancient Babylonians, Egyptians or Greeks. He considered that his primary mission, therefore, was to eliminate individual fancy and expose the bare bones of the first "true" religion, which began with Noah. Newton refers to "Monstrous legends, false miracles, veneration of reliques, charms, doctrines of Ghosts or Demons, and their intercession, invocation and worship and other heathen superstitions as were then brought in."[261]

At no time did Newton approach the Old and New Testaments as the revelation of truths above human reason.[262] Indeed, historian of science Richard Westfall (1924–1996), suggests that Book I of the *Principia* was an implicit argument for the existence of God through Newton's inverse-square law of attraction, empirically proven in Book III.[263] Another eminent Newtonian scholar, Betty J. T. Dobbs (1930–1994) further proposed that:

> Perhaps because of the remarkable success of the *Principia* itself in restoring natural philosophy, Newton shifted his focus to more study of natural philosophy as the best way to restore true religion. He sought the border where natural and divine principles met and fused.[264]

In fact, Newton appears not to have worried about maintaining tidy boundaries between reason and faith because the "holy alliance" of science and religion was cemented by his Lord God of supreme dominion, who not only created the universe but directed nature through divine intervention.[265]

THE RISE OF WESTERN SCIENCE: FROM STRUGGLE TO TRIUMPH

> It is difficult for a modern person to appreciate the unity of science and Christian religion that existed at the time of Renaissance and far into the eighteenth century. The reason why there was no conflict between science and theology was that the two had been synthesised as natural theology (physio-theology), the science of the day. The natural theologian studied the works of the creator for the sake of theology. Nature for him was convincing proof for the existence of a supreme being, for how else could one explain the harmony and purposiveness of the creation?   E. Mayr[266]

Rethinking of the physical object in a natural world

Although part of Western science had deep roots extending as far back as ancient Mesopotamia and Egypt, the enterprise did not become "natural" until the Greeks (Ch. 4). After more than a thousand-year hiatus in the European West, renewed interest in the natural world and science began with the medieval theologian-natural philosophers, and their successors. The revival occurred within the scholastic university, where Aristotle's original corpus was rediscovered, and where God was seen to have conferred the power on physical objects to directly act upon each other to bring about change.[267] Importantly, God was not the direct and immediate cause of every action, as many Islamic theologians and natural philosophers had believed, but had empowered physical objects to act by themselves through his natural laws.

This "re-thinking" of physical objects in the natural world, along with seeing the workings of the world as a product of secondary causation involving inter-actions among them, was a momentous step towards renewed interest in Western science. Recall that in the ancient Near East, the Sumerians and Egyptians had no concept of the physical and believed a sense-object, such as a reed, could take on magical powers and be transformed into a basket or writing stylus under the guidance of a particular god (Chs 2 and 3). This mythopoeic view was rejected by early Greek philosophers, who gave the sense-object a physical makeover; the Presocratics produced a bewildering array of theories from the four basic elements (water, air, fire and earth) to atomism, and to these four elements Aristotle added the concepts of matter and form (Ch. 5). Aristotle also added the abstraction of substance or essence, which existed independent of the object, and provided the later Islamic and Christian scholars with an important literary tool to link the physical and divine (Ch. 5). In contrast, the early Christian philosophers, apologists and theologians paid less attention to the physical object as matter stood in opposition to God, and forever thwarted his plan and purpose of the "divine *logos*". Matter was the furthest away from God and in some instances the source of human sin and evil (Ch. 6).

From back yards to laboratories and greater public acceptance

In the sixteenth century, the "New Science" grew as part of the Renaissance culture that swept western Europe. It was a period when enterprising capitalism spawned wealth and leisure; a burgeoning technology with patent protection stimulated inventiveness; a print industry empowered the public with new knowledge; increased decentralization of the Church led to greater social diversity and independence, and last, but not least, the growth of universities ensured new ideas and knowledge dissemination with a wider interest in the classics (Plato, in particular) and mathematics.[268] Within this new culture, science shifted slowly from the secrecy of gifted back-yard hobbyists, magicians and charlatans to more formal laboratories.[269] The institutionalization of science with scientific societies and journals was unique to the West. The scope that existed by the middle of the seventeenth century is illustrated in the founding aims of the Royal Society[270] of London (*c*.1662): "to improve the knowledge of natural things, and all useful Arts, Manufactures, Mechanic practices, Engines and Inventions by Experiment – (not meddling with Divinity, Metaphysics, Morals, Politics, Grammar, Rhetoric or Logic)".

Another factor responsible for the broadening scope of science in the seventeenth century was its wider public acceptance. Westfall argues that Galileo was among the first to build such an audience after achieving hero status for his telescopic astronomy.[271] Although Bacon's skills as science spokesperson were significant, Galileo described his experiments and his point of view so clearly that he won over the European learned community.[272] Thus modern Western science must not be seen as a simple extension of medieval science; it was a new endeavour within a new cultural mosaic.

Different methodologies: towards finding a "middle ground"

In the evolution of philosophical thought, the following question has played a major role: what knowledge is pure thought able to supply independently of sense perception. Is there any such knowledge?   Albert Einstein[273]

In the quote above, Einstein raises an interesting question. Some of these philosophical boundaries were revisited in the seventeenth century, as illustrated by Bacon's empiricism and Descartes's rationalism.[274] However, as discussed earlier in the chapter, both methodologies had shortfalls; the empiricist in Bacon argued for observation, some sort of test and a logical method of induction, whereas the rationalist in Descartes began with a set of a priori propositions that he believed *actually existed as certainties,* and proceeded to derive scientific truths using reason alone.[275] Eighteenth-century science popularizer Bernard de Fontenelle (1657–1757) summed up Descartes as someone who "set out from what he knew clearly, in order to find the cause of what he saw" and Newton as the experimenter who "set out from what he saw, in order to find the cause".[276] In the end, Descartes's method erred towards idealism because it could not be independently checked and agreed upon, and while Bacon's methodology was closer to the mark, it relied too heavily on observational facts, and not enough on stressing the importance of raw intuition and mathematics. Not surprisingly, it was left to the scientists themselves, not the philosophers, to find a middle ground. There was no single scientific method that emerged in the seventeenth century, nor is there, 400 years later, a single way of doing science today. I know of no professional scientist who would prescribe to "one" method. Scientists simply do not carry out their business in this way (see Ch. 1).

Science as a tool to open new worlds within worlds

Despite its complex philosophical underpinnings, the "New Science" won favour because it provided a key to open new worlds within worlds. The telescope, microscope, barometer, calculator, air pump, pendulum clock and thermometer all helped to extend the human senses beyond their "normal" physiological limits. These inventions were the source of great intrigue and wonder and helped to popularize scientific research. The microscope, for example, with a magnification power of 275, permitted Anton van Leeuwenhoek (1632–1723) to describe life in a drop of ditchwater: never witnessed before by any human being. He spent days and months marvelling at free-living single-celled protozoa, bacteria and "hairlike" blood capillaries with red cells moving inside.[277] Marcello Malpighi (1628–1694) was another who witnessed first-hand the frantically swimming sperm in search of an egg and the life stages in a developing chick embryo. He also described strange tiny spiral "breathing" openings in insects and holes on the underside of leaves. Seventeenth-century microscopists, with their new-found technology, were in a state of high exhilaration and reported to London's Royal Society that the world of the very small was just as grand as the world of the heavens.[278]

Mathematical mechanization of nature

Philosophy is written in this most grand book, the universe, which stands continually open to our gaze. But the book cannot be understood unless one first learns to comprehend the language and read the letters in which it is composed. It is written in the language of mathematics, and its characters are triangles, circles, and other geometrical figures without which it is humanly impossible to understand a single word of it.

Galileo[279]

The so-called scientific revolution, which traditionally dates from 1543 to 1687, went hand in hand with advances in mathematics. Mathematics comprised not only formal logic as in medieval scholasticism,[280] but it embodied the natural order of the workings of the world. Before this time, the academic world drew a clear line of demarcation between mathematics and physical theory, with mathematics being subordinate to Christian theology and philosophy. And because physical theories belonged to the realm of natural philosophy, a mathematician was free to postulate highly abstract concepts, but as soon as he attempted to make claims about physical reality, the idea could easily be discredited as coming from an inferior discipline.[281] We saw this division in the reception of Copernicus, Kepler and Galileo, and to a far lesser extent in Newton, as science became more popular and began to assert its authority towards understanding the physical world.

We saw how Copernicus and Kepler constructed their mathematical models, which defined an "ideal case" against which phenomena and relations in the real world could be compared and tested. The construction of the idealized case was also a powerful tool for Galileo and Newton. Specifically, Galileo used mathematics to codify the connections between theory, observations and measurements, which he masterfully applied to the kinematics of free fall, relations of time, distance and velocity, and uniformly accelerated motion.[282] Likewise, in his *Principia* Newton explained that his axioms of motion were purely mathematical abstractions without any physical, metaphysical or ontological commitment. However, in Book III he ingeniously demonstrated the mathematical correspondence between these abstractions, physical objects and natural phenomena. Newton realized that mathematical abstractions, while having no physical meaning in themselves, provided a powerful language to link God and physical phenomena through potentially measurable concepts.

In the "New Science" much of Aristotle's *physics* of motion or his physical sublunary and divine celestial regions was superfluous. The Greek dualistic world comprising the physical and divine was transformed into a grand mathematical "celestial machine", a seventeenth-century metaphor borrowed from the late medievalists.[283] Indeed, Kepler made the analogy between the world and a clock,[284] and by the end of the century Newton had extended the idea to the workings of life itself, including human beings. Newton imagined that the forces of attraction and repulsion governed the chemical and physiological processes of life and thus made nature "very conformable unto herself".[285]

Another major advance in the correspondence between mathematics and physical reality was recognition of the importance of "proportionality constants" as part of God's natural laws. Despite earlier contributions on the algebraic relations of Aristotelian kinematics by medieval people like Gerard of Brussels and Thomas

Bradwardine,[286] the wider significance of the proportionality constant was not fully recognized until the seventeenth century. The power of the proportionality constant was illustrated in Kepler's third law of harmony, where he showed that the ratio between the time for one revolution of a planet to its mean radius of orbit was "a constant" for all planets. Galileo's free-fall experiments had distance varying as the square of time, linked by a "constant" of acceleration. Boyle's law dealt with proportionality between the pressure of a gas and its volume at different temperatures. And Newton's second law of motion and inverse-square law of gravitation illustrated perhaps the highest degree of mathematical elegance containing proportionality constants. The fundamental importance of proportionality constants in the "New Science" appear to have received little attention from historians of science.

While it is true that the ancient Greeks had elaborate reasoning methods and theories, most failed to capitalize on the power of experiment, mathematics and measurement to link their concepts through proportionalities. With few exceptions, the Greek natural philosophers seemed satisfied with the beauty and aesthetics of pure Aristotelian logical deduction in demonstrating a truth. The fundamental importance of nature's "constants" was summed up by Astronomer Royal Martin Rees when he wrote: "The entire physical world, not just atoms, but stars and people as well, is essentially determined by a few basic "constants"; the masses of some so-called elementary particles, and the strength of the forces – electric, nuclear and gravitational – that bind them together and govern their motions."[287]

A deathblow to Aristotelian causation

In Aristotlelian physics, terrestrial models were deemed irrelevant because celestial bodies were made of an entirely different material. In Galileo's unified cosmos, analogies from familiar objects can be used to explain features of the moon and the planets, but the limitations of his method are made clear. Galileo's caution is dictated by the prudence of the experimentalist for whom the world always holds surprises.

W. Shea[288]

After nearly 2000 years, Aristotle's physics and theory of causation[289] came to an abrupt halt. Kepler had no time for the concepts of efficient or final causation and he and Galileo preferred the term "relations" between phenomena.[290] "Between cause and effect", Galileo wrote, "there exists a firm and constant relation, such that necessarily each time we observe a variation in the effect there must be a firm and constant alteration in the cause."[291] For Galileo, this intermediate stage of seeking relations between cause and effect was a process of active construction and deconstruction, of testing, investigating, experimenting, measuring and eliminating all other possibilities, and then working backwards to the effect in nature. A good example of this approach is Galileo's kinematics and his use of telescopic astronomy to argue for a Copernican universe (even though he could not eliminate Tycho Brahe's earth-centred model). Galileo used the term "*regressus*" for working backwards and rebuilding the phenomenon.[292]

Importantly, in order for scientific researchers to employ their new methods, they had to invent innovative ways to reduce the complexities in the natural world into simpler systems. Certainly, this process of reduction did not do away with the phenomena under investigation, as some critics of science have charged, but made the system simpler and more amenable to study. The way Galileo "diluted" gravity using a low-angled inclined board to study free-falling objects of different weights is a good example of reductionism. And in those cases where analogic devices or machines could not be built, researchers resorted to examples already found in nature, such as Newton's moon–apple analogy.

The other emerging feature of the "New Science", and one fully appreciated by Galileo and Newton, was that the more science became involved in the quest for certainty, *the fewer things it could explain*. A good example was when Huygens declared that Newton's *Principia* was incomplete because it lacked a mechanical explanation of gravity's "first" cause. Huygens, a great scientist in his own right, clearly missed the underlying power of science. Newton openly admitted that he could not provide a physical explanation of gravity's "first" cause, and further made the point that it was unknown to the "New Science". The force of gravity, Newton explained, does not "cause" a planet to move around the sun, but is a measure of the strength of its motion. Natural science could go no further and many seventeenth-century scientists knew this, as did many of the medievalists, including Grosseteste and Ockham. The grand irony of early modern science was that it emerged triumphant as a provisional body of knowledge more along the lines of Plato's *Timaeus* than Aristotle's *Physics*.

God, natural laws and world governance

The idea of nature as a system governed by laws, and the idea that one of the main aims of a scientist should be the discovery of these laws, is therefore historically quite specific … Though they first emerge as centrally important to scientific thinking in the seventeenth century, they inevitably have an earlier history, and without some attention to this, their later development cannot properly be understood.

J. R. Milton[293]

The main job of the seventeenth-century natural philosopher was to discover the laws of nature. In Chapters 4 and 5 we saw that most Greek philosophers equated the "laws of nature" with divine order and harmony. Among the later Stoics, the "laws of nature" meant leading the good life in accordance with nature (*physis*).[294] This moral association reappeared in Aquinas's *Summa Theologia*, in which Christian life was linked to nature's law as part of God's creation,[295] and in the twelfth century the natural laws (or "common course of nature") were viewed as part of an orderly, harmoniously operating machine.[296] In addition to rethinking the physical object and causal relations, the concept of world harmonies became very popular, if not an obsession, in the "New Science". However, there was one big question that generated much speculation and debate: what precisely was God's role in world governance? That is, how did God influence world harmony and human events?

Three main viewpoints were expressed in the seventeenth century. The first held that God left the world to run by itself through natural (or "secondary") causes, except to return now and again to execute the odd miracle which could change the course of natural and human history.[297] For Newton, the universe was highly unstable, and if there were no God the world would eventually run down. Newton felt that the planets might slow down from frictional drag and the sun itself could lose matter through vaporization. The second view, popular among theologians, held that God acted "continually" to maintain world order and human events. And the third, more extreme, view held that after the creation, God left, never to return, leaving the universe to fend for itself (and human beings to fend for themselves).[298] Despite these different positions about God's possible role in the world, the one framing foundation of seventeenth-century thought that rarely came into question was the belief in God and his transcendence.

Faith and reason: separate roads but one journey

Two extremes: to exclude reason, to admit reason only.   Blaise Pascal[299]

As we leave the sixteenth and seventeenth centuries, it seems a fitting time to reflect upon the interactions between science and religion. They were wholly compatible in the grand scheme of things. A popular metaphor in Galileo's and Newton's time was to speak of God as the author of "the book of nature" and "the book of Scripture". For most natural philosophers, the job of science was to discover and explain how things worked, and religion was the means of placing their discoveries in an all-embracing worldview. In general, faith and reason operated in separate domains but were part of one journey. The above quote from Blaise Pascal sums it up nicely: knowledge has "two extremes", which meet at some point and enable human beings fully to understand the world. Science advocate Bacon believed that science was "the most approved nourishment for faith".[300] Kepler's search for celestial harmony was an exploration into the geometrical archetype in the mind of God.[301] Galileo saw every scientific discovery contributing to a proof of God: "to make myself better understood, I say that the truth we know through mathematical demonstrations is the same as that truth the divine wisdom knows".[302] Boyle regarded all mechanical images as proof of God and a defence of Christianity. And, finally, Newton believed that the job of natural science was to affirm God's design and sovereignty.

Accordingly, at least in principle, there was little or no conflict between science and religion during the development of early modern science. Conflicts arose when individuals were charged by the Holy Office with *disobeying Church authority*, as illustrated by Galileo's experience with the Inquisition.[303] As science grew in strength and began to stamp its authority on unveiling God's secrets, faith in God did not weaken, but strengthened and diversified. Religion too became more diversified and personal. To illustrate the changing times in western Europe there is a marvellous story about English poet Alexander Pope in the closing hours of his life in 1744. Alexander was asked by a friend if he wished to see a priest and he replied: "I do not think it essential but it will be very right and I thank you for putting me in mind of it."[304]

CHAPTER 9

The Big Bang: starlight to superstrings

INTRODUCTION: OUR CHANGING UNIVERSE

> The world of our senses is a world of matter and energy, space and time. After
> centuries of philosophical and scientific study, these, the very logical elements of
> science, are no doubt still without final description.   L. J. Henderson [2]

In the centuries that followed Newton's *Principia*, more startling discoveries were made in mathematical and observational astronomy. Simon Laplace (1749–1827) proposed that the solar system was not created by God, but formed from a cloud of dust and gas (the so-called Laplace–Kant nebular hypothesis). When asked by Napoleon why he had not included God, Laplace replied, "Sir, I do not need this hypothesis."[3] Laplace's solar system was self-stabilizing and would not wind down like a giant clock in the absence of God's intervention, as Newton had proposed.[4]

Armed with larger, more powerful telescopes, and the invention of spectroscopy (1814) and photography (1826), the next generation of astronomers showed that the universe was much larger than anyone had imagined. By the early to mid-nineteenth century, it was clear that the Newtonian system was an over-simplification. The sun was not motionless, as Copernicus and others had envisaged, but part of a solar system that was moving at around $250 \, \text{km s}^{-1}$ in the Milky Way galaxy and completing a "galactic" orbit every 200 million years.[5] It is now known that the Milky Way galaxy is one of over 100 billion galaxies in the universe.

The other startling discovery in the early twentieth century was that the universe itself was not stationary, but expanding in all directions, and the most distant galaxies were moving away at speeds exceeding $100\,000 \, \text{km s}^{-1}$, or one-third the speed of light. The concept of the expanding universe was so incredible that not even Einstein himself believed it at first. The expanding universe, together with the finite speed of light, meant that the further astronomers looked out into the night sky, the closer they were to its creation. When you look out into the starry night sky, you are really looking back in time, and the biggest telescopes have detected objects more than 12 billion light-years away.

If the gigantic cosmic clock was run backwards, everything in the universe would end up in an infinitely small, infinitely dense hot spot called a mathematical singularity. At time zero, you, I, your mother and father, every individual who has ever lived, all animals and plants, every solar system, galaxy and black hole would be there. Of course, in the beginning matter and energy did not exist in the same forms as they exist today, but in an extremely unstable state. Some highly respected physicists, such as Astronomer Royal Sir Martin Rees, further propose that following the Big Bang explosion, the present universe may be one of many.[6] The present visible universe could, at least theoretically, lie on a membrane floating within a higher-dimensional space containing parallel universes that cannot be detected using current technology. Our most powerful telescopes may in fact be looking at a region of space called a "Hubble bubble" within an infinite system of bubbles that might be contracting or expanding, all having different laws describing their behaviour. This chapter traces some of these extraordinary developments in cosmology and challenges for the future.

THE HOT BIG BANG

Strictly speaking, the Big Bang theory does not describe the birth of the universe, but its growth and maturation.   M. A. Bucher & D. N. Spergel[7]

The universe originated some 15 billion years ago (bya)[8] from the hot Big Bang. The Milky Way galaxy formed about 10 billion years *later* and our solar system and Earth 4.6 bya.[9] The term "Big Bang" was coined in 1950 by English physicist Fred Hoyle (1915–2001) during one of his popular BBC radio broadcasts.[10] Hoyle used the term somewhat disparagingly to describe the explosion and expansion theory[11] of Belgian priest George Lemaitre (1894–1966) and George Gamow (1904–1968).[12] Hoyle jokingly described the theory "as about as elegant as a party girl jumping out of a cake".[13]

The Big Bang theory is not one model but represents a whole class of cosmogonical theories that predict an extremely small hot early universe.[14] The theory proposes a highly unstable state or singularity, which mathematicians and quantum cosmologists prefer to think of as a mathematical point with no dimensions (as we understand them). Lemaitre visualized the state as a "cosmic atom" in the form of an incredibly dense "egg", whereas Gamow called it the "ylem".[15]

What happened during the first moments?

Scientists can only speculate about what occurred in the first ten million, billion, billion, billion, billionths of a second (10^{-43} s). The exceptionally high temperatures were in excess of 10^{32} K, or over a billion, billion, billion times the temperatures of a thermonuclear explosion.[16] This early gestation period was followed by the longest cosmic period (from 10^{-43} s to 4.5 billion years), leading to galaxy formation and our solar system. Unlike the state of singularity, cosmologists have a fairly good idea about what happened during this period, although many pieces of the puzzle are still missing.[17] From 10^{-43} to 10^{-34} s there was a period of rapid, accelerating expansion

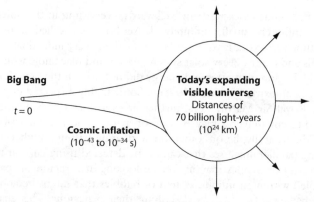

Figure 9.1 One of the reasons proposed for the universe being so large and flat is accelerated expansion of space called cosmic inflation. It went from being infinitesimally small to the size of a basketball in a fraction of a second and continued to expand to the extraordinary large scale today involving intergalactic distances of up to 70 billion light-years. (Modified after Barrow 1994: 65, fig. 4.4.)

called cosmic inflation. The open inflationary theory explains why the visible universe is so very large and flat in all directions with tiny density fluctuations amounting to a few atoms per cubic metre.[18]

During this inflationary period space expanded faster than the speed of light as the universe increased from a point to about the size of a basketball (and the temperature dropped by over one million K) (Fig. 9.1). By around one million millionths of a second (10^{-12} s) the universe was uniform. Differences in the density of matter in the early universe amounted to only one part in 100 000. A millionth of a second later (10^{-6} s) the universe had grown to nearly the size of our solar system and cooled to a temperature of 10 billion K. At the age of 35 minutes, the average temperature was 300 million K.

Furthermore, not only was the size and shape of the universe decided very early, but so too was its structure and "physical constants". These constants include the masses of the elementary particles and the strengths of gravitational force, electromagnetic force and two nuclear forces inside atoms that operate over extremely small distances.[19] From 10^{-34} s to 3 min, the universe changed from a plasma of quarks, electrons and other particles to predominantly 75 per cent hydrogen and 24 per cent helium.[20]

About 300 000 years after the Big Bang, the temperature had dropped to 3000 K and the primordial "seeds" began to form galaxies and galaxy clusters.[21] This was a critical stage of development because matter and the cosmic background radiation began to separate,[22] and the universe became transparent for the first time (see Fig. 9.2). Before it was 300 000 years old the universe was too hot for electrons and protons to combine and form hydrogen or helium atoms. This is why in 1992 the COBE satellite could map the universe back to 300 000 years after the Big Bang, but no earlier because the instruments were not sensitive enough to detect any matter from before then (see later). The temperature continued to fall to its present-day cold interstellar value of about 3 K (~ −270 °C). The universe evolved from a smooth state to one of clumpiness as matter began to form, which in turn gave rise to the billions of galaxies and stars driven by the force of gravitation. The first stars are believed to have formed about 200 million years after the Big Bang, which is the time when the lights of the universe were literally turned on.[23]

As a scientist working in a very different field, that of heart biochemistry and physiology, I find it extraordinary that most of the early cosmic events from about 10^{-43} s to the present can be described mathematically and fit, albeit cautiously, within the current physical laws. Equally extraordinary are the predictions that our universe may be only one of a huge number of universes. Rees argues that many universes (or a "multiverse") are theoretically possible, but each would have different physical constants and laws leading to different dimensional structures that we cannot detect with our current technologies.[24] He argues that some universes may have been stillborn because the gravitational force was stronger than the force that the present visible universe experienced, while other universes may have remained in higher dimensions beyond the human reach (see later string theory).[25]

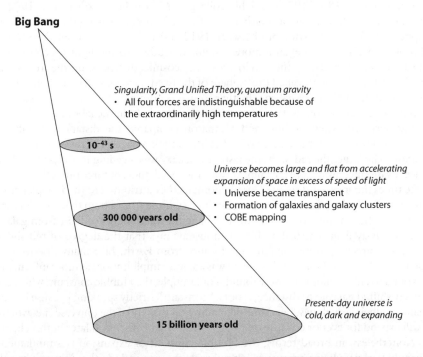

Figure 9.2 Schematic representation of major events after the Big Bang (modified after Smoot 1993: 150e). Our physical laws can describe what happened down to 10^{-43} s after which a period of cosmic inflation occurred leaving a very large flat universe. As the temperature dropped the primordial seeds in space-time formed galaxies and galaxy clusters. Today the universe is very old, dark and getting bigger all the time. It has been estimated that faint distant galaxies such as Hydra (3960 million light-years from Earth) are moving away from Earth at velocities up to 61 000 km s^{-1} (one-fifth of the speed of light). In the next 5 s the universe will expand by about the volume of our own Milky Way galaxy. Stephen Hawking put the whole system in perspective when he calculated from the Hubble constant that the universe is expanding only at a rate of 5–10 per cent every billion years.

EVIDENCE FOR A HOT BIG BANG

So far we have concentrated on events that are believed to have occurred in the formation of the early universe. We have not discussed the genesis of the Big Bang itself. The Big Bang is a theory that explains three independent observations:

- the expansion of the visible universe;
- the existence of background microwave radiation; and
- the present-day abundance of the light and heavy elements.

Expansion of the universe

The expansion of the universe was discovered in 1929 by attorney-turned-astronomer Edwin Hubble (1889–1953) and his colleague Milton Humason (1891–1972) at Mount Wilson Observatory in southern California.[26] After reviewing the work of Vesto Slipher (1875–1969) carried out between 1912 and 1917 at the Lowell Observatory, Hubble and Humason began a more systematic study into the light spectra of faint superclusters of galaxies, their velocities and cosmic distances in the region the medievalists and ancients called the "sphere of the fixed stars" (Ch. 8). To their surprise, they found that light from galaxies further away was dominated by longer wavelengths, or red-shifted, compared to the spectral lines of white light in the laboratory.[27]

Furthermore, when Hubble and Humason compared the distances of different galaxies from Earth to the degree of red-shift, to their amazement they found a linear relation. The larger the red-shift, the faster the galaxy was receding from Earth; galaxies twice the distance away were receding at twice the speed, those at three times the distance, three times the speed and so on. This phenomena they attributed to the Doppler effect, which normally describes the changing pitch of a whistle from a train that speeds past an observer,[28] but in this case applies to the changing wavelengths of light from galaxies speeding away from Earth. Hubble's famous law says that the degree of red-shift of galaxies is directly proportional to the distance from Earth. Like many discoveries in science, Hubble and Humason's scheme was an over-simplification; as more information was obtained more anomalies were found. For example, the Hubble constant, which links the red-shifted galaxies to distance, is not a "constant" strictly speaking because its value changes, albeit very slowly, over time depending on the fate of the universe (i.e. whether it will expand for ever or collapse on itself), which will be discussed later in this chapter.

Nonetheless, in broad terms, the Hubble constant or expansion is a fundamental cosmological parameter because it not only sets the size-scale of the universe, but also indirectly its timescale.[29] Hubble and Humason's original value was $500 \, \text{km s}^{-1}$ per megaparsec, corresponding to a universe age of 2 billion years.[30] Current estimates have the value ten times lower, in the range $50–100 \, \text{km s}^{-1} \, \text{Mpc}^{-1}$, giving an age of 10–20 billion years. Some theorists believe the constant may be as low as $30 \, \text{km s}^{-1} \, \text{Mpc}^{-1}$, which, if true, means that our universe could be much older, perhaps around 30 billion years.[31] It is extremely difficult to estimate the age of the universe from the Hubble constant, given that the most recent measurements show the rate of expansion has been increasing during the life of the universe.[32]

How did an expanding universe lead to the notion of a beginning?

By winding back the cosmic clock to time zero, all the galaxies would end up in a single dot (the singularity). In the early 1930s, Eddington presented a two-dimensional balloon analogy to help visualize the events.[33] He drew a number of small black dots, which represented the galaxies, on a deflated balloon, and then slowly inflated the balloon (Fig. 9.3). As the balloon expands the dots representing galaxies move away from one another. *An observer on any galaxy would observe all the other galaxies moving away relative to their position.*[34] If, now, the clock was wound backwards by deflating the balloon, all the black dots would become one and indistinguishable.[35] It was precisely this sort of deductive reasoning from Hubble and Humason's observations that led to Gamow to propose the Big Bang theory.[36]

Importantly, the balloon analogy does not mean that there was a *single* dot *in space* at time zero because in the beginning there was no space. Nor do the galaxies literally fly apart *through* space as you might throw a rock from point A to point B; rather, they are carried along as *space itself* expands. The red-shifted light of distant galaxies is therefore due to the space expanding or stretching, not the galaxies moving through space. The same phenomenon exists for stars closer to our own Milky Way, but the red-shift is much smaller and difficult to measure than distant nebulae.

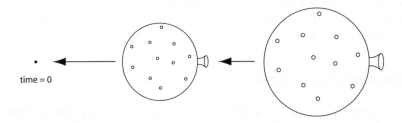

Figure 9.3 Two-dimensional balloon analogy of the Big Bang and winding back the cosmic clock to a point known where all the present matter, space and time were compacted into an infinitesimally small point ($t = 0$).

How fast are the galaxies (or space) moving away from us?

Faint distant galaxies such as Hydra (about 3000 million light-years from Earth) have been estimated to be moving away from Earth at up to $61\,000\,km\,s^{-1}$, or one-fifth of the speed of light.[37] To give you some feeling for these speeds, sound travels at $0.34\,km\,s^{-1}$, a bullet at $0.3–1\,km\,s^{-1}$, and the escape velocity of a NASA rocket leaving Earth is more than $11\,km\,s^{-1}$. At the most distant reaches of the visible universe, cosmologists estimate that galaxies may exceed 90 per cent of the speed of light.[38] The universe is expanding at such extraordinary speeds that in the next 5 seconds it will expand by about the volume of our own Milky Way galaxy (100 000 light-years across).[39] However, Stephen Hawking has put the whole picture into perspective when he calculated from the Hubble constant that the universe itself is only getting bigger by a rate of 5–10 per cent every billion years.[40] The universe is *huge*![41]

Einstein predicted universe expansion but didn't believe his calculations

Like it or not, empty space is not empty at all.   L. M. Krauss[42]

An interesting footnote to the discovery of the expanding universe is that Einstein himself had mathematically predicted it from his own field equations a decade earlier in 1916/17. He thought the idea was so dimwitted that he added an extraneous term for a long range "repulsive" force (a cosmological constant) so that the universe would "stand still" in all directions.[43] Einstein's equations appeared in the *Proceedings of the Prussian Academy* under the title "Cosmological Considerations in General Relativity Theory". Some years later, when George Gamow was discussing the subject, Einstein conceded "that the introduction of the cosmological term was the biggest blunder he had ever made in his life".[44]

Einstein's point is one that should not go unnoticed because it speaks to the immense power of mathematics in *exploring, describing and predicting phenomena* (Ch. 1). Ironically, in recent years, Einstein's cosmological constant has attracted a great deal of attention. The constant, or something just like it, turns out to be related to the expansion and fate of the universe.[45] There is also growing consensus that the cosmological constant relates to the energy density of the vacuum that comprises around 70 per cent of the "missing" matter of the universe.[46] It might also be involved in quantum fluctuations,[47] which evoke putative "wormhole" connections to other possible universes.

Background microwave radiation

It is a suspicious feature of the explosion theory that no obvious relics of a superdense state of the Universe can be found ... An ingenious answer has been offered to these questions by George Gamow, who argues that during the early phases of a superdense Universe radiation was the predominant form of energy, not matter.

Fred Hoyle[48]

The second piece of evidence for a hot Big Bang comes from the uniform cosmic background radiation.[49] If background radiation were present, the short-wavelength, high-energy gamma radiation[50] from the Big Bang should now be stretched or diluted over time and detected as longer-wavelength microwaves. Microwaves would represent the afterglow relics of the cosmic fireball. Hoyle and Gamow discussed the possibility in the summer of 1956 while cruising around California in a Cadillac convertible. If background radiation were present, as Gamow argued, a background temperature of about 5 K would be predicted, but if Hoyle were correct and there was no Big Bang, the background temperature would be absolute zero.[51]

Like many discoveries in science, background microwave radiation was discovered by accident. In 1964/65, AT&T Bell Laboratories engineers Arno Penzias (b. 1933) and Robert Wilson (b. 1936) were testing sensitive antenna intended for use with the Echo communication satellites.[52] To their amazement, they detected anomalous "excess antenna temperature": "excess" meaning a few degrees above 0 K, which is still extraordinarily cold at about −270 °C.[53] The cosmological significance of their discovery was not recognized until Penzias phoned physicist Robert Dicke (b. 1916) of Princeton university (30 miles away). The irony was that Robert Dicke was just about to begin his own search for background radiation.[54]

Amazingly, Dicke himself had worked on radar some 20 years earlier and had developed an instrument to measure background radiation. Dicke actually detected a weak background radio noise that corresponded to a temperature of below 20 K (the instrument's detection limits).[55] Dicke obviously forgot about his own previous work on radar, which was published in 1946 in the journal *Physical Review*. Dicke's publication, and later publications by Soviet scientists in obscure journals, obviously did not reach cosmologists (or himself!) until many years later. These historical events emphasize again the unpredictable nature of the scientific process and why basic science should not be overshadowed by targeted science.

Gamow's prediction was correct. Cosmic background microwave radiation was coming to us from all directions, strongly suggesting that our universe was once hot, dense and opaque. If there were no Big Bang, there would be no background radiation, and the temperature would be absolute zero, as Hoyle argued. You can actually see some of these primordial photons left over from the "fireball" on any television channel receiving no programmes. About 1 per cent of the white "fuzz" is the actual cooled, red-shifted primordial "relic" photons formed a few hundred thousand years after the Big Bang, which have travelled some 15 billion years to our television sets;[56] the other 99 per cent is noise interference from modern-day transmission communications.

Abundance of light and heavy elements

A star is a kind of cosmic kitchen inside which atoms of hydrogen are cooked into heavier atoms … If you wish to make an apple pie from scratch, you must first invent the universe.
Carl Sagan[57]

The third piece of evidence in support of a hot Big Bang comes from the abundance of light and heavy elements in the "ordinary" visible matter of the universe. Although astronomers are still looking for the remaining 90 per cent of matter (see "'Visible' and 'dark' matter", below), spectroscopic analysis of the stars shows that the most abundant light elements are hydrogen (about 75 per cent by mass) and helium (about 24 per cent by mass).[58] The heavy elements such as carbon, oxygen, nitrogen, phosphorus, magnesium and calcium are extremely rare (less than 1 per cent). This one-sidedness of ordinary matter is thought to have come within the first 3 minutes after the Big Bang, when nearly all of the light elements had formed from a plasma of quarks, electrons and other particles.[59]

In fact, it was the abundance of light elements that led Gamow to propose a hot Big Bang in the first place. The heavy elements appeared much later because they have to be made from successive nuclear fusions in the furnace of stars.[60] Our sun, for example, is slowly converting helium into the heavy elements, a process that will rapidly accelerate when hydrogen becomes limited and the star begins to die.[61] More massive stars (10 times the size of the sun) can make elements up to iron, after which there is a gigantic outer-layer supernova explosion with the core collapsing to form a highly compressed "neutron star" or a "black hole".[62] Nucleogenesis, or cooking light elements to make heavier ones, was one of the great triumphs of twentieth-century astrophysics.[63]

In short, the oxygen we breathe, the food we eat, the earth we stand on and the calcium phosphate in our bones are all produced in the furnace of dying stars in the distant past. Human beings are, to paraphrase astronomer Carl Sagan (1934–1996), "star dust with consciousness". Sagan went on to write: "We are a local embodiment of a Cosmos grown to self-awareness … starstuff pondering the stars … these are some of the things that hydrogen atoms do, given fifteen billion years of cosmic evolution."[64]

THE 1992 COBE SATELLITE OBSERVATIONS AND THE BIG BANG THEORY

What COBE found really was a "missing link" in the Big Bang theory of creation, a piece of the jigsaw puzzle that had to be there if the theory was correct, but which had proved extremely difficult to locate.
                                                                                    J. Gribbin[65]

While great strides were made in the latter half of the twentieth century on what happened during the first moments of the Big Bang and the growth and maturation of the early universe, there were some big questions that remained unanswered. Although the cosmic background radiation indicates an incredibly smooth universe, there must be some "ripples" in the past to account for the building of galaxies and galaxy clusters. This missing piece of the puzzle was found in April 1992. The public announcement that NASA's Cosmic Background Explorer satellite (COBE) had discovered the first indication of wrinkles in space caused a worldwide media frenzy.[66]

One of the predictions of the Big Bang theory was that tiny energy differences should be detected when the matter and radiation separated, making the universe transparent, around 300 000 years after the explosion.[67] After mapping the background energy for four years, involving some 70 million measurements, COBE detected areas in space that were 30 millionths of a degree hotter and colder than the average background temperature of 2.735 K.[68] COBE gave support to the Big Bang theory by measuring tiny energy (or temperature) fluctuations from an era when the universe was only 300 000 years old.

The measurements were not uniform, however, but corresponded to clouds of matter spreading across distances of around 500 million light-years.[69] The density fluctuations were responsible for the gentle curvature of space-time in the universe. The ripples are believed to be hydrogen and helium gas concentrated into hot-spots brought together by a gravitational tug from the "dark" or "missing" matter. It is this dark matter that many cosmologists think provided the primordial seeds for the formation of galaxies, clusters of galaxies and superclusters.[70] More will be said about "dark" matter in the next section. The COBE ripples, however, must not be confused with hypothetical gravitational waves propagating through space-time.[71] To put the COBE discovery into perspective, what COBE did for the Big Bang theory is what Eddington's 1919 expedition to equatorial Africa did for Einstein's theory of relativity:[72] it provided good agreement between prediction and observation.

WILL THE UNIVERSE EXPAND FOR EVER OR END IN A BIG CRUNCH?

What might our entire universe be like when it is ten times older than today – after, say, another 100 billion years? Cosmic expansion is being slowed by the gravitational pull that each galaxy exerts on everything else. If the density doesn't exceed the critical value ... our universe is fated to continue expanding. But if the density is substantially higher, gravity would have decelerated the expansion enough to bring it to a halt ... and have been engulfed in a final "crunch."   Martin Rees[73]

Open or closed universe?

If the universe is open (or "flat"[74]), then it will expand for ever and the temperature will gradually decrease, ending in a Big Chill (see Fig. 9.4). On the other hand, if the universe is closed, it will eventually collapse on itself in a Big Crunch. In the latter case, the Big Bang may not be one creation, but one of many creations (as the ancient Hindus and Neo-Confucians believed) because the potential is there for it to be repeated.[75] The Big Chill and Big Crunch scenarios arise directly from the solutions to Einstein's "field equations" formulated in 1922 by mathematician Alexander A. Friedmann (1888–1925).[76]

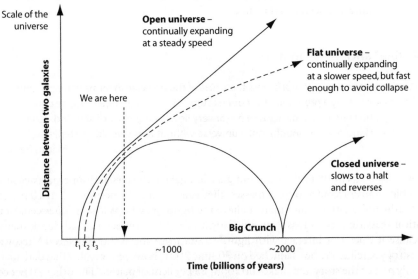

Figure 9.4 Three cosmological models for the fate of the universe (adapted from Kutter 1989: 63, fig. 1.20). For an open universe (which expands for ever) the Hubble constant remains the same or increases with time; and for a closed universe (which eventually collapses on itself), the Hubble constant will decrease over time, reaching zero and then becoming negative, ending in a Big Crunch. Note that the three models are close to one another at the present time in scale of distance. With a Hubble constant of 15 km s^{-1} per million light-years, for an open universe the Big Bang occurred more than 13 bya (t_1); for a flat universe it occurred 13 bya (t_2); and for a closed universe it occurred less than 13 bya (t_3).

Whether the universe is open or closed depends on critical estimates of the amount of matter present in the universe. If the density is below or equal to the critical mass, the universe is open and will expand for ever. If the density of a matter-filled universe exceeds the critical value, the universe is closed and will eventually collapse and perhaps begin another cycle. For this to happen, the universe must contain at least ten to a hundred times more matter than is currently detected by astronomers. That is, the critical density must be in excess of about 25 hydrogen atoms per average size room ($5\,m^3$) (greater than $5 \times 10^{-30}\,g\,cm^{-3}$).[77]

The critical density of matter is also related to the "Hubble expansion", which, as mentioned before, links red-shifted galaxies speeding away from us in all directions. Recent observations of supernovae (exploding stars) at different distances, have led astronomers to conclude that the universe has not been expanding at a constant expansion rate but is getting faster and faster as the universe gets older.[78] In other words, something else is giving the universe a push, quite separate from the force of the Big Bang itself, which began 10–20 bya.

The mysterious force pushing everything apart in the universe is related to Einstein's "fudge factor", or cosmological constant, which he added into his equations to keep the universe stationary. Notwithstanding many deep mysteries remaining, all indications point towards an infinite universe that will expand for ever.[79] This should be of little concern to human existence, because if the sun continues to eat 700 million tons of hydrogen each second, it will die in about 5 billion years, long before the universe decides on its fate.[80]

"Visible" and "dark" matter

> Ordinary atoms may comprise less than 10% of the universe in terms of mass ... But atoms are plainly a prerequisite for our existence. Without them, a universe could harbour no stars, no chemistry and no (or very little) complexity of any kind. Atoms may be a kind of afterthought, but a universe without them would be sterile.
>
> Martin Rees[81]

If astronomers count all the stars and galaxies, galaxy clusters and supergalaxies in the "visible" universe and add their masses, they can account for no more than 10 per cent of "ordinary" matter,[82] and many believe the figure may be as low as 5 per cent of the critical mass density.[83] This "missing" form of matter has been called "dark matter" because it does not interact with light.[84] Data from the WMAP Satellite (Microwave Anistropy Satellite Probe), launched on 30 June 2001, however, revealed that dark matter is only part of the story and makes up about 25 per cent of matter. The other 70 per cent is a kind of vacuum energy called "dark energy", which is related to Einstein's cosmological constant. The generally accepted tally of matter in the universe today is 5 per cent "ordinary", 25 per cent dark matter and the remaining 70 per cent dark energy. Dark energy is not really matter *per se*; rather, it possesses energy density and is very unusual.

Cosmologists have no idea what form this "dark" matter might take, as it does not give off any detectable light or other radiation. And the composition of dark energy is more problematic. The existence of "dark matter" has been inferred from the behaviour of gases and stars around galaxies, rotational speeds of galaxies that otherwise cannot be explained by the theory of gravity, and the existence of "dark energy" from the observation of gravitational repulsion responsible for the accelerated expansion of the universe.

- Astronomers have discovered that enormous pancake-shaped spiral galaxies rotate about their centres at a rate much higher than could be sustained gravitationally if they only contained the matter that is visible. In order to explain the high rates of rotation, another form of matter we cannot currently detect must be holding the spiral galaxy together and preventing it from flying apart into space.[85]
- The second piece of evidence for dark matter comes from galaxy clusters themselves. From the mapping of our skies the galaxies are not uniformly distributed in space, but are "clustered" in groups numbering from a few to millions. Like the rotating spiral galaxy, astronomers find that the speeds at which these galaxies are moving in their clusters are so high that other forms of matter must be present.[86] Explaining how individual galaxies move within galaxy clusters requires a pull of more than ten times more matter than in stars and galaxies.[87]

Where might all this "dark" matter be located? Probable places include black holes,[88] brown dwarfs, outside galaxies and galaxy clusters, neutron stars, faint stars or extremely dim galaxy clusters that cosmologists can't detect.[89] Cosmologists estimate that there might be at least twice as many galaxies than previously thought in the visible universe. Dark matter might also reside in parallel universes, affecting the large-scale structure of our universe through gravitational effects.[90]

THE FIRST MOMENTS OF THE BIG BANG: THE CHALLENGE FOR THE FUTURE

How was the power of atoms first made known and what could they accomplish with their combinations, if Nature herself did not give the blueprint of creation?

… At that time the sun's bright disc was not to be seen soaring on high with ample light, nor the constellations of the heavens, nor sea, nor sky, nor earth nor air, or any things that we see and know today; but a strange wind and a newly-gathered mass of atoms of every sort, whose discord brought a mighty conflict of intervals and pathways and connections and weights, and blows and impacts, and many motions and conjunctions; due to the different shapes and variations of form, they could not all remain locked in the combinations or make the necessary motions when combined. Then they began to be sorted out, and like combined with like, so that the world began to take its shape.

Lucretius[91]

The three main physical theories that currently describe the relations between space, time, matter and energy are:

- the theory of special relativity (1905)
- the theory of general relativity (1915)
- quantum mechanical theory (1920s).[92]

The two theories of relativity describe gravity and the large-scale structure of the universe,[93] whereas the quantum theory describes events on a subatomic scale[94] (less than the size of a proton).[95] The three theories are only partial theories; general relativity was built on special relativity, and quantum field theory has inputs from both (Fig. 9.5).

A further advance was made in the 1970s by Nobel laureate Steven Weinberg and Abdus Salam (d. 1996), who independently built a unified theory of electricity and magnetism, light and radioactivity called "electroweak force theory". The theory was the first to link electromagnetic and "weak" forces at very high temperatures, which has been supported in big particle accelerators.[96] A bigger challenge for twenty-first-century physics is to formulate a theory that merges the "strong" force that holds the bulk of matter together at the nuclear level and the "weak" forces: the so-called grand unified theory (GUT).[97] The energies involved are many thousands of millions times greater than the energies generated by current particle accelerators. An even greater challenge is to form a theory of everything (TOE), which describes conditions where the "strong", "weak", electromagnetic and gravitational forces are indistinguishable (see Fig. 9.5).

The major difficulty in unifying the four forces is how to reconcile the "probabilistic" or "chance" nature of the quantum predictions at the sub-atomic level with the large-scale reality of the universe.[98] Niels Bohr (1885–1962) favoured the quantum theory and Einstein the larger-scale reality. Einstein abhorred Bohr's idea of leaving the events in the universe to "blind chance": "God does not play at dice with the world."[99] This infuriated Bohr so much that at a meeting he stood and replied, "Albert! Stop telling God what he can do!"[100] The philosophical debate between these two schools continues today. A debate on the subject was held in 1994 at the University of Cambridge between Roger Penrose (taking Einstein's position) and Stephen Hawking (taking Bohr's position).[101] Hawking concluded: "Unfortunately, however, these two theories are known to be inconsistent with each other – they cannot both be correct. One of the major endeavours in physics today … is the search for a new theory that will incorporate them both – a quantum theory of gravity."[102]

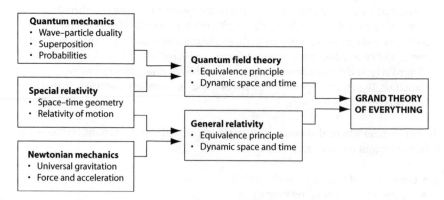

Figure 9.5 The challenge for physics in the twenty-first century (modified after Weinberg 1999: 39).

Can science and technology recreate the first moments of the Big Bang?

When two protons travelling at 99.999999 percent of the speed of light collide head-on, the ensuing subatomic explosion provides nature with 14 trillion electron volts (TeV) of energy to play with.   C. Llewellyn Smith[103]

The biggest stumbling block in formulating a *theory of everything* is the inability of cosmologists to mimic the extremely high temperatures (and energies) involved in the first fractions of a second of the Big Bang. Studying events in stars like our sun (up to 10^7 K) is of little value because the temperatures of thermonuclear reactions are too low by many orders of magnitude.[104] A partial solution may be possible, however. In December 1994, a number of countries joined together and agreed to build the world's most powerful particle accelerator.[105] The European large hadron collider (LHC) particle accelerator is being built astride the Franco-Swiss border west of Geneva in the existing 27 km tunnel housing the large electron-positron (LEP) collider.[106] The LHC is expected to operate up to 14 TeV and should enable physicists to accelerate and smash particles at temperatures of 10^{15} K.

The LHC project may provide the window into the first moments of the universe formation by duplicating conditions 10^{-12} s after the Big Bang.[107] At these temperatures, the electromagnetic and weak forces are believed to unify and may permit physicists to gain insights into the elusive Higgs boson,[108] the postulated origin of mass.[109] By colliding proton beams of unprecedented intensity to increase the number of rare collisions, the LHC will help scientists understand nature's strong force, the glueballs (made of gluons).[110] The gluons carry the strong force that binds quarks together to make up protons and neutrons. The potential further exists for the LHC to create "micro" black holes by smashing protons at high energy. The accelerator is expected to be completed around 2007 at a cost of over 2–5 billion US dollars.[111] Unfortunately, a similar initiative in the US (a superconducting supercollider-SSC accelerator operating at 40 TeV) planned for the late twentieth century was cancelled due to lack of congressional support.

Superstring theory: the best hope for unifying the four forces

The idea of extra dimensions in effect continues the Copernican tradition in understanding our place in the world: The earth is not the center of the solar system, the sun is not the center of our galaxy, our galaxy is just one of billions in the universe that has no center, and now our entire three-dimensional universe would be just a thin membrane in the full space of dimensions. If we consider slices across the extra dimensions, our universe would occupy a single infinitesimal point in each slice, surrounded by a void.   N. Arakani-Hamed et al.[112]

Growing consensus in recent decades is that our huge four-dimensional, incredibly smooth, flat universe may have grown out of higher dimensions in our early history.[113] In the first moments of creation, some ten dimensions may have curled up or flipped over into the four dimensions we experience today (three for space and one for time). Recently, physicists recognized that some of these extra dimensions may be as "big" as a millimetre, but remain invisible to the human senses.[114] Experiments are underway to detect signs of extra dimensions by studying gravity over distances smaller than a millimetre. These extra dimensions may also give rise to the production of bizarre quantum gravity objects such as "micro" black holes, graviton particles and super-strings detected in the high-energy particle accelerators.[115]

Superstrings come in many forms, but they all share the property of a line-like topology (the so-called strings) where all the forces were compacted and unified; the strings are tiny (10^{20} times smaller than an atomic nucleus!).[116] The superstring theory describes mathematically the temperature-dependent phase transitions in the first moments of the creation.[117] It proposes that elementary particles of quantum gravity act as vibrational multi-dimensional modes of infinitesimal strings, not as dot points.[118] The different "notes" that the tiny loops of string vibrate equate to a new exotic particle.[119] It was not until the temperature dropped after the Big Bang that the strings "compactified" and acted as a source of gravitational mass from which were seeded the galaxies. Six of the ten dimensions are believed to have compacted so tightly as to become effectively "invisible" today, which left the present four-dimensional visible universe.[120] Unfortunately, the equations to describe these events have tens of thousands of six-dimensional solutions, leaving at least that many four-dimensional present-day universes.[121] This has led some theorists to propose that our universe itself may lie within a higher-dimensional realm. The interface separating our universe from other universes may be what string theorists call membranes, which gravity (gravitons) can pass, but not much else.[122]

Trying to match one of these universes with our own is no easy task and requires a new kind of mathematics.[123] Mathematical physicists believe the "string" theory represents one of the best candidates to help unify Einstein's gravity with quantum forces (weak, strong and electromagnetic). Importantly, as with many scientific theories, if the new unified theory turns out to be wrong, it will undoubtedly lead to many new and exhilarating predictions and technologies that will drive the scientific process forwards.

The origin of life was necessarily the beginning of organic evolution
and it is among the greatest of all evolutionary problems.

G. G. Simpson[1]

CHAPTER 10

Origins of life: from molecules to machines

INTRODUCTION: THE DYNAMICS OF LIVING MATTER

What we anticipate seldom occurs;
What we least expected generally happens.   Henrietta Temple[2]

Having discussed the Big Bang, we now turn our attention to another deep mystery: life and its origins. In the earliest Near Eastern river-valley civilizations, the creation of life was deeply mythologized around the all-powerful creator-gods and many hundreds of "helper" gods. More physical accounts of life and its origins did not appear until those of the ancient Greek philosophers. Thales, for example, removed the creator-gods and believed everything originated from water. Anaximander reasoned that living creatures originated from moisture evaporated by the sun and that human beings developed from the transmutation of lower animals, and saw life and nature as a self-regulating system of cycles, as did most Presocratics (see Ch. 4). Life was a microcosm of the larger living, breathing, thinking *cosmos*. Likewise, Empedocles believed that natural diversity arose from some kind of evolution and taught that the world order was connected through immanent law, just as the living body was connected to its constituent parts. Plato, on the other hand, believed that everything in nature was divinely created from a "blueprint" comprising non-physical, eternal Ideas (see Ch. 5). Aristotle disagreed, and believed that the world was eternal and that some animals had always been able to generate spontaneously from dead matter, others spawning from parent animals according to their kind.[3] In the fifth and fourth centuries BC, the Hippocratic doctors similarly taught the idea of natural cycles and combined this idea with the doctrine of four elements in order to diagnose and treat human sickness.

In early Christian Europe, the study of life, nature and medicine was not popular and did not become so in Europe until the Renaissance (see Chs 6, 7 and 8). The world and everything in it were increasingly viewed in mechanistic terms, and thought to operate like a giant clock as part of God's laws. In the eighteenth century, mechanistic thinking was still prevalent, but there was less emphasis on God's laws. A turning point came in

1780 when Lavoisier and Laplace showed that animal respiration was analogous to the burning of fuels in a steam engine. Both body and engine required food for their combustion.[4] Next came the discovery of the conservation and degradation of energy, and its relation to heat and power. The human body was now seen as a *heat* engine that converts fuel into work and heat.[5]

Equally sensational was Friedrich Wöhler's (1800–1882) demonstration of the synthesis of urea in his laboratory in 1828. The manufacture of an organic compound "outside" the living body left many vitalists in a state of disbelief, although most (including Wöhler himself) continued to use the concept of vitalism for a number of years, arguing that such a synthesis could not imitate living processes. Vitalism held that life could not be explained by physical or chemical laws alone, but required some external principle from the outside, such as a soul, to endow the body with vital properties necessary for life. It remained a popular doctrine in the nineteenth century with leading exponents Henri Bergson (1859–1941), Hans Driesch (1867–1941) and Justin von Liebig (1803–1873).[6]

Another challenge to vitalism came from Jakob Berzelius (1779–1848), who proposed that living systems are self-regulating, use organic compounds, and possess chemical reactions and catalysis. Berzelius wrote in 1836: "In animals and plants there occur thousands of catalytic processes between the tissues and fluids."[7] Vital forces turned out not to be metaphysical forces, but "physical", catalytic forces of physical or material origin. John Dalton's (1766–1844) chemical theory of atoms also emerged in the early nineteenth century (1808), and around 31 new elements were discovered between 1790 and 1830, further indicating a more physical basis for life. A mechanistic conception of life was also championed by Claude Bernard (1813–1878), Charles Darwin (1809–1882), Emile Du Bois-Reymond (1818–1896), Thomas Huxley (1825–1895), Jacques Loeb (1859–1924), Louis Pasteur (1822–1895) and Theodor Schwann (1810–1882).[8] The human body was now seen as a heat-producing, *chemical* machine that used cellular metabolism to convert food into useful energy and work.

As scientists delved deeper into life's processes, many more questions were raised than could be answered. Freshwater hydra could be chopped up and, miraculously, each individual piece grew into an entirely new individual; no external supernatural forces were required. Frog muscles were shown to contract by stimulating the sciatic nerve, giving rise to the concept of animal electricity. These bizarre new discoveries, together with Darwin's theory of natural selection, Charles Lyell's (1797–1875) geology, Charles Walcott's (1850–1927) fossil record and Theodor Schwann's cell theory (see p. 319), demanded a new look into life's origins, processes and the underpinnings of natural diversity.[9] An unfortunate outcome of the growing enthusiasm for science, however, was a dramatic rise in biblical literalism that often portrayed science as the enemy of religion.[10]

In the last century, in spite of background rumblings from literalism, extraordinary advances were made in understanding life's origins and processes.[11] In this chapter I discuss a number of these advances, and the formidable challenges that lie ahead.

WHAT GAVE LIFE ITS CHANCE?

> However improbably we regard this event, or any of the steps which it involves, given
> enough time it will almost certainly happen at least once. G. Wald[12]

Today most scientists believe the "chance" of life came from the trillions upon trillions upon trillions of atoms,[13] molecules and ions interacting in some watery environment nearly 4 bya. In a single drop of water[14] there are over 100 billion atoms (10^{11} atoms). This is about the same number of stars in the Milky Way galaxy, and galaxies in our visible universe. In the seven oceans, the number of atoms increases to a mind-boggling 10^{36}.

Given the extraordinary number of chance interactions, it is no wonder many theoretical biologists like Stuart Kauffman claimed that the origin of life was not a "chance" event (as most scientists believe) but a "near certainty".[15] Kauffman's computer simulations reveal that self-organization of catalytic polymers and life assemblies arose out of primordial chaos as a result of increasing natural complexity. Kauffman further proposed that once underway, evolving systems would tend towards a special ordered state representing the ideal balance between stability and propensity to explore change; in other words, they evolve "evolveability".[16] He argued that the origin of multicellular life from single cells, including human beings, applied equally well as the origin of first life from non-living matter. Kauffman summarized his views: "If life were bound to arise, not as an incalculably improbable accident, but as an expected fulfillment of the natural order, then we truly are at home in the universe."[17] From the scientific evidence, physicist Freeman J. Dyson summed-up the past history of life in the following way: "Looking at the past history of life, we see that it takes about a million years to evolve a new species, 10 million years to evolve a new genus, 100 million years to evolve a class, a billion years to evolve a phylum, and *less* than 10 billion years to evolve all the way from the primaeval slime to *Homo sapiens*."[18]

THEORIES ON THE ORIGINS OF LIFE

> Today you are a walking collection of about 10^{14} cells, coordinated in origin and
> function. Each of your cells bears strong family resemblance in size, function and
> chemistry to contemporary protozoa. The principle of evolution has allowed us to
> understand how this increase in complexity has occurred. Carl Sagan[19]

Over the past 5000 years, explanations for the origin of life fall into at least one of five categories: spontaneous generation; divine creation; vitalism; panspermia; and evolution.[20]

Spontaneous generation: life from non-life *without* divine creation

Spontaneous generation is the creation of life out of non-living matter such as putrefying bogs, mounds, decaying flesh or riverbed ooze.[21] According to this theory all living forms were created by the generative power of dead matter and many continued to be created by spontaneous generation (i.e. not by seeds or parents).[22] It was first documented by the early Mesopotamians and ancient Egyptians around 3000–2500 BC, and later by the ancient Indians and Chinese.[23] The ancient Egyptians vividly describe the creation of beetles, worms, frogs and toads out of the sun-warmed mud and mounds on the banks of the Nile. Other reports can be found in the writings of the Presocratic Greeks and later by Aristotle and the Stoics.[24] The Roman poet-philosopher Lucretius (c.95–55 BC) also reported on the phenomenon, stating that: "For clearly, animals did not fall from the sky, nor can land-dwelling creatures come from salty sea-pools ... Even now, many creatures come out of the ground, formed by the rain and by the warmth of the shining sun."[25] The theory that many organisms originated from dead matter without divine creation was taught in the West for almost 2000 years.[26] In the seventeenth century, Johannes Baptista van Helmont (c.1579–1644) published a recipe for spontaneously generating mice in 21 days from open jars stuffed with soiled underwear and kernels of wheat.[27] He believed that the combination of odour, ferment from the underwear and the husks transformed the wheat into adult male and female mice.[28]

Over the next 200 years, spontaneous generation was met with increasing scepticism and finally disproved with the experiments of Tuscan physician Francisco Redi (1626–1697). Redi showed that maggots in putrefying meat were a result of the eggs laid by flies.[29] A century later, Italian biologist Lazzaro Spallanzani (1729–1799) repeated Redi's experiments and wrote:

> a great man, this fellow Redi ... See how easy he settles it! He takes two jars and puts some meat in each one. He leaves one jar open and puts a light veil over the other one. He watches and sees flies go down into the meat in the open pot – and in a little while there are maggots there, and then new flies. He looks at the jar which has a veil over it – and there are no maggots or flies in that one at all. How easy![30]

In the nineteenth century, spontaneous generation received its death blow from physicist John Tyndall (1820–1893) and biologist Louis Pasteur (1822–1895).[31] In 1860 Pasteur demonstrated that bacteria, fungal spores or any other microbial life could not be spontaneously generated from sterilized broth. Life only appeared in his specially designed flasks when exposed to contaminants in the air. In his famous victory address to the French Academy of Science (7 April 1864), Pasteur said: "Never will the doctrine of spontaneous generation recover from the mortal blow of this simple experiment."[32] Living systems could arise only from other living systems: "Omni vivum ex vivum, omni ovo ex ovo."[33] This is another good example of how, through method, experiment and measurement, science can dramatically change the way we think.

Divine creation

Divine creation has a long history. The most popular version in the West is found in Genesis, which describes how Yahweh created the world within six days: light on the first day; the stars on the second day; the Earth on the third day; the sun and moon on the fourth day; the fish in the sea and the fowl in the air on the fifth day; and the first man, Adam, from some inanimate material like clay, and then woman, Eve, from Adam's rib, on the sixth day (Ch. 2). The Genesis story has been adopted by the three major world religions of Judaism, Christianity and Islam. Serious attempts in the nineteenth century tried to work out whether this six-day creation was tenable and whether Noah's ark had room for representatives of all species. Twentieth-century French Jesuit paleontologist and philosopher Pierre Teilhard's (1881–1955) heroic attempt to unite Christian creation beliefs with the scientific facts of evolution met with mixed reactions.[34] Nobel immunologist Peter Medawar (1915–1987) dismissed Teilhard's theory as a "bag of tricks".[35] Some other prominent scientists are more sympathetic to Teilhard's finalism. Nobel neurophysiologist Sir John Eccles (1903–1998) wrote: "I believe that there is a Divine Providence operating over and above the materialist happenings of biological evolution that eventually resulted in the creation of the human genotype."[36] Nobel physicist Erwin Schrödinger (1887–1961) also supported the idea of divine creation when he wrote: "life is the work of the fine and precise creation of the quantum mechanics of our Lord".[37] As we have maintained throughout, the subject of divine creation lies outside the domain of science and in its most literal interpretation remains a matter of faith (see Chs 11 and 12).

Vitalism and cell theory

As mentioned earlier, vitalism states that life cannot be explained by the physical laws of science alone, but requires an external vital force such as soul or spirit (e.g. mind–body dualism; see Ch. 11).[38] The vitalistic perception of life dates back to the ancient Greeks (and probably earlier) and was revived in the West by physician George Stahl (1660–1734) in 1707.[39] For a long time, chemists had taught that a "vital force" manufactured all compounds in the living animal, and therefore the compounds could not be made in the laboratory. In addition to Wöhler synthesizing urea in the laboratory, Hermann Kolbe (1818–1884) synthesized acetic acid from its inorganic constituents in 1845, a feat thought to be impossible. In light of these experiments, and others, the concept of vitalism was slowly abandoned.

Vitalism was eventually eclipsed by the cell theory of Theodor Schwann (1810–1882) and his idea of metabolism as a physicochemical process in living tissue.[40] Life now represented a continuous line of descent involving chemistry, physics, biology and physiology, with less emphasis on a supernatural act of creation. The cell theory of 1839 says that all living things are made up of cells, and that all cells arose from the same fundamental reproductive processes of division and multiplication: "All cells from cells [*Omnis cellula e cellula*]".[41] Without doubt, the cell theory gave biology its long sought after unity among the sciences. Today the cell theory holds for the simplest of single cells like protozoa and bacteria up to the human being, which contains a staggering 10^{14} cells (one hundred thousand billion).

Cosmic panspermia: life from outer space

> To consider the Earth as the only populated world in infinite space is as absurd as to assert that in an entire field sown with millet, only one grain will grow.
>
> Metrodorus of Chios[42]

The name "panspermia" was coined in 1907 by Swedish chemist Svante Arrhenius (1859–1927) and literally means "seeds everywhere".[43] The panspermia hypothesis dates back to the Greek natural philosopher Anaxagoras.[44] Life may have arrived on Earth from outer space in the form of spores or microorganisms in cosmic dust propelled by the radiation pressure from the sun or by facilitated passage on meteorites and comets.

Panspermia is a real possibility, given that hundreds of tons of extraterrestrial matter (mostly dust) visits Earth daily, and considerably more during the Earth's compaction and bombardment over 4 bya.[45] Of the hundreds of tons reaching Earth each day, some 30 tons is organic matter.[46] These tiny freezing flecks litter the inner solar system,[47] and we sometimes see them streaking across the sky as shooting stars.

In addition, biologist George Wald (1906–1997) estimated that the number of planetary systems similar to ours in the Milky Way is around 1–5 per cent of the stars present.[48] This amounts to no less than a staggering 1–5 billion possible "Earth" systems. Even if only a fraction of these were similar to ours, a reasonable prediction would be that we are not alone. The question of other worlds has recently been revisited by Charles Lineweaver and Daniel Grether at the University of New South Wales in Australia. The two astrophysicists support Wald's calculations, and believe the number could be higher, based on the number of Jupiter-like planets orbiting sun-like stars in our galaxy.[49] More accurate information is expected from NASA's space telescope Kepler, approved to be launched in 2006. Although the probe will not take photographs, it will monitor the light of about 100 000 stars, and look for any signature drops in light or periodic dimming that might indicate Earth-sized planets in an Earth-like orbit in front of a "sun-like" star. The four-year Kepler mission is expected to detect up to 500 Earth-sized planets and up to 1000 Jupiter-sized planetary systems, and help us to map our solar system among the 100–400 billion other stars and their planets in the galaxy.

In the twentieth century, a number of cosmic panspermia scenarios emerged. Nobel laureate Francis Crick (1916–1984) and chemist Leslie Orgel (b. 1927) believe that the "life seeds" were sent to Earth from other intelligent extra-terrestrials.[50] Fred Hoyle and Chandra Wickramasinghe (b. 1939) further propose that interstellar dust is a "life cloud" composed largely of bacteria.[51] Others argue that only the raw ingredients reached us, leaving life to form on Earth unassisted. This is a separate hypothesis from panspermia,[52] and one that has received some support with the discovery of amino acids in meteorites and organic compounds hydrogen cyanide (HCN), formaldehydes, acetaldehydes, quinones and cyanamide in interstellar clouds.[53] Seventy-four amino acids have been discovered in the 1969 Murchison meteorite.[54] Eight of these are in life's proteins. All proteins in living organisms are composed of different arrangements of 20 basic amino acids. On other meteorites, scientists have found evidence of the nucleotide bases themselves that make up the genetic information encoded on our DNA (deoxyribonucleic acid).

The possibility of extraterrestrial colonization of Earth received a further boost in August 1996 with the discovery of fossil remnants found on a meteorite, ALH84001, that came from Mars around 13 000 years ago. NASA scientists announced that the "life forms" resembled bacteria but were some 100 times larger. Unfortunately, in March 1999 the claims were disproved. A few months later, NASA scientists again announced they had uncovered even stronger evidence on different meteorites for life on Mars. In the same year, Russian scientists claimed the presence of microfossil communities on the Murchison meteorite that hit Australia in 1969. These are all exciting possibilities. The problem is that Mars shared similar planetary conditions with Earth around 3.5 bya,[55] thus making it difficult to decide if the life remnants came from Mars or *originated* from the Earth itself.[56] Future planned visits to comets by satellites and lander probes from NASA (comet Tempel 1 in 2005) and from the European Space Agency (comet Wirtanen in 2013) will undoubtedly enhance knowledge on these key questions. I think what will emerge is that the origins of life on Earth, and the origins of life *per se* (e.g. from outer space domiciles), will turn out to be very different.

Evolution by natural selection: a paradigm for life

Darwin's theory of evolution by natural selection … is the idea that, in nature, those individuals best able to survive and reproduce will transmit the characteristics that enabled them to do so to their children, leading to the evolution of traits beneficial to the organism itself, rather than to the breeder.   J. Maynard Smith & E. Szathmary[57]

Evolution proceeds in two stages: chemical and biological. Chemical evolution occurs when inorganic substances self-associate to form more complex molecules and compounds. Over many millions of years and almost infinite opportunities, these products of chemical evolution in turn combined to form independent cells capable of self-regulation, growth and reproduction. Biological evolution refers to the cumulative changes that occur in a population over time. Sometimes, individuals inherit new traits that provide a survival and reproductive advantage in their local environments. As paleobiologist J. William Schopf (b. 1941) pointed out, two of the greatest inventions evolution devised were: oxygen-forming photosynthesis, which was key to the development of oxygen-consuming respiration and anaerobic-aerobic transitions of the living world; and eukaryotic sex, the main source of genetic variation in higher organisms, giving rise to their remarkable diversity and rapid evolution over the past 500 million years.[58]

An important point is that evolution by itself is not a theory of "random" chance, but contains "random" chance. Random chance occurs at the level of the genes as they mutate and/or combine in different ways during reproduction and are passed on to subsequent generations. These small mutations occur to one or more of four nucleotide bases of DNA that are arranged in triplets and strung together in long coded sequences. These tiny changes, and their differential expression during stages of embryonic development, lead to the endless variation of life.[59] Another point of emphasis is that these mutations are often more harmful to survival than adaptive.[60] That is, they are not in themselves goal-directed toward adaptive improvement of an organism in the Aristotelian sense; that job is left to natural selection (see Ch. 11).[61]

The link between the evolution of the inanimate world and the first cells or life forms remains an enormous challenge for future science.

WHAT IS LIFE?

Life, however varied in its appearance, is built on the same simple principles.

A. Szent-Györgyi[62]

Like the concept of time, everyone seems to know what life is until someone asks them the question. The difficulty is much like what philosopher Gilbert Ryle (1900–1976) called a category error. Ryle gave the example of a first-time visitor to the University of Oxford. The visitor was shown the lecture theatres, conference rooms, library, student union, offices, maintenance buildings, swimming pool and sports arenas. The visitor then met the students, lecturers and office staff. When the tour was over the visitor politely said, "Thank you for showing me all these things, but where is the university?" Ryle's point was that the visitor mistakenly thought that the "university" belonged to the same category as all the other entities he was shown. The visitor failed to realize that the university was the sum of all things.[63] Similar problems arise when trying to define life. Life exhibits many unique characteristics such as microstructural self-assembly, boundaries, cell organization, self-regulation, growth, repair, metabolism, adaptation, responsiveness, heredity and reproduction.[64] Assembling these in a definition is problematic because, for example, viruses cannot reproduce by themselves; they need the machinery of a living cell to carry out reproduction and replication. Are viruses alive or potentially alive?

A more satisfying definition of life can be sought by first asking what separates the living from the non-living. Inanimate objects or entities like a snowflake, an opal or the air we breathe are all made of the same elemental stuff as you, me or a tree. The only difference is the way matter is organized in three-dimensional space and the degree to which energy is required to maintain that organization over time. Living systems require a continual "flow" of matter and energy to maintain their cellular, tissue and whole body integrity. For most, this "flow" comes from food and oxygen, which in turn are dependent on light and heat from the sun. Ninety-nine per cent of all living things are made up of the elements carbon, hydrogen, oxygen and nitrogen. If we add calcium, sulphur, phosphorus, silicon, potassium, magnesium, iron and sodium we have accounted for 99.98 per cent. The heavy elements, as discussed in Chapter 9, were manufactured in the furnaces of old stars.

A second distinguishing feature of life is that it does not exist in a vacuum. Each of the projected 30 million species on Earth[65] is part of a vast ecological network of small- and large-scale matter–energy conversion cycles linking our terrestrial, marine and cosmic environments (including the formation and destruction of stars, galaxies and black holes). Unfortunately, we have taken far too long to recognize that a break in any one of these cycles can eventually return all living systems to the non-living. The hole in the ozone layer, the accumulation of greenhouse gases, the burning of fossil fuels and global warming are some examples of this interdependence that may in time lead to our own extinction.

Any minimum definition of life must take these matter–energy exchanges into account; which brings us to the first and second laws of thermodynamics. The first law states that the total amount of energy in the universe is constant or conserved.[66] Energy can neither be created nor destroyed. The difference between 15 bya and the present is the form in which energy appears. Moments after the Big Bang, all the energy was in a high-grade form called potential energy. Potential energy and its lower-grade product, heat energy, drive the small- and large-scale matter–energy cycles. As time progresses, the amount of potential energy in the universe decreases as it converts to a non-useable temperature-dependent "by-product" called entropy. The term "entropy" is often used as a measure of the disorder of a system. And it is this "directionality" of energy conversions *with respect to time* that embodies the second law of thermodynamics.

This directionality was first recognized in 1857 by the German physicist Hermann von Helmholtz (1821–1894). He viewed the entire universe as a huge machine with a finite stock of fuel that must eventually run out. Thus the second law predicts that the universe will slowly wind down like a giant clock spring at the expense of these high-grade matter–energy conversions (Fig. 10.1).

The second law is wholly consistent with our universe coming into being from a small hot singularity exploding some 15 billion years ago and becoming larger and cooler with time. Too often we read that life itself violates the second law of thermo-dynamics. This is nonsense. Some biblical creationists further argue that evolution is anti-entropic and violates the second law. The confusion arises when the perpetrators forget that the second law relates to *isolated systems*, which the physical universe is

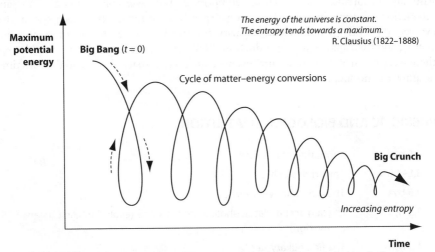

Figure 10.1 The second law of thermodynamics tells us that the universe is slowly winding down like a giant clock spring. This is happening as a consequence of all the small- and large-scale matter–energy conversions. The second law states that "isolated" systems are moving towards a state of increasing entropy (or disorder). The maximum potential energy that ever existed occurred at the time of the Big Bang. At the Big Crunch (or Chill) there will be no more high-grade energy because the system will be at maximum entropy.

believed to be,[67] but life and evolution are most definitely not.[68] Life and evolution are open systems driven by high-grade energy from the surroundings. Life is only possible at the expense of greater disorder occurring somewhere else in the universe, yet *the overall net result is a decrease in high-grade energy and an increase in entropy.* As physicist James Trefil (b. 1938) pointed out, if the creationists were right, you would never be able to make ice cubes from water.[69] The ice cube forms from the increase in order of the water molecules on freezing, but this is matched by a greater disorder at the power plant burning high-grade fuel. The second law of thermodynamics satisfactorily explains why hot objects become cold but cool objects never become hot (without some form of added energy), why rivers don't flow uphill and why we grow older not younger.

Life does not violate the second law of thermodynamics, *but is a product of it.* A definition of life taking this into account was formulated by biophysicist A. Katchalsky, who emphasizes that living systems are not equilibrium systems but steady-state systems:

> Life is a constant struggle against the tendency to produce entropy. The synthesis of large and information rich macromolecules, the formation of intricately structured cells, the development of organisation, all these are all-powerful anti-entropic forces. But since there is no possibility of escaping the entropic doom imposed on all natural phenomena under the second law of thermodynamics, living organisms choose the least evil – they produce entropy at a minimum rate by maintaining a steady state.[70]

If I were asked to define life I would offer the following: "Life may be defined as that naturally occurring phenomenon comprising the assembly, organization and interaction of atoms in three-dimensional space and in time; which, as a system, has evolved the entropy-minimising capacity for steady-state exchange of matter and energy, and the capacity for reproduction."[71] Within the realm of our physical laws, if there were no succession of natural events contained in space there would be no time, no universe, no life: nothing.

PREBIOTIC AND BIOLOGICAL EVOLUTION

4.6 bya	Formation of the Earth
3.8–4 bya	The origins of life
3.5 bya	The oldest known fossils
2.5 bya	Oxygen accumulates, photosynthesis starts (evolution's first great innovation)
1.5 bya	The first eukaryotes
1.1 bya	Sex appears (evolution's second great innovation, increasing the potential for variation, diversity and survival of a population)
0.63 bya	Soft-bodied multicellular life
0.53 bya	Hard-bodied multicellular life

Earth is believed to have formed from "clumps" of cosmic dust and gas over a period of about a 100 million years,[72] and first life appeared about 650 million years later. The earliest atmosphere[73] was composed of hot hydrogen gas from the out-gassing of rocks during the Earth's compaction and bombardment by asteroids, comets and meteorites.[74] At 4 billion years things started to settle down. Hydrogen was lost to space due to its small size, or alternatively self-associated with other elements on Earth to form heavier compounds.[75] What happened next is not clear. One view is that the Earth's atmosphere was strongly reducing from high levels of methane, nitrogen, ammonia, carbon dioxide, sulphur, water vapour, hydrogen and carbon monoxide.[76] This composition is similar to the gases from modern volcanoes, and fumaroles such as the deep-sea hydrothermal vents discovered in 1977.[77]

Another popular view is that the early atmosphere was much less reducing, and made up of nitrogen, carbon dioxide and water.[78] Most of its methane and ammonia was broken down by the ultraviolet light from the sun.[79] In the first model, atmospheric methane and ammonia may have formed a blanket and kept the Earth's surface warm, whereas in the second, the world's oceans (covering up to 97 per cent of its surface) would have been frozen to depths of up to 300 m. Whether the top layer of the world's oceans was frozen and for how long remain contentious issues, although according to geochemist Jeffrey L. Bada and colleagues, a 1-km-diameter asteroid or meteor could have melted the ice.[80] Like the origins of life, the state of the early atmosphere is hotly debated.

Earliest life and free oxygen

Over the last three decades, the evolutionary Tree of Life has been extended sevenfold. An immense early fossil record, unknown and thought unknowable, has been discovered. For the first time we have firm knowledge that life originated, evolved, and rose to become a flourishing success during the infancy of planet Earth.

J. W. Schopf[81]

The earliest biochemical evidence for life comes from around 3.8 bya. The date is based on isotopic fingerprints of carbon found in "banded iron" rocks at Isua in southern Greenland.[82] Most experts agree that the remnants could have belonged only to living organisms. The oldest known life forms are fossilized stromatolites dated around 3.5 bya, discovered near Warrawoona in Western Australia and South Africa.[83] The well-preserved microscopic fossils were discovered by Schopf and Elso Barghoorn from Harvard in the early 1960s. With the help of other scientists, Schopf and Barghoorn had solved Darwin's puzzle of "why we do not find rich fossiliferous deposits belonging to these assumed earliest periods".[84] The deposits *do exist but are hard to find*. Other cellular thread-like microbes from Marble Bar in Western Australia have been dated as 3.5 billion years old.[85] These earliest life forms are strikingly similar to the primitive ancestors of today's photosynthetic cyanobacteria and the amazing archaebacteria that we shall discuss shortly.

More recently, Rasmussen reported early microbial life in deep-sea volcanic rocks that are 3.2 billion years old.[86] The thread-like filaments may be fossilized bacteria that lived below the light penetration zone at high temperatures and used inorganic matter as their energy source.[87] Thus the current scenario from the available Precambrian geological and fossil evidence points to life's origins occurring within a tiny window of 500 million years or less, and may have started and stopped many times between the early cataclysmic meteorite bombardments of Earth.

As early life forms increased in number, the atmosphere slowly transformed from a reducing or mildly reducing to an oxidizing one containing free oxygen.[88] Oxygen first appeared around 4.3 bya by photodissociation,[89] an ultraviolet light-driven process that splits the abundant atmospheric water vapour into oxygen and hydrogen.[90] A second more dramatic way oxygen levels rose in the atmosphere was from the first oxygen-producing organisms around 2.8–3 bya.[91] By around 2.5 bya, oxygen-producing bacteria like the cyanobacteria were thriving.[92]

As free oxygen accumulated, the ozone layer[93] slowly formed. Today, the ozone layer is 25–30 km above the Earth's surface and shields us against harmful ultraviolet rays.[94] The problem facing biologists today is if free oxygen formed around 2.5 bya, why did it take land vertebrates another 2 billion years to appear on the Earth's surface (about 500 million years ago (mya))? A possible reason is that it may have taken that long for free oxygen to build up to sufficient levels compatible with the high oxygen demands of terrestrial life. It appears that oxygen did not reach today's steady-state value of 21 per cent until about 200 mya.

"PRECELLULAR" EVOLUTION: THE FIRST BUILDING-BLOCKS

> It is often said that all the conditions for the first production of a living organism are now present, which could ever have been present. But if (and oh what a big if) we could conceive in some warm little pond, with all sorts of ammonia and phosphoric acids, light, heat, electricity, etc., present, that a protein compound was chemically formed, ready to undergo still more complex changes, at the present day such matter would be instantly devoured or absorbed, which would not have been the case before living creatures were formed.
>
> Charles Darwin[95]

Location of Darwin's "warm little pond"

The location of Darwin's "warm little pond" is not known. It may have been on the Earth's hard crusted surface, in the open ocean, within coastal sediment mats, in lake communities or in some shallow backwater intertidal pool. Other possible sites include near deep-sea hydrothermal vents, dark volcanic bogs or perhaps in space, as discussed earlier. The possibility that has received a great deal of attention recently is deep-sea hydrothermal vents. Given the sterilizing bombardments from asteroids and meteorites during and after the Earth's compaction, the deep-sea "safe havens" may have escaped the global calamities from which first life arose. The heat fuelling first life may not therefore have been from the sun, but from the internal oven of Earth's molten core.[96]

Life's building-blocks

The next crucial question to ask in understanding the origins of life is how might the "precellular" micro-self-assembly structures – namely, the amino-acids, simple sugars, fatty acids, nucleotides and first cells – have formed? The study of life's origins began in earnest in the 1920s with Alexander Oparin (1894–1980) and J. B. S. Haldane (1892–1964). They believed that life arose naturally and slowly in the vast chemical factory of the primordial terrestrial seas overlayed by an atmosphere rich in methane and ammonia powered by the sun.[97]

Oparin and Haldane's idea was not tested until 1953, at the University of Chicago, by Stanley Miller on the advice of supervisor Harold Urey.[98] The results were dramatic. By simulating the Earth's early atmosphere, these scientists demonstrated the synthesis of at least four amino acids (building-blocks of proteins) from a selection of chemical elements, not unlike how Darwin had envisioned in his "warm little pond".[99] The ingenious experiment began by introducing an electric spark into a closed flask of heated water below a gaseous mixture of hydrogen, methane and ammonia, with a cooling condenser below to cool the chamber atmosphere. The electric spark discharges mimicked lightning and the cooling mimicked rain formation.[100]

The Urey and Miller experiment was modified nearly ten years later by Juan Oró, who synthesized all the 20 amino acids that exist in living systems.[101] Further, Oró found that if hydrogen cyanide (HCN) was bubbled into the "primordial" soup, trace amounts of the purine adenine could be synthesized.[102] This was an important discovery because adenine is one of the two purines that are the building-blocks of our information-laden genetic library in DNA and RNA and passed on from generation to generation.[103] Adenine is also a vital component of the energy currency of life, known as ATP (adenosine-5'-triphosphate), and it is not inconceivable that if phosphate and other precursors were added to the mixture a number of nucleosides and nucleotides could be synthesized.

In 1985, Sidney Fox and colleagues made another important discovery. They synthesized another essential feature of a cell: its membrane.[104] By heating and drying a mixture of amino acids and re-dissolving them with other molecules, small stable spheres were formed.[105] While synthesizing life's building-blocks or a synthetic membrane in the laboratory is a far cry from solving the mystery of life's origins 3.8–4 bya, they are important first steps demonstrating the natural tendency of atoms to associate and support the idea of chemical evolution as one explanation for the origin of life. Among the shortfalls of the Urey–Miller-type experiments are the low yield of material, a lack of specificity of the reactions and lack of informational transfer to build longer polymers necessary for life.

The first replicators: information and action

> To go from a bacterium to people is less of a step than to go from a mixture of amino acids to a bacterium. Margulis[106]

Biological information is stored in the DNA of the genes,[107] which in eukaryotes are located on chromosomes in the nucleus of a cell. Each chromosome contains a different molecule of DNA, and human beings have 46 chromosomes in every cell (except sperm and egg cells and mature red blood cells). The DNA molecule looks like a twisted rope ladder, a double helix; this was discovered by James Watson, Francis Crick and Rosalind Franklin in 1953.[108] All the DNA contained in the cells of an organism including its genes is called a genome. The human genome contains around 32 000 genes, and only about 1 per cent of the code for proteins that make up the living organism (see Ch. 11). If you could unwind the entire length of DNA in each cell (connect all 46 chromosomes end to end), it would be approximately 2 m long. And if all the DNA in the 10^{14} cells of our body were put end to end, they would reach the sun and back more than 600 times!

Living organisms are extraordinary replicating machines. Human beings turn over (lose and replace) about 300 million cells in their bodies per minute, or 5 million cells per second. The regulation of transfer of genetic information to maintain body functions occurs with high accuracy. DNA information is transcribed into single-stranded RNA, and the RNA is then translated into the amino acid language of the proteins. Chromosomes ensure that when one gene is replicated, all genes are replicated, and facilitate easy arrangement when the cell divides during replacement or reproduction. For decades each gene was thought to contain the instructions for the building of one protein, but it now appears, at least in human beings, that genes can produce several different proteins per gene.[109]

The need for enzymes

Without enzymes, information transfer and indeed life would be impossible. Thermo-dynamics, while essential for assessing energy relations, tell us virtually nothing about how "fast" things go. The living accelerators are called "catalysts", a term introduced by Jakob Berzelius in 1836.[110] The catalysts or enzymes are special proteins that speed up chemical reactions by as much as a trillionfold but are not consumed in the process.[111] Each of our 10^{14} cells contains over 50 000 enzymes. The carbohydrates, proteins and fats we eat every day are broken down by a specific set of metabolic enzymes.

If there were no enzymes, the food we eat and the oxygen we breathe could not produce sufficient rates of energy (ATP) to keep the machine running smoothly. Life is very expensive. Every day, the adult human being turns over (uses and replaces) about 35 kg of ATP energy. A marathon runner can nearly turn over his or her own body weight in ATP in just over two hours (up to 56 kg ATP)! Compare this to the largest 100 000 kg blue whale with a turnover of 10 000 kg ATP per day or the smallest mammal, the 2 g shrew (or bumblebee bat), with 0.1 kg ATP per day (50 times its body weight of ATP each day). Enzymes are so versatile that they permit the 0.4 kg human heart (the size of a clenched fist) to beat at a rate of around 70 beats per minute, the 600 kg whale heart (the size of small car) to beat at around 6 beats per minute and that of the the tiny shrew (bumblebee bat or hummingbird) (the size of a pencil point) to beat at up to 1500 beats per minute.[112]

Enzymes represent the largest class of proteins in the body and are not only involved in harnessing energy but are vital for all cell functions including informational transfer between DNA and RNA. The problem is that proteins cannot replicate and require information in DNA and RNA for their production in the cell. As Leslie Orgel wrote, "The replication of DNA requires the pre-existence of protein enzymes, but the formation of protein enzymes requires the pre-existence of DNA."[113] This sets up the famous chicken-and-egg question: which came first, nucleic acids or proteins? In 1982, Nobel laureates Tom Cech (b. 1947) and Sydney Altman (b. 1939) may have solved the dilemma by discovering a new class of (non-protein) enzymes called RNA catalysts or ribozymes.[114] Understanding the functions of these RNA catalysts provided an important clue in "precellular" chemical evolution.

RNA: the first non-protein catalysts and genetic replicators?

Growing evidence supports the idea that the emergence of catalytic RNA was a crucial early step. How that RNA came into being remains unknown.   L. E. Orgel[115]

The curious idea of RNA existing *before* DNA in a "precellular" biological system was proposed in the early 1960s by Carl R. Woese and Leslie E. Orgel.[116] Francis Crick made the further suggestion that RNA might catalyze its own self-replication.[117] Cech subsequently showed that ribozymes could indeed snip out regions from their own nucleotide sequence. This discovery raised many eyebrows because it meant that RNA could have been the first self-replicator of heredity *before* being relegated to its present role as the DNA-protein go-between.[118]

The possibility exists, therefore, that RNA may have been the original "precellular" pathway to life before DNA appeared. Nobel laureate Manfred Eigen (b. 1927) has further suggested that short proteins may have coexisted before self-replicating RNA-cleaving ribozymes appeared.[119] Once formed, these small proteins and RNA may have helped make other RNA molecules, before taking on other catalytic functions in the primitive cell.[120] In 1992, Eigen's RNA model was partially reproduced in the test-tube.[121] The tentative conclusion from the available evidence is that *nature does not need to have proteins and translating machinery to have enzymes.* This protein-independent stage of early biological evolution when living systems used RNA both as a catalyst and as an informational macromolecule is known as the "RNA world".[122]

Clay origins: fact or fiction?

The difficulty with RNA occurring before DNA is figuring out how it formed and how the information was transferred. Did RNA naturally self-associate or was it a product of some earlier proto-genetic system. In the early 1950s, biophysicist J. D. Bernal (1901–1971) proposed that life's first catalytic reactions might have begun on clay surfaces.[123] Bernal suggested that "pre-existing" organic compounds may have concentrated on to the surfaces of clay, and the early reactions were catalyzed on its mineral surface or within the layers.[124] One of the problems with Darwin's "warm little pond" is that it is difficult to form long polymers of RNA (or proteins) in water.[125]

Clays, therefore, may have helped the informational transfer to build the longer polymers of life (a limitation of the Urey–Miller type experiments). Clays have been shown to catalyze the building of carbohydrates, nucleotides, and even fats.[126] Kaolinite[127] and montmorillonite have been shown to catalyze the building of protein chains on their active surfaces in the presence of energy compound ATP or AMP.[128] Remarkably, in 1992 Ferris and Ertem successfully supported Bernal's hypothesis by forming RNA fragments containing 6–14 monomer units by binding to and polymerizing activated monomers of the nucleotides of adenine and uracil on mont-morillonite clay.[129] This amazing experiment was performed in the absence of RNA, DNA or protein enzymes. However, the data should not be over-interpreted. Ferris summed it up when he wrote, "Probably, the formation of short RNA oligomers by catalysis on montmorillonite was not sufficient to initiate the RNA world ... but it is possible to use the life-on-the-rock approach to generate fairly long RNAs by elongating short oligomers."[130]

Graham Cairns-Smith has further suggested that the defects on clays may have served as the original genetic material *before* RNA and DNA.[131] He argues that it was unlikely that a molecule as complex as RNA could have appeared *de novo* 3.8 bya.[132] A self-replicating clay could have solved this problem. The Cairns-Smith "clay world" therefore appears to have clay first, enzymes second, cells third and genes fourth.[133] To date there is little or no experimental support for the Cairns-Smith model.

What are we to believe?

Notwithstanding RNA's extraordinary ability to catalyze new complementary strands, the practical difficulty to overcome in setting the early stage for life is its very low efficiency and low specificity. No RNA has been found to make a complete copy of itself. While the so-called RNA world is widely accepted, its existence remains unproved.[134] Clays also fall down from a lack of efficiency and specificity, and again the evidence for a clay world is lacking.[135] In contrast, we know that protein enzymes are more stable than RNA and possess high affinities for their reactants, and these properties combined with their catalytic power underpin the high degree of regulation and coordination of information in the cell. Enzymes, with their efficiencies and specificities, would also help to solve the problem of a finite solvent capacity inside cells and permit the packaging of a lot of chemistry into tiny volumes.[136] But this still does not answer the question about how their catalytic efficiency and high specificity arose in the first place.

The other difficulty with the current models is that "something" is still required to kick-start the catalytic process. A more recent proposal is a pre-RNA (PNA) world containing small chain proteins, RNA, DNA, clay and other molecules with varying degrees of catalytic capacity. The PNA world is postulated to have existed for less than 100 million years before RNA and DNA dominated all life forms. Nobel laureate Christian de Duve has added energy-rich metabolites such as ATP to the PNA world.[137] These high-energy compounds, known as thioesters, could have helped build the long polymers in the Haldane–Oparin primordial soup. In de Duve's "thioester world", inorganic pyrophosphate (PPi) could have preceded ATP as the energy donor to drive life's beginnings.[138] A possible scenario of the stages of building-block formation and assembly, and the evolution of informational transfer is shown in Figure 10.2.

What if science could create life?

We must, however, admit that nothing contradicts the possibility that artificial production of living matter may one day be accomplished.   Jacques Loeb[139]

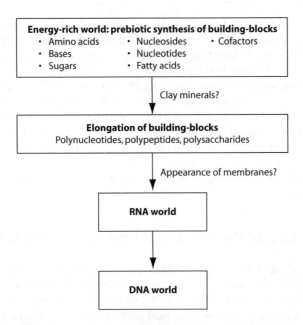

Figure 10.2 Possible early events in the origins of life. The energy-rich (thioester) world represents a hypothetical stage where atomic and molecular components progressively self-organized and, in the presence of a catalytic framework, formed primitive reactions that led to life's first building-blocks. RNA could have been the first self-replicator of heredity before protein catalysts and DNA. The transition from an RNA to a DNA world was not abrupt but probably involved the conversion of RNA to a mixed copolymer of RNA and DNA then to distinct RNA and the more stable DNA.

Even if science could *create* life, the question of origins 3.8 bya would remain. Don't get me wrong: a "cookbook" creation, which may be possible in 20 years or so, would profoundly alter the way scientists think about origins, not least further diminish God's involvement. But it would not *directly* answer what happened. This is not just a play on words, but stresses why "first causes" such as the origins of life and the origins of the universe are beyond the scope of science. Science works because it sharpens our knowledge by confirming and rejecting theories. With respect to origins, scientists have to be content with developing plausible "scenarios" that mimic primordial conditions and assume there is continuity between extant organisms and the earliest life forms.

There is a long road ahead, but great strides are being made. To recap, from paleobiology we know that life originated and evolved very early after the Earth had formed. From astronomy we know that the light elements that form the basis of life originated shortly after the Big Bang, and the heavy elements originated much later in the furnace of dying stars. From chemistry we know more about the elements and how they self-associate and combine to form organic compounds. From supra-molecular chemistry we know how molecules aggregate by weakly binding to one another, which we can use to manufacture new designer molecules and assemblies. From biochemistry we know a lot about how enzymes control metabolism, and how energy transformations occur in the cell. From physiology we know the importance of homeostasis and how the 11 or so organ systems work in a coordinated manner to maintain a dynamic steady-state. From molecular biology we know that RNA can act both as an enzyme and as a replicator. We know in general terms how information is coded in the DNA, and how it is transcribed to RNA, which in turn is translated into functional protein sequences that constitute the basic stuff of living-day organisms. We also know a great deal about the part of DNA that represents the chemical code for a certain protein, and what parts start or stop many of the cell's operations. The interruption of any of these control systems, for example by viral infection or other disease states, can disrupt the homeostasis of the body, leading to sickness or death. Despite all this knowing and extraordinary advances in recent years, we are still a long way from assembling a unifying conceptual scheme surrounding the emergence of life on Earth 3.8 bya.

BIOLOGICAL EVOLUTION: ORGANIZATION OF EARLY LIFE SYSTEMS

Although the origin of life cannot be dated precisely, Schopf has theorized that life may have originated as early as 4.2 bya, a claim based on extrapolation methods of how fast organisms evolved 2.5–3.5 bya.[140] The earliest life forms were probably like an oil-droplet with no easily preserved hard parts. In addition, the rocks where they might reside have been destroyed by plate tectonics, biological recycling or pressure cooking from the sterilizing early bombardments.[141]

The earliest organisms we know about are bacteria. Bacteria lived unchallenged on Earth for nearly 2.5 billion years and, in terms of numbers, they still reign supreme as the dominant life form; there are more bacteria inhabiting a handful of dirt or in the human mouth or on the skin than the total number of human beings that have ever lived! Their extraordinary large numbers and wide diversity are related to their short generation times, which range from 20 minutes to 3 hours.[142] What follows is a brief account of some of the amazing features of the extant archaebacteria, cyanobacteria and nanobacteria that have provided scientists with important clues to better understand what kinds of organisms might have been present early in Earth's history.

Archaebacteria: the first to synthesize organic compounds in a reducing atmosphere

Archaebacteria are the modern branch of survivors that may be related to the earliest bacteria.[143] These remarkable bacteria can flourish in hostile environments of no oxygen, high temperatures (in excess of 100 °C), high salinity (Great Salt Lakes and the Dead Sea), high pressure to depths of 5 km (up to 300 atm) and high acidity (pH 2–4). These extreme conditions support the idea that first life may have formed in the vicinity of deep-sea hydrothermal vents or subterranean sediments. Like all bacteria, today's archaebacteria are single cells, lack mitochondria, use ATP as their energy currency and possess DNA as their heredity material.[144]

Unlike most bacteria, however, archaebacteria possess ribozymes. Ribozymes are the catalytic RNA mentioned earlier that can cut pieces off themselves or off other RNA molecules, and catalyze the breaking and reforming of new RNA molecules. Archae-bacteria possess so many unique features that in 1996 they were reclassified into their own kingdom. The other two kingdoms house the "true" bacteria (eubacteria) and the eukaryotes (animals, plants, fungi and many unicellular life forms).[145] The three main types of the surviving archaebacteria are: methane-producing archaebacteria (methano-gens); hydrogen-sulphide producing archaebacteria (halophiles); and a type that can tolerate extremes in temperature and acidity (thermoacidophiles).

- **The methanogens**. This first type of archaebacteria living without oxygen possesses the ability to reduce carbon dioxide in the presence of hydrogen to form methane (or natural gas) and water. Recently they have also been shown to reduce elemental sulphur to form hydrogen sulphide, as with the other two sulphur-reducing bacteria below. The methanogens are the most prominent. They can be found today in sewage outlets, bogs, swamp mud, lake- and ocean-bottom sediments and rotting manure, and in the stomachs of ruminants and other herbivores, where they produce methane from the fermentation processing of organic compounds such as formic acid and methyl alcohol. These bacteria are responsible for a cow releasing as much as 250–500 L of methane per day.[146] Early in the history of the Earth, these methanogens may have helped to keep the Earth's surface warm through the greenhouse effect, and thereby promoted other life forms.[147] They are also responsible for a major portion of our natural gas reserves found in subterranean pockets. These bacteria, and the extreme halophilic and thermoacidophilic bacteria below, may have entered the more stable subterranean habitats at a time when the Earth's surface was being bombarded by meteors/asteroids. It has been known for many years, for example, that certain micro-organisms can eat through rocks and excrete minerals and are responsible for many of the iron-ore (Fe_3O_4) and lead-zinc deposits around the world. A recently found metal-reducing bacteria is *Shewanella putrefaciens* (or *oneidensis*), which, in the absence of oxygen, can eat iron oxides or manganese oxides as "oxygen substitutes" for respiration.[148] Their life revolves around the respiration of rocks!
- **The extreme halophilic archaebacteria**. These bacteria are capable of combin-ing hydrogen gas with elemental sulphur to form hydrogen sulphide and then using this (instead of water) as the hydrogen source for the manufacture of carbohydrate from carbon dioxide to sustain life.[149] These exotic bacteria are found in the fumaroles of the world, such as in the deep-sea hydrothermal vents, where hot hydrogen and sulphur gases and noxious chemicals spew out from cracks in the ocean floor at temperatures up to 350 °C. Some of these amazing bacteria and their products have even been found up to 5 km beneath the Earth's surface. This extraordinary finding invites new questions on the origin of life and its location, as mentioned earlier. In addition to being found in volcanic mud pots they thrive in salt flats such as the Great Salt Lakes and the Dead Sea.[150]
- **The thermoacidophiles**. The third bacteria are very similar to the second but can withstand high acidity (pH of around 2) and thrive in hot temperatures (greater than 90 °C). These are found today in the hot sulphur springs of Yellow-stone National Park.[151]

Some methanogen and halophilic bacteria do possess photosystems, that is, specialized membranes to trap light energy and fix carbon dioxide and make organic compounds. However, the big difference from the photosynthetic cyanobacteria (see below) is that they *do not produce oxygen.*

Cyanobacteria: the first photosynthetic life forms

Cyanobacteria appeared at least 2.5 bya during the hostile Archean era (2.5–3.8 bya). Generally, we know them today as the greenish slime on the side of a damp flower pot or on the damp side of the house or seasonal (sometimes toxic) blooms in our waterways. These single-celled organisms have the ability to trap solar light and manufacture sugars from carbon dioxide and produce oxygen, a process known as photosynthesis.[152] Cyanobacteria have made an enormous contribution to the evolution of green plants because a chloroplast is actually a cyanobacterium living inside the green plant cell. Cyanobacteria have additional blue or red pigments, hence their original name "blue-green algae". Cyanobacteria lack internal organelles such as a discrete nucleus.

Depending on the species and the environment, cyanobacteria may live a solitary life or in colonies as filaments, sheets or even hollow balls. The most famous living colonies are at Hamelin Pool, Shark Bay and Lake Clifton in Western Australia. Another living colony can be found in the salty marshes of the Baja California lagoons. Cyanobacteria are also thought to have been largely responsible for colonies of layered mats in ancient times, that eventually formed sedimentary fossilized structures known as stromatolites.[153] Stromatolites range in size from a few centimetres to large domes or branching columns several metres across and one metre high. These fascinating structures dominate the fossil record about 1–2 bya. Today stromatolites can be found in Russia, China and in the Warrawoona Group in Western Australia.

Studying the evolution and history of cyanobacteria is key to understanding the origins of life because it was not until they increased in numbers, around 2.8–3 bya, that molecular oxygen was produced at a much faster rate than it was consumed.[154] During the early transition from a reducing to an oxidizing atmosphere, it is believed that the increased oxygen levels led to the emergence of an unprecedented number of new life forms, most of which would have died out from intense competition.[155]

Nanobacteria: "life, life everywhere ..."

> The most salient feature of life has been the stability of its bacterial mode from the beginning of the fossil record until today, and with little doubt, into all future time so long as the Earth endures. This is truly the "age of bacteria" – as it was in the beginning, is now and ever shall be.
>
> S. J. Gould[156]

Bacteria vary tremendously in size. The smallest are called nanobacteria (or nannobacteria), and appear as spheres or ellipses, often occurring in chain-like assemblies. The first mineralized forms were discovered in 1990 by geologist Robert Folk.[157] Folk proposed that these tiny organisms may be more abundant than normal bacteria by an order of magnitude and may form the bulk of living organisms in soils, sediments, minerals and rocks. Moreover, he asserted that they may be responsible for most of the Earth's surface chemistry (i.e. ore deposition, mineralization and corrosion of metals). They also appear to be involved in the construction of the calcium carbonate of shells of clams, foraminifera, and possibly birds' eggs.[158]

Nanobacteria range in size between 0.02 µm and 0.15 µm (about one-tenth the diameter and one-thousandth the volume of ordinary bacteria). The smallest were described in 1997/98 by Philippa Uwins, along with University of Queensland colleagues Richard Webb and Anthony Taylor. Uwins was analysing sandstone core samples from an oil-drilling site 3.5 km below the Australian sea bed.[159] These organisms had cellular structures similar to actinomyces (filamentous soil-inhabiting bacteria and disease-producing plant and animal parasites) and fungi (spores, hyphae and fruiting bodies) with the exception of being up to ten times smaller in diameter. The team, however, resisted calling their discovery "nanobacteria", preferring "nanobes" because of their imprecise phylogeny.

Little is known of the genetics, metabolism or reproductive strategies of nano-bacteria. Apparently they can be cultured in the laboratory and look similar to those occurring in ancient rocks and minerals. They also have unusually slow metabolic rates, are often resistant to antibiotics and can support autonomous replication under suitable conditions.[160] When grown in serum, alone or with mammalian cells, they often form a white biofilm. These tiny organsims also appear to be able to trick some cells into taking them into their internal environment (perhaps similar to how endo-symbiotic cyanobacteria were engulfed by archaic plant cells to become chloroplasts, or purple photosynthetic bacteria into archaic plant and animal cells to become mitochondria; see Fig. 10.4).

Nanobacteria are so tiny that they could conceivably pass through skin and enter our bodies. In 1998, Finnish biochemist E. Olavi Kajander and colleague Neva Ciftcioglu reported that nanobacteria can live in urine and, by precipitating calcium and other minerals around themselves, might induce the formation of kidney stones.[161] Some scientists have also suggested that illnesses as diverse as heart disease, cancer, diabetes, arthritis and multiple sclerosis might be related to bacterial or viral infections. What role nanobacteria play, if any, remains to be established.[162]

Further interest in nanobacteria occurred in 1996 with the exciting discovery of similar nano-sized structures in the Martian meteorite ALH84001. As mentioned earlier, the Mars findings have not been conclusive.[163] Other possible sites for nanobacteria (and perhaps other exotic life forms) include the unexplored waters of Lake Vostok, a vast body of water beneath about 4 km of glacial ice in Antarctica. Tiny viable bacteria, fungi and algae have already been found in the deep ice cores adjacent to the lake.[164]

Despite these fascinating discoveries, many scientists are still struggling to under-stand how these tiny organisms could be classified as life. How could the complex enzymatic and reproductive machinery of life's processes fit into such a small space? Perhaps these bizarre microbes might be transitional stages to life, where the dividing lines between what is alive and what is not are blurred. Certainly, there is no doubt that the existence of nanobacteria and their possible role in nature and origins of life will remain a hot topic for many years to come.

THE GEOLOGICAL TIMESCALE: APPEARANCE OF DIFFERENT LIFE FORMS

Life remained almost single-celled for over 80 per cent of the past 3.8 billion years. Single-cell prokaryotes (no nucleus), were the first life forms, followed by eukaryotic cells (having a nucleus) about 1.5 bya.[165] Multicellular organisms did not appear until about 630 mya, followed by the first terrestrial plants and insects 410–50 mya. The first corals and first vertebrates appeared 430–500 mya, the first bony fishes 400–50 mya, amphibians 360 mya, reptiles 200–300 mya, birds 150–200 mya and mammals about 200 mya.[166] The genus *Homo,* of which we are the only surviving species, began with the protohumans appearing about 4 mya. Our own *Homo sapiens* arose 200–300 thousand years ago.[167]

An informative way to view the appearance of these various life forms on Earth is to equate 15 billion years, the age of the universe, to an imaginary 12-month period (Fig. 10.3). The Earth did not form until 12 September, and there was no life until 7 October (the appearance of the prokaryotes). The eukaryotes did not appear until around 28 October. The first bony fish appeared on 20 December, amphibians on 22 December, reptiles on 24 December, the first dinosaurs at 3.36 pm on Christmas Day, 25 December (220 mya), and the birds and first mammals appeared a day later around 26 December. The first protohumans appeared on Earth at 9.40 pm on 31 December (4 mya) and modern humans appeared 2 h 13 min later at 11.53 pm on 31 December of this imaginary year (~200 000 years ago).

Homo sapiens	**31 December 11.53pm**
First protohumans	31 December 9.40pm
Birds and first mammals	26 December
Dinosaurs	25 December 3.36pm
Reptiles	24 December
Amphibians	22 December
First bony fish	20 December
First eukaryotes	28 October
FIRST LIFE	**7 October**
Formation of Earth	12 September
BIG BANG	**t = 0**

Figure 10.3 A useful way to obtain a time perspective on the appearance of the various life forms on Earth is to equate 15 billion years to an imaginary 12-month period. Of the total 30 billion species that are believed to have existed over the past 3.5 billion years (from 7 October of our imaginary year), some 30 million species of plants and animals exist today. With respect to origins, the link between the inanimate world and first life forms still remains an enormous challenge for science.

From the "ladder of life" to a "low-lying bush"

Until the 1960s, most scientists viewed species relatedness on the basis of their anatomy and physiology.[168] Nobel laureate Linus Pauling of the California Institute of Technology and Emile Zuckerkandl were among the first to suggest a rethink of this method to construct the "tree of life". In addition to anatomy and physiology they proposed using the differences of the order of the building-blocks in selected genes or proteins.[169] Today, using new molecular methodologies, the model of the evolutionary "tree of life" or Aristotle's "ladder of life" (Fig. 5.8) are no longer tenable.[170] Ladders are not representative of the path of evolution: evolution is not a continuous sequence of ancestors and descendants, from lowest to highest.[171] The shape is more like a low-lying bush with many interconnecting roots and no single trunk (Fig. 10.4). Accurate dating of the early branching points remains a challenge.

The interconnecting roots are thought to have merged as a "web" or "unit" of communal, loosely knit, diverse conglomeration of primitive cells. This "unit" would probably be the Pre-RNA or RNA worlds mentioned earlier, which possess relatively few

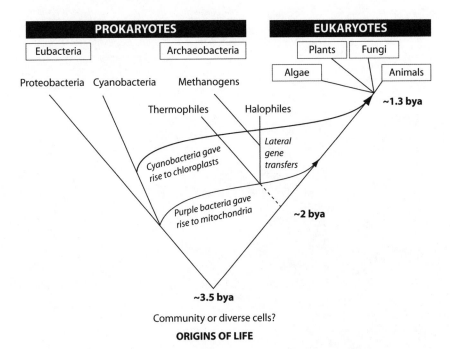

Figure 10.4 Broad schematic of recent work from molecular biology and systematics shows that the prokaryotes split into at least two divergent lineages very early in the history of life (modified after Gerhart & Kirschner 1997: 6). One branch produced the eubacteria and the other the archaebacteria. Archaebacteria appear to have been direct ancestors of eukaryotes, which include plants, fungi and animals. Only a few genera of archaebacteria survive today and they are found in the most extreme environments. In contrast, eubacteria are thought to have split earlier and they include cyanobacteria and nearly all contemporary prokaryotes.

genes but may have swapped them freely in what is known as lateral gene transfer.[172] From these primitive cells the three basic domains – the archaebacteria, bacteria and eukaryotes – formed (Fig. 10.4). Today the concept of higher organisms being "more highly evolved" or "more perfect" is wrong. Darwin's world was not a ladder of progress but one based on variants, which occurred randomly and selected for or against an extraordinarily complex array of conditions and behaviours. In Chapter 11 we shall focus on the origins of human beings and ask what factors gave us the selective advantage over our nearest relatives, the chimps and apes.

It has often and confidently been asserted, that man's origin can never be known: but ignorance more frequently begets confidence than does knowledge: it is those who know little, and not those who know much, who so positively assert that this or that problem will never be solved by science.

Charles Darwin[1]

CHAPTER 11

Humankind's evolutionary origins and emergence of mind

OUR HUMAN HERITAGE

Genesis and geology: irreconcilable differences

For it was in geology that the idea of evolution left the domain of speculative philosophy where it had stayed for over two thousand years, and first entered into the domain of science. The central idea in evolutionary philosophy is that the organization of the world is in a state of flux.

J. Howard[2]

The final leg of our journey will concentrate on the origins of humankind and emergence of mind. Before the nineteenth century, most people in the West believed that God created human beings with fully developed minds, consciousness, reason and speech, and that all species were fixed and unchangeable.[3] English naturalist John Ray (1627–1705) summed up the traditional view in 1686 when he wrote: "the number of true species in nature is fixed and limited and, as we may reasonably believe, constant and unchangeable from the first creation to the present-day".[4] Among the early naturalists who officially queried the contemporary view was diplomat John Hookham Frere (1769–1846). In 1797, Frere sent a letter to the Society of Antiquities of London documenting his discovery of early human stone and flint implements in a local brick-quarry at Hoxne in England.[5] Frere suggested that the stone implements were "weapons of war, fabricated and used by a people who had not yet the use of metals ... The situation in which these weapons were found may tempt us to refer them to a very remote period indeed, even beyond that of the present world."[6] Frere's reasoned insight preempted the discovery of Paleolithic human beings, who had lived tens of thousands of years before Adam and Eve, something the ancient Greeks also speculated on when they examined stone tools.[7]

In an attempt to calm the growing tensions between natural science and Christianity, Swedish botanist and taxonomist Carolus Linnaeus (1707–1778) set out to show God's revealed plan by classifying animals, plants and human beings. Linnaeus's starting-point was the belief that one of Adam's chief responsibilities in the Garden of Eden was the naming of animals and plants. His system of naming became known as the Linnaeus method.[8] However, after decades of study Linnaeus himself began to doubt the traditional doctrine of a single creation.[9] His observations and classifications were not consistent with a "fixity of species" predetermined by God's divine order.

A more outspoken critic of the "fixity of species" concept was French naturalist Jean Baptiste Lamarck (1744–1828), who believed that evolution was the best explanation for the order and diversity of species, and that the historical process was brought about by acquired inheritance.[10] Lamarck became famous for thinking that giraffes possessed long necks because they had to stretch higher to reach a diminishing food resource. Over the generations, adults passed on these "acquired long neck characters" to their offspring.[11] In his *Philosophie zoologique* (1809), Lamarck further postulated that human beings were also the product of evolution, not a single creation.[12] Although some aspects of Lamarck's views on cultural inheritance have recently received favourable support (see p. 350),[13] Lamarckism in general has not stood the test of time as a theory to explain natural diversity and change. Animals do not respond creatively to their needs and pass acquired traits to their offspring; variation is not predirected in favourable ways.[14] Lamarck was correct in proposing evolution but fundamentally mistaken on its mechanism.

Lamarck's views on evolution stirred up a great deal of controversy in the late eighteenth and early nineteenth centuries. His main rival was naturalist-Christian George Cuvier (1769–1832), who believed that the diversity was the result of sudden, devastating catastrophes such as Noah's flood and not because of an evolutionary process.[15] Cuvier maintained that every species was created by God for its own special purpose and each organ was "fixed" for one specific function and invariant over time.[16] The abundance of marine fossils also offered proof of a great flood, a flood that carved out mountain ranges and valleys in days and deposited sea shells near their summits. Cuvier's "catastrophic" views gained wide acceptance, including support from paleontologist Jean Louis Agassiz (1807–1873), who viewed glaciers as "God's great plough".[17]

The difficulty with Cuvier's "catastrophic" theory was its failure to explain the facts from geology. For example, after careful analysis of minerals, fossils and rock strata, Scottish geologist James Hutton (1726–1797) recognized that there was slow cyclical change everywhere. He argued in his *Theory of the Earth* (1795) that, given enough time, the natural agents such as sedimentation, volcanic activity and erosion could explain the Earth's present geological features. Hutton's uniformitarianism (or gradualism) theory proposed that the mountains and valleys were slowly formed over vast periods of geological time, a principle that was diametrically opposed to the doctrine of catastrophism. Hutton concluded that the Earth was very old and "[in geology] we find no vestige of a beginning – no prospect of an end".[18]

Hutton's theory was endorsed by French naturalist Georges-Louis Buffon (1707–1788), but with one modification. In a desperate attempt to keep hold of tradition, Buffon shoehorned the immense geological time period into six grand epochs corresponding to the six biblical days – each of around 35 000 years – plus another epochical day extending to the present.[19] Based on experiments on the cooling rate of metal spheres, Buffon estimated life had begun in the past 35 000 years, and that the Earth had taken some 74 832 years to cool from its molten state.[20]

Buffon's seven-day "compaction" theory horribly backfired and sparked off the first of a series of heated debates on the accuracy of the Church's widely accepted date of creation 23 October 4004 BC, which was calculated by Archbishop James Ussher in the early 1650s.[21] The Church had so much confidence in the date that it was inserted in the margin of the authorized version of the Bible around 1701 and remained there for over 100 years. The Church considered Buffon's timescale of events flagrant heresy. On 12 March 1751, the theological faculty of the Sorbonne forced Buffon to recant his views and he conceded: "I declare that I had no intention of contradicting the text of the Scriptures ... and, that I abandon everything in my book respecting the formation of the Earth, and generally all which may be contrary to the narrative of Moses."[22]

The conflict between Genesis and geology grew deeper early in the nineteenth century, when highly respected geologist Sir Charles Lyell entered the debate. Lyell told his audience that he, too, had arrived at Hutton's gradualism principle from natural events. In his famous three-volume *Principles of Geology* (1830–33), Lyell maintained that the Earth's physical features were not created by the Flood but were the result of slow action over geological time. Lyell suggested that the age of the Earth was around 240 million years. The emerging scientific worldview angered the biblical literalists, who viewed all geologists as staunch enemies of God and Christianity. In his *Scriptual Geology* (1826/27), George Bugg wrote:

Geology is the *last* subject to which the adversaries of *Revelation* have resorted, and from which as a science of an ambiguous and not very tangible character, they perhaps hoped to derive some objections to its truth ... And no doubt when the subject should have been sufficiently general and adequately rooted, they would ... have turned our Geology against the Bible, and made us pay dearly for our unwise and easy credulity.[23]

Charles Darwin and the place of human beings in nature

Can we doubt ... that individuals having an advantage, however slight, over others, would have the best chance of surviving and procreating their own kind? On the other hand, we may feel sure that any variation in the least degree injurious would be rigidly destroyed. This preservation of favourable variations ... I called Natural Selection.

Charles Darwin[24]

The decisive blow to a literal Genesis came on 22 November 1859. Charles Darwin's *The Origin of Species by Means of Natural Selection* (1859) demonstrated three interdependent scientific facts:

- that evolution (or "theory of descent with modification",[25] as he called it) had occurred *without purpose, spirit or direction*;[26]
- that natural selection was its driving force; and
- that survival through adaptation was its reward.[27]

Evolution is thus a mixture of chance and necessity: chance at the level of variation and necessity through natural selection.[28] Darwin's theory of natural selection provides the best explanation for the appearance of existing and new adaptations, and why some 99.9 per cent of all species that ever existed are now extinct. That is, it explains why, of the total 30 *billion* species of animals and plants believed to have existed over the past 3.5–3.8 billion years, only 15–30 *million* are around today.

Importantly, Darwin did not set out to challenge the existence of God, repudiate the Church or deny the sacred Scriptures. His early passion was to document God's "fixity" of species, rather as Linneaus had attempted a hundred years earlier.[29] After many years of meticulous study, Darwin maintained that the extraordinary diversity of life and uncanny perfection was not God's creation, but the end-result of a slow, blind, natural process where individuals struggle to increase their participation in future generations, and that is all.[30] Evolution works via selection through "descent", and not through divine intervention "from the outside". The notions that God operated as the first cause at the species level, and reproduction as the secondary cause, were replaced with the formative principles of differential reproduction, selection and adaptation.[31] Darwin's true legacy, therefore, is not only his lengthy argument for the process of evolution, his theory of natural selection or his condemnation of the contemporary worldview that human beings were far superior to any animal, all of which were revolutionary, but the manner in which he interrogated the world and changed his opinions as new observations emerged. This will be discussed further in Chapter 12.

Early school and university years

Charles Darwin was born on 12 February 1809 in Shrewsbury, England. His father, Robert Darwin II, was a physician, and his grandfather, Erasmus Darwin, was a distinguished physician, poet, inventor and speculative evolutionist who, in many ways, foreshadowed his grandson's theory of evolution.[32] His mother, Susannah Wedgwood, was the daughter of Josiah Wedgwood, founder of Wedgwood pottery, but died when Darwin was 8 years old.[33] Charles had an older brother, Erasmus, and four sisters (Caroline, Marianne, Susan and Emily). He was a great collector of insects and beetles and was fascinated with natural history. Darwin hated school with its rote-learning classical emphasis. In later life he was sent a questionnaire about his early education, which elicited the following responses. "How taught?" Darwin answered, "I consider that all I have learnt of any value has been self-taught … Peculiar merits of education? None whatever. Chief omissions? No mathematics or modern languages, nor any habits of observation or reasoning."[34]

Like Newton, in his early years Darwin showed little academic genius. "When I left school", Darwin wrote, "I believed that I was considered by my masters and by my father as a very ordinary boy, rather below the common standard in intellect."[35] His lacklustre approach to education led his father to remark angrily, "You care for nothing but shooting, dogs and rat-catching, and you will be a disgrace to yourself and all your family."[36] In 1825, Darwin went to the prestigious University of Edinburgh for two preparatory sessions for a career in medicine, but left after two years. In 1828, his father sent him to Christ's College, University of Cambridge, to complete a Bachelor of Arts, because he wanted Charles to become an Anglican priest. Again, young Darwin showed no great aptitude for the arts, and struggled to complete his degree by 1831.[37] Despite his family's growing concern about his future, Darwin privately persisted with his love of natural history. At the age of 21, he wrote in his personal journal "continued to collect insects; to hunt, to shoot and be *quite idle*".[38] Darwin was also fond of poetry and music.[39]

Despite Darwin's struggle to find a suitable profession, university life was a vast improvement over his school years. He became deeply interested in the conflict between science and religion, and the use of scientific evidence against the various forms of atheistic materialism. Darwin was a great admirer of theologian William Paley (1743–1805), who, in his *Natural Theology* (1802) advanced the teleological argument of God's existence from design: "Design must have a designer. That designer must be a person. That person is God."[40] Darwin was particularly enthralled by Paley's book, *View of the Evidences of Christianity* (1794), which was compulsory reading for undergraduates. Fifty years later Darwin recalled "getting up Paley's Evidences and Moral Phil., thoroughly well as I did, I felt was an admirable training, and everything else bosh".[41]

Darwin also became fascinated with geology, and the works of Buffon, Hutton and Lyell, and the expeditionary work of naturalist Friedrich Humboldt (1769–1859). Lyell was to become one of Darwin's closest lifelong friends (as was botanist Joseph Hooker). Darwin was also an admirer of Sir John Herschel's classic volume *Preliminary Discourses on the Study of Natural Philosophy* (1830). After finishing his degree, Darwin remained at Cambridge for two extra terms to study geology under Reverend Professor Adam Sedgwick (1785–1873), who was an ardent catastrophist. It was during this period that his life changed and put him on the path to the voyage of HMS *Beagle*.

The voyage of HMS *Beagle*

> Philosophy in Darwin's day, and virtually to the present, was dominated by essentialism, that is a belief in a world of discontinuities, and of constant, underlying essences, sharply separated from all others. Darwin, by contrast, introduced population thinking, a conceptualization in which the uniqueness of every individual plays a major role.
>
> E. Mayr[42]

While at Cambridge, Darwin received a letter from his botany mentor and friend Professor John Henslow in Edinburgh. Henslow urged Darwin to apply for an unpaid position as "gentleman naturalist" on the old 100-foot, three-masted, refitted ten-gun warship HMS *Beagle*. Ironically, Darwin was not selected as the ship's "official" naturalist, but as companion to Captain Robert FitzRoy (1805–1865); British naval tradition held that a captain was to have very little social contact with the crew and a companion was necessary for intellectual stimulation, mostly at mealtimes.[43] Darwin was chosen because of his congenial manner and interest in natural history. The position of naturalist was originally held by the ship's surgeon, Robert McKormick. At the age of 22, Darwin accepted the job after his uncle Josiah Wedgewood convinced his father that the journey would be a positive experience and ideal training for a man of God.[44] The voyage began on 27 December 1831 and ended five years later in 1836, three years later than originally planned. The mission was to complete a survey of the world's lesser-known waters around South America, and to carry out a chain of chronometrical measurements around the world.

Within eight weeks of setting sail, Darwin was so taken with the natural beauty and diversity of life in a Brazilian rainforest (near Salvador) that he wrote in his diary: "The mind is a chaos of delight."[45] He compiled some 3000 pages of notes documenting an extraordinary number of plant and animal species, living and fossilized, from jungles, plains, tropical forests and mountains and from the famous Galapagos Archipelago. Three observations had a profound effect on Darwin:

- the way closely related species appeared and replaced one another;
- the relationships between island and continent species; and
- the close relationship between surviving and extinct species.

Well-versed in Lyell's *Principles of Geology*, Darwin soon became convinced of evolution, but the mechanism of diversity – of differential survival and reproduction – remained elusive. Fossils were no longer the animal remains that did not make it on to the ark, as Captain FitzRoy had believed.[46] They were remnants of life preserved in rocks, some many hundreds of millions of years old, which provided Darwin with compelling evidence that evolutionary processes had occurred. FitzRoy became so incensed with Darwin's writings and interpretation of the voyage, that he countered with a 25-page narrative "confirming" Noah's flood.[47]

It is truly amazing how two people can see identical phenomena and devise totally opposing sets of beliefs. Darwin was open to change because he desired to remain flexible in thought, whereas FitzRoy was more conservative. Darwin wrote: "I have steadily endeavoured to keep my mind free so as to give up any hypothesis, however much beloved (and I cannot resist forming one on every subject), as soon as the facts are shown to be opposed to it."[48] He further wrote that his success grew from "the love of science – unbounded patience in long reflecting over any subject – industry in observing and collecting facts – and a fair share of invention as well as of common sense".[49] The turning point in Darwin's life was unquestionably the voyage on the *Beagle*, which provided his restless mind with the limitless opportunity to explore new ideas.

Natural selection

I came to the conclusion that selection was the principle of change from the study of domesticated productions; and then, reading Malthus, I saw at once how to apply this principle.
Charles Darwin[50]

After returning home, Darwin lived and breathed science. He came to his theory of natural selection from observations, collections, wide reading and raw genius. Fascinated with how each species could be so admirably adapted to its environment, Darwin began systematically to study domesticated animals and cultivated plants. He concluded that the mechanism of selection lay in the methods used by animal and plant breeders to improve their stock.[51] But how could the same mechanism work in nature? In September 1838, two months before he married his cousin, Emma Wedgwood, Darwin solved the mystery "by fortunate chance" after re-reading Malthus' population theory.[52] In his autobiography, Darwin wrote that he picked up Malthus's book "for amusement" only.[53] What immediately caught Darwin's attention was that populations of animals (including human beings) tended to increase geometrically ($1 \rightarrow 2 \rightarrow 4 \rightarrow 8 \rightarrow 16 \rightarrow 32$), while their ability to supply food increased arithmetically ($1 \rightarrow 2 \rightarrow 3 \rightarrow 4 \rightarrow 5 \rightarrow 6$).[54] This out-of-step progression between growth and subsistence meant "struggle for existence" was imminent, if left unchecked.[55] Furthermore, Malthus knew that natural populations did not continue to increase geometrically but levelled off, indicating some sort of regulation.

The final piece of the puzzle was solved by Darwin. He knew that every parent species produced more offspring than reached maturity, and this excess pointed to a "struggle for existence". He further reasoned that if offspring varied among themselves, any favoured trait would have a greater chance of surviving past maturity, and thereafter be passed on to the next generation. Each generation would differ slightly from the one before, and the more extreme the environment, the tougher the competition for survival.[56] In his autobiography, Darwin wrote that the idea of natural selection came to him in October 1838:

> it at once struck me that under these circumstances favourable variations would tend to be preserves and unfavourable ones to be destroyed. The result of this would be the formation of new species. Here then I had at last got a theory by which to work, but I was so anxious to avoid prejudice, that I determined not for some time to write down the briefest sketch.[57]

For Darwin, natural selection was the mechanism responsible for selecting the heritable variations of a species for a particular environment. Some of the environmental pressures that can lead to a species' adaptation (or extinction) include predation, competition for food, water availability, temperature, physical geography, disease, natural disasters and exploitation by human beings. As mentioned earlier, Darwin's theory was that natural selection is a process that has no direction, which helps to explain why some 99.9 per cent of all species that ever existed are now extinct. The phrase "survival of the fittest" is often used as a substitute for "natural selection". It was coined by English biologist and sociologist Herbert Spencer (1820–1903) in 1851.[58] However, Darwin chose not to adopt the phrase in the first five editions of *Origins of Species*, presumably because it was somewhat ambiguous. If "fittest" implies survival then the phrase reads "survival of the survivors". "Survival of the fittest" also fails to adequately convey the blind nature of the selection process, which leads more often to death than survival.

An interesting story surrounding the theory of natural selection is that Darwin was not its sole discoverer. On 18 June 1858, Darwin received a 4000-word manuscript from a young field naturalist, Alfred R. Wallace (1823–1913), who was working in Borneo.[59] To his amazement, Wallace's essay outlined, in the most concise terms, the theory of natural selection. Darwin immediately sought solace from Lyell and Hooker, who both suggested that he and Wallace present a paper on natural selection at the July meeting of the Linnean Society.[60] As so often appears to be the case, the society was unimpressed, to say the least, by their selection theory. So much so, that at year's end, the president wrote: "The year has not, indeed, been marked by any of those striking discoveries which at once revolutionise, so to speak, the department of science on which they bear."[61] How wrong they were.

Darwin avoided human descent

To establish his 20-year priority over Wallace, Darwin wrote his 450-page *Origin of Species* in the next 15 months. In the first edition, Darwin was extremely cautious not to discuss human origins. Apparently, he did not want to stir up religious opposition and diminish the hopes of his book being a success.[62] It was obvious from what he wrote, however, that human beings were not divinely created in 4004 BC, but shared a common ancestor with the modern apes. The human species was one of the animals, but endowed with a larger brain and heightened reason than the other animals. Darwin conceded 15 years later that he had avoided entering the human debate:

> It seemed to me sufficient to indicate, in the first edition of my "Origin of Species", that by this work "light would be thrown on the origin of man and his history"; and this implies that man must be included with other organic beings in any general conclusion respecting his manner of appearance on this earth. [63]

In the interim, English biologist Thomas Henry Huxley (1825–1895) entered where Darwin refused to go. Huxley, in contrast to Darwin, thrived on controversy as he applied the selection theory to human origins based on evidence from comparative anatomy, embryology and fossils. In a little over three years Huxley published his celebrated *Evidence as to Man's Place in Nature* (1863). He became so convinced that natural selection was correct that, in the ninth edition of the *Encyclopedia Britannica* he wrote, "the evolution of many existing forms of animal life from their predecessors is no longer an hypothesis, but an historical fact". German biologist Ernst Haeckel (1834–1919) agreed with Huxley and applied Darwin's theory to the entire animal kingdom.[64]

Among the scientists who rejected the idea that human beings descended from the apes were some of Darwin's closest friends: Hooker, Lyell, Agassiz, botanist Asa Gray (1810–1888) and co-discoverer of natural selection, Wallace. Wallace would not rule out divine intervention in the origin of human beings, and he used terms such as "some other power", "some intelligent power", or a "superior intelligence".[65] He felt that natural selection could not endow human beings with a large brain and a mind for morality, without the intervention from some superior power.[66]

The great Oxford debate: is the hairy ape from your grandfather's or grandmother's side?

> If I did not think you a good-tempered, and truth-loving man, I should not tell you that … I have read your book with more pain than pleasure. Parts of it I admired greatly, parts I laughed at till my sides were almost sore; other parts I read with absolute sorrow, because I think them utterly false and grievously mischievous.
>
> Adam Sedgwick[67]

This quote is an extract from a letter sent to Darwin in 1859 from his friend and former geology professor, Adam Sedgwick (1785–1873). The controversy came to a head on 30 June 1860 at the British Association Meeting held at Oxford, and chaired by Henslow. The debate was between the Bishop of Oxford, Samuel Wilberforce, and Darwin's "bulldog", Thomas Huxley. In the official version, the bishop concluded his attack on human evolution by saying to Huxley, "It would be interesting to know whether the ape in question was on your grandfather's or your grandmother's side."[68] After the laughter had subsided, Huxley responded. One version of his rejoinder goes:

> I asserted ... that a man has no reason to be ashamed of having an ape for his grandfather. If there were an ancestor whom I should feel shame in recalling, it would be a man, a man of restless and versatile intellect, who, not content with an equivocal success in his own sphere of activity, plunges into scientific questions with which he has no real acquaintance, only to obscure them by aimless rhetoric, and distract the attention of his hearers from the real point at issue by eloquent digressions, and skilled appeals to religious prejudice.[69]

Huxley's own account of the incident, discovered in a letter 60 years later, differed somewhat from the above account.[70] Huxley claimed that following the bishop's *ad hominem* attack, he leaned over to a colleague and whispered, "the Lord hath delivered him into mine hands". Huxley then rose to his feet with the following crushing rebuke:

> If then, said I, the question is put to me would I rather have a miserable ape for a grandfather or a man highly endowed by nature and possessing great means of influence and yet who employs those faculties and that influence for the mere purpose of introducing ridicule into a grave scientific discussion – I unhesitatingly affirm my preference for the ape.[71]

Huxley further recounted that "there was unextinguishable laughter among the people", and then "they listened to the rest of my argument with the greatest attention".[72] Apparently, at the height of the excitement, Lady Brewster was overcome and fainted as Huxley addressed the good bishop.[73] And Captain FitzRoy is reported to have become so angry that he waved the Bible above his head and screamed at the top of his lungs that the Scriptures alone were the source of all truth.[74] Five years later, FitzRoy committed suicide by slitting his throat.

There remains considerable doubt about the actual events that occurred in the furore.[75] Darwin was not in attendance, but in a letter of 3 July 1860 he commended Huxley for standing up to the bishop. Darwin wrote "I honour your pluck, I would as soon have died as tried to answer the Bishop in such an assembly."[76]

Darwin finally entered the debate in 1871

In his *Descent of Man*, Darwin wrote that human beings were not divinely created but a descendent from some "hairy, tailed quadruped, probably arboreal in its habits, and an inhabitant of the Old World".[77] Human beings were "one of several exceptional forms of Primates" that had evolved chiefly as the great development of their brain and erect posture.[78] In addition, based on the fossil evidence, Darwin argued that the birthplace and antiquity of humankind was on the African continent.[79] Again, Darwin recognized that his views would be controversial:

> The main conclusion arrived at in this work, namely, that man is descended from some lowly organised form, will, I regret to think be highly distasteful to

many … For my own part, I would as soon be descended from that heroic little monkey who braved his dreaded enemy in order to save the life of his keeper, or from that old baboon, who descending from the mountains, carried away in triumph his comrade from a crowd of astonished dogs – as from a savage who delights to torture his enemies, offers up bloody sacrifices, practices infanticide without remorse, treats his wives like slaves, knows no decency, and is haunted by the grossest superstitions.[80]

Despite the bitter controversy and *ad hominem* attacks, there were some lighter moments. In 1860, the wife of the Bishop of Worcester is reputed to have said, on first hearing of Darwin's theory of human descent, "Descended from the apes! My dear, we hope that it is not true. But if it is, let us pray that it may not become generally known!"[81]

Darwin's reflections on religion

Accordingly I read with great care *Pearson on the Creeds*, and a few other books on divinity; and as I did not then in the least doubt the strict and literal truth of every word in the Bible, I soon persuaded myself that our [Church of England's] creed must be fully accepted.   Charles Darwin[82]

Darwin wrote the above in his autobiography as he was reflecting on his years at Cambridge (1828–31) after he had failed to qualify for medicine and, following the suggestion of his father, turned his sights to become a minister of the Church. In the end, Darwin did qualify with a degree but he was never ordained. What is interesting is that when Darwin wrote these words he added another sentence, but decided against its inclusion. The omitted sentence, found 72 years later by his devoted granddaughter Nora Barlow was: "It never struck me how illogical it was to say that I believed in what I could not understand and what is in fact unintelligible. I might have said with entire truth that I had no wish to dispute any dogma; but I was never such a fool as to feel and say '*credo quia incredible* [I believe the impossible]'."[83]

It was not until returning from his epic voyage that Darwin totally abandoned the Christian faith. He wrote: "disbelief crept over me at a very slow rate, but it was at last complete. The rate was so slow that I felt no distress, *and have never doubted for a single second that my conclusion was correct … and this is a damnable doctrine.*"[84] The italics were censored from Darwin's original autobiography by his wife, Emma.[85] Any shred of belief in Christianity was finally stripped from Darwin when his beloved 10-year-old daughter, Annie, died from typhoid in 1851. While he personally condemned conventional orthodoxy, Darwin never refused help to any religious institution doing good and he maintained close friends in religious circles. In 1879, after being asked if he believed in God, Darwin replied in a letter:

What my own views may be is a question of no consequence to anyone but myself. But as you ask, I may state that my judgment often fluctuates … In my most extreme fluctuations, I have never been an Atheist in the sense of denying the existence of a God. I think that generally (and more and more as I grow older), but not always, that an Agnostic would be the more correct description of my state of mind.[86]

As Darwin grew older, a particular focus of his thinking concerned human nature. Deeply hurt from the loss of his daughter, the "struggle" of existence in his own personal life led him to emphasize love and affection as the true meaning of life. Over time, sadly, he also appears to have lost interest in poetry, art and music.[87] For 45 years of his life, he was plagued by ill health. He died on the afternoon of Wednesday 19 April 1882 at the age of 73. The pallbearers included Huxley, Wallace, Hooker and Lowell. Darwin was buried in Westminster Abbey, fittingly a few feet away from Isaac Newton.

How have Darwin's ideas stood the test of time?

Let me lay my cards on the table. If I were to give an award for the single best idea anyone ever had, I'd give it to Darwin, ahead of even Newton or Einstein and everyone else. In a single stroke, the idea of evolution by natural selection unifies the realm of life, meaning and purpose with the realm of space and time, cause and effect, mechanism and physical law.   D. C. Dennett[88]

Ever since the first 1250 copies of *The Origin of Species* rolled off the presses nearly 150 years ago, there has been overwhelming observational, embryological, fossil and molecular evidence supporting evolution by natural selection.[89] Single-handedly, Darwin founded a new branch of life science: evolutionary biology. The four pillars were built on:

- his demonstration of the non-constancy of species extending far into the distant past (the modern concept of evolution);
- his introduction of the idea of branched evolution from a single common ancestor (the rejection of Lamarckian "linear" evolution or Aristotle's concept of *Scala Naturae*);
- his concept of the gradualness of evolution over vast periods of time; and
- his mechanism of natural selection.[90]

Darwin was also correct in inferring that human beings evolved from some extinct stock of apes in Africa. He would have been delighted at his theory's extraordinary success, given that he knew little or nothing about genes, gene frequencies or underlying mechanisms of heredity and adaptive change. He thought that parental characteristics were transmitted in the blood, not in the nuclear DNA as we know today. The success of Darwin's theory lies in the extraordinary number of facts he obtained to support it, which have been corroborated over the past 150 years. A point of emphasis is that natural selection is not a principle of progress from simple to more complex but a principle of adaptation.

As with any scientific theory, however, there are legitimate concerns with Darwinism and evolution.[91] Although Darwin envisaged the tree of life descending in linear fashion without exchange of inheritable elements between species, it is now known that the tree is more like a bush and that lateral transfers do occur among parallel lines of descent (see Ch. 10). These lateral transfers may occur via symbiogenesis and can involve tiny insertion sequences, genes, gene islands or portions of whole genomes.[92] Another legitimate concern is whether natural selection through random mutation is the only way to invoke change in an organism. Can characteristics be acquired during one's lifetime and inherited by future generations in a truly Lamarckian fashion? Can a parent incorporate a new DNA sequence in its sex cells and transmit the change to its progeny? The answer is apparently yes. The biological community is increasingly accepting of *E. coli* bacteria undergoing non-random changes in response to environmental stresses and passing on the advantage to the next generation. Indeed, the mutation rate in *E. coli* has been estimated to be around 100 million times greater than can be statistically expected if it came by random chance. Another example may be the rapidly changing human immunodeficiency virus (HIV or AIDS) or the increasing problem of bacterial drug resistance. Lamarckian behaviour is also found in the immune system, where antibodies can undergo rapid mutation in response to invaders resulting in a "soma to germ flow of genetic information" or acquired inheritance.[93] In an era of jumping genes, paramutation and genomic imprinting, it does appear that the genome may direct itself in ways that require modification of Darwin's theory of natural selection. However, it is important to remember that Darwin himself, although having tried to refute Lamarck's theory of "acquired inheritance", later admitted that the heritable effects of use and disuse might be important in evolution. In *The Origin of Species*, Darwin conjectured that the vestigial eyes of moles and of cave-dwelling bats were "probably due to gradual reduction from disuse, but aided perhaps by natural selection".[94] It is therefore incorrect to assume that Darwin believed his theory was the only theory to explain the grand diversity; he was always open to reasoned argument and criticism.

In a different sense, but no less challenging was Darwin's idea of the origins of humankind from the apes in Africa. Anthropologists know with a fair degree of accuracy when the Old World monkeys split from a common ancestor (around 30 mya). However, until recently they did not know precisely when the hominids split off from the chimpanzee line. Up until the early 1990s the hominid fossil record went back a little over 4 million years, whereas the split from the chimpanzee line is thought to have occurred around 7–9 mya, leaving a 3–5 million year gap (see below). Is the gap in the fossil record the window where God conferred the first "human-like" beings with "fully developed minds, consciousness, reason and speech", as argued by Sir John Eccles?[95] The "God of the gaps" hypothesis would also fit nicely with the ideas of many of Darwin's adversaries, including Wallace, and many twentieth- and twenty-first-century beliefs from a wide number of religions. We shall now trace the protohuman legacy and show how the once deep mysteries have been slowly whittled away using the power of modern science.

The protohuman legacy: the direct path to humanity

> One no longer has the option of considering a fossil specimen older than about 8 million years a hominid, *no matter what it looks like*.   Vincent Sarich[96]

Our early ancestors split from the apes around 7–9 million years ago
Before 1967, anthropologists believed that the human–African ape divergence occurred about 20–25 mya.[97] This date has now been pushed forwards to 7–9 mya, due, in part, to the pioneering work of physical anthropologist Vincent Sarich and

biochemist Allan Wilson. Sarich and Wilson teamed up and compared the amino acid sequence of a protein called serum albumin in the blood[98] of human beings and of a variety of living apes. To their surprise, they found the difference between human beings and chimpanzees was only one-sixth of the difference between human beings and Old World monkeys (the latter, which has been reliably dated at 30 million years, were used as a reference).[99] The split between the human being and the chimpanzee, according to Sarich and Wilson's calculations, was around 30 divided by 6, or 5 million years ago. If Sarich and Wilson's molecular dating method was correct, there was no "God of the gaps". However, things in science are never quite that simple. More accurate molecular clock data have pushed the Sarich and Wilson value back to 7–9 million years, leaving a 3–5 million year gap.[100]

Probing the human–ape relatedness: from genes to protein–protein interactions

Differences among species may also be found in the numbers of genes in their cells. Based on their different looks and lifestyles, one might reasonably predict that human beings have a slightly larger genome than the chimpanzee, and the chimpanzee may have a larger genome than the rat, and the worm may have a larger genome than either an insect or a single-celled bacteria. Since the 1980s, experts believed that mammals, including primates and human beings, had around 80 000–150 000 genes.[101] However, to the surprise of most scientists, it was announced on 12 February 2001 (fittingly, Darwin's birthday) that the number is considerably smaller: around 32 000 genes.[102] This means that the human genome contains fewer genes than corn and wheat (at around 40 000 genes), and 1.2 times the number of genes in the thale cress mustard plant (at 26 000 genes), 1.7 times those of a worm (a nematode has 19 000 genes), about 2.5 times those of an insect or slime mould (12 500–13 000 genes), over 5 times those of yeast (6000 genes), and 8 times those of bacteria (4000 genes).[103] This comparison illustrates that the difference in the number of genes in bacteria and human beings[104] is not large given their widely diverse morphologies and habits. Moreover, more than 220 of human genes have been shown to have come directly, and in some cases quite recently, from bacteria, and another 1 per cent from viral invaders. To complicate matters further, of the total number of genes in the genome, only about 1 per cent code directly for proteins, the stuff of life; the remaining 99 per cent of the human genome is made up of repeat sequences (49 per cent) and "junk" genes (50 per cent), which are now known to underpin the whole structure of the cell by controlling and interacting with the coding genes .[105]

Today scientists are unclear about what further information on human–ape relatedness will be provided by these new gene-finding programmes. In the meantime, the early work of Charles Sibley and Jon Ahlquist remains of great interest. In 1984, by probing the informational content of DNA, Sibley and Ahlquist found that human beings share an astonishing 98.4 per cent of DNA with the common chimp.[106] A technique called DNA hybridization (where DNA fragments bind to one another and the degree of binding reflects genetic similarities) showed there is only a 1.6 per cent difference between our DNA and chimpanzee DNA; human DNA differs from gorilla DNA by 2.3 per cent; orang-utan DNA by 3.6 per cent; and gibbon DNA by 4.8 per cent (Fig. 11.1). These findings have subsequently been supported by more detailed studies using actual nuclear coding DNA sequences,[107] not just fragments.[108]

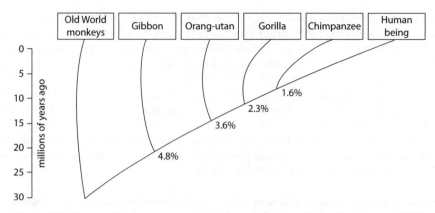

Figure 11.1 Human relatedness among the living primates (modified after Diamond 1991). Genetic relatedness is based on genetic differences in their DNA. Central to the analysis is the reliability of fossil evidence for the split of the Old World monkeys from apes 30 mya. The percentages shown are the differences in primate DNA and human DNA. In other words, human genes contain 98.4 per cent chimpanzee genes. Results are from Sibley & Ahlquist (1984).

Even more amazingly, the DNA of the pygmy chimpanzee from Zaire, North Africa, is closer to us than to the common chimp, and has only 0.7 per cent difference from human DNA (a 99.3 per cent match).[109] This startling result means that human beings are closer to chimpanzees than chimpanzees are to gorillas.

The story does not end there. Our knowledge of human origins and relatedness to other species is also being enriched by another rapidly developing area in molecular biology: the study of "homeobox" genes.[110] "Homeobox" genes act like programming "master" chips that code for identical protein sequences and lay down our body plans during development.[111] The remarkable thing is that the *same* "homeobox" controllers are found in diverse species from insects to human beings,[112] which indicates that the *same* complicated processes have been solved only once (or at least a few times).[113] You only have to look around to see that most vertebrates have two eyes, a nose, two ears, a backbone, a heart, a brain, a liver, blood, two or four appendages and so on. Whether an animal or insect has legs to jump, wings to fly, fins to swim, or arms and legs to climb and walk appears to involve only minor differences in the primitive zootype master plan, which dates back some 540 million years.[114] Evolution seems to have worked with the same master genes in new combinations leading to new forms; there exist about 35 different body plans today. Likewise, many elementary cellular functions in life's grand design such as transcription of DNA into RNA, translation of RNA into protein, DNA replication, cell signalling and basic metabolism have been highly conserved throughout evolution from single-celled yeast and bacteria to human beings. Many hundreds of "homeobox" genes have been identified in the orchestration of development in vertebrates and invertebrates.

In summary, all life is linked spatially and through time. If our computer technologies are accurate, the human–ape relatedness does not appear to lie in the number of genes, but in the kinds of genes turned "on" and "off" during different stages of embryonic development. Scientists want to know how each gene is controlled, and how the product of each gene affects the expression of other genes. In addition, it appears that differences among closely related species may reside in protein–protein interactions and assemblies. Human proteins contain many more domains than proteins in worms and insects, which can lead to an extraordinary array of combinations and may well be the answer to human complexity. Whether these differences play a role in human–ape comparisons is not known. Sorting out human–ape relatedness from the perspective of genomics and proteomics is extraordinarily complex and the subtleties will no doubt take many years to unravel.

The first hominids

Bipedalism is thought to have appeared in the fossil record around 7–9 mya, specialized tool manufacture and a bigger brain (potentiality for heightened consciousness and social behaviours) around 2.5 mya, and eventually the emergence of modern human beings around 0.2 mya.

Genus *Australopithecus*:"Lucy in the Sky with Diamonds"

A hominid is an upright-walking ape.[115] Members are believed to have lived in small social foraging groups in Africa from 1–6 mya or more.[116] The oldest hominids are believed to have had lightly pigmented skin covered with dark black hair, similar to that of the modern chimpanzee.[117] They belong to the genus *Australopithecus*, or "southern apes". The first fossilized remains were unearthed in 1924 from a limestone quarry in South Africa by Australian anatomist Raymond Dart. Dart named the incomplete skull "Taung Baby" and recognized that it was intermediate between ape and human being. He later named the species *Australopithecus africanus*, and it is known to have lived about 2.3–3 mya. Since Dart's time, at least four other australopithecines have been discovered: *A. robustus* (1–1.8 mya, discovered in 1938); *A. boisei* (1.3–2.1 mya, discovered in 1959); *A. afarensis* (2.8–4 mya, discovered in 1974); *A. aethiopicus* (2.3–2.7 mya, discovered in 1985); and *A. garhi* (2.5 mya, discovered in 1999).[118] In the middle of the 1990s anthropologists agreed to assign the more robust, large-toothed, australopithecines (*robustus*, *boisei* and *aethiopicus*) to the genus *Paranthropus*.[119]

Without doubt, the most famous australopithecine is Lucy (*A. afarensis*), who was discovered in 1974 by paleoanthropologist Don Johanson in a remote part of the Hadar desert in Ethiopia.[120] Johanson named her Lucy after hearing Elton John's version of the Beatles's "Lucy in the Sky with Diamonds" on his tape recorder. Lucy stood about 1.1 m (3'8") and her 40 per cent complete skeleton prompted a major reevaluation of human origins. She lived around 3.2 mya, and later fragments of her species have been dated to just over four million years.

Until 1994, Lucy was the oldest hominid discovered. Then came the surprising discovery of a 4.2-million-year-old species called *A. anamensis* in the Lake Turkana region of East Africa. *A. anamensis* appears contemporaneous with *A. afarensis*, but little can be inferred about its life habits from the few bone fragments found.[121] A year later, an older potential hominid was discovered at Aramis (just south of Hadar in Ethiopia), and dated at 4.4–5.8 million years old. The bones belong to a new genus *Ardipithecus* (*A. ramidus*) on the assumption that it was not bipedal.[122] However, the jury is still out on whether *ramidus* stood upright and constitutes a hominid.[123] In 2000 an even older potential hominid, *Orrorin tugenensis*, was reported in Kenya and dated at about 6 million years old, and recent evidence suggests that it was bipedal.[124] Perhaps the most startling discovery of a potential hominid was announced by French scientists in 2002.[125] The team uncovered a skull from Sahel in Central Africa and dated it at 6–7 million years old, the period when the earliest protohumans and chimpanzee lineages diverged. The new discovery (*Sahelanthropus tchadensis*), nicknamed Toumai (a name often given to children born close to the dry season), has a short face, jaw, canines and pronounced brow ridges similar to an australopith hominid and the back more like that of a large monkey. Indeed, some highly respected anthropologists believe the skull is of an ancient female gorilla. Because no limbs were preserved, it is difficult to tell whether Toumai was a biped or a quadraped. A generalized lineage for the paths of early human evolution is presented in Figure 11.2.

Despite the increasing number of new hominids discovered over the past decade, most paleoanthropologists appear to agree that relatively few existed before 3 million years ago. After this time, 2–3 mya, a cluster of hominid species appear to have emerged in eastern and southern Africa (*Australopithecus arafensis, A. africanus, Paranthropus aethiopicus, A. garhi, Homo rudolfensis*). A contributing factor for their emergence was a cooler, drier and more seasonal climate, which eventually led to a thinning of the forests and favoured hominid radiation on the savannah. Of profound significance was the discovery of *A. garhi*, who apparently butchered mammals and presumably ate meat. The transition to meat-eating was not abrupt but probably involved many grades of species sharing a common landscape: climbing trees and eating fruit or opportunistically scavenging and butchering on the African savannahs.[126] Paleoanthropologist Tim White aptly summarized the transition: "You go into this period with, in essence, bipedal big-toothed chimps and come out with meat-eating large-brained hominids – that is a big change in a relatively short time."[127] Fire and cooking did not appear until much later in human prehistory, around 800 000 years ago. (Two sites have been dated at around 1.6 mya, but there was no evidence of bones.)

Along with meat availability, another possible selection pressure limiting hominid radiation on the savannah was longer exposure times to damaging ultraviolet (UV) radiation. Some anthropologists believe increased UV radiation would have favoured darker over lighter skin and a larger number of sweat glands so that individuals could forage longer before the heat forced them back into the shade.[128] A darker skin would protect sweat glands from UV induced injury, thus helping with temperature regulation.[129] Thus another big change 2–3 mya is that hominids in eastern and southern Africa may have entered with white skin, similar to a modern chimp, and left with darker pigmentation and more sweat glands better suited for life on the savannah.

Early *Homo*: from handy man to upright man

The first human species of the genus *Homo* lived in eastern and southern parts of Africa at least 2.5 mya. This highly diverse genus includes *Homo rudolfensis* (1.8–2.4 mya), *H. habilis* (1.6–1.9 mya), *H. ergaster* (1.5–1.9 mya), *H. erectus* (0.2–1.5 mya), *H. neanderthalensis* (0.03–0.5 mya) and the last surviving member, our own *H. sapiens* (0.2 mya to the present).[130] *H. rudolfensis* and *H. habilis* appear to be transitional between the Lucy-like, ape-faced, hominid and *H. ergaster*.[131] Because their morphology (and probably behaviour) is closer to the australopithecines than to

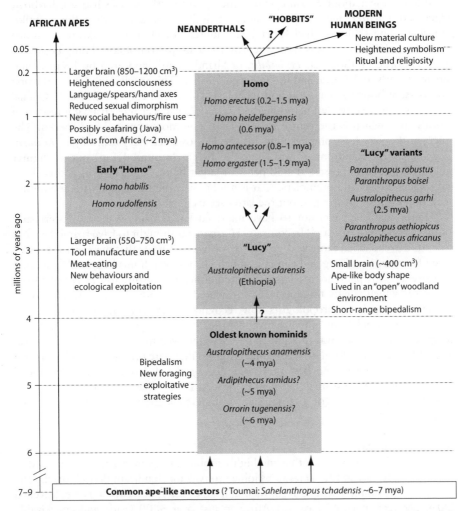

Figure 11.2 Simplified scheme of hominid evolution. The hominid lineage diverged from the chimpanzee lineage some 7–9 mya exclusively on the African continent. *Ardipithecus ramidus* and *Australopithecus anamensis* are considered the most probable ancestors of later hominids. The "Lucy" variants include the gracile forms (australopithecines) and robust forms (paranthropines). Early *Homo* are believed to have emerged from a relative of *A. africanus* or *A. garhi*. Presently, it is unclear what species gave rise to *H. ergaster* around 1.9 mya. The emergence of modern human beings has not been linear, but rather a highly branched evolution shaped more like a bush than either the classical evolutionary tree or a ladder. Modern human beings are the only surviving species of the genus *Homo*; two closely related species were the Neanderthals and the newly discovered "hobbits", *Homo floresiensis*. Preliminary dating places the "hobbits" at around 70 000 years ago, but they may extend back as far as 800 000 years.

Homo, paleoanthropologist Bernard Wood has argued that both *H. rudolfensis* and *H. habilis* is better suited to a new taxonomic subdivision of "early *Homo*" (Fig. 11.2).[132]

Little is known about *H. rudolfensis*, other than that the species had smaller brow ridges and a flatter, narrower and more vertically sloping face than the australopithecines. The skull also had fewer heavy muscle attachments.[133] More is known about *H. habilis*, which was discovered in 1959 by paleontologist Louis Leakey at Olduvai Gorde in Tanzania. *H. habilis*, or "handy man", appeared by 1.9 mya, and perhaps as early as 2.3 mya, and was last seen 1.6 mya. This species was among the first tool-users, although stone tools and technical skills date back to 2.5 mya.[134] Cranial endocasts show that the left hemisphere of *H. habilis* had a characteristic impression of Broca's area, which is the centre for oro-facial fine motor control and speech. The bulge, at the very least, implies that this species possessed *the potential for rudimentary language*. "Handy man" was similar in height (around 1.1 m) but of slighter build than Lucy and possessed a 50 per cent larger brain, larger incisors and canines, and smaller molars and premolars.[135] It is not known whether *H. habilis* was a hunter or an opportunistic scavenger, but the latter seems more likely.

"Handy man" appears not to have migrated far, remaining in the eastern and southern regions of Africa.[136] In contrast, *H. ergaster* is thought to have roamed far and wide. Its barrel-shaped thoracic cage and narrow waist indicate that this species was well suited for bipedal walking and running, much like modern human beings.[137] Because their overall body plans are modern, it is often difficult to distinguish *H. ergaster* from *H. erectus*, which is why this species is considered the "early African" *H. erectus*. In general, many paleoanthropologists now recognize early "African" *H. erectus* as *H. ergaster*, and populations *after* 1.5 mya in Africa, Asia and Europe as *H. erectus*. For many years, *H. ergaster* was thought to have have evolved from *H. habilis* (or relative) around 1.9 mya, but this now seems unlikely given the more primitive ape-like features of *H. habilis*. One of the best preserved *H. ergaster* skeletons is "Turkana Boy" discovered by Leakey's team in 1984 along the west Turkana basin in northern Kenya.[138] Presumably, *H. ergaster*, or a close relative, undertook the first grand exodus from Africa.[139]

Exodus from Africa

By 1.8 mya, there is evidence that the highly mobile *H. ergaster* may have reached as far as China, Russia and Java (Java was joined to Asia for significant periods during the Ice Age).[140] A simple calculation shows that if *H. ergaster*, or a close relative, travelled 200 m per year, it could have left Africa in just over 5000 years, and conceivably reached parts of Asia by 1.8 mya. No one knows what prompted the waves of migration both within and out of Africa, but they were probably related to the species venturing into new territory in search of new resources.

Around 1.5 mya, *H. ergaster* became extinct and was displaced by the next rising star, the highly esteemed *H. erectus* or "upright man", who possessed a larger brain relative to body size compared to any of its predecessors.[141] *H. erectus* resembled contemporary human beings except for a long, low cranium, with prominent brow ridges, thick skull bones and a more robust build. The species was present in the Middle East (Israel, Turkey and Iran) around 1.5 mya, and in Europe by about a million years ago.[142]

H. erectus reigned supreme in both Africa and Eurasia one million years ago, with population numbers estimated at around 125 000.[143] For a few hundred thousand years, this highly successful adventurer and tool manufacturer shared its territory with at least two other species: *H. antecessor* (0.8–1 mya in Spain) and later *H. heidelbergensis* (0.6 mya, throughout the Old World).[144] The most recent evidence suggests that *H. heidelbergensis* gave rise to the Neanderthals, at least in Europe.[145] It is unclear, however, whether any of these species gave rise to modern human beings.

The first *H. erectus* skeleton was found in Java in 1891 by French paleontologist Eugene Dubois (1858–1940). Dubois believed that "Java man" was the long-sought "missing link" between human beings and the apes.[146] Many fossils have since been discovered in Africa, the Middle East, Europe, Russia and China (Peking man). *H. erectus* was not only an intrepid wanderer but may have been a seafarer as well. This proposal is based on the discovery of tools on the Indonesian islands of Lombok (25 km from Bali) and Flores (500 km east of Bali), which have been dated at around 800 000 years.[147] If *H. erectus* was not a seafarer, experts are puzzled as to how the tools arrived on the islands. Although much of the area was joined into a single land mass during the last Ice Age, which included Borneo, Java and Sumatra, Flores was separated by three deep-water channels, the narrowest of which was 19 km wide. Traditionally, seafaring has been associated with our species during the last 100 000 years, not 800 000 years ago.

Paleoanthropologists generally agree that *H. erectus* probably conversed through some form of language, hunted large game and learned to keep warm and cook meat by fire.[148] Unlike many of their antecedents (e.g. the australopithecines, *Paranthropus* species and *H. ergaster*), the males and females were about the same size; Lucy was about half the size of the male. From studies on primates, a reduction in sexual dimorphism indicates the emergence of new behavioural and social changes within a group, such as less competition among males for access to females. Dimorphism is not generally seen in monogamous species.[149]

Homo erectus is believed to have become extinct around 200 000 years ago owing to changes in climate, but recent evidence from Java suggests that this species (and possibly other grades) may have still been around as late as 40 000–100 000 years ago.[150] Notwithstanding the ongoing debates on early human origins, extraordinary strides have been made in recent decades. Forty years ago, for example, the theory of human origins progressed from *Australopithecus africanus* through *Homo erectus* to *Homo sapiens*.

The ascent of modern human beings: the final journey

Until the 1970s, physically modern people (*Homo sapiens sapiens*) were thought to have evolved at about the same time as the appearance of Upper Paleolithic blade technology in Europe, around 35,000 years ago. Then new dating techniques and new fossils from southern and East Africa as well as Israel showed that modern, or near-modern, people were present in these areas from 120,000 years ago, at a time when archaic Neandertals occupied western Europe. P. G. Bahn[151]

By 200 000 years ago, *Homo sapiens* (or "thinking man") and *H. neanderthalensis* (Neanderthals[152]) were on the landscape. The oldest human fossils have been dated to around 160 000 years ago and were found in Herto, Ethiopia.[153] Other human evidence, including deliberate human burials, dated to around 90 000 to 120 000 years ago, come from South Africa and the Middle East.[154] Between 50 000 and 60 000 years ago, human beings had reached Australia, and by 40 000 years ago they were in western Europe (Fig. 11.3), as indicated by different kinds of material culture: art, refined fish hooks, new types of spear heads and more advanced tools.[155] By 30 000 years ago, the stocky Neanderthals were extinct in northern and western Europe. Reasons for their disappearance are not known, but it was probably caused by climatic changes and increased population numbers of human beings.[156] The world population of human beings around this time has been estimated at around 3 million.[157]

While we remain the sole surviving species of the genus *Homo*, a recent discovery has complicated matters, as science invariably does. In 2004, archaeologists Peter Brown and Mike Morwood reported the discovery of a new 1 m tall people, nicknamed "hobbits", who are believed to have lived before 38 000 years ago until at least 18 000 years ago, hunted pygmy elephants and other animals and used sophisticated tools.[158] The skeletal

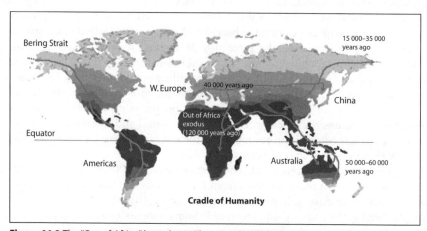

Figure 11.3 The "Out of Africa" hypothesis. There were at least three waves of migrations out of Africa: the first to the Middle East between 90 000 and 120 000 years ago; the second was eastwards to Asia where human beings had reached Australia by around 50 000–60 000 years ago; and the third was to western Europe, where they appeared around 40 000 years ago. The timing and the number of waves of immigrants that shaped populations in the Americas are still controversial, but it appears that significant flows of people occurred 15 000–35 000 years ago. Skin colour of peoples migrating to the different regions of the world has also been predicted based on exposure to levels of UV radiation. The data reveal three distinct skin tone zones. Zone 1 falls within the tropics, including most of Africa, Mexico, Central America, Amazonia, Asia, Australia and Oceania, and contains indigenous peoples with highly melanized or dark skin (dark regions). Zone 2 encompasses large parts of the northern hemisphere, including most of the US and southern Europe (lighter shades). Historical residents of Zone 2 have moderately pigmented skin but possess great potential to alter their skin tone through tanning; they can increase melanin to prevent folate loss and then lighten their tan in autumn and winter in order to take advantage of the dimmer, shorter days. Zone 3 includes high-latitude and polar regions (lightest shade), where people face the greatest risk of vitamin D deficiency and compensate for the diminished light with paler skin and by eating vitamin D-rich foods (Jablonski & Chaplin 2000).

remains from eight individuals were unearthed on the remote Indonesian island of Flores, and it appears they lived around the same time that modern human beings were colonizing the area. The "hobbits", about the size of the smallest known australo- pithecines (e.g. Lucy), were adult members of the genus *Homo*, had a brain about one- third the size of modern human beings, and are believed to have arisen from an ancestral *H. erectus* population (see Fig. 11.2).[159] The new species has been named *H. floresiensis*. This amazing discovery further questions the uniqueness of *H. sapiens* and adds to the unfolding complexity of the evolutionary story of modern human beings. It will be interesting to learn more on the genetic history of these fascinating individuals, their lifestyle and their culture. There has even been the extraordinary suggestion that the "hobbits" may have lived on Flores island as recently as 200 years ago. Although this remains a remote possibility, one inescapable conclusion of the new discovery is that we coexisted with another *Homo* species until much more recently than first thought.

A "single" African origin or multiregional origins?

A hotly debated question is whether human beings had a "single" African origin, as Darwin had envisaged, or a "multiregional European" origin. The "Out of Africa" hypothesis proposes that human beings arose in Africa around 200 000 years ago and did not spread to the rest of the world until about 120 000 years ago, long after the African exodus of *H. ergaster* and later *H. erectus*.[160] In contrast, the multiregional hypothesis proposes that human beings *arose* in Asia and Europe from the interbreeding of different grades of *Homo* populations in the different regions.[161] Thus, the "Out of Africa" hypothesis posits that human beings *had a more recent African origin*, and from a smaller number of individuals, although occasional interbreeding cannot be excluded.

In recent years, the single African origin has gained increasing support from the fossil record, from archaeological digs and from DNA analysis of human remnants and from people living today.[162] The fossil evidence shows that modern human beings did not arrive in western Europe until around 40 000–45 000 years ago, and perhaps 10 000– 20 000 years earlier in parts of Asia and Australia. David Harris of University College London, believes the discrepancy is explained by human beings moving "Out of Africa" along the coastal areas to Australia and the Pacific Rim, and not inland, as previously thought (see Fig. 11.3). The discovery of fossil shells and bones from terrestrial animals along the Red Sea, for example, supports the idea that human beings were living on the Red Sea coast 120 000 years ago, the approximate time when early modern human beings began to leave northeast Africa. Going inland would have been a lot harder, and more dangerous, than moving along the coast with its abundance of food. White's momentous discovery of human cranial material from three individuals in Herto, Ethiopia, dated to about 160 000 years ago, has provided fresh evidence for the "Out of Africa" model.[163] It therefore appears that human beings were scattered in Africa from about 260 000 to 130 000 years ago, after which they dispersed to other parts of the world.

The "Out of Africa" hypothesis has also received support from mitochondrial DNA studies.[164] Mitochondrial DNA is present in every cell in the body and carries genetic information (about 17 000 base pairs compared to 3 billion in the nuclear DNA genome); it is *inherited solely from the mother*, not both parents (i.e. not mixing male and female genes at the time of fertilization). Mitochondrial DNA remains virtually unchanged (aside from random mutations) as it passes from mother to daughter. By quantifying and analysing the mutations of this relatively stable circle of DNA, scientists can chart population histories down the maternal line.

Detailed analysis of mitochondrial DNA from existing human populations points to a single "Eve" in Africa around 200 000 years ago.[165] Li Jin of the University of Texas has further examined mitochondrial DNA from 28 ethnic groups across China and his findings also support a single-origin hypothesis.[166] The number of migrations from "Eve" in Africa is still unknown. At least three distinct prehistoric dispersals have been proposed: one to Oceania, one to Asia and subsequently to America, and a third predominantly to Europe.[167] According to Oxford geneticist Bryan Sykes, most people of European ancestry can trace their mitochondrial DNA back to one of seven female groups who lived between 45 000 and 8000 years ago.[168] It is noteworthy that if a grade of human did not have any daughters, and vanished from the landscape, there would be no transference of mitochondrial genes in today's population (which appears to be the case for the discovery of Mungo Man in Australia).

Further support for the "Out of Africa" hypothesis has come from nuclear DNA studies. One study on different genes on the male sex Y chromosome, which are only passed from father to son, has proposed a human "Adam", also living about 200 000 years ago.[169] More recently, Peter Underhill and colleagues report that more than 95 per cent of all Caucasian men are descendants of ten men who migrated separately to Europe tens of thousands of years ago.[170] Comparing 22 genetic markers on the Y chromosome of 1007 European and Middle Eastern men, the researchers found two of the ten lineages migrated to Europe from the Near East sometime in the Paleolithic period, and the others arrived between 7000 and 3000 BC.[171] It would be interesting to analyse and compare mitochondrial and genomic DNA taken from other existing populations and, if possible, compare them with skeletal remains from different ancient burial sites around the world. If only minor genetic variations are found, the data would suggest human populations had little time to diverge, and would support the "Out of Africa" hypothesis.

Although the full implications of the human genome project have not been realized, the early data on DNA sequence variation support the "Out of Africa" model. The data postulate that a very small number of people expanded rapidly to populate the earth in the last 50 000–100 000 years.

Evolution of skin colour: not black and white

Another outcome of the human genome project, and molecular biology and genetics in general, is that "race" is no longer a valid term to determine phylogenetic relationships among modern human groups. Races such as Mongoloids, Caucasoids and Negroids are no longer distinct biological categories defined by differences in genes that people inherit from their parents. For much of the twentieth century race was a social, cultural and political concept based largely on conspicuous appearances such as skin texture, eye shape and skin colour. In his *The Origin of the Races* (1962), anthropologist Carleton Coon wrote that that there were five major human races and each had evolved independently from *Homo erectus* to *H. sapiens* with dark-skinned people making the last transition. Even the intelligence quotient (IQ) test has been used by some people to infer genetic differences in intelligence among races.

In order to address the evils of racism in light of the new scientific data, the American Anthropological Association has recently adopted a statement declaring that "differentiating species into biologically defined 'races' has proven meaningless and unscientific as a way of explaining variation (whether in intelligence or other traits)".[172] In 1997 the association strongly recommended that the US government scrap the term "race" on official forms because it holds "no scientific justification in human biology". Race and traits such as skin colour are of no value in determining phylogenetic relationships among modern human groups.

The latest scientific evidence on skin colouration suggests that when modern *Homo sapiens* left the tropics of eastern Africa around 120 000 years ago, they were dark skinned from a higher melanin (a natural sunblock) level, which protected their bodies from the damaging effects of UV light.[173] As groups migrated from East Africa into the Middle East, Indonesia and Australia, western Europe and parts of Asia, they would have undergone various degrees of changes in skin colour (Fig. 11.3). According to Jablonski and Chapman, two key pieces of evidence link UV intensity to skin colour. First, skin synthesizes vitamin D, which is essential for the management of calcium and building of strong bones and, secondly, a correct amount of melanin is required to help prevent the breakdown of blood folate. Folate is a member of the vitamin B complex and is critical in normal development; too much UV radiation can break down blood folate, and this has been correlated with neural-tube defects such as spina bifida and anencephaly.[174]

Indigenous people who live in the tropics (Zone 1) have developed dark skin to block out the sun from harmful UV rays and to protect their body's folate reserves. Indigenous people who live far from the equator (Zone 3) have developed fair skin, which soaks up the sun to produce adequate amounts of vitamin D during the long winter months (Fig. 11.3). Inuit have darker skin than predicted due to their relatively recent occupation of the Arctic but make up for any vitamin D deficiencies by eating fish oil and marine mammal blubber. Although we don't see human skin changing in response to environmental changes because our time frame is too short, we do know that people who move from high intensity UV regions (Africa or India) to lower intensity UV countries (Canada or northern Europe) are more susceptible to vitamin D deficiencies (rickets and osteoporosis).[175] In addition, the lighter colour of female skin in any given population may be required to permit synthesis of the relatively higher amounts of vitamin D necessary during pregnancy and lactation.

Jablonski and Chapman further believe that some groups during the various migrations may have lost pigmentation as they migrated north from the tropics then regained pigmentation as they moved back into more intense UV regions, such as in southern India.[176] Skin colour genes therefore appear to have turned "off" and "on" very quickly in evolution, and the human species could have changed from black to white, or white to black, in 10 000–25 000 years (about 200–500 generations), and then back again in the same time period. The important conclusion is that skin colour, and probably skin texture, eye shape, nasal flaring and shape of forehead, are highly adaptive features of the human body.[177] Skin colour is purely a biochemical and physiological response to UV intensity that has changed over thousands of years to reflect environmental conditions. Thus whether a person is black or white depends on biochemical and physiological adaptations, and not differences in genetics.

To summarize a fascinating and complex story, the scientific evidence suggests that the hominid lineage began over 6 million years ago in Africa with our distant relatives having white skin covered with thick hair, like a modern-day chimpanzee. Some time between 2 million and 3 million years ago conditions on the savannah favoured darker pigmentation, and not long after that the first *Homo* species appeared. Dark skin probably became an essential human trait at least 1.5 million years ago, when our ancestors first attained human-like body proportions and perhaps had less body hair, more sweat glands, and lived in more exposed habitats than their predecessors. The "Out of Africa" migrations that gave rise to modern human beings resulted in skin colour change depending on where on the globe they lived. The change in pigmentation, which can take anywhere between 10 000–30 000 years, is not a consequence of genetic differences among modern human beings but a feature of the body's biochemical and physiological responses (i.e. optimizing vitamin D production and folate reserves) to UV light, which is the strongest in the tropics and weakest in the higher latitudes.

EMERGENCE OF MIND AND CONSCIOUSNESS

In the past 12 000 years, human potentiality has been realized from a hunter–gatherer existence to builders of a succession of grand civilizations with the most elaborate language and cultural systems. But there is one tantalizing mystery that continues to "boggle the mind", and that is the mind itself.

Brain size is not the whole story

Having traced the patterns of human evolution, it is still not clear what features gave us a selective advantage over our rivals. For a long time, the advantage was thought to reside in a larger brain.[178] Over the past four million years, the average absolute brain size from "Lucy" through "handy man" and "upright man" to "thinking man" has tripled in volume (Fig. 11.4), and doubled when body size increases[179] is taken into account. Brain size, however, is not the whole story because Neanderthals had larger brains on average than we do today,[180] and "hobbits" had a brain size similar to the australopithecines (e.g. Lucy), yet were adult members of the genus *Homo* (see Figs 11.2 and 11.4).[181]

The selective advantage of human beings appears to reside in the internal organization of the brain, particularly in the cerebrum or forebrain (see below). Neanderthals possessed low protruding brow ridges and had longer slanting foreheads with a bulge in the rear.[182] They also had a different vocal tract with a larynx that sat higher in the throat than in modern human beings,[183] which would suggest a slow, limited form of speech.[184] Increased forebrain organization and different shaped vocal apparatus are important factors that have contributed to our species' extraordinary potential for problem-solving, symbolic language and socialization. This is not to say that the Neanderthals were stupid, or lacked some form of language, only that they may not have had the *same in-built potential* for language, problem-solving and socialization as modern human beings.

The forebrain: from fish to philosopher

The forebrain (or cerebrum) is the most prominent feature of the human brain. It is composed of two halves: the right and left hemispheres. The importance of the

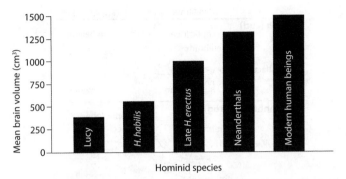

Figure 11.4 Absolute brain size from "Lucy" to modern human beings. Absolute brain size has more than tripled, and the relative size (taking into account the increase in body size), has more than doubled. Lucy had a relative brain size close to a modern chimpanzee. Neanderthals, on average, had a higher absolute brain size than modern human beings, and a lower relative brain size, arising from a heavier body. The average body mass of "Lucy", *H. habilis*, late *H. erectus*, *H. sapiens* and *H. neanderthalis* are 37, 34, 57, 58 and 76 kg respectively (Wood & Collard 1999b: 69). The recently discovered *H. floresiensis* (nicknamed "hobbits") on the remote Indonesian island of Flores has challenged this scheme, as these 1 m-high individuals had body and brain size similar to that of Lucy, yet lived as little as 18 000 years ago (see text). Anthropologists speculate, however, that the "hobbits" brain (380 cm^3) was packed more tightly, leading to their sophisticated tool manufacture and use compared to their distant relatives.

hemispheres was recognized as early as 1824 by eminent physiologist Marie Jean Pierre Flourens (1794–1867). Flourens found that when both cerebral hemispheres were surgically removed (about 80 per cent of brain mass) from birds and mammals, the animals did not die, but entered into a perpetual sleep. When awakened they could move around, but could only eat if hand-fed. In one particular case, Flourens noticed that the pigeon could fly if thrown into the air, but was devoid of a number of perceptions, motor and intellectual functions.[185] Flourens concluded that the cerebrum was not concerned with locomotion, but with higher mental faculties. This observation in the middle of the nineteenth century was highly significant, and led to early research into cerebral localization and human epilepsy.

The forebrain has undergone a number of major changes throughout vertebrate evolution (Fig. 11.5). In fishes and amphibians, it is a pair of swellings concerned primarily with smell and covered by a smooth, undifferentiated pallium (or cloak). The forebrain appears to serve as a relay station between the olfactory bulb and more posterior parts of the brain. In reptiles, it is more developed and takes over the control of vision and other sensations. Birds exhibit a further shift, and the forebrain becomes a central command centre. By far the greatest changes in the forebrain are found in the mammals, monkeys, apes and human beings. As the forebrain increased in size, the relative area devoted to locomotory activities became smaller and smaller, giving way to increased intellect, language, curiosity, self-awareness and emotion.[186]

In human beings (as well as hominids, higher primates and other animals) there has also been hemispheric specialization called lateralization. In 90 per cent of human beings the left hemisphere is thought to be dominant (right-handed people). From split-brain and other research, we know that the left hemisphere has greater capacities

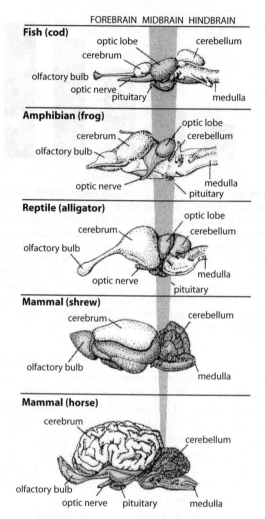

FOREBRAIN MIDBRAIN HINDBRAIN

Fish (cod)
optic lobe
cerebrum
cerebellum
olfactory bulb
optic nerve
pituitary
medulla

Amphibian (frog)
optic lobe
cerebrum
cerebellum
olfactory bulb
optic nerve
medulla
pituitary

Reptile (alligator)
optic lobe
cerebrum
cerebellum
olfactory bulb
optic nerve
medulla
pituitary

Mammal (shrew)
cerebrum
cerebellum
olfactory bulb
medulla

Mammal (horse)
cerebrum
cerebellum
olfactory bulb
optic nerve
pituitary
medulla

Figure 11.5 Expansion of the forebrain from fish to mammals (modified after Keeton (1980: fig. 10.49), based on Romer (1962: figs 381–3, 385) and Simpson *et al.* (1957: fig. 9.15, 214) by permission of E. L. Simpson). The relative size of the midbrain in fish to mammals shows a marked decrease, and that of the cerebrum (forebrain) an enormous increase. There has also been a gradual shift in the control and integration from the lower brainstem to the higher cerebral cortex.

for symbolic language, logic, considered responses and problem-solving tasks, and the right for facial recognition, awareness, emotions, attention monitoring, artistic and musical skills.[187] Neuroscientist Michael Gazzaniga believes that with the evolution of symbolic language, many of the visual-spatial centres in the left hemisphere were taken over by the right hemisphere.[188] Thus hemispheric specialization in human beings did not mean pre-existing capacities were lost, but that they were transferred to the other hemisphere, which improved the overall processing capacity.[189]

The cerebral cortex: the window of the soul

The fact that man can have the idea "I" raises him infinitely above all beings living on Earth.
Immanuel Kant[190]

The outer area of the forebrain is the cerebral cortex (meaning outer bark). In human beings it is about is 3–5 mm thick, contains ten billion nerve cells arranged in six layers and trillions and trillions of nerve interconnections, and constitutes over two-thirds of the total brain mass. The highly differentiated area in the adult has a large surface area of about 2500 cm², arising from folds or convolutions,[191] which were observed by the Greek physician Erasistratus of Chios as long ago as the third century BC.[192] Erasistratus was comparing the brains of a monkey and a human being, and correctly reasoned that the large number of convolutions was related to "superior" intelligence.

In broad terms, intelligence is defined as the capacity of an animal to learn a new response pattern. Chimpanzees, and even bees, can learn many new complex behaviours, quite separate from instinctive behaviours. However, human beings appear to be the only species that can take these learning skills to a much higher level of understanding. Laboratory tests have demonstrated that monkeys, apes, dolphins and pigs are extraordinarily intelligent but, in the wild, their daily lives are relatively undemanding compared to their inherent capacity.[193] The possibility exists that the higher degree of intelligence in primates, and in our own species, may have developed from the selection pressure of social group interactions. The pioneering work of Jane Goodall (b. 1934) shows that many primates devote much time to developing "friendships" and observing others' alliances, which bolsters reproductive success.

The place where social alliance-building occurs is the cerebral cortex, and particularly the left hemisphere. The left hemisphere, as mentioned, provides the heightened mental capacity for intelligence and self-awareness, and is the place where we store, process, program and transmit information; it permits us to speak, think, abstract, reason, manipulate, invent, love, hate and decide right from wrong. The right hemisphere is also concerned with socialization, but mainly through facial recognition and attention monitoring.[194] Overall, the left hemisphere seems to be the place where we construct theories about relationships between perceived events, actions and feelings and where systems like science, religion and myth are born and housed.

The problem of consciousness

Consciousness is the having of perceptions, thoughts, and feelings; awareness. Many fall into the trap of confusing consciousness with self-consciousness – to be conscious it is only necessary to be aware of the external world. Consciousness is a fascinating but elusive phenomenon: it is impossible to specify what it is, what it does, or why it evolved.
N. S. Sutherland[195]

Mind is synonymous with brain function and development

Most people are intimidated by the terms "mind" and "consciousness" because of the deep mysteries surrounding their functions. We must not forget, however, that despite the present difficulties, the terms were invented to help explain what the brain "is" and what it "does". Neuroscientist Susan Greenfield has tried to demystify "mind" by considering it as synonymous *with brain function, neurological development and sensory input*.[196] A baby, for example, has fewer connections between brain cells than a 6-year-old or adult, and so has a different subjective sense of awareness, ownership and identity. The concept of mind, therefore, has a time component and is the product of interactions between ourselves, the environment, community, people's attitudes towards us, and the making of choices. Neurophysiologists claim that the human brain during early stages of development forms about 1 million new connections per second!

Mind is where matter and energy become consciousness. Consciousness is *mind in action* and defines our existence and responsibility; it is responsible for outward expressions, feelings, social behaviour and self-awareness.[197] John Allman of the California Institute of Technology has recently found an area of nerve cells in the anterior cingulate cortex of the frontal lobe that appears to be implicated in self-awareness in chimpanzees, gorillas and orang-utans.[198] The spindle-shaped nerve cells serve no known function, other than as a "centre of self". Of great clinical interest is that these cells in Alzheimer's patients have irrevocably degenerated. Most neuroscientists today, however, do not accept the idea of a single conscious control centre in human beings.

The alternative emerging view is that consciousness is part of a subconscious continuum across a collection of neural circuits devoted to specific capacities. The conscious experience is simply the awareness or feelings that we have these capacities, not the capacities themselves.[199] Our conscious thoughts are only the tip of an iceberg. How a problem that was formulated days, weeks or even months ago suddenly pops into our heads with an answer remains a complete mystery. Moreover, the ability of the brain to be conscious is not dependent wholly on the cerebral cortex, but on many associated linkages,[200] including the primitive "reptilian" region in part of the brainstem (see Fig. 11.5). Neurosurgeons have known for decades that large parts of the human cortex can be removed without loss of consciousness, as long as the lower brainstem is not damaged.[201] Moreover, consciousness can be switched "on" or "off" when we fall asleep, or can be modified by alcohol, anaesthetics or drugs.

Dreaming is also a form of consciousness, but differs by not relying directly on the external senses for its activity. Neuroscientist Rodolfo Llinas has proposed a controversial scheme where the brain might be a dream machine, and where everything runs backwards. The brain creates preformed images, which are transformed into reality from our sense-perceptions, and not as a by-product of sensory input, as traditionally taught.[202] Llinas argues that everything may begin in the subconscious and perceptions may serve to identify reality from fiction. That the subconscious world governs the conscious world is partially supported by the experiments of Benjamin Libet.[203] He proposes that conscious awareness of the sensory world is delayed by up to 0.5 s, and believes that the unconscious brain prepares to act *before* we are consciously aware of a decision to act.[204] The implication here is that human free will may conceivably arise from an unconscious "afterthought", and not from a conscious act.[205] Whether or not Llinas or Libet's ideas are borne out by future studies, modern science has made great strides in understanding the human mind since the ancient Greeks, who viewed it as the special "reasoning" portion (*nous*) of the life-soul (*psyche*) linked to the divine (Chs 4 and 5).

The mind–body problem: spiritual units or physical continuum

An entertaining play on words runs: "What is Matter? Never mind. What is Mind? No matter!"[206] Sir John Eccles believed that the human mind remained an enigma "as long as it is regarded as *an exclusively natural process in an exclusively materialist world*".[207] Eccles appears to have sided with many of the ancient Greek philosophers, and Descartes,[208] who divided mind into physical and divine components.[209] Eccles suggested that the fossil "gap" between the first hominids and the chimpanzee line was the period when God intervened. He claimed it was God who gave rise to the first consciousness in a "hitherto mindless world".[210]

Eccles's giant leap to God's intervention is not necessary. The fossil "blackout", as he calls it,[211] might simply be the result of small errors in modern dating methods or simply be that our direct ancestors were too few in number and so are now too difficult to find.[212] Although, to his credit, Eccles conceded low hominid numbers several millions of years ago, he nonetheless refused to rule out divine intervention. In 1989 Eccles wrote:

> Since materialist solutions fail to account for our experienced uniqueness, I am constrained to attribute the uniqueness of Self or Soul to a supernatural spiritual creation. To give the explanation in theological terms: each soul is a new Divine creation which is implanted into the growing fetus at some time between conception and birth. It is the certainty of the inner core of unique individuality that necessitates the "Divine creation". I submit no other explanation is tenable.[213]

There is no need to invoke uniqueness of soul or spiritual units to explain the present mystery of early human origins. I am not suggesting that part of the mind does not contain spiritual ideas, but the real question is how did the ideas get there? Recent laboratory experiments by neuroscientist Michael Persinger and others show that by stimulating the temporal lobe, a person can experience out-of-body sensations, and see tunnels and bright lights. Moreover, if weak magnetic fields are applied to the same area, a person can experience a number of sensations ranging from a "sensed" presence in the room – some entity standing nearby – an induction of a synthetic ghost, to a number of mystical experiences and conversions.[214] Out-of-body sensations were also reported by a 45-year-old woman suffering epilepsy after part of the parietal lobe of her brain was electrically stimulated.[215] Although the genuine religious experience has not yet been recreated, many of the building-blocks of the sensations have been. Further, it is not too far-fetched to envisage a spiritually enlightened person, or even a deranged multi-personality thinking he or she is God, having differences in this region of the brain. Spiritual enlightenment may turn out to be a wholly physical process.

Indeed, a number of evolutionary psychologists have recently sought to explain the origin of spiritual and religious ideas on a wholly physical basis. Steven Mithen and Pascal Boyer view "religion" as a natural by-product of accumulated ordinary experiences that have occurred over millions of years.[216] The naturalness-of-religion hypothesis states that religious ideas are *almost* hard-wired in the mental machinery of the evolved human brain and activated by events in the external world as part of normal development. Importantly, these evolutionary psychologists do not believe in "built-in" ready-made concepts of god or supernatural agency, only that the *potential* for these concepts is present in our neural circuits at birth and activated from environmental/

social cues during development. At birth, part of the brain is not a "clean slate" from which ideas enter via learning from culture. Rather, the psychologists *believe that there exist multiple, content-rich, domain-specific modules that are naturally receptive to religious concepts.*[217] And it is not only religious modules that respond to particular stimuli: very early in life the face recognition area is activated by seeing a face; the spoken language acquisition area (as opposed to reading and writing) is activated by hearing language; and religious modules are activated by the spatiotemporal events we experience around us.[218] Religious ideas such as god, supernatural agencies, spirits, ghosts, miracles, the afterlife, revelation and even ritual, all belong to the human condition as part of an evolutionary process.[219] Thus, the brain's capacity for spiritual and religious ideas has been partly conserved throughout hominid evolution presumably because of a positive effect on the overall survival of the species, such as promoting personal well-being and communal socialization.[220] The inherent neural adaptations that advanced social cooperation would be candidates for natural selection, and may have, for example, contributed to the extinction of the Neanderthals. While the new empirically grounded picture of religion is in its infancy, there is no need to invoke supernatural intervention from "the outside", as many philosophers and religious scholars have maintained for over 2500 years.

In short, the main difficulty with arguments such as those of Eccles, is that once a religious bias is admitted into science, the enquiry is unduly limited because the conclusion is predetermined by faith. Eccles was a brilliant neurophysiologist and I have used his views only to illustrate this point. History is full of examples where mythopoeic, religious or other biases have been replaced by scientific ones. Another good example is exemplified by what German pathologist Rudolf Virchow (1821–1902) wrote in the late nineteenth century about our human–ape ancestry: "The idea that men arose from animals is entirely unacceptable in my view, for if such transitional men had lived there would be evidence of it, and such evidence does not exist. The creature preliminary to man just has not been found."[221] Virchow was absolutely correct in stating that *in his time* there were few, if any, intermediate forms of human beings, but quite wrong today, based on the scientific evidence.

A more objective approach on the existence of "spiritual units" or "physical continuum" was provided many years ago by Karl Popper, who incidentally was a good friend of Eccles. Popper wrote, "The emergence of consciousness in the animal kingdom is perhaps as great a mystery as the origin of life itself. Nevertheless, one has to assume, despite the impenetrable difficulty, that it is a product of evolution, of natural selection."[222] Today's emerging scientific evidence shows that consciousness is not specific to human beings, but represents a continuum from lower to higher animals with the greatest development in human beings.[223] Your pet dog, cat or bird has a consciousness, albeit a very different type of self-awareness than experienced by you or me. And now as a result of the efforts from neurobiologists and neuropsychologists, religious ideas themselves appear to be the product of that natural continuum as part of the evolutionary processs.

Quantum consciousness: a new frontier?

Even if quantum mechanics does not explain consciousness, perhaps a theory of consciousness might shed some light on the problems of quantum mechanics. After

all, it is widely agreed that these problems have something to do with observership
and experience.   D. J. Chalmers[224]

Because of the brain's complex organization, consciousness continues to baffle
modern science. How does a group of nerve cells generate, store, reflect and release
ideas and emotions? One of the more challenging physical theories comes from
quantum physics.[225] The connection between quantum mechanics and consciousness
began a long time ago with Bohr, Eddington and Heisenberg.[226]

Quantum mechanics, as mentioned in Chapter 9, deals with tiny local matter–
energy interactions on a subatomic scale. Since atoms make up the hundreds of
billions of nerve cells in our brains, there may be a connection between consciousness
and the quantum phenomenon.[227] Bohr recognized that some regulatory sites in the
brain may constitute quantum mechanical systems.[228] Eddington examined Bohr's
hypothesis and concluded that the quantum magnitudes were too small to regulate
brain functions.[229] Eddington preferred to think of regulation at a higher level,
namely among the billions of nerve cells and their trillions of interconnections.
Eddington raised a good question. Is consciousness occurring at the level of quantum
space or the nerve cell, or in larger circuit networks? The answer appears to be larger
circuit networks,[230] but this does not rule out smaller quantum space and time effects.

The development of the theory of quantum consciousness goes something like this.
In the early 1930s, mathematician John von Neumann (1903–1957) proposed that light
particles or photons, which obey the laws of quantum mechanics, enter the eye of the
observer and interact with the retina.[231] The signal passes down the observer's optic
nerve and enters the brain. Only when the signal enters the conscious brain does the wave
function[232] of quantum mechanics "collapse", which, von Neumann argues, is part of the
consciousness process.[233] At all times, the wave function "collapse" requires a conscious
observer. In 1994, Penrose, after Stuart Hameroff, further suggested that the "collapse"
may occur in the brain's microtubules, which are tiny protein structures found in the
skeleton of a nerve cell.[234] Microtubules therefore have one foot in quantum mechanics
and the other in conscious thought. In the Hameroff–Penrose model, the source of
consciousness arises from an orchestrated series of "collapses" in the neurone.

Unfortunately, many of these ideas have not yet been raised to the level of a
"testable" hypothesis. Fundamentally, how can the statistical methods of quantum
theory predict the results of experimental measurements? How can the quantum state
of the position or momentum of a particle or groups of particles translate into an idea,
reflection, image, sensation and feelings or emotions? Even Penrose himself concedes
that a new physics is required to answer these basic questions. Like the problem of
singularity, he believes that the answers may be forthcoming when the two partial
theories of quantum mechanics and general relativity merge to form a "theory of
everything".[235] As with many of the big problems in science, a major limitation is
often not the ideas, but the technology required to test them.

When you are on a journey, and the end keeps getting further and further away, then you realize that the real end is the journey.

Emile Durkheim (1858–1917)[1]

CHAPTER 12

Tradition at the crossroads: seeking unity in diversity

BACK TO THE FUTURE

History is the witness of the times, the torch of truth, the life of memory, the teacher of life, the messenger of antiquity.   Cicero[2]

We have now come to the end of our 5000-year journey. How would you sum up the underlying reasons for the extraordinary diversity in mythopoeic, religious and scientific thought? How can greater harmony be reached when barriers are erected and conflicts arise? What follows are my personal reflections of the past 5000 years, and some speculation about seeking truth, meaning and purpose in life.

From an evolutionary standpoint, the main feature that underlies human diversity and success is the brain's extraordinary ability to reflect, create and problem-solve. As discussed in Chapter 11, human diversity and success do not appear to reside in the number of genes or the number of brain cells, but in the number and kinds of brain circuits devoted to specific tasks or capacities; the human brain has many more neural circuits than the chimp, which has more than a monkey, which has more than a dog, bird, reptile or fish.

Increased brain circuitry is key to our species uniqueness; it confers the ability for speech, writing, counting, mathematics, art, music and some spatiotemporal measurement to help explain, explore and understand the world around us. Accepting that the human brain is loaded with evolutionary potential, which underpins the ability for heightened symbolism, its circuitry does not, however, directly determine what particular language a person might speak or what mythopoeic, religious or scientific worldview a person might hold. A child brought back from the Upper Paleolithic period would have the same potentiality for solving the great mysteries of the world as a child today, even though that child 40 000 years ago never advanced beyond being a hunter-gatherer. A cloned human being has the same potentiality as the parent yet, in all likelihood, would grow up with a totally different sense of awareness, ownership and identity. The difference between potentiality and actuality is culture.

Over tens of millennia, culture has changed dramatically as people have moved from the plains and forests to villages, through to a more urbanized lifestyle. Increasingly, as populations have grown, the drive to make sense of experience and advance culture has been shaped by a changing framework of occupational and class distinctions with different communication skills, forms of art, music and architecture, myths and religious practices and techno-scientific skills.

What stands out in the succession of ways that human beings have sought to make sense of experience is the relentless search for order and harmony in the world. From the Sumerians to contemporary cultures, human beings have sought to discover the underlying world order, which has been linked to social and political harmony through the interactions of hundreds of gods, one god or no god at all. The diversity of world-views between cultures, or within a culture, arises largely from the different emphasis placed on myth, religion and science, and their respective philosophies. The framing of a worldview incorporating these different systems determines not only how knowledge is ordered, but how meaning and purpose are realized.

New ideas and revolutionary worldviews appear in a society when free thinkers confront tradition; most of these individuals have a passionate drive to explore beyond the present. If the human genome and proteome projects or NASA's space explorations are any indication, the twenty-first century and third millennium promises to be one in which the human being will be redefined, ethical standards challenged and worldviews transformed. One way to help to prepare for these changes is for our educational systems to convey that human knowledge, from a cross-cultural perspective, is provisional, and it is through its provisional power that the richness of human potentialities can be realized *without* losing sight of the truth. Truth, as we have shown throughout our 5000-year journey, rests upon many factors such as cultural traditions, authority, language, abstract generalization, methods of criteria and, at the end of the day, some sort of consensus. Everyone's truths, to some degree, have been shaped by the ideas of the past. By opening and connecting the mind's eye to history, people can achieve a deeper understanding into the different ways human beings have made sense of the world, how people through the ages have sought and responded differently to new paradigms, and how a particular worldview fits into the larger picture.

Despite recent polls demonstrating that the public has a profound yearning for the latest scientific and technological discoveries, the enthusiasm appears insufficient for the majority to break free from past traditions. For example, in the US over 80 per cent of the public still believe that God created human beings; 44 per cent accept the literal account of Genesis and 38 per cent believe that God has guided evolution. About 50 per cent believe in the power of astrology, 75 per cent believe in angels, 93 per cent believe in heaven and 75 per cent believe in life after death.[3] Unfortunately, despite extraordinary advances, there seems to be a growing distrust of science when the information overlaps religious beliefs. Worldwide, it has been estimated that only one in seven people (or 14 per cent) believes in biological evolution.

IN THE FULLNESS OF TIME ...

To put aside hints and speak plainly, and dealing with science as a method of demonstration and reasoning capable of human pursuit, I hold that the more this partakes of perfection, the smaller the number of propositions it will promise to teach, and fewer yet will it conclusively prove. Consequently the more perfect it (science) becomes, the less attractive it will be and the fewer be its followers. Galileo[4]

The reasons for most people being reluctant to change or modify their worldviews are complex and multi-layered. An important component appears to be a lack of understanding of the power of the provisional basis of knowledge, and the wider problem of certainty. We all want to be right in our thinking. However, from the vantage point of history, certainty (and truth) emerges as a culturally conditioned construct, and not an absolute. Bronowski ably put it when he wrote: "we have to cure ourselves of the itch for absolute knowledge and power".[5] Similarly, the general conclusion from our long journey is that human knowledge can never be complete or final; but must be continually scrutinized and criticized. This is not suggesting that many statements in our knowledge are untrue or that individuals cannot know truth – everyone has formulated truths – but every truth has a framework from which it was constructed. Truth is shaped by rules within a set of boundaries and consensus is achieved within those boundaries.

In the world of reason, there is no absolute language, no absolute certainty, no absolute truth, no absolute law, no absolute perfection and no absolute ethical good. There is no "certain" way of telling truth from falsehood that everyone can agree upon. Popper felt that the inability of our methods to tell truth from falsehood was the deepest reason for the fallibility of man. However, the limitation to which Popper refers is not a weakness but a great strength because it provides the wellspring of new ideas essential for human beings to realize their potentiality. Socrates partially recognized this empowerment when he taught that wisdom was *knowing that we don't know*.[6]

Regardless of whether we are considering a small group of nomadic hunters sitting around the campfire or the intricate workings of the grandest of civilizations, patterns of human thought and action have been socially conditioned from a complex interplay of altruism, leadership, languages, myths, religions, rituals, technologies and eventually science. Our story particularly focused on the relations between science and religion. Science, in contrast to religion, does not deal with "first causes", a view fully recognized by Kepler, Galileo, Newton, Descartes, Faraday, Maxwell, Einstein and *bona fide* scientists today. An area of confusion in recent times is fundamental Creationism,[7] and its various forms, which recount an extremely narrow window of Hebrew history, and allow literal interpretations of Scripture to enter the domain of science. Contrary to what is presented by advocates of the Creationist movement, at centre stage is neither evolution nor natural selection *per se*, but the scientific *process* about how ideas and knowledge are formed, transformed and verified (or falsified). The public needs to be aware that a Creationist victory in the law courts is a legal victory not a scientific one. Certainly, no judge in any court has the jurisdiction to make an "absolute" knowledge base out of a discipline such as science that does not have one. Nineteenth-century biblical scripturalist George Bugg again provides an excellent example of an "absolute" thinker confusing science and religion. Bugg wrote: "I allow ... that Sacred writers may (have been) silent about science and even ignorant of it ... They were under divine and supernatural guidance, and therefore personal *ignorance* in the writer is no *defect*, and *error* is impossible."[8]

What most literalists fail to grasp is that Darwin himself did not set out to repudiate the authority of the Bible. As discussed in Chapter 11, his early passion was to document God's "fixity" of species, not to refute the idea. It was only after years of exhaustive observations, deep learning and reflection, and encouragement from close friends that Darwin finally broke silence and claimed that evolution had occurred through natural selection and that human beings were biologically evolved creatures, not lost souls. In short, no one should blindly accept (or refute) what Darwin, Copernicus, Kepler, Galileo, Newton or Einstein discovered, but rather understand how they made their discoveries; how they interrogated the world and how they changed their views and overarching boundaries as new observations and truths emerged. The key to innovation and discovery in science is keeping one's thoughts and discussions free and open.

The important message to convey about modern science is that it ceases to exist in a world of absolutes. Indeed, one could argue that science has released us, intellectually, from the past mythopeic and authoritarian eras by continually shifting and challenging the boundaries of our thinking. Science entertains many more starting-points than religion in the sense that each of its premises in the physical realm is open to doubt and empirical assessment. Proving God's existence, the Incarnation, Last Judgement, Holy Trinity, Descartes's mind–body dualism, Peacock's "God in action"[9] or Polkinghorne's divine action channelled through quantum "indeterminacies"[10] are all intractable in the world of science because there is no empirical observable link between the divine and the physical, outside the belief itself. The problem of the divine and the physical is beyond the intellectual reach of human reason, and resides exclusively in the domain of faith.

Religion, on the other hand, thrives in the super-sensory dimension. In theistic argument, articles of faith are unknowable from a scientific or philosophic standpoint. Most theologians would regard the articles of faith (or intractable questions) as supra-natural and supra-rational, but they are not irrational and never in conflict. Below the deep mysteries of faith, theistic argument is just as dynamic as argument in science and philosophy. Extending from the supra-rational in God's grace and perfection to reason in scriptural interpretation is one of the cornerstones of Christian, Judaic or Islamic religious belief. Religion's "top-down" approach of faith seeking understanding is suitably illustrated by Anselm when he wrote: "*I do not seek to understand so that I may believe; but I believe so that I may understand. For this too I believe, that unless I believe, I shall not understand.*"[11] This "top-down" approach contains all the hallmarks of Platonism, moving from eternal, absolute perfection to the "necessary" reasons.[12] Even Aquinas, who took the opposite Aristotelian direction of proceeding from a particular object in nature to a more universal understanding of the world in mind, had to furnish the necessary reasons to reach the God he knows exists.[13] In modern science, there is no perfection beyond reason and proof of theory or experiment. Natural science may be regarded as "proof without certainty" and religion (and myth) "certainty without proof".

Today we live on the cusp of one of the most profound intellectual and techno-logical revolutions ever, with our knowledge-base doubling every ten years or so. School children in 2050 will probably take for granted answers to the many deep mysteries that captivate our imaginations today, and today's truths may well be the source of tomorrow's myths. Despite the many surprises that lie ahead, my optimistic prediction is that the world will never be totally demystified. If I have represented anything in this long journey, it is the promotion of free enquiry to generate more questions than can be solved, because it is this restless search that advances knowledge, sharpens the truth and enriches our lives. Free and open enquiry traditionally began with the Greeks, who single-handedly injected philosophical reasoning and higher standards of criticism into Western thought; it meant that you could be wrong but still be highly productive in advancing knowledge through endless imagination, innovation and discovery.

For me, seeking meaning and purpose in life begins with recognition that life and nature are one: infinitely creative and infinitely changeable. Life and nature are not events but processes, not independent but a continuum. I do not believe in a personal god, heaven or hell, the afterlife or the notion that human beings are special creations of God. I endorse Voltaire's sentiment when he wrote: "If God created us in his own image, we have more than reciprocated."[14] The idea of a personal god, heaven or hell, the afterlife or the act of special creation are "truths of the past" and, along with the concepts of spirit and soul, belong to the history of ideas. Together they serve as a grand testimony to our species' extraordinary evolutionary potential, imagination and inventiveness. I do however share with all Christians the disbelief in the thousands of gods in ancient Sumer, Mesopotamia, Egypt, Greece, India and elsewhere, while at the same time recognizing that there are 33 800 denominations of Christianity in 238 countries around the world, each believing the other is wrong on some fundamental interpretation of Scripture or Judeo-Christian history,[15] not to mention the 1.3 billion Muslims and 0.9 billion Hindus each believing the 2 billion Christians are just plain wrong, and vice versa. In no way do my agnostic views suggest doing away with religion; I only want to emphasize, from a cross-cultural perspective, that one's religious beliefs are firmly bounded by articles of faith derived from history and, within these highly prescribed boundaries, there exists a system that is just as dynamic as science and other systems of human thought.

The best human potentiality can do is offer provisional truths, whether they are historical, mythopoeic, religious, scientific, philosophical, legal or ethical. Unity in diversity will not be found by attacking peoples' traditional beliefs or inciting hatred and violence, as the world tragically witnessed in the USA on 11 September 2001 or in Indonesia on 12 October 2002. It is my belief that new inroads can be made through education using programmes designed to bridge the past with the present and future. These new programmes must include a commitment to better understand different points of view by tapping into the history of ideas. The assertion and blind acceptance that there is one truth is an anathema to human potentiality. In a rapidly changing world, where many still cling to the hope of finding one timeless truth, the message I want to shout from the highest mountain is that the most certain thing about reasoned knowledge in general, and science, religion or myth in particular, is its uncertainty.

Notes

Preface

1. Pascal, *Pensées, II: The Misery of Man without God*, no. 172 (1952: 203).
2. Barrett & Freeman (1986: 38). The full quote can be found in Chapter 11, note XX.
3. Geertz (1973: 140).
4. Auden (1999: 3). The quote is the abbreviated form of: "It is perfectly true, as philosophers say, that life must be understood backwards. But they forget the other proposition, that it must be lived forwards."

Chapter 1. Science, religion and myth: making sense of the world

1. In 384 BC Symmachus wrote to the Christian Emperor Valentinian II pleading for the continuation of pagan ceremonies (Hooper & Schwartz 1991).
2. Aristotle, *Metaphysics* I 982b10–15, translated in Barnes (1984: 1554).
3. Kant (1973: 10).
4. Da Vinci (1975: no. 1150).
5. Cassirer (1944: 76).
6. Myth is an early nineteenth-century word derived from the Greek *mythos* meaning "story" (Hinnels 1984; Barnhart 1988). "Mythology" is a much older word and dates back to the Greek Thucydides (*c.*471–400 BC). Thucydides used mythology to describe the epic poetry of Homer and Hesiod (Jaeger 1936). A non-religious story of mythical character is generally called a fable.
7. Scarborough (1994).
8. Kirk (1970a); Campbell (1988, 2004).
9. Scarborough (1994).
10. Campbell (1988: 31).
11. *Ibid.*, 28.
12. Leeming & Leeming (1994).

13. Supernatural animal spirits might have ranged from giant snakes to bears, fish to birds and sea monsters to winged super-creatures. These may have been constructed in the ancient mind from the magnificent star patterns in the night sky and abstracted into their reality (Stott 1991).
14. Renfrew & Bahn (1996).
15. Fagan (1995); Renfrew & Bahn (1996).
16. Frankfort & Frankfort (1951: 15).
17. Kahn (1979: 137).
18. Jacobsen (1976: 3).
19. Needham (1955).
20. Westermann (1984); Renfrew (1994); Renfrew & Zubrow (1994); Cohn (1996).
21. Speiser (1960).
22. Hick & Knitter (1987).
23. According to Barnhart (1988) the word "religion", as the belief in God employing a system of faith and service worship, first appeared in *Curso Mundi* published around AD 1325. The word itself dates back to the Roman orator and statesman Marcus Tullius Cicero (106–43 BC), who taught that religion was compounded from *religere* meaning "to gather together" and "the idea of obligation" (Onions 1966). Later, Christian apologist Firmianus Lactantius (AD 240–320), Latin grammarian Servius (fl. AD 350) and Saint Augustine of Hippo (AD 354–430) asserted that religion was derived from the Latin *religare* meaning "to bind strongly" in the sense of obligation to a source as it related to one's faith and morals (Barnhart 1988).
24. Barnhart (1988); Clarke & Byrne (1993).
25. Tylor (1958b: 8).
26. Frazer (1922: vol. 1, 222); see also Ward (1994).
27. Campbell (1988).
28. Whitehead (1926: 6–7).
29. Durkheim (1954), quoted in Abercrombie *et al.* (1988: 207); see also Bullock *et al.* (1988).
30. An extreme view of religion's social function was

taught by Karl Marx (1818–1883), who argued that its development was based on class antagonisms by the social elite for the manipulation of the masses (Renfrew 1994; Rappaport 1971). Another comes from Sigmund Freud (1856–1939), who treated all religious beliefs as an unhealthy pathological illusion (Bullock *et al.* 1988).

31. Yinger (1970: 7).
32. Bergounioux & Goetz (1966); Eliade (1979).
33. McBrearty & Brooks (2000).
34. This is highly speculative.
35. McBrearty & Brooks (1998).
36. Some 30 000 miniature figurines from the Neolithic period have been excavated to date in such faraway places as the Fertile Crescent to the Indus valley (Baring & Cashford 1991) and China (Christie 1968). The Mother Goddess appears to have presided over the creation with animals and plants and human beings as her children (Baring & Cashford 1991). The small figurines are carved from stone, bone, clay, wood and ivory and have a featureless face but exaggerated breasts and genitalia (Renfrew & Bahn 1996; Baring & Cashford 1991; Brandon 1963). The Mother Goddess dates back some 25 000 years before Christ and appears to have survived until the end of the Neolithic period with extensions into Minoan Crete (2600–1400 BC) (Ferguson 1989; Dickinson 1994). Figurines have been found in the excavated remains of Mesopotamia from the early second millenium BC. The Mother Goddess of fertility also appears in early Chinese folk history (*c.*2000), later to become integrated into the Taoist philosophy around 300 BC (Christie 1968; Ronan 1978). In some aspects of Hinduism she has ascended to such power as to be at the same level as the three great gods of the triad: Brahma, Vishnu and Shivu (Vitsaxis 1977). More remarkable was the 1981 discovery of a "figurine" excavated at Berekhat Ram on the Golan Heights, Israel, which dates back at least 230 000 years. It is only 2.5 cm long and shaped like the "Venus" figurines of 25 000 years ago (Renfrew & Bahn 1996). No one knows who made the figurine or for what purpose.
37. Paleolithic cave art is found across the world (Valladas *et al.* 2001). In western Europe, one of the oldest underground art galleries was discovered in 1994 in the Chauvet Cave in southern France, and dates to around 30 000 years ago (Chauvet 1996). Art traditions were also known to have existed in the Levant, eastern Europe, southern Africa, India and Australia. They included complex finger markings, paintings of animals or animal forms and hand stencils (Conrad 2003). In the older European Mousterian period (c.50 000 BC) fewer art traditions have been found (Marshack 1990). Many anthropologists believe that the reduced number of symbolic objects (i.e. images that stand for ideas) reflects a less developed language among the peoples of this period, but this is highly controversial (*ibid.*; Corbalis 1992).

38. Morell (1995).
39. Baring & Cashford (1991).
40. *Ibid.*; Brandon (1963).
41. "Shaman" is derived from a name for a religious specialist among Siberian tribes. Many ethnologists restrict the term to individuals who acquire supernatural power and access to the gods through inspiration, revelation, vision or other personal experience (Norbeck 1961). Shamanism is found in hunter–gatherer/nomadic groups of human beings and still survives today among the Inuit of Alaska, and among the reindeer herders and fishers of northeastern Asia. The shaman is a religious specialist (man or woman) who links human beings to the spirit world in times of trouble, anticipation or sickness. The link is usually through a trance from which the soul leaves the body and communicates with the gods in the spirit world (Crofton 1995).
42. Durkheim (1954).
43. Renfrew (1994: 47).
44. Buddhism teaches that there is no permanent "self". Nothing exists permanently – only perpetual change – paralleling the philosophy of Greek contemporary Heraclitus (*c.*533–475 BC) (see Ch. 4). What we see is only a product of the transitory factors of existence; our views are mental constructions shaped by the senses (Smart 1991). Buddha reportedly did not believe in a personal god. Different strands of Buddhism spread to China, Korea, Japan and Tibet.
45. Solomon & Higgins (1996). Confucianism was founded on an ethical system to harmonize social relations in the Chinese state during gross civil disorder (Smart 1991). In the sixth century, Confucius taught that the duty of human beings and their happiness lay in conforming to the "Will of Heaven", a supreme spiritual principle (the *li*) that orders the world and relationships among people. The *tao* (the Way) is to live within the structures of social order.
46. Solomon & Higgins (1996); Barnes (1997).
47. Smart (1991).
48. Solomon & Higgins (1996). Hinduism contains different manifestations of an ultimate reality, an impersonal transcendent being. The oldest Vedic scriptures of around 1000 BC sing praise to a supreme god, Varuna, the sustainer of the creation and guardian of universal order. A second generation of Vedic gods appear as manifestations of world order and quite separate from the creation. A later treatise in the Vedic literature has the ultimate reality as Brahman and his many helper gods, who are inferior manifestations; they continue to play an important role in the life of many Hindus today (Smart 1991; Sutherland *et al.* 1988).
49. Smart (1989).
50. Sutherland *et al.* (1988); Smart (1989, 1991).
51. Sutherland *et al.* (1988); Smart (1989, 1991).
52. Frend (1984).
53. Davis & Moore (1945: 244, 246); Merton (1968).

54. Kearns (1995).
55. Postgate (1992).
56. Baines & Malek (1984).
57. Christie (1968).
58. Exodus 24:12–18.
59. Isaiah 2:2–4.
60. Kramer (1963).
61. H. Smith (1952).
62. Barrett *et al.* (2001).
63. Darwin (1874: 636).
64. J. Taylor (1990); Famighetti (1996).
65. Bacon (1597).
66. Ross (1962).
67. The word "science" appeared in print in 1834 in the *Quarterly Review* as part of a book review written by Whewell himself, who, at the time, chose to remain anonymous (Ross 1962). In 1840, Whewell properly introduced the term "scientist" in his famous two-volume book, *The Philosophy of the Inductive Sciences* (1840). Despite early opposition from eminent people such as Sir John Lubbock (1834–1913), Thomas H. Huxley (1825–1895), Michael Faraday (1791–1867), Lord Kelvin (1824–1907) and John W. Rayleigh (1842–1919), who preferred "natural philosopher", the word "scientist" was eventually accepted (Knight 1981: 381, 494).
68. Koyre (1956); Kuhn (1970); Dobson (1997).
69. Dobson (1997).
70. Kuhn (1970).
71. Duchovnay & Joyce (2000).
72. Logic is the art of inference-building via persuasion using good and bad argument. Since Aristotle's time, there are two basic types of inference-drawing: inductive and deductive (Popper 1959). The following example illustrates both types. From throwing many balls in the air, we know that they all go up, reach a maximum height and then fall. This general truth was obtained by the logical process of *induction*. From this general principle, it can be *deduced* that any object thrown in the air will show the same tendency. If the premise is true then the conclusion deduced concerning the throwing of an object will also be valid. However, the general principle that all objects dropped will tend to fall to the earth is never certain or "absolute". For example, if the experiment was performed 200 km above the Earth's surface in a gravity-free environment, a very different premise would have been inductively obtained. Moreover, in practice, the logical operations in science are more complex. In the nineteenth century, many philosophers of science argued that Newton inductively arrived at his law of gravitation from Galileo or Kepler's laws of motion. Nothing could be further from the truth. As Karl Popper (1902–1994) pointed out, it was "only after we are in possession of Newton's theory can we find out in which sense the older theories were approximations to it ... It is only ingenuity which can make this step" (1957: 29; see also Cohen 1977: 335). Albert Einstein (1879–1955) concurred when he wrote: "There is no logical way to discovery of the elementary laws. There is only the way of intuition, which is helped by a feeling for the order lying behind the appearances" (Holton & Roller 1958: 251). English Nobel prize-winning immunologist Peter B. Medawar (1915–1987) further concluded "there is no rigorous procedure by which an inductive truth can be proved to be so" (Medawar 1984: 14, 1991). Medawar claimed that towards the end of his career Whewell was in two minds about the role of induction in science, and even suggested abandoning the word altogether (Medawar 1984, Fruton 1992). The logical structure of science was best summed up by Bertrand Russell (1872–1970) when he wrote: "I am convinced that induction must have validity of some kind in some degree, but the problem of showing how or why it can be valid remains unsolved" (1927: 14).
73. At the root of new discovery lies the potential of improving the quality of human life. Scientific knowledge provides intellectual power and a means to technological power. Basic curiosity-driven, as opposed to "targeted" (directed or goal-orientated) research, must continue to be supported by governments (Wong 1996). A good example of "basic" science is the discovery of the antibiotic penicillin. In 1928, Alexander Fleming (1881–1955) was working in the laboratory with bacterial cultures of Staphylococci and separately with *penicillium* mould cultures (Fleming 1946; MacFarlane 1985). One day the bacterial cultures were "accidentally" contaminated with *penicillium* spores. While Fleming was in the process of throwing out the contaminated bacterial plates, he noticed there were spots in the culture where the bacteria did not grow. The *penicillium* mould had produced something that killed the bacteria. In 1929, after an exhaustive number of experiments of validation, Fleming called the antibacterial substance "penicillin", and the rest is history. A statement from Arthur Kornberg further distinguishes the difference between basic and targeted research:

> The truly major discoveries that have altered the face of medicine ... for example, x-rays, penicillin, recombinant DNA ... have all come from the pursuit of curiosity about nature without relevance to medicine ... No matter how counter-intuitive it may seem ... to the scientist as well as to the layman ... the most sure and cost-effective route to discovery is through creative activity of the scientist or inventor rather than the pursuit of a defined goal. (1992: 859)

The history of science is replete with examples of how accidents have led to profound discoveries. That "basic" science is full of surprises is a feature not widely publicized.
74. Carnap (1966).
75. Bridgman (1927).
76. Howard (1982); Mayr (2000).
77. Gould (1986b).

78. Mayr (2000).
79. Gould (1986b).
80. From a letter from Charles Darwin to J. D. Hooker, 23 April 1861, in Darwin (1888: vol. 11, 155).
81. Koyre (1956); Kuhn (1970).
82. Einstein (1950a).
83. Infeld (1950).
84. Einstein & Infeld (1954); Gamow (1962).
85. Harrow (1920); Gamow (1962).
86. Barnett (1948).
87. Hawking (1996).
88. *Ibid.*
89. Veggeberg (1992).
90. Thorne (1991).
91. Rees (1998).
92. Dobson (1997).
93. Davies (1977).
94. Rolston (1987).
95. Mach (1893: 483).
96. Ziman (1978).
97. Galileo wrote that, without mathematics, "it is impossible to comprehend a single word of the great book of the universe" (Baumer 1960: 252). He wrote further: "Philosophy (natural science) is written in that great book which ever lies before our eyes – I mean the universe – but we cannot understand it if we do not learn the language and grasp the symbols in which it is written. This book is written in the mathematical language, and the symbols are triangles, circles, and other geometrical figures without whose help it is impossible to comprehend a single word of it, without which one wanders in vain through a dark labyrinth" (Holton 1952: 227). Darwin too was captivated by the power of mathematics, although he freely admitted that he had no special aptitude for numbers. Darwin claimed that "mathematics seems to endow one with something like a new sense" (Bell 1937).
98. Koyre (1956); Kuhn (1970).
99. Rees (1998: 57).
100. Having formulated a question, the next step is to propose a tentative solution or hypothesis. Why doesn't the moon fall to the Earth like the apple? One reason may be that the attraction force between the moon and Earth is weak over the vast distance separating them. Another hypothesis may be that the attractive force is the same, but the moon doesn't fall because it orbits the Earth. Therefore, if the moon ever stopped moving, even for a fraction of a second, it would come crashing down to Earth like the apple. After centuries of observations and testable physical theory, the latter explanation is true: the moon is 384 400 km above the Earth, has a mean orbital velocity of 10 km s^{-1} and completes one orbit around Earth about every 28 days.
101. Popper (1957, 1959).
102. In the 1930s, when Popper proposed his idea of falsification, the prevailing philosophy was logical empiricism. Logical empiricism held that scientific unity and method was built on verification. Any statement that was not verifiable was denied of literal or cognitive meaning. Popper, however, objected to confining science (and philosophy) to only verifiable statements, at least in principle, and proposed his falsifiability idea (1959; Bronowski 1977).
103. Bronowski (1977: 87).
104. Mill (1843: 11).
105. Popper (1959); Ziman (1978).
106. Rolston (1987); Barbour (1990).
107. Bernard (1957: 38).
108. It is often reported that on 31 October 1992 Pope John Paul II "officially" announced that Galileo was right in affirming that the Earth was moving around the sun and the Church was wrong (Pedersen 1983; Blackwell 1998). Unfortunately, the world media wrongly took this out of context. Catholic authorities had long accepted the Earth's motion around the sun because the Copernican texts were removed from the Catholic Index of Prohibited Books early in the nineteenth century.
109. Blackwell (1998: 350).
110. Whitehead (1933); Ziman (1978); Medawar (1984).

Chapter 2. Life among the gods, part I: the Sumerians

1. Tylor (1958a: 1).
2. Street (1980).
3. *Ibid.*; Renfrew & Bahn (1996).
4. Street (1980).
5. Lewin (1998).
6. Renfrew & Bahn (1996).
7. *Ibid.*; Lewin (1998).
8. Archaeologist Gordon Childe (1964, 1967) coined the term Neolithic revolution in 1941. It literally meant the "New Stone Age". Nowadays, the word "revolution" has been replaced by "process" (Renfrew & Bahn 1996).
9. Fagan (1995); Schwartz (1995).
10. How farming spread through Europe is highly controversial. One school argues that the farmers migrated into Europe with the skills of farming in hand. Another more recent suggestion is that the European farmers were not new arrivals but descended from the first human beings, who moved into Europe some 50 000 years ago in the Upper Paleolithic (Lewin 1997).
11. Renfrew & Bahn (1996).
12. The word "culture" encompasses the sum total of human achievement. It was first applied by the ancient Romans to the cultivation of their fields (*agri cultura*), cultivation of the mind (*anima cultura*) and cultivation of religion and God (*Dei cultus or cultura*). In the nineteenth century the term was introduced into the anthropological literature by Tylor (1958a,b, 1960) after the German-Swedish historian and jurist, Samuel Pufendorf (1632–1694).
13. Economy is defined as "those aspects of human

behaviour that concern the production, management, distribution, and consumption of material wealth as well as structural relations that determine commodity transaction" (Yoffee 1995: 1387).

14. "Civilization" is derived from the Latin *civis* meaning "a citizen", and *civilis*, "pertaining to a citizen and a city". The "civilized" condition or state was first recorded in James Boswell's *Life of Samuel Johnson* (1791) in a conversation about entering the meaning of the word into Johnson's *Dictionary* (fourth edition) (Barnhart 1988). For our purposes, civilization is defined as a distinctive type of urban society with a population numbering in the thousands, usually with a food surplus, a system of writing, politics, myth, religion, mathematics and a system of weighing, measuring and counting.

15. Renfrew & Bahn (1996).

16. Lewin (1998).

17. Abraham's home was near the ancient city of Haran in northern Mesopotamia (Genesis 11:31–2). In Judaism and Christianity, Abraham migrated to Israel and it was in Jerusalem that he prepared to sacrifice Isaac and where Adam was created and buried. In Islamic tradition, Abraham was regarded as the rebuilder of Ka'ba in Mecca after the Flood. He was the propagator of pure monotheism, from which Judaism and Christianity developed (McManners 1990: 175).

18. Greek historian and geographer Strabo (*c.*64 BC–AD 23) referred to Mesopotamia as the northern part of the fertile plain and quite separate from southern "Babylonia" (Woolley 1963). Later Pliny (*c.* AD 23–79) extended Mesopotamia's physical limits to the Arabian Gulf, which was about equal to modern-day Iraq (established 1921) (Lloyd 1978). Earlier in the nineteenth century, James Henry Breasted (1865–1935) termed the enormous arc connecting southeast Asia to the shores of the Mediterranean sea "the Fertile Crescent" (1938).

19. Lloyd (1978).

20. Babylonia roughly corresponds to the plain between modern Baghdad and the Persian Gulf in southern Iraq, while Assyria corresponds to the region located around present-day Mosul in northern Iraq. Assyria was originally designated as the stretch of land situated between the Tigris River and the eastern mountains of Iran. Babylonia and Assyria were named after their capital cities, Babylon and Ashur (Ashshur). The name Babylon is the Greek form of Babel or Babili, meaning "the Gate of the Gods". The ancient city was located near the modern town of Hilla, 93 km south of Baghdad. The capital city of Assyria, Ashur, was located near the modern village of Sharqat on the Tigrus River 96 km south of Mosul in northern Iraq (Stevenson 1972).

21. Oppenheim (1977); Postgate (1992).

22. In the Book of Genesis (11:2–4): "And it came to pass, as they journeyed from the east, that they found a plain in the land of Shinar; and they dwelt there. And they said one to another, Go to, let us make brick, and burn them thoroughly. And they had brick for stone, and lime had they for mortar. And they said, Go to, let us build us a city, and a tower, whose top may reach unto heaven; and let us make us a name, lest we be scattered abroad upon the face of the whole earth."

23. Kramer (1983).

24. Kramer (1980: 169).

25. Daniels (1995).

26. See Speiser (1960); Margueron (1965); Wellard (1972); Lansing (1974); Renfrew & Bahn (1996).

27. Bottero (1992); Edzard (1995).

28. Kramer (1963); Pope (1975); Daniel (1968).

29. In an agglutinative language, the words run together into compounds in which the form and meaning of the constituent parts undergo little or no change, whereas in Indo-European or Semitic languages words are constructed using shorter sequences, where the basic element or root of the word may change (e.g. sing, sang, sung).

30. Indo-European people (Aryans) belonged to a linguistic family, not a racial group. In prehistoric times, they occupied a portion of northeastern Europe, and began to migrate throughout Europe around 6000 BC. These peoples established Indo-European languages in Asia Minor, Persia, India, Greece, Italy and other parts of Europe. Among the modern languages of Indo-European origins are Greek, Latin, Slavic, Germanic, Celtic, Sanskrit, Iranian and Armenian (Renfrew & Bahn 1996).

31. Edzard (1995).

32. Postgate (1992); Eyre (1995).

33. Bottero (1992).

34. Kramer (1963).

35. Quoted from Doblhofer (1961: 121).

36. Postgate (1977); Daniels (1995).

37. Larsen (1995); Saggs (1995).

38. Pope (1975); Bottero (1992); Bahn (1996).

39. Hincks proposed that the signs represent syllables, meaning usually one vowel sound with or without consonant(s) preceding or following. America (A–mer–i–ca) has four syllables. Syllables were arranged in different combinations to make a word, or each sign might be the word (e.g. man, tree, etc.). The phonemic system of the Sumerians appears to have consisted of four vowels – a, i, e, u – and 15 consonants – b, d, g, h, k, l, m, n, p, r, s, s´, s^, t, z (Kramer 1963).

40. Margueron (1965); Daniels (1995).

41. Daniel (1968); Bottero (1992).

42. Pope (1975).

43. Glassner (2003).

44. Daniels (1995).

45. Kramer (1963); Daniel (1968); Romer (1989).

46. Kramer (1963); Daniel (1968).

47. Kramer (1963); Lloyd (1978).

48. In addition to hundreds of gods, each city had one patron or favourite god –Ur had goddess Nanna; Uruk had Ishtar/Inanna; Eridu had Enki; Lagash had Ningirsu; and Larsa had Babba –

which led to slight differences in social organization of each city-state (Wellard 1972).

49. The priests were the principal overseers of people organization, knowledge acquisition and protection, agriculture, time-keeping and divine scholarship. There is some evidence that an assembly of citizens may have had some influence over priestly rule during the Early Dynastic I period (2900–2750) but very little is known (Postgate 1992; Crawford 1991).

50. Kramer (1963); Oppenheim (1977); Lloyd (1978); Fagan (1995). The system of castes in Mesopotamia appears to have developed from rapid agricultural prosperity and military power. The top of the caste system was the king (military leader) followed by the high priests, politicians and palace officials, merchants and landowners. The largest fraction of the population comprised farmers, peasants and slaves, and children were mostly bound to follow their parents. Slavery was a recognized institution of Sumerian society (Kramer 1983). Women had, for the most part, equal rights with men of the same class; they could own land and conduct business.

51. Crawford (1991).

52. Kramer (1963, 1983); Postgate (1992).

53. Jacobsen (1976); Kramer (1983).

54. Ziggurats were flat-topped staged pyramids of about seven storeys high and were part of a huge temple complex. They became known as the "Hill of Heaven" or "Mountain of God" and had a long stairway that led at the top to the gate of the gods, the entrance to the divine house. Nearly 30 ziggurats have been discovered by archaeologists in the Mesopotamian region; the largest is in Babylon. The Ziggurat of Babylon became known in the Hebrew tradition as the Tower of Babel (see Genesis 11:1–9). Unlike the pyramids of Egypt, the Sumerian temples were built not of stone but of mud-baked bricks and have weathered extensively. The best preserved of the Sumerian temples is the Ziggurat of Ur, which is estimated to have been around 90 m high with a temple about 15 m high on a 60 m × 90 m base. The ziggurat can be traced back to the Al 'Ubaid people, who had cultural ties with Elam (western Iran). The Egyptians may (this is highly controversial) have borrowed the idea of the pyramid from the Sumerian ziggurat and temple complex.

55. Oppenheim (1977).

56. Jacobsen (1976); Postgate (1992).

57. Daniel (1968).

58. Daniel (1968: 73).

59. Quoted from Doblhofer (1961: 13).

60. Pope (1975); Cooper (1989).

61. Kramer (1963).

62. Phonetic writing appears to have evolved from pictographic carvings on stone or cave walls. In contrast, pictorial writing possessed no connection between the graphic image and phonetic value (sound of the spoken language).

63. Bottero (1992); Whitt (1995).

64. Edzard (1995); Glassner (1995). Bottero (1992) believes that the construction of the cuneiform script may have influenced other archaic writing systems introduced into the West (Egypt around 3000 BC) and the East (India, around 2500 BC and China around 2000–1500 BC).

65. Cooper (1989); Bottero (1992); Schmandt-Besserat (1992). Of the 500 000 tablets excavated, about 80 per cent deal with business documents (Bottero 1992).

66. Besserat (1995).

67. Kramer (1963).

68. Pearce (1995).

69. *Ibid.*; Baines (1983); Powell (1995).

70. Scribes were mostly adult males who learned the skill of writing from their fathers (Pearce 1995). There is evidence that on rare occasions females were trained in the scribal schools as well (Postgate 1992; Pearce 1995). Writing and scribes were under the control of the priests and kings.

71. Black & Tait (1995).

72. The Nippur temple library reportedly housed over 30 000 tablets. In January 1986, archaeologists uncovered new tablets in the library at Sippar located in northern Babylon (Black & Tait 1995). The tablets were found in a small room and were stacked in their original pigeonholes. The texts were copies of literary works, hymns, prayers, divination procedures and astrological omens. There was also a text with a unique circular "astrolabe" containing interstellar distances and arrangement of stars (*ibid.*). The discovery is significant because the astrolabe was originally thought to have been a Greek invention of around 200 BC (Evans 1998).

73. Breasted (1938).

74. Kramer (1956: 20).

75. Bottero (2001). The cuneiform sign for "a divinity" was a sketch of a star. It also means "on high" or "what is elevated", and, concretely, the upper level of the universe – "heaven". Thus the divine world was "superior" to anything that existed below (Bottero 1992: 211; 2001: 58–68).

76. Kramer (1956); Wiggermann (1995).

77. Wiggermann (1995).

78. Kramer (1956); Bottero (1992); Lesko (1995); Scurlock (1995).

79. Wiggermann (1995).

80. Frankfort & Frankfort (1951); Bottero (1992).

81. Green (1995).

82. Jacobsen (1976).

83. Westermann (1984).

84. Most of the information on the Sumerian worldview comes from their art, myths, epic tales and hymns (Kramer 1963). There is no one poem or book dedicated to the topic of the creation and structure. Today's accounts have been compiled from scattered sources usually located at the beginning of a poem or story (Glassner 1995; Lambert 1995).

85. Kramer (1963); Bottero (1992).

86. Brandon (1973a).

87. Some of the other powerful deities were the moon god, Nanna, his son the sun god, Utu, and

his daughter, Inanna. Inanna was the goddess of love and war (known to the Semites as Ishtar) (Kramer 1983; Glassner 1995; Lambert 1995). Her name in Sumerian was literally "Queen of Heaven", later changed to "Queen of Heaven and Earth". She was responsible for the Morning Star and Evening Star, the growth of plants and animals and fertility in humankind (Wolkstein & Kramer 1983). Other gods were: Gibil, god of fire; Iskur, god of storms; and Sirus, god of transforming barley into the national drink, beer.

88. Kramer (1983).
89. Kramer (1963); Bottero (1992); Glassner (1995).
90. Jacobsen (1951); Kramer (1963); Westermann (1984).
91. Only a few fragments of Sumerian creation texts have survived and I have used the literary translations and interpretations of Sumerologist Samuel Kramer (1963).
92. Glassner (1995); Lambert (1995); Wiggermann (1995). The later Babylonian creation myth *Enuma Elish* [*When on High*], so-named after the first two words of the poem on Tablet 1, was written in Akkadian on seven tablets around 1500BC (Pritchard 1958b). In *Enuma Elish*, before heaven and earth were formed there were two vast bodies of water: the male freshwater ocean was called Apsu ("the sweet waters") and the female saltwater ocean was called Tiamat (the Akkadian word *tiamat* means "sea"). Through the fusion of the waters of Apsu and Tiamat, successive generations of gods came into being, including the supreme god-king of Babylon, Marduk. As in the Genesis story (Genesis 1), water is the primeval element, but here it is identified with the gods (Lambert 1995). The story is believed to have been recited at New Year festivals in Babylon to honour the gods; in particular how the hero-god Marduk, the city-god of Babylon, became the supreme deity, king over all gods of heaven and earth (Frankfort *et al.* 1951: 184; Munitz 1957: 8–20). In many ways, *Enuma Elish* recounts the constant struggle between cosmic order and chaos, a recurring theme in many creation epics, including Genesis.
93. Kramer (1963).
94. The word "chaos" often appears in ancient cosmogonies to denote the primeval "disorder" or "ultimate beginning in itself" (Cornford 1952). In the Old Testament, the separation of the waters is immediately followed by the description of "chaos" (Westermann 1984). The separation is not an add-on; it *is the creation*. Later in Greek Homer and Hesiod's epics, the meaning of "chaos" changed to a "yawning gap" or "empty space" between the fiery heaven and earth (see Ch. 4).
95. Kramer (1956: 133).
96. Kramer (1956).
97. Jacobsen (1978); Bottero (1992).
98. Kramer (1963). As earth began to form, Ki took on the name Ninhursag, in whose womb all precious things grow: the great gods and goddesses, metals, animals and plants. Ninhursag had temples at Kish, Lagash and Tell Obeid. Some scholars combine the names: Ninhursag-Ki.

99. Lambert (1995).
100. *Ibid.*
101. Wiggermann (1995: 1858).
102. Glassner (1995: 1820).
103. Kramer (1956: 169).
104. Kramer (1956); Jacobsen (1976).
105. Kramer (1963).
106. Kramer (1963, 1956, 1980). Other variations can be found in Jacobsen (1976).
107. Kramer (1963).
108. Genesis 2:14–19.
109. Pritchard (1958a); Kramer (1963); Lansing (1974); Westermann (1984).
110. Kramer (1963).
111. Genesis 2:7–14.
112. Speiser (1951).
113. Wellard (1972).
114. Genesis 2:5–8. Biblical passages are taken from the revised standard version (e.g. New York: Thomas Nelson, 1952).
115. Genesis 2:21–3.
116. Lansing (1974).
117. Baring & Cashford (1991).
118. Kramer (1963); Lansing (1974); Green (1995).
119. Strong (1978).
120. Kramer (1963). According to the *The Oxford Dictionary of the Christian Church* (Cross 1961), the Hebrew word for Eve may have also meant "serpent", and was associated with the primitive myth that all life originated from a primeval serpent (Baring & Cashford 1991; Cross 1961). Eve was tempted by the serpent to eat the fruit of the tree of knowledge; she and Adam disobeyed and were driven out of the Garden of Eden. Eve was punished with the pain of childbirth.
121. Westermann (1984).
122. Kramer (1956, 1963); Wiggermann (1995).
123. Kramer (1963: 150).
124. *Ibid.*
125. Eliade (1979). For a more detailed comparative analysis of the different creation myths consult Claus Westermann's *Genesis 1–11* (1984) and Theodor Gaster's *Myth, Legend and Custom in the Old Testament* (1969).
126. Peacocke (1979).
127. Westermann (1984).
128. Albright (1957).
129. Westermann (1984: 49).
130. In addition to Genesis, the Flood is mentioned in two other places of the Old Testament. The first is in Ezekiel (14:14, 20), where the biblical writer emphasizes the heroic life of Noah, and the second is in Isaiah (54:9), which combines Yahweh's promise of no more destruction after Noah's flood with the assurance that he will stop being angry with the generation of the exile (Schmidt 1995). These latter passages are believed to have been written around the time of the Babylonian Exile (586–538 BC), a period when the Jews were forcibly deported

to, and detained in, Babylon. In Jewish history, the Exile was second in importance to the Exodus, and was believed to have been God's punishment against the Jews (through the Babylonians) for worshipping idols and corrupting the Mosaic laws.

131. Rappaport (1978); Cohn (1996); Best (1999).
132. Pritchard (1958a).
133. Kramer (1956).
134. Kramer (1956: 201).
135. Kramer (1956: 203).
136. Cohn (1996); Best (1999). The Old Testament presents Noah (Genesis 6:11–9:19). In a test of obedience to God's command, Noah and his family were saved in the ark made of gopher wood, while the rest of mankind was destroyed. According to Genesis, the entire surviving human race and history descended from Noah's three sons.
137. Cohn (1996).
138. Kramer (1956: 204).
139. Kramer (1956: 205).
140. Cohn (1996).
141. Quoted in Doblhofer (1961: 121).
142. The Babylonian myth appears to have strong Sumerian roots but was changed slightly by their successors by having Semitic names substituted for the Sumerian gods (Cohn 1996).
143. Moran (1995); Schmidt (1995); Cohn (1996); Best (1999).
144. Moran (1995); Cohn (1996). The Epic of Gilgamesh was written between 2500 BC and 2000 BC, and should not be confused with the second famous Epic of the Babylonians, the *Enuma Elish*, written around 1500 BC (Frankfort *et al.* 1951; Munitz 1957).
145. Moran (1995).
146. Pritchard (1958a).
147. George Smith began a distinguished career as an apprentice engraver for the firm Bradbury and Evans in London. In his spare time, Smith spent evenings reading the works of the great archaeologists Layard and Rawlinson and visited the British Museum. Eventually the museum gave Smith the job as repairer of the cuneiform tablets from Nineveh. Smith came to Assyriology with no formal training, only raw enthusiasm. In ten years, he learned how to decipher the texts. It was at the British Museum that Smith made one of the most spectacular discoveries in Assyriology. In the poorly lit room of Assyrian King Assurbanipal's royal library, Smith found the account of the Babylonian flood (Pritchard 1958a). His claim to fame, however, was not limited to the discoverer of the Epic of Gilgamesh, but later included the discovery of a seven-tablet unrelated epic on the Babylonian Creation, the *Enuma Elish*. On 4 March 1875, Smith wrote a letter to the *Daily Telegraph* newspaper claiming that these new tablets "join or form parts of a continuous series of legends, giving the history of the world from the Creation down to some period after the Fall of Man" (McCall 1990: 14).
148. Pritchard (1958a: 161).
149. Sayce (1872); McCall (1990: 14).
150. Pritchard (1958a).
151. Thomas (1958).
152. Kramer (1963); Oppenheim (1977); Rappaport (1978).
153. According to the ancient Greek flood myth, Deucalion, the son of Prometheus, is the Greek counterpart to the Babylonian Utnapishtim or the Sumerian flood hero Ziusudra. When Zeus decided to wipe out mankind by releasing a great flood on earth, Deucalion, warned by his father, made an ark, which saved both he and his wife, Pyrrha, daughter of Epimetheus. After nine days, the flood subsided and the ark came to rest on the top of Mount Parnassus (Barker & Cook 1976: 117).
154. Koran; Sura 11:25–48; Schmidt (1995); Cohn (1996).
155. It is generally agreed that the Flood was not part of the original epic but was added later (Moran 1995).
156. Pritchard (1958b); Moran (1995).
157. Pritchard (1958b).
158. *Ibid.*, 168.
159. Ashurnasirpal II of Assyria (883–859 BC) knew of Mount Nisir and believed it was located south of a tributary of the Tigris (south of Little Zab River), which may be the existing Mount Pira Magrun (about 2,750 m high). Mount Ararat is about 5,180 m high (Cohn 1996).
160. McCall (1990).
161. Cohn (1996: 1).
162. Today Ur is about 320 km from the sea and a little over 4 m above sea level. The shift inland is due to the deposition of silt that has occurred over the millennia.
163. Woolley (1954, 1963); Raikes (1966).
164. Woolley (1954).
165. Best (1999).
166. Ryan & Pitman (1998).
167. *Ibid.*
168. *Ibid.*
169. Woolley (1954: 34).
170. Cohn (1996).
171. Bailey (1977); Cohn (1996).
172. Robbins (1990).
173. *Ibid.*
174. Plimer (1997).
175. *Ibid.*
176. Pockley (1997).
177. Scmidt (1995).
178. Bottero (1992: 7).
179. Jacobsen (1976).
180. *Ibid.*; Toy (1913).
181. Woolley (1963); Jacobsen (1976).
182. Jacobsen (1951).
183. Jacobsen (1976).
184. Kramer (1963); Bottero (1992).
185. Green (1995); Scurlock (1995).
186. Wiggermann (1995).
187. Kramer (1963); Bottero (1992).
188. Bottero (1992: 211).
189. Scurlock (1995).
190. Kramer (1956); Scurlock (1995).

191. Scurlock (1995).
192. Oppenheim (1977).
193. *Ibid.*, 199–200.
194. *Ibid.*
195. Postgate (1992).
196. Glassner (1995); Wiggermann (1995).
197. Eamon (1990).
198. McNeill (1963); Oppenheim (1977); Baring & Cashford (1991); Farber (1995).
199. Woolley (1928: 126).
200. Jacobsen (1976).
201. Bottero (1992: 39).
202. Powell (1995: 1941).
203. Mathematics grew from early human beings wanting better ways to count, weigh and measure. In addition, mathematics was used for surveying and dividing the land; construction and repairing dykes, dams, irrigation and drainage channels; developing a system of commodity exchange, including coinage; organization of public affairs; building of homes, schools, libraries and the grand ziggurat temples; and measuring the passage of time.
204. Childe (1967).
205. Wellard (1972).
206. The Sumerians used the cubit (0.5 m) and the danna (10.8 km) for units of length. Area was computed in *iku* (1 *iku* = 0.36 ha). Their unit of weight was the *mina* (1 *mina* = 500 g). The *mina* was divided into 60 *shekels*, and 60 *minas* was equal to one *talent* (or 30 kg) (Breasted 1938). Volume or capacity in Sumer was 1 *sila* (1 litre). These weights and measures were used by the ancients for tens of centuries until the times of the Greeks. For a more complete breakdown see Postage (1992).
207. Dilke (1987).
208. Beale and Carter (1983).
209. Crawford (1991).
210. Powell (1995: 1945).
211. Analysis of the thousands of clay tablets from later Mesopotamian excavation sites show that their school texts comprised tables that contained mathematical problems. Most of the clay tablets containing these tables and problems are Semitic Akkadian, dating back to 2600 BC, although we believe they have much earlier Sumerian roots.
212. *Ibid.*; Kramer (1963).
213. Pythagoras' theorem is $c^2 = a^2 + b^2$ where c, a, b are the sides of the right-angled triangle and c is the length of the longest side, the hypotenuse. As a matter of record, there is no clay tablet providing any formal proof. Nor is there any direct evidence that Pythagoras himself provided the proof (see Ch. 4).
214. The Babylonians surpassed the Egyptians and later Greeks in recognizing the importance of algebraic mathematical proofs. Unlike the Egyptians of the same time period, the Babylonians solved linear and quadratic equations with two variables, and problems involving cubic and biquadratic equations (Struik 1987).
215. Powell (1995); Saggs (1962).
216. Struik (1987: 10).
217. Kramer (1963); Powell (1995).
218. Powell (1995). The concept of zero appeared much later in the first millennium BC and is usually attributed to the Hindus (*c.*700 BC), who established the first decimal positional system, substituting the names of the ranks with zero (Bynum *et al.* 1981: 304). The invention of the concept of zero was a logical extension of the positional or place-value system, but only after the technique of computation reached a high degree of perfection (Struik 1987).
219. *Ibid.*
220. Kramer (1963: 91).
221. Kramer (1963); Neugebauer (1975); Powell (1995).
222. Struik (1987).
223. Rochberg (1995: 1925).
224. Robin (1992). The oldest records of timekeeping date back to the Upper Paleolithic period (20 000–30 000 years ago). A reindeer antler was discovered early in the twentieth century in Le Blanchard rock shelter in the Dordogne district of France. The bone displays a series of incisions and shallow pits with five turns (Robin 1992). The five turns appear to be the ancient connection between the moon and the mythical serpent (Baring & Cashford 1991). As the moon dies and returns to life; the serpent sheds its skin. In 1965, French paleontologist Alexander Marshack discovered that the markings were not decorations but represented a record of the changing phases of the moon (invisible, waxing, full, and waning), extending to three lunar months (Robin 1992). If Marshack's interpretation is correct, human beings were writing notations on time-keeping some 25 000 years before the Sumerians.
225. Kramer (1963: 90).
226. Kramer (1963).
227. The lunar calendar was inherited by the Jews and Persians and it is still used in modern times by some oriental Jews and Mohammedans (Neugebauer 1952). The word "calendar" comes from the Latin *kalendae* (calends), which literally means "the day on which the accounts were due".
228. Kramer (1963).
229. Fraser (1966).
230. Saggs (1962).
231. *Ibid.*
232. Williams (1930); Farber (1995).
233. Rochberg (1995).
234. McLeish (1992).
235. Rochberg (1995: 1925).
236. Powell (1995). Astrology (from the Greek *astron* meaning star and *logos* meaning discourse) is the ancient art of divining the fate and future of human beings and their activities through the study of the celestial positions of the sun, moon and planets relative to one another.
237. Farber (1995).
238. Rochberg (1995).
239. Kramer (1963).
240. Rochberg (1995).
241. Kramer (1963).
242. Kramer (1963).

243. Neugebauer (1952).
244. The term "Chaldean" for Greek Hellenistic writers means both Persian and Babylonian, and for the later Romans every astrologer was a "Chaldean" (Partington 1970). Babylonian astrology reached Persia after the conquest of Babylon by Cyrus in 539 BC. The Greeks became acquainted with astrology during the Persian wars in the fifth century BC.
245. Rochberg (1995).
246. *Ibid.*
247. Neugebauer (1952).
248. Astrology in Roman and medieval Europe was essentially the practice of predicting the future and performing exorcisms involving charms, witches, evil spirits and the devil. An astrologer in medieval Europe was known as a Chaldean, and it is believed some of our toe-counting methods – "eeny, meeny, meyny, moe" – evolved from a form of divination used by the Chaldean magicians (West 1904: 46). The Chaldeans foretold eclipses, made star maps, and marked out the heavens as well as the apparent yearly path of the sun. Every great city had its lofty observatory and its royal astronomer. For over 1700 years, astrology was linked to the ancient alchemical art of making of gold from base metals. Although the practice of astrology has no scientific foundation, it is still practised today.
249. Haggard (1933: 9).
250. Biggs (1995).
251. Woolley (1954); Kramer (1963).
252. Lansing (1974).
253. Kramer (1963).
254. *Ibid.*
255. Levey (1959).
256. Kramer (1963); Oppenheim (1977); Farber (1995).
257. Temkin (1991); Longrigg (1993); Nutton (1995).
258. Farber (1995).
259. The British Museum possesses a clay model of a liver divided up into 50 squares, and within each square was written an omen for a particular condition that was used for the diagnosis of illness (Farber 1995).
260. *Ibid.*; Singer (1944).
261. Farber (1995).
262. Biggs (1995: 1923).
263. Kramer (1963); Biggs (1995).
264. Presumably the aim of this prescription was to empty the patient's bowels, but why an enema should be so elaborate is not clear.
265. Wellard (1972: 134).
266. In early Babylonian times, there seems to have been no shortage of physicians. Yet according to Greek historian Herodotus, who visited Babylonia in the fourth century BC, the Babylonians had no regular doctors. Herodotus claimed when a person was sick he or she was placed in the street so that anybody who came along could listen to the symptoms, make a diagnosis and provide a cure (Wellard 1972).

267. Oppenheim (1977).
268. Kramer (1963).
269. Oppenheim (1977).
270. Biggs (1995).
271. Woolley (1928); Biggs (1995).
272. The Code of Hammurabi was discovered in 1902 by Jaques de Morgan during a French expedition excavating the ancient city of Susa, Elam in southwest Iran (Bottero 1992). Today, the 2.26-m high pillar of hard black diorite stone is housed in the Louvre Museum, Paris. The inscription was written in cuneiform/Semitic language and contained some 280 laws arranged under headings of trade, family, labour, real estate and personal property. Although written in the second millennium BC, the Sumerian words clearly indicate that the laws date back centuries earlier. The code was a systematic compilation of the laws in medical practice, commerce, property rights, marriage, divorce, acts of violence, theft and most aspects of daily life. King Hammurabi called his work "verdicts of the just order" and, in the prologue inscribed on the pillar, he declared that he was acting on behalf of the gods Anum and Enlil with the purpose of promoting justice and the welfare among his people:

At that time Anum and Enlil named me
to promote the welfare of the people,
me, Hammurabi, the devout, god-fearing prince,
to cause justice to prevail in the land,
to destroy the wicked and the evil,
to prevent the strong from oppressing the weak,
to rise like the sun over the black-headed people,
and to light up the land.
(Pritchard 1958a: 210)

273. Biggs (1995).
274. Woolley (1963).
275. Walker (1955: 27).
276. Powell (1995: 1943).
277. Muhly (1995).
278. Levey (1959); Oates (1980).
279. Copper ore and other metals were obtained from trading cloth and other manufacturing products with the peoples of the Persian Gulf region and neighbouring Asian countries (Muhly 1995). Copper came from Oman in the south of the Persian Gulf, and the early Mesopotamians obtained their tin from eastern Iran, Asia Minor and Syria (Daniel 1968). Gold came from Elam, Cappadocia and the region of Antioch, and silver from Elam and the Taurus mountains. An extensive trade existed in the fourth millennium BC, long before the invention of coinage.
280. Childe (1967); Muhly (1995).
281. Levey (1959: 182).
282. Levey (1959).
283. *Ibid.*
284. Levey (1959); Crawford (1991); Postgate (1992).
285. Childe (1964); Snell (1995). Grain was probably the first conventional value standard of trade among neighbouring states and nations before

metal, mostly silver (or copper for small transactions) (Childe 1964; Snell 1995). The switch to a metal currency marked the transition from a natural economy to a money economy. A money economy was necessary for international trade because it provided a common standardization of value for different kinds of goods.

286. Crawford (1991).
287. Levey (1959); Snell (1995).
288. Levey (1959).
289. Postgate (1992).
290. Snell (1995).
291. Glassner (1995: 1815).
292. Kramer (1956); Bottero (1992).
293. Kramer (1956).
294. Evans (1998).
295. In general, something is said to be objective when the observer detaches himself from the observed (Ayer 1979). Strictly speaking, there is no such thing as "objective" sense-perception: only "objective" reflection.
296. Oppenheim (1977: 202).
297. *Ibid.*, 203.
298. See Long (1999b: 11).
299. Peacocke (1979: 355–66).
300. *Ibid.*, 366.

Chapter 3. Life among the gods, part II: ancient Egyptians

1. Quoted in Lesko (1994: 88).
2. Herodotus (1928: Bk 2, 93).
3. Herodotus (1928).
4. In his famous epic poem the *Odyssey*, Homer used the name Aigyptos collectively for the Nile River plus the "Black country" it watered. Aigyptos was the name from which Egypt was later derived (Gardiner 1961). Misr, the Arabic name for Egypt, is of Semitic origin and possibly means "a country" or "a state"; the Assyrian name was Musru, meaning "Far Land" or "Frontier Land" (Peck 1898). In the Bible, the Hebrews often referred to ancient Egypt as Mizraim, which means "the two territories" (Quirke & Spencer 1992).
5. Kemp (1989); Postgate (1992).
6. Baines & Malek (1984); Quirke & Spencer (1992).
7. Morenz (1973).
8. The name "Nile" comes from the Greek *Neilos*, which is believed to have come from the Semitic root *nahal*, meaning "a valley" or "river valley". The ancient Egyptians called the Nile, Ar or Aur (meaning "black") on account of the rich colour of its soil. Some Egyptian texts refer to the Nile as *iteru*, "the river" or *iteru aa*, "the great river" (Quirke & Spencer 1992). The Arabs preserved the name "the Nile of Misr [Egypt]". The Nile River (6650 km) is marginally longer than the Amazon (6437 km) and the Mississippi (6212 km).
9. Postgate (1992).
10. Gardiner (1961).

11. Woolley (1963); Trigger (1993).
12. Quirke & Spencer (1992).
13. *Ibid.*
14. The Institute of Egyptian Antiquities remained under French direction for many years and published the famous multi-volume tome *Description de l'Egypte* (1809–1830) (Quirke & Spencer 1992). French control of the institute was in name only because much of its vast archaeological collection found its way to London's British Museum, not the Louvre in France.
15. The Rosetta Stone (1.14 m × 0.71 m) was discovered in August AD 1799 by Brigadier-General Boussard, a French officer under Napoleon during the French invasion of Egypt (Budge 1929; Pope 1975). It was found near Fort St Julien, 8 km from the small city of Rosetta, or Rashid, located on the left branch of the Nile in the western Delta, about 48 km from Alexandria. Boussard dislodged the large slab of basalt with a lucky blow from his pick (Budge 1929). The trilingual slab passed into British hands with the French surrender of Egypt in 1801 and became part of the British Museum's Egyptian collection in 1802 (Pope 1975).
16. Budge (1929); Daniel (1968).
17. James (1995).
18. Quirke & Spencer (1992). From 8000 BC, the maximal rate of alluvium accumulation is estimated to be of the order of 10 cm every 100 years, which means that by the time of the Aswan Dam construction it had reached an average depth of 9 m (Watterson 1997).
19. Quirke & Spencer (1992).
20. Daniel (1975).
21. Quirke & Spencer (1992).
22. Baines & Malek (1984).
23. *Ibid.*
24. Quirke & Spencer (1992); Spencer (1993).
25. Quirke & Spencer (1992).
26. Spencer (1993); Watterson (1997).
27. Frankfort *et al.* (1951); Woolley (1963); Kemp (1989). Some Egyptian motifs of hunting scenes, lions devouring cattle, composite animals (e.g. serpent-necked felines or serpopards), winged griffins and snakes interlaced together have a distinctive Mesopotamian character (Gardiner 1961; Daniel 1968). There is even a decorated ivory knife handle (now in the Louvre) from predynastic Egyptian Gebel-el-Arak, which bears a heroic figure subduing two lions (Watterson 1997). This motif, some suggest, bears striking similarities to the grand Mesopotamian Epic of Gilgamesh (Gardiner 1961; Spencer 1993). A similar Egyptian scene was discovered on the walls of the "Painted Tomb" at Hierakonpolis (Spencer 1993).
28. In 1957, German archaeologist Werner Kaiser reassessed the cultural divisions in the Late-predynastic period and proposed a new division, Naqada III. This new division had the advantage of emphasizing continuity of the Naqada culture through to dynastic times. From these three

A CHAOS OF DELIGHT

broad divisions, numerous subdivisions were proposed to more accurately depict the complex archaeological record (Spencer 1993).

29. Kemp (1995).
30. Watterson (1997).
31. Daniel (1968).
32. Leahy (1995).
33. Leahy (1995); Roberts (1995).
34. Roberts (1995).
35. Recent archaeological evidence suggests that Upper and Lower Kingdoms in the late fourth millennium BC grew out of a common way of life throughout Egypt. The two halves did not comprise two separate kingdoms but were paired opposites (valley and delta, life and death, river and desert). Thus the "Two Lands" or "Two Countries", referred to in older texts, was really a common synonym for "the Beloved Land" of Egypt (Quirke 1990).
36. Quirke & Spencer (1992); Kemp (1995).
37. Roberts (1995).
38. Hornung (1995).
39. De Burgh (1955).
40. Roberts (1995); Te Velde (1995).
41. Wilson (1951b: 50).
42. Griffiths (1986).
43. Shaw & Nicholson (1995).
44. Quoted from Wilson (1951b: 42).
45. The most common way for young boys to advance within the ancient Egyptian class structure was through the learned profession of writing. Most scribes found employment in clerical book-keeping, but those who were gifted became secretaries to nobles and a few became the highest dignitaries of the land. In Mesopotamia, members of a caste had no such freedom and could not extend beyond the limits of the caste, with the young practising the occupations of their fathers.
46. Wilson (1951b).
47. Quirke & Spencer (1992); Roberts (1995).
48. Quirke & Spencer (1992).
49. Dilke (1987).
50. Quirke & Spencer (1992).
51. Pliny, *Natural History*, 5.58; Watterson (1997).
52. Pope (1975); Davies (1987).
53. Gardiner (1961).
54. Spencer (1993).
55. *Ibid.*
56. Gardiner (1961); Pope (1975); Davies (1987); Quirke & Spencer (1992).
57. Gardiner (1961).
58. Davies (1987).
59. *Ibid.*; Quirke & Spencer (1992).
60. Gardiner (1961); Davies (1987).
61. Gardiner (1961).
62. Quirke & Spencer (1992).
63. Vercoutter (1992).
64. Budge (1929); Pope (1975); Watterson (1997).
65. Black & Tait (1995). Egyptian papyrus was a flowering marsh plant found in great quantities along the Nile. Its hard outer shell was used by the Egyptians to make sandals, baskets, and rope

and the soft inside for paper (Quirke & Spencer 1992).
66. Quirke & Spencer (1992).
67. The association between papyrus and *byblos* appears to have arisen in Egypt under Greco-Roman rule. Papyrus at the time was becoming scarce and had to be imported from Byblos (or Jubayl), a coastal village of Phoenicia about 30 km north of present-day Beirut, Lebanon. The process of paper-making was a Chinese invention around the second century BC. Paper-making was introduced into western Europe by the Arabs via Spain in the eighth and ninth centuries AD. Apparently, the Arabs had learned the pulping process from the Chinese prisoners they had captured in AD 751 after an attempted Chinese invasion of Turkistan, now part of Uzbekistan, Russia.
68. Breasted (1938); Black & Tait (1995).
69. Breasted (1938).
70. *Ibid.*
71. Black & Tait (1995).
72. The Rosetta Stone was a memorial stone commissioned by the Council of Priests at Memphis around 200 BC (Doblhofer 1961; Andrews 1981). The stone was a gift from the Egyptian people to honour the 22-year reign of Ptolemy V Epiphanes (*c.*210–180 BC) and his success in helping the people by reversing the many abuses of the previous government. In particular, Ptolemy helped restore the privileges, power and ancient rites to the priests when the country was being Hellenized (see Ch. 5) (Budge 1929).
73. Budge (1929).
74. Pope (1975); Andrews (1981).
75. Doblhofer (1961); Andrews (1981). Thomas Young was a remarkable scholar. He discovered the nature of optical astigmatism and resurrected Huygen's wave theory of light in opposition to Newton's corpuscular theory. Young was the first to use the term energy in its modern sense: as a property of a system capable of performing work (Asimov 1964).
76. Budge (1929: 202).
77. Doblhofer (1961).
78. Budge (1929).
79. Allen (1988a: 57).
80. Allen (1988a).
81. Silverman (1991).
82. Morenz (1973); Assmann (1995).
83. Wilson (1951b); Allen (1988a); Van Dijk (1995).
84. Frankfort (1948); Frankfort & Frankfort (1951); Allen (1988a); Assmann (1995). Atum was the supreme creator-god and source of all existence. He was the "total of the gods' forms" and contained all the elements of the creation on one level, but independent or outside the creation, on another (Frankfort 1948; Frankfort & Frankfort 1951; Allen 1988a).
85. Allen (1988a); Wilson (1951a).
86. Allen (1988a); Silverman (1991).
87. Shaw & Nicholson (1995).
88. The sun generally is understood as the source of the Ennead and identified with Atum. Sometimes

386

the sun is also the product of the Ennead and identified with Horus (Allen 1988a). These complex issues are beyond the scope of the present discussion but a full discussion can be found in Allen (1988a) and Assmann (1995).

89. Allen (1988a).
90. Assmann (1995); Van Dijk (1995).
91. Allen (1998a: 47).
92. Assmann (1995: 157).
93. Frankfort (1948).
94. Assmann (1995: 171); Allen (1998a).
95. Assmann (1995: 172).
96. Van Dijk (1995).
97. Assmann (1995: 159).
98. Lesko (1991); Allen (1998a).
99. Wilson (1951b). All these terms describing the outermost rim are believed to have been prototypes for the Greek word *Okeanos* (Wilson 1951b).
100. *Ibid.*
101. Grimal (1992); Shaw & Nicholson (1995).
102. Pyramid Texts are funerary inscriptions of stories/spells about the creation, life and the afterlife. They are the oldest funerary inscriptions and were first found on the interior chambers of several of the Old Kindgom pyramids at Saqqara, hence the name (Silverman 1991). Egyptologists use the texts to better understand how the ancient Egyptians made sense of the world and events. The ancient Egyptians also recorded their beliefs and rituals in other collections of spells that adorned the walls of temples, tombs and coffins (Shafer 1991). These books of spells are known as Coffin Texts and were used by the Egyptian privileged class (Silverman 1991). Coffins were painted with magical spells to help the soul on its journey through the underworld to the next life. Some of the incantations date as far back to the first dynasty after the unification around 3000 BC (Shafer 1991).
103. Allen (1998a). God said, "Let there be a vault through the middle of the waters to divide the waters in two". God made the vault, and it divided the waters under the vault from the waters above the vault. God called the vault "heaven" (Genesis 1:6–7).
104. Allen (1998a).
105. Wilson (1951b).
106. Wilson (1951b).
107. *Ibid.*
108. Shaw & Nicholson (1995).
109. Wilson (1951b).
110. *Ibid.*
111. Allen (1988a: 58).
112. Kramer (1963).
113. Allen (1988a: 24).
114. Eliade (1979); Shaw & Nicholson (1995).
115. Trigger (1993).
116. Smyth (1880).
117. *Ibid.*
118. Wilson (1951b).
119. Wilson 1951b: 65).
120. Grimal (1992).
121. Morenz (1973).

122. Quirke & Spencer (1992).
123. Lesko (1991: 92).
124. The *Book of the Dead* was an Egyptian collection of mortuary texts comprising spells or magic formulas. The collection was recorded predominantly on papyri but some spells were found on coffins, amulets and tomb walls and are thought to have helped and protected the dead in the afterlife (Baines & Malek 1984).
125. Wilson (1951b).
126. *Ibid.*
127. Brandon (1963); Westermann (1984); Van Dijk (1995). Westermann argues that the creation of the world and that of human-kind were independent events and passed on by different traditions, which he believes has direct bearing on understanding the biblical creation narratives. For a most interesting discussion on this point see his *Genesis 1–11* (1984: 24).
128. Wilson (1951b).
129. *Ibid.*, 64.
130. Van Dijk (1995).
131. Grimal (1992).
132. Van Dijk (1995).
133. Hornung (1983).
134. Grimal (1992).
135. Osiris was worshipped as an early ruler of ancient Egypt. He is said to have ruled wisely and benevolently in a golden age, bringing civilization to the land. Isis was his sister and devoted wife. Osiris was murdered by his brother Seth, who coveted his throne, and avenged by Horus, son of Isis and Osiris (see text). Although Osiris was celebrated by the ancient Egyptians as risen, he became god of the dead or underworld.
136. Baines & Malek (1984).
137. The Egyptians deified the moon usually under the name of Thoth. Thoth was powerful and represented by an ibis or baboon, crowned with a lunar disc and crescent moon. Thoth was sacred to Hermopolis and became the god of knowledge and wisdom, and the lord of magic (Quirke & Spencer 1992: 65). As in Mesopotamia, he was the scribe of the gods and was the patron god of the scribal profession (Silverman 1991). The Egyptian and Mesopotamian association of the moon with writing and learning is fascinating in light of the immense importance of moon worship by the earlier Sumerians, the purported inventors of writing (*ibid.*).
138. The beetle was a symbol for the morning sun (Wilson 1951b: 58).
139. Grimal (1992).
140. Shaw & Nicholson (1995).
141. Quirke & Spencer (1992).
142. Wilson (1951b).
143. *Ibid.*; Silverman (1991).
144. Morenz (1973).
145. Edwards (1947).
146. Quirke & Spencer (1992).
147. Wilson (1951b); Silverman (1991).
148. Wilson (1951b); Griffiths (1986); Silverman (1991).

149. Foster (1995: 1753).
150. Hornung (1983); Assmann (1995); Shaw & Nicholson (1995); Whitehouse (1995).
151. Frankfort (1948); Hornung (1983); Shaw & Nicholson (1995).
152. Hornung (1983); Silverman (1991); Phillips (1998).
153. Williams (1958); Foster (1995).
154. Williams (1958).
155. Foster (1995).
156. Ibid.
157. Shaw & Nicholson (1995).
158. Griffiths (1986); Silverman (1991).
159. Foster (1995: 1754).
160. Hornung (1983: 248).
161. Freud (1939).
162. Maier (1995).
163. Phillips (1998).
164. Albright (1957).
165. Exodus 2:10.
166. Numbers 26:59.
167. Shaw & Nicholson (1995); Assmann (1997).
168. Albright (1957); Shaw & Nicholson (1995); Phillips (1998).
169. Foster (1995); Maier (1995); Shaw & Nicholson (1995).
170. Shaw & Nicholson (1995).
171. Breasted (1912: 49).
172. Morenz (1973); Hart (1990); Quirke (1992).
173. Griffiths (1986).
174. Wilson (1951b).
175. Hornung (1983); Pinch (1994).
176. Hornung (1983); Te Velde (1995).
177. Temples were gods' houses and were decorated with profound cosmological symbolism. The roof represented the sky and the sanctuary represented the horizon where the sun rose and set, symbolizing the eternal renewal, decline and rebirth in the universe (O'Connor 1980).
178. Unlike the human sacrificial rituals of early Mesopotamia (Daniel 1968), there is no strong evidence that the practice occurred in pharaonic Egypt (Shaw & Nicholson 1995).
179. The shrines of gods were not gods but the image or emblem of the god made from stone, wood, metal or clay. One creation myth states: "The creator-god acted for all other gods, and he made their bodies like that with which their hearts were satisfied. So the gods entered into their bodies of every (kind of) wood, of every (kind of) stone, or every (kind of) clay ... in which they had taken form" (Wilson 1951b: 73).
180. Silverman (1991); Shaw & Nicholson (1995).
181. Shafer (1991); Hornung (1995).
182. Hornung (1995).
183. Hornung (1983); Silverman (1991); Watterson (1997).
184. Cicero (1877: Bk 1, XXIX).
185. Hornung (1995).
186. Ibid.
187. 8 December 1818, quoted in Adams (1971, vol. 10, 362–3).
188. Johnson (1978).
189. Williams (1958); Shaw & Nicholson (1995).
190. Te Velde (1995: §1119); see also O'Connor (1980).
191. Silverman (1991); Quirke & Spencer (1992).
192. Griffiths (1986).
193. Roberts (1988).
194. Steedman (1995).
195. For comparative purposes, immortality was part of the early folk religion of China, and in India reincarnation was part of the time cycle ((Vitsaxis 1977; Moore 1928). The idea of immortality (and reincarnation) was continued by Orphic and other cult religions of archaic Greece (see Ch. 4). A possible variation on this basic theme was incorporated into Western Christian tradition with the opposites of heaven and hell.
196. Silverman (1991).
197. Shaw & Nicholson (1995).
198. Shafer (1991).
199. Borghouts (1995); Roberts (1995).
200. Shaw & Nicholson (1995).
201. Shafer (1991).
202. Shaw & Nicholson (1995).
203. Hornung (1995: 1721).
204. Baines (1991).
205. Lesko (1995); Shaw & Nicholson (1995).
206. Baines (1991).
207. Quirke & Spencer (1992).
208. Morenz (1973); Lesko (1995).
209. Drenkhahn (1995: 339).
210. Grimal (1992).
211. Drenkhahn (1995).
212. Grimal (1992); Drenkhahn (1995).
213. Schafer (1974); Shafer (1991).
214. Quoted in Shafer (1991: 6).
215. Quoted in Davis & Hersh (1981: 113).
216. Robins (1995).
217. Gillings (1980).
218. The Rhind Papyrus is also sometimes called the Ahmes (or Ahmose) Papyrus, after the scribe who copied it from a papyrus in the nineteenth century BC (Dilke 1987). The Rhind Papyrus was purchased in Luxor on the Nile in AD 1858 by Scottish banker and antiquarian A. Henry Rhind (1833–1863) (Struick 1987: 21). The papyrus is housed at the British Museum. The Moscow Papyrus was translated in AD 1930 (Baines & Malek 1984).
219. Robins & Shute (1987).
220. The numeration of the ancient nations of Egypt, China and India, and later the Mayas and Aztecs, and Romans, was decimal.
221. Struik (1987).
222. Dilke (1987); McLeish (1992).
223. Lindberg (1992).
224. Neugebauer (1952).
225. Ibid.
226. McLeish (1992).
227. Gillings (1980). Frustum (from the Latin frustum, a piece or bit) in geometry is the bottom part of a square pyramid or conical shaped solid, formed by cutting off the top with a plane parallel to the base.

228. Bell (1945).
229. Bell (1937); Robins (1995).
230. Burkert (1972); Hussey (1997).
231. Ball (1960); Dilke (1987); Robins (1995).
232. Dilke (1987).
233. Stadelmann (1995).
234. Spence (2000). Khufu was the Egyptian name for the second pharoah-king of the Old Kingdom (2664–2155 BC). Khufu was an abbreviated version of Khnum-khuefui (*Khnum* meaning "protecting me") (Grimal 1992). Cheops was the Greek name for Khufu.
235. Stadelmann (1995).
236. Grimal (1992).
237. *Ibid.*
238. Edwards (1947).
239. Roberts (1995).
240. The quarrying, cutting and transporting methods of the ancient Egyptians are still a matter of controversy. Some of the blocks embodied in the Mortuary Temple of Mycerinus weigh around 200 tons. Transport of the blocks along the waterways was presumably by barge. Overland the Egyptians used sledges, rollers, ropes, levers and cradles to transport the huge blocks (Edwards 1947). They also employed high heat followed by cold, which left superficial cracks that could easily be chipped away to the desired shape and size (Edwards 1947: 214).
241. Edwards (1947).
242. Smyth (1880: 15).
243. *Ibid.*, i, 331–58.
244. Cole (1925); Edwards (1947).
245. Smyth (1880); Edwards (1947).
246. Smyth (1880: 21).
247. Smyth (1880); Petrie (1883); Edwards (1947); Wilson (1951, 1972).
248. Petrie (1940: 89).
249. Sarton (1952).
250. Wilson (1951a).
251. Edwards (1947).
252. Spence (2000).
253. Gingerich (2000).
254. Petrie (1940).
255. *Ibid.*, 89.
256. Edwards (1947).
257. Smyth (1880); Watterson (1997).
258. Lesko (1991).
259. Herodotus (1814: 82).
260. Robins (1995).
261. Parker (1974); Shaw & Nicholson (1995).
262. Parker (1978).
263. *Ibid.*
264. Parker (1950).
265. Parker (1978).
266. *Ibid.*
267. The ancient Egyptians probably adopted an arbitrary year by counting the number of days between each Nile flood, which, over many centuries, averaged 365 days, the average Nile year. However, there was a problem. The start of the flood came at different times with variable strength. As they refined their calendar with more accurate celestial observations, the priest-astronomers adopted the "heliacal rising" of Sirius (the Dog Star) as the basis of their civil calendar. Three thousand years ago, Sirius appeared just above the horizon at dawn on 19 July. This event was a very reliable predictor of the recurring flood and closely matched the solar year (the time for the Earth to revolve once around the sun). Today, the heliacal rising of Sirius is a few weeks later due to the wobble of the Earth on its axis.
268. Gardiner (1961).
269. Robins (1995). The three seasons comprising four lunar months were: *Akhet*, "the inundation" (mid-July to mid-November); *Peret*, "the emergence or coming forth" (meaning the sprouting of the seeds after the inundation; mid-November to mid-March); and the *Shomu*, "the low water" or "the harvest" (mid-March to mid-July) (Breasted 1938; Parker 1978; Watterson 1997).
270. Neugebauer (1942).
271. Gingerich (2000).
272. Parker (1978).
273. Quoted in Parker (1978: 725).
274. Neugebauer & Parker (1968).
275. Haggard (1933: 26).
276. Grimal (1992); Nunn (1996).
277. Oppenheim (1977).
278. Nunn (1996).
279. Herodotus (1928: Bk 2, 108).
280. Robinson (1931: 25).
281. Imhotep means "He who cometh in peace" and he was not only the first Egyptian physician but also a great architect vizier, sage, astrologer and engineer. There are many bronze statuettes of Imhotep, seated and looking at a papyrus.
282. Nunn (1996); Steedman (1995).
283. Murnane (1995); Steedman (1995).
284. Walker (1955); Johnson (1978); Longrigg (1989).
285. Weeks (1995).
286. Nunn (1996).
287. Borghouts (1995).
288. Shaw & Nicholson (1995).
289. Pinch (1994).
290. Maspero (1891), quoted in Walker (1955: 30).
291. The Edwin Smith Surgical Papyrus is about 5 m long and 33 cm high, and was discovered at Luxor in 1862, on the east bank of the Nile in Upper Egypt. The papyrus is housed in the New York City Museum. The Ebers Medical Papyrus is a longer roll, 20.23 m long and 30 cm high and organized in 108 columns of 20–22 lines, each containing some 877 ailments and remedies. It was discovered in Thebes in 1862 by the German Egyptologist George Moritz Ebers (1837–1898), and is now kept at Leipzig University Library (Temkin 1938). There are other extant papyrus rolls such as the Kahun Papyrus (1898) and the Berlin Papyrus (1909) (Lefebvre 1963).
292. Wilson (1951a); Clendening (1960); Lefebvre (1963); Nunn (1996).
293. Harris (1971); Shaw & Nicholson (1995); Weeks (1995).

294. Temkin (1938); Wilson (1951a).

295. An eighteenth-century AD French Pharmacopoeia used the following products from humans as remedies for ailments: "All parts of man, his excrescences and excrements, contain oil and sal volatile, combined with phlegm and earth. Skull, brain, and calculus are employed in medicine, and are referred to in their proper places. Burning hair, smelt by patients, will counteract the vapors. Moss of the human skull, human blood, and human urine all have their places in medicine ... Fresh urine, two or three glasses drunk in the morning fasting, is good against gout, hysterical vapors, and obstructions. It may also be applied externally in gout and in skin complaints. Excrement of man can be applied to anthrax, plague bubos, and quinsies. Dried and powdered, it is recommended in epilepsy and intermittent fevers. Dose, one scruple to one drachm" (quoted from Robinson 1931: 14).

296. Weeks (1995).

297. Nunn (1996).

298. Sarton (1952).

299. Clendening (1960).

300. Sarton (1931).

301. Hornung (1983).

302. Sarton (1931); Lefebvre (1963).

303. Lefebvre (1963); Woolley (1963); Weeks (1995).

304. Lefebvre (1963); Weeks (1995).

305. Some 2000 years passed before Herophilos of Alexandria (c.300 BC) began to count the heart rate by means of a small clepsydra as timer (Lefebvre 1963: 47).

306. Robinson (1931: 22).

307. *Ibid.*, 22.

308. Lefebvre (1963); Woolley (1963).

309. Weeks (1995).

310. Shaw & Nicholson (1995); Te Velde (1995); Weeks (1995).

311. According to Herodotus, the Egyptians priests bathed twice a day and twice again during the night; they were clean shaven and had no body hair. He also says they were obliged to be circumcised and abstained from sexual intercourse during their period of office. When not confined to the temple, priests could have intercourse but, according to Diodorus Siculus, were limited to having one wife (Te Velde 1995). Priests wore only the finest linen and were prohibited from wearing wool or leather (Shaw & Nicholson 1995). Their sandals had to be made of papyrus.

312. Te Velde (1995).

313. Quoted in Robinson (1931: 25).

314. Edwards (1947); Hart (1991); Lesko (1995).

315. Edwards (1947); Hart (1991).

316. Hart (1991).

317. Smyth (1880); Quirke & Spencer (1992).

318. Lesko (1995); Shaw & Nicholson (1995).

319. Hart (1991). The modern word "mummy" was derived from the Arab *mummiya*, meaning bitumen or pitch (Bahn 1992; Quirke & Spencer 1992). The word "mummy" is really a misnomer because bitumen was not widely used until well into the Middle Kingdom (Quirke & Spencer 1992). The Arabs interpreted the blackening of the resins as the effects of bitumen, from which the word "mummy" was derived (Shaw & Nicholson 1995). Another possibility for the origin of the word "mummy" may be from a primary material of mummification: wax. In Egyptian Coptic one word for wax is *mum*.

320. Bahn (1992); Durand & Lichtenberg (1994).

321. Hart (1991); Watterson (1997).

322. Quirke & Spencer (1992).

323. Watterson (1997).

324. Shaw & Nicholson (1995).

325. Robinson (1931).

326. Quirke & Spencer (1992).

327. See Lesko (1995).

328. *Ibid.*

329. Herodotus (1814: 109).

330. The later Taoists of the second and third centuries BC believed in the attainment of physical immortality. Immortality was achieved during life by particular techniques working with environmental events and not against them (Ronan 1978). Since human beings possessed souls, the Chinese believed that it was not possible to possess immortality without some form of bodily component (Christie 1968; Smith 1968). In the Chinese system, being reincarnated in animal form was punishment for human errors in life.

331. Christie (1968); Smith (1968).

332. Morenz (1973).

333. Quoted in Johnson (1978: 111).

334. Quoted in Mason (1962: 23).

335. Leicester (1956).

336. Alchemy became very popular during the Hellenization of Egypt at Alexandria in Egypt (c.300 BC). It was widely practised with astrology by many nations in the East from the fourth century AD up until the sixteenth century AD. In the seventh century AD, alchemy entered the West via the Arabs, who conquered Egypt, and from there transferred to Spain and Italy. From Spain and Italy it spread to the Christian West at the beginning of the thirteenth century (Read 1961).

337. Pinch (1994).

338. The Leiden Papyrus and the Stockholm Papyrus are the surviving documents after Roman Emperor Diocletian (AD 245–313) decreed that all written works pertaining to the alchemical arts must be destroyed. The order was issued in AD 290 in an attempt to prevent the makers of gold and silver accumulating wealth and overthrowing the empire (Stillman 1960: 79).

339. Partington (1957); Pinch (1994).

340. Stillman (1960).

341. In addition to alloying gold and silver in their furnaces, the Egyptians found and quarried electrum in Egypt (Quirke & Spencer 1992). Electrum contained 25–50 per cent silver and the different blends led to different colours ranging from deep yellow to pale yellowish-white (*ibid.*). By the second millennium, Egypt was a major exporter of gold and it gave the country tremen-

dous economical and political wealth (Johnson 1978). Gold mining in Upper Egypt dates back to predynastic times.

342. Cayley (1926, 1927).

343. Partington (1957: 17).

344. Stillman (1960).

345. *Ibid.*

346. Quoted in Stillman (1960: 97).

347. Spencer (1993).

348. The widespread production of bronze did not occur in Egypt until the New Kingdom (*c.*1500 BC), although it was known in Byblos (Egypt's gateway to Asia) as early as the Eleventh Dynasty of the Middle Kingdom (2040 BC) (Johnson 1978). It appears that the efficient Sumerian furnace (up to 1100 °C) required for smelting and alloying was not utilized by the Egyptians until around 2000 BC.

349. Quirke & Spencer (1992). The source of tin in ancient Egypt is unknown, but it may have come from mines in Drangiana (now included in western Afghanistan and eastern Iran), mentioned by the Greek historian and geographer Strabo of Amaseia (*c.*64 BC–AD 21) (Partington 1957).

350. Quirke & Spencer (1992). The Hyksos were Asiatic invaders (thought to be of Semitic origin) who ruled Egypt from about 1670 to 1570 BC. They were finally driven out of Egypt by Ahmosis, founder of the Eighteenth Dynasty of the New Kingdom (Warren 1975). A second school argues that there was no great invasion of Egypt by the Hyksos, but that they gradually filtered from the east, which eventually led to their control over Lower Egypt and the Nile Delta (Watterson 1997).

351. Quirke & Spencer (1992).

352. Roberts (1995).

353. Shaw & Nicholson (1995).

354. Tylecote (1975); Quirke & Spencer (1992).

355. Shaw & Nicholson (1995).

356. Allen (1988a: ix).

357. Frankfort & Frankfort (1951); Allen (1988a).

358. Allen (1988a).

359. Kramer (1948: 41).

360. Frankfort & Frankfort (1951: 15).

361. Kramer (1948: 42).

362. Gaster (1955: 423–4).

363. Kramer (1948); Gaster (1955).

364. Frankfort & Frankford (1951: 16).

Chapter 4. The Presocratics: from myth to philosophical reason

1. Russell (1959: 10).

2. Burnet (1930).

3. Most (1999: 333).

4. Barnes (1987).

5. Kahn (1960); Hussey (1972). Greek science and philosophy began around 585 BC with Thales of Miletus, and ended in AD 529, when Christian Emperor Justinian banned the teaching of pagan philosophy at the University of Athens.

6. Kahn (1960); Guthrie (1971, 1974); Hussey (1972); Kirk *et al.* (1983); Barnes (1987). The idea of the "divine" probably began as a belief in an external spirit, power or force, which later became synonymous with the gods. According to Greek scholar Werner Jaeger (1888–1961), the word "divine" did not appear in Greek literature before Anaximander (before 600 BC), but was a frequent substitute for "the god(s)" by the time of Herodotus, 150 years later (Jaeger 1936).

7. Originally the Greek *polis* was a fortified site or acropolis located on the highest ground (Snodgrass 1980). It was a community with new forms of self-government and citizenship, from which the word *politics* is derived.

8. Democracy is a Greek word derived from *demos*, meaning "the people" and *kratos*, meaning "rule" or "power". Democracy developed from "rule of the people" by way of elected representatives under a legal constitution. It was the Greek people who made the laws in a democracy as opposed to the god-incarnate pharaoh in ancient Egypt, or the priestly class in Sumer. In the fourth century BC, the Athenian concept of democracy waned and city-states returned to oligarchy ("rule of the few") or tyranny ("rule of one").

9. Emlyn-Jones (1980); Snodgrass (1980); Long (1999b). Notwithstanding the importance of geography and multiculturalism, archaeologist Anthony Snodgrass (1980) thinks a far more likely scenario to the new way of Greek thinking was increased leisure time among the people. Snodgrass (1980) argues that urbanization and increased leisure time came earlier to Ionia than on the mainland (Emlyn-Jones 1980). Aristotle too believed that leisure was an important factor in the development of Presocratic thinking. Some Ionians were farmers, others were businessmen and trade merchants, and others preferred to contemplate the world and reality. Herodotus also reported that the early Ionian thinkers travelled extensively and studied in Egypt and other Near Eastern cultures (Kirk *et al.* 1983). To do this, however, individuals must have had personal wealth (perhaps from a business), a patronage or some form of consultancy.

10. Bury & Meiggs (1975).

11. Warren (1975).

12. *Ibid.*

13. Woolley (1928: 193).

14. Cotterell (1979); Renfrew & Bahn (1996).

15. Cotterell (1979).

16. Bury & Meiggs (1975); Warren (1975).

17. Hollister (1972: 70).

18. Homer was a blind minstrel who is thought to have been a native Ionian and sang of the warrior aristocracy (Stapleton 1978; Emlyn-Jones 1980). Hesiod was a farmer in Ascra in central Greece. A contemporary of Homer, Hesiod was more concerned with the peasant base in society and improving their way of life (Morford & Lenardon 1999).

19. Jaeger (1936).

20. Most (1999).

21. Jaeger (1936); Kirk *et al.* (1983); Lamberton (1988); Vegetti (1995).
22. Morgan (1992); Penglase (1994).
23. Vegetti (1995).
24. Emlyn-Jones (1980).
25. Hinnels (1984).
26. Troy was located along a major trade route and was a vital player in the cultural exchange between the East and the West. The fortified city of Troy had massive stone walls and was surrounded by an enormous ditch (*ibid.*).
27. Lang *et al.* (1950); Stapleton (1978).
28. Lang *et al.* (1950); Morford & Lenardon (1999).
29. Butcher & Lang (1950).
30. Hesiod, from West (1978: 276 ff.).
31. Lloyd (1983: 11).
32. Solon of Athens (*c.*640–560 BC) was a Greek statesman and poet who reformed the Athenian constitution by permitting the citizens to voice their opinions about the governing of the *polis*. He held an election in 594 BC to improve conditions for the peasants and won. Solon was the first to set limits of land ownership among the powerful land nobles and established in law that all free men were given equal rights in the courts of law. He also offered citizenship to immigrant craftsmen to encourage industry and commerce.
33. Kirk *et al.* (1983).
34. Jaeger (1936).
35. Kirk *et al.* (1983).
36. Herodotus, translated by G. Rawlinson, in Jaeger (1936: 183).
37. Homer (*Iliad*: xiv).
38. Hesiod, *Theogony*, 26–28 (Clay 2003). See also Kirk *et al.* (1983: 35).
39. According to Hesiod, the Muses were the daughters of Zeus, created after the victory of the Olympians over the Titans (see Stapleton 1978). The Muses were considered goddesses of wisdom and guardian spirits of writers and artists, and especially of song. The Muses, like all goddesses, did not tolerate competition and anyone found challenging their authority was severely punished.
40. Cornford (1952: 192).
41. Jaeger (1936).
42. Emlyn-Jones (1980).
43. Algra (1999).
44. Hesiod, *Theogony*, 116–33, translated in Cornford (1952: 193).
45. This interpretation of Hesiod's *Theogony* has been compiled from a number of sources: Jaeger (1936); Cary *et al.* (1950); Cornford (1952); Brandon (1963); Guthrie (1971); Algra (1999); Morford & Lenardon (1999); Clay (2003).
46. In Sumerian cosmogony, Heaven and Earth were separated by the god Enlil (Ch.r 2). In Egyptian mythology the separation was ascribed to the air god, Shu, who separated the bodies of Geb (Earth god) and Nut (sky goddess): "The arms of Shu are under Nut, that he may carry her" (Wilson 1951b) (Ch. 3).
47. See Dickinson (1944); Nilsson (1950); Guthrie (1952); Brandon (1963); Brandon (1973a); Warren (1975, 1987); Chadwick (1976); Burkert (1985); Vegetti (1995).
48. The name Zagreus is thought to have been derived from Mount Zagron, which is part of a mountain system of Mesopotamia and Persia (western Iran) (see Fig. 2.2) (Guthrie 1952).
49. Zeus has a long ancestry and has been associated with *Dyaus pitar* in the Indian Vedas (Chadwick 1976). In ancient Greece, Zeus was the king of all Olympian gods. He was born to Rhea, the wife and sister of Kronos. Rhea also bore Poseidon, Pluto, Hestia, Hera, and Demeter (Morford & Lenardon 1999). Rhea's worship was associated with fertility rites, particularly prominent in Crete in Minoan times. The Greeks often identified her with Gaea and Cybele. Among the Babylonians and Assyrians, the "goddess of fertility" was identified as Ishtar (Ch. 2), and among the Egyptians she was called Isis (Ch. 3).
50. Vegetti (1995).
51. Brandon (1963).
52. *Ibid.*
53. *Ibid.*
54. Vegetti (1995).
55. Brandon (1973a).
56. Clay (2003).
57. Morford & Lenardon (1999).
58. Cornford (1952).
59. *Ibid.*
60. Homer, *Odyssey*, XI: 204–22.
61. Hack (1931: 27).
62. Foster (1934).
63. Long (1999b).
64. Aristotle, *Metaphysics* I 983b20–1.
65. Vlastos (1975a); Most (1999).
66. The first rhapsodist on record was Theagenes of Rhegion (fl. 525 BC), who reportedly gave the first allegorical interpretation of Homer (Cary *et al.* 1950). Theagenes' new use of myth appears to have been a reply to Xenophanes' relentless attack on anthropomorphic polytheism (Burkert 1985: 321).
67. Most (1999).
68. Etymologically the word "philosophy" originated from the composite Greek noun, *philosophia*, which means "love or pursuit of wisdom" (Nahm 1964; Taylor 1997a). Although the first Presocratics (Thales, Anaximander and Anaximenes) are often referred to as natural philosophers, the word "philosopher", according to Diogenes Laërtius (fl. AD 250), did not enter the Greek language until around the time of Pythagoras (*c.*572–497 BC) (Nahm 1964). Pythagoras was the first to call himself a philosopher (or lover of wisdom), distinct from those sages before him who were called *sophoi* (or "wise men"). Pythagoras is reported to have said: "Life is like a festival; just as some come ... to compete, some to ply their trade but the rest come as spectators, so in life, the slavish men go hunting for fame or gain, the philosophers for the truth" (Gjertsen 1989: 14).

In general, the term "philosopher" applies to any person who possesses not only practical wisdom, but one who exercises profound speculative insight into the unifying principles of life and the order of the universe. One of the best descriptions of a philosopher is that by Francis M. Cornford, who separated the reasoning processes from the older myth-making practices:

> A philosopher relies for his vision of divinity and of the real nature of things on the assumed identity of his own reason with a portion of the cosmic consciousness. The power of thought immediately discerns a reality akin to itself, which is hidden from the senses. The intuitive reasons or nous replaces that supernormal faculty which had formerly been active in dreams and prophetic visions; the supernatural becomes the metaphysical. All philosophy is based on the postulate that world must be an intelligible order, not a mere welter of sights and sounds flowing in upon the senses from moment to moment.
>
> Cornford (1952: 154)

69. The major cities were Miletus, Colophon, Ephesus, Myus, Priene, Clazomenae, Erythrae, Teos, Lebedos and Phocaea on the Ionian coast, and the two island cities Chios and Samos (Emlyn-Jones 1980).
70. Emlyn-Jones (1980); Snell (1995).
71. Hussey (1972); Emlyn-Jones (1980).
72. Guthrie (1971); Hussey (1995). Where possible in the text that follows, the Fragment number and line numbers of text quoted have been given, together with the details of the translation.
73. Guthrie (1971: 37).
74. Wightman (1953); Guthrie (1971).
75. Jacobsen (1951); Hussey (1995).
76. Barnes (1987).
77. Weisheipl (1954); Hussey (1972, 1995); Bynum *et al.* (1981); Campbell (1992).
78. Oppenheim (1977: 202).
79. Cornford (1991).
80. Aristotle, *Metaphysics* I 983b20; Barnes (1984: 1556).
81. Hussey (1972); Schofield (1997).
82. Malcolm Schofield (1997) points out that Aristotle's information on Thales' idea of water was principally obtained from the authority of Hippias of Elis (*c.*481–411 BC).
83. Guthrie (1971).
84. *Ibid.*; Luce (1992).
85. Popper (1970).
86. Dreyer (1956).
87. *Ibid.*; Lloyd (1973).
88. Mueller (1997).
89. Mueller (1997).
90. Compiled from Genesis 1:2; Jaeger (1936); Sambursky (1956); Guthrie (1971); Hussey (1972); Furley (1973); Long (1973); Kahn (1979); Bynum *et al.* (1981); Corrigan (1986); Barnes (1987); Gerson (1990); Luce (1992); Blackburn (1994); Stead (1994).
91. Dicks (1970).
92. Panchenko (1994: 277).
93. Guthrie (1971).
94. Jaeger (1936); Barnes (1979, 1987).

95. As discussed in Chapter 2, the Mesopotamians had *simtu*: one of the four protective souls (or spirits) associated with specific powers of precious stones (Oppenheim 1977: 203). One wonders if Thales learned of this during his travels to Babylonia.
96. Cherniss (1970); Barnes (1987).
97. Aristotle, *De Anima* I 404a19–21 in Barnes (1984: 645–6).
98. Cherniss (1970).
99. Aristotle, *Metaphysics* I 3983b20; Barnes (1984: 1556).
100. Kirk *et al.* (1983).
101. Schofield (1997: 55).
102. Anaximander was an associate (some say pupil) of Thales (Kahn 1960; Schofield 1997). He wrote on cosmogony, cosmology, astronomy, meteorology, geology, geography and on the evolution of animals and human beings (Kahn 1960; Cherniss 1970).
103. Kahn (1960).
104. The term "unlimited" means that which goes beyond any fixed boundary. Unlimited or boundless is different from the mathematical "infinite" (infinitude of space or time; lines and surfaces; collection of objects). Strictly the "infinite" did not appear until some 100 years later with Zeno and Anaxagoras (Reymond 1927; Blackburn 1994). Where the mathematical analysis of infinity is concerned it was not developed until the nineteenth century, when Georg Cantor (1845–1918) developed his infinite theory of numbers (Bynum *et al.* 1981).
105. Kahn (1960); Kirk *et al.* (1983).
106. Aristotle, *Physics* 4, iii 203b11.
107. Jaeger (1936).
108. *Ibid.*; Kahn (1960).
109. Guthrie (1950); Vlastos (1970).
110. Kahn (1960).
111. *Ibid.*
112. Reymond (1927).
113. Kahn (1960).
114. Schofield (1997: 64).
115. Kirk *et al.* (1983).
116. Hussey (1972).
117. Anaximander offered no solution on how the *apeiron* was continually rotating. It appears that the Milesian philosophers accepted motion as a basic property of world order (Sambursky 1956: 11).
118. Sambursky (1956); Kahn (1960).
119. Plutarch (*c.* AD 46–120) wrote: "at the birth of this world a germ (or seed) of hot and cold is separated off from the eternal (or boundless) and from this a sphere of flame grew around the air surrounding the earth, like bark around a tree" (Lloyd 1970: 21).
120. Algra (1999).
121. Cavendish (1964); Farrington (1964).
122. Sambursky (1956); Schofield (1997).
123. Kirk *et al.* (1983).
124. *Ibid.*
125. Sambursky (1956); Kirk *et al.* (1983).

126. Aristotle, *De caelo* II 295b10–16.
127. Algra (1999).
128. Popper (1970: 133).
129. Hussey (1972); Schofield (1997).
130. McLean & Aspell (1970: 15).
131. Hippolytus, translated in Kirk *et al.* (1983: 141).
132. Cornford (1952); Hussey (1972).
133. Barnes (1979, 1987).
134. Kirk *et al.* (1983).
135. Haeckel (1900, 1905) .
136. Hussey believes that Anaximenes and Anaxagoras did not follow Anaximander's sequence. These two philosophers appear to have recognized the divine and the physical and from there worked on their different world constructions (Hussey, personal communication).
137. Jaeger (1936).
138. Hippolytus described Anaximenes' position:

> He [Anaximenes] said that limitless Air was the principle, from which arises what comes into being, what has become, and what will be, and gods and things divine; but other things arise from its offspring. The form of air is as follows: when it is most uniform it is invisible to sight (atmospheric air); but it is made manifest by cold and heat and moisture and motion. It moves continually; for it would not change as much as it does if it were not in motion. As it thickens or rarefies it appears as different. For when it spreads out into rarer form it becomes fire; winds on the other hand are air as it thickens; from air cloud is produced by compression; and water still by more compression; when further thickened it becomes earth and in its thickest form stones. Kahn (1979: 137)

139. Algra (1999).
140. Samburesky (1956); Hussey (1972).
141. This line of reasoning helped explain how air was released from boiling water; which then formed clouds and may either form rain or snow, which falls again upon earth in a cycle.
142. Anaximenes, *Aetius* I. 3.4, translated in Kirk *et al.* (1983: 158).
143. Jaeger (1936); McLean & Aspell (1970).
144. Dreyer (1956); Kirk *et al.* (1983).
145. Algra (1999).
146. Apparently Anaximenes' system was the first in Greek astronomy where the planets had been distinguished from the stars or heavenly bodies (Dreyer 1956).
147. Schofield (1997).
148. Aristotle, translated in Schofield (1997: 49).
149. Algra (1999).
150. Hussey (1972); Schofield (1997).
151. Xenophanes, at the age of 25, reportedly fled from his hometown of Colophon after its occupation by the Lydians. Xenophanes travelled to Babylon, Egypt, Greece, and Sicily. Although he lived most of his life in Elea (below present-day Naples), his natural philosophy remained essentially Ionian (Schofield 1997).
152. Barnes (1987). The term "theologian" is often associated with Xenophanes to signify his ability to study or discourse about the history of god(s). The earliest use of the term "theologia" seems to be by Plato (*Republic* 379a5) where it is understood as a set of principles based on mythopoeic pronouncements (Gerson 1990: 240). Aristotle used "theologia" to describe the world of mythology but in his *Metaphysics* (VI.1.1026a18–21) he used the term to distinguish *physis* from myth (Gerson 1990). Modern Western thought uses the term theology in two ways: natural theology, meaning accessible to human reason; and revealed theology, based on divine revelation. Others argue that such a two-pronged distinction is misleading because all theology is based principally on revelation (Hinnels 1984; Bullock *et al.* 1988).
153. Jaeger (1936).
154. Xenophanes' world was composed of two regions: the earth and the air. The heavenly bodies were burning masses of vapour or ignited clouds, not gods. He believed that the sun did not revolve around the earth but went in a straight line and disappeared in the evenings. The next morning a new sun was formed from small sparks (Stace 1920; Barnes 1987). Xenophanes thought that he had solved the puzzle of what kept the earth in place by declaring that the earth had roots that extended to infinity (Evans 1998). In addition, Xenophanes anticipated the science of palaeontology and geology (Barnes 1987). The mystery of shells and petrified marine animals found on the inland mountains and quarries of Syracuse were explained in the following way. Long ago the land was covered by the sea and, as it gradually rose it left inland marine fossil deposits. Xenophanes believed that the uplifted land would again sink and take with it the entire human race. The earth would then rise again as part of a grand cycle and the human species would be regenerated (Pease 1942). Hippolytus wrote on Xenophanes' views:

> Xenophanes thinks that a mixture of the Earth with the sea is going on, and that in time the Earth is dissolved by the moist. He says that he has demonstrations of the following kind: shells are found inland, and in the mountains, and in the quarries in Syracuse he says that an impression of a fish and of seaweed has been found, while an impression of a bay-leaf was found in Paros in the depth of the rock, and in Malta flat shapes of all marine objects. These, he says, were produced when everything was long ago covered in mud, and that the impression was dried in the mud. All mankind is destroyed when the earth is carried down to the sea and becomes mud; then there is another beginning of coming-to-be, and this foundation happens for all the worlds.
> (translated in Kirk *et al.* 1983)

155. Kirk *et al.* (1983).
156. Quoted in *ibid.*, 169.

157. *Ibid.*, 168.
158. Nahm (1964).
159. Algra (1999).
160. Aristotle, *Metaphysics* 986b21; Jaeger (1936).
161. *Fragment* 23, translated in Kirk *et al.* (1983: 169).
162. Stead (1994).
163. According to Simplicius:
    Always he remains in the same place, moving not at all; nor is it fitting for him to go to different places at different times, but without toil he shakes all things by the thought of his mind ... All of him sees, all thinks, and all hears.   (translated in Kirk *et al.* 1983: 169)
164. *Fragments* 25–26; Kirk *et al.* (1983: 169).
165. Jaeger (1936: 44).
166. *Fragments* 25–6; Kirk *et al.* (1983: 169).
167. Heraclitus was a native of the Ionian port city of Ephesus, located about 50 km north of Miletus. Unlike Miletus, Ephesus was spared from the attacks by the Persians (they surrendered to them shortly after 540 BC) and continued as one of the major trade cities of Asia Minor.
168. Kahn (1979). Heraclitus is often grouped (and contrasted) with the Eleatics (Parmenides and Zeno) because of his obsession with the problem of change (Burnet 1930). Zeller and Burnet grouped him with the Ionians because his philosophy is best understood against the Ionian worldviews (Burnet 1930; Kahn 1979).
169. Kahn (1979).
170. For Plato, Heraclitus was the originator of the idea of universal flux, which he contrasted with Parmenides, who denied change altogether (*ibid.*).
171. Kirk *et al.* (1983), Blackburn (1994).
172. Cherniss (1970); Kahn (1979).
173. Kirk (1960).
174. Guthrie (1971); Kahn (1979).
175. Kahn (1979).
176. *Ibid.*
177. Cornford (1932); Jaeger (1936).
178. Kahn (1979).
179. Kirk (1960); Kahn (1979).
180. Kirk (1970b: 173).
181. Hussey (1999).
182. Cornford (1952); Kahn (1979).
183. Kahn (1979).
184. *Ibid.*
185. Luce (1992).
186. Barnes (1987).
187. Nahm (1964).
188. Guthrie (1974).
189. Kahn (1979).
190. Jaeger (1936); Russell (1959).
191. Guthrie (1971).
192. Guthrie (1950).
193. Hussey (1999).
194. *Ibid.*, 101.
195. Clement of Alexandria, translated in Hussey (1999: 99).
196. Burnet (1930).
197. Hussey (1999: 100).
198. *Fragment* 31, translated in Jaeger (1936: 123).
199. Barnes (1987).
200. Luce (1992: 31).
201. Huffman (1999).
202. Gorman (1979).
203. Guthrie (1950).
204. Plato, *Republic*, X 600a9–b5.
205. Gorman (1979); Clark (1994); Hussey (1997).
206. Huffman (1999).
207. Kirk *et al.* (1983).
208. Burkert (1985).
209. Burkert (1972); Kingsley (1995); Hussey (1997); Huffman (1999); Long (1999b).
210. Hippasus, according to Aristotle, was one of the Pythagoreans, who "first laid hold of mathematics and advanced it" (*Metaphysics* I.5 985b24). His work appears to have demonstrated the relations between whole number ratios and the concordant musical intervals (Huffman 1999).
211. Huffman (1999).
212. Burkert (1972); Huffman (1999).
213. Guthrie (1974: 270).
214. Cavendish (1964).
215. Aristotle, *Metaphysics* I.5 985b23.
216. Gorman (1979).
217. Sambursky (1956).
218. Farrington (1964); McLean & Aspell (1970); Haar (1973).
219. The ancient Greeks lacked the number zero as well as the arithmetic notation that enabled them to add, subtract and multiply. The Greeks commonly used the cumbersome letters of the alphabet to symbolize numerical quantities, as did the later Romans. In contrast, the Pythagoreans used arithmetical manipulation in groups of tens (interestingly 10 and 60 was the basis of the sexagesimal system of the Sumerians 2500 years earlier). Since no zero existed, the Pythagorean unity (a single pebble) performed two functions: it was both a one-dimensional unit of construction and a non-dimensional mathematical point of contact between two sections (Sambursky 1956).
220. Sambursky (1956); Cavendish (1964); Cherniss (1970); Guthrie (1971); Kirk *et al.* (1983).
221. Aristotle, *De Caelo* II 13 293a16–35; 293b1–6.
222. Huffman (1999).
223. *Ibid.*
224. Sambursky (1956).
225. Abetti (1952); Guthrie (1971).
226. Huffman (1999).
227. Abetti (1952); Kirk *et al.* (1983).
228. Dreyer (1956).
229. Kuhn (1957).
230. Aristotle wrote the following on Pythagoras's "harmony of the spheres":
    From all this it is clear that the theory that the movement of the stars produces harmony, i.e. that the sounds they make are concordant, in spite of the grace and originality with which it has been stated, is nevertheless untrue. Some think that the motion

of bodies of that size must produce noise, since on our earth the motion of bodies far inferior in size and in speed of movement has that effect. Also, when the sun and moon, they say, and all the stars, so great in number and size, are moving with so rapid motion, how should they not produce a sound immensely great. Starting from this argument and from the observation that their speeds, as measured by their distances, are in the same ratios as musical concordances, they assert that the sound given forth by the circular movement of the stars is a harmony. Since, however, it appears unaccountable that we should not hear this music, they explain this by saying that the sound is in our ears from the very moment of birth and is thus indistinguishable from its contrary silence, since sound and silence are discriminated by mutual contrast.

Aristotle (*De Caelo* II 9 290b12)

231. The Pythagoreans, especially Hippasus (fl. *c.*470 BC), investigated the relations between the lengths of strings in musical instruments and the harmonic combinations they produce. They used a monochord, which was a string that can be varied in length and subjected to different tensions caused by a suspended weight. Using the same weight, and varying the length of the string, the Pythagoreans reportedly found that the pairs of harmonic tones were described by a simple mathematical relation: the length ratio 2:1 corresponded to an octave; the ratio 3:2, a fifth; and the ratio 4:3, a fourth (Russell 1959; Nahm 1964). Pythagoreans extended their philosophy from harmony of strings to the movement of the heavenly bodies. They postulated that since the motion of the planets must be "harmonious" their distance from the earth must stand in the same relation as the lengths of the strings of the Greek musical instrument, the lyre, under equal tension.

232. Cavendish (1964).
233. Stead (1994).
234. Herodotus (1928: Bk II, 123).
235. Burkert (1985).
236. McLean & Aspell (1970: 27); Luce 1992: 34.
237. Huffman (1999).
238. Guthrie (1971).
239. *Ibid.*, 470.
240. Cherniss (1970).
241. Sedley (1999).
242. Barnes (1987).
243. Hussey (1997).
244. *Ibid.*
245. Sedley (1999).
246. Cherniss (1970).
247. Translated in Kirk *et al.* (1983: 244).
248. Simplicius's translation of Parmenides' *Fragment* 8 is:

There is only one description of the way remaining, (namely), that (What is) Is. To this way there are very many sign-posts: that Being has no-coming-into-being and no destruction, for it is whole of limb, without motion, and without end. And it never Was, nor Will Be, because it Is now, a Whole all together, One, continuous; for what creation of it will you look for? How, whence (could it have) sprung? Nor shall I allow you to speak of it from springing from Not-Being; for it is neither expressible nor thinkable that What-Is-Not Is. Also what necessity impelled it, if it did spring from Nothing, to be produced later or earlier? This it must Be absolutely, or not at all. Nor will the force of credibility ever admit that anything should come into being, beside Being itself, out of Non-Being. So far as that is concerned, Justice has never released (Being) in its fetters and set it free either to come into being or to perish, but holds it fast. The decision on these matters depends on the following: IT IS, or IT IS NOT. IT is therefore decided-as it inevitable-(that one must) ignore the one way as unthinkable and inexpressible (for it is no true way) and take the other as the way of Being and Reality. How could Being perish? How could it come into Being? It came into being, it IS NOT, and so too if it is about to be at some future time. Thus Coming-into-Being is quenched, and Destruction also into the unseen.

Nor is Being divisible, since it is all alike. Nor is there anything (here or) there which could prevent it from holding together, nor any lesser thing, but all is full of being. Therefore it is altogether continuous; for Being is close to Being.

But it is motionless ... And remaining the same in the same place, it rests by itself and thus remains there fixed ... because it is decreed by divine law that Being shall not be without boundary. For it is not lacking; but if it were (spatially infinite), it would be lacking everything.

But there is a (spatial) Limit, it is complete on every side, like the mass of a well rounded sphere, equally balanced from its centre in every direction ... For, in all directions equal to itself, it reaches its limits uniformly.

(*Physica*, 145, 1–27; 146, 7–15; translated in McLean & Aspell 1970: 42)

249. Sedley (1999: 115).
250. Barnes (1987).
251. *Ibid.*
252. Algra (1999).
253. Russell (1959: 29).
254. Russell (1945: 49).
255. Barnes (1987); McKirahan (1999).
256. Kasner & Newman (1940); Russell (1956).
257. Asimov (1966).
258. Bell (1945).
259. Kingsley (1995). Empedocles was a charismatic figure; a popular, self-professed prophet of god who could heal the sick, control the winds, produce the

rain and bring the dead back to life (Most 1999: 355). After accusing his fellow natural philosophers of having "wandered everywhere", he declared that he would reveal as much of the divine as the law allowed. Empedocles' true legacy, however, was not in prophecy, but in philosophy.

260. Wright (1997).
261. Kingsley (1995).
262. Algra (1999).
263. Kingsley (1995).
264. Cherniss (1970).
265. Wright (1997).
266. Jaeger (1936).
267. Luce (1992); Wright (1997).
268. Barnes (1987).
269. *Fragment* 17, lines 27–35, translated in Kirk *et al.* (1983: 290).
270. Wright (1997: 181).
271. Barnes (1987).
272. Hussey (1972).
273. *Ibid.*
274. Luce (1992).
275. *Fragment* 17, lines 7–13; translated in Kirk *et al.* (1983: 287).
276. Kirk *et al.* (1983).
277. Hack (1931).
278. Kirk *et al.* (1983).
279. Barnes (1987: 42).
280. Dreyer (1956).
281. Kirk *et al.* (1983).
282. Hussey (1972).
283. Aetius, translated in Kirk *et al.* (1983: 303).
284. *Fragment* 61, translated in Kirk *et al.* (1983: 303).
285. Hussey (1972).
286. *Ibid.*
287. *Fragment* 134, translated in Kirk *et al.* (1983: 312).
288. *Fragment* 135, translated in Hack (1931: 96).
289. Hack (1931); Hussey (1972); Cornford (1975).
290. Guthrie (1974).
291. Barnes (1987).
292. Hussey (1972). Empedocles believed that human thought took place primarily in the blood, which was composed of a near perfect mixing of the four elements (Long 1973).
293. Hack (1931).
294. Long (1973).
295. Luce (1992).
296. *Fragment* 134, translated in Kirk *et al.* (1983: 312).
297. Luce (1992).
298. Barnes (1987).
299. Hack (1931); Russell (1959).
300. Barnes (1987: 45).
301. Anaxagoras was an Ionian. He was a contemporary of Empedocles, and several fragments of his "Treatise on Nature" have survived (Barnes 1987). In his early forties, Anaxagoras moved to Athens, where he befriended and taught Pericles, the inventor of Western democracy.
302. *Ibid.*
303. Luce (1992: 67–8).

304. Anaxagoras believed that there was infinite diversity beyond our senses (Hussey 1972).
305. *Fragment* 1, translated in Kirk *et al.* (1983: 358).
306. Translated in Kirk *et al.* (1983: 360).
307. Long (1973).
308. Cornford (1975); Strang (1975); Vlastos (1975b).
309. Cornford (1975).
310. In Anaxagoras's own words:

> and Mind controls all things … Mind controlled also the whole rotation, so that it began to rotate in the beginning. And it began to rotate first from a small area, but it now rotates over a wider and will rotate over a wider area still. And the things that are mingled and separated and divided off, all are known by Mind. And all things that were to be – those that were and those that era now and those that shall be – Mind arranged them all, including that rotation that in which are now rotating the stars, the sun and moon, the air and the aether that are being separated off. And this rotation caused the separating off. And the dense is separated off from the rare, the hot from the cold, the bright from the dark and the dry from the moist. But there are many portions of many things, and nothing is altogether separated off nor divided one from the other except Mind. Mind is all alike, both the greater and smaller quantities of it, while nothing else is like anything else, but each single body is and was most plainly those things of which it contains most.   (*Fragment* 12, translated in Kirk *et al.* 1983: 363)

311. Kirk *et al.* (1983).
312. Cornford (1975).
313. Kirk *et al.* (1983: 363).
314. McLean & Aspell (1970: 58).
315. Hussey (1972).
316. Guthrie (1974: 277).
317. Kahn (1960).
318. Vlastos (1991).
319. Taylor (1997b).
320. McDougall (1911).
321. Dreyer (1956).
322. Kahn (1979).
323. Kirk *et al.* (1983).
324. *Ibid.*
325. Kirk *et al.* (1983: 378).
326. Barnes (1987).
327. Taylor (1999).
328. Algra (1999).
329. Guthrie (1974).
330. Taylor (1999: 185).
331. Aristotle, *De gen. et corr.* 325a2, translated in Kirk *et al.* (1983: 403).
332. Guthrie (1974).
333. Taylor (1999).
334. Kirk *et al.* (1983).
335. *Fragment* 9, translated in McLean & Aspell (1970: 68).
336. Cornford (1975); Vlastos (1975b).

337. Guthrie (1974).
338. Aristotle, *De Caelo* 295 11; translated in McLean & Aspell (1970: 65).
339. Kirk *et al.* (1983).
340. Kahn (1960); Schofield (1997).
341. Taylor (1999).
342. Guthrie (1974).
343. Aetius, translated in Kirk *et al.* (1983: 428).
344. Kirk *et al.* (1983); Barnes (1987).
345. Taylor (1999).
346. Kirk *et al.* (1983).
347. Guthrie (1974).
348. Stead (1994).
349. Barnes (1987).
350. Guthrie (1974).
351. Taylor (1999).
352. McGibbon (1965); Gerson (1990).
353. Guthrie (1974); Stead (1994).
354. *Fragment* 166, translated in McLean & Aspell (1970: 67).
355. Guthrie (1974).
356. Cavendish (1964).
357. Guthrie (1974: 480).
358. Guthrie (1974).
359. Cornford (1952: 154).
360. Algra (1999).
361. Einstein (1950b: 59).
362. Cherniss (1970: 12).
363. Translated in Kirk *et al.* (1983: 179).
364. Denyer (1991).
365. Lesher (1999).
366. *Fragment* 34, translated in Popper (1970: 152).
367. Translated in Popper (1970: 153).
368. Popper (1970: 153).
369. Barnes (1987).
370. Burnyeat (1982, 1983).
371. Denyer (1991).
372. Popper (1965: 26).
373. Popper (1970).
374. Vlastos (1975a: 20).
375. Most (1999).
376. Xenophanes seems to have escaped harsh criticism, but Anaxagoras was not so lucky. Anaxagoras was tried in Athens for treason for claiming that the heavenly bodies were not gods, but made of physical matter (Vlastos 1975a). Similarly, in the fifth century Protagoras was banished from Athens for the following statement: "About the gods I am not able to know whether they exist or do not exist, nor what they are like in form; for the factors preventing knowledge are many: the obscurity of the subject, and the shortness of human life" (*Fragment* 4, translated in McLean & Aspell 1970: 82).
377. Cherniss (1970: 153).
378. Kahn (1960).

Chapter 5. Classical philosophy: different roads to truth

1. Quoted in Hollister (1972: 87).
2. Cassirer (1950: 5).
3. Cornford (1952).
4. Cornford (1932: 50).
5. Vlastos (1991).
6. McLean & Aspell (1970); Barabas (1986).
7. Luce (1992: 91). Socrates reportedly spoke these words to the jury in the court of Athens in 399 BC. He believed that the purpose of human life was to examine one's inner self and strive for personal and spiritual growth.
8. In his *Phaedo* (97 & 98), Plato tells how Socrates was excited on first hearing about Anaxagoras's idea of a world caused and ruled by mind or intelligence, but after reading Anaxagoras's book he became bitterly disappointed and turned his enquiry from nature to the human condition (Cornford 1932).
9. Guthrie (1950); Cornford (1952); Nahm (1964).
10. Taton (1963).
11. Smith (1995).
12. Plato, *Apology* 32.
13. Under the Roman Empire, the term "Sophist" applied to professors of rhetoric, orators, and prose writers. As a result of Plato and Aristotle's fierce opposition to the profession, the meaning in modern times usually is taken to be a "captious or fallacious reasoner or quibbler" (Stevenson 1972).
14. Brickhouse (1989).
15. Most (1999).
16. Guthrie (1950).
17. Patterson (1985: 100–101).
18. Aristotle, *Ethics. Eud.* I 1216b3, translated in Barnes (1984: 1925).
19. Cornford (1932: 37).
20. Benson (1997).
21. Guthrie (1950).
22. Socrates believed that the seat of this faculty of insight, the place where we can know good from evil or right from wrong, was found not in the body but in the immortal soul. The truth was stored in a "memory" from a former state of existence before it came into the body at birth. Tapping into this new kind of knowledge was essential in promoting moral excellence and social well-being (Cornford 1932).
23. Vlastos (1991).
24. Aristotle described Socrates' preoccupation with definitions:

    Socrates, however, was busying himself about ethical matters and neglecting the world of nature as a whole but seeking the universal in these ethical matters, and fixed thought for the first time on definitions; Plato accepted his teaching, but held the problem applied not to sensible things but to entities of another kind.

    (*Metaphysics* I 6 987b1–4)
25. Guthrie (1950).
26. Plato, *Apology*, 31; *Republic*, 496.
27. McLean & Aspell (1970); Gjertsen (1989).
28. Vlastos (1991).
29. *Ibid.*
30. *Ibid.*, 158.

31. Plato, *Euthyphro* 2B1–4; translated in Vlastos (1991: 293).
32. Brickhouse & Smith (1989).
33. R. L. Nettleship, quoted in Becker & Barnes (1961: 68).
34. Kraut (1992).
35. Crombie (1962).
36. The word "academy" is believed to have derived from the legendary Attic hero *Academos* (or Hecademus), who was instrumental in helping Castor and Pollux rescue Helen of Sparta after she was kidnapped (Ronan 1982). Plato's Academy was located about 2 km outside the city walls and was intended to provide an education suitable for legislators and administrators. Students at the Academy walked about while in discussion, hence the name "Peripatetic" School (from the Greek word "walking about"). The name "Peripatetic" is also associated with Aristotle's school in the Lyceum (see text).
37. The curriculum was similar to that in Pythagorean schools: arithmetic, geometry, astronomy and harmonics (sound), philosophy and the art of dialectic. The Academy was a place where scholars could study how to shift from the world of sense to the world of ideas that lay hidden behind.
38. Plato, *Republic* V.473c6–7. See also Taylor (1934); Furley (1973); Price (1997).
39. Furley (1973); Hare (1982).
40. Vlastos (1975a: 23).
41. Crombie (1962: 153).
42. Cornford (1941); Kraut (1992).
43. Rowe (1997).
44. Taylor (1934: 2).
45. Taylor (1934); Bynum *et al.* (1981); Heinaman (1997).
46. Mathews (1972).
47. Cornford (1941: xxvii, 180); Huby (1964: 18).
48. Heinaman (1997).
49. Plato, *Republic*, Bk 5, para. 89.
50. Cross & Woozley (1979); Blackburn (1994).
51. Cross & Woozley (1979).
52. Lloyd (1968); Denyer (1991).
53. Denyer (1991).
54. Crombie (1962); Mathews (1972).
55. Huby (1964); Denyer (1991).
56. Cooper (1970).
57. Taylor (1997a).
58. Ross (1927).
59. Taton (1963); Cross & Woozley (1979).
60. Finney (1973: 390).
61. Cornford (1935); Crombie (1964); Craig (1980); Hare (1982).
62. Crombie (1964).
63. Schuhl (1973).
64. Philip (1973); Sorabji (1988); Rowe (1997).
65. Plato, *Phaedrus* 245 e.
66. Furley (1973); Rowe (1997).
67. Plato, *Laws*, 896 a.
68. Burkert (1985: 329).
69. Vlastos (1975a: 26).
70. Taylor (1934); Cornford (1937); Vlastos (1975a).
71. Cornford (1937: 34).
72. Burkert (1985: 328).
73. Crombie (1962, 1964); Vlastos (1975a).
74. Stewart (1965).
75. Crombie (1962).
76. Stewart (1965).
77. Burkert (1985: 328).
78. Cornford (1937: 34).
79. That the soul survives death was Plato's way of separating mind from body (Taylor 1997a). Plato believed the wise and the good would enjoy a better life after death than the ignorant and the bad, an idea that gained increasing acceptance among the Greek people in the late fifth and early fourth centuries BC (Price 1997). The highest honour for anyone's soul was to be reincarnated on one of the planets.
80. Cornford (1935).
81. Plato, *Timaeus* 42 a–d.
82. Finney (1973).
83. Burkert (1985).
84. Taylor (1934); Craig (1980).
85. Cornford (1937).
86. Hussey (1986: 19–20).
87. Cornford (1937); Stewart (1965); Furley (1973).
88. Furley (1973).
89. Sorabji (1988).
90. Cornford (1937: 361).
91. Brandon (1963); Jones (1969).
92. Taylor (1934).
93. Plato appears to have rejected the concept of the innumerable coexisting worlds (or *cosmoi*) implied by Anaximander, and explicitly stated by the later atomists, Leucippus and Democritus (Hussey 1972). In addition, Plato did not believe in the succession of cycles of universes as proposed by Empedocles, and some older Hindu cosmogonic myths.
94. Cornford (1937); Craig (1980); Burkert (1985).
95. Ronan (1961); Chadwick (1991).
96. Ross (1950).
97. Gorman (1979).
98. Vlastos (1975a).
99. Furley (1973); Vlastos (1975a).
100. Crombie (1994).
101. Hussey (1986: 19–20).
102. Hussey (1986).
103. Ronan (1982).
104. Stewart (1965); Vlastos (1975a).
105. Solmsen (1960).
106. Vlastos (1975a).
107. Plato, *Timaeus* 55C.
108. Owen (1970); Johnson (1973); Hussey (1986).
109. Hussey (1986: 20).
110. Hussey (1986); Luce (1992).
111. Vlastos (1975a).
112. Cornford (1937: 28).
113. Vlastos (1975a: 65).
114. Crombie (1962: 153).
115. *Ibid.*, 392.
116. Crombie (1962); Vlastos (1975a).
117. Mathews (1972).
118. Burkert (1985); Morgan (1992).

119. Quoted in Farrington (1965: 22).
120. Crombie (1962: 365).
121. Vegetti (1995).
122. Ross (1927: v).
123. Guthrie (1981).
124. Barnes (1991).
125. It is not clear why Aristotle left Athens. It may have been out of great disappointment at Plato leaving the headship of the Academy to nephew Speusippus, or it might have been a reaction to the rapid rise in anti-Macedonian sentiment that had arisen after Philip II of Macedon had sacked the city-state of Olynthus. Nonetheless, Aristotle relocated to the coastal town of Assos, which grew to become a scholarly community under the authority of Hermias. After some time Aristotle came to be the most prominent among the scholars and married Hermias's niece, Pythias. After Assos, Aristotle moved to the nearby island of Lesbos, which was noted for the foundations of the biological sciences.
126. Barnes (1991).
127. Aristotle and his pupils philosophized (or discoursed) among themselves in a covered walkway. The root of own word "discourse" literally means "running from one place to another".
128. Early in Aristotle's career, he wrote on a number of ethical themes that greatly influenced Plato (only fragments remain). Some of his most famous works are in physics (natural philosophy), metaphysics (theology), logic, biology, psychology (*On the Soul*), ethics, politics and literary criticism (Ross 1959; Huby 1985; Lloyd 1987; Barnes 1991).
129. Jaeger (1934); Stahl (1962).
130. Ross (1950: 95).
131. Barnes (1991).
132. Quoted in Knowles (1999: 25).
133. Aristotle, *On the Soul* III 432a5–7, in Barnes (1984: vol. 1, 687).
134. Aristotle, *Analytic Posterior* II 19 99b, translated in Barnes (1984: 166).
135. Aristotle, *De interpretatione* I 16a4.
136. Allen (1970: 17).
137. O'Connor (1964a).
138. Aristotle repeatedly argued that nature was purposeful and goal-directed without postulating a divine mind governing and controlling the world from the outside. Physical objects in Aristotle's system have their "ends" within themselves; the "Earth naturally seeks its own place, and the young boy naturally grows into a man" (Lloyd 1968: 62).
139. Allen (1970: 84).
140. Aristotle, *Metaphysic* VII (Z) 1–4, translated in Barnes (1984: 1623–5).
141. Frede (1985); Corrigan (1986).
142. Blackburn (1994); Wagner (1996).
143. Allen (1970: 29).
144. J. Owens, quoted in Craig (1980: 41).
145. A full understanding of Aristotle's "four causes" is somewhat hampered because he did not precisely define what he meant by the term "cause".

Most scholars believe he meant the factor responsible for *B* forming from *A*, which is different from the modern scientific sense of *A* causes *B*. In his *Metaphysics* a cause is "the maker of what is made and the change of what is changed" (V.2 1013a31–2). Thus a "cause" in early Greek philosophy is usually translated as that which was "responsible" for something happening or why something was as it was (O'Conner 1964; Wallace 1972). Clearer definitions of "cause" were used by the Hippocratic doctors (Vegetti 1999), and did not reappear in the West until the rebirth of natural science in the late medieval period and specifically in the seventeenth century, in the work of Galileo (Drake 1981).
146. Aristotle believed that the sensible properties of objects fall within ranges of extremes such as light and dark, sweet and bitter, hard and soft, and so on. Human beings detect objects differently because they take up different positions on the scale of opposites. Any change in the world implies a passage between two contraries – from one to the other, or somewhere between the two – and for this to occur there must be a substrate that changes and survives the change (Owen 1970). On this point, Aristotle does not believe that new types emerge in nature. In *Physics* (II8), he rejected the idea of evolution (Owen 1970: 254).
147. Grant (1996).
148. Kahn (1985).
149. Craig (1980).
150. O'Connor (1964a).
151. Kahn (1985).
152. Lloyd (1968).
153. Smith (1995).
154. *Ibid.*
155. The *Organon* comprised six parts: (i) *Categories* (classification of the classes into which all concepts are derived, e.g. substance, quantity, quality, relation, action, passion, place, time, situation and habits); (ii) *De interpretatione* (proposition and judgement); (iii) *Prior Analytic* (reasoning – deductive and inductive); (iv) *Posterior Analytic* (discussion on demonstrative knowledge and science); (v) *Topics* (concerned largely with probabilities); and (vi) *Sophistic fallacies* (containing an attack on the Sophists).
156. O'Connor (1964b).
157. Farrington (1965); Owen (1970).
158. Smith (1995).
159. C. C. W. Taylor (1990).
160. Aristotle, *Analytics Pr.* I 1 24a18–20, translated in Barnes (1984: 126); for more details see Smith (1995).
161. Hussey (1986); Hankinson (1995a).
162. Aristotle, *Post Analytics* I 12 71a21–33, translated in Barnes (1984: 126); for more details see Hankinson (1995a).
163. Wherever possible, Aristotle used mathematical axioms and theorems to describe physical and mechanical relations among objects. Mathematics captured certain qualities of physical things, but

left unexplained their true natures, such as their natural tendency for change (which could not be reduced by mathematics) (Deason 1986: 168). Aristotle viewed number, proportion, quantity and geometrical shapes as pure human abstraction of sense-experience (Hussey 1983).

164. Sorabji (1988); Crombie (1994).
165. Hankinson (1995a).
166. For Aristotle, the most perfect kind of logical demonstration (*or quia*) was proof through the proper, immediate, and commensurate *cause* of an effect or fact. The process he called *propter quid* demonstration reduced complex phenomena to simple principles by either definition or demonstration (Weisheipl 1978). The *propter quid* demonstration was proof of a fact through a true cause or reason for the fact.
167. Wallace (1972); Smith (1995).
168. Hussey (1983: xxxiii).
169. Hussey (1983).
170. Craig (1980); Hussey (1983).
171. Aristotle used three pieces of evidence for a spherical Earth: (i) heavy bodies tend to fall toward the centre of the Earth; (ii) a curved shadow is cast during eclipses; and (iii) for small changes in north–south movements on Earth the star map changes dramatically. Aristotle accepted that the circumference of the Earth was about 64 000 km.
172. Farrington (1964, 1980).
173. Crombie (1964).
174. Farrington (1964).
175. Evans (1998).
176. Farrington (1964).
177. Allen (1970).
178. Farrington (1965); Allen (1970).
179. Ross (1959); Farrington (1965); Lloyd (1968); Allen (1970).
180. Owen (1970).
181. "Planet" was derived from the Greek word meaning "vagabond" from the wanderings of the planets in the night sky (Farrington 1965: 21). Aristotle solved the problem by putting more spheres in place, to help to account for the erratic changes observed (*ibid.*). Years earlier, Plato had questioned the divinity of planets and the Academy's astronomers also added a number of different motions to "save the appearances".
182. Hankinson (1995b).
183. Farrington (1965).
184. Ross summarized Aristotle's cosmology:

The universe consists of a series of concentric spheres. The earth is a sphere of no great relative size, at rest at the centre of the universe. The outer shell of the universe – the "first" heaven – is a finite sphere containing what we now call the fixed stars. These stars have no motion of their own but are carried round by the uniform rotation of the first heaven once in twenty-four hours. With regard to the more complex movements of the sun, the moon, and the planets Aristotle adopts with a modification the theory of Eudoxus as it had been developed by his own friend Callippus …

… Aristotle assigns (intermediary) spheres moving in directions contrary to those of the original spheres and allowing only the movement of the outermost sphere of each system (the daily rotation from east to west) to be carried through to the system inside it. He thus gets 55 spheres in all …

The movement of the first heaven is due to the action of God, operating as an object of love and desire … But the proper motions of the sun, moon, and planets involve spheres rotating in directions different from that of the first heaven, and this movement he explains by the action not of God but of a separate motive agent for each sphere – the "intelligences" of the schoolmen. He (Aristotle) certainly means to reach a monistic system; he adopts as his own the Homeric maxim "the rule of many is not good; one ruler let there be". The intelligences must be inferior to the prime mover, but their actual relation to God is quite obscure, as is also their mode of operation on the spheres. As they are incorporeal (non-physical) beings, presumably they too act not as physical agents but as objects of desire.
(1924: 96–8; 384–7)

185. Johnson (1973).
186. Hussey (1986); Johnson (1973).
187. Ross (1959: 159).
188. Guthrie (1950).
189. Adapted from Craig (1980: 24).
190. As Ross explains: "He (God) moves directly the 'first heaven' ie., He causes the daily rotation of the stars around the Earth. Since He moves by inspiring love and desire, it seems to be implied that the 'first heaven' has soul. And this is confirmed by statements elsewhere that the heavenly bodies are living beings" (1959: 181).
191. Guthrie (1950); Ross (1959); Gerson (1990).
192. Campbell (1992).
193. O'Connor (1964a); Kahn (1985); Gerson (1990).
194. Kahn argues a more direct involvement of God in the sublunary spheres. He believes that "everything in Nature aspires to the condition of deity; but each kind of thing can attain this goal only in a limited, specific way" (1985: 184). God is the source of actualization in the sublunary sphere and all motion and change were brought about by God's *direct* actions (e.g. day and night, the seasons). Kahn concludes: "And so the prime mover has a special role as mover of the simple, uniform motion of the First Heaven, in addition to its more general role as the goal of the universal tendency of nature to move from potency to act, from unrealised matter to realised form" (1985: 203). Ross, a traditionalist, would have agreed with Kahn to some extent, but would not have agreed that God permeated nature. Ross summarized his position:

The conception of god presented in Aristotle is certainly an unsatisfactory one. God, as conceived by Aristotle, has a knowledge which is not knowledge of the universe, and an influence on the universe which does not flow from His knowledge; an influence on the universe which can hardly be called an activity since it is the sort of influence that one person may unconsciously have on another, or even a statue or a picture may have on its admirer. Little wonder that commentators have found it hard to believe that this is really Aristotle's view, and have tried to read something different into what he says.
(1959: 183)

195. Kahn (1985).
196. Aristotle, *De Anima* II 1 412b5, translated in Barnes (1984: 657); for further discussion see Barnes (1991: 156).
197. Barnes (1991).
198. Aristotle, *De Anima*, translated in Barnes (1984: 641–92).
199. Atherton (1986: 125).
200. Barnes (1991).
201. Farrington (1964); Lloyd (1968); Allen (1970).
202. Mayr (1982).
203. See Aristotle's *History of the Animals* 539a18–33, translated in Barnes (1984: 852); 547b13–22, translated in Barnes (1984: 864); 569a21–569b3, translated in Barnes (1984: 894).
204. Allen (1970).
205. Lloyd (1968); McHenry (1969).
206. Gruenberg (1929).
207. Allen (1988b); Assmann (1995); Lesko (1995); Van Dijk (1995).
208. McHenry (1969).
209. Marenbon (1983).
210. Roger (1986).
211. Corrigan (1986).
212. *Ibid.*; Barnes (1991).
213. Farrington (1965); Barnes (1991).
214. Haren (1985).
215. Farrington (1965).
216. Barnes (1991).
217. Farrington (1965: 84).
218. Gerson (1990: 140).
219. Barnes (1991).
220. *Ibid.*, 158.
221. Weisheipl (1954: 388).
222. The term "metaphysics" appears to have originated in the first century BC when Andronicus of Rhodes edited Aristotle's works. Andronicus placed Aristotle's "first philosophy" after (*meta*) his physics (Hatfield 1990). Kant questioned this interpretation and argued that *meta* meant "trans", meaning the science of things beyond the physical, thus providing a link between "first philosophy" and the study of God (*ibid.*). To Aristotle, his *Metaphysics* represented the knowledge of the first, highest or most general principles of the universe. All other branches were subordinate in the sense that they dealt with principles less universal in scope, but not in importance. The modern name for metaphysics is "ontology" or the science of being. In short, metaphysics attempts to claim truths of existence by reason beyond human experience (*ibid.*).
223. Allen (1970: 118).
224. Owen (1970).
225. Cornford (1991: 261).
226. Aristotle, *Metaphysics* XI 1074b1–10, translated in Barnes (1984: 1698).
227. Hamilton (1957: 103).
228. Edelstein (1966); Longrigg (1993).
229. Longrigg (1993: 2).
230. Davey (2001).
231. Edelstein (1966: 208).
232. Edelstein (1937); Kudlien (1968); Longrigg (1993).
233. Longrigg (1989).
234. The relevant passage of Homer's account runs as follows:

> The arrows rattled on the shoulders of the angry god when he moved and his coming was like the night. Then he sat down apart from the ships and let fly a shaft. Terrible was the twang of the silver bow. He attacked the mules first and the swift dogs, but then he loosed his piercing shafts upon the men themselves and shot them down and continually the pyres of the dead thickly burned. For nine days the missiles of the god ranged throughout the host ...
> (*Iliad*, I, 46–53; translated in Longrigg 1989: 2)

235. Longrigg (1989).
236. Joly (1970); Temkin (1991).
237. Edelstein 1966: 208.
238. Edelstein (1937); Longrigg (1989); Nutton (1995).
239. Longrigg (1980).
240. Longrigg (1989); Temkin (1991).
241. *Thucydides* Book II 53, quoted in Glendening (1960: 31).
242. In the first century BC, historian Diodorus reported that the Great Plague was due to some people breathing corrupted air from overcrowding in Athens. A later account attributed it to the heavy rains of the previous winter and other natural causes (Longrigg 1993).
243. Longrigg (1993).
244. *Ibid.*
245. Joly (1970); Nutton (1995).
246. Longrigg (1993).
247. Plato, *Protagoras,* 311b–c.
248. Aristotle, *Politics* 7 1326a15–16; Joly (1970).
249. Temkin (1991: 197).
250. McHenry (1969).
251. Longrigg (1993).
252. Hippocrates, quoted in McHenry (1969: 8).
253. Edelstein (1952); Vegetti (1999).
254. From the sixth century, the Greek physicians had acquired a great reputation. Democedes (521–485 BC) dissected animals and made important discoveries such as the sensory nerves, which were considered as empty canals (Reymond 1927;

Longrigg 1993). He also explained illness as a disturbance of equilibrium between the opposing elements that constitute the body: cold and heat, dryness and moisture, and so on (Longrigg 1993).

255. Vegetti (1999).

256. Hippocrates, quoted in C. G. Starr (1991: 331).

257. Nutton (1995).

258. Temkin (1991); Nutton (1995).

259. Nutton (1995: 16).

260. Although this widely quoted passage is usually attribute to Hippocrates, it is a composite from a variety of treatises (e.g. *Aphorisms* III.1, which depends on *Airs, Waters, Places*). The notion that diseases have individual manifestations is typically Hippocratic, but that the nature of a disease is derived solely from external causes would be contested vigorously by almost all writers in the Hippocratic corpus (Vivan Nutton, personal communication).

261. Nutton (1995: 24).

262. Nutton (1995).

263. Aetius wrote:

Alcmaeon holds that what preserves health is the equality of the powers – moist and dry, cold and hot, bitter and sweet and the rest – and the supremacy of any one of them causes disease; for the supremacy of either is destructive. The cause of disease is an excess of hot or cold; the occasion of it surfeit or deficiency of nourishment; the location of it blood, marrow or the brain. Disease may come about from external causes, from the quality of water, local environment or toil or torture. Health, on the other hand, is a harmonious blending of the qualities.

(translated in Longrigg 1993: 52)

264. Longrigg (1993).

265. Vegetti (1999).

266. Temkin (1991: 190).

267. Sedley (1980: 3).

268. Alexandria was founded and pronounced capital of Egypt in 331 BC by Alexander the Great. Alexander was the Macedonian warrior who, in the same year, had completed his two-year conquest of the Orient. The city of Alexandria was laid out by the architect Dinocrates of Rhodes (fl. 330 BC) in the shape of a parallelogram with its streets crossing at right angles (Van Wagenen 1924: 20). Alexandria remained the capital of Egypt for nearly 1000 years until it was captured and sacked by the Arabs in AD 642.

269. Bowman (1986).

270. Greek Hellenism is described as the intellectual culture that developed between the death of Alexander the Great in 323 BC and the accession of the Roman emperor, Augustus (63 BC–AD 14). The period should not be confused with the Greco-Roman period from 323 BC to the fall of Rome in AD 476. The term is somewhat misleading because the majority of scientific achievements were not Greek but a mixture of Greek, Egyptian and Near Eastern influences.

271. Fraser (1972).

272. Long & Sedley (1987); Shaw & Nicholson (1995).

273. Long & Sedley (1987); Longrigg (1993).

274. Amun was united with Zeus; Isis assimilated with Demeter (or Aphrodite), Horus with Apollo, Imhotep with Asklepios, Osiris with Dionysis and Thoth with Hermes (Shaw & Nicholson 1995; Vegetti 1995).

275. Shaw & Nicholson (1995); Vegetti (1995).

276. Kakosky (1995).

277. Green (1990).

278. Taton (1963); Green (1990).

279. Clagett (1955); Taton (1963); Green (1990).

280. Clagett (1955).

281. Proclus, quoted in Bulmer-Thomas (1970–80: 423).

282. Bulmer-Thomas (1970–80: 529).

283. McLeish (1992).

284. According to one story, King Ptolemy asked Euclid if there was no shorter way in geometry than that contained in his *Elements*. Euclid replied, "Sire, there is no royal road to geometry."

285. Proclus, quoted in Bulmer-Thomas (1970–80: 423).

286. McLeish (1992).

287. Quoted in Misner *et al.* (1973: 5).

288. Boyer (1991).

289. Quoted in *Pappas Alexander* (Clagett 1970–80: 213).

290. Heath (1911); Boyer (1991).

291. Clagett (1970–80).

292. Archimedes was killed at the age of 75 during the second Punic War, by the sword of a Roman soldier. Archimedes apparently was trying to solve a problem of circles in the sand when the soldier approached. The soldier is reported to have stepped on the diagram and Archimedes angrily said, "Don't disturb my circles", after which he was swiftly slain (Heath 1911). The Roman general Marcellus, who had ordered his men not to harm the famous sage, directed an honourable burial for Archimedes and had a sphere in a cylinder inscribed on his tomb, as Archimedes had requested in the event of his death (Heath 1911).

293. Taton (1963).

294. Bell (1937); Clagett (1970–80).

295. Archimedes, *On the Method*, quoted in Clagett (1970–80: 221).

296. Heath (1911).

297. Rees (1998).

298. Jenkins-Jones (1996).

299. Bell (1937).

300. Archimedes believed that mechanical inventions were beneath the dignity of pure science and he declined to leave written records of them. Archimedes is reported to have invented elaborate weapons of war for the King of Syracuse, which were responsible for the successful defence of the city against the Romans. The weapons included super catapults flinging quarter-ton shots, a crane-like beak with iron claws to reach over the walls and thwart approaching ships, and

his famous burning mirrors. He also invented the lever to facilitate the loading and unloading of cargo on tó merchant ships.

301. Clagett (1970–80: 213–14).
302. Grant (1996).
303. Archimedes, *Psammites* 1, 1–10, quoted in Heath (1991: 105).
304. Stahl (1970–80).
305. Clagett (1955).
306. Kuhn (1957); Heath (1991).
307. Reymond (1927); Cary *et al.* (1950).
308. Plutarch, *De facie in orbe lunae*, Ch. 6, quoted in Heath (1991: 108).
309. Stahl (1970–80).
310. *Ibid.*
311. Kuhn (1957); Neugebauer (1975, 1983).
312. Dreyer (1956); Dicks (1970–80).
313. Dicks (1970–80).
314. Dilke (1987).
315. Cleomedes, *De motu cirulari* I, 10; (Dicks 1970–80).
316. Van Helden (1985).
317. Dicks (1970–80).
318. Dilke (1987).
319. Dicks (1970–80).
320. Toomer (1970–80a).
321. Neugebauer (1975).
322. *Ibid.*
323. Neugebauer (1975); Evans (1998).
324. Robins & Shute (1987).
325. Neugebauer (1952: 145).
326. Dreyer (1956).
327. Ptolemy's original work was called the "Great Composition", from the Greek *megiste* meaning "the greatest". The later Arabs referred to it as, "Al Magisti", from which *Almagest* was derived (Abetti 1952: 43).
328. Toomer (1970–80b); Van Helden (1985).
329. Kuhn (1957).
330. Dreyer (1956).
331. Holton & Roller (1958); Ionides & Ionides (1939).
332. Abetti (1952: 43).
333. Dreyer (1956).
334. *Ibid.*
335. Lloyd (1987: 48).
336. Ptolemy, quoted in Boyer (1991: 158).
337. Plato, *Laws*, Bk 3, Pt 4.
338. Frede (1985).
339. Frede (1990: 225).
340. Frede (1990).
341. *Ibid.*
342. *Ibid.*
343. Vegetti (1999).
344. Guthrie (1971: 29).
345. Although Aristotle claimed that he began with common-sense intuition and observations, his standard syllogistic method in science was highly restrictive. For the most part, Aristotle's science began with an absolute and ended with an absolute. Equally problematic was that there was no agreement among Greek scientists on what constitutes a scientific proof (Clagett 1955;

Crombie 1994). "Proof" meant different things to different people and while experiments may have been performed (Crombie 1994), they appeared to lack the level of testability and verifiability evident in modern science (see Ch. 8). The major limitation, therefore, in Greek science in general, and in Aristotle's science in particular, seems not be in the logical method *per se*, but how it was applied to the overall process of analysis, synthesis and validation (see below).

346. Aristotelian science failed to appreciate the descriptive and predictive power of mathematics (Crombie 1994). Aristotle appeared satisfied with Euclidean axiomatic geometry and simple mathematics, which supported his geocentric, anthropocentric and dualistic worldview. That is, Aristotle defined place not as a three-dimensional extension, as we do today, but as a two-dimensional perimeter (Sorabji 1988: 187). Although the Greeks possessed the concepts of up and down, side to side (east–west) and backwards and forwards (north–south), they never described a place in space by putting numbers or coordinates to them (Weyl 1949; Jammer 1954; Sorabji 1988). Nor did Aristotle realize the importance of superimposing the fourth dimension of time on these three spatial coordinates to describe motion. Aristotle granted mathematics only a hypothetical status and thought it was inappropriate in the natural sciences (Crombie 1994). He preferred observation and demonstration, a view which dominated Western thought until the high Middle Ages and early modern era (*ibid.*). Plato, on the other hand, encouraged the study of mathematics but shared the view that it was inappropriate for studying nature.

Aristotle and most Greek scientists failed to discover the interconnectedness running through their concepts by not developing algebraic manipulation (and other numerical methods). Aristotle held that gravity was a property of a body's weight, not a property of the cosmos. If a body was left unsupported, it would naturally fall towards the centre of the earth (Cornford 1937; Cooper 1970).

347. Aristotle's primary focus was on the gravitating body, not on the place in space where it was located. He also believed that a heavy object would fall at a faster rate than a lighter one because he reasoned that it would have a greater pull towards the earth. By thinking this way, Aristotle missed discovering the constant acceleration with which "all" free-falling bodies accelerate towards earth. He failed to link the concepts of weight, velocity, distance, force, resistance and time in algebraic form and to test his predictions. Aristotle did not possess mathematical skill with respect to algebraic relations and proportionality constants (Cornford 1937). To give a modern example, Einstein's famous $E = mc^2$ tells us that energy (E) is proportional to mass (m) with the proportionality constant being the square of the speed of light (c^2). It is mind-boggling to think that 1 kg

of flowers has the same "cosmic energy" as 1 kg of rocket fuel with respect to the speed of light. I am not suggesting that Greek science wholly lacked mathematics and proportions: Anaximander taught a geometrical cosmology with its 3:2:1 ratio for the sun, moon and fixed stars with respect to the Earth; the Pythagoreans studied musical scales with a relationship between the lengths of vibrating strings and the pitch of notes (ratio of the octave is 1:2, of the fourth, 4:3; and the fifth, 3:2) (Barnes 1979); Archimedes performed experiments in mechanics and on floating bodies (Van Wagenen 1924); and much earlier the Babylonians discovered the relationship between the circumference and the diameter of a circle, π (Burnet 1930; Farber 1995).

348. Outside aspects of Greek astronomy, Aristotelian science generally lacked predictability (Crombie 1994). Aristotle's theory (after Empedocles) that everything was made of four elements (water, earth, air and fire) was useful, but it made few, if any, predictions outside those discussed in Hippocratic medicine. Democritus's atomic theory was equally ingenious, but predicted nothing like John Dalton's (1766–1844) chemical atomism. Greek science simply did not have the mathematical algebraic mindset to predict as modern science does today.
349. Popper (1957); Medawar (1984).
350. Clagett (1955: 45).
351. Kenny (1986: 281).
352. Frankfort (1948); Assman (1995).
353. Crombie (1962).
354. Gerson (1990).
355. Jaeger (1934: 159).
356. Aristotle required an unmoved mover for every eternal movement in the celestial region of the *cosmos*. The first unmoved mover was the supreme being, because it moved the first heaven (Craig 1980). Kahn argues, however, that Aristotle does not appear to be moving towards monotheistic thinking (1985: 201).
357. Kenny (1986); Gerson (1990).
358. The Stoic Zeno reportedly declared "the entire universe and heaven is the substance of god" (Gerson 1990). The past dilemmas associated with the separation of the physical and divine appear much less important to the Stoics, as their God was material. All matter was totally imbued with the intelligent divine comprising the *pneuma* (which was also equated with soul) (Pepin 1986; Long & Sedley 1987; Crombie 1994). Stoicism's rival philosophy was Epicureanism. The Epicureans, headed by Epicurus (341–270 BC), banished all their gods from the physical world and placed them in spaces between the worlds (Long & Sedley 1987). There the gods lived in peace and assumed no responsibility for influencing world events (Dover 1980). The physical world, one of innumerable worlds, was a product of complex atomic collisions in space coming into being from spontaneous movement. The Epicurean world was a world of chance with no purposeful origin

and no "mind of God" (Long & Sedley 1987). They did not deny the existence of gods, but thought that the gods (if they existed) cared little about human beings and world events. Human beings had to take responsibility for the good and evil in the world. The soul was purely "physical" and perished with the body at death. There was no life after death and therefore nothing to fear (Long & Sedley 1987).
359. Peters (1972); Dover (1980); Long & Sedley (1987).
360. Nothing in Greek philosophy is straightforward. Other Stoic deities were mentioned and this was reconciled by treating air, water, and so on, as referents of divine names Hera, Poseidon and others (Long & Sedley 1987). Thus imperfections in Stoic "monotheism" existed only when the parts were studied in isolation from the bigger picture (Long & Sedley 1987). Another problem for the Stoics was that they, like Plato, never satisfactorily proposed how the perfect unitary principle in God allowed for evil in the world (Peters 1972).
361. Peters (1972); Pepin (1986).
362. Long & Sedley (1987).

Chapter 6. Early Christianity: the historical road to one God

1. Clement, *Stromateis*, 1.5.29.
2. Stead (1994: 79).
3. Balson (1970); Merdinger (1991).
4. Merdinger (1991).
5. Brown (1992); Grant (1996); Colish (1997).
6. In the first century AD, Seneca studied meteorological phenomena and geography, drawing heavily on Aristotle, Posidonius and Theophrastus and other Greek sources (Grant 1996). His *Natural Questions* was particularly popular among early Christian scholars because he often linked morality with natural phenomena. Seneca taught that studying science would eventually reveal nature's secrets (*ibid.*). Pliny's 37-volume *Natural History* examined about 2000 volumes from 100 primary past authors and hundreds of secondary authors. He covered topics from astronomy through geography to zoology. In general, the encyclopedic authors wrote on Plato, Aristotle, Archimedes, Euclid, Theophrastus and others, but in reality their sources were often second or third hand, which led to gross distortions over the centuries (*ibid.*).
7. Stahl (1962); Grant (1996).
8. Merdinger (1991).
9. Grant (1996).
10. Brown (1981).
11. Constantine converted to Christianity, and the edict of Milan in 313 gave civil rights to Christians throughout the empire.
12. H. Chadwick (1967a); Frend (1984); Lynch (1992).
13. Burkill (1971: 1).
14. The Hebrews of earliest times are referred to as

"Israelites"; the generations after about 500 BC became known as the "Jews". "Hebrew" means "wanderer", after their nomadic lifestyle, and "Jew" comes from the people from Judah after the Babylonian Exile.
15. See also Genesis 11:31.
16. Genesis 17:4–7.
17. See Joshua 24:2–14.
18. Palestine was a trading gateway between Mesopotamia (the Babylonians), Asia Minor (the Hittites), the deserts of Arabia (the Semitic nomads) and Egypt (the Egyptians).
19. Exodus 3:8–17.
20. Exodus 3:2–4.
21. Stead (1994: 142).
22. Cornford (1932); Jaeger (1936).
23. Stead (1994).
24. According to the Old Testament, the Hebrews arrived in Egypt because of drought and famine in Canaan. A few generations after arriving in Egypt, they were enslaved by the New Kingdom pharaohs (c.1550–1070 BC). The Egyptians had become extremely suspicious of all foreigners after finally defeating the invading Hyksos, who had ruled northern Egypt from about 1720 to 1570 BC (Shaw & Nicholson 1995). It appears that slavery was an accepted practice, but the slaves were to be treated with respect and kindness (ibid.: 272). Eventually Moses persuaded Pharaoh Rameses II to release his captives from bondage (Exodus 12: 31).
25. Exodus 3:8–11.
26. Richard Dawkins calculated that if the Israelites had no stops during the exodus they would move approximately 22 m per day, or 90 cm h⁻¹, which is much slower than the fastest snail, which according to the Guiness Book of Records was clocked at a record speed of 50 m h⁻¹ (Dawkins 1991). The Israelites must have camped for very long periods along the way or got themselves horribly lost. Whatever the reasons, the exodus was an extremely slow journey for a group fleeing a country.
27. Exodus 24:12–18.
28. Exodus 20–30.
29. Most ancient codes of law were of divine origin. We saw this in ancient Sumer, Babylonia and Egypt. Greek historian Diodorus Siculus wrote: "they did all this because they believed that a conception that would help humanity was marvellous and wholly divine; or because they held that the common crowd would be more likely to obey the laws if their gaze were directed towards the majesty and power of those to whom their laws were ascribed" (Diodorus Siculus I sciv, 1–2, translated in Durant 1935: 331).
30. Armstrong (1993).
31. Brandon (1973a); Exodus 3:14.
32. Albright (1957); Peacocke (1979).
33. Albright (1957); Westermann (1984).
34. Exodus 20:7.
35. Albright (1957). In the Old Testament Adonai occurs 434 times.
36. See Judges 5:4; Psalms 77:17.
37. Exodus 15:3,6; 23:27–30; 2 Samuel 22: 35.
38. Albright (1957).
39. Brandon (1973a).
40. Exodus 20:2–3.
41. Psalms 89:11.
42. During the Babylonian Exile (586–538 BC) over 200 000 Israelites were captured and moved to Babylonia. It was one of the turning points in Hebrew history. After the exile, the Prophets depicted Yahweh as a single God, eternal, and the creator of all things (Isaiah 40–55). He was also a God of justice and pity who had created human beings in his image as companions, not as slaves.
43. Brandon (1973a).
44. Ezekiel 18, 32; Moore 1928; Sandmel 1979.
45. Sandmel (1979).
46. Jeremiah 31:33; see also Ezekiel 36:26.
47. Peacocke (1979: 41).
48. Gnuse (1999).
49. Saggs (1978).
50. According to Old Testament scholar William F. Albright, "Nowhere is there any hint of cosmic speculation in the prophetic writings of the pre-exilic times (before about 600 BC). They were not so interested in the creation or how the forces of nature operated only that God controlled them" (1957: 328).
51. Isaiah 40–55.
52. Peacocke (1979); Westermann (1984).
53. Isaiah 49:6; and see Isaiah 48–49.
54. Deuteronomy 4:19.
55. Isaiah 42, 49.
56. Genesis 1:27.
57. Micah 6:8
58. Albright (1957).
59. Also of profound influence on the Jews in the fifth century BC was the Persian conception of a judgement at death, not just for human beings but the world itself (Moore 1928: 55). The Persian religion Zoroastrianism taught that all evil would eventually be destroyed, with renewed life for the righteous. Greek Platonism and the immortality of the soul (following the Pythagorean concept) also filtered among the intellectual circles of the Jews during Hellenistic times. The Persians and the Greeks therefore heavily influenced the Jewish conception of death and retribution in the first century BC. The Jewish Pharisees, for example, believed in the resurrection, in rewards and punishments after death, and in the coming of the messiah (Albright 1957). Their rivals, the Sadducees, did not believe in resurrection and of rewards and punishments in the afterlife (ibid.; Moore 1928).
60. Buccellati (1995).
61. Exodus 20:4–6.
62. Deuteronomy 4:15–19; Isaiah 40; Albright (1957).
63. Micah 6:8.
64. Daniel 9:24–7; Isaiah 9:6, 11:1–2; Micah 5:2.
65. Albright (1957).
66. Revelation is defined as a divine act of God in

history which celebrates His "will" and final triumph over evil in the world (Chadwick 1982: IV, 159).

67. Albright (1957); Armstrong (1993).

68. H. Chadwick (1967a).

69. Williams (1991).

70. Jaeger (1961).

71. *Ibid.*

72. Schalit (1969: 48).

73. Toynbee (1969).

74. Sandmel (1979).

75. Frend (1984).

76. Goodness came through God's judgement; each person must study the Torah and seek God's "divine will". The problem that arose within the Jewish community, however, was a lack of consensus on how to interpret the scriptural laws, and deep divisions arose (*ibid.*; H. Chadwick 1967a).

77. Chadwick (1990: 22).

78. Lynch (1992).

79. Frend (1984).

80. Acts 10, esp. v. 45.

81. Jaeger (1961).

82. Acts 11:26.

83. Jesus never openly proclaimed himself "the Messiah". His closest disciples, however, saw him as the new Joshua or "saviour", hence the Greek name "Jesus" from the Hebrew "Joshua", and "Christ" from the Greek *Christos* for Messiah (*Mashiah*) or "anointed one" (Albright 1957). John 14:6 tells of Jesus saying "I am the way, and the truth, and the life; no one comes to the Father but by me". The apostles variously reported Jesus claiming to speak for God (John 14:12; Mark 9:2–7; Luke 7:28, 10:23–4), whereas the prophets, or even Moses, reported the commands and utterances of God directly – "The Lord spake to Moses" (Exodus 34:1)

84. John 1:41.

85. Price (1992).

86. H. Chadwick (1967a); Meeks (1983).

87. Barret *et al.* (2001).

88. Riches (1990).

89. The word "Gospel" comes from the Greek *evangelion*, meaning "good news". In their gospels, Matthew and Luke record the birth and early childhood of Jesus; Mark is more concerned with Christ's mission, beginning with the baptism of the adult Jesus by John the Baptist in the Jordan River. John also records Christ's mission to promote love and speaks of his divinity. The original function of the gospels was as an instrument to help the 12 disciples present Jesus and his mission to the non-Jewish community (Metzger 1988). There are contradictions among the four gospels in the New Testament.

90. Metzger (1988); Williams (1991).

91. The content of the Old Testament of the Christian Bible was approved by a council of rabbis around AD 90. The books of the Old and New Testaments did not appear until early in the third century (Metzger 1988). Some of the details of the origin of each of the 27 books of the New Testament (gospels, letters and apocalypse) are provided in those books, but the origin of the New Testament as a whole is controversial (Albright 1957; Frend 1984). Unlike the Old Testament, the New Testament was written relatively quickly (in about a century), and there are many outstanding questions about how it was compiled. It is generally agreed that the New Testament containing the gospels (the "good news" of Jesus Christ) is a compilation of literature that early Christians found inspiring in worship and teaching, relevant to the times in which they lived, yet still totally in agreement with the Old Testament (see Metzger 1987). Most, if not all, of the books' authors believed that they had been inspired with the same true Spirit that inspired the prophets of the Old Testament. For example, Paul often refers to his writings as inspired by the Holy Spirit (I. Cor. 7:40b). For further discussion of this controversial subject see Metzge (1987).

92. Schubert (1969); Thering (1992); Stead (1994).

93. Jesus is presented in the New Testament as being born to Mary under the influence of the Holy Spirit. An angel contacted Mary and told her of her pending birth of "a son of the Most High" (Luke 1:32 see also Matthew 1:18–25). St Paul also mentions the birth and believed Jesus was "of the seed of David" (Romans 1:3). In stark contrast, John 17:5 presents Jesus as "divine", and as having descended from Heaven to "become flesh" and to speak of "the glory which he had with his Father before the world existed" (Stead 1994). The connection between these two very different accounts is left unexplained. However, most Christians seem little concerned with these logical inconsistencies.

94. Mark 12:29–31.

95. Matthew 5:43–8.

96. Matthew 17:20; Mark 11:22–3.

97. Albright (1957).

98. Before Jesus was born, the Jewish nation was divided into three main Judaeic sects: the Pharisees (formed around 150 BC), the Sadducees (150 BC–AD 70) and the Essenes (130 BC–AD 60) (Schubert 1969). The Pharisees mostly comprised the middle class, who developed ideas about resurrection from the dead, reward after death for the good and punishment of the wicked, and believed in the coming of the Messiah (but not Jesus). According to them, Israel's observance of the Torah had a profound influence on the salvation of the world because the Torah was God's instrument of creation. The Sadducees were the upper class and included the priests, who were staunch literalists and did not believe in rewards and punishments in the afterlife (Acts 23:8). The Sadducees disappeared from history after the destruction of the Second Temple in Jerusalem in AD 70 (Schubert 1969). The third group, the Essenes, were from the lower classes; they practised asceticism and emphasized the spiritual aspects of religion. The community Jesus

founded was comparable in some respects with the Essene movement. Primary sources on the Essenes were unveiled in AD 1947 with the discovery of the Dead Sea Scrolls (*ibid.*). Searching for his lost sheep, a shepherd threw a stone down a hole in some rocks and heard a tremendous noise. He returned with a friend and discovered a cave with about 50 cylindrical earthern jars containing leather scrolls. They tell of a people of a monastic community between 130 BC and AD 67, who lived a life of humility and studied the Old Testament. The scrolls also make repeated mention of a reforming movement within Judaism and a teacher of righteousness. Because of the differences in dates, the teacher of righteousness was not Jesus, but some unknown forerunner, believed by some to be the Messiah. These people seemed to be linked to the same movement that led to the growth of the Essenes (*ibid.*). The New Testament makes no mention of the Essenes.

99. Albright (1957).
100. Toynbee (1969).
101. The rabbi is not a priest, but a teacher and spiritual guide. Rabbis studied and worshipped in a synagogue, not a temple. Synagogues were found throughout Galilee (Mark 1:39) and were also houses of healing. Followers lived strictly by a literal interpretation of the Torah and believed that God would one day send the real Messiah to issue retribution on the world and to punish those who had lived outside Torah law. Jesus also worshipped in the synagogue (Luke 4:16ff.) and continued to do so after he disagreed with some of their practices (Matthew 23:6, 6:2,5; Price 1992).
102. The Pharisees should not however be thought of as a reactionary party; on the contrary, they were far less literal and absolute than the high priesthood (Sadducees), and some other breakaway Jewish sects.
103. Armstrong (1993).
104. The Palestinian Jews revolted against the Romans in AD 66. Up to this time, the Roman generals largely tolerated their worship of God. What they did not tolerate, however, was violence. In response to the Jewish attempt to preserve their "chosen" identity by staging their revolt, the Romans sent an army to Jerusalem in AD 70 and destroyed the city and its famous temple. If it had not been for small Jewish communities thriving elsewhere, such as in Asia Minor, Jewish traditions might have been lost for ever (Butterfield 1973).
105. Jesus is said to have healed the sick, raised the dead and performed other miracles. Miracles were one way of fulfilling the Old Testament's promise of salvation by combining forgiveness of sins with curing of illnesses (and exorcisms of demons).
106. Jesus was sentenced to be crucified by Roman governor Pontius Pilate, on the advice of the chief priests, for sedition against the Roman government in Judaea.

107. Acts 1:6.
108. Before AD 66, the high priests of Jerusalem desperately tried to preserve Torah law and "hit men" were employed to persecute defectors (Meeks 1983). One persecutor was the Pharisee Paul (originally named Saul) of Tarsus. The biblical book The Acts of the Apostles portrays Paul as an enthusiastic supporter of the stoning of the first Christian martyr, St Stephen. Paul's life turned around completely in AD 33. While walking on the road to Damascus, Paul was suddenly blinded by a light and, as he fell to the ground, he heard a voice (later identified as the risen Jesus Christ) saying, "Saul, Saul, why do you persecute me?" (Acts 9:3–4). Paul was then firmly convinced that Jesus Christ, God's anointed Messiah, represented the fulfilment of historic Judaism. Paul talks about the event in his epistle to the Galatians and explains how he became convinced that the person who had died on the cross was the Messiah. Alongside the Pauline mission was the ministry of the apostles, and other successful missionary efforts, as part of the spread of Hellenized Jewish communities throughout Europe and beyond (Meeks 1983; Frend 1984).
109. In the Old Testament, the term "Gentile" was commonly used to describe a non-Israelite person or people, that is, those not descended from Abraham. Gentiles were respected by the Israelites: "Love the sojourner therefore; for you were sojourners in the land of Egypt" (Deuteronomy 10:19). The Israelites sympathized with them: "For you shall not oppress a stranger; you know the heart of a stranger, for you were strangers in the land of Egypt" (Exodus 23:9). However, during the early Christian era this attitude towards the Gentiles changed. Gentiles were detested by orthodox Jews, who regarded them as unclean and depraved; see Albright (1957); Toynbee (1969); Frend (1984); Price (1992).
110. Meeks (1983).
111. Wolfson (1969).
112. Meeks (1983).
113. Stead (1994).
114. *Ibid.*, 96.
115. Romans 6:3ff.; Brandon (1973b). Although there is no explicit reference in the Old Testament to baptism in the Christian sense of repentance for the forgiveness of sins, there are accounts of the use of water for ceremonial purification, the pouring out of the Holy Spirit onto individuals and, possibly, circumcision. For example, Isaiah (1:16) states: "Wash yourselves; make yourselves clean; remove the evil of your doings before my eyes." Furthermore, in Zechariah (13:1) the Lord says: "In that day there shall be a fountain opened to the house of David and to the inhabitants of Jerusalem for sin and for uncleanness." These passages clearly point to the baptismal promise, as does King David in Psalms (51:2): "Wash me thoroughly from my iniquity, and cleanse me from my sin." Finally, Isaiah (12:2–3) appears to link water and salvation: "Behold, God is my salvation; I will trust, and will not

be afraid, for the Lord God is my strength and my song, and He has become my salvation. With joy you will draw water from the wells of salvation." There are also commentaries about a form of baptism that was practised just before the Christian era by Jews initiating Gentile converts in Judaism (Frend 1984).

116. Galatians 2:20.
117. St Paul's death remains a mystery. On his last visit to Jerusalem around AD 59, he apparently was mobbed by orthodox Jews and then arrested. He was charged (and perhaps prosecuted) with violating the sanctity of the synagogue/temple. As a Roman citizen, he requested to be returned to Rome for a fair trial. One story has Paul being executed on the Ostian Way near Rome, and another has him housed in a Roman prison until his death around AD 65. Paul is reportedly buried close to Peter in the catacombs of Rome.
118. Pope John Paul II (1998: 33).
119. Wolfson (1969); Stead (1994).
120. Cross (1997).
121. Hebrews 11:2–27.
122. Wolfson (1969).
123. *Ibid.*, 311.
124. The concept of paganism is a Jewish–Christian construct. The term "pagan" comes from the Latin *paganus*, which has many meanings. In early Roman times, Christians distinguished civilians from the military by calling them *paganai*, so since Christians often called themselves "soldiers of Christ", or *miles Christi*, non-Christians became *paganai*. Others have interpreted *paganai* as "outsider" (O'Donnell 1977). The term was used by Latin-speaking Christians from about AD 300 onwards to describe the cults of the Roman, Greek or Punic traditions. In general, "paganism" described all non-monotheist unbaptised "civilians" who were potentially recruitable by the Church (H. Chadwick 1967a).
125. 1 Corinthians 2:5–7.
126. Wolfson (1969).
127. Stead (1994: 224).
128. Armstrong (1969).
129. Quoted in Sandmel (1979: 163).
130. Sandmel (1979).
131. H. Chadwick (1967b).
132. Armstrong (1969); Copleston (1972).
133. H. Chadwick (1967b).
134. Platonism claims that "abstract" objects, such as those in mathematics, or the concept of number or justice actually exist. They are real, independent, timeless and objective entities expressed in Plato's Ideas (or Forms) (Blackburn 1994).
135. Jaeger (1961), H. Chadwick (1967b). Philo arrived at this view after recognizing that Plato introduced a number of contradictions in his doctrine of Ideas (Wolfson 1969). Sometimes Plato wrote that Ideas were "uncreated" and coeternal with his supreme god; at other times they were "created" by God and at other times they were God's eternal thoughts (*ibid.*). Philo settled on

Plato's Ideas being the eternal "thoughts" of God (Campbell 1992).
136. Wolfson (1969).
137. Frend (1984).
138. Schurer & Bigg (1911: 410).
139. Wolfson points out that since the *logos* was not uncreated, and God is, the *logos* cannot be called God. Wolfson believes that when Philo applied "*logos*" to God, he was using the term loosely in the sense of being "divine" (1969: 312).
140. Wolfson (1969).
141. Stead (1994).
142. Psalms 33:6.
143. Copleston (1972).
144. Sandmel (1979).
145. *Ibid.*, 93.
146. The *logos* also gave rise to the heavens, with spirits and angels who helped God govern the world (Stead 1994). Other lower spirits and angels resided in the air and some become incarnate in our bodies. Philo appears to be associating manifestations of the "divine *logos*" with the "daemons" of ancient Greece, and perhaps the "angels" of the Jews, who were servants and messengers of God in the physical world (Schurer & Bigg 1911). This scheme also has some parallels with Plato's worldview; the big difference was that Plato linked the divine and physical via the soul.
147. Sandmel (1979).
148. Stead (1994).
149. Schurer & Bigg (1911).
150. Sandmel (1979).
151. G. P. Fisher, quoted in Cunliffe-Jones (1978: 4).
152. Lynch (1992).
153. Matthew 28:18–20; Mark 16:15.
154. Roman philosopher Celsus (fl. AD 178) wrote *True Discourse*, wherein he discussed the practices of various Christian groups and described their heated debates during the second century (Hoffmann 1987). After criticizing the belief that God descended to Earth to favour the "chosen few", he proceeded to attack Christianity on two levels (Frend 1988). First, Christians belonged to a secret society, whose members were bound by "dreadful oaths", and hence the society was illegal. Secondly, Christians were apostates from Judaism; they were simply "apostate Jews" (*ibid.*). In short, Christianity was nothing more than an opposition sect to subvert established society inspired by Judaism. Jesus was an impudent quack who learned his magic from Egypt and was unable to save himself from death at the hands of his enemies (Frend 1984: 177).
155. Gnosticism (from the Greek *gnosis*, meaning "knowledge") was a second-century breakaway movement of the Church (Frend 1984; Rudolph 1987). The different Gnostic schools shared the basic belief that the material world was evil, and the spirit world was good. This cosmological dualism arose from two different creator-gods. The physical world, the human body and all matter were all created by a demiurge, an artisan

God, and the world was created by the supreme God of truth and knowledge. According to the Gnostics, knowledge was the way to salvation (Rudolph 1987). Gnosticism, for the most part, ignored the historical events on which Church tradition and Old Testament traditions were based (*ibid.*).

156. Rudolph (1987). Another Christian breakaway movement in the middle of the second century was Marcionitism (Frend 1984; Rudolph 1987). Marcion of Sinope (*c.*100–165), an anti-Jewish heretic, believed that he was the restorer of an apostolic movement relying heavily on St Paul's works. He argued for a complete breakaway from Judaism, Yahweh and the Old Testament. He was excommunicated in AD 144. Marcion maintained that Christianity was a completely new revelation with a new God. He denied the God of the Jews and taught that only asceticism could bring human beings to the good God of the spirit who first revealed himself to Jesus (Armstrong 1993).

157. Frend (1984).
158. Chambers *et al.* (1987).
159. Wolfson (1969).
160. Hellenization is a term broadly meaning sharing Greek thought and culture. Christianity was born into a Hellenized world from Syria in the north, Egypt in the south, and Palestine in between. Greek remained the language of the Western Church well into the third century, before Latin became the official language. The development of early Church theology appears to have gone through three stages: a period of uncertainty and vagueness, a period of intense debate and argument, and the final emergence of explicit statements of doctrine.
161. Frend (1984).
162. H. Chadwick (1967a: 75).
163. Barnard (1967); Chadwick (1982).
164. Frend (1984).
165. Chadwick (1982).
166. Justin, II *Apologies*, xviii, 1, quoted in Lebreton (1913: 581).
167. Chadwick (1982).
168. Chadwick (1990).
169. Translated in Helm (1999: 57).
170. Frend (1984).
171. Burkill (1971).
172. Chadwick (1982).
173. On the Creation, Clement rejected the Aristotelian eternal world. God created the world, which began as a formless state of "non-being", reconciling both Genesis and Plato's *Timaeus* (Chadwick 1982: **4**, 171). To Clement this was sufficient evidence for God's transcendence and the contingency of the created world (Chadwick 1982).
174. Roberts & Donaldson (1995).
175. Chadwick (1990).
176. Frend (1984).
177. Burkill (1971).
178. Chadwick (1990).
179. Translated in Helm (1999: 60).

180. Other apostolic writers of Clement's time were: St Irenaeus of Lyon (*c.*130–*c.*200), *Against Heresies*; Tertullian (see below); and St Hippolytus (170–235), *Apostolic Tradition*. Hippolytus was among the last in antiquity to write commentaries in Greek and preserved the many fragments of the Presocratic and classical philosophers referred to in Chapters 4 and 5.
181. Frend (1984); Haren (1985).
182. Burkill (1971).
183. Frend (1984: 376).
184. Armstrong (1993: 128).
185. Chadwick (1990).
186. Frend (1984).
187. Berchman (1984).
188. *Ibid.*
189. Chadwick (1990).
190. Chadwick (1982); Armstrong (1993: 119).
191. Chadwick (1982: **4**, 171).
192. Quoted in Frend (1984: 377).
193. Chadwick (1982: **4**, 191).
194. Haren (1985).
195. Colish (1997: 11).
196. Colish (1997).
197. Jaeger (1961: 33).
198. Tertullian, translated in Helm (1999: 62).
199. The word "orthodoxy" became popular for mainstream Christian theology in the second and third centuries.
200. Colish (1997: 11).
201. Translated in McLean & Aspell (1970: 321).
202. According to Plotinus's biographer and student, Porphyry (c.232–305), Plotinus was born in Lycopolis, Egypt and spent his formative years in Alexandria. There Plotinus became acquainted with Greek philosophy and with Christian theology, presumably from his teacher Ammonius (Gatti 1996).
203. Armstrong (1969).
204. Frend (1984).
205. Armstrong (1967b).
206. Armstrong (1969: 214).
207. Haren (1985: 31).
208. Campbell (1992).
209. Stead (1994).
210. Rist (1996).
211. Campbell (1992)
212. Chadwick (1990).
213. Armstrong (1969: 213a).
214. Armstrong (1969).
215. Leaman (1985: 58).
216. In the Platonic tradition, the world, *logos* and reason were less important to Plotinus than the soul. The *logos* was part of the essence of matter, but immaterial itself; it was the forming principle of the physical world that gave substances their coming-to-be potency and life, as opposed to the soul, which gave things movement (Corrigan 1996; Wagner 1996). Unfortunately, he provided few details on how the *logos* was linked to the soul in the generative causes of the physical world (Corrigan 1996; Wagner 1996).
217. Armstrong (1969).

218. Hinnels (1984); Blackburn (1994).
219. Armstrong (1969).
220. *Ibid.*
221. Stead (1994).
222. Haren (1985).
223. Armstrong (1969).
224. Theodosius (347–395), translated in Gardner-Smith (1932: 10).
225. Instead of uniting Rome, moving the capital from Rome to Constantinople only fanned greater divisions between the East and the West, which set the stage for the European Middle Ages. In AD 395, the Roman Empire was divided into the Western and Eastern Empires. Rome became progressively weaker and was sacked by the Visigoths in 410, and by 476 the entire Western Empire was destroyed. The Eastern Empire continued as a state until 1453, when Constantinople was conquered by the Turks (after which it was called Istanbul).
226. Lynch (1992).
227. Diocletian (245–313) became emperor after the mysterious death of Emperor Numerian on his return from a Persian expedition. According to historian Flavius Eutropius (fl. 4th century): "Diocletian's first act was to swear in front of an assembly of soldiers that Numerian had not died from any plots of his". In the half century before Diocletian there were no fewer than 19 emperors, all of whom were either killed in battle or assassinated (Merdinger 1991). Rome's vast bureaucracy was slowly imploding because of devastating plagues, crippling inflation, famine, brutal wars and a sense of hopelessness. Between AD 256 and AD 280 the cost of living rose by over 1000 per cent.
228. Rusch (1977).
229. Markus (1990).
230. In addition to translating works by Plato, Aristotle and Porphyry, Marius Victorinus (fl. 361) was a highly original thinker. His teachings became so popular in Rome that in 353 a statue was erected in his honour in the Forum of Trajan.
231. Kelly (1975); Markus (1990).
232. Lynch (1992).
233. Pelagianism was a radical fifth-century breakaway Christian movement. Followers believed that Jesus's word should be obeyed literally, that each person was responsible for his or her own sin and salvation, and that Adam's sin had affected Jesus alone, and not the entire human race (i.e. they denied the concept of original sin) (Hazlett 1991). St Augustine fiercely opposed the monk Pelagius and Pelagianism. Partly because of this, Pelagius was excommunicated in 417 by Pope Innocent I (410–17) and Pelagianism was condemned by a number of regional and ecumenical councils in subsequent decades (see Lampe 1978: 160–62).
234. Followers of Donatism formed a North African Christian splinter group in the fourth century (Hazlett 1991). This schismatic movement arose when an apostatic archdeacon was ordained Bishop of Carthage, and the Donatists protested his consecration by appointing their own Bishop of Carthage: Majorinus in 311 and Donatus in 315 (after whom the movement was named). Donatists believed that those involved with apostasy, such as those who renounced their Christian faith or handed sacred books and relics over to the authorities during the Roman persecution, should not be part of the Church or perform baptisms (Frend 1984). By 350, Donatists outnumbered orthodox Christians in Africa, and each city had opposing Donatist and orthodox bishops. The Church became very concerned with the growing power of the Donastic movement, and held an imperial commission in Carthage in 411 to resolve the issues. The commission, comprising both orthodox and Donatist bishops, discredited and condemned Donatism, and the movement slowly vanished (Frend 1984; Hazlett 1991).
235. Rusch (1977).
236. *Ibid.*
237. The name "Latin Doctors of the Church" was ratified on 20 September 1295 by Pope Boniface VIII (Kelly 1975: 33).
238. Albright (1957: 394).
239. Wolfson (1969).
240. Gerson (1990); Stead (1994).
241. Wolfson (1969).
242. Quoted in Lampe (1978: 25).
243. *Ibid.*
244. *Ibid.*
245. Epistle of St Ignatius to the Magnesians (Magnesians 13).
246. Quoted in Lampe (1978: 26).
247. Arius was a priest who rejected the idea that Jesus was equal to God. Instead, Jesus was the Son created by God and therefore not co-eternal with Him or formed of the same substance (Chadwick 1990). Arius assumed the incarnation of the *logos* as a body, not as a human soul. Arianism was condemned as heretical in the fourth-century councils of Nicae and Constantinople.
248. Other agenda items included fixing the date of Easter, independent of Jewish calculations, and a clearer separation of Christianity from Judaism (Frend 1984).
249. Chadwick (1982); Frend (1984).
250. Chadwick (1982) believes that the voting was so one-sided because the Nicene Creed was written in an ambiguous manner (although not intentionally). The bishops, who may have normally disagreed, could interpret the highly generalized creed without conflict. The other reason for a one-sided vote was that the emperor was present and wanted a majority decision for the unity of the Church (*ibid.*).
251. Chadwick (1990).
252. Emperor Constantine, translated in Frend (1984: 500).
253. Stead (1994).
254. Stead (1994).
255. Dudden (1935: vol. 2, 561), quoting Ambrose, Id. *Hexaem.* i, 9.

256. Dudden (1935).
257. Colish (1997).
258. Dudden (1935: 558).
259. *Ibid.*
260. Ambrose's command of prose was extraordinary. Although not the first to do so, Ambrose popularized a range of poetry to make a statement of communal faith articulated in Church services, including the singing of hymns (Colish 1997).
261. Dudden (1935: 560).
262. Dudden (1935).
263. Frend (1984).
264. Rusch (1977).
265. Kelly (1975: 337).
266. Kelly (1975).
267. Jerome was a complex, restless and troubled man. Kelly (1975: 335) describes him as follows:
   Far cleverer and more versatile than Rufinus, more learned and acute than Augustine … His affection for his friends, while they were his friends, was unstinted though possessive; once they ceased to be friends, he could pursue them with a rancour and spitefulness which still dismay. Warm-hearted, kind to the poor and the distressed, easily reduced to tears by their sufferings, he was also inordinately vain and petty, jealous of rivals, morbidly sensitive and irascible, hag-ridden by imaginary fears.
268. Jerome chose to translate from the original Hebrew because of the many changes made to the Old Testament over the centuries. He believed that the apologists could better silence their Jewish critics if they used the original Hebrew text (Kelly 1975: 160). Unfortunately, Jerome did not know that the original Septuagint had preserved many more ancient passages than the accepted Hebrew text he chose to translate.
269. Kelly (1975).
270. Colish (1997).
271. Some of Jerome's disciples were widows and maidens, which raised many suspicions among his fellow priesthood. On the question of marriage Jerome had extreme views, claiming that the institution was the way of "bringing more virgins into the world" (Pelikan 1971; Kelly 1975). Marriage, he taught, kept men from "burning" and facilitated the propagation of species (Markus 1990). Jerome regarded women as capable of serious intellectual pursuits and important independent contributions to theology, if permitted (Colish 1997). One sees in Jerome the extremes of Christian asceticism, on one hand, and Christian feminism, on the other (Kelly 1975).
272. St Augustine of Hippo should not be confused with St Augustine of Canterbury (d. *c.*607), the founder of the Christian Church in southern England. St Augustine of Canterbury was born in Rome and, under the direction of Gregory I (*c.*540–604), led a mission to return Christianity to paganized England after the British Christians had fled following the Anglo-Saxon invasions.
273. Quoted in Rist (2001: 38).
274. Chadwick (1991).
275. Brown (1967); Chadwick (1991). Augustine was a prolific writer with some 105 books and numerous letters to his name. He once described himself as "a man who writes as he progresses and who progresses as he writes" (Chadwick 1991).
276. Augustine was born in Thagaste now Souk-Ahras, Algeria.
277. Colish (1997).
278. Stead (1994).
279. *City of God* (**8**, 5); Brown (1967).
280. Augustine's restless search for truth ended one day after listening to one of St Ambrose's sermons. Ambrose incorporated a passage from Romans calling for the abandonment of the urges of the flesh, which changed Augustine's life: "Let us conduct ourselves becomingly as in the day, not in reveling and drunkeness, not in debauchery and licentiousness, not in quarreling and jealously. But put on the Lord Jesus Christ, and make no provision for the flesh, to gratify its desires" (Romans 13:13–14). Augustine converted to Christianity at the age of 32, and was baptized the following year by Ambrose (Lesaar 1931).
281. Frend (1984).
282. *Ibid.*
283. Haren (1985).
284. Jones (1969: 88).
285. Translated in Markus (1964: 97).
286. Markus (1964: 84).
287. Chadwick (1991).
288. *Ibid.*
289. *Ibid.*
290. Based on his reading of Isaiah 7:9, translated in Markus (1964: 82).
291. The concept of goodness was at the heart of Augustine's faith and ultimate reality in God (Haren 1985).
292. Chadwick (1991).
293. Price (1992: 77).
294. Campbell (1992).
295. Chadwick (1991).
296. *Ibid.*
297. *Ibid.*
298. *Ibid*
299. *Ibid.*
300. *Ibid.*, 231.
301. *De Doctrina: Christiana* (1.7.7), quoted in MacDonald (2001: 79).
302. Macdonald (2001: 78).
303. Craig (1980); MacDonald (2001).
304. Campbell (1992).
305. Jones (1969).
306. Translated in Cahn (1977: 248).
307. Augustine, *Confessions*, Bk XI, sec. XIV, quoted in Cahn (1977: 249); see also Knuuttila (2001).
308. Augustine, translated in Cahn (1977: 248).
309. Sorabji (1983).
310. Evans (1993).
311. Jones (1969).
312. Evans (1993).
313. Chadwick (1991).
314. Evans (1993).

315. Lynch (1992: 284).
316. Mann (2001).
317. Stead (1994).
318. If Adam and Eve had not sinned by eating the forbidden apple, they, and we, would have been immortal. As discussed in earlier chapters, the search for immortality is something human beings have been obsessed with for millennia. In ancient Mesopotamia, the Epic of Gilgamesh saw Gilgamesh set out on a long journey in search of immortality (which he never found). In ancient Egypt, there was another set of elaborate beliefs and practices surrounding death, with each person judged by Osiris. The idea of immortality was also prevalent among the Greek Orphic religion and other cult religions, culminating in the Pythagorean theory of transmigration of souls. Immortality continued to be a main theme in the mystery religions of the Roman Empire before they were eclipsed by the salvation religion of Christianity.
319. Augustine, *Confessions* 8.16.
320. Chadwick (1991).
321. Frend (1984).
322. Augustine became hopelessly obsessed with sin, perhaps because of his rather dissolute life in his teenage years and early adulthood (O'Meara 1980). In one passage in his *Confessions*, he acknowledged that he "did not know to what temptation he might next submit" (10.5.7). He considered babies at the mother's breast to be full of sin based on possessiveness, gluttony and other vices (*Confessions* 1.7.11; Stead 1994). In addition, Augustine viewed marriage as "lawful wedlock" only for the purpose of procreation, and thought that sex should not be enjoyed. He appears to have judged rape victims harshly, suggesting that God permitted rapes because some women were too proud of their own chastity (Russell 1945: 356). However, rape of a pious virgin was not seen as loss of virginity (*ibid.*; Lamp 1978: 162–3). In *City of God* Augustine wrote, "the sanctimony of the will, if it remain firm and inviolate, what way soever the body be disposed of or abused … this sufferance layeth no crime upon the soul … Tush, another's lust cannot pollute thee" (Bk I, Chs 15–19, 20–25). The one proviso to the exoneration of virtuous women who are raped is that they must not have enjoyed the experience, as that would have constituted a sin (Russell 1945: 356).
323. Augustine's *City of God* was also about the sacred history of Judaism, the secular history of contemporary Europe and the Christian expectation of a future resurrection.
324. Chadwick (1991).
325. Chadwick (1991: 279).
326. Evans (1993).
327. Lynch (1992).
328. Burkill (1971).
329. Helm (1999: 3).
330. Helm (1999: 47–9).
331. *Ibid.*, 48.
332. Tertullian, *Praescr. Haer.* 7.9, quoted in Barnes (1971: 210).
333. H. Chadwick (1967a).
334. Solomon & Higgins (1996).
335. Jaeger (1961); Brown (1992).
336. Brown (1992: 122).

Chapter 7. Medieval Christendom: faith and reason

1. Lord Acton in a letter to Bishop Mandell Creighton, 3 April 1887.
2. Price (1992: vii).
3. The term "Middle Ages" (*media tempestas*) was introduced in the late fifteenth century by the humanist historians to describe the prolonged millennium of spiritual and cultural stagnation separating the fall of Rome and the Italian Renaissance (Lynch 1992). In a sense, the humanists invented the Middle Ages in order to separate themselves from what they perceived as a dark, barbaric period unworthy of a name of its own. A similar attitude was echoed by sixteenth-century Protestant reformers, philosophers of the French Enlightenment, and many historians of the nineteenth and early twentieth centuries.
4. Burrows (1981).
5. The origin of the Byzantine Empire is usually dated to about AD 330, after Constantine I, the first Christian emperor, moved the Roman capital from Rome to Byzantine or Constantinople (present-day Istanbul). By the fifth century these two parts of the empire had become virtually two separate states. The eastern half developed from the classical Greco-Roman culture to a unique medieval Eurasian-Christian civilization that integrated the Slavic people with the Greco-Roman tradition. The Byzantine Empire survived about 1000 years longer than its Western counterpart, and was finally destroyed by the Turks in 1453.
6. The Islamic civilization began in the seventh century AD on the Arabian peninsula (located south of the Byzantine Empire). It began with Muhammad of Mecca (*c.*570–*c.*632), who the Muslims believe to be the last prophet of God (Allah), after Adam, Noah, Moses and Jesus. The word Islam literally means "surrender", and the religion is so-named because the believer, namely the Muslim, "surrenders" to the absolute will of Allah, the creator, sustainer and restorer of the universe. In the Middle Ages, one of the great strengths of Islam was the promotion of learning and understanding to advance its theology. Islamic philosophy played a pivotal role in the reawakening of Latin Christian Europe to the Greek classics.
7. Holmes (1988); Colish (1997). The Western Europeans were a highly heterogeneous group, comprising Christian, classical Greco-Roman and Germanic cultures. The term Germanic (from Germany, Italy, Spain, Gaul, Britain and later Islam) described a branch of Indo-Europeans of unknown origin (Holmes 1988). In prehistoric

times, they are thought to have inhabited north-ern Germany and Scandinavia. By the time of Emperor Julius Caesar (100/102–44 BC), some groups had migrated southwards and occupied a broad area between the Baltic Sea and the North Sea and the Rhine–Danube Rivers. The Romans named the first tribes to cross the Rhine "the Germani", a name that later applied to the Ger-mans (Greer 1982). In addition to the Germanic tribes, there were the Berbers in North Africa, Iberians in Spain, Gauls in France and Britons in England. Of all the tribes, only two succeeded in building permanent states: the Anglo-Saxons and the Franks. The former successfully invaded Brit-ain during the fifth century, after Rome had with-drawn its forces; and finally in the tenth century the separate Anglo-Saxon states were united into a single kingdom, known as England. The most powerful state to rise in the West following the fall of Rome was Frankland, part of which became France.

8. The term "Dark Ages" appears to have been coined by Petrarch after he had discovered the wonders of antiquity in two previously unknown orations of Cicero at Liege (discovered in 1333) (Mommsen 1942). Petrarch was referring to the catastrophic intellectual and literary impoverish-ment of the period compared to earlier Greek tra-ditions. Today, it is more appropriate to think of the "Dark Ages" as a reconstructive phase of insti-tutional assimilation and transformation (Brown 1988).

9. Lynch (1992).

10. James (1988). Three possible reasons for the Catholic Church's survival are: (i) the Church was already established as an institution and posed no political or physical threat to the barbarian pres-ence; (ii) it was an heir to the great Greco-Roman culture and possessed great power in wisdom and learning that greatly impressed the barbarian war-lords; and (iii) the warlords were highly supersti-tious people and may have feared divine recourse from the God of the Christians (James 1988; Brown 1988).

11. St Gregory the Great (c.540–604) is often grouped with the three great Latin Church fa-thers for his practical work in bringing institution-alized Christianity to the ordinary Christian and conversion of the heathen (Markus 1997). Gregory built on the work of Augustine by teach-ing that the Catholic Church was the sole media-tor of saving grace, and that its teachings must be accepted without question (ibid.). In 592, he as-sured the survival of the papacy in Rome by nego-tiating a peace settlement with the warring Lombards, again demonstrating papal authority over other rule. In a very real sense Gregory was the last of the Romans, because in the next four centuries papal power underwent even more dra-matic changes to keep God's word alive (ibid.).

12. Benedictine monasticism was made up of the con-federated congregations of monks and lay broth-ers of early medieval Italy and Gaul. It grew out of

Western monasticism, founded by St Benedict of Nursia (c.480–c.547), who wrote a 73-chapter directory on how to regulate communal religious life for government and spiritual learning. Gregory adapted Benedict's Rule to his monas-tery in Rome, and from there the monastic move-ment reached England, where it helped to Christianize Anglo-Saxon England (nearly com-plete around AD 700) (Marenbon 1983).

13. Holmes (1988); Markus (1997).

14. McMurrin (1982); Marenbon (1983).

15. Grant (1996).

16. Holmes (1988).

17. Colish (1997).

18. Riley-Smith (1997).

19. Kretzmann et al. (1988); Grant (1996).

20. Grant (1996).

21. Marenbon (1983: 3).

22. Knowles (1962); Marenbon (1983, 1987); Colish (1997).

23. Marenbon (1983: 45).

24. Gibson (1981).

25. McMurrin (1982).

26. Chadwick (1981).

27. The "seven liberal arts" comprised two major di-visions of language and mathematics after the an-cient Greek and Roman classifications. The language disciplines were grammar, rhetoric and dialectic (or logic), collectively known as the trivium (the three ways to knowledge) (Gibson 1981).

28. Hyman & Walsh (1973).

29. In ancient Greece (~400 BC), arithmetic, geom-etry, astronomy and music had been recognized as distinct studies, collectively known as the mathemata, meaning "disciplines", from which the word "mathematics" was derived. Mathemat-ics in the early Middle Ages comprised arithmetic, geometry, astronomy and music, and was called the quadrivium (the four ways to knowledge), a term introduced by Boethius himself (Chadwick 1981).

30. Ibid.

31. Ibid.

32. Gibson (1981); Marenbon (1983).

33. Pedersen (1978).

34. Gibson (1981).

35. Pedersen (1978); Chadwick (1981).

36. Fichtenau (1968); Contreni (1984, 1995).

37. The Lombards were Arian heretics and past en-emies of the papacy. These Germanic peoples had invaded and defeated the Byzantine forces in Italy about AD 568 and ruled there until Charle-magne's victory in AD 774.

38. Contreni (1995).

39. Leff (1970).

40. McKitterick (1989).

41. Hyman & Walsh (1973: 12).

42. Marenbon (1983).

43. James (1988).

44. Price (1992).

45. Annals of Saint Vaast (AD 884), quoted in Cubberley (1948: 146).

46. Feudalism was primarily a political system as well an economic system that arose in the middle of the ninth century when the central authority of the West Frankish kingdom was beginning to collapse and lose its power base (Contreni 1984). Feudalism was a complicated communal network of rights and obligations between the overlords or kings and their lesser lords.
47. Contreni (1984).
48. *Ibid.*
49. *Ibid.*
50. *Ibid.*
51. James (1988).
52. "Scotus" was a commonly used surname for many Irish monks emigrating to Europe; it meant "Irishman" (Marenbon 1983).
53. Carabine (2000).
54. Colish (1997).
55. *On the Division of Nature* was a large, systematic work in four books, presenting a vision of reality that was strongly Neoplatonic. The work, written between 862 and 867, was strongly influenced by St Augustine. It appears most unlikely that Eriugena had direct knowledge of the original texts of the pagan Neoplatonists, including Plotinus, Porphyry and Proclus, but he did have some direct knowledge of a portion of a translation of Plato's *Timaeus* and some of Augustine's works (Carabine 2000).
56. Marenbon (1983).
57. *Ibid.*
58. Haren (1985).
59. Marenbon (1983).
60. Hyman & Walsh (1973).
61. Eriugena, *Periphyseon*, IV.759a–b (see Marenbon 1983).
62. Eriugena went to great pains to explain why we can never know God, which left him with little to say about understanding the universe because it seemed bound to end in the realm of the "inexpressible and incomprehensible" (Marenbon 1983: 62). He also believed that the intellect could not be identified with the "second person" in the Trinity because the Son would be less than equal to the Father.
63. Carabine (2000).
64. Johns (1990: 189–90).
65. Leaman (1999).
66. Mohammed was orphaned by the age of 6 and raised by his grandfather and uncle. In later life he was married and had two children. At about the age of 40 his life was transformed and the new world religion, Islam, was formed (Robinson 1996).
67. Hourani (1991); Robinson (1996).
68. Robinson (1996).
69. *Ibid.*
70. Islam officially condemned forced conversions. However, Muslim leaders instructed their people to ensure that the world was under the political domination of the faithful, which justified the use of the sword to reach this noble goal. In addition to the common association of Jihad with "Holy War", the Arabic word in the Koran literally means "struggle" or "striving" to become a better Muslim. However, there are a few passages in the Koran where Allah orders Muslims to terrorize non-Muslims; see Surah 8:60, 9:14, 8:12–17, 9:123.
71. Robinson (1996); Hourani (1991).
72. "Saracen" was a term applied around AD 100–300 by the Romans to describe the Arab peoples living in the Sinai Peninsula. In the Middle Ages, the Saracen armies comprised both Arabs and Turks. After the establishment of the caliphate, the Byzantines referred to all Muslim subjects of the Caliph as Saracens.
73. Knight (1964).
74. Bakar (1996).
75. Leaman (1985); Robinson (1996).
76. Leaman (1999).
77. Walzer (1967).
78. Kennedy-Day (1998); Netton (1998).
79. Craig (1980).
80. Kennedy-Day (1998).
81. Leaman (1999). The Muslims were not as interested in Greek literature and history as the early Latin Neoplatonic philosophers in the West.
82. *Ibid.*
83. Leaman (1985).
84. Craig (1980).
85. *Ibid.*, 48.
86. Haren (1985).
87. Leaman (1999).
88. Walzer (1967); Leaman (1985).
89. Leaman (1985).
90. Leaman (1999).
91. Walzer (1967: 650).
92. Walzer (1967).
93. Haren (1985).
94. Copleston (1972).
95. Craig (1980).
96. Copleston (1972).
97. Ivry (1972: 130).
98. Colish (1997).
99. Barnes (1991).
100. *The Soul* (429a 10 ff.).
101. Farrington (1965).
102. Inati (1998a).
103. *Ibid.*
104. Haren (1985).
105. Walzer (1967).
106. Quoted in Walzer (1967: 655).
107. Kennedy-Day (1998).
108. Craig (1980: 76).
109. Walzer (1967).
110. Copleston (1972).
111. Walzer (1967).
112. Westfall (1980).
113. Inati (1998b).
114. Walzer (1967); Haren (1985).
115. Inati (1998a).
116. *Ibid.*
117. Walzer (1967).
118. Leaman (1985).
119. Walzer (1967: 650).

120. Walzer (1967); Evans (1993).
121. Copleston (1972).
122. Avicenna's approach to medicine was used as a guide in twelfth- to seventeenth-century Europe, although fundamentally he added little to Galen's approach.
123. As a natural philosopher, he partly agreed with Aristotle that we derive valid information from sense-data, from which the mind forms concepts and propositions, allowing us to study cause–effect relations. He added a further step, that of judgement. Avicenna believed certainty was possible, but involved more than having an idea; it required a correspondence with the sensible world (Colish 1997).
124. Goodman (1992).
125. Walzer (1967).
126. Copleston (1972).
127. Walzer (1967); Haren (1985).
128. Walzer (1967).
129. Craig (1980); Colish (1997).
130. Colish (1997).
131. Kemal (1998).
132. Goodman (1992: 109).
133. Goodman (1992).
134. Colish (1997).
135. Goodman (1992).
136. Kemal (1998).
137. Walzer (1967).
138. Haren (1985: 128).
139. Leaman (1998b).
140. Copleston (1972); Colish (1997).
141. Copleston (1972).
142. Fakhry (1983); Haren (1985).
143. Colish (1997).
144. Nakamura (1998).
145. Walzer (1967).
146. Leaman (1999).
147. Colish (1997).
148. Unfortunately, Averroes never explains how the material intellect, also one and eternal for all human beings, divided and became individualized in different people. The implication was that different thinking in different people was only possible when the material intellect was in direct communication with the material forms in the human body (Leaman 1998b).
149. Ibid.
150. Leaman (1999: 170).
151. Leaman (1998b).
152. Copleston (1972: 126).
153. Katz (1980).
154. Sirat (1985).
155. Haren (1985).
156. Ibid.
157. Copleston (1972); Katz (1980).
158. Leff (1970).
159. Sirat (1985).
160. Ibid.
161. Leaman (1990).
162. Sirat (1985).
163. Leaman (1990).
164. Goodman (1998).
165. Leaman (1999).
166. Craig (1980).
167. Leaman (1990).
168. Katz (1980).
169. Goodman (1998).
170. Haren (1985).
171. Craig (1980); Katz (1980).
172. Leaman (1998a: 7–8).
173. Surah 10:5–6; Sardar (1998).
174. Marenbon (1996).
175. Johns (1990).
176. Russell (1945: 429).
177. As the Arabs and Jews were flourishing in Spain (and North Africa), the Latin West remained in a state of social unrest. It was not until the eleventh century that the Church formed a unified political and military alliance in the West to ensure greater harmony. In his landmark address of 27 November 1095 to the Council of Clermont, in southern France, Pope Urban II (c.1042–1099) called on the lords, knights and foot soldiers of the Church to stop feuding with each other. "It is the will of God!", he proclaimed, that the West should be united against those who were destroying the Holy Land (Hyman & Walsh 1973). His appeal was more successful than anyone could have imagined, with the nobles of France and England uniting, but not those of Germany. The unification culminated in a series of military expeditions known as the Crusades (1095–c.1450), which were designed to reclaim the Holy Sepulchre from the Seljuk Turkish hordes (Muslims and Jews) in Jerusalem, and to return power, order and dignity to the West, including better relations between the churches (Riley-Smith 1997). The "Great Crusade" to recapture the Holy Land began in 1096 (called the People's Crusade), and this was followed by a second Crusade in 1144, and a third in 1187. Five other Crusades, principally undertaken by the French in the thirteenth century, were of much less consequence. The Crusade movement did not restrict itself to fighting Muslims, but was also directed against Europe's Jewish population and non-Catholic Christians (Constantinople was pillaged in 1204, and parts of southern France were attacked in 1209). The two winners of the Crusades were the Church in the West and Islam in the East (ibid.).
178. The feudal society was slowly transformed by a new "middle" class of townspeople, who ranked between the nobles and peasants: the burghers in Germany, burgesses in England and the bourgeoisie in France (Mayer 1972; Riley-Smith 1977). The term "burgher" was used in Germany to describe a citizen of a "borough" or "burgh", which was a community with a charter that involved, among others, exemptions from manorial duties or landholding in payment for rent. A burgher possessed the rights and privileges of citizenship rather than heredity, as in the feudal society. After the twelfth century feudalism was dying out as the people left the feudal estates and escaped to the towns. From the increased number

of towns, industry and wealth in western Europe grew and an influential class of people called the "burgher class" developed.

179. Riley-Smith (1977).

180. The word "scholasticism" is derived from Latin *scholasticus*, which in the twelfth century meant "master of a school".

181. Morris (1990); Colish (1997).

182. Cobban (1988); Grant (1996). It is near impossible to assign accurate dates to the origin of the early universities in Europe because they were outgrowths of pre-existing schools established in the eleventh and twelfth centuries. Like the cathedral and monastic schools, universities were legal corporations: associations of teachers and students with collective legal rights under legal charters. Membership meant that you were exempt from the rule of civil law. Other universities sprang up in the thirteenth century and modelled themselves on Bologna, Paris, Oxford and Cambridge. The most important were Naples (*c.*1224) under the patronage of Frederick II (1215–1250); Toulouse (*c.*1229) and Montpelier (*c.*1220) in France; Salamanca (*c.*1230) and Valladolid (*c.*1230) in Spain, and Prague (*c.*1347) in Germany. The universities encouraged a great diffusion of knowledge and scholars came from all corners of Europe to advance their learning. Paris, for example, was unrivalled for its scholastic theology; Bologna, Orleans and later Bourges, specialized in Roman jurisprudence; and Montpelier in medicine.

183. Burnett (1998); Kretzmann *et al.* (1988).

184. Grant (1996).

185. Knowles (1962).

186. Goodwin (1965).

187. Quoted in Hyman & Walsh (1973: 150) and Haren (1985: 101).

188. Anselm, translated in Evans (1989: vii).

189. Evans (1989).

190. Southern (1963); Hopkins (1972); Evans (1989).

191. Southern (1963); Liebeschutz (1967).

192. Evans (1989: 37).

193. Evans (1989).

194. Southern (1963).

195. Evans (1989: 56–66).

196. *Ibid.*, 41.

197. Anselm, *De Concordia* (III.6), quoted in Marenbon (1983: 97). Also see Evans (1989: 40).

198. Malcolm (1960); Hyman & Walsh (1973).

199. Cahn (1977); Helm (1999).

200. Helm (1999).

201. Marenbon (1983).

202. Copleston (1972).

203. Hyman & Walsh (1973).

204. Colish (1997).

205. Liebeschutz (1967).

206. Davies (1993); Armogathe (1998).

207. Jones (1969: 201–6); Davies (1993: 63).

208. Quoted in Price (1992: 86).

209. Aquinas was born at the castle of Roccasecca, near Aquino, between Rome and Naples. His parents sent him to the Benedictine Abbey at Monte Cassino for his education, and then to the University of Naples in 1239. While in Naples, Aquinas was deeply influenced by the newly created Order of Preachers founded by St Dominic (1170–1221). Aquinas's family were outraged that he wanted to join a lowly Dominican order, and not the wealthy, highly influential Benedictines. Legend has it that Aquinas's family offered him a prostitute to change his mind but he refused and joined the Dominican Order in 1243 at the age of 18 (Cahn 1977).

210. Aquinas's philosophy and theology were so profound that many of his views remain the basis of the Catholic tradition today. At first, the Franciscans had convinced the Pope to condemn Aquinas and his writings. But the Dominicans rallied to his defence, and officially accepted Thomism in 1278; Aquinas was canonised 44 years later (1323). In the sixteenth century, Aquinas was ranked with the four great Latin Church fathers: Ambrose, Jerome, Augustine and Gregory the Great. In 1879 Pope Leo XIII pronounced Thomism the basic theory of the Roman Catholic Church. In his encyclical *Aeterni Patris [On the Restoration of Christian Philosophy]* (nos 21, 31), Pope Leo wrote: "we exhort you, venerable brethren, in all earnestness to restore the golden wisdom of St Thomas, and to spread it far and wide for the defense and beauty of the Catholic faith, for the good of society, and for the advances in the sciences ... Let carefully selected teachers endeavour to implant the doctrine of Thomas Aquinas in the minds of students, and set forth clearly his solidarity and excellence over others. Let the universities already founded or to be founded by you illustrate and defend this doctrine, and use it for the refutation of prevailing errors."

211. Goodwin (1965).

212. "Thomas Aquinas", in Herbermann *et al.* (1913: vol. 14, 671).

213. Tranoy (1964); Aertsen (1993); Kretzmann & Stump (1993).

214. Colish (1997).

215. MacDonald (1993).

216. *Ibid.*

217. *Summa Theologica* (Ia.1.9).

218. Aertsen (1993).

219. *Ibid.*

220. Tranoy (1964).

221. McCracken (1998).

222. *Ibid.*

223. Aquinas, *Summa Contra Gentiles* (II, nos. 83–90).

224. Blackburn (1994: 22).

225. McCracken (1998).

226. Colish (1997).

227. Wippel (1993).

228. Goodwin (1965).

229. Jones (1969: 234).

230. Wippel (1993).

231. Kenny (1969).
232. Craig (1980).
233. *Ibid.*
234. *Ibid.*
235. William of Conches (*c.*1121), quoted in Grant (1996: 21).
236. Aertsen (1993).
237. Wippel (1977).
238. Marenbon (1987).
239. Grant (1979); Aertsen (1993).
240. Decades earlier, Pope Innocent III (*c.*1160–1216) had convinced the civil authorities that treason to the Christian God was treason to the State.
241. Aertsen (1993).
242. Baldwin (1970); Aertsen (1993).
243. St Bernard of Clairvaux (1091–1153), quoted in Jones (1969: 200).
244. Luscombe (1970).
245. Jones (1969: 200). See also Abelard, "Prologue" to *Sic et Non [Yes and No]*, lines 330–50, quoted in Boyer & McKeon (1976).
246. Colish (1997).
247. Blackburn (1994).
248. Jones (1969: 193).
249. Abelard, quoted in Hyman & Walsh (1973: 183).
250. Owen (1993: 49).
251. Crombie (1959: 12).
252. Crombie (1953).
253. Marenbon (1987).
254. Hyman & Walsh (1973: 432).
255. Crombie (1959).
256. Crombie (1970–80b); Wallace (1972).
257. Wallace (1972).
258. Crombie (1994).
259. *Ibid.*
260. *Ibid.*
261. Wallace (1972).
262. Southern (1986).
263. Grosseteste may have also been the first to deal with the fundamental methodological problem of error, something the vast majority of Greeks paid little attention to. He was also fascinated by the rainbow and concluded that the colours were caused by refraction of light through the cloud. The drops of water in the cloud acted like tiny spherical lenses, which he supported in his laboratory experiments on lenses. Grosseteste was the first Latin scholar to realize the importance of magnification, and its possible application to correct human eyesight (Crombie 1953, 1994).
264. Crombie (1959).
265. Taton (1963).
266. Marrone (1983).
267. Crombie (1969).
268. *Ibid.*
269. Sardar (1988, 1998).
270. Sardar (1988, 1998).
271. Marrone (1983: 148).
272. Marrone (1983).
273. *Ibid.*
274. *Ibid.*
275. Light was the original physical form created by God and the cause of natural change. Beginning as a "point" source, it radiated into a sphere, which gave rise to the spatial dimensions human beings experience. Light was the mediator for the interaction between the human soul and the physical body and the senses (Crombie 1994: 319). Visible light was just one manifestation of this divine power. In the third century, Plotinus had argued that light was the visible manifestation of power and goodness and many effects of causes could be described as their "reflections" and knowledge as "illumination" (Lloyd 1970–80).
276. Quoted in Crombie & North (1970–80: 377).
277. Jones (1969).
278. Unfortunately, Bacon fell into the same trap as those he was criticizing by unknowingly using mistranslated passages. In his *Opus Majus* (1268) Bacon wrote:

> Every translator ought to understand the author's subject, and the two languages from which and unto which he is to render the work. But none hitherto, except Boethius, have sufficiently known the languages; nor has one, except Robert Grosseteste (the famous bishop of England), had a competent acquaintance with science. The rest make egregious errors in both respects. And there is so much misapprehension and obscurity in the Aristotleian writings as thus translated, that no one understands them.
>
> (Vol. 1, p. 45)

279. Lindberg (1983).
280. *Ibid.*
281. Bacon, quoted in Jones (1969: 290).
282. Bacon (1928: 587).
283. Crombie (1994).
284. Lindberg (1983).
285. Crombie (1994).
286. Hyman & Walsh (1973).
287. Bacon, quoted in Wallace (1972: 47).
288. Crombie (1994).
289. Lindberg (1983).
290. Crombie (1994).
291. Lindberg (1983).
292. Crombie (1994: 392).
293. Spade (1999a).
294. Saw 1964; Moody 1970–80.
295. Marenbon (1987); McCord-Adams (1987).
296. Helm (1999).
297. Goddu (1999).
298. *Ibid.*
299. Crombie (1994: 392).
300. Goddu (1999).
301. Ockham, quoted in Wallace (1972: 54).
302. Wallace (1972).
303. Goddu (1999).
304. Wallace (1972).
305. Goddu (1999: 156).
306. Crombie (1994).
307. Goddu (1999).
308. Spade (1999b).
309. Marenbon (1987).
310. Goddu (1999).

311. Jones (1969).
312. Spade (1994).
313. Marenbon (1987).
314. Spade (1999b).
315. Ockham, quoted in Moody (1970–80: 173).
316. Spade (1999b: 101).
317. *Ibid.*
318. Moody (1970–80).
319. Saw (1964).
320. Russell (1945).
321. Grant (1996: inside cover).
322. Peters (1968: 157).
323. Grant (1996).
324. *Ibid.*

Chapter 8. The triumphant rise of Western science: methodologies, mathematics and measurement

1. Quoted in Koestler (1963: 261).
2. F. Guicciardini (1483–1540), quoted in Russell (1945: 501).
3. Riley-Smith (1977).
4. Parkinson (1993). The word "Renaissance" (*Rinascita*) was invented by Italian painter and architect Giorgio Vasari (1511–1574). It first appeared in his book *Lives of the Most Excellent Italian Architects, Painters and Sculptors from Cimabue to our own Times* (1550) (Hay 1973). The concept of "Renaissance", in its modern aspect, is attributed to the nineteenth-century Swiss historian Jacob Burckhardt after the French historian Jules Michelet and Engish poet, essayist and literary historian John Addington Symonds. The Renaissance is commonly dated from the year 1453, the year Constantinople was captured by the Turks.
5. It was Italy, and not some other location in Europe, for complex reasons. First, Italy was strategically located as a trade link between the West and East (particularly after the fall of Constantinople). Secondly, independent city-states in northern Italy had grown out of the struggle between the holy emperors and popes. Florence, for example, had its own army and government, as did Venice, Padua, Milan and Genoa. A third factor was historical scholarship. Italy had been the centre of classical Greco-Roman learning; the home of scholars and manuscripts of the Byzantine Empire after the Turks invaded the eastern Mediterranean (Pumfrey 1991). Lastly, Italy retained a strong secular tradition and interest in worldly affairs despite being the home of the Pope and long Christian traditions (Hay 1961, 1973).
6. The term "humanist" originated in Italy in the fifteenth century and was used to refer to a teacher or student of the *studia humanitati* – the humanities – which included the study of classical texts, mainly grammar, rhetoric, poetics, moral philosophy and history (Parkinson 1993: 3).
7. Petrarch, quoted in Kraye (1993: 17).
8. Whitfield (1943).
9. Kraye (1993).
10. Brown (1993).
11. Ferguson (1948); Westfall (1971); Cohen (1985).
12. Kenny (1983).
13. Although it was not Luther's intent, his actions provoked widespread revolt. The major goal of the Lutheran Protestants was to denounce Catholic orthodoxy and return the authority to the Scriptures and teachings of Jesus, who believed in the "original goodness" of all human beings. Luther was joined by other humanists Erasmus (*c.*1466–1536) and Calvin (1509–1564). Ecclesiastical supremacy eventually broke down and gave way to greater Christian diversity.
14. Within the Aristotelian system, nearly all disciplines could lay claim to being a science. The word "science" meant any systematic body of knowledge dealing with a discrete field of enquiry depending upon logic and/or authority. During the Renaissance, the meaning of "science" was being sharpened to include only physical phenomena, not supernatural/magical phenomena.
15. Butterfield (1957); Hall (1962); Westfall (1971); Biagioli (1993).
16. The earliest mention of a printing press with a metal typeface and ink was found in a lawsuit in Strasbourg in 1439. The lawsuit described the construction of a printing press with a moveable type invented by the German, Johann Gutenberg (*c.*1400–*c.*1468).
17. Grant (1996: 171).
18. Bacon (1902: 12).
19. Bacon (1902); Hesse (1964); Cohen (1985).
20. Bacon, *Novum Organum* (Book II, 10); Perez-Ramos 1993.
21. Quinton (1980).
22. Eamon (1990).
23. Koyre (1943: 401).
24. Quinton (1980); McMullin (1990).
25. Horton (1973); Quinton (1980); McMullin (1990).
26. Popper (1957, 1959); Urbach (1982); Cohen (1985).
27. Hesse (1970–80); Brooke (1991).
28. Hesse (1970–80).
29. Brooke (1991).
30. Parkinson (1993: 7).
31. Gaukroger (1993).
32. *Republic* (510–11, 532–4); Cottingham (1984).
33. Cohen (1985).
34. McMullin (1990).
35. Cohen (1985).
36. Quinton (1980).
37. Crombie (1970–80a).
38. Cottingham (1993).
39. Grant (1996: 104).
40. Kuhn (1957); Evans (1998).
41. Rosen (1971); Smith (1972).
42. Kuhn (1957).
43. Clark (1969).
44. Grant (1996).

45. *Ibid.*
46. Grant (1996).
47. Koyre (1957).
48. Kuhn (1957); Evans (1998).
49. Kuhn (1957).
50. Evans (1998).
51. Kuhn (1957).
52. Koyre (1957).
53. The alchemists taught that one could transform "prime" matter into another kind, for example, making gold from silver.
54. Nadler (1998).
55. Evans (1998: 145).
56. Molland (1993).
57. Rosen (1971).
58. Kuhn (1957); Evans (1998).
59. Cohen (1960: 35).
60. Cohen (1960).
61. Grant (1996).
62. Ravetz (1990).
63. Evans (1998: 422).
64. Pannekoek (1961).
65. Rosen (1970–80: 404; 1971).
66. Copernicus, quoted in Armitage (1990: 77).
67. Crombie (1994).
68. North (1994).
69. In ancient and medieval times, the movement of the sun was explained by the slow revolution of the whole field of fixed stars from east to west about the poles of the equator. Copernicus provided a better explanation by having the slightly tilting Earth move in the opposite direction (Evans 1998).
70. Rosen (1970–80, 1971).
71. Evans (1998). The equinox refers to the north–south motion of the sun over the year. The sun moves north from the equator from 21 March to 22 June, when it reaches its most northerly point (giving the longest day of the year in the Northern Hemisphere or summer solstice). The sun then moves south, reaching the equator again, and proceeds to its most southerly point on 22 December (the shortest day of the year in the Northern Hemisphere or winter solstice) (*ibid.*). During the annual movement of the sun, it crosses the Earth's equator twice, on the spring equinox (21 March) and the autumn equinox (23 September). On these dates, the sun's rays are directly above the equator and therefore give a ("equi-") 12-hour day and a 12-hour night. Beyond the Arctic and Antarctic Circles the sun does not set in summer or rise in winter (*ibid.*).
72. North (1994).
73. Westman (1986).
74. Kuhn (1957).
75. Kuhn (1957: 144).
76. Rosen (1971).
77. In Chapter 1 of Copernicus's book he begins with a general sketch of his theory and ends with the mathematics of plane and spherical triangles. The second chapter dealt with spherical astronomy. The third chapter was concerned with the motions of the Earth about its axis and around the sun. The fourth chapter was a theory of the moon's motion; the fifth was on the motions of the planets in longitude (inner planets); and the sixth chapter was on planetary motion in latitude (outer planets) (Dreyer 1956; Kuhn 1957; Rosen 1971).
78. Swerdlow & Neugebauer (1984).
79. Armitage (1990).
80. Copernicus's dedicatory preface to the Pope, *De Revolutionibus Orbium Coelestium*, quoted in Kuhn (1957: 138). See also Hall (1972: 60–61); Rosen (1971).
81. Westman (1986).
82. Hall (1962); Evans (1998); Silver (1998).
83. Luther, quoted in Tappert (1967: 359).
84. There is some doubt among historians of science that Calvin and Luther made these comments. Doubts about the Luther quote are addressed by Norlind (1953), and the comments ascribed to Calvin are discussed in some detail by White (1980).
85. White (1922).
86. Pannekoek (1961: 222).
87. Evans (1998).
88. Molland (1993).
89. Sobel & Andrews (1999).
90. Ravetz (1990).
91. Hatfield (1990).
92. Evans (1998: 417); see also Rosen (1971).
93. Evans (1998).
94. Gingerich (1993).
95. *Ibid.*
96. Molland (1993).
97. Osiander, quoted in Armitage (1990: 66).
98. Westman (1986).
99. Dreyer (1956).
100. Evans (1998).
101. Cohen (1985); Armitage (1990).
102. Hall (1962: 65).
103. The Earth's daily rotation was not demonstrated until 1851, when Jean Foucault (1819–1868) devised an ingenious experiment with a large iron-ball pendulum suspended by a 61 m wire from the dome of the Pantheon in Paris (North 1994). The pendulum was set oscillating along a fixed-swing line marking the meridian on a giant fixed table. Those who watched saw the plane of the pendulum turn slowly in a clockwise direction, which was due to the progressive change in the direction of the meridian caused by the Earth's rotation. The direct demonstration of the Earth's yearly orbit was a separate measurement made by F. W. Bessel (1784–1846). Bessel observed a nearby star called 61 Cygni for 18 months in relation to two much fainter stars. By the end of 1838, Bessel had enough data to calculate the stellar parallax (annual displacement) of the star viewed from opposite ends of a long baseline, such as the diameter of the Earth's orbit around the sun (North 1994). If the Earth were motionless, such calculations would be impossible.
104. Ravetz (1990).
105. Molland (1993).

106. Hall (1962).
107. Kuhn (1957); Koyre (1957); Kraye (1993: 49).
108. Quoted in Singer (1968: 58–9).
109. Singer (1968: 158–80).
110. Kuhn (1957: 210).
111. North (1994).
112. Kuhn (1957).
113. Lear (1965).
114. Holton (1960).
115. North (1994).
116. *Ibid.*
117. Kepler, quoted in McMullin (1998: 301).
118. Westfall (1971).
119. North (1994).
120. Danilov & Smorodinskii (1975: 702).
121. Cohen (1985: 128).
122. Molland (1993).
123. Lear (1965: 7); Koestler (1963: 312).
124. Quoted in Koestler (1963: 345).
125. Lear (1965).
126. Cohen (1985).
127. *Ibid.*
128. Kepler, quoted in Holton & Roller (1958: 150).
129. Westfall (1971: 5).
130. Westfall (1971).
131. North (1994).
132. Kepler, "Harmonice mundi", translated in Gingrich (1972: 595).
133. Cohen (1985: 134).
134. Machamer (1998a).
135. Swerdlow (1998).
136. Drake (1980).
137. Swerdlow (1998: 244).
138. Galileo did not invent the telescope, but he did revolutionize its use. The telescope was a Dutch invention of around 1600. In 1609, while on a trip to Venice, Galileo learned of the discovery and rushed back to Padua. By the end of that year he had built his own (Shea 1998).
139. Drake (1957); Shea (1998).
140. Swerdlow (1998).
141. *Ibid.*
142. Shea (1998).
143. Molland (1993: 120).
144. Swerdlow (1998).
145. Galileo, quoted in Reichenbach (1952: 21).
146. Drake (1970–80).
147. Molland (1993).
148. William Shakespeare, *Hamlet*, I.iv.166.
149. Swerdlow (1998).
150. Fermi & Bernardini (1961).
151. McMullin (1998).
152. *Ibid.*, 277.
153. Holton (1960); Armitage (1990).
154. Quoted in Drake (1957: 182, 86–7).
155. McMullin (1998: 279).
156. McMullin (1998).
157. Blackwell (1998: 348).
158. Blackwell (1998).
159. *Ibid.*, 252.
160. Fermi & Bernardini (1961: 75).
161. *Ibid.*
162. *Ibid.*
163. Drake (1980a: 66).
164. McMullin (1998).
165. Brooke (1991).
166. It is hard to believe that Galileo would have deliberately targeted Pope Urban VIII in the last pages of his *Dialogue Concerning the Two Chief Systems of the World*. Historian of science John Hedley Brooke agrees, and argues that because Simplicio's argument was endorsed by Salviati, Galileo was using a simple literary device to ensure impartiality in both parties to accept the Pope's argument (Brooke 1991: 104). Thus there was no intention on Galileo's part to confront the papacy. However, his approach tragically backfired.
167. As mentioned in Chapter 7, the Inquisition emerged in the middle of the thirteenth century and again in the middle of the sixteenth century during the Counter-Reformation (Fermi & Bernardini 1961). The movement worked in secrecy in the cities and reported to Catholic officials on those suspected of heresy (Drake 1980). The intent of the Church was always to contain any problems before they developed into more widespread issues.
168. de Santillana (1955).
169. Blackwell (1998).
170. Drake (1980).
171. Quoted in de Santillana (1955: 312).
172. Milton (1998).
173. Sagan (1980: 142).
174. Drake (1980: 33).
175. Shea (1998).
176. Cohen (1985); Sorabji (1988).
177. Cohen (1985).
178. Drake (1981); Sorabji (1988); Crombie (1994).
179. Drake (1980: 33).
180. Drake (1980); Westfall (1990).
181. Cohen (1985).
182. Drake (1981).
183. Settle (1961).
184. Hankins (1990).
185. Redondi (1998: 201).
186. Machamer (1998a).
187. Drake (1957); Holton (1960).
188. Cohen (1985: 142).
189. Drake (1980).
190. McMullin (1998: 302).
191. Galileo, quoted in Fermi & Bernardini (1961: 73).
192. The term "demonstration" meant a progression from "effect to cause" separated by an "intermediate" stage involving the mental examination of the "cause" (Wallace 1998). The "intermediate" stage was a process of active construction and deconstruction, of testing, investigating, experimenting, measuring, eliminating the possibilities and working backwards to the effect. Galileo used the term *regressus* for working backwards (*ibid.*).
193. McMullin (1998).
194. Machamer (1998b: 20).
195. McMullin (1998).
196. *Ibid.*: 306.

197. Alexander Pope (1688–1744), quoted in Silver (1998: 62).
198. Drake (1980: 92).
199. Drake (1981).
200. Drake (1980).
201. Drake (1970–80).
202. Drake (1980: 93).
203. Attributed to French mathematician Joseph Lagrange, who also said, "There is only one law of the universe and Newton discovered it" (Cohen 1960: 189).
204. Pope wrote this epitaph soon after Newton's death in 1727 (quoted in Cohen 1960: 184).
205. Funkenstein (1986).
206. Westfall (1980).
207. Chittenden (1848).
208. Westfall (1980).
209. *Ibid.*
210. Chittenden (1848).
211. Westfall (1980: 39).
212. Cohen (1960); Westfall (1980).
213. Cohen (1985).
214. Westfall (1980).
215. *Ibid.*, 143.
216. Newton, letter to Robert Hooke, 5 February 1675.
217. Quoted in Westfall (1980).
218. Quoted in Chittenden (1848: 58); Bell (1937: 90); Westall (1980: 863).
219. Westfall (1980).
220. Karp (1972: 170).
221. Quoted in Cohen & Smith (2002: 15). Newton's letter was a reply to Hooke's letter sent a month earlier as part of a goodwill gesture for having openly criticized Newton's theory of light (*ibid.*: 31).
222. Gribbin (1993a: 6).
223. Bragg (1998).
224. Hooper (1998: 150).
225. Newton's definitions were abstractions designed to simplify otherwise complex phenomena and appear in the first of the three books of *Principia*.
226. Cohen (1985).
227. Newton's first law of motion states that *a body at rest will remain at rest, and a body in motion will remain in motion in a straight line unless acted upon by an external force.* The book on your desk will remain at rest until someone or something moves it. Arrows would move in a straight line, if there were no air resistance or gravity. Planets would move through empty space (no resistance), but not in straight lines. Instead, they would carve out a Keplerian ellipse because the sun–planet gravitational tug bends the line of motion into that shape. The second law states that *a change of motion of a body is proportional (a) to the force acting upon it and (b) inversely on the mass of the body.* If you hit a ball twice as hard it will go twice as far. Or if you hit a ball that is twice as heavy, the ball will go half as far. Newton's third law states that *for every action there is an equal and opposite reaction.* If the Earth tugs at the moon with a given force, then the moon tugs at the Earth with an equal force, but in the opposite direction.
228. North (1994).
229. Cohen (1985: 165).
230. Newton (1848: 383).
231. To quote Newton biographer R. S. Westfall, the story of the apple "has contributed to the notion that universal gravitation appeared to Newton in a flash of insight in 1666 and that he carried the Principia about with him essentially complete for twenty years until Halley pried it loose and gave it to the world ... The story vulgarizes universal gravitation by treating it as a bright idea" (1980: 155).
232. Cohen (1960).
233. McMullin (1978).
234. Molland (1993: 118).
235. Crombie (1994).
236. North (1994).
237. Sir Christopher Wren (1623–1723) had an extraordinary intellect. He was Professor of Astronomy at Oxford from 1661 to 1673 and a charter member of the Royal Society. He met regularly with Halley and Hooke, and offered a prize for whoever solved the long-standing problem of planetary motion, which they all agreed had to be some kind of inverse-square law (Cohen 1960: 155; Ronan 1961: 110). Hooke claimed to have solved the problem, but never produced the proof. Halley visited Newton, who had solved the problem (see Cohen 1960: 155 and text). In later years, Sir Christopher Wren devoted himself more to architecture and was instrumental in planning the rebuilding of the city of London after the Great Fire in 1666, and later designed St Paul's Cathedral (1675–1716).
238. North (1994).
239. Newton (1848: 506).
240. Hawking (1996).
241. *Ibid.*
242. See Westfall (1986: 229). Westfall noted that when Newton studied the nature of Christ and God he came to the belief that the early Christian theologians of the fourth and fifth centuries had committed a monstrous fraud by perverting the nature of Christianity.
243. Quoted in Westfall (1986: 233).
244. Newton (1848: 504–7).
245. Westfall (1986).
246. Force (2000).
247. Holton (1960).
248. Force & Popkin (2000).
249. Westfall (1986).
250. Popkin (2000).
251. Westfall (1980).
252. Force & Popkin (2000).
253. Westfall (1986).
254. Popkin (2000).
255. Popkin (1998).
256. Westfall (1980).
257. Westfall (1986).
258. Westfall (1980).
259. Newton, quoted in Westfall (1980: 354).

260. Westfall (1986).
261. *Ibid.*, 231.
262. Westfall (1986).
263. *Ibid.*
264. Dobbs (1991: 170).
265. Force (2000).
266. Mayr (1982: 103).
267. Grant (1996).
268. Butterfield (1957); Hall (1962); Rossi (1970); Westfall (1971).
269. Eamon (1990).
270. The Royal Society started in weekly meetings in London that began around 1645. It was followed by the French Academy of Science of Paris (founded in 1666). Both societies actively promoted the diffusion of scientific knowledge by publishing and distributing journals on a regular basis.
271. Westfall (1991).
272. *Ibid.*
273. Einstein (1954: 19).
274. Bacon was an empiricist, along with Gassendi and Hobbes (followed by Locke, Berkeley and Hume). The rival rationalists were Descartes, Spinoza and Leibniz, who believed that reality can be understood by purely a priori reasoning without any appeal to the senses.
275. Brooke (1991).
276. Quoted in Crombie (1970–80a).
277. Dobell (1958: 112).
278. Dobell (1958: 192).
279. Galileo, quoted in Drake (1957: 237).
280. Murdoch (1982); Grant (1996).
281. Biagioli (1993).
282. Shea (1998).
283. The celestial machine metaphor was not Kepler's innovation but can be traced back to the twelfth century, when natural science was reintroduced as a path to the glorification of God. The metaphor arose when the conception of the world changed from being unpredictable and capricious to a harmonious smoothly operating, self-sufficient machine (or *machine*, as it was frequently called) (Grant 1996).
284. Kepler wrote in 1605 (quoted in Mahoney 1998: 706) that the model of the world was:

    not on the model of a divine, animate being, but on the model of a clock – if you think a clock to be animate, you attribute glory to the world of the craftsman. In [that machine] almost all the variety of motions [stems] from one most simple, physical magnetic force just as in the clock all motions stem from a most simple weight. And I mean to call this form of reasoning "physics" [done] with numbers and geometry.
285. Mahoney (1998).
286. Crombie (1994); Grant (1996).
287. Rees (1998: 236).
288. Shea (1998: 231).
289. Galileo wrote that Aristotelian axioms "were not only not obvious to the senses, but have never been proved, and cannot be proved because they are completely false" (Galileo 1960: 42). Galileo, and Newton, believed the task of science was to discover truth from the preponderance of evidence, not from moving from one absolute to another, as Descartes had proposed. Although Newton defined "absolute" quantities, he rarely made explicit use of them (Holton 1952). In Newton's own words, "the parts of that immovable [absolute] space, in which these motions are performed, do by no means come under the observation of our senses" (quoted in Holton 1952: 174).
290. Drake (1981).
291. Fermi & Bernardini (1961: 37).
292. Wallace (1998).
293. Milton (1998: 681).
294. Milton (1998).
295. *Ibid.*
296. Grant (1996).
297. Force (2000).
298. Milton (1998).
299. Pascal, *Pensées, IV: Of the Meaning of Belief*, no. 253 (1952: 220).
300. Eamon (1990).
301. Hatfield (1990: 109).
302. Marion (1998: 269).
303. Blackwell (1998).
304. Quoted in Silver (1998: 62).

Chapter 9. The Big Bang: starlight to superstrings

1. Longfellow, "The Day is Done", lines 19–20 (Longfellow 1909–14).
2. Henderson (1913: 8).
3. Koyre (1957: 276).
4. Hahn (1986); Brooke (1991).
5. Rees (1998).
6. Rees (1998); Tegmark (2003).
7. Bucher & Spergerl (1999: 45).
8. Today's estimates of the age of the universe is between 10 and 20 billion years. The universe's great age and size explain many past mysteries. For example, why is the sky dark at night? If there are so many stars, why don't they act like a floodlight leaving the sky continually bright? The question was raised by mathematician Thomas Digges in 1576 and was known to Kepler, Halley and Herschel. In 1826, astronomer Heinrich Olbers (1758–1840) observed that in the clear night sky some stars were faint and others were bright. He reasoned that the night sky was dark because the universe was very large and very old, and not enough time had passed for light from all the stars to reach us on Earth. The problem was solved and is known as Olber's paradox.
9. Weinberg (1988); Silk (1989).
10. Hogan (1998).
11. The expansion theory was put forward in 1933 by George Lemaitre as part of his attempt to predict the large-scale structure and evolution of the universe (Rees 1998). Lemaitre examined the various

models predicted from Einstein's field equations. Fifteen years later Gamow proposed a similar scenario, but it was part of his theory of the origin of the light elements and structure and evolution of stars (Gamow 1948; Hoyle 1955; Bondi *et al.* 1960; Silk 1989).

12. Rees (1998).

13. Gribbin (1993b).

14. Kragh (1996); Hogan (1998).

15. The "ylem" (pronounced *ilem*) of George Gamow was a name for the primordial mixture of matter and energy just before the huge explosion. The word is a revival of an obsolete noun that, according to *Webster's Dictionary*, meant "the first substance from which the elements were formed" (Gamow 1952: 57).

16. The zero on the Kelvin scale (K) is called absolute zero. At this temperature all thermal motion of atoms and molecules is halted. On the Celsius scale, absolute zero is equal to −273 °C. The cosmic background radiation that fills interstellar space (between stars and galaxies) has a temperature of around 3 K (or −270 °C). The temperatures involved in the splitting of the atom are similar to the temperatures of thermonuclear reactions occurring in the sun (around 10^7 K).

17. Davis (2001).

18. Bucher & Spergel (1999).

19. Rees (1998). Gravity is the weakest of the four forces (10^{40} times weaker than the electrical forces inside an atom). Gravity operates on a large scale; all particles feel the effect of gravity but the force dominates the universe when matter is on a large scale. Electromagnetic force is the next strongest force and arises between electrically charged particles. A comb can attract small pieces of paper through electromagnetism and the forces of attraction and repulsion are more powerful than the force of gravity. Electromagnetic force can also operate on a large scale. The third kind of force is the weak nuclear force responsible for radioactive decay in the neutron. The fourth, and the strongest, is the nuclear forces in which gluons hold the quarks together in the proton and neutron, and hold the protons and neutrons together in the nucleus to form atoms (Hawking 1996). Within the proton the strong nuclear force is about 100 times stronger than the electromagnetic force. Both weak and strong nuclear forces act inside the atom and operate over extremely short distances. The strong nuclear force is responsible for the large amounts of energy released in atomic bombs.

20. Weinberg (1988).

21. Rowan-Robinson (1993).

22. When matter changed state from plasma to permanent atoms, the removal of the free electrons resulted in the universe becoming "transparent", meaning that light could now pass through space. Before then, light was scattered (or deflected) by the free "plasma" electrons washing out any directional information. If an electron fell into orbit around an atom during the "opaque" period, it would probably have been knocked off by a collision with another speeding particle. As the temperature dropped, the electrons and protons formed hydrogen atoms, allowing light to pass for the first time, giving a transparent universe.

24. Rees (1998).

25. *Ibid.*

26. Hogan (1998).

27. *Ibid.*

28. The Doppler effect was named after its discoverer, Austrian physicist Christian Johann Doppler (1803–1853). Most of us have experienced the effect. As a train approaches sounding its whistle, a very distinct and sudden increase in pitch occurs, and as it moves away from us, the pitch becomes lower. The increase in pitch occurs because the approaching train is pushing sound waves against the air making their wavelengths shorter. As the train moves away, it drags the sound waves along producing longer wavelengths and a lower pitch. Hubble was not concerned with sound, but with different wavelengths of light from different galaxies speeding away from us on Earth. The galaxies speeding away are pulling or stretching the wavelengths of light, resulting in a red-shift.

29. Bartlett *et al.* (1995).

30. There are 3.09×10^{19} km in a megaparsec (Mpc), and 3.16×10^7 s in a year. Hubble's original value corresponds to an expansion time-scale of $3.09 \times 10^{19}/(500 \times 3.16 \times 10^7) = 2$ billion years, the age of the universe.

31. Freedman (1992); Bartlett *et al.* (1995).

32. Davis (2001).

33. Eddington (1933).

34. The two-dimensional model is not fully accurate because the black dots representing nebulae would expand too as the balloon increased in size (Barnett 1948). Importantly, the galaxies are moving away from each other and their recession velocities increase as they recede further from the observer.

35. Eddington (1933).

36. Gamow (1948); Hoyle (1955).

37. Kutter (1989).

38. Rees (1998: 36).

39. Atkins (1992). A light-year is the distance travelled by light moving at $300\,000$ km s^{-1} in space for a period of one tropical year.

40. Hawking (1988: 45).

41. Willem de Sitter was among the first to calculate the size of the universe from knowledge of the universe's curvature using Einstein's field equations. He estimated a radius of about 2 billion light-years (Howard 1951: 411). Most of us cannot imagine a radius of 2 billion light-years; it is equivalent to about 19 thousand billion kilometres (19×10^{21} km). The sun is only about a thousandth of one light-year away from Earth (or $149\,700\,000$ km). This means that light takes 8.3 minutes to reach Earth from the sun. More recent estimates on the size of the universe have

shown that de Sitter's calculations no longer apply. Today, intergalactic distances of 70 billion light-years (10^{24} km) are not out of the ordinary in the cosmological sense.

42. Krauss (1999: 37).

43. Pais (1982); Atkins (1992); Krauss & Turner (2004).

44. Clark (1971: 215).

45. Kirshner (2002).

47. Rees (1998); Baggot (1992).

48. Hoyle (1955: 32).

49· The background radiation is remarkably constant except that it looks brighter in one direction and slightly dimmer in the opposite direction (1/1000 dimmer). This is because our Milky Way galaxy is moving at a speed of around 600 km s^{-1} (Rowan-Robinson 1993).

50. A universe compressed into a single point 15 billion years ago would emit most of its energy in the shortest most energetic wavelengths, the gamma rays. Gamma rays are the most energetic of a family of photons, which range across very weak radio waves, microwaves, infrared radiation, visible light, ultraviolet and x-ray radiation.

51. Gribbin (1993b).

52. Wilson (1979).

53. Rees (1998).

54. Gribbin (1993b).

55. Ibid.

56. Emilani (1992).

57. Sagan (1980: 218).

58. Gamow (1952); Burbidge et al. (1957).

59. Silk (1989); Smoot (1993).

60. Rees (1998).

61. The sun spends most of its life fusing hydrogen to form helium (one helium nucleus requires the fusion of four hydrogen nuclei) (Rees 1998). As hydrogen becomes depleted, the sun will contract, heat up and begin the fusion process to heavier elements up to about carbon. After the initial contraction, the sun would then expand to become a red giant and eject its outer layers to form a planetary nebula. The exposed core would cool off to form a "white dwarf" remnant.

62. Rowan-Robinson (1993); Rees (1998).

63. Rees (1998: 17).

64. Sagan (1980: 338, 345).

65. Gribbin (1993b: 19).

66. Some experts were so excited that they claimed that it was the "discovery of the century, perhaps of all time", "the Holy Grail of cosmology" or "a certain Nobel prize"; see Rowan-Robinson (1993: 5); Gribbin (1993b: 18).

67. Smoot (1993).

68. Gribbin (1993b); Rees (1998).

69. A question often asked is: how can the clouds of matter detected by COBE be 500 million light-years across if the universe is only 300 000 years old? How can its dimensions exceed 300 000 light-years? The answer is that during those 300 000 years, space itself was expanding faster than the speed of light. The assumption that nothing travels through space faster than the speed

of light is not violated (Gribbin 1993b).

70. Bartlett et al. (1995).

71. Weinberg (1988); Rowan-Robinson (1993). Ripples are local irregularities of mass in the space-time fabric arising from matter in the stars, galaxies and clusters of galaxies (Hawking 1993). Gravitational waves are disturbances in the curvature of space-time produced by "matter in motion" arising from massive physical bodies or even black holes colliding with one another. Gravitational waves do not really travel through space-time, but "oscillate" the fabric of space-time (Hawking 1996).

72. Einstein & Infeld (1954); Gamow (1962).

73. Rees (1998: 204).

74. "Flat" refers to a special kind of space that extends infinitely far in any direction, and represents an "open" universe that will go on expanding for ever, as opposed to a closed universe, which will eventually re-collapse on itself.

75. Vitsaxis (1977); Ronan (1978); North (1994).

76. Friedman successfully solved Einstein's "field equations", as did Georges Lemaître five years later. Friedman obtained three different solutions to Einstein's equations, each of which predicted a universe beginning with an explosion. The three solutions were: infinite expansion; an infinite cycle of expansions and contractions; and an intermediate between these two (Hawking 1996: 54–9).

77. Rees (1998); Silk (1989).

78. Davis (2001); Kirshner (2002).

79. Davis (2001).

80. Hawking (1993); Hazen & Trefil (1991); Barrow (1994).

81. Rees (1998: 204).

82. Hawking (1993).

83. Davis (2001).

84. Rees (1998).

85. Hawking (1993: 147).

86. Hawking (1993).

87. Hellemans (1995).

88. Black holes are regions of space-time where the matter is so dense that not even light can escape; the light-trapping gravity conceals everything inside. Astronomers attempt to see black holes in much the same way as we observe the wind: by observing objects it moves (Hawking 1996). Black holes arise from the death or burning cycle of a massive star where the gravitational forces become so strong that the star collapses inwards. In 1978, theorists proposed that M87, an enormous galaxy some 52 million light-years away from Earth, had a black hole at its core. In 1992, the Hubble Space Telescope, even with its flawed mirror, sent back images that appear to support this claim. The black hole is estimated to be about 2.6 billion times the mass of the sun and would explain the extraordinary clustering near M87's core. Many black holes have been identified in the past decade.

89. Hellemans (1995); Rees (1998).

90. Arkani-Hamed et al. (2000).

91. Lucretius (1965: 137, 148).
92. Hawking (1996); Rees (1998).
93. Einstein (1950); White & Gribbin (1994). Special relativity deals with constant velocity systems compared to general relativity's accelerating or inertial system (Einstein 1950; Einstein & Infield 1954).
94. Quantum mechanics arose from the theory of Max Planck (1858–1947), Niels Bohr (1885–1962), Erwin Schrödinger (1887–1961), Werner Heisenberg (1901–1976) and Paul Dirac (1902–1984). In addition to proposing that energy is absorbed or released by systems in discrete small packets or "quanta", the quantum theory predicts that when the property of an electron or another particle is measured, the state of that particle changes in some "unpredictable" way (Weinberg 1977). The more accurate the measurement, the more unpredictable the mechanical system becomes. The Heisenberg "uncertainty principle" states that the more precisely you know the value of a particle's position in space, the less sure you are about how fast it is going and where it is moving, and vice versa (Heisenberg 1971). The uncertainty principle has helped physicists describe quantum mechanical systems in terms of probabilities, known as wave functions. In contrast to the solid billiard balls envisaged by Newton; quantum particles exist as a blur without the certainty of being at one place at a particular time (Taylor 1993). Quantum particles are not only prone to uncertainties with respect to their position but also in their energy, speed and sometimes existence (Baggot 1992; Taylor 1993, Weinberg 1994). It logically follows that if a "virtual" particle could appear and disappear out of nothing (the vacuum) by chance, so too could the universe (Taylor 1993). However, if the universe is a quantum fluctuation, the theory needs to explain how time, space, matter and energy were created out of nothing (Barrow 1994).
95. Weinberg (1977).
96. Rees (1998); Greene (1999); Kirshner (2002).
97. Rees (1998: 168); Greene (1999); Kirshner (2002).
98. Rowan-Robinson (1993); Hawking & Penrose (1996); Greene (1999); Kirshner (2002).
99. Clarke (1971: 19).
100. Clark (1971).
101. Hawking & Penrose (1996).
102. Hawking (1996: 18).
103. Llewellyn Smith (2000: 59).
104. See Arkani-Hamed et al. (2000).
105. Clery (1995).
106. Llewellyn Smith (2000).
107. Ibid.
108. The properties of the Higgs boson(s) form the basis for the various models of cosmic inflation, in addition to providing a mechanism for generating the mass of particles.
109. Clery (1995); Rees (1998).
110. Stone (1995); Llewellyn Smith (2000).
111. Arkani-Hamed et al. (2000).
112. Ibid.: 54.

113. Hawking (1996); Rees (1998); Greene (1999); Arkani-Hamed et al. (2000); Kirshner (2002).
114. Greene (1999); Arkani-Hamed et al. (2000); Kirshner (2002); Bousso & Polchinski (2004); Veneziano (2004).
115. Ibid.
116. Rees (1998); Greene (1999).
117. Weinberg (1994).
118. Rees (1998); Silk (1989).
119. Greene (1999); Arkani-Hamed et al. (2000); Kirshner (2002); Bousso & Polchinski (2004); Veneziano (2004).
120. Greene (1999).
121. Ibid.
122. Arkani-Hamed et al. (2000).
123. Rees (1998).

Chapter 10. Origins of life: from molecules to machines

1. Simpson (1949: 14).
2. Henrietta Temple (1837), quoted in Bartlett (1992: 434).
3. See Aristotle, Generation of Animals, Bk 3, Ch. 11, in Barnes (1984: 1178–81) for an explanation of why he believed that some animals generate spontaneously.
4. Fruton (1972: 262–73).
5. Fruton (1972: 266); Lahav (1999).
6. Bynum et al. (1981: 439).
7. Loeb (1906: 7); Fruton (1972: 67).
8. Loeb (1906); Fruton (1972: 266); Bynum et al. (1981: 439).
9. Brooke (1991).
10. Draper (1898); White (1922); Brooke (1991: 152–91).
11. Schopf (1999).
12. Wald (1954: 45–53).
13. Atoms are the building-blocks of molecules and compounds, the stuff of matter and of life. On Earth there are 92 kinds of "naturally" occurring elements made from one type of atom, hydrogen numbered 1 and uranium 92. Except for the rare radioactive elements like uranium, atoms cannot be created or destroyed by the natural processes on Earth (Rees 1998).
14. In a public lecture, Lord Kelvin used a different example to illustrate the extraordinary number of possibilities. Suppose you marked all the water molecules in a glass of water, poured the contents into the seven seas, and then thoroughly mixed the oceans (some 1.4 billion km^3) with a big spoon. Kelvin calculated that if you visited any one of the world's oceans and collected a glass of water you would detect about 100 marked molecules (Schrödinger 1992: 6). This amazing calculation tells us there are many more molecules in a glass of water than there are glasses of water in the sea, and further that we are dealing with very large numbers with respect to chance interactions of life-forming atoms, molecules and compounds in a watery environment.

15. Kauffman (1993; 1995).
16. Kauffman (1995); Southgate (1999).
17. Kauffman (1995: 20).
18. Dyson (1979: 453); also quoted in Atkins (1992: 12).
19. Sagan, in Sagan & Shklovskii (1966: 186).
20. Lull (1917); Oparin (1955, 1962); Keosian (1964); Bernal (1967); de Duve (1990a); Schopf (1999).
21. Bernal (1967); Farley (1977); Mayr (1982).
22. Lahav (1999).
23. Farley (1977).
24. Lahav (1999).
25. Lucretius (1965: vol. 5, 158, lines 793–8).
26. Harris (2002: 5). Although the range of species thought to be generated spontaneously narrowed over the centuries to more primitive animals and insects, the continued popularity of spontaneous generation was largely due to the endorsement of Aristotle's works by St Augustine's and the Christian Church until the time of the Protestant Reformation and Renaissance (ibid.: 6).
27. Oró (2002: 13).
28. Harris (2002).
29. Farley (1977).
30. Quoted in de Kruif (1926: 30).
31. de Kruif (1926); de Duve (1990a); Geison (1995); Harris (2002).
32. Quoted in Geison (1995: 120); Harris (2002: 118); see also Duve (1990b); Orgel (1994).
33. Oró (2002: 13).
34. Teilhard (1955).
35. Medawar (1961: 100).
36. Eccles (1989: 239).
37. Quoted in Schopf (2002a: 13).
38. Geison (1969); Maienschein (1990).
39. Lahav (1999).
40. Maienschein (1990); Harris (1002: 94–100).
41. Geison (1969: 273); Harris (2002: 99).
42. Drake & Sobel (1992: 1). Metrodorus of Chios (331–278 BC) was a Greek atomist and philosopher in the Epicurean school.
43. de Duve (1995).
44. Anaxagoras accounted for the origin of life by "seeds" coming to Earth from the atmosphere, brought down by rainwater into the terrestrial slime, which is not too dissimilar from the panspermia hypothesis (Kirk et al. 1983).
45. Mason (1991); Gribbin (1993b); Bernstein et al. (1999).
46. Bernstein et al. (1999).
47. Ibid.
48. Wald (1973).
49. Lineweaver and Grether are trying to estimate the number of Jupiter-like planets orbiting sun-like stars in the Milky Way galaxy. They chose Jupiter-like planets orbiting sun-like stars because Jupiter is the largest planet, and has by far the bulk of our solar system's mass (with the exception of the sun). It is known that Jupiter shielded Earth from an even heavier bombardment of debris that made its way from the outskirts of the new system toward its central star around 4–4.6 billion years ago. The astrophysicists estimate that there are about 300 billion stars in the Milky Way galaxy, of which about 10 per cent (or 30 billion) are roughly sun-like. Of these, they maintain that at least 5 per cent (1.5 billion) could be solar systems similar to ours.
50. Crick (1981); Hoyle & Wickramasinghe (1981).
51. Hoyle & Wickramasinghe (1981); Schopf (2002a: 14).
52. Bada (1995).
53. Oró (1997); Bernstein et al. (1999).
54. Bada (1995).
55. About 3.5 billion years ago, Mars lost its magnetosphere, hydrosphere and atmosphere, making it an extremely hostile environment for life compared to conditions on Earth. Because of its subzero temperatures and low atmospheric pressures, there is no liquid water on the surface of the planet. But the presence of bacterial life occurring deep in Mars's interior remains a distinct possibility given that the early conditions were similar to Earth (i.e. before 3.5 billion years ago) (Rye & Holland 1998).
56. Schopf (1999).
57. Maynard-Smith & Szathmary (1999: 1).
58. Schopf (1999).
59. Watson et al. (1987).
60. Maynard-Smith & Szathmary (1999: 1).
61. Evolution by way of natural selection is a huge lottery with only a few survivors. If a change in an organism is suitable for a particular environment, it may be selected. If not, the organism will die. Evolution is unidirectional, meaning that if the Earth's clock were wound back to time zero and the process started over again, the evolutionary outcomes would probably be very different (Dawkins 1989; 1991). Over the millennia, human beings have added another "non-random" dimension to the equation by altering the natural balance of the environment.
62. A. Szent-Györgyi (1948: 9).
63. Ryle (1949: 17–18).
64. Margulis & Sagan (1995).
65. In the cycle of life, more than 99.9 per cent of everything alive on the planet is eventually recycled to some other living system; the small fraction of dead organisms left over is the pool from which fossils form (Schopf 1999: 72).
66. Schrödinger (1992).
67. An isolated universe is not to be confused with the "closed" or "open" universe discussed in Chapter 8. In thermodynamic terminology, an "isolated" universe refers to a "contained" system where no matter–energy is exchanged with any other system. In cosmological terminology, a "closed" and "open" universe refers only to the fate of the universe, which is determined by the total amount of matter it contains. Both a "closed" and "open" universe are isolated systems in a thermodynamic sense.
68. Blum (1955).
69. Trefil (1994).
70. Quoted in Lehninger (1975: 413).
71. Dobson (2004: 470).

72. During the Earth's compaction, the denser molten material (iron and nickel) sank to the centre, forming the core. The less dense material stratified in different layers at the top, forming the mantle. The core and mantle constitute about 99 per cent of the total mass of the Earth and the remaining 1 per cent is in the outer crust (Mason 1958). The average thickness of the Earth's crust is 35 km (ranging from 7 km in deep oceanic basins to 60–80 km under mountain ranges, e.g. Tibet). The world's continents attach to the constantly moving plates of the mantle. The temperature gradient from the outer crust to the inner core is 15 °C–6000 °C (Emiliani 1992).

73. The word "atmosphere" is derived from the Greek meaning "ball of vapour". Today, the atmosphere is about 100 km deep and constitutes 0.0001 per cent of the Earth's total mass. Half of the atmosphere by weight lies in the first 5.5 km above the Earth's surface (Mason 1958). The air above 100 km is a near-vacuum, exerting only one millionth of the barometric pressure at sea level (Lovelock 1991). The atmosphere keeps the Earth's surface warm and watery and protects it from incoming harmful high-energy radiation.

74. The solar system is believed to have formed from a cloud of swirling matter remaining after a supernova explosion of burnt-out stars. The sun formed from the condensing gas about 5 bya, and its nine orbiting planets around 400 million years later (Emiliani 1992).

75. Ibid.

76. Bernal (1967); Dyson (1999).

77. Cairns-Smith (1985); Lahav (1999).

78. Kasting (1993). The nitrogen level in primordial times is thought to be similar to the level today but the level of carbon dioxide was tens of thousands times greater (Bada 1995). The present-day atmosphere is highly oxidizing and comprises 20.95 per cent oxygen, 78.10 per cent nitrogen, 0.09 per cent argon, 0.035 per cent carbon dioxide and 0.0002 per cent methane.

79. Mason (1991); Bada (1995).

80. Bada et al. (1994); Wills & Bada (2001).

81. Schopf (1999: 3).

82. Holland (1997).

83. Mason (1991); Holland (1997).

84. Schopf (1999: 271; 2002b).

85. Schopf (1999: 271; 2002b).

86. Rasmussen (2000).

87. Nisbet (2000).

88. Rye & Holland (1998). The principal oxidants in the lower atmosphere are ozone (O_3) and photodissociation by-products, the hydroxyl radical (OH) and hydrogen peroxide (H_2O_2) (Thompson 1992).

89. The inorganic mechanism of photolysis is capable of producing only trace amounts of free atmospheric oxygen. Schopf believes that the biologically mediated photodissociation of water to oxygen by photosynthesizers was much more important to the release of oxygen into the atmosphere (Schopf 1983).

90. Emiliani (1992).

91. Rye & Holland (1998).

92. Rye & Holland (1998); Nisbet (2000).

93. Ozone is formed at altitudes above 16.8 km with maximum concentrations occurring around 20–25 km (Emiliani 1992). After a thunder shower, the smell of ozone can be detected. In the Odyssey, and again in the Iliad, Homer refers to the characteristic odour of ozone after a storm. The first investigation into ozone began in 1785, a little over 10 years after the discovery of oxygen. The Dutch chemist Van Murem reported that he could generate the characteristic smell at the anode in the electrolysis of water. In 1840, the smelly gas was named ozone by C. F. Schonbein after a Greek word meaning "to smell" (Asimov 1964).

94. Folsome (1979).

95. Darwin (1871) in a letter to botanist friend Joseph Hooker (1817–1911).

96. Wills & Bada (2001); Miller & Lazcano (2002: 100–102).

97. Haldane (1954); Oparin (1955).

98. Miller (1955); Miller & Lazcano (2002: 78–112).

99. Orgel (1994).

100. Miller & Orgel (1974); Cohen (1996).

101. Oró et al. (1973); Miller & Lazcano (2002: 92–4); Oró (2002: 7–45, and references).

102. Oró & Kimball (1961); Oró (2002: 23–5). Oró was able to synthesize over a billion adenine molecules in a week.

103. Orgel (1994).

104. Fox (1986).

105. Smith & Roohk (1985); Fox (1988).

106. Quoted in Horgan (1996: 140).

107. Genes are the basic units of heredity. They are built of a chain-like sequence of hundreds of nucleotides. Each nucleotide is composed of three subunits: a sugar, a phosphate and a base. The base may be a purine (adenine "A", or guanine "G") or a pyrimidine (cytosine "C", or thymine, "T"). Each DNA molecule consists of two strands wound in a double helix and is made up of genes joined like a string of beads. The gene-bearing DNA is housed in the chromosomes. The sequence of the order A, G, C and T bases contains the chemical code required for the manufacture of proteins.

108. Ayala (1995b).

109. Pennisi (2001).

110. Fruton (1972: 47, 67).

111. Price & Stevens (1982).

112. Dobson (2003).

113. Orgel (2002: 141).

114. Cech (1986a,b).

115. Orgel (1994: 53).

116. Orgel (1994).

117. Cech (1986a).

118. Eigen (1992); Orgel (1994). DNA seems to have been selected over RNA because of its greater evolvability giving rise to multicellular organisms (Gerhart & Kirshner 1997). In single-cell life

forms, the DNA exists as a single strand, while more advanced forms of life have their DNA packaged into bundles called chromosomes.

119. Eigen (1992).
120. Cohen (1996).
121. Beaudry & Joyce (1992).
122. Gilbert (1986); Orgel (2002: 142).
123. Bernal (1967). Freeman Dyson and James Ferris explain that the microcrystals of clay have an irregular distribution of minerals (e.g. kaolinite, illite, montmorillonite) or metal ions (e.g. uranyl ion, Mg^{2+}, Ca^{2+}, Mn^{2+}) on their surface, and it is these minerals or metal ions that can operate as catalysts and carriers of information for building the nucleotide bases in a molecule such as RNA (Dyson 1999: 43; Ferris 2002: 124).
124. *Ibid.*
125. Ferris (2002).
126. Ferris *et al.* (1996).
127. Kaolinite forms from the deep weathering of feldspars and other aluminosilicates. Other major clay types are illite and montmorillonite (Emiliani 1992).
128. Cairns-Smith (1985); Ferris *et al.* (1996).
129. Ferris & Ertem (1992); Ferris (2002: 121).
130. Ferris (2002: 123).
131. Cairns-Smith (1982); Asimov (1987).
132. Orgel (2002).
133. Cairns-Smith (1982); Dyson (1999: 43–4).
134. Orgel (2002: 142).
135. *Ibid.*, 151.
136. Hochachka & Somero (2002: 273).
137. de Duve (1990a).
138. Lahav (1999); Miller & Laxcano (2002: 105).
139. Loeb (1906: 1).
140. Schopf (1999).
141. Rye & Holland (1998).
142. Theoretically, if a doubling occurred every 20 minutes, a single cell could give rise to a colony weighing 10^6 kg in 24 hours. Food availability and other regulatory factors do not permit this vast potential to be realized in nature.
143. Woese (1981).
144. *Ibid.*
145. Doolittle (2000).
146. The total number of cows on Earth produce about 50 million metric tons of methane per year. Other methane producers include sheep, goats, camels, deer, elk, buffalo and caribou. As methane rises in the atmosphere, it converts into carbon dioxide, contributing to the greenhouse effect, however, the biggest culprit to the greenhouse effect is not animal flatulence, but humans burning fossil fuels (Lovelock 1991).
147. *Ibid.*
148. Rye & Holland (1998).
149. Mason (1991).
150. Postlethwait & Hopson (1992).
151. Campbell (1996).
152. The term "photosynthesis" was introduced in 1893. In the eighteenth century, English chemist Stephen Hales believed that leaves of plants "perspired" during the day and absorbed "imbibed" air, which formed some kind of nourishment at night. A little later, Dutch plant physiologist Jan Ingenhousz discovered that white light was essential for the process by which green plants absorb carbon dioxide and release oxygen. Ingenhousz's findings made a great deal of sense and confirmed the self-regulating cycle and economy of nature proposed earlier by Joseph Priestley (Bynum *et al.* 1981). That is, green plants absorb carbon dioxide and release oxygen and animals do the opposite in a self-perpetuating cycle.
153. Stomatolites are fossilized mats of alternating organically rich and poor laminated layers (1.0 mm thick) of sediment (Schopf 1999). Microscopic spherical and filamentous cyanobacteria have been found in the organic layers and calcium carbonate or silicon oxide in the alternate layers. Stromatolites resemble the layered mats constructed by present-day colonies of bacteria. The layers are sediments that stick to the jelly coats of bacteria, which then migrate, reproduce and move out and form a new layer, producing the characteristic banding pattern (*ibid.*). Stromatolites are found in Newfoundland, Canada; Minnesota, USA; the Bahamas, and Shark Bay, Australia.
154. Rye & Holland (1998).
155. Schopf (1999).
156. Gould (1994: 65).
157. Folk (1997).
158. *Ibid.*
159. Uwins *et al.* (1998).
160. Kajander *et al.* (2001).
161. Kajander & Ciftcioglu (1998).
162. Wainwright (1999); Cisar *et al.* (2000).
163. McKay *et al.* (1996).
164. Karl *et al.* (1999).
165. Rye & Holland (1998).
166. Asimov (1987); Raven & Johnson (1996).
167. Leakey & Lewin (1992).
168. Doolittle (2000).
169. *Ibid.*
170. Schopf (1999).
171. Gould (1973).
172. Woese (1999).

Chapter 11. Humankind's evolutionary origins and emergence of mind

1. Darwin (1874: 18–19).
2. Howard (1982: 15).
3. Lewin (1998).
4. Raven (1942: 234).
5. Whitehouse (1980); Bahn (1996).
6. Quoted in Whitehouse (1980: 16–24).
7. Malefijt (1974).
8. Linnaeus's method of classifying a species was binomial. The binomial system denoted an animal's (or plant's) immutability (genus) and its distinctiveness (species): for example, *Homo sapiens* = human thinking (established 1758). Linnaeus believed that every species was created

by God simultaneously. Immutability meant that species could not merge with another, nor were they related genetically.

9. Mayr (1982).
10. Simpson (1949); Mayr (1982).
11. Mayr (1982); Dobzhansky & Boesiger (1983).
12. Mayr (1982).
13. Medawar (1991: 5).
14. Gould (1973).
15. Cohn (1996); Whitehouse (1980).
16. Coleman (1973).
17. Clark (1984).
18. Quoted in White (1970: 128). The full passage in Hutton's *Theory of the Earth* involving geological processes occurring over long periods is as follows:

> We have now got to the end of our reasoning; we have no data further to conclude immediately from that which actually is: But we have got enough; we have the satisfaction to find, that in nature there is wisdom, system, and consistency. For having, in the natural history of this earth, seen a succession of worlds, we may from this conclude that there is a system in nature; in like manner as, from seeing revolutions of the planets, it is concluded, that there is a system by which they are intended to continue those revolutions. But if the succession of worlds is established in the system of nature, it is in vain to look for any thing higher in the origin of the earth. The result, therefore, of our present enquiry is, that we find no vestige of a beginning, – no prospect of an end.

19. Cohn (1996).
20. Mayr (1982).
21. James Ussher's (1581–1656) calculation was very complicated and was based on the most up-to-date chronological methods and a critical synthesis of biblical, Middle Eastern and Mediterranean sources (Craig & Jones 1982; Cohn 1996). His analysis can be found in Volume 4 of his famous *Annals of the World* (1650). In highly abbreviated form, Ussher compared the six days of God's creation with the 6000 years envisaged for the Earth's duration ("one day with the Lord was a thousand years") (see Bahn 1996). Since the first and second days saw the creation of air and the stars, that leaves four days or 4000 years before Christ. The extra four years were added because Herod had died in 4 BC, making that the year of the birth of Christ (*ibid.*).

Ussher began his chronology with the creation of light on early Saturday evening after the autumnal equinox (October in the old Roman calendar), followed by the creation of the world on Sunday. He never specified a time as is often reported (i.e. 9.00am), only that "the creation and first motion" occurred on "the evening preceding that first day of the Julian year", which would make it the evening of 22 October (Brice 1982). Ussher calculated other important dates in biblical history, concluding, for example, that

Adam and Eve were expelled from Paradise on Monday 10 November 4004 BC, and that the ark landed on Mt Ararat on 5 May 1491 BC, "on a Wednesday".

Dr John Lightfoot (1602–1675), one of the most eminent Hebrew scholars of his time, believed, after an exhaustive study of the Scriptures, that human beings were created at 9.00am and that the world was created on Sunday 12 September 3928 BC (Brice 1982). These computations were performed in 1642 and 1644, six to eight years *before* the publication of Ussher's *Annals of the World*. The time of 9.00am often associated with Ussher's date of world creation was an apparent conflation of Ussher's chronology with that of Lightfoot's computations (see Brice 1982). Further criticisms of Ussher's work by a number of nineteenth-century Bible scholars, who were trying to harmonize Genesis with the new discoveries in the geology of the Earth and human antiquity, can be found in Numbers (2000).

It is also worth noting that in the three forms in which Genesis appears – the Hebrew text, the Samaritan Pentateuch and the Septuagint (ancient Greek translation) – no two estimates of the creation of the world agree (see Westermann 1984). For example, the Jewish date for the creation of the Earth is 3760 BC; Eusebius of Caesarea (AD 260–340) calculated it as 3184 BC, Kepler calculated it as 3993 BC and Newton calculated it as 3998 BC using numerous biblical and classical texts.

22. White (1922: 9); see also Dobzhansky & Boesiger (1983).
23. Quoted in Cohn (1996: 123).
24. Darwin (1859: 70).
25. Darwin (1859: 149). To Darwin, "descent with modification" meant changes that occur in a population over the generations. In the introduction to his *Origin of Species*, Darwin wrote:

> As more individuals of each species are born than can possibly survive; and as, consequently, there is a frequently recurring struggle for existence, it follows that any being, if it vary however slightly in any manner profitable to itself, under the complex and sometimes varying conditions of life, will have a better chance of surviving, and thus be naturally selected. From the strong principle of inheritance, any selected variety will tend to propagate its new and modified form.
> (*Ibid.*: 3–4)

26. See *ibid.*, 100–112.
27. See Mayr (1988: 216–32); Gould (1973: 11–12, 40–41); Dawkins (1991: 43–76).
28. Gould (1973).
29. Gillespie (1979); Mayr (1982).
30. Gould (1973).
31. Howard (1982).
32. Erasmus Darwin practised medicine for some 40 years, and his magnum opus, *Zoonomia* (1794–96), was mostly a work of medical theory. For much of his life, Erasmus rejected Christianity in

favour of Deism. He often asked how a truly loving Father could allow terrible diseases to be inflicted upon innocent children. Erasmus also developed a theory of biological evolution, asking: "Would it be too bold to imagine, that in the great length of time, since the earth began to exist, perhaps millions of ages before commencement of the history of mankind ... that all warm-blooded animals have arisen from one living filament, which THE GREAT FIRST CAUSE endued with animality?" (quoted in King-Hele 1968: 87).

33. Desmond & Moore (1994).
34. Darwin (1888: vol. 2, 355).
35. Darwin (1888: vol. 1, 30).
36. Clark (1984: 6).
37. Desmond & Moore (1994).
38. Clark (1984: 12).
39. Darwin (1888).
40. Quoted in Clark (1984: 13); see also Darwin (1888: vol. 1, 41). Darwin was in awe of Paley's logical method and wrote in his autobiography that it "gave me as much delight as did (reading) Euclid" (Darwin 1888: vol. 1, 41). Paley used the analogy of a watch and watchmaker to argue the need for an intelligent designer, and that designer was God. The famous analogy can be found in the opening paragraph of his *Natural Theology* (1802):

> In crossing a heath, suppose I pitched my foot against a *stone*, and were asked how the stone came to be there; I might possibly answer, that, for anything I knew to the contrary, it had lain there for ever: nor would it perhaps be very easy to show the absurdity of this answer. But suppose I had found a *watch* upon the ground, and it should be inquired how the watch happened to be in that place; I should hardly think of the answer which I had before given, that for any thing I knew, the watch might have always been there.

In his analogy, Paley emphasizes the difference between a physical object such as a stone and a designed, manufactured object, such as a watch. Paley concludes: "that the watch must have had a maker; that there must have existed, at some time, and at some place or other, an artificer or artificers, who formed it for the purpose which we find it actually to answer; who comprehended its construction, and designed its use" (quoted in Dawkins 1991: 4).

41. Clark (1984: 13); see also Darwin (1888: vol. 1, 40–41).
42. Quoted in Ruse (1982: *xi*).
43. Gould (1973).
44. Ruse (1982); see also Darwin (1888: vol. 1, 50).
45. Darwin wrote these beautiful words in his diary on 28 February 1832, when he first experienced a Brazilian rainforest near All Saints Bay. He wrote:

> The delight one experiences in such times bewilders the mind; if the eye attempts to follow the flight of a gaudy butter-fly, it is arrested by some strange tree or fruit; if

watching an insect one forgets it in the stranger flower it is crawling over; if turning to admire the splendour of the scenery, the individual character of the foreground fixes the attention. The mind is a chaos of delight, out of which a world of future & more quiet pleasures will arise" (quoted in Barrett & Freeman 1986: 38).

46. Clark (1984).
47. *Ibid.*
48. Darwin (1888: vol. 1 83).
49. *Ibid.*, vol. 1, 86; see also Poulton (1911); Pekin (1938).
50. Charles Darwin in a letter to Alfred Russel Wallace, quoted in Clark (1984: 53).
51. Ruse (1982).
52. Thomas R. Malthus (1766–1834) was an English clergyman and political economist. Malthus's sociological treatise was a response in part to the views of philosopher and mathematician Marquis de Condorcet (Mayr 1982: 493). Condorcet believed in a social Utopia where all people, regardless of race, creed or colour, were to be equally assured of freedom and opportunity, either by law or by custom. Malthus agreed with Condorcet's vision, but believed that it would rarely be realized in real life.
53. Darwin (1888: vol. 1, 68); for more information see Mayr (1988: 216–17); Clark (1984: 53–7).
54. *Ibid.*
55. Malthus argued that the mismatch between population growth and food supply helped explained human suffering such as disease, famine, homelessness and war. Malthus's actual sentence that aroused Darwin's interest was: "It may safely be pronounced, therefore, that population, when left unchecked, goes on doubling itself every twenty-five years, or increases in a geometrical ratio" (quoted in Clark 1984: 54).
56. Mayr (1982).
57. Darwin (1888: vol. 1, 68). Darwin's briefest "sketch" on natural selection appeared in 1842, and was followed by a 230-page essay in 1844 (Howard 1982).
58. Mayr (1982: 386).
59. Howard (1982).
60. Darwin & Wallace (1958); Ruse (1982).
61. Howard (1982: 6).
62. Clark (1984).
63. Darwin (1874: 17).
64. Haeckel (1906).
65. Wallace (1871: 372); Eccles (1989: 235).
66. Gould (1973); Mayr (1982).
67. From a personal letter from Sedgwick to Darwin, written after he read *The Origin of Species*. The letter was dated 24 December 1859 and can be read in its entirety in Darwin (1888: vol. 2, 42–5). For further discussion see Ritland (1982).
68. Darwin (1888: vol. 2, 115). See also Huxley (1901: 192–204); Lucas (1979: 324); Gould (1986a).
69. Darwin (1888: vol. 2, 115).
70. Lucas (1979: 324–30).

71. Quoted in Gardner (1963: 126); see also Lucas (1979: 324). For more details see Thomson (2000: 210).
72. Gardner (1963: 126); Darwin (1888).
73. Clark (1984).
74. *Ibid.*
75. Brooke (1991).
76. Darwin (1888: 117).
77. Darwin (1874: 633).
78. *Ibid.*, 170.
79. *Ibid.*, 171.
80. *Ibid.*, 643.
81. Dobzhansky (1956: 3).
82. Darwin (1888: vol. 1, 39).
83. Quoted in Clark (1984: 12).
84. Darwin (1959: 85–7).
85. Clark (1984: 58).
86. Darwin (1888: 275).
87. Later in his life Darwin wrote, "I have said that in one respect my mind has changed during the last twenty or thirty years. Up to the age of thirty, or beyond it, poetry of many kinds, such as the works of Milton, Gray, Byron, Wordsworth, Coleridge, and Shelley, gave me great pleasure, and even as a schoolboy I took intense delight in Shakespeare, especially in the historical plays. I have also said that formerly pictures gave me considerable, and music very great delight. But now for many years I cannot endure to read a line of poetry: I have tried lately to read Shakespeare, and found it so intolerably dull that it nauseated me. I have also almost lost my taste for pictures or music. Music generally sets me thinking too energetically on what I have been at work on, instead of giving me pleasure. I retain some taste for fine scenery, but it does not cause me the exquisite delight which it formerly did" (Darwin 1888: vol. 1, 81).
88. Dennett (1995: 21).
89. Simpson (1949); Gould (1973); Dobzhansky *et al.* (1977); *Nature* (1981); Ruse (1982); Dobzhansky & Boesiger (1983); Dawkins (1991); Leakey (1994).
90. Mayr (2000).
91. Ruse (1982); Lewin (1998).
92. See Gerhart and Kirshner (1997); Gehring (1999).
93. Steele (1998).
94. Darwin (1859: 123).
95. Eccles (1979, 1989, 1990).
96. Vincent Sarich, quoted in Leakey & Lewin (1992: 76).
97. Leakey & Lewin (1992).
98. Sarich and Wilson's method involved accepting that the apes split from the Old World monkeys 30 mya. The two scientists then analysed blood albumin (and other proteins) in a range of living apes (and human beings) that split from this established line (Gribbin 1985). If the species under investigation were closely related, then one would expect a very good biochemical match. And from measuring the degree of genetic differences between two related species, a divergence time can be estimated. A major assumption of the method was that any changes on a protein were random and occurred at a constant rate. If, for example, the rate were faster in the past 5 million years compared to the previous 25 million years, errors would be present in the estimates (Sibley *et al.* 1990; Diamond 1991; Leakey 1994).
99. Sarich & Cronin (1977).
100. Diamond (1991).
101. The often mentioned 100 000 human genes was postulated by Harvard Nobel laureate Walter Gilbert in the middle of the 1980s (Pennisi 2001).
102. The project was carried out by a publicly funded consortium of international researchers (International Human Genome Sequencing Consortium) administered by the National Institutes of Health (IHGS Consortium 2001), and by a second privately funded US company, Celera Genomics (Venter *et al.* 2001), using new methodologies and supercomputing power.
103. Maynard-Smith & Szathmary (1999); Pennisi (2001).
104. Another amazing discovery of the human genome project is that human beings share up to 233 genes with bacteria. These genes do not exist in the worm, fly or yeast. The vertebrate genome seems to have taken on bacterial genes in the same way bacterial genes take on genes that confer antibiotic resistance (Pennisi 2001). These bacterial genes probably entered the human genome directly (or in one of our vertebrate ancestors), not by evolution from bacteria (Baltimore 2001). Another most interesting feature is that human beings have incorporated the genetic information from bacteria into vital physiological functions, including the immune system.
105. Repeat sequences are patterns of bases that have been "repeated", sometimes for long stretches along the chromosome, and may represent ancient remnants (like a fossil record) that have shaped the evolution of the human genome (Baltimore 2001). Repeats are thought to be involved in turning "on" and "off" genes, which can lead to new rearrangements and possibly new developmental processes. Interestingly, the human genome has many more repeats than most organisms studied: the mustard plant has 11 per cent repeats, the worm has 7 per cent repeats and the fly has 3 per cent repeats. Curiously, the extra baggage is not present in the deer or bat, which has a genome about one-sixth to one-tenth the size of the human genome. The non-coding "junk" genes (50 per cent) were so named because no one really knows their function. Recent consensus is that the non-coding "junk" genes underpin the whole structure of the cell by controlling and interacting with the coding genes.
106. Sibley & Ahlquist (1984); Sibley *et al.* (1990).
107. Morris Goodman reported in 1987 that there was about 1.6 per cent difference between human beings and chimpanzees in non-coding regions of the globin cluster (Goodman *et al.* 1989).

Goodman used linear sequence DNA information comprising some 10 000 bases (different arrangements of the bases adenine, cytosine, guanine and thymine). In light of the recent mapping of the human genome, at least in terms of protein-coding genes, human beings may be more closely related to chimpanzees than the 1.6 per cent difference of "total" DNA implies. Indeed, the differences may be so subtle that simple genomic comparisons may not be sufficiently sensitive.

108. Goodman *et al.* (1989); Lewin (1998).
109. Diamond (1991); Lewin (1998).
110. McGinnis *et al.* (1984); Scott & Weiner (1984).
111. Gehring (1999).
112. Holland & Fernandez (1996).
113. Gehring (1999).
114. Slack *et al.* (1993); de Rosa *et al.* (1999); Baltimore (2001).
115. Hominids are thought to have been exclusively ground-dwelling and bipedal, used tools, possessed an enlarged brain relative to body weight, shared food, displayed pair-bonding, were continuously sexually active and had nuclear families. In contrast, the apes are largely arboreal, quadrupeds, display minimal use of tools, are not pair-bonded, display little food sharing, mate only during oestrus and care for a single infant (Johanson & Edey 1982; Wood 1991). Although some differences remain controversial, particularly tool use, the two most distinguishing features between a hominid and an ape are the large brain size to body weight ratio and the reliance on bipedal or erect-walking.
116. Leakey & Lewin (1992).
117. Jablonski & Chaplin (2000).
118. Asfaw *et al.* (1999).
119. Wood (1996).
120. Johanson & White (1979); Johanson & Edey (1982); Johanson *et al.* (1996).
121. Leakey *et al.* (1995).
122. White *et al.* (1995).
123. Harcourt-Smith & Aiello (2004).
124. Galik *et al.* (2004).
125. Brunet *et al.* (2002).
126. Asfaw *et al.* (1999).
127. *Ibid.*, 632.
128. Jablonski & Chaplin (2000).
129. *Ibid.*
130. Wood & Collard (1999b).
131. Wood & Brooks (1999); Tattersall (2000).
132. Wood & Collard (1999a); Elton *et al.* (2001).
133. Tattersall (2000).
134. Wood & Brooks (1999).
135. Leakey & Lewin (1992).
136. *Ibid.*
137. Wood & Collard (1999b).
138. Leakey & Lewin (1992).
139. Tattersall (2000).
140. Balter (2001).
141. Wood (1996); Tattersall (2000).
142. Balter (2001).
143. Deevey (1960).
144. Tattersall (2000).
145. *Ibid.*
146. Leakey & Lewin (1992).
147. Moorwood *et al.* (1998).
148. Balter (1995).
149. Leakey & Lewin (1992).
150. Tattersall (1999, 2000).
151. Bahn (1996: 324).
152. Neanderthal people were approximately 1.5 m tall, with low sloping heads that bulged at the rear, low heavy brows, massive jaws, thick-set bodies with short forearms and a large brain capacity (Tattersall 2000). They were prolific hunters and lived in caves and rock shelters, participated in burying the dead and other rituals, used elaborate tools, and used fire to cook and protect themselves from the extreme cold (Leakey & Lewin 1992; Stringer & Gamble 1993). What caused the disappearance of Neanderthals remains a mystery.
153. White *et al.* (2003).
154. Ayala (1995a); McBreaty & Brooks (2000). Some of the oldest human fossils have been found in the Levant at the site of Qafzeh Cave in Palestine (near Nazareth). There was also a controversial report in 1994 from Chinese scientists of a re-dated skull of a modern-looking human being, which they date to at least 200 000 years ago.
155. There was a major advance in understanding human evolution on the discovery of a new symbolic language that appeared around 40 000 years ago in the Upper Paleolithic. The time corresponds to the emergence in western Europe of a different kind of art, refined fish hooks, new types of spear heads, more advanced tools, carved figurines and evidence of burial of the dead with adornments and plants (Fagan 1994; Renfrew 1994; Burkert 1996; Renfrew & Bahn 1996; Lewin 1998; McBreaty & Brooks 2000). In the Middle East, around the same time, there appears to be no comparable activity, which is somewhat paradoxical if modern human beings migrated out of Africa along the northeastern route. More understandable is the later arrival of new inventions in Asia because of the long distances that had to be travelled (Lewin 1998).
156. Akazawa *et al.* (1998).
157. Deevey (1960).
158. Brown *et al.* (2004); Morwood *et al.* (2004).
159. Brown *et al.* (2004).
160. Wilson & Cann (1992); Ingman *et al.* (2000).
161. Thorne & Wolpoff (1992); Leakey (1994); Stringer & McKie (1996); Stringer (2003).
162. Lahr (1994); Hedges (2000); Stringer (2003).
163. White *et al.* (2003).
164. Hedges (2000); Ingman *et al.* (2000).
165. Ingman *et al.* (2000).
166. Jin *et al.* (1999).
167. Balter (2001).
168. Sykes (2001)
169. Lewin (1998); Pough *et al.* (1999).
170. Semino *et al.* (2000).
171. *Ibid.*
172. American Anthropological Association Statement

on "Race" and Intelligence, adopted December 1994. For details see www.aanet.org/stmts/race.htm (accessed Feb. 2005).

173. Jablonski & Chaplin (2000).

174. *Ibid.*

175. *Ibid.*

176. *Ibid.*

177. *Ibid.*

178. The vertebrate brain is a conspicuous lobed enlargement of neural tissue housed in the cranial cavity of the skull and continuous with the anterior end of the spinal cord. The function of the brain is to integrate and coordinate behaviour and experience. The first recorded reference to the brain and its description is found in ancient writings of Egypt in the Edwin Smith Surgical Papyrus (McHenry 1969; Skinner 1970).

179. In addition to measuring brain size by volume there is an equation relating brain volume and body size, which leads to a parameter called the encephalization constant Jerison 1973 [1016]. The encephalization constant is 1.53 for a gorilla, 1.63 for an orang-utan (male), 2.48 for a chimpanzee and 7.79 for human beings (Jerison 1973; Stein & Rowe 1989). Interestingly, the porpoise's brain is 3–4 times the value for a Californian sea-lion of equal body weight (Jerison 1988: 452). In addition, although human beings do have larger brains for their body size than primates, there appears to be nothing disproportionate about many of its major parts. For example, the volume of the frontal lobes expressed as a percentage of the hemispheres is 37 per cent in human beings and 35 per cent in bonobos, chimps and gorillas. Expansion of hominid brain size is thought to be related to a species' response to niche-specific cognitive challenges (Finlay *et al.* 2001).

180. Stringer & Gamble (1993: 480).

181. Brown *et al.* (2004).

182. Leakey & Lewin (1992); Stringer & Gamble (1993).

183. The vocal tract in early hominids (and possibly Neanderthals) is located behind the base of the tongue. In modern human beings, the vocal tract is much lower and shifts to the front between one and two years of age, with the creation of a much larger resonating chamber for speech. This also allows greater space above the larynx housing the voice box and permits a wider modification of sounds. Non-human mammals (and newborn human beings up to 1.5–2 years old) are limited to modifying laryngeal sounds by altering the shape of the oral cavity and the lips (Leakey 1994). When human beings reach 2 years old, the larynx begins to migrate lower in the neck, achieving the adult position at around 14 years of age. Some paleoneurologists believe that the position of the larynx in *Homo erectus*, and perhaps *H. ergaster*, was similar to about an 8-year-old human being (Lewin 1998). Human beings also possess the ability to voluntarily breathe through their mouths, something other mammals are unable to

achieve (Pough *et al.* 1999). Fine respiratory control is a necessary component for fully developed modern language, which is also believed to have evolved between 0.1–1.6 mya (Maclarnon & Hewitt 1999).

184. Stringer & Gamble (1993).

185. McHenry (1969).

186. Crook (1980); Denton (1993); Singer (1995).

187. Gazzaniga (1998, 2000).

188. Gazzaniga (1998, 2000).

189. Corballis *et al.* (2000).

190. Kant (1974: I, 9).

191. The other animals showing similar increases in cortical folding to human beings are porpoises and dolphins (2500–3000 cm^2). Some speculate the extra brain volume in dolphins relates to advanced echo communication (McMahon & Bonner 1983; Jerison 1988).

192. McHenry (1969).

193. Lewin (1998).

194. Gazzaniga (1998).

195. Sutherland (1989: 90).

196. Greenfield (1995).

197. Searle (1992); Chalmers (1996); Dennett (1996).

198. Allman (1999).

199. Gazzaniga (1998).

200. This is not strictly true because the cortex, as discussed, is not an entity in its own right but is functionally linked to other parts of the brain.

201. Penfield (1961).

202. Llinas & Pare (1991).

203. Libet (2000).

204. *Ibid.*

205. Libet (1999).

206. Attributed to Thomas H.Key (1799–1875), in *Punch* **29** (14 July 1855): 19.

207. Eccles (1989).

208. The concept of mind–body dualism is inherited from the ancient Greeks. Seventeenth-century philosopher René Descartes maintained that the physical substance that makes up the bulk of the body, including the nervous system, is of three dimensions and can be measured and divided. Animals, according to Descartes, were *mechanical automata* (or machines) that lacked consciousness, reason and souls (Dobzhansky & Boesiger 1983). The second kind of substance that separated human beings from animals was confined to the part of the brain involved in thought, desires and volitions. This non-physical substance comprises the region known as the mind or soul. The substance of mind, unlike that of the body, cannot be extended or divided. The mind, Descartes wrote, "is of a nature that has no relation to the extent nor to the dimensions or properties of matter of which the body is made" (*ibid.*). A major problem with Descartes's dualism relates to "causal interaction". For example, how do such substances in mind coordinate sense-perception and become an idea? We know from walking down the street or driving down a winding road that the mind and body do not operate

in isolation. Descartes himself was aware of this problem but reconciled it by saying that in many cases mind and body "intermingle" to form a kind of unit. He thought the two communicated in the pineal gland. The doctrine of Cartesian dualism has received little scientific support.

209. Warner (1994).
210. Eccles (1989: 176, 237); Eccles (1979, 1990).
211. Eccles (1989: xi).
212. Leakey *et al.* (1995).
213. Eccles (1990: 237).
214. Persinger (1993a, 1993b); Persinger *et al.* (2000).
215. Blanke *et al.* (2002).
216. Mithen (1996); Boyer (2001).
217. Barrett (2000).
218. *Ibid.*
219. Boyer (2003).
220. Barrett (2000).
221. Virchow, quoted in Wendt (1974: 57–8).
222. Quoted in Eccles (1989: 176); Popper (1978).
223. Gazzaniga (1998); Laland (1998); Lewin (1998).
224. Chalmers (1996: 334).
225. Chalmers (1996).
226. Wigner (1961); Pelletier (1978); Lockwood (1989); Hameroff (1994).
227. Cairns-Smith (1996).
228. Bohr (1961).
229. Eddington (1935).
230. Crick & Koch (1992); Crick (1995).
231. von Neumann (1955); Baggot (1992).
232. The core of quantum physics rests on two principles. The first describes the dynamics of the wave function; the Shrödinger equation which is a linear differential equation dealing with amplitudes of wave functions. The second is the measurement postulate (when a measurement is made, the wave function collapses into a more definite form) (Chalmers 1996). Quantum wave function collapse refers to the description of wave functions of a group of particles producing a particular result for a particular experimental arrangement (Baggot 1992). The collapse of wave function does not represent a physical change in a quantum system but rather a change in the state of knowledge of that system (*ibid.*). It is a mind invention, which allows physicists to predict the outcomes of measurements in quantum space. Some argue that the collapse is the only way in which the "real world" of classical objects (Newtonian/Einstein) can be related to the "unreal" world of quantum particles (*ibid.*).
233. von Neumann (1955); Baggot (1992).
234. Penrose (1994).
235. *Ibid.*

Chapter 12. Tradition at the crossroads: seeking unity in diversity

1. Quoted in Campbell (1988: 230).
2. Quoted in Menken (1962: 36) and Bartlett (1992: 87).
3. Plimer (1997); Raymo (1998).
4. Galileo Galilei, quoted in Drake (1980: 12). For the full text of Galileo's *The Assayer* (1623) see Drake (1957: 239–40).
5. Bronowski (1973: 374).
6. See Plato's *Apology* 20c–d (Plato 2003: 45); Penner (1992: 139). A common quote attributed to Socrates is: "I am the wisest man alive, for I know one thing, and that is that I know nothing". Another is: "True knowledge exists in knowing that you know nothing". These quotes appear to be constructed from the passage in Plato's *Apology.*
7. Creationism relies upon a literal interpretation of Scriptures, and has as its foundation the view that God's Mind (Will) lies directly behind all physical phenomena. Anything that occurs in the universe must take place because it is immediately part of God's plan. Christian creationists believe that the physical world should, and does, provide proof of God's existence, goodness and grace. The Creationist movement is an ideological movement and Creationists claim their truths to be "scientific", and believe that as such they should be taught alongside evolutionary theory in schools (Plimer 1997). As explained in the main body of the text, the movement provides a good example of "certainty seeking" that has gone awfully wrong by teaching bad history, bad religion and bad science.
8. George Bugg (d. 1851), quoted in Cohn (1996: 122).
9. Peacocke (1986).
10. Polkinghorne (1996).
11. Quote from Anselm's personal address to God in *Proslogion 1*, which can be found in Hyman & Walsh (1973: 150) and Haren (1985: 101). As we saw in Chapter 7, Anselm's deep conviction about "faith seeking understanding" was borrowed from Augustine and his interpretation of Isaiah 7:9, from a pre-Vulgate translation of the Bible (see Markus 1964: 82; Haren 1985: 222).
12. Hyman & Walsh (1973: 147); Marenbon (1983: 98).
13. Kenny (1969); Aertsen (1998: 19, 30); Kretzmann & Stump (1998).
14. Voltaire (1770), quoted in Bartlett (1992: 306).
15. Barrett *et al.* (2001).

Bibliography

Abercrombie, N., Hill, S. & Turner, B. S. 1988. *The Penguin Dictionary of Sociology*, 2nd edn. Harmondsworth: Penguin.

Abetti, G. 1952. *The History of Astronomy*. New York: Henry Shuman.

Adams, J. 1971 [1856]. *The Works of John Adams*, C. F. Adams (ed.). New York: AMS Press.

Aertsen, J. A. 1993. *Aquinas's Philosophy in its Historical Setting*, in Kretzmann & Stump (eds) (1993), 12–37.

Akazawa, T., Aoki, K. & Bar-Yosef, O. (eds) 1998. *Neandertals and Modern Humans in Western Asia*. New York: Plenum Press. 427–38.

Albright, F. 1957. *From Stone-Age to Christianity*. New York: Doubleday.

Algra, K. 1999. "The beginnings of cosmology", in Long (ed.) (1999), 45–65.

Allen, D. J. 1970. *The Philosophy of Aristotle*, 2nd edn. Oxford: Oxford University Press.

Allen, J. P. 1988a. *Genesis in Egypt: The Philosophy of Ancient Egyptian Creation Accounts*. New Haven, CT: Yale University Press. 38–49.

Allen, J. P. 1988b. "Funerary texts and their meaning", in *Mummies and Magic: The Funerary Arts of Ancient Egypt*, P. Lacovara, S. D'Auria & C. H. Roehrig (eds), 38–49. Boston: Museum of Fine Arts.

Allman, J. M. 1999. *Evolving Brains*. New York: W. H. Freeman.

Andrews, C. A. 1981. *The Rosetta Stone*. London: British Museum Press.

Andrews, R., Biggs, M. & Seidel, M. (eds) 1996. *The Columbia World of Quotations*. Princeton, NJ: Princeton University Press.

Arkani-Hamed, N., Dimopoulos, S. & Dvali, G. 2000. "The universe's unseen dimensions", *Scientific American* **283** (August), 48–55.

Armitage, A. 1990. *Copernicus:The Founder of Modern Astronomy*. New York: Dorset Press.

Armogathe, J.-R. 1998. "Proofs of the existence of God", in Garber & Ayers (eds) (1998), 305–30.

Armstrong, A. H. (ed.) 1967a. *The Cambridge History of Later Greek and Early Medieval Philosophy*. Cambridge: Cambridge University Press.

Armstrong, A. H. 1967b. "Plotinus", in Armstrong (ed.) (1967), 195–271.

Armstrong, A. H. 1969. "Greek philosophy in the age of Cicero to Plotinus", in Toynbee (ed.) (1969), 209–14.

Armstrong, A. H. (ed.) 1986. *Classical Mediterranean Spirituality*. New York: Crossroad Publishing Company.

Armstrong, K. 1993. *A History of God From Abraham to the Present: The 4000-Year Quest for God*. London: Mandarin.

Asfaw, B., White, T., Lovejoy, O. *et al.* 1999. "*Australopithecus garhi*: a new species of early hominid for Ethiopia", *Science* **284**, 629–34.

Asimov, I. 1964. *Asimov's Biographical Enclyopedia of Science and Technology*. Garden City, NY: Doubleday.

Asimov, I. 1966. *Understanding Physics, volume 3*, 3 vols. London: George Allen and Unwin.

Asimov, I. 1987. *Beginnings: The Story of Origins of Mankind, Life, the Earth, and the Universe*. New York: Walker and Company.

Assmann, J. 1995. *Egyptian Solar Religion in the New Kingdom: Re, Amun and the Crisis of Polytheism*. New York: Columbia University Press.

Assmann, J. 1997. *Moses the Egyptian: The Memory of Egypt in Western Monotheism*. Cambridge, MA: Harvard University Press.

Atherton, P. 1986. "Aristotle", in Armstrong (ed.) (1986), 121–34.

Atkins, P. 1992. *Creation Revisited: The Origin of Space, Time and the Universe*. Harmondsworth: Penguin.

Auden, W. H. (ed.) 1999. "The living thoughts of Kierkegaard", *New York Review of Books*.

Ayala, F. J. 1995a. "Genes and origins: the story of modern humans", *Journal of Molecular Evolution* **41**, 683–8.

Ayala, F. J. 1995b. "The myth of Eve: molecular biology and human origins, *Science* **270**, 1930–36.

Ayer, A. J. 1979. "Construction of our theory of the physical world", in *Philosophy As It Is*, T. Honderich & M. Burnyeat (eds), 311–47. Harmondsworth: Penguin.

Bacon, F. 1902. *Novum organum*, J. Devey (ed.). New York: P. F. Collier.

Bacon, R. 1928 [1268]. *The Opus Majus of Roger Bacon*, R. B. Burke (trans.). Philadelphia, PA: University of Pennsylvania Press.

Bada, J. L. 1995. "Cold start", *The Sciences* **35**(3), 21–5.

Bada, J. L., Bigham, C. & Miller, S. L. 1994. "Impact melting of frozen oceans on the early earth: implication for the origin of life", *Proceedings of the National Academy of Sciences (USA)*, **91**, 1248–50.

Baggot, J. 1992. *The Meaning of Quantum Theory*. Oxford: Oxford University Press.

Bahn, P. G. 1992. "The making of a mummy", *Nature* **356**, 109.

Bahn, P. G. (ed.) 1996. *The Cambridge Illustrated History of Archaeology*. Cambridge: Cambridge University Press.

Bailey, L. R. 1977. "Wood from Mt Ararat: Noah's Ark", *The Biblical Archaeologist* **40**, 137–46.

Baines, J. R. 1983. "Literacy and ancient Egyptian society", *Man* **18**, 572–99.

Baines, J. 1991. "Society, morality, and religious practice", in Shafer (ed.) (1991), 123–200.

Baines, J. & Malek, J. 1984. *Atlas of Ancient Egypt*. New York: Time Life Books.

Bakar, O. 1996. "Science", in *History of Islamic Philosophy*, S. H. Nasir & O. Leaman (eds), 926–46. London: Routledge.

Baldwin, M. W. 1970. *Christianity through the Thirteenth Century*. London: Macmillan.

Ball, W. W. 1960 [1908]. *A Short Account of the History of Mathematics*, 4th edn. New York: Dover Publications.

Balson, J. P. V. D. 1970. *Rome: The Story of an Empire*. New York: McGraw Hill.

Balter, M. 1995. "Did *Homo erectus* tame fire first?", *Science* **268**, 1570.

Balter, M. 2001. "In search of the first Europeans", *Science* **291**, 1722–5.

Baltimore, D. 2001. "Our genome unveiled", *Nature* **409**, 814–16.

Barabas, M. 1986. "The strangeness of Socrates", *Philosophical Investigations* **9**, 89–110.

Barbour, I. G. 1990. *Religion in the Age of Science*. London: SCM Press.

Baring, A. & Cashford, J. 1991. *The Myth of the Goddess: Evolution of an Image*. London: Viking.

Barker, M. & Cook, K. (eds) 1976. *Pears Encyclopaedia of Myths and Legends*. London: Book Club Associates.

Barnard, L. W. 1967. *Justin Martyr: His Life and Thought*. Cambridge: Cambridge University Press.

Barnes, T. D. 1971. *Tertullian: A Historical and Literary Study*. Oxford: Oxford University Press.

Barnes, J. 1979. *The Presocratic Philosophers: The Arguments of the Philosophers*. London: Routledge & Kegan Paul.

Barnes, J. 1984. *The Complete Works of Aristotle*. Princeton, NJ: Princeton University Press.

Barnes, J. 1987. *Early Greek Philosophy*. Harmondsworth: Penguin.

Barnes, J. 1991. "Aristotle", in *Founders of Thought*, R. M. Hare, J. Barnes & H. Chadwick (eds), 85–183. Oxford: Oxford University Press.

Barnes, J. 1995a. "Metaphysics", in Barnes (ed.) (1995b), 66–108.

Barnes, J. (ed.) 1995b. *Aristotle*. Cambridge: Cambridge University Press.

Barnes, M. H. 1997. "Rationality in religion", *Religion* **27**, 375–90.

Barnett, L. 1948. *The Universe and Dr. Einstein*. New York: William Sloane Associates.

Barnhart, R. K. (ed.) 1988. *The Barnhart Dictionary of Etymology*. New York: H. W. Wilson.

Barrett, J. L. 2000. "Exploring the natural foundations of religion", *Trends in Cognitive Science* **4**(1), 29–34.

Barrett, P. H. & Freeman, R. B. (eds) 1986. *The Works of Charles Darwin, volume 1: Diary of the Voyage of* HMS *Beagle*, N. Barlow (ed.). London: William Pickering.

Barrett, D. B., Kurian, G. T. & Johnson, T. M. (eds) 2001. *World Christian Encyclopedia: A Comparative Survey of Churches and Religions in the Modern World*. Oxford: Oxford University Press.

Barrow, J. D. 1994. *The Origin of the Universe*. London: Phoenix.

Bartlett, J. 1992. *Familiar Quotations*, 16th edn. Boston, MA: Little, Brown and Company.

Bartlett, J. G., Blanchard, A., Silk, J. & Turner, M. S. 1995. "The case for a Hubble constant of 30 km s^{-1}Mpc^{-1}", *Science* **267**, 980–83.

Baumer, F. L. (ed.) 1960. *Main Currents of Western Thought*. New York: Alfred A. Knopf.

Beale, T. W. & Carter, S. M. 1983. "On the track of the Yahya Large Kush", *Paleorient* **9**, 81–8.

Beaudry, A. A. & Joyce, G. F. 1992. "Directed evolution of an RNA enzyme", *Science* **257**, 635.

Becker, H. & Barnes, H. E. 1961 [1938]. *Social Thought: From Lore to Science*, 3rd edn. New York: Dover Publications.

Bell, E. T. 1937. *Men of Mathematics*. New York: Simon and Schuster.

Bell, E. T. 1945. *The Development of Mathematics*. New York: McGraw-Hill.

Benson, H. H. 1997. "Socrates and the beginnings of moral philosophy", in Taylor (ed.) (1997), 323–55.

Berchman, R. M. 1984. *From Philo to Origen: Middle Platonism in Tradition*. Chico, CA: Scholar Press.

Bergounioux, F. M. & Goetz, J. 1966. *Primitive and Prehistoric Religions*. New York: Hawthorn Books.

Bernal, J. D. 1967. *The Origin of Life*. London: Weidenfeld and Nicolson.

Bernard, C. 1957. *An Introduction to Experimental Medicine*. New York: Dover Publications.

Bernstein, M. P., Sandford, S. A. & Allamandola, L. J. 1999. "Life's far-flung raw materials", *Scientific American* **281** (July), 26–33.

Besserat, D. S. 1995. "Record keeping before writing", in Sasson *et al.* (eds) (1995), 2097–106.

Best, R. M. 1999. *Noah's Ark and the Ziusudra Epic: Sumerian Origins of the Flood Myth*. Winona Lake, IN: Eisenbrauns.

Biagioli, M. 1993. *Galileo Courtier: The Practice of Science in the Culture of Absolutism*. Cambridge, IL: University of Chicago Press.

Biggs, R. D. 1995. "Medicine, surgery and public health in ancient Mesopotamia", in Sasson *et al.* (eds) (1995), 1911–24.

Black, J. A. & Tait, W. J. 1995. "Archives and libraries in the ancient Near East", in Sasson *et al.* (eds) (1995), 2197–210.

Blackburn, S. 1994. *The Oxford Dictionary of Philosophy*. Oxford: Oxford University Press.

Blackwell, R. 1998. "Could there be another Galileo case?", in Machamer (ed.) (1998), 348–66.

Blanke, O. *et al.* 2002. "Stimulating illusory own-body perceptions", *Nature* **419**(6904), 269–70.

Blum, H. F. 1955. *Time's Arrow and Evolution*. Princeton, NJ: Princeton University Press.

Bohr, N. 1961 [1934]. *Atomic Theory and the Description of Nature: Four Essays with an Introductory Survey*. Cambridge: Cambridge University Press.

Bondi, H., Bonner, W. B., Lyttleton, R. A. & Whitrow, G. J. 1960. *Rival Theories of Cosmology*. Oxford: Oxford University Press.

Borghouts, J. F. 1995. "Witchcraft, magic, and divination in ancient Egypt", in Sasson *et al.* (eds) (1995), 1775–85.

Bottero, J. 1992. *Mesopotamia: Writing, Reasoning and the Gods*. Chicago, IL: University of Chicago Press.

Bottero, J. 2001. *Religion in Ancient Mesopotamia*, T. L. Fagan (trans.). Chicagor, IL: University of Chicago Press.

Bousso, R. & Polchinski, J. 2004. "The string theory landscape", *Scientific American* **291**(3), 61–9.

Bowman, A. K. 1986. *Egypt After the Pharaohs: 332 BC–AD 642 from Alexander to the Arab Conquest*. London: British Museum Press.

Boyer, C. B. 1991. *A History of Mathematics*, U. C. Merzbach (rev.). New York: John Wiley.

Boyer, P. 2001. *Religion Explained: The Evolutionary Origins of Religious Thought*. New York: Basic Books.

Boyer, P. 2003. "Religious thought and behaviour as by-products of brain function", *Trends in Cognitive Sciences* 7(3), 119–24.

Boyer, B. B. & McKeon, R. (eds) 1976. *Sic et Non*, W. J. Lewis (trans.). Chicago, IL: University of Chicago Press.

Bragg, M. 1998. *On Giant's Shoulders: Great Scientists and their Discoveries from Archimedes to DNA*. London: Hodder & Stoughton.

Brandon, S. G. F. 1963. *Creation Legends of the Ancient Near-East*. London: Hodder and Stoughton.

Brandon, S. G. F. 1973a. "Idea of God from prehistory to the middle ages", in Wiener (ed.) (1973), 331–46.

Brandon, S. G. F. 1973b. "Sin and salvation", in Wiener (ed.) (1973), 224–34.

Breasted, J. H. 1912. *Development of Religion and Thought in Ancient Egypt*. New York: Harper & Row.

Breasted, J. H. 1938. *The Conquest of Civilization*, E. W. Ware (ed.). New York: Harper & Brothers.

Brice, W. R. 1982. "Bishop Ussher, John Lightfoot and Age of Creation", *Journal of Geological Education* **30**, 18–24.

Brickhouse, T. C. & Smith, N. D. 1989. "Socrates on good, virtue and happiness", *Oxford Studies in Ancient Philosophy* **5**, 1–27.

Brickhouse, T. C. & Smith, N. D. 1989. *Socrates on Trial*. Oxford: Oxford University Press.

Bridgman, P. W. 1927. *The Logic of Modern Physics*. New York: Macmillan.

Bronowski, J. 1973. *The Ascent of Man*. Boston: Little Brown.

Bronowski, J. 1977. *A Sense of the Future: Essays in Natural Philosophy*. Cambridge, MA: MIT Press.

Brooke, J. H. 1991. *Science and Religion: Some Historical Perspectives*. Cambridge: Cambridge University Press.

Brown, P. 1967. *Augustine of Hippo: A Biography*. Berkeley, CA: University of California Press.

Brown, P. 1981. *The Cults of the Saints: Its Rise and Function in Latin Christianity*. Chicago, IL: University of Chicago Press.

Brown, T. 1988. "The transformation of the Roman Mediterranean", in *The Oxford Illustrated History of Medieval Europe*, G. Holmes (ed.), 1–62. Oxford: Oxford University Press.

Brown, P. 1992. *Power and Persuasion in Late Antiquity: Towards a Christian Empire*. Madison, WI: University of Wisconsin Press.

Brown, S. 1993. "Renaissance philosophy outside Italy", in Parkinson (ed.) (1993), 70–104.

Brown, P., Sutikna, T., Morwood, M.J. *et al.* 2004. "A new small bodied hominin from the Late Pleistocene of Flores, Indonesia", *Nature* **431**, 1055–61.

Brunet, M., Guy, M., Pilbeam, F. *et al.* 2002. "A new hominid from the upper Miocene of Chad, Central Africa", *Nature* **418**(6894), 145–51.

Buccellati, G. 1995. "Ethics and piety in the ancient Near East", in Sasson *et al.* (eds) (1995), 1685–96.

Bucher, M. A. & Spergel, D. N. 1999. "Inflation in low-density universe", *Scientific American* **280** (January), 43–9.

Budge, E. A. W. 1929. *The Rosetta Stone in the British Museum*. London: The Religious Tract Society.

Bullock, A., Stallybrass, O. & Trombley, S. (eds) 1988. *The Fontana Dictionary of Modern Thought*. London: Fontana Press.

Bulmer-Thomas, I. 1970–80. "Euclid", in Gillispie (ed.) (1970–80), **4**, 414–37.

Burbidge, E. M., Burbidge, G. R., Fowler, W. A. & Hoyle, F. 1957. "Synthesis of the elements in stars", *Review of Modern Physics* **29**, 547–56.

Burkert, W. 1972. *Lore and Science in Ancient Pythagoreanism*. Cambridge, MA. : Harvard University Press.

Burkert, W. 1985. *Greek Religion: Archaic and Classical*. Oxford: Basil Blackwell.

Burkert, W. 1996. *Creation of the Sacred: Tracks of Biology in Early Religion*. Cambridge, MA: Harvard University Press.

Burkill, T. A. 1971. *The Evolution of Christian Thought*. Ithaca, NY: Cornell University Press.

Burnet, J. 1930. *Early Greek Philosophy*, 4th edn. London: A. & C. Black.

Burnett, C. 1998. "Islamic philosophy: transmission into western Europe", in Leaman (ed.) (1998), 21–5.

Burnyeat, M. 1982. "Idealism and Greek philosophy: what Descartes saw and Berkeley missed", *Philosophical Review* **91**, 3–40.

Burnyeat, M. 1983. *The Skeptical Tradition*. Berkeley, CA: University of Berkeley Press.

Burrows, T. 1981. "Unmaking 'the middle ages'", *Journal of Medieval History* **7**, 127–34.

Bury, J. B. and Meiggs, R. 1975. *A History of Greece*, 4th edn. London: Macmillan.

Butcher, S. H. and Lang, A. (ed.) 1950. *The Odyssey of Homer*. New York: Random House.

Butterfield, H. 1957 [1949, London]. *The Origins of Modern Science, 1300–1800*, 2nd edn. New York: Macmillan.

Butterfield, H. 1973. "Christianity in history", in Wiener (ed.) (1973), 373–412.

Bynum, W. F., Browne, E. J. & Porter, R. (ed.) 1981. *Dictionary of the History of Science*. Princeton, NJ: Princeton University Press.

Cahn, S. M. (ed.) 1977. *Classics of Western Philosophy*. Indianapolis, IN: Hackett Publishing Company.

Cairns-Smith, A. G. 1982. *Genetic Takeover and the Mineral Origins of Life*. Cambridge: Cambridge University Press.

Cairns-Smith, A. G. 1985. "The first organisms", *Scientific American* **252** (June), 90–98.

Cairns-Smith, A. G. 1996. *Evolving the Mind: On the Nature of Matter and the Origin of Consciousness*. Cambridge: Cambridge University Press.

Campbell, J. 1988. *The Power of Myth*, B. Moyers & B. S. Flowers (eds). New York: Doubleday.

Campbell, R. 1992. *Truth and Historicity*. Oxford: Oxford University Press.

Campbell, N. A. 1996. *Biology*, 4th edn. Redwood City, CA: Benjamin Cummings Publishing.

Campbell, J. 2004 [1948]. *The Hero with a Thousand Faces*. Princeton, NJ: Princeton University Press.

Carabine, D. 2000. *John Scotus Eriugena*. Oxford: Oxford University Press.

Carnap, R. 1966. *Philosphical Foundations of Physics*, M. Gardner (ed.). New York: Basic Books.

Cary, M., Nock, A. D., Denniston, J. D. *et al.* (eds) 1950. *The Oxford Classical Dictionary*. Oxford: Clarendon Press.

Cassirer, E. 1944. *An Essay of Man*. New Haven, CT: Yale University Press.

Cassirer, E. 1950. *The Problem of Knowledge*. New Haven, CT: Yale University Press.

Cavendish, A. P. 1964. "Early Greek philosophy", in O'Connor (ed.) (1964), 1–13.

Cayley, M. 1926. "Leyden and Stockholm papyri", *Journal of Chemical Education* **3**, 1149.

Cayley, M. 1927. "Leyden and Stockolm papyri", *Journal of Chemical Education* **4**, 979.

Cech, T. R. 1986a. "A model for the RNA-catalyzed replication of RNA", *Proceedings of the National Academy of Sciences (USA)* **83**, 4360–63.

Cech, T. R. 1986b. "RNA as an enzyme", *Scientific American* **255**, 64–75.

Chadwick, J. 1967. *The Decipherment of Linear B*, 2nd edn. Cambridge: Cambridge University Press (1st edn 1958).

Chadwick, H. 1967a. *The Early Church*. London: Penguin (rev. 1993).

Chadwick, H. 1967b. "Philo and the beginnings of Christian thought", in Armstrong (ed.) (1967), 133–94.

Chadwick, J. 1976. *The Mycenaean World*. Cambridge: Cambridge University Press.

Chadwick, H. 1981. *Boethius: The Consolations of Music, Logic, Theology and Philosophy*. Oxford: Oxford University Press.
Chadwick, H. 1982. *History and Thought of the Early Church*. London: Variorum Reprints.
Chadwick, H. 1990. "The early Christian community", in McManners (ed.) (1990), 21–61.
Chadwick, H. 1991. "Augustine", in *Founders of Thought*, T. Thomas (ed.), 191–297. Oxford: Oxford University Press.
Chalmers, D. J. 1996. *The Conscious Mind: In Search of a Fundamental Theory*. Oxford: Oxford University Press.
Chambers, M., Grew, R., Herlihy, D. *et al.* 1987. *The Western Experience to 1715*, 4th edn. New York: Alfred A. Knopf.
Chauvet, J. -M., Deschamps, E. B., Hillaire, C. & Bahn, P. G. 1996. *Dawn of Art: The Chauvet Cave: The Oldest Known Paintings in the World*. New York: Harry N. Abrams.
Cherniss, H. F. 1970. "The characteristics and effects of presocratic philosophy", in Furley & Allen (eds) (1970), 1–28.
Childe, V. G. 1964. *What Happened in History*. London: Book Club Associates.
Childe, V. G. 1967. "The advent of civilization", in *Ancient Civilization*, N. F. Cantor & M. S. Werthman (eds), 4–63. New York: Thomas Y. Crowell.
Chittenden, N. W. 1848. "Life of Isaac Newton", in *Newton's Principia: The Mathematical Principles of Natural Philosophy*, A. Motte (trans.), 9–61. New York: D. Adee.
Christie, A. 1968. *Chinese Mythology*. London: Hamlyn.
Cicero, M. T. 1877. *The Nature of the Gods*, C. D. Yonge (trans.). New York: Harper and Brothers.
Cisar, J. O., Xu, D. Q., Thompson, J. *et al.* 2000. "An alternative interpretation of nanobacteria-induced biomineralisation", *Proceedings of the National Academy of Sciences (USA)* 97, 11511–15.
Clagett, M. 1955. *Greek Science in Antiquity*. New York: Abelard-Schuman.
Clagett, M. 1970–80. "Archimedes", in Gillispie (ed.) (1970–80), 1, 213–31.
Clark, J. T. 1969. "The philosophy of science and the history of science", in *Critical Problems in the History of Science*, M. Clagett (ed.), 103–40. Madison, WI: University of Wisconsin Press.
Clark, R. W. 1971. *Einstein: The Life and Times*. Cleveland, OH: World Publishing Company.
Clark, R. W. 1984. *The Survival of Charles Darwin: A Biography of a Man and an Idea*. New York: Random House.
Clark, S. R. L. 1994. "Ancient philosophy", in *The Oxford Illustrated History of Western Philosophy*, A. Kenny (ed.), 1–53. Oxford: Oxford University Press.
Clarke, P. B. & Byrne, P. 1993. *Religion Defined and Explained*. New York: St. Martin's Press.
Clay, J. S. 2003. *Hesiod's Cosmos*. Cambridge: Cambridge University Press.
Clendening, L. 1960 [1942]. *Source Book of Medical History*. New York: Dover Publications.
Clery, D. 1995. "CERN's LHC gets the go-ahead", *Science* 267, 26.
Cobban, A. B. 1988. *The Medieval Universities: Their Development and Organisation*. Berkeley, CA: University of California Press.
Cohen, I. B. 1960. *The Birth of a New Physics*. New York: Doubleday.
Cohen, I. B. 1977. "History and the philosopher of science", in *The Structure of Scientific Theories*, F. Suppe (ed.), 308–49. Urbana, IL: University of Illinois Press.
Cohen, I. B. 1985. *Revolution in Science*. Cambridge, MA: Belknap Press of Harvard University Press.
Cohen, P. 1996. "Let there be life", *New Scientist* 151 (6 July), 22–7.
Cohen, I. B. & Smith, G. E. 2002. "Introduction", in *The Cambridge Companion to Newton*, I. B. Cohen & G. E. Smith (eds), 1–32. Cambridge: Cambridge University Press.
Cohn, N. 1996. *Noah's Flood*. New Haven, CT: Yale University Press.
Cole, J. H. 1925. *Determination of the Exact Size and Orientation of the Great Pryamid at Giza*. Cairo: Government Press.
Coleman, W. 1973. "Cuvier and evolution", in *Science and Religious Belief: A Selection of Recent Historical Studies*, C. A. Russell (ed.), 224–37. London: University of London Press.
Colish, M. L. 1997. *Medieval Foundations of the Western Intellectual Tradition 400–1400*. New Haven, CT: Yale University Press.
Consortium, I. H. G. S. 2001. "Initial sequencing and analysis of the human genome", *Nature*, 409, 860–921.
Contreni, J. J. 1984. "The Carolingian Renaissance", in *Renaissances Before the Renaissance: Cultural Revivals of Late Antiquity and Middle Ages*, W. Treadgold (ed.), 57–74. Palo Alto, CA: Stanford University Press.
Contreni, J. J. 1995. "The Carolingian Renaissance: education and literary culture", in *The New Cambridge Medieval History*, R. McKitterick (ed.), 709–57. Cambridge: Cambridge University Press.
Cooper, J. M. 1970. "Plato on sense perception and knowledge", *Phronesis* 15, 123–46.
Cooper, J. S. 1989. "Writing", in *International Encylopedia of Communications*, E. Barnouw (ed.), 321–31. Oxford: Oxford University Press.
Copleston, F. C. 1972. *A History of Medieval Philosophy*. London: Methuen.

Corballis, P. M., Funnell, M. G. & Gazzaniga, M. S. 2000. "An evolutionary perspective on hemispheric asymmetries", *Brain and Cognition* **43**, 112–17.
Cornford, F. M. 1932. *Before and after Socrates*. Cambridge: Cambridge University Press.
Cornford, F. M. 1935. *Plato's Theory of Knowledge*. London: Routledge & Kegan Paul.
Cornford, F. M. 1937. *Plato's Cosmology: The Timaeus of Plato*. London: Routledge.
Cornford, F. M. 1941. *The Republic of Plato*. Oxford: Oxford University Press.
Cornford, F. M. 1952. *Principium Sapientia: The Origins of Greek Philosophical Thought*. Cambridge: Cambridge University Press.
Cornford, F. M. 1975. "Anaxagoras' theory of matter", in Furley & Allen (eds) (1975), 275–322.
Cornford, F. M. 1991 [1912]. *From Religion to Philosophy: A Study of the Origins of Western Speculation*. Princeton, NJ: Princeton University Press.
Corrigan, K. 1986. "Body and soul in ancient religious experience", in Armstrong (ed.) (1986), 360–83.
Corrigan, K. 1996. "Essence and existence in the Enneads", in Gerson (ed.) (1996), 105–29.
Cotterell, A. 1979. *The Minoan World*. London: Guild Publishing.
Cottingham, J. 1984. *Rationalism*. London: Paladin.
Cottingham, J. 1993. "Descartes: metaphysics and the philosophy of mind", in Parkinson (ed.) (1993), 201–34.
Craig, W. L. 1980. *The Cosmological Argument from Plato to Leibniz*. London: Macmillan.
Craig, E. (ed.) 1988. *Islamic Philosophy: The Routledge Encyclopedia of Philosophy*. London: Routledge.
Craig, G. Y. & Jones, E. J. 1982. *A Geological Miscellany*. Princeton, NJ: Princeton University Press.
Crawford, H. 1991. *Sumer and the Sumerians*. Cambridge: Cambridge University Press.
Crick, F. 1981. *Life Itself: Its Origin and Nature*. London: MacDonald.
Crick, F. 1995. *The Astonishing Hypothesis: the Scientific Search for the Soul*. New York: Touchstone.
Crick, F. & Koch, C. 1992. "The problem of consciousness", *Scientific American* **267** (September), 111–17.
Crofton, I. (ed.) 1995. *The Guinness Enclyopedia*. Enfield: Guinness Publishers.
Crombie, A. C. 1953. *Robert Grossetestes and the Origin of Experimental Science 1100–1700*. Oxford: Oxford University Press (3rd rev. edn 1971).
Crombie, A. C. 1959. *Medieval and Early Modern Science*. Garden City, NY: Doubleday.
Crombie, I. M. 1962. *An Examination of Plato's Doctrines*. London: Routledge & Kegan Paul.
Crombie, I. M. 1964. *Plato: the Midwife's Apprentice*. New York: Barnes and Noble.
Crombie, A. C. 1969. "The significance of medieval discussions of scientific method for the scientific revolution", in *Critical Problems in the History of Science*, M. Clagett (ed.) (1969), 79–102. Madison, WI: University of Wisconsin Press.
Crombie, A. C. 1970–80a. "Descartes, Rene (1596–1650)", in Gillispie (ed.) (1970–80), **4**, 51–5.
Crombie, A. C. 1970–80b. "Grosseteste, Robert (c 1168–1253)", in Gillispie (ed.) (1970–80), **5**, 548–54.
Crombie, A. C. 1994. *Styles of Scientific Thinking in European Tradition*. London: Duckworth.
Crombie, A. C. & North, J. D. 1970–80. "Bacon, Roger (c 1219–1292 AD)", in Gillispie (ed.) (1970–80), vol. 1, 377–85.
Crook, J. H. 1980. *The Evolution of Human Consciousness*. Oxford: Clarendon Press.
Cross, F. L. (ed.) 1997. *Oxford Dictionary of the Christian Church*, 3rd edn. Oxford: Oxford University Press.
Cross, R. C. & Woozley, A. D. 1979. *Plato's Republic: A Philosophical Commentary*. New York: St Martin's Press.
Cubberley, E. P. 1948. *The History of Education*. Cambridge, MA: The Riverside Press.
Cunliffe-Jones, H. (ed.) 1978. *A History of the Christian Doctrine*. Edinburgh: T. & T. Clark.
Daniel, G. 1968. *The First Civilizations: The Archaeology of their Origins*. New York: Thomas Y. Crowell Company.
Daniel, G. 1975. *A Hundred and Fifty Years of Archaeology*, 2nd edn. London: Duckworth (first printed 1951).
Daniels, P. T. 1995. "The decipherment of ancient Near Eastern scripts", in Sasson *et al.* (eds) (1995), 81–93.
Danilov, Y. A. & Smorodinskii, Y. A. 1975. "Kepler and modern physics", *Vistas in Astronomy* **18**, 699–708.
Darwin, C. 1859. *The Origin of Species*. Reprinted from the sixth London edition, with additions and corrections. New York: Hurst and Company.
Darwin, C. 1874. *The Descent of Man and Selection in Relation to Sex*, 2nd edn. New York: Hurst and Company.
Darwin, F. 1888. *The Life and Letters of Charles Darwin*, 2 vols. New York: D. Appleton and Company.
Darwin, C. 1959. *The Autobiography of Charles Darwin 1809–1882 with Original Omissions Restored*, N. Barlow (ed.). New York: Collins.
Darwin, C. & Wallace, A. R. 1958. *Evolution by Natural Selection*. Cambridge: Cambridge University Press.
Davey, L. M. 2001. "The oath of Hippocrates: an historical review", *Neurosurgery* **49**(30), 554–66.
Davies, P. C. W. 1977. *Space and Time in the Modern Universe*. Cambridge: Cambridge University Press.
Davies, W. V. 1987. *Egyptian Hieroglyphics*. London: British Museum Publications.
Davies, B. 1993. *An Introduction to the Philosophy of Religion*. Oxford: Oxford University Press.

Da Vinci, L. 1975. *The Notebooks of Leonardo Da Vinci*, J. P. Richter (ed.). New York: Dover Publications.

Davis, M. 2001. "Weighing the universe", *Nature* **410**, 153–4.

Davis, P. J. & Hersh, R. 1981. *The Mathematical Experience*. Boston, MA: Birkhäuser.

Davis, K. & Moore, W. E. 1945. "Some principles of stratification", *American Sociological Review* **10**, 242–9.

Dawkins, R. 1989. *The Selfish Gene*, 2nd edn. Oxford: Oxford University Press.

Dawkins, R. 1991. *The Blind Watchmaker*. Harmondsworth: Penguin.

Deason, G. B. 1986. "Reformation theology and the mechanistic conception of nature", in Lindberg & Numbers (eds) (1986), 167–91.

de Burgh, W. G. 1955 [1923]. *The Legacy of the Ancient World*, vol. 1. London: Penguin.

de Duve, C. 1990a. *Blueprint for a Cell: The Nature and Origin of Life*. Burlington, NC: Neil Patterson Publishers.

de Duve, C. 1990b. "Prelude to a cell", *The Sciences* **30**, 22–8.

de Duve, C. 1995. *Vital Dust: Life as a Cosmic Imperative*. New York: Basic Books.

Deevey, E. S. 1960. "The human population", *Scientific American* **203**(3), 194–206.

de Kruif, P. 1926. *Microbe Hunters*. New York: Harcourt, Brace and Co.

Dennett, D. C. 1995. *Darwin's Dangerous Idea: Evolution and the Meanings of Life*. New York: Simon and Schuster.

Dennett, D. C. 1996. *Kinds of Minds: Toward an Understanding of Consciousness*. New York: Basic Books.

Denton, D. 1993. *The Pinnacle of Life: Self-Awareness in Humans and Animals*. Sydney: Allen and Unwin.

Denyer, N. 1991. *Language, Thought and Falsehood*. London: Routledge.

de Rosa, R., Grenier, J. K., Andreeva, T. *et al.* 1999. "Hox genes in brachiopods and priapulids and protostome evolution", *Nature* **399**, 772–6.

de Santillana, G. 1955. *The Crime of Galileo*. Chicago, IL: University of Chicago Press.

Desmond, A. & Moore, J. 1994. *Darwin: Life of a Tormented Evolutionist*. New York: W. W. Norton & Co.

Diamond, J. 1991. *The Rise and Fall of the Third Chimpanzee*. New York: Random House.

Dickinson, O. 1994. *The Aegean Bronze Age*. Cambridge: Cambridge University Press.

Dicks, D. R. 1970. *Early Greek Astronomy to Aristotle*. Ithaca, NY: Cornell University Press.

Dicks, D. R. 1970–80. "Eratosthenes", in Gillispie (ed.) (1970–80), **4**, 388–93.

Dilke, O. A. W. 1987. *Mathematics and Measurement*. London: British Museum Publications.

Dobbs, B. J. T. 1991. *The Janus Faces of Genius: The Role of Alchemy in Newton's Thought*. Cambridge: Cambridge University Press.

Dobell, C. 1958. *Antony van Leeuwenhoek and his "Little Animals"*. New York: Russell and Russell.

Doblhofer, E. 1961. *Voices in Stone: The Decipherment of Ancient Scripts and Writings*, M. Savill (trans.). New York: Viking.

Dobson, G. P. 1997. "Reshaping the teaching of science: a scientist's perspective", *Journal of Chemical Education* **74**(4), 453–4.

Dobson, G. P. 2003. "On being the right size: heart design, mitochondrial efficiency, and lifespan potential", *Clinical Experimental Pharmacology and Physiology* **30**(8), 590–97.

Dobson, G. P. 2004. "Organ arrest, protection and preservation: natural hibernation to cardiac surgery", *Comparative Biochemistry and Physiology B. Biochemistry Molecular Biology* **139**(3) (November), 469–85.

Dobzhansky, T. 1956. *The Biological Basis of Human Freedom*. New York: Columbia University Press.

Dobzhansky, T. & Boesiger, E. 1983. *Human Culture: A Movement in Evolution*. New York: Columbia University Press.

Dobzhansky, T. H., Ayala, F. J., Stebbins, G. L. & Valentine, J. W. 1977. *Evolution*. San Francisco: W. H. Freeman.

Doolittle, W. F. 2000. "Uprooting the tree of life", *Scientific American* **282**(2), 73–7.

Dover, K. J. 1980. *The Greeks*. London: BBC Publications.

Drake, S. 1957. *Discoveries and Opinions of Galileo*. Garden City, NY: Doubleday.

Drake, S. 1970–80. "Galileo Galilei (1564–1642 AD)", in Gillispie (ed.) (1970–80), **5**, 237–49.

Drake, S. 1980. *Galileo*. New York: Hill and Wang.

Drake, S. 1981. *Cause, Experiment and Science*. Chicago, IL: University of Chicago Press.

Drake, F. & Sobel, D. 1992. *Is Anyone Out There?*. New York: Delacorte Press.

Draper, J. W. 1898. *History of the Conflict between Religion and Science*. New York: D. Appleton and Co.

Drenkhahn, R. 1995. "Artisans and artists in pharaonic Egypt", in Sasson *et al.* (eds) (1995), 331–44.

Dreyer, J. L. E. 1956 [1906]. *A History of Astronomy from Thales to Kepler*. New York: Dover Publications.

Duchovnay, B. & Joyce, C. 2000. "The spirit of discovery", *Science* **287**, 1595–7.

Dudden, F. H. 1935. *The Life and Times of St. Ambrose*. Oxford: Clarendon Press.

Durand, F. & Lichtenberg, R. 1994. *Mummies: A Journey through Eternity*. London: Thames & Hudson.

Durant, W. 1935. *The Story of Civilisation*, vol. 1. New York: Simon and Schuster.

Durkheim, É. 1954. *The Elementary Forms of Religious Life*. Glencoe: The Free Press.

Dyson, F. J. 1979. "Time without end: physics and biology in an open universe", *Reviews in Modern Physics* **51**, 447–60.

Dyson, F. 1999. *Origins of Life*, rev. edn. Cambridge: Cambridge University Press.

Eamon, W. 1990. "From the secrets of nature to public knowledge", in Lindberg & Westman (eds) (1990), 333–65.

Eccles, J. 1979. *The Human Mystery*. New York: Springer International.

Eccles, J. C. 1989. *Evolution of Brain: Creation of the Self*. London: Routledge.

Eccles, J. 1990. "Evolution of the human brain: creation of the conscious self", *International Journal on the Unity of the Sciences* 3, 123–38.

Eddington, A. 1933. *The Expanding Universe*. Cambridge: Cambridge University Press.

Eddington, A. S. 1935. *New Pathways in Science*. Cambridge: Cambridge University Press.

Edelstein, L. 1937. "Greek medicine and its relation to religion and magic", *Bulletin of the Institute of the History of Medicine* 5(3), 201–46.

Edelstein, L. 1952. "The relation of ancient philosophy to medicine", *Bulletin of the Institute of the History of Medicine* 26(4), 299–316.

Edelstein, L. 1966. "The distinctive Hellenism of Greek medicine", *Bulletin of the Institute of the History of Medicine* 40(3), 197–255.

Edwards, I. E. S. 1947. *The Pyramids of Egypt*. Baltimore, MD: Penguin.

Edzard, D. O. 1995. "The Sumerian language", in Sasson *et al.* (eds) (1995), 2107–16.

Eigen, M. 1992. *Steps Towards Life*. Oxford: Oxford University Press.

Einstein, A. 1950a. *The Meaning of Relativity*. Princeton, NJ: Princeton University Press.

Einstein, A. 1950b. *Out of My Later Years*. New York: Philosophical Library.

Einstein, A. 1954. *Ideas and Opinions*, based on *Mein Weltbild*, C. Seelig *et al.* (eds), S. Bargmann (rev. and trans.). New York: Crown Publishers.

Einstein, A. & Infeld, L. 1954. *The Evolution of Physics: The Growth of Ideas from Early Concepts to Relativity and Quanta*. New York: Simon and Schuster.

Eliade, M. 1979. *A History of Religious Ideas*. London: William Collins.

Elton, S., Bishop, L. C. & Wood, B. 2001. "Comparative context of plio-pliestocene hominin brain evolution", *Journal of Human Evolution* 41, 1–27.

Emiliani, C. 1992. *Planet Earth*. Cambridge, MA: Cambridge University Press.

Emlyn-Jones, C. J. 1980. *The Ionians and Hellenism*. London: Routledge & Kegan Paul.

Evans, G. R. 1989. *Anselm*. Wilton, CT: Morehouse-Barlow.

Evans, G. R. 1993. *Philosophy and Theology in the Middle Ages*. London: Routledge.

Evans, J. 1998. *The History and Practice of Ancient Astronomy*. Oxford: Oxford Unviersity Press.

Eyre, C. J. 1995. "The agricultural cycle, farming and water management in the ancient Near East", in Sasson *et al.* (eds) (1995), 175–90.

Fagan, B. M. 1994. *In the Beginning: An Introduction to Archaeology*, 8th edn. New York: HarperCollins.

Fagan, B. M. 1995. *People of the Earth: An Introduction to World Prehistory*, 8th edn. New York: HarperCollins.

Fakhry, M. 1983. *A History of Islamic Philosophy*, 2nd edn. New York: Columbia University Press.

Famighetti, R. (ed.) 1996. *The World Almanac and Book of Facts*. Mahwah, NJ: World Almanac Books.

Farber, W. 1995. "Witchcraft, magic and divination in ancient Mesopotamia", in Sasson *et al.* (eds) (1995), 1895–909.

Farley, J. 1977. *The Spontaneous Generation Controversy: From Descartes to Oparin*. Baltimore, MD: Johns Hopkins University Press.

Farrington, B. 1964. "Greek science", in *Science in its Context*, J. Brierley (ed.), 139–54. London: Heinemann.

Farrington, B. 1965. *Aristotle: Founder of Scientific Philosophy*. New York: Praeger.

Farrington, B. 1980. *Greek Science: Its Meaning for Us*. Nottingham: Spokesman.

Ferguson, W. K. 1948. *The Renaissance in Historical Thought:Five Centuries of Interpretation*. Boston, MA: Houghton Mifflin.

Ferguson, J. 1989. *Among the Gods: An Archaeological Exploration of Ancient Greek Religion*. London: Routledge.

Fermi, J. & Bernardini, G. 1961. *Galileo and the Scientific Revolution*. New York: Basic Books.

Ferris, J. P. 2002. "From building blocks to the polymers of life", in Shopf (ed.) (2002a), 113–39.

Ferris, J. P. & Ertem, G. 1992. "Oligomerization of ribonucleotides on montmorillonite: reaction of the 5'-phosphorimidazolide of adenosine", *Science* 257, 1387.

Ferris, J. P., Hill, A. R., Liu, R. & Orgel, L. E. 1996. "Synthesis of long prebiotic oligomers on mineral surfaces", *Nature* 381, 59–61.

Fichtenau, H. 1968. *The Carolingian Empire*. Oxford: Oxford University Press.

Finlay, B. L., Darlington, R. B. & Nicatro, N. 2001. "Developmental structure in brain evolution", *Behavioural and Brain Sciences* 24(2), 263–78.

Finney, G. L. 1973. "Harmony or rapture in music", in Wiener (ed.) (1973), 388–95.

Fitton, J. K. 2002. *Minoans*. London: British Museum Press.

Fleming, A. 1946. "History and development of penicillin", in *Penicillin: Its Practical Application*, A. Fleming (ed.), 1–23. Philadelphia, PA: The Blakiston Co.

Folk, R. L. 1997. "Nanobacteria: surely not figments, but what under heaven are they?" *Natural Science* 1, 1–5.

Folsome, C. E. 1979. *The Origin of Life: A Warm Little Pond*. San Francisco: W. H. Freeman.

Force, J. E. 2000. "The nature of Newton's 'holy alliance' between science and religion: from the scientific revolution to Newton (and back again)", in *Rethinking the Scientific Revolution*, M. J. Osler (ed.), 247–70. Cambridge: Cambridge University Press.

Force, J. E. & Popkin, R. H. (ed.) 2000. *Newton and Religion*. Dordrecht: Kluwer.

Foster, M. B. 1934. "The Christian doctrine of creation and the rise of modern natural science", *Mind* 43, 446–68.

Foster, J. L. 1995. "The hymn to Aten: Akhenaten worships the sole god", in Sasson *et al.* (eds) (1995), 1751–62.

Fox, S. W. 1986. "The evolutionary sequence: origins and emergences", *The American Biology Teacher* 48, 140–49.

Fox, S. 1988. *The Emergence of Life: Darwinian Evolution from the Inside*, vol. 48. New York: Basic Books.

Frankfort, H. 1948. *Ancient Egyptian Religion*. New York: Harper & Row.

Frankfort, H. & Frankfort, H. A. 1951. "Myth and reality", in Frankfort *et al.* (eds) (1951), 11–38.

Frankfort, H., Frankfort, H., Wilson, J. A. and Jacobsen, T. 1951. *Before Philosophy: The Intellectual Adventure of Ancient Man*. Harmondsworth: Penguin.

Fraser, J. T. (ed.) 1966. *The Voices of Time*. New York: George Braziller Publisher.

Fraser, P. M. 1972. *Ptolemic Alexandria*. Oxford: Oxford University Press.

Frazer, J. 1922. *The Golden Bough*. London: Macmillan.

Frede, M. 1985. "Substance in Aristotle's metaphysics", in Gotthelf (ed.) (1985), 17–26.

Frede, M. 1990. "An empiricist view of knowledge: memorism", in *Epistemology*, S. Everson (ed.), 225–72. Cambridge: Cambridge University Press.

Freedman, W. L. 1992. "The expansion rate and size of the universe", *Scientific American* 267 (November), 54–60.

Frend, W. H. C. 1984. *The Rise of Christianity*. London: Darton, Longman & Todd.

Frend, W. H. C. 1988. *Archaeology and History in the Study of Early Christianity*. London: Variorum Reprints.

Fruton, J. S. 1972. *Molecules and Life*. New York: John Wiley.

Fruton, J. 1992. *A Sceptical Biochemist*. Cambridge, MA.: Harvard University Press.

Funkenstein, A. 1986. *Theology and the Scientific Imagination from the Middle Ages to the Seventeenth Century*. Princeton, NJ: Princeton University Press.

Furley, D. 1973. "Rationality among the Greeks and Romans", in Wiener (ed.) (1973), 46–51.

Furley, D. J. & Allen, R. E. (eds) 1970. *Studies in Presocratic Philosophy: The Beginnings of Philosophy*. London: Routledge & Kegan Paul.

Furley, D. J. & Allen, R. E. (eds) 1975. *Studies in Presocratic Philosophy: The Eleatics and Pluralists*. London: Routledge & Kegan Paul.

Galik, K., Senut, B., Pickford, M. *et al.* 2004. "External and internal morphology of the BAR 1002'00 Orrorin tugenensis femur", *Science* 305(5689), 1450–53.

Galileo Galilei 1960. *On Motion and on Mechanics*, I. E. Drabkin & S. Drake (trans.). Madison, WI: University of Wisconsin Press.

Gamow, G. 1948. "Galaxies in flight", *Scientific American* 179 (July), 21–5.

Gamow, G. 1952. *The Creation of the Universe*. New York: Viking Press.

Gamow, G. 1962. *Gravity*. Garden City, NY: Doubleday.

Garber, D. & Ayers, M. (eds) 1998. *The Cambridge History of Seventeenth-Century Philosophy*. Cambridge: Cambridge University Press

Gardiner, A. 1961. *Egypt of the Pharaohs*. Oxford: Clarendon Press.

Gardner, M. (ed.) 1963. *Great Essays in Science*. New York: Washington Square Press, p. 126.

Gardner-Smith, P. 1932. *The Church in the Roman Empire*. Cambridge: Cambridge University Press.

Gaster, T. H. 1955. "Mythic thought in the ancient Near East", *Journal of the History of Ideas* 16, 422–6.

Gaster, T. 1969. *Myth, Legend and Custom in the Old Testament*. New York: Harper & Row.

Gatti, M. L. 1996. "Plotinus: the Platonic tradition and the founder of Neoplatonism", in Gerson (ed.) (1996), 10–37.

Gaukroger, S. 1993. "Descartes's methodology", in Parkinson (ed.) (1993), 167–200.

Gazzaniga, M. S. 1998. "Brain and conscious experience", *Advances in Neurology* 77, 181–92.

Gazzaniga, M. S. 2000. "Cerebral specialisation and interhemispheric communication: does the corpus callosum enable the human condition?", *Brain* 123, 1293–326.

Geertz, C. 1973. *The Interpretation of Cultures*. New York: Basic Books.

Gehring, W. J. 1999. *Master Control Genes in Development and Evolution: The Homeobox Story*. New Haven, CT: Yale University Press.

Geison, G. L. 1969. "The protoplasmic theory of life and the vitalist-mechanist debate", *Isis* 60, 273–92.

Geison, G. L. 1995. *The Private Science of Louis Pasteur*. Princeton, NJ: Princeton University Press.

Gentner, D., Brem, S., Ferguson, R. W. *et al.* 1997. "Analogical reasoning and conceptual change: a case study of Johannes Kepler", *The Journal of the Learning Sciences* 6(1), 3–40.

Gerhart, J. & Kirschner, M. 1997. *Cells, Embryos and Evolution.* Oxford: Blackwell Scientific.

Gerson, L. P. 1990. *God and Greek Philosophy: Studies in the Early History of Natural Theology.* London: Routledge.

Gerson, L. P. (ed.) 1996. *The Cambridge Companion to Plotinus,* Cambridge: Cambridge University Press.

Gibson, M. (ed.) 1981. *Boethius, His Life, Thought and Influence.* Oxford: Oxford University Press.

Gilbert, W. 1986. "The RNA world", *Nature* 319, 618.

Gillespie, N. C. 1979. *Charles Darwin and the Problem of Creation.* Chicago, IL: University of Chicago Press.

Gillings, R. J. 1980. "The mathematics of ancient Egypt", in Gillispie (ed.) (1970–80) 15, 681–705.

Gillispie, C. C. (ed.) 1970–80. *Dictionary of Scientific Biography.* New York: Charles Scribner's Sons.

Gingerich, O. 1972. "The origins of Kepler's Third Law", in *Vistas in Astronomy,* A. Beer & P. Beer (eds). Oxford: Pergamon.

Gingerich, O. 1993. *The Eye of Heaven: Ptolemy, Copernicus, Kepler.* New York: American Institute of Physics.

Gingerich, O. 2000. "Plotting the pyramids", *Nature* 408, 297–8.

Gjertsen, D. 1989. *Science and Philosophy: Past and Present.* Harmondsworth: Penguin.

Glassner, J. J. 1995. "The use of knowledge in ancient Mesopotamia", in Sasson *et al.* (eds) (1995), 1815–23.

Glassner, J. J. 2003. *The Invention of Cuneiform: Writing in Sumer,* M. van de Mieroop & Z. Bahrani (trans. and ed.). Baltimore, MD: Johns Hopkins University Press.

Glendening, L. 1960 [1942]. *Source Book of Medical History.* New York: Dover Publications.

Gnuse, R. 1999. "The emergence of monotheism in ancient Israel: a survey of recent scholarship", *Religion* 29, 315–36.

Goddu, A. 1999. "Ockham's philosophy of nature", in *The Cambridge Companion to Ockham,* P. V. Spade (ed.), 143–67. Cambridge: Cambridge University Press.

Goodman, L. E. 1992. *Avicenna.* London: Routledge.

Goodman, L. E. 1998. "Moses Maimonides", in *Routledge Encyclopedia of Philosophy* 6, 40–49. New York: Routledge.

Goodman, M., Koop, B. F., Czelusniak, J. *et al.* 1989. "Molecular phylogeny of the family of apes and humans", *Genome* 31, 316–35.

Goodwin, R. P. 1965. *Selected Writings of St. Thomas Aquinas.* Indianapolis, IN: Bobbs-Merill Publishing.

Gorman, P. 1979. *Pythagoras: A Life.* London: Routledge & Kegan Paul.

Gotthelf, A. (ed.) 1985. *Aristotle on Nature and Living Things.* Bristol: Bristol Classical Press.

Gould, S. J. 1973. *Ever Since Darwin: Reflections in Natural History.* New York: W. W. Norton.

Gould, S. J. 1986a. "Knight takes bishop: the facts about the Wilberforce–Huxley debate don't always fit the legend", *Natural History* 95(5), 18–33.

Gould, S. J. 1986b. "Soapy Sam's logic: a true scoundrel but with redeeming value", *Natural History* 95(4), 16–26.

Gould, S. J. 1994. "The evolution of life on earth", *Scientific American* 271(4), 63–9.

Grant, E. 1979. "The condemnation of 1277, God's absolute power and physical thought in the late middle ages", *Viator* 10, 211–44.

Grant, E. 1996. *The Foundations of Modern Science in the Middle Ages.* Cambridge: Cambridge University Press.

Green, A. 1995. "Ancient Mesopotamian religious iconography", in Sasson *et al.* (eds) (1995), 1837–55.

Green, P. 1990. *Alexander to Actium: The Hellensitic Age.* London: Thames & Hudson.

Greene, B. 1999. *The Elegant Universe: Superstrings, Hidden Dimensions and the Quest for the Ultimate Theory.* New York: W. W. Norton.

Greenfield, S. 1995. *Journey to Centres of Mind: Toward a Science of Consciousness.* New York: W. H. Freeman.

Greer, T. H. 1982. *A Brief History of the Western World,* 4th edn. New York: Harcourt Brace Jovanovich.

Gribbin, J. 1985. *In Search of the Double Helix: Quantum Physics and Life.* Harmondsworth: Penguin.

Gribbin, J. 1993a. *In Search of the Edge of Time.* London: Black Swan.

Gribbin, J. 1993b. *In the Beginning: The Birth of the Living Universe.* Harmondsworth: Penguin.

Griffiths, J. G. 1986. "The faith of the pharaonic period", in Armstrong (ed.) (1986), 3–38.

Grimal, N. 1992. *A History of Egypt.* Oxford: Blackwell Publishers.

Gruenberg, B. C. 1929. *The Story of Evolution: Facts and Theories on the Development of Life.* Garden City, NY: D. Van Nostrand.

Guthrie, W. K. C. 1950. *The Greek Philosophers: From Thales to Aristotle.* New York: Harper and Row.

Guthrie, W. K. C. 1952. *Orpheus and Greek Religion.* Princeton, NJ: Princeton University Press.

Guthrie, W. K. C. 1971 [1962]. *A History of Greek Philosophy: The Earlier Presocratics and the Pythagoreans,* vol. 1. Cambridge: Cambridge University Press.

Guthrie, W. K. C. 1974 [1965]. *A History of Greek Philosophy: The Presocratic Tradition from Parmenides to Democritus,* vol. 2. Cambridge: Cambridge University Press.

Guthrie, W. K. C. 1981. *A History of Greek Philosophy: Aristotle, An Encounter*, vol. 6. Cambridge: Cambridge University Press.

Haar, J. 1973. "Pythagorean harmony of the universe", in Wiener (ed.) (1973), 38–42.

Hack, R. K. 1931. *God in Greek Philosophy to the time of Socrates*. Princeton, NJ: Princeton University Press.

Haeckel, E. 1900. *The Riddle of the Universe*. New York: Harper and Brothers.

Haeckel, E. 1905. *The Wonders of the Universe*. New York: Harper and Brothers.

Haeckel, E. 1906. *The Evolution of Man: A Popular Scientific Study*, 5th edn. New York: Peter Eckler.

Haggard, H. W. 1933. *Mystery, Magic and Medicine: The Rise of Medicine from Superstition to Science*, 1st edn. Garden City, NY: Doubleday.

Hahn, R. 1986. "Laplace and the mechanistic universe", in Lindberg & Numbers (eds) (1986), 256–76.

Haldane, J. B. S. 1954. "The origin of life", *New Biology* 16, 12–27.

Hall, A. R. 1962. *The Scientific Revolution, 1500–1800: The Formation of the Modern Scientific Attitude*, 2nd edn. Boston, MA: Beacon Press.

Hall, M. B. 1972. "Copernicus", in *Makers of Modern Thought*, J. Thorndike (ed.), 50–63. New York: American Heritage.

Hameroff, S. R. 1994. "Quantum coherence in microtubules: a neural basis for an emergent consciousness", *Journal of Consciousness Studies* 1, 91–118.

Hamilton, E. 1957. *The Echo of Greece*. New York: W. W. Norton.

Hankins, T. L. 1990. "Newton's 'mathematical way' a century after *Principia*", in *Some Truer Method: Reflections on the Heritage of Newton*, F. Durham & R. D. Purrington (eds), 89–112. New York: Columbia University Press.

Hankinson, R. J. 1995a. "Philosophy of science", in Barnes (ed.) (1995), 109–39.

Hankinson, R. J. 1995b. "Science", in Barnes (ed.) (1995), 140–67.

Harcourt-Smith, W. E. H. & Aiello, L. C. 2004. "Fossils, feet and the evolution of human bipedal locomotion", *Journal of Anatomy* 204, 403–16.

Hare, R. M. 1982. *Plato*. Oxford: Oxford University Press.

Haren, M. 1985. *Medieval Thought: The Western Intellectual Tradition from Antiquity to the Thirteenth Century*. Basingstoke: Macmillan.

Harris, J. R. (ed.) 1971. *The Legacy of Egypt*, 2nd edn. Oxford: Clarendon Press.

Harris, H. 2002. *Things come to Life: Spontaneous Generation Revisited*. Oxford: Oxford University Press.

Harrow, B. 1920. *From Newton to Einstein: Changing Conceptions of the Universe*. New York: Van Nostrand.

Hart, G. 1990. *Egyptian Myths*. London: British Museum Press.

Hart, G. 1991. *Pharaohs and Pyramids*. London: British Museum Press.

Hatfield, G. 1990. "Metaphysics and the new science", in Lindberg & Westman (eds) (1990), 93–166.

Hawking, S. W. 1988. *A Brief History of Time*. New York: Bantam Books.

Hawking, S. 1993. *Black Holes and Baby Universes*. London: Bantam Press.

Hawking, S. W. 1996. *The Illustrated A Brief History of Time*. Toronto and New York: Bantam Books.

Hawking, S. & Penrose, R. 1996. *The Nature of Space and Time*. Princeton, NJ: Princeton University Press.

Hay, D. 1961. *The Italian Renaissance*. Cambridge: Cambridge University Press.

Hay, D. 1973. "Idea of Renaissance", in Wiener (ed.) (1973), 121–9.

Hazen, R. M. & Trefil, J. 1991. *Science Matters: Achieving Scientific Literacy*. Garden City, NY: Doubleday.

Hazlett, I. (ed.) 1991. *Early Christianity: Origins and Evolution to AD 600*. London: SPCK Publications.

Heath, T. L. 1911. "Archimedes", in *Encyclopedia Brittanica*, 368–9. New York: Encyclopedia Brittanica.

Heath, T. L. 1991 [1932]. *Greek Astronomy*. New York: Dover Publications.

Hedges, S. B. 2000. "Human evolution: a start for population genomics", *Nature* 408, 652–3.

Heinaman, R. 1997. "Plato: metaphysics and epistemology", in Taylor (ed.) (1997), 356–93.

Heisenberg, W. 1971. *Physics and Beyond: Encounters and Conversations*. New York and London: Harper Torchbooks.

Hellemans, A. 1995. "Dwarfs and dim galaxies marks limits of knowledge", *Science* 268, 366–7.

Helm, P. (ed.) 1999. *Faith and Reason*. Oxford: Oxford University Press.

Henderson, L. J. 1913. *The Fitness of the Environment*. New York: Macmillan.

Herbermann, C. G., Pace, E. A., Pallen, C. B. *et al.* (eds) 1913. *The Catholic Encyclopaedia: An International Work of Reference on the Constitution, Doctrine, Discipline, and History of the Catholic Church*. New York: The Encyclopaedia Press.

Herodotus 1928. *The History of Herodotus*, M. Komroff (ed.). New York: Tudor Publishing.

Herschel, J. F. W. 1830. *A Preliminary Discourse on the Study of Natural Philosophy*. London: Longman, Rees, Orme, Brown, Green, & Longman, and John Taylor.

Hesse, M. B. 1964. "Francis Bacon", in O'Connor (ed.) (1964), 141–52.

Hesse, M. 1970–80. "Bacon, Francis (1561–1626)", in Gillispie (ed.) (1970–80), 1, 372–7.

Hick, J. & Knitter, P. F. (eds) 1987. *The Myth of Christian Uniqueness*. London: SCM Press.

Hinnels, J. R. (ed.) 1984. *The Penguin Dictionary of Early Religions*. Harmondsworth: Penguin.

Hochachka, P. W. & Somero, G. N. 2002. *Biochemical Adaptation: Mechanism and Process in Physiological Evolution*. Oxford: Oxford University Press.

Hoffmann, R. J. (ed.) 1987. *Celsus: On The True Doctrine*. Oxford: Oxford University Press.

Hogan, C. J. 1998. *The Little Book of the Big Bang*. New York: Springer Verlag.

Holland, H. D. 1997. "Evidence for life on earth more than 3850 million years ago", *Science* **275**, 38–9.

Holland, P. W. H. & Fernandez, J. G. 1996. "Hox genes and chordate evolution", *Developmental Biology* **173**, 382–95.

Hollister, C. W. 1972. *Roots of the Western Tradition: A Short History of the Ancient World*, 2nd edn. New York: John Wiley.

Holmes, G. (ed.) 1988. *The Oxford Illustrated History of Medieval Europe*. Oxford: Oxford University Press.

Holton, G. 1952. *Introduction to Concepts and Theories in Physical Science*. Cambridge, MA: Addison-Wesley.

Holton, G. 1960. "Notes on the religious orientation of scientists", in *Science Ponders Religion*, H. Shapley (ed.), 52–64. New York: Appleton-Century-Crofts.

Holton, G. 1973. *Thematic Origins of Scientific Thought: Kepler to Einstein*. Cambridge: Cambridge University Press.

Holton, G. & Roller, D. H. D. 1958. *Foundations of Modern Physical Science*, D. Roller (ed.). Reading, MA: Addison-Wesley.

Hooper, W. 1998. "Inertial problems in Galileo's preinertial framework", in Machamer (ed.) (1998), 146–74.

Hooper, F. & Schwarts, M. (eds) 1991. *Roman Letters: History from a Personal Point of View*. Detroit, MI: Wayne State University Press.

Hopkins, J. 1972. *A Companion Study of St Anselm*. Minneapolis, MN: University of Minnosota Press.

Horgan, J. 1996. *The End of Science*. New York: Addison-Wesley.

Hornung, E. 1983. *Conceptions of God in Ancient Egypt*. London: Routledge & Kegan Paul.

Hornung, E. 1995. "Ancient Egyptian religious iconography", in Sasson *et al.* (eds) (1995), 1711–29.

Horton, M. 1973. "In defense of Francis Bacon", *Studies in the History and Philosophy of Science* **4**, 241–78.

Hourani, A. 1991. *Islam in European Thought*. Cambridge: Cambridge University Press.

Howard, A. V. 1951. *Chamber's Dictionary of Scientists*. New York: E. P. Dutton.

Howard, J. 1982. *Darwin*. Oxford: Oxford University Press.

Hoyle, F. 1955. *Frontiers of Astronomy*. London: Heinemann.

Hoyle, F. & Wickramasinghe, N. C. 1981. *Evolution from Space*. New York: Simon and Schuster.

Huby, P. H. 1964. "Socrates and Plato", in O'Connor (ed.) (1964), 14–35.

Huby, P. 1985. "Theophrastus in the Aristotelian corpus, with particular reference to biological problems", in Gotthelf (ed.) (1985), 313–26.

Huffman, C. A. 1999. "The Pythagorean tradition", in Long (ed.) (1999), 66–87.

Hussey, E. 1972. *The Presocratics*. London: Duckworth.

Hussey, E. 1983. *Aristotle's Physics: Books III and IV*. Oxford: Oxford University Press.

Hussey, E. 1986. "Matter theory in ancient Greece", in *The Physical Sciences Since Antiquity*, R. Harré (ed.), 10–28. London and Sydney: Croom Helm.

Hussey, E. 1995. "Ionian inquiries: on understanding the Presocratic beginnings of science", in *The Greek World*, A. Powell (ed.), 530–49. London: Routledge.

Hussey, E. 1997. "Pythagoreans and Eleatics", in Taylor (ed.) (1997), 128–74.

Hussey, E. 1999. "Heraclitus", in Long (ed.) (1999), 88–112.

Huxley, L. 1901. *Life and Letters of Thomas Henry Huxley*, 2 vols. New York: D. Appleton.

Hyman, A. & Walsh, J. J. 1973. *Philosophy of the Middle Ages*. Indianapolis, IN: Hackett.

Inati, S. C. 1998a. "Concept of soul in Islamic philosophy", in Leaman (ed.) (1998), 40–44.

Inati, S. C. 1998b. "Epistemology in Islamic philosophy", in Leaman (ed.) (1998), 384–8.

Infeld, L. 1950. *Albert Einstein*. New York: Charles Scribner's Sons.

Ingman, M., Kaessmann, H., Paabo, S. & Gyllensten, U. 2000. "Mitochondrial genome variation and the origin of modern humans", *Nature* **408**, 708–13.

Ionides, S. A. & Ionides, M. L. 1939. *Stars and Men*. New York: Bobbs-Merrill Publishing.

Ivry, A. L. 1972. "Al-Kindi as philosopher: the Aristotelian and Neoplatonic dimensions", in *Islamic Philosophy and the Classical Tradition: Essays Presented to Stern*, A. Hourani & V. Brown (eds), 117–39. Oxford: Oxford University Press.

Jablonski, N. G. & Chaplin, G. 2000. "The evolution of human skin colouration", *Journal of Human Evolution* **39**(1), 57–106.

Jacobsen, T. 1951. "Mesopotamia: the cosmos as a state", in Frankfort *et al.* (eds) (1951), 137–234.

Jacobsen, T. 1976. *The Treasures in Darkness: A History of Mesopotamian Religion*. New Haven, CT: Yale University Press.

Jaeger, W. 1934. *Aristotle: Fundamentals of the History of his Development*. Oxford: Clarendon Press.

Jaeger, W. 1936. *The Theology of the Early Greek Philosophers: The Gifford Lectures*. Oxford: Oxford University Press.

Jaeger, W. W. 1961. *Early Christianity and Greek Paideia*. Cambridge, MA: The Belknap Press of Harvard University Press.

James, E. 1988. "The northern world in the dark ages", in *The Oxford Illustrated History of Medieval Europe*, G. Holmes (ed.), 63–114. Oxford: Oxford University Press.

James, T. G. H. 1995. "Rediscovering Egypt of the Pharaohs", in Sasson *et al.* (eds) (1995), 2753–64.

Jammer, J. 1954. *Concepts of Space: The History of Theories of Space in Physics*. Cambridge, MA: Harvard University Press.

Jenkins-Jones, S. (ed.) 1996. *The Hutchinson Dictionary of Scientists*. Oxford: Helicon.

Jerison, H. J. 1973. *Evolution of the Brain and Intelligence*. San Diego: Academic Press.

Jerison, H. J. 1988. "Evolutionary biology of intelligence: the nature of the problem", in *Intelligence and Evolutionary Biology*, H. J. Jerison & I. Jerison (eds), 1–11. Berlin: Springer-Verlag (in cooperation with NATO scientific affairs division).

Jin, L., Underhill, P. A., Vishal, D. *et al.* 1999. "Distribution of haplotypes from a chromosome 21 region distinguishes multiple prehistoric human midrations", *Proceedings of the National Academy of Sciences (USA)* **96**, 3796–800.

Johanson, D. C. & Edey, M. A. 1982. *Lucy: The Beginnings of Humankind*, 1st edn. New York: A Warner Communications Company.

Johanson, D. C. & White, T. D. 1979. "A systematic assessment of early African hominids", *Science* **203**(4378), 321–30.

Johanson, D. C., Edgar, B. & Brill, D. 1996. *From Lucy to Language*, 1st edn. New York: Simon and Schuster.

Johns, J. 1990. "Christianity and Islam", in McManners (ed.) (1990), 163–95.

Johnson, H. J. 1973. "Changing concepts of matter from antiquity to Newton", in Wiener (ed.) (1973), 185–96.

Johnson, P. 1978. *The Civilization of Ancient Egypt*. London: Weidenfeld & Nicolson.

Joly, R. 1970. "Hippocrates of Cos", in Gillispie (ed.) (1970–80), **6**, 418–31.

Jones, W. T. 1969. *The Medieval Mind*. New York: Harcourt Brace Jovanovich.

Kahn, C. H. 1960. *Anaximander and the Origins of Greek Cosmology*. New York: Columbia University Press.

Kahn, C. H. 1979. *The Art and Thought of Heraclitus: An Edition of the Fragments with Translation and Commentary*. Cambridge: Cambridge University Press.

Kahn, C. 1985. "The place of the prime mover in Aristotle's teleology", in Gotthelf (ed.) (1985), 183–205.

Kajander, E. O. & Ciftcioglu, N. 1998. "Nanobacteria: an alternative mechanism for pathogenic intra- and extracellular calcification and stone formation", *Proceedings of the National Academy of Sciences (USA)* **95**, 8274–9.

Kajander, E. O., Ciftcioglu, N., Miller-Hjelle, M. A. & Hjelle, J. T. 2001. "Nanobacteria: controversial pathogens in nephrolithiasis and polycystic kidney disease", *Current Opinions in Nephrology and Hypertension* **10**, 445–52.

Kakosy, L. 1995. "Egypt in ancient Greek and Roman thought", in Sasson *et al.* (eds) (1995), 3–14.

Kant, I. 1974. *Anthropology from a Pragmatic Point of View*, M. J. Gregor (trans.). The Hague: Martinus Nijhoff.

Karl, D. M., Bird, D. F., Björkman, K. *et al.* 1999. "Microorganisms in the accreted ice of Lake Vostok, Antarctica", *Science* **286**, 2144–7.

Karp, W. 1972. "Isaac Newton", in *Makers of Modern Thought*, J. Thorndike (ed.), 161–79. New York: American Heritage.

Kasner, E. & Newman, J. 1940. *Mathematics and the Imagination*. New York: Simon and Schuster.

Kasting, J. F. 1993. "Earth's early atmosphere", *Science* **259**, 920–26.

Katz, S. T. (ed.) 1980. *Medieval Jewish Philosophy*. New York: Arno Press.

Kauffman, S. A. 1993. *The Origins of Order: Self-Organisation and Selection in Evolution*. Oxford: Oxford University Press.

Kauffman, S. A. 1995. *At Home in the Universe*. Harmondsworth: Penguin.

Kearns, E. 1995. "Order, interaction, authority: ways of looking at Greek religion", in *The Greek World*, A. Powell (ed.), 511–29. London: Routledge.

Keeton, W. T. 1980. *Biological Science*. New York: W. W. Norton.

Kelly, J. N. D. 1975. *Jerome: His Life, Writings and Controversies*. London: Duckworth.

Kemal, S. 1998. "Ibn Sina 'Ali al-Husayn (980–1037)", in Leaman (ed.) (1998), 647–54.

Kemp, B. J. 1989. *Ancient Egypt: Anatomy of a Civilisation*. London: Routledge.

Kemp, B. J. 1995. "Unification and urbanisation of ancient Egypt", in Sasson *et al.* (eds) (1995), 679–90.

Kennedy-Day, K. 1998. "Aristotelianism in Islamic philosophy", in Leaman (ed.) (1998), 382–6.

Kenny, A. 1969. *The Five Ways*. London: Routledge & Kegan Paul.

Kenny, A. 1983. *Faith and Reason*. New York: Columbia University Press.

Kenny, J. P. 1986. "Monotheistic and polytheistic elements in classical Mediterranean spirituality", in Armstrong (ed.) (1986), 269–92.

Keosian, J. 1964. *The Origin of Life*. New York: Reinhold Book Corporation.

Kepler, J. 1940 [1618]. "Harmonice mundi", *Gesammelte Werke*, vol. 6. Munich.

King-Hele, D. 1968. *The Essential Writings of Erasmus Darwin*. London: MacGibbon and Kee.

Kingsley, P. 1995. *Ancient Philosophy, Mystery and Magic: Empedocles and Pythagorean Tradition*. Oxford: Oxford University Press.

Kirk, G. S. 1960. "Popper on science and Presocratics", in Furley & Allen (eds) (1970), 154–77.
Kirk, G. S. 1970. *Myth: Its Meaning and Functions in Ancient and Other Cultures*. Cambridge: Cambridge University Press.
Kirk, G. S., Raven, J. E. & Schofield, M. 1983 [1957]. *The Presocratic Philosophers*, 2nd edn. Cambridge: Cambridge University Press.
Kirshner, R. P. 2002. *The Extravagant Universe: Exploding Stars, Dark Energy, and the Accelerating Cosmos*. Princeton, NJ: Princeton University Press.
Knight, M. 1964. "Science and religion: by a non-theist", in *Science in its Context*, J. Brierley (ed.), 121–36. London: Heinemann.
Knight, D. M. 1981. "Scientist", in *Dictionary of the History of Science*, W. F. Bynum, E. J. Browne & R. Porter (ed.), 381. Princeton, NJ: Princeton University Press.
Knowles, D. 1962. *The Evolution of Medieval Thought*. London: Longmans, Green.
Knowles, E. 1999. *The Oxford Dictionary of Quotations*, 5th edn. Oxford: Oxford University Press.
Knuuttila, S. 2001. "Time and creation in Augustine", in Stump & Kretzmann (eds) (2001), 103–15.
Koestler, A. 1963. *The Sleepwalkers*. New York: Grosset & Dunlop.
Kornberg, A. 1992. "Science is great, but scientists are still people", *Science* 257, 859.
Koyre, A. 1943. "Galileo and Plato", *Journal of the History of Ideas* 4, 400–428.
Koyre, A. 1956. "The origins of modern science: a new interpretation", *Diogenes* 16, 1–22.
Koyre, A. 1957. *From the Closed World to the Infinite Universe*. Baltimore, MD: Johns Hopkins University Press.
Kragh, H. 1996. *Cosmology and Controversy: The Historical Development of Two Theories of the Universe*. Princeton, NJ: Princeton University Press.
Kramer, S. N. 1944. "The epic of Gilgamesh and its Sumerian sources: a study in literary tradition", *Journal of the American Oriental Society* 64, 7–23.
Kramer, S. N. 1948. "Review of *The Intellectual Adventure of Ancient Man: An Essay on Speculative Thought in the Ancient Near East*", *Journal of Cuneiform Studies* 2, 39–70.
Kramer, S. N. 1956. *History Begins at Sumer*. London: Thames & Hudson.
Kramer, S. N. 1963. *The Sumerians: Their History, Culture and Character*. Chicago, IL: University of Chicago Press.
Kramer, S. N. 1980. *History Begins at Sumer*, 3rd edn. London: Thames & Hudson.
Kramer, S. N. 1983. "Sumerian history, culture and literature", in *Inanna: Queen of Heaven and Earth*, D. Wolkstein & S. N. Kramer (eds), 115–26. London: Rider and Company.
Krauss, L. M. 1999. "Cosmological antigravity", *Scientific American* 280 (January), 35–41.
Krauss, L. M. & Turner, M. S. 2004. "A cosmic conundrum", *Scientific American* 291(3), 53–9.
Kraut, R. (ed.) 1992. *The Cambridge Companion to Plato*. Cambridge: Cambridge University Press.
Kraye, J. 1993. "The philosophy of the Italian Renaissance", in Parkinson (ed.) (1993), 16–69.
Kretzmann, N. & Stump, E. (eds) 1993. *The Cambridge Companion to Aquinas*. Cambridge: Cambridge University Press.
Kretzmann, N., Kenny, A. & Pinborg, J. (ed.) 1988. *The Cambridge History of Later Medieval Philosophy*. Cambridge: Cambridge University Press.
Kudlien, F. 1968. "Early Greek primitive medicine", *Clio Medica* 3, 305–36.
Kuhn, T. S. 1957. *The Copernican Revolution*. Cambridge, MA: Harvard University Press.
Kuhn, T. S. 1970. *The Structure of Scientific Revolutions*, 2nd edn. Chicago, IL: University of Chicago Press.
Kutter, G. S. 1989. *Origin and Evolution of the Universe*. Boston, MA: Jones and Bartlett.
Lahav, N. 1999. *Biogenesis: Theories of Life's Origin*. Oxford: Oxford University Press.
Lahr, M. M. 1994. "The multiregional model of modern human origins: a reassessment of its morphological basis", *Journal of Human Evolution* 26, 23–56.
Laland, K. N. 1998. "The evolution of culture", in *Neandertals and Modern Humans in Western Asia*, T. Akazawa *et al.* (eds), 427–38. New York: Plenum Press.
Lambert, W. G. 1995. "Myth and mythmaking in Sumer and Akkad", in Sasson *et al.* (eds) (1995), 1825–35.
Lamberton, R. 1988. *Hesiod*. New Haven, CT: Yale University Press.
Lampe, G. W. E. 1978. "Christian theology in the Patristic period", in *A History of Christian Doctrine*, H. Cunliffe-Jones (ed.), 23–180. Edinburgh: T. & T. Clark.
Lang, A., Leaf, W. & Meyers, E. (eds) 1950. *The Iliad of Homer*. New York: Random House.
Lansing, E. 1974. *The Sumerians*. London: Cassell.
Larsen, M. T. 1995. "The 'Babel/Bible' controversy and its aftermath", in Sasson *et al.* (eds) (1995), 95–106.
Leahy, A. 1995. "Ethnic diversity in ancient Egypt", in Sasson *et al.* (eds) (1995), 225–34.
Leakey, R. 1994. *The Origin of Humankind*. London: Weidenfeld & Nicolson.
Leakey, R. & Lewin, R. 1992. *Origins Reconsidered*. London: Abacus.
Leakey, M. G., Feibel, C. S., McDougall, I. & Walker, A. 1995. "New four-million year old hominid species from Kanapoi and Allia Bay, Kenya", *Nature* 376, 565–71.

Leaman, O. 1985. *An Introduction to Medieval Islamic Philosophy*. Cambridge: Cambridge University Press.

Leaman, O. 1990. *Moses Maimonides*. London: Routledge.

Leaman, O. 1998a. "Concept of philosophy in Islam", in Craig (ed.) (1998), 5–9.

Leaman, O. 1998b. "Ibn Rushd, Abu'l Walid Muhammad (1126–98)", in Craig (ed.) (1998), 638–46.

Leaman, O. 1999. *A Brief Introduction to Islamic Philosophy*. Cambridge: Polity Press.

Lear, J. 1965. *Kepler's Dream*. Berkeley, CA: University of California Press.

Lebreton, J. 1913. "St Justin Martyr", in C. G. Herbermann *et al.* (eds), 580–86.

Leeming, D. A. & Leeming, M. A. 1994. *A Dictionary of Creation Myths*. Oxford: Oxford University Press.

Lefebvre, G. 1963. "Egyptian medicine", in *History of Science: Ancient and Medieval Science*, R. Taton (ed.), 44–64. New York: Basic Books.

Leff, G. 1970. *Medieval Thought: St. Augustine to Ockham*. Harmondsworth: Penguin.

Lehninger, A. 1975. *Biochemistry*, 2nd edn. New York: Worth.

Leicester, H. M. 1956. *The Historical Background of Chemistry*. New York: Dover Publications (reprinted 1971).

Leroi-Gourhan, A. 1967. *Treasures of Prehistoric Art*. New York: Harry N. Abrams.

Lesaar, H. H. 1931. *Saint Augustine*. London: Burns Oates & Washbourne.

Lesher, J. H. 1999. "Early interest in knowledge", in Long (ed.) (1999), 225–49.

Lesko, L. H. 1991. "Ancient Egyptian cosmogonies and cosmology", in Shafer (ed.) (1991), 88–122.

Lesko, L. H. 1994. *Pharaoh's Workers: The Villagers of Deir el Medina*. Ithaca, NY: Cornell University Press.

Lesko, L. H. 1995. "Death and the afterlife in ancient Egyptian thought", in Sasson *et al.* (eds) (1995), 1763–74.

Levey, M. 1959. *Chemistry and Chemical Technology in Ancient Mesopotamia*. Amsterdam: Elsevier.

Lewin, R. 1997. "Ancestral echoes", *New Scientist* 155(2089), 32–7.

Lewin, R. 1998. *Principles of Human Evolution: A Core Textbook*. Cambridge, MA: Blackwell Science.

Libet, B. 1999. "Do we have free will?", *Journal of Consciousness Studies* 6, 47–57.

Libet, B. 2000. "Time factors in conscious processes: reply to Gilberto Gomes", *Consciousness and Cognition* 9, 1–12.

Liebeschutz, H. 1967. "Anselm of Canterbury: the philosophical interpretation of faith", in Armstrong (ed.) (1967), 611–42.

Lindberg, D. C. (ed.) 1983. *Roger Bacon's Philosophy of Nature*. Oxford: Oxford University Press.

Lindberg, D. C. 1992. *The Beginnings of Western Science*. Chicago, IL: University of Chicago Press.

Lindberg, D. C. & Numbers, R. L. (eds) 1986. *God and Nature: Historical Essays on the Encounter between Christianity and Science*. Berkeley, CA: University of California Press.

Lindberg, D. C. & Westman, R. (eds) 1990. *Reappraisals of the Scientific Revolution*. Cambridge: Cambridge University Press.

Llewellyn Smith, C. 2000. "The large hardron collider", *Scientific American* 283 (July), 59–63.

Llinas, R. R. & Pare, D. 1991. "Of dreaming and wakefulness", *Neuroscience* 44, 521–35.

Lloyd, G. E. R. 1968. *Aristotle: The Growth and Structure of his Thought*. Cambridge: Cambridge University Press.

Lloyd, G. E. R. 1970. *Early Greek Science: From Thales to Aristotle*. New York: W. W. Norton.

Lloyd, A. C. 1970–80. "Plotinus (c 204–270 AD)", in Gillispie (ed.) (1970–80), 11, 41–2.

Lloyd, S. 1978. *The Archaeology of Mesopotamia*. London: Thames & Hudson.

Lloyd, G. E. R. 1983. *Science, Folklore and Ideology: Studies in the Life Sciences in Ancient Greece*. Cambridge: Cambridge University Press.

Lloyd, G. E. R. 1987. *The Revolutions of Wisdom: Studies in the Claims and Practice of Ancient Greek Science*. Berkeley, CA: University of California Press.

Lockwood, M. 1989. *Mind, Brain and the Quantum*. Cambridge, MA: Basil Blackwell.

Loeb, J. 1906. *The Dynamics of Living Matter*. New York: Columbia University Press.

Long, A. A. 1973. "Psychological ideas in antiquity", in Wiener (ed.) (1973), 1–9.

Long, A. A. (ed.) 1999a. *The Cambridge Companion to Early Greek Philosophy*. Cambridge: Cambridge University Press.

Long, A. A. 1999b. "The scope of early Greek philosophy", in Long (ed.) (1999), 1–21.

Long, A. A. & Sedley, D. N. 1987. *The Hellenistic Philosophers: Translations of the Principal Sources with Philosophical Inquiry*, vol. 1. Cambridge: Cambridge University Press.

Longfellow, H. W. 1909–14. "The Day is Done", in *English Poetry III: From Tennyson to Whitman*, vol. 42 of 51, C. W. Eliot (ed.). New York: P. F. Collier & Son.

Longrigg, J. N. 1980. "The great plague of Athens", *History of Science* 18, 209–25.

Longrigg, J. 1989. "Presocratic philosophy and Hippocratic medicine", *History of Science*, 27, 1–39.

Longrigg, J. N. 1993. *Greek Rational Medicine*. London: Routledge.

Lovelock, J. 1991. *Gaia: The Practical Science of Planetary Medicine*. Hong Kong: Allen and Unwin.

Lucas, J. R. 1979. "Wilberforce and Huxley: a legendary encounter", *The Historical Journal* 22, 313–30.

Luce, J. V. 1992. *An Introduction to Greek Philosophy*. London: Thames & Hudson.

Lucretius 1965. *On the Nature of the Universe (De Rerum Natura)*, J. H. Mantinband (trans.). New York: Frederick Ungar.

Lull, R. S. 1917. *Organic Evolution*. New York: Macmillan.
Luscombe, D. E. 1970. *The School of Peter Abelard*. Cambridge: Cambridge University Press.
Lynch, J. H. 1992. *The Medieval Church: A Brief History*. London and New York: Longman.
MacDonald, S. 1993. "Theory of knowledge", in Kretzmann & Stump (eds) (1993), 160–95.
MacDonald, S. 2001. "The divine nature", in Stump & Kretzmann (eds) (2001), 71–90.
MacFarlane, G. 1985. *Alexander Fleming: The Man and the Myth*. Oxford: Oxford University Press.
Mach, E. 1893. *The Science of Mechanics: A Critical and Historical Exposition of its Principles*. La Salle, IL: Open Court.
Machamer, P. (ed.) 1998a. *The Cambridge Companion to Galileo*. Cambridge: Cambridge University Press.
Machamer, P. 1998b. "Introduction", in Machamer (ed.) (1998), 1–26.
Maclarnon, A. M. & Hewitt, G. P. 1999. "The evolution of human speech: the role of enhanced breathing control", *American Journal of Physical Anthropology* **109**(3), 341–63.
Mahoney, M. 1998. *The Mathematical Realm of Nature*, in Garber & Ayers (eds) (1998), 702–55.
Maienschein, J. 1990. "Cell theory and development", in *Companion to the History of Modern Science*, R. C. Olby *et al.* (eds), 357–73. London: Routledge.
Maier, J. 1995. "The ancient Near East in modern thought", in Sasson *et al.* (eds) (1995), 107–22.
Malcolm, N. 1960. "Anselm's ontological arguments", *Philosophical Review* **69**, 41–62.
Malefijt, de Waal, A. 1974. *Images of Man: A History of Anthropological Thought*. New York: Alfred A. Knopf.
Mann, W. E. 2001. "Augustine on evil and original sin", in Stump & Kretzmann (eds) (2001), 40–48.
Marenbon, J. 1983. *Early Medieval Philosophy (480–1150)*. London: Routledge & Kegan Paul.
Marenbon, J. 1987. *Later Medieval Philosophy (1150–1350)*. London: Routledge & Kegan Paul.
Marenbon, J. 1996. "Medieval Christian and Jewish Europe", in *History of Islamic Philosophy*, K. Nasir & O. Leaman (eds), 1001–12. London: Routledge.
Margueron, J.-C. 1965. *Mesopotamia*. Cleveland, OH: World Publishing Company.
Margulis, L. & Sagan, D. 1995. *What is Life?* New York: Simon and Schuster.
Marion, J.-L. 1998, *The Idea of God*, in Garber & Ayers (eds) (1998), 265–304.
Markus, R. A. 1964. "Augustine", in O'Connor (ed.) (1964), 79–97.
Markus, R. 1990. "From Rome to the barbarian kingdoms", in McManners (ed.) (1990), 62–91.
Markus, R. A. 1997. *Gregory the Great and his World*. Cambridge: Cambridge University Press.
Marrone, S. P. 1983. *William of Auvergne and Robert Grosseteste: New Ideas of Truth in the Early 13th Century*. Princeton, NJ: Princeton University Press.
Mason, B. 1958. *Principles of Geology*. New York: John Wiley.
Mason, S. F. 1962. *A History of the Sciences*. New York: Collier Books (new revised edition).
Mason, S. F. 1991. *Chemical Evolution: Origin of the Elements, Molecules and Living Systems*. Oxford: Clarendon Press.
Mathews, G. 1972. *Plato's Epistemology*. London: Faber and Faber.
Mayer, H. E. 1972. *The Crusades*, J. Gillingham (trans.). Oxford: Oxford University Press.
Maynard Smith, J. & Szathmary, E. 1999. *The Origins of Life: From the Birth of Life to the Origin of Language*. Oxford: Oxford University Press.
Mayr, E. 1982. *The Growth of Biological Thought: Diversity, Evolution and Inheritance*. Cambridge, MA: The Belknap Press of the Harvard University Press.
Mayr, E. 1988. *Towards a New Philosophy of Biology*. Cambridge, MA: Harvard University Press.
Mayr, E. 2000. "Darwin's influence on modern thought", *Scientific American* **283** (July), 67–71.
McBrearty, S. & Brooks, A. S. 2000. "The revolution that wasn't: a new interpretation of the origin of modern human behaviour", *Journal of Human Evolution* **39**, 453–563.
McCall, H. 1990. *Mesopotamian Myths*. Austin, TX: British Museum Publications with University of Texas Press.
McCord-Adams, M. 1987. *William Ockham*. Notre Dame, IN: Notre Dame University Press.
McCracken, C. 1998. "Knowledge of the soul", in Garber & Ayers (eds) (1998), 796–832.
McDougall, W. 1911. *Body and Mind: A History and a Defense of Animism*. London: Methuen.
McGibbon, D. 1965. "The religious thought of Democritus", *Hermes* **93**, 385–97.
McGinnis, W. R., Garber, R. L., Wirz, J. *et al.* 1984. "A homologous protein coding sequence in drosophila homeotic genes and its conservation in metazoans", *Cell* **37**, 403–8.
McHenry, L. C. 1969. *Garrison's History of Neurology*. Springfield, IL: Charles. C. Thomas.
McKay, D., Gibson E. K., Thomas-Keprta, K. L. *et al.* 1996. "Search for past life on Mars: possible relic biogenic activity in Martian meteorite ALH84001", *Science* **273**, 924–30.
McKirahan, R. D. 1999. "Zeno", in Long (ed.) (1999), 134–58.
McKitterick, R. 1989. *The Carolingians and the Written Word*. Cambridge: Cambridge University Press.
McLean, G. F. & Aspell, P. J. (eds) 1970. *Readings in Ancient Western Philosophy*. New York: Appleton-Century-Crofts.
McLeish, J. 1992. *Number: From Ancient Civilizations to the Computer*. London: Flamingo Press.
McMahon, T. A. & Bonner, J. T. 1983. *On Size and Life*. New York: Scientific American Library.
McManners, J. (ed.) 1990. *The Oxford Illustrated History of Christianity*. Oxford: Oxford University Press.

McMullin, E. 1978. *Newton on Matter and Activity*. Notre Dame, IN: University of Notre Dame Press.

McMullin, E. 1990. "Conceptions of science in the scientific revolution", in Lindberg & Westman (eds) (1990), 27–92.

McMullin, E. 1998. "Galileo on science and scripture", in Machamer (ed.) (1998a), 271–347.

McMurrin, S. M. 1982. *Religion, Reason and Truth: Historical Essays in the Philosophy of Religion*. Salt Lake City, UT: University of Utah Press.

McNeill, W. H. 1963. *The Rise of the West: A History of the Human Community*. Chicago, IL: University of Chicago Press.

Medawar, P. 1961. "Review of the phenomenon of man", *Mind* 70, 99–106.

Medawar, P. 1984. *The Limits of Science*. Oxford: Oxford University Press.

Medawar, P. 1991. *The Threat and the Glory: Reflections on Science and Scientists*, D. Pyke (ed.). Oxford: Oxford University Press.

Meeks, W. 1983. *The First Urban Christians: The Social World of the Apostle Paul*. New Haven, CT: Yale University Press.

Mencken, H. L. (ed.) 1962. *A New Dictionary of Quotations on Historical Principles: From Ancient and Modern Sources*. New York: Alfred A. Knopf.

Merdinger, J. 1991. "The world of the Roman Empire", in *Early Christianity: Origins and Evolution to AD 600*, I. Hazlett (ed.), 17–27. London: SPCK.

Merton, R. K. 1968. *Social Theory and Social Structure*. New York: Macmillan and The Free Press.

Metzger, B. M. 1987. *The Canon of the New Testament: Its Origin, Development and Significance*. Oxford: Clarendon Press.

Mill, J. S. 1843. *A System of Logic, Ratiocinative and Inductive, Being a Connected View of the Principles of Evidence, and the Methods of Scientific Investigation*. London: J. W. Parker.

Miller, S. L. 1955. "Production of some organic compounds under possible primitive conditions", *Journal of the American Chemical Society* 77, 2351–61.

Miller, S. L. & Lazcano, A. 2002. "Formation of the building blocks of life", in Schopf (ed.) (2002a), 78–112.

Miller, S. L. & Orgel, L. E. 1974. *The Origins of Life on Earth*. Englewood Cliffs, NJ: Prentice-Hall.

Milton, J. R. 1998. "Laws of nature", in Garber & Ayers (eds) (1998), 680–701.

Misner, C. W., Thorne, K. S. & Wheeler, J. A. 1973. *Gravitation*. San Francisco: Freeman.

Mithen, S. 1996. *The Prehistory of Mind*. London: Thames & Hudson.

Molland, G. 1993. "Science and mathematics from the Renaissance to Descartes", in Parkinson (ed.) (1993), 104–39.

Mommsen, T. E. 1942. "Petrarch's conception of the 'Dark Ages'", *Speculum* 17, 226–42.

Moody, E. A. 1970–80. "Ockham, William (1285–1349)", in Gillispie (ed.) (1970–80), 10, 171–5.

Moore, G. F. 1928. *History of Religions*. New York: Charles Scribner's Sons.

Moran, W. 1995. "The Gilgamesh Epic: a masterpiece from ancient Mesopotamia", in Sasson *et al.* (eds) (1995), 2327–36.

Morell, V. 1995. "The earliest art becomes older – and more common", *Science* 267, 1908–9.

Morenz, S. 1973. *Egyptian Religion*. Ithaca, NY: Cornell University Press.

Morford, M. P. & Lenardon, R. J. 1999. *Classical Mythology*, 6th edn. Oxford: Oxford University Press.

Morgan, M. L. 1992. "Plato and Greek religion", in *The Cambridge Companion to Plato*, R. Kraut (ed.), 227–47. Cambridge: Cambridge University Press.

Morris, C. 1990. "Christian civilisation", in McManners (ed.) (1990), 196–266.

Morwood, M. J., O'Sullivan, P. B., Aziz, F. & Raza, A. 1998. "Fission track ages of stone tools and fossils in Central Flores, Indonesia", *Nature* 392, 173–6.

Morwood, M. J., Soejono, R. P., Roberts R. G. *et al.* 2004. "Archaeology and age of a new hominin from Flores in eastern Indonesia", *Nature* 431, 1087–91.

Most, G. W. 1999. *The Poetics of Early Greek Philosophy*, in Long (ed.) (1999), 332–62.

Mueller, I. 1997. "Greek arithmetic, geometry and harmonics: Thales to Plato", in Taylor (ed.) (1997), 271–322.

Muhly, J. D. 1995. "Mining and metalwork in ancient Western Asia", in Sasson *et al.* (eds) (1995), 1501–22.

Munitz, M. K. 1957. *Theories of the Universe: From Babylonian Myth to Modern Science*. Glencoe, IL: The Free Press.

Murdoch, J. 1982. "The analytic character of late medieval learning: natural philosophy without nature", in *Approaches to Nature in the Middle Ages*, L. D. Roberts (ed.), 171–213. New York: Binghamton.

Murnane, W. J. 1995. "The history of ancient Egypt: an overview", in Sasson *et al.* (eds) (1995), 691–718.

Nadler, S. 1998. "Doctrines of explanation in late scholasticism and in the mechanical philosophy", in Garber & Ayers (eds) (1998), 513–52.

Nahm, M. C. 1964. *Selections from Early Greek Philosophy*, 6th edn. New York: Appleton-Century-Crofts.

Nakamura, K. 1998. "Al-Ghazali, Abu Hamid (1058–1111)", in Leaman (ed.) (1998), 61–8.

Nature 1981. "How true is the theory of evolution?", *Nature* 290, 75–6.

Needham, J. (ed.) 1955 [1925]. *Science, Religion and Reality*. New York: George Braziller.

Netton, I. A. 1998. "Neoplatonism in Islamic philosophy", in Leaman (ed.) (1998), 804–8.

Neugebauer, O. 1942. "The origin of the Egyptian calendar", *Journal of Near Eastern Studies* **1**, 396–403.
Neugebauer, O. 1952. *The Exact Sciences in Antiquity*. Princeton, NJ: Princeton University Press.
Neugebauer, O. 1975. *A History of Ancient Mathematical Astronomy*. New York: Springer-Verlag.
Neugebauer, O. 1983. *Astronomy and History: Selected Essays*. New York: Springer-Verlag.
Neugebauer, O. & Parker, R. 1968. "Two demotic horoscopes", *Journal of Egyptian Archaeology* **54**, 231–5.
Newman, J. R. 1956. *The World of Mathematics*, vol. 1. New York: Simon and Schuster.
Newton, I. 1848. *Newton's Principia: The Mathematical Principles of Natural Philosophy*. New York: D. Adee.
Nilsson, M. P. 1950. *The Minoan-Mycenaean Religion and its Survival in Greek Religion*, 2nd edn. Lund: Gleerup.
Nisbet, E. 2000. "The realms of Archaean life, *Nature* **405**, 625–6.
Norbeck, E. 1961. *Religion in Primitive Society*. New York: Harper & Row.
Norlind, W. 1953. "Copernicus and Luther: A Critical Study", *Isis* **44**, 273–6.
North, J. 1994. *The Fontana History of Astronomy and Cosmology*, R. Porter (ed.). London: Fontana Press.
Numbers, R. L. 2000. "'The Most Important Biblical Discovery of Our Time': William Henry Green and the demise of Ussher's chronology", *The American Society of Church History* **69** (June), 2–22.
Nunn, J. 1996. *Ancient Egyptian Medicine*. London: British Museum Press.
Nutton, V. 1995. "Medicine in the Greek world, 800–50 BC", in *The Western Medical Tradition: 800 BC to AD 1800*, L. I. Conrad *et al.* (eds), 11–38. Cambridge: Cambridge University Press.
Oates, J. 1980. "The emergence of the Near-East", in Sherratt (ed.) (1980), 112–19.
O'Connor, D. J. 1964a. "Aristotle", in O'Connor (ed.) (1964), 36–61.
O'Connor, D. J. (ed.) 1964b. *A Critical History of Western Philosophy*. New York: Free Press of Glencoe.
O'Connor, D. 1980. "Egypt and the Levant in the Bronze Age", in Sherratt (ed.) (1980), 128–35.
O'Donnell, J. J. 1977. "Paganus", *Classical Folia* **31**, 163–9.
O'Meara, J. J. 1980. *The Young Augustine: An Introduction to the* Confessions *of St Augustine*. London: Longman.
Onions, C. T. (ed.) 1966. *Oxford Dictionary of English Etymology*. Oxford: Clarendon Press.
Oparin, A. J. 1955. *The Origin of Life*. Moscow: Foreign Languages Publishing House.
Oparin, A. I. 1962. *Life: Its Nature, Origin and Development*. New York: Academic Press.
Oppenheim, A. L. 1977. *Ancient Mesopotamia*. Chicago, IL: University of Chicago Press.
Orgel, L. E. 1994. "The origin of life on earth", *Scientific American* **271** (October), 53–61.
Orgel, L. E. 2002. "The origin of biological information", in Schopf (ed.) (2002a), 140–57.
Oró, J. 1997. "Comets and the origin and evolution of life", in *Comets and the Origin and Evolution of Life*, P. J. Thomas *et al.* (eds), 3–27. New York: Springer-Verlag.
Oró, J. 2002. "Historical understanding of life's beginnings", in Schopf (ed.) (2002a), 7–45.
Oró, J. & Kimball, A. P. 1961. "Synthesis of purines under primitive earth conditions. I. Adenine from hydrogen cyanide", *Archives of Biochemistry and Biophysics* **94**, 221.
Oró, J., Miller, S. L., Ponnamperuma, C. & Young, R. D. S. (eds) 1973. *Cosmochemical Evolution and the Origins of Life*. Dordrecht: D. Reidel.
Owen, G. E. L. 1970. "Aristotle", in Gillispie (ed.) (1970–80), **1**, 250–58.
Owen, J. 1993. "Aristotle and Aquinas", in Kretzmann & Stump (eds) (1993), 38–59.
Pais, A. 1982. *Subtle is the Lord*. Oxford: Oxford University Press.
Paley, W. 1794. *A View of Evidences of Christianity* (2 vols). London: R. Faulder Publishers.
Panchenko, D. 1994. "Thales' prediction of a solar eclipse", *Journal for the History of Astronomy* **24**, 275–88.
Pannekoek, A. 1961. *A History of Astronomy*. New York: Interscience.
Parker, R. A. 1950. *The Calendars of Ancient Egypt*. Chicago, IL: University of Chicago Press.
Parker, R. A. 1974. "Ancient Egyptian astronomy", *Philosophical Transactions, Royal Society London* **276**, 51–65.
Parker, R. A. 1978. "Egyptian astronomy, astrology, and calendrical reckoning", in Gillispie (ed.) (1970–1980), **15**, 706–27.
Parkinson, G. H. R. (ed.) 1993. *The Renaissance and Seventeenth-Century Rationalism*. London: Routledge. vol. 4.
Partington, J. R. 1957 [1937]. *A Short History of Chemistry*, 3rd edn. New York: Harper and Brothers.
Partington, J. R. 1970. *A History of Chemistry, Part I: Theoretical Background*, vol. 1. London, New York: Macmillan and Company.
Pascal, B. 1952. *Provincial Letters, Pensées, Scientific Treatises*, W. F. Trotter (trans.). Chicago, IL: William Benton.
Patterson, R. 1985. *Image and Reality in Plato's Metaphysics*. Indianapolis, IN: Hackett.
Paul II, J. 1998. *Faith and Reason: Encyclical Letter to the Bishops of the Catholic Church*. Strathfield: St. Pauls Publications.
Peacocke, A. R. 1979. *Creation and the World of Science*. Oxford: Oxford University Press.
Peacocke, A. R. 1986. *God and the New Biology*. San Francisco: Harper & Row.
Pearce, L. E. 1995. "The scribes of and scholars of ancient Mesopotamia", in Sasson *et al.* (eds) (1995), 2211–21.

Pease, A. S. 1942. "Fossil fishes again", *Isis* **33**, 689–90.

Peck, H. T. (ed.) 1898. *The International Cyclopedia*. New York: Dodd, Mead & Co.

Pedersen, O. 1978. "Astronomy", in *Science in the Middle Ages*, D. C. Lindberg (ed.), 303–36. Chicago, IL: The University of Chicago Press.

Pedersen, O. 1983. "Galileo and the Council of Trent: the Galileo affair revisited", *Journal of the History of Astronomy* **14**, 1–29.

Pekin, L. B. 1938. *Darwin*. New York: Stackpole Sons.

Pelikan, J. 1971. *The Christian Tradition: A History of the Development of Doctrine*, vol. 1 (5 vols). Chicago: University of Chicago Press.

Pelletier, K. R. 1978. *Toward a Science of Consciousness*. New York: Delta Books.

Penfield, W. 1961. "The physiological basis of the mind", in *Man's Civilization: Control of the Mind*, S. M. Farber & R. H. L. Wilson (eds), 3–17. New York: McGraw-Hill.

Penglase, C. 1994. *Greek Myths and Mesopotamia: Parallels and Influence in the Homeric Hymns and Hesiod*. London: Routledge.

Penner, T. 1992. "Socrates and the Early Dialogues", in *The Cambridge Companion to Plato*, R. Kraut (ed.), 121–69. Cambridge: Cambridge University Press.

Pennisi, E. 2001. "The human genome", *Science* **291**(5507), 1177–80.

Penrose, R. 1994. *Shadows of the Mind*. Oxford: Oxford University Press.

Pepin, J. 1986. "Cosmic piety", in Armstrong (ed.) (1986), 408–35.

Perez-Ramos, A. 1993. "Francis Bacon and man's two-faced kingdom", in Parkinson (ed.) (1993), 140–66.

Persinger, M. A. 1993a. "Paranormal and religious beliefs may be mediated differentially by subcortical and cortical phenomenological processes of the temporal (limbic) lobes", *Perceptual and Motor Skills* **76**, 247–51.

Persinger, M. A. 1993b. "Vectorial cerebral hemisphericity as differential sources for the sensed presence, mystical experiences and religious conversions", *Perceptual and Motor Skills* **76**, 915–30.

Persinger, M. A., Tiller, S. G. & Koren, S. A. 2000. "Experimental simulation of a haunt experience and elicitation of paroxymal electroencephalographic activity by transcerebral complex magnetic fields: induction of a synthetic 'ghost'?", *Perceptual and Motor Skills* **90**, 659–74.

Peters, F. E. 1968. *Aristotle and the Arabs: The Aristotlelian Tradition in Islam*. New York: New York University Press.

Peters, F. E. 1972. *The Harvest of Hellenism*. London: George Allen and Unwin.

Petrie, W. M. F. 1883. *The Pyramids and Temples of Gizeh*. London: Field and Tuer.

Petrie, W. M. F. 1940. *Wisdom of the Egyptians*. London: British School of Archaeology.

Philip, J. 1973. "Pythagorean doctrines to 300 BC", in Wiener (ed.) (1973), 30–38.

Phillips, G. 1998. *Act of God: Moses, Tutankhamun and the Myth of Atlantis*. London: Sidgwick and Jackson.

Pinch, G. 1994. *Magic in Ancient Egypt*. London: British Museum Press.

Plato 2003. *Plato: The Last Days of Socrates: Euthyphro, Apology, Crito & Phaedo*, H. Tredennick & H. Tarrant (trans.). Harmondsworth: Penguin.

Plimer, I. 1997. *Telling Lies for God*. Sydney, Toronto and New York: Random House Australia Pty. Ltd.

Pockley, P. 1997. "Geologist loses creation challenge", *Nature* **387**, 540.

Polkinghorne, J. 1996. *Beyond Science*. Cambridge: Cambridge University Press.

Pope, M. 1975. *The Story of Decipherment: From Egypt Hieroglyphic to Linear B*. London: Thames & Hudson.

Popkin, R. 1998. "The religious background of the seventeenth-century philosophy", in Garber & Ayers (eds) (1998), 393–422.

Popkin, R. H. 2000. "Newton and Spinoza and the bible scholarship of the day", in *Rethinking the Scientific Revolution*, M. J. Osler (ed.), 297–311. Cambridge: Cambridge University Press.

Popper, K. R. 1957. "The aim of science", *Ratio* **1**, 24–35.

Popper, K. R. 1959 [1934, Vienna]. *The Logic of Scientific Discovery*. New York: Basic Books.

Popper, K. R. 1965. *Conjectures and Refutations*. London: Routledge & Kegan Paul.

Popper, K. 1970. "Back to the Presocratics", in Furley & Allen (eds) (1970), 130–53.

Popper, K. 1978. "Natural selection and emergence of mind", *Dialectica* **32**, 339–55.

Postgate, J. N. 1977. *The First Empires*. London: Elsevier.

Postgate, J. N. 1992. *Early Mesopotamia: Society and Economy at the Dawn of History*. London: Routledge.

Postlethwait, J. H. & Hopson, J. L. 1992. *The Nature of Life*. New York: McGraw-Hill.

Pough, F. H., Janis, C. M. & Heiser, J. B. 1999. *Vertebrate Life*, 5th edn. Englewood Cliffs, NJ: Prentice Hall.

Poulton, E. B. 1911. "Darwin, Charles Robert", in *Encyclopedia Britannica*, 11th edn, 840–43. New York: Encyclopedia Britannica.

Powell, M. A. 1995. "Metrology and mathematics in ancient Mesopotamia", in Sasson *et al.* (eds) (1995), 1941–57.

Price, A. W. 1997. "Plato: ethics and politics", in Taylor (ed.) (1997), 394–424.

Price, B. B. 1992. *Medieval Thought: An Introduction*. Oxford: Blackwell.

Price, N. C. & Stevens, L. 1982. *Fundamentals of Enzymology*. Oxford: Oxford University Press.

Pritchard, J. B. 1958a. *Archaeology and the Old Testament*. Princeton, NJ: Princeton University Press.
Pritchard, J. B. (ed.) 1958b. *The Ancient Near-East: An Anthology of Texts and Pictures*, vol. 1. Princeton, NJ: Princeton University Press.
Pumfrey, S. 1991. "The history of science and the renaissance science of history", in *Science, Culture and Popular Belief in Renaissance Europe*, S. Pumfrey *et al.* (eds), 48–70. Manchester: Manchester University Press.
Quinton, A. 1980. *Francis Bacon*. Oxford: Oxford University Press.
Quirke, S. 1990. *Who Were the Pharaohs?* New York: Dover Publications.
Quirke, S. 1992. *Ancient Egyptian Religion*. London: British Museum Press.
Quirke, S. & Spencer, J. (ed.) 1992. *The British Museum Book of Ancient Egypt*. London: British Museum Press.
Raikes, R. L. 1966. "The physical evidence for Noah's flood", *Iraq* **28**, 52–66.
Rappaport, R. A. 1971. "Ritual, sanctity and cybernetics", *American Anthrolopogist* **73**, 59–76.
Rappaport, R. 1978. "Geology and orthodoxy: the case of Noah's Flood in eighteenth-century thought", *British Journal for the History of Science* **37**, 1–18.
Rasmussen, B. 2000. "Filamentous microfossils in a 3,235-million-year-old volcanogenic massive sulphide deposit", *Nature* **405** (8 June), 676–9.
Raven, C. E. 1942. *John Ray, Naturalist: His Life and Works*. Cambridge: Cambridge University Press.
Raven, P. H. & Johnson, G. B. 1996. *Biology*, 4th edn. St. Louis, Boston and London: Mosby Year Book.
Ravetz, J. R. 1990. "The Copernical revolution", in *Companion to the History of Modern Science*, R. C. Olby *et al.* (eds), 201–16. London: Routledge.
Raymo, C. 1998. *Sceptics and True Believers: The Exhilarating Connection Between Science and Religion*. New York: Allen and Unwin.
Read, J. 1961. *Through Alchemy to Chemistry*. London: G. Bell and Sons.
Redondi, P. 1998. "From Galileo to Augustine", in Machamer (ed.) (1998), 175–210.
Rees, M. 1998. *Before the Beginning*. London: Touchstone.
Reichenbach, H. 1952. *From Copernicus to Einstein*. New York: The Philosophical Library.
Renfrew, C. 1994. "The archaeology of religion", in *The Ancient Mind*, C. Renfrew & E. B. W. Zubrow (eds), 47–54. Cambridge: Cambridge University Press.
Renfrew, C. & Bahn, P. 1996. *Archaeology: Theories, Methods and Practices*, 2nd edn. London: Thames & Hudson.
Reymond, A. 1927. *History of the Sciences in Greco-Roman Antiquity*. New York: Dutton and Co.
Riches, J. K. 1990. *The World of Jesus: First Century Judaism in Crisis*. Cambridge: Cambridge University Press.
Riley-Smith, J. 1977. *What were the Crusades?* London: Rowman & Littlefield.
Riley-Smith, J. (ed.) 1997. *The Oxford Illustrated History of the Crusades*. Oxford: Oxford University Press.
Rist, J. 1996. "Plotinus and Christian philosophy", in Gerson (ed.) (1996), 386–413.
Rist, J. 2001. "Faith and reason", in *The Cambridge Companion to Augustine*, E. Stump & N. Kretzmann (eds), 26–39. Cambridge: Cambridge University Press.
Ritland, R. 1982. "Historical development of the current understanding of the geological column: part II", *Origins* **9**(1), 28–50.
Robbins, L. H. 1990. *Stones, Bones and Ancient Cities*. New York: St. Martin's Press.
Roberts, J. M. 1988. *The Penguin History of the World*. Harmondsworth: Penguin.
Roberts, D. 1995. "Egypt's Old Kingdom", *National Geographic* **187**(1), 2–44.
Roberts, A. & Donaldson, J. (eds) 1995. *The Anti-Nicene Fathers, II*. Peabody, MA: Hendrickson.
Robin, H. 1992. *The Scientific Image: From Cave to Computer*. New York: Harry N. Abrams.
Robins, G. 1995. "Mathematics, astronomy and calendars in pharaonic Egypt", in Sasson *et al.* (eds) (1995), 1799–1813.
Robins, G. & Shute, C. 1987. *The Rhind Mathematical Papyrus*. London: British Museum Publications.
Robinson, V. 1931. *The Story of Medicine*. New York: The New Home Library.
Robinson, F. (ed.) 1996. *The Cambridge Illustrated History of the Islamic World*. Cambridge: Cambridge University Press.
Rochberg, F. 1995. "Astronomy and calendars in ancient Mesopotamia", in Sasson *et al.* (eds) (1995), 1925–40.
Roger, J. 1986. "The mechanistic conception of life", in Lindberg & Numbers (eds) (1986), 277–95.
Rolston, H. 1987. *Science and Religion: A Critical Survey*. Philadelphia, PA: Temple University Press.
Romer, A. S. 1962. *The Vertebrate Body*, 3rd edn. New York: W. B. Saunders.
Romer, J. 1989. *Testament: The Bible and History*. New York: Henry Holt.
Ronan, C. A. 1961. *Changing Views of the Universe*. New York: Macmillan.
Ronan, C. A. 1978. *The Shorter Science and Civilisation in China*, vol. 1. Cambridge: Cambridge University Press.
Ronan, C. A. 1982. *Science: Its History and Development among the World's Cultures*. New York: Facts on File.
Rosen, E. 1970–80. *Copernicus*, in Gillispie (ed.) (1970–80), **3**, 401–11.

Rosen, E. 1971. *Three Copernican Treatises*, 3rd edn. New York: Octagon Books.

Ross, W. D. (ed.) 1924. *Aristotle's Metaphysics*. Oxford: Oxford University Press.

Ross, W. D. (ed.) 1927. *Aristotle Selections*. New York: Charles Scribner's Sons.

Ross, W. D. 1950. "Aristotle", in *The Oxford Classical Dictionary*, M. Cary et al. (eds), 94–7. Oxford: Clarendon Press.

Ross, W. D. (ed.) 1959. *Aristotle*, 5th edn. New York: Meridian Books.

Ross, S. 1962. "Scientist: the story of the word", *Annals of Science* **18**, 65–85.

Rossi, P. 1970. *Philosophy, Technology and the Arts in the Early Modern Era*. New York: Harper & Row.

Rowan-Robinson, M. 1993. *Ripples in the Cosmos*. Oxford: W. H. Freeman Spektrum.

Rowe, C. 1997. "Plato: aethestics and psychology", in Taylor (ed.) (1997), 425–55.

Rudolph, K. 1987. *Gnosis: The Nature and History of Gnosticism*. New York: Harper & Row.

Rusch, W. G. 1977. *The Latin Fathers*. London: Duckworth.

Ruse, M. 1982. *Darwin Defended: A Guide to Evolutionary Controversies*. London: Addison-Wesley.

Russell, B. 1927. *Philosophy*. New York: W. W. Norton.

Russell, B. 1945. *A History of Western Philosophy*. New York: Simon and Schuster. (Copyright renewed 1972 Edith Russell)

Russell, B. 1956. "Mathematics and the metaphysicians", in *The World of Mathematics*, J. R. Newman (ed.), 1576–92. New York: Simon and Schuster.

Russell, B. 1959. *Wisdom of the West*, P. Foulkes (ed.). Garden City, NY: Doubleday.

Ryan, W. & Pitman, W. 1998. *Noah's Flood: The New Scientific Discoveries about the Event that Changed History*. New York: Simon & Schuster.

Rye, R. & Holland, H. D. 1998. "Paleosols and the evolution of atmospheric oxygen: a critical review", *American Journal of Science* **298**, 621–72.

Ryle, G. 1949. *The Concept of Mind*. Harmondsworth: Penguin.

Sagan, C. 1980. *Cosmos*. New York: Random House.

Sagan, C. & Shklovskii, I. 1966. *Intelligent Life in the Universe*. San Francisco: Holiden-Day.

Saggs, H. W. F. 1962. *The Greatness that was Babylon*. New York: Hawthorn Books.

Saggs, H. W. F. 1978. *The Encounter with the Divine in Mesopotamia and Israel*. London: Athlone.

Saggs, H. W. F. 1995. *The Babylonians: Peoples of the Past*. London: British Museum Press.

Sambursky, S. 1956. *The Physical World of the Greeks*. London: Routledge & Kegan Paul.

Sandmel, S. 1979. *Philo of Alexandria: An Introduction*. Oxford: Oxford University Press.

Sardar, Z. 1988. *Exploration in Islamic Science*. New York: Mansell Publishers.

Sardar, Z. 1998. "Science in Islamic philosophy", in Leaman (ed.) (1998), 561–5.

Sarich, V. M. & Cronin, J. E. 1977. "Molecular systematics of the primates", in *Molecular Anthropology*, M. Goodman & R. E. Tashan (eds), 141–70. New York: Plenum Press.

Sarton, G. 1931. "James Henry Breasted. The Edwin Smith Surgical Papyrus", *Isis* **15**, 355–67.

Sarton, G. 1952. *Ancient Science through the Golden Age of Greece*. Cambridge, MA: Harvard University Press.

Sasson, J. M., Baines, J., Beckman, G. & Rubinson, K. S. (eds) 1995. *Civilisations of the Ancient Near East*. New York: Charles Scribner's Sons.

Saw, R. L. 1964. "William of Ockham", in O'Connor (ed.) (1964), 124–40.

Sayce, A. H. 1872. "The Chaldean Account of the deluge and its relation to the Old Testament", *Theological Review* **10**, 364–77.

Scarborough, M. 1994. *Myth and Modernity: Postcritical Reflections*. New York: SUNY Press.

Schabas, M. 1990. *A World Ruled by Number: William Stanley Jevons and the Rise of Mathematical Economics*. Princeton, NJ: Princeton University Press.

Schafer, H. 1974. *Principles of Egyptian Art*. Oxford: Oxford University Press.

Schalit, A. 1969. "A clash of ideologies", in Toynbee (ed.) (1969), 48–76.

Schmandt-Besserat, D. 1992. *Before Writing: From Counting to Cuneiform*. Austin, TX: University of Texas Press.

Schmidt, B. B. 1995. "Flood narratives of ancient Western Asia", in Sasson et al. (eds) (1995), 2337–51.

Schofield, M. 1997. "The Ionians", in Taylor (ed.) (1997), 47–87.

Schofield, M., Burnyeat, M. & Barnes, J. 1980. *Doubt and Dogmatism: Studies in Hellenistic Epistemology*. Oxford: Oxford University Press.

Schopf, J. W. (ed.) 1983. *Earth's Earliest Atmosphere: Its Origin and Evolution*. Princeton, NJ: Princeton University Press.

Schopf, J. W. 1999. *Cradle of Life: The Discovery of Earth's Earliest Fossil*. Princeton, NJ: Princeton University Press.

Schopf, J. W. (ed.) 2002a. *Life's Origins: The Beginnings of Biological Evolution*. Berkeley, CA: University of California Press.

Schopf, J. W. 2002b. "When did life begin?", in Schopf (ed.) (2002a), 158–79.

Schrodinger, E. 1992 [1944]. *What is Life? With Mind and Matter and Autobiographical Sketches*. Cambridge: Cambridge University Press.

Schubert, K. 1969. "Jewish religious parties and sects", in Toynbee (ed.) (1969), 87–98.
Schuhl, P. M. 1973. "Myth in antiquity", in Wiener (ed.) (1973), 272–5.
Schurer, E. & Bigg, C. 1911. "Philo", in *The Encycopedia Britannica*, 11th edn, 409–12. New York: The Encycopedia Britannica.
Schwartz, G. M. 1995. "Pastoral nomadism in ancient Western Asia", in Sasson *et al.* (eds) (1995), 249–58.
Scott, M. P. & Weiner, A. J. 1984. "Structural relationships among genes that control development: sequence homology between antennapdeia, ultrabithorax and fushi tarazu loci of drosophila", *Proceedings of the National Academy of Sciences (USA)* **81**, 4115–19.
Scurlock, J. A. 1995. "Death and afterlife in ancient Mesopotamian thought", in Sasson *et al.* (eds) (1995), 1883–93.
Searle, J. R. 1992. *The Rediscovery of the Mind.* Cambridge, MA: MIT Press.
Sedley, D. 1980. "The protagonists", in *Doubt and Dogmatism: Studies in Hellenistic Epistemology*, M. Schofield, M. Burnyeat & J. Barnes, 1–19. Oxford: Oxford University Press.
Sedley, D. 1999. "Parmenides and Melssus", in Long (ed.) (1999), 113–33.
Semino, O., Passarino, G., Oefner, P. J. *et al.* 2000. "The genetic legacy of Paleolithic *Homo sapiens sapiens* in extant Europeans: a Y chromosome perspective", *Science* **290**(5494), 1155–9.
Settle, T. B. 1961. "An experiment in the history of science", *Science* **133**, 19–23.
Shafer, B. E. (ed.) 1991. *Religion in Ancient Egypt: Gods, Myths, and Personal Practice.* Ithaca, NY: Cornell University Press.
Shaw, I. & Nicholson, P. 1995. *British Museum Dictionary of Ancient Egypt.* London: British Museum Press.
Shea, W. 1998. "Galileo's Copernicanism: the science and the rhetoric", in Machamer (ed.) (1998), 211–43.
Sherratt, A. (ed.) 1980. *The Cambridge Encyclopedia of Archaeology.* New York: Crown Publishers and Cambridge University Press.
Sibley, C. G. & Ahlquist, J. E. 1984. "The phylogeny of hominoid primates, as indicated by DNA-DNA hybridisation", *Journal of Molecular Evolution* **20**, 2–15.
Sibley, C. G., Comstock, J. A. & Ahlquist, J. E. 1990. "DNA hybridisation evidence of hominoid phylogeny: a reanalysis of the data", *Journal of Molecular Evolution* **30**, 202–36.
Silk, J. 1989. *The Big Bang.* New York: W. H. Freeman.
Silver, B. L. 1998. *The Ascent of Science.* Oxford: Oxford University Press.
Silverman, D. P. 1991. "Divinity and deities in ancient Egypt", in Shafer (ed.) (1991), 7–87.
Simpson, G. G. 1949. *The Meaning of Evolution.* New Haven, CT: Yale University Press.
Simpson, G. G., Pittendrigh, C. S. & Tiffany, L. H. 1957. *Life: An Introduction to Biology.* New York: Harcourt, Brace & World.
Singer, C. 1944. *A Short History of Medicine.* Oxford: Clarendon Press.
Singer, D. W. 1968. *Giordano Bruno: His Life and Thought.* New York: Greenwood Press.
Singer, W. 1995. "Development and plasticity of cortical processing architectures", *Science* **270**, 758–64.
Sirat, C. 1985. *A History of Jewish Philosophy in the Middle Ages.* Cambridge: Cambridge University Press.
Skinner, H. A. 1970. *The Origin of Medical Terms*, 2nd edn. New York: Hafner Publishing.
Slack, J. M. W., Holland, P. W. H. & Graham, C. F. 1993. "The zootype and the phylotypic stage", *Nature* **361**, 490–92.
Smart, N. 1989. *The World's Religions.* Cambridge: Cambridge University Press.
Smart, N. 1991. *The Religious Experience*, 4th edn. New York: Macmillan.
Smith, H. W. 1952. *Man and His Gods.* Boston, MA: Little, Brown.
Smith, D. H. 1968. *Chinese Religions.* London: Weidenfeld and Nicolson.
Smith, A. G. R. 1972. *Science and Society in the Sixteenth and Seventeenth Centuries.* London: Harcourt Brace.
Smith, R. 1995. "Logic", in Barnes (ed.) (1995), 27–65.
Smith, L. M. & Roohk, B. L. 1985. *Introducing Biology*, 2nd edn. Dubuque, IA: Kendall Hunt.
Smoot, G. 1993. *Wrinkles in Time.* Berkeley, CA: Little, Brown and Company.
Smyth, P. 1880. *The Great Pyramid.* New York: Bell Publishing Company (reprinted 1980, W. Isbister, London).
Snell, D. C. 1995. "Methods of exchange and coinage in ancient Western Asia", in Sasson *et al.* (eds) (1995), 1487–97.
Snodgrass, A. 1980. *Archaic Greece: The Age of Experiment.* London: J. M. Dent and Sons.
Solmsen, F. 1960. *Aristotle's System of the Physical World: A Comparison with His Predecessors.* Ithaca, NY: Cornell University Press.
Solomon, R. C. & Higgins, K. M. 1996. *A Short History of Philosophy.* Oxford: Oxford University Press.
Sorabji, R. 1983. *Time, Creation and the Continuum.* London: Duckworth.
Sorabji, R. 1988. *Matter, Space and Motion: Theories in Antiquity and their Sequel.* London: Duckworth.
Southern, R. W. 1963. *Saint Anselm and His Biographer.* Cambridge: Cambridge University Press.
Southern, R. W. 1986. *Grosseteste.* Oxford: Clarendon Press.
Southgate, C. (ed.) 1999. *God, Humanity and the Cosmos.* London: T. &T. Clark.
Spade, P. V. 1994. "Medieval philosophy", in *The Oxford Illustrated History of Western Philosophy*, A. Kenny (ed.), 55–105. Oxford: Oxford University Press.

Spade, P. V. (ed.) 1999a. *The Cambridge Companion to Ockham*, P. V. Spade (ed.). Cambridge: Cambridge University Press.

Spade, P. V. 1999b. "Ockham's nominalist metaphysics: some main themes", in Spade (ed.) (1999a), 100–117.

Speiser, E. A. 1951. "Ancient Mesopotamia, a light that did not fail", *National Geographical Magazine* **49**, 41–105.

Speiser, E. A. 1960. "Three thousand years of Bible study", *The Centennial Review* **4**, 206–22.

Spence, K. 2000. "Ancient Egyptian chronology and the astronomical orientation of pyramids", *Nature* **408**, 320–24.

Spencer, A. J. 1993. *Early Egypt: The Rise of Civilization in the Nile Valley*. London: British Museum Press.

Stace, W. T. 1920. *A Critical History of Greek Philosophy*. London: Macmillan.

Stadelmann, R. 1995. "Builders of the pyramids", in Sasson *et al.* (eds) (1995), 719–34.

Stahl, W. H. 1962. *Roman Science*. Madison, WI: University of Wisconsin Press.

Stahl, W. H. 1970–80. "Aristarchus of Samos", in Gillispie (ed.) (1970–80), **1**, 246–50.

Stanley, S. M. 1981. *The New Evolutionary Timetable: Fossils, Genes, and the Origin of Species*. New York: Basic Books.

Stapleton, M. 1978. *The Hamlyn Concise Dictionary of Greek and Roman Mythology*. London: Hamlyn (reprinted 1992).

Starr, C. G. 1991. *A History of the Ancient World*. Oxford: Oxford University Press.

Stead, C. 1994. *Philosophy in Christian Antiquity*. Cambridge: Cambridge University Press.

Steedman, S. 1995. *Ancient Egypt*. London: Dorling Kindersley.

Steele, E. J., Lindley, R. A. & Blanden, R. V. 1998. *Lamarck's Signature: How Retrogenes are Changing Darwin's Natural Selection Paradigm*. St Leonards, NSW: Allen & Unwin.

Stein, P. L. & Rowe, B. M. 1989. *Physical Anthropology*, 4th edn. New York: McGraw-Hill.

Stevenson, A. J. (ed.) 1972. *Webster's New Geographical Dictionary*. Springfield, MA: G. & C. Merriam Company.

Stewart, D. J. 1965. "Man and myth in Plato's universe", *Bucknell Review* **13**, 72–90.

Stillman, J. M. 1960 [1924]. *The Story of Alchemy and Early Chemistry*. New York: Dover Publications.

Stone, R. 1995. "Mastering nature's strong force", *Science* **270**, 1756–7.

Stott, C. 1991. *Celestial Charts: Antique Maps of the Heavens*. London: Studio Editions.

Strang, C. 1975. "The physical theory of Anaxagoras", in Furley & Allen (eds) (1975), 361–80.

Street, F. 1980. "Ice age environments", in Sherratt (ed.) (1980), 52–6.

Stringer, C. 2003. "Human evolution: out of Ethiopia", *Nature* **423**(6941), 692–3.

Stringer, C. & Gamble, C. 1993. *In Search for the Neanderthals: Solving the Puzzle of Human Origins*. London: Thames & Hudson.

Stringer, C. & McKie, R. 1996. *African Exodus*. New York: Henry Hold.

Strong, J. 1978 [1894]. *Strong's Exhaustive Concordance of the Bible*. Nashville, TN: Abingdon Publishers.

Struik, D. J. 1987 [1948]. *A Concise History of Mathematics*, 4th rev. edn. New York: Dover Publications.

Stump, E. & Kretzmann, N. (eds) 2001. *The Cambridge Companion to Augustine*. Cambridge: Cambridge University Press.

Sutherland, N. S. (ed.) 1989. *Macmillan Dictionary of Psychology*. London: Macmillan.

Sutherland, S., Houlden, L., Clarke, P. & Hardy, F. (eds) 1988. *The World's Religions*. London: Routledge.

Swerdlow, N. M. 1973. "The derivation and first draft of Copernicus's planetary theory: a translation of the *Commentariolus* with commentary", *Proceedings of the American Philosophical Society* **117**(6), 423–512.

Swerdlow, N. M. 1998. "Galileo's discoveries with the telescope and their evidence for the Copernican theory", in Machamer (ed.) (1998), 244–70.

Swerdlow, N. & Neugebauer, O. 1984. *Mathematical Astronomy in Copernicus' De Revolutionibus*. New York: Springer.

Sykes, B. 2001. *The Seven Daughters of Eve: The Science that Reveals our Ancestry*. New York: W. W. Norton.

Szent-Gyorgyi, A. 1948. *Nature of Life: A Study of Muscle*. New York: Academic Press.

Tappert, T. G. (ed.) 1967. *Luther's Works, Vol. 54: Table Talk*. Philadelphia, PA: Fortress Press.

Taton, R. (ed.) 1963. *History of Science, Volume 1: Ancient and Medieval Science from the Beginnings to 1450*. New York: Basic Books.

Tattersall, I. 1999. *The Last Neanderthal: The Rise, Success and Mysterious Extinction of our Closest Human Relative*. Boulder, CO: Westview Press.

Tattersall, I. 2000. "Once we were not alone", *Scientific American* **282**, 39–44.

Taylor, A. E. 1934 [1926]. *Plato: The Man and his Work*, 4th edn. London: Metheun.

Taylor, C. C. W. 1990. "Aristotle epistemology", in *Epistemology*, S. Everson (ed.), 116–42. Cambridge: Cambridge University Press.

Taylor, J. 1990. "The future of Christianity", in McManners (ed.) (1990), 628–65.

Taylor, J. 1993. *When the Clock Struck Zero: Science's Ultimate Limits*. London: Picador.

Taylor, C. C. W. (ed.) 1997a. *Routledge History of Philosophy, Volume 1: From the Beginning to Plato*. London: Routledge.

Taylor, C. C. W. 1997b. "Anaxagoras and the atomists", in Taylor (ed.) (1997), 208–43.
Taylor, C. C. W. 1999. "The atomists", in Long (ed.) (1999), 181–204.
Tegmark, M. 2004. "Parallel universes", *Scientific American* **288**(5), 31–41.
Teilhard, P. 1955.*The Phenomenon of Man*. London: Collins.
Temkin, O. 1938. "The Papyrus Ebers – the greatest Egyptian document", *Isis* **28**, 126–31.
Temkin, O. 1991. *Hippocrates in a World of Pagans and Christians*. Baltimore, MD: Johns Hopkins University Press.
Te Velde, H. 1995. "Theology, priests and worship in ancient Egypt" in Sasson *et al.* (eds) (1995), 1731–49.
Thering, B. 1992. *Jesus the Man: A New Interpretation from the Dead Sea Scrolls*. Sydney: Doubleday.
Thomas, D. W. (ed.) 1958. *Documents from Old Testament Times*. New York: Thomas Nelson and Sons.
Thompson, A. M. 1992. "The oxidizing capacity of the earth's atmosphere: probable past and future changes", *Science* **256**, 1157–65.
Thomson, K. S. 2000. "Huxley, Wilberforce and the Oxford Museum", *American Scientist* **88**(3), 210–13.
Thorne, K. S. 1991. "Do the laws of physics permit closed timelike curves?", *Annals of the New York Academy of Science* **631**, 182–93.
Thorne, A. G. & Wolpoff, M. H. 1992. "The multiregional evolution of humans", *Scientific American* (April), 76–83.
Toomer, G. J. 1970–80a. "Hipparchus", in Gillispie (ed.) (1970–80), **6**, 207–24.
Toomer, G. J. 1970–80b. "Ptolemy (Claudius Ptolemaeus)", in Gillispie (ed.) (1970–80), **11**, 186–206.
Toy, C. H. 1913. *Introduction to the History of Religions*. Boston, New York, London: Ginn and Company.
Toynbee, A. (ed.) 1969. *The Crucible of Christianity: Judaism, Hellenism and Historical Background to the Christian Faith*. Cleveland, OH: World Publishing.
Tranoy, K. 1964. "Thomas Aquinas", in O'Connor (ed.) (1964), 98–123.
Trefil, J. 1994. *1001 Things Everybody Should Know about Science*. London: Cassell.
Trigger, B. G. 1993. *Early Civilizations: Ancient Egypt in Context*. Cairo: The American University in Cairo Press.
Tylecote, R. F. 1975. "The origin of iron smelting in Africa", *West African Journal of Archaeology* **5**, 1–9.
Tylor, E. B. 1958a [1873]. *Primitive Culture I: The Origins of Culture*. New York: Harper & Brothers.
Tylor, E. B. 1958b [1873]. *Primitive Culture II: Religion in Primitive Culture*. New York: Harper & Brothers.
Tylor, E. B. 1960 [1881]. *Anthropology (abridged and with a foreword by Leslie A. White)*. Ann Arbor, MI: University of Michigan Press.
Urbach, P. 1982. "Francis Bacon as a precursor to Popper", *British Journal of the Philosophy of Science* **33**, 113–32.
Uwins, P. J. R., Webb, R. I. & Taylor, A. P. 1998. "Novel nano-organisms from Australian sandstones", *American Mineralogist* **83**, 1541–50.
Van Dijk, J. 1995. "Myth and mythmaking in ancient Egypt", in Sasson *et al.* (eds) (1995), 1697–709.
Van Helden, A. 1985. *Measuring the Universe*. Chicago, IL: University of Chicago Press.
Van Wagenen, T. F. 1924. *Beacon Lights of Science: A Survey of Human Achievement from Earliest Recorded Times*. New York: Thomas Crowell.
Vegetti, M. 1995. "The Greeks and their gods", in *The Greeks*, J.-P. Vernant (ed.), 254–84. Chicago, IL: University of Chicago Press.
Vegetti, M. 1999. "Culpability, responsibility, cause: philosophy, historiography, and medicine in the fifth century", in Long (ed.) (1999), 271–89.
Veggeberg, S. 1992. "Cosmic wormholes: where science meets science fiction", *The Scientist* **6**(5) (July), 15–16.
Veneziano 2004. "The myth of the beginning of time", *Scientific American* **290**(5), 30–39.
Venter, J. C. *et al.* 2001. "The sequence of the human genome", *Science* **291**(5507), 1304–51.
Vercoutter, J. 1992. *A Search for Ancient Egypt*. London: Thames & Hudson.
Vitsaxis, V. G. 1977. *Hindu Epics, Myths and Legends in Popular Illustrations*. Delhi: Oxford University Press.
Vlastos, G. 1970. "Theology and philosophy in early Greek thought", in Furley & Allen (eds) (1970), 92–129.
Vlastos, G. 1975a. *Plato's Universe*. Seattle, WA: University of Washington Press.
Vlastos, G. 1975b. "The physical theory of Anaxagoras", in Furley & Allen (eds) (1975), 323–53.
Vlastos, G. 1991. *Socrates: Ironist and Moral Philosopher*. Cambridge: Cambridge University Press.
von Neumann, J. 1955 [1932]. *Mathematical Foundations of Quantum Mechanics*. Princeton, NJ: Princeton University Press.
Wagner, M. F. 1996. "Plotinus on the nature of physical reality", in Gerson (ed.) (1996), 130–70.
Wainwright, M. 1999. "Nanobacteria and associated 'elementary bodies' in human disease and cancer", *Microbiology* **145**, 2623–4.
Wald, G. 1954. "The origin of life", *Scientific American* **191**, 45–53.
Wald, G. 1973. "Fitness in the universe: choices and necessities", in *Cosmological Evolution and the Origins of Life*, J. Oró *et al.* (eds), 7–27. Dordrecht: D. Reidel.

Walker, K. 1955. *The Story of Medicine*. Oxford: Oxford University Press.

Wallace, A. R. 1858. "On the tendency of varieties to depart indefinitely from the original type", *Proceedings of the Linnean Society of London* **3** (1 July), 53–62.

Wallace, A. R. 1871. *Contributions to the Theory of Natural Selection: A Series of Essays*, 2nd edn. New York: Macmillan.

Wallace, W. A. 1972. *Causality and Scientific Explanation*, vol. 1. Ann Arbor, MI: University of Michigan Press.

Wallace, W. E. 1998. "Galileo's Pisan studies in science and philosophy", in Machamer (ed.) (1998), 27–52.

Walzer, R. 1967. "Early Islamic philosophy", in *The Cambridge History of Later Greek and Early Mediaeval Philosophy*, A. H. Armstrong (ed.), 643–69. Cambridge: Cambridge University Press.

Ward, K. 1994. *Religion and Revelation: A Theology of Revelation in the World's Religions*. Oxford: Clarendon Press.

Warner, R. 1994. "Introduction: the mind–body debate", in *The Mind–Body Problem*, R. Warner & T. Szubka (eds), 1–16. Oxford: Blackwell.

Warren, P. 1975. *The Making of the Past: The Aegean Civilization*. Oxford: Elsevier.

Warren, P. 1987. "Crete: The Minoans and their gods", in *Origins: The Roots of European Civilization*, B. Cunliffe (ed.), 30–41. London: BBC Books.

Watson, J. D., Hopkins, N. H., Roberts, J. W. *et al.* 1987. *Molecular Biology of the Gene*, 4th edn. Menlo Park, CA: The Benjamin/Cummings Publishing Co.

Watterson, B. 1997. *The Egyptians*. London: Blackwell Publishers.

Weeks, K. R. 1995. "Medicine, surgery and public health in ancient Egypt", in Sasson *et al.* (eds) (1995), 1787–98.

Weinberg, S. 1977. "The search for unity: notes for a history of quantum field theory", *Daedalus* (Fall), 17–36.

Weinberg, S. 1988. *The First Three Minutes*. New York: Basic Books.

Weinberg, S. 1994. "Life in the universe", *Scientific American* (October), 22–7.

Weinberg, S. 1999. "A unified physics by 2050", *Scientific American* **281**(6), 36–43.

Weisheipl, J. A. 1954. "The concept of nature", *The New Scholasticism* **28**, 377–408.

Weisheipl, J. A. 1978. "The nature, scope, and classifications of the sciences", in *Science in the Middle Ages*, D. C. Lindberg (ed.), 461–82. Chicago, IL: University of Chicago Press.

Wellard, J. 1972. *Babylon*. New York: Saturday Review Press.

Wendt, H. 1974. *From Ape to Adam: The Search for the Ancestry of Man*. London: Book Club Associates.

West, M. L. 1978. *Hesiod's Works and Days*. Oxford: Clarendon Press.

West, W. M. 1904. *The Ancient World*. Boston, MA: Norwood Press.

Westermann, C. 1984 [1974, Germany]. *Genesis 1–11: A Commentary*. London: SPCK.

Westfall, R. S. 1971. *The Construction of Modern Science: Mechanisms and Mechanics*. New York: Wiley and Sons.

Westfall, R. S. 1980. *Never at Rest: A Biography of Isaac Newton*. Cambridge: Cambridge University Press.

Westfall, R. S. 1986. "The rise of science and the decline of orthodox Christianity: a study of Kepler, Descartes and Newton", in Lindberg & Numbers (eds) (1986), 218–37.

Westfall, R. S. 1990. "Making a world of precision: Newton and the construction of a quantitative worldview", in *Some Truer Method: Reflections on the Heritage of Newton*, F. Durham & R. D. Purrington (eds), 59–88. New York: Columbia University Press.

Westfall, R. S. 1991. "Galileo and Newton: two different rhetorical strategies", in *Persuading Science: The Art of Scientific Rhetoric*, M. Pera & W. Shea (eds), 107–22. Canton, MA: Science History Publications.

Westman, R. S. 1986. "The Copernicans and the Churches", in Lindberg & Numbers (eds) (1986), 76–113.

Weyl, H. 1949. *Philosophy of Mathematics and Natural Science*. Princeton, NJ: Princeton University Press.

Whewell, W. 1840. *Philosophy of the Inductive Sciences: Founded upon their History*. London: Harrison.

White, A. D. 1922. *A History of the Warfare of Science with Theology in Christendom*. New York and London: D. Appleton and Co.

White, G. W. 1970. *Contributions to the History of Geology, volume 5: James Hutton's System of the Earth (1785)*, *Theory of the Earth (1788)*, *Observations on Granite (1794)*, *together with Playfair's Biography of Hutton*, intro. by V. A. Eyles. New York: Hafner Press.

White, R. 1980. "Calvin and Copernicus", *Calvin Theological Journal* **15**, 233–43.

White, T. D., Asfaw, A., De Gusta, D. *et al.* 2003. "Pleistocene *Homo sapiens* from Middle Awash, Ehtiopia", *Nature* **423**(6941), 742–7.

White, M. & Gribbin, J. 1994. *Einstein: A Life of Science*. London: Simon and Schuster.

White, T. D., Suwa, G. & Asfaw, B. 1995. "*Australopithecus ramidis*, a new species of early hominid from Aramis, Ethiopia", *Nature* **375**, 88.

Whitehead, A. N. 1926. *Religion in the Making*. New York: Macmillan.

Whitehead, A. N. 1933 [1926]. *Science and the Modern World*. Cambridge: Cambridge University Press.

Whitehouse, D. 1980. "The origins and growth of archaeology", in Sherratt (ed.) (1980), 16–24.

Whitehouse, H. 1995. "Egypt in European thought", in Sasson *et al.* (eds) (1995), 15–32.

Whitfield, J. H. 1943. *Petrarch and the Renaissance*. Oxford: Oxford University Press.

Whitt, W. D. 1995. "The story of the Semitic alphabet", in Sasson *et al.* (eds) (1995), 2379–97.

Wiener, P. P. (ed.) 1973. *Dictionary of the History of Ideas: Studies of Selected Pivotal Ideas*. New York: Charles Scribner's Sons.

Wiggermann, F. A. M. 1995. "Theologies, priests, and worship in ancient Mesopotamia", in Sasson *et al.* (eds) (1995), 1857–70.

Wightman, W. P. D. 1953. *The Growth of Scientific Ideas*. New Haven, CT: Yale University Press.

Wigner, E. P. 1961. "Remarks on the mind–body question", in *The Scientist Speculates*, I. J. Good (ed.), 284–302. New York: Basic Books.

Williams, H. S. 1930. *The Great Astronomers*. New York: Simon & Schuster.

Williams, R. J. 1958. "The Hymn to Aten", in *Documents from Old Testament Times*, D. W. Thomas (ed.), 142–50. London: Thomas Nelson.

Williams, R. 1991. "The Bible", in *Early Christianity: Origins and Evolution to AD 600*, I. Hazlett (ed.), 81–91. London: SPCK.

Wills, C. & Bada, J. L. 2001. *The Spark of Life: Darwin and the Primeval Soup*. New York: Basic Books.

Wilson, J. A. 1951a. *The Culture of Ancient Egypt*. Chicago, IL: University of Chicago Press.

Wilson, J. A. 1951b. "Egypt", in Frankfort *et al.* (eds) (1951), 39–103.

Wilson, R. W. 1979. "The cosmic microwave background radiation", *Science* **205**, 866–74.

Wilson, A. C. & Cann, R. L. 1992. "The recent African genesis of humans", *Scientific American* (April), 68–73.

Wippel, J. F. 1977. "The condemnation of 1270 and 1277 at Paris", *Journal of Medieval and Renaissance Studies* **7**, 169–210.

Wippel, J. F. 1993. "Metaphysics", in Kretzmann & Stump (eds) (1993), 85–127.

Woese, C. R. 1981. "Archaebacteria", *Scientific American* **244**, 94–107.

Woese, C. 1999. "The universal ancestor", *Proceedings of the National Academy of Sciences (USA)* **95**(12), 6854–9.

Wolfson, H. A. 1969. "Greek philosophy in Philo and the church fathers", in Toynbee (ed.) (1969), 309–16.

Wolkstein, D. & Kramer, S. N. 1983. *Inanna: Queen of Heaven and Earth*. London: Rider and Company.

Wong, E. 1996. "An economic case for basic research", *Nature* **381**, 187–8.

Wood, B. 1992. "Origin and evolution of the genus Homo", *Nature* **355**, 783–90.

Wood, B. 1996. "Human evolution", *Bioessays* **18**(12), 945–54.

Wood, B. & Brooks, A. 1999. "We are what we eat", *Nature* **400**, 219–20.

Wood, B. & Collard, M. 1999a. "The changing face of genus Homo", *Evolutionary Anthropology* **8**, 195–207.

Wood, B. & Collard, M. 1999b. "The human genus", *Science* **284**(5411), 65–71.

Woolley, C. L. 1928. *The Sumerians*. Oxford: Clarendon Press.

Woolley, L. 1954. *Excavations at Ur*. New York: Thomas Y. Crowell.

Woolley, L. 1963. "The beginnings of civilization", in *History of Mankind: Prehistory and the Beginnings of Civilization*, J. H. A. L. Woolley (ed.), 359–854. New York: Harper & Row.

Wright, M. R. 1997. "Empedocles", in Taylor (ed.) (1997), 175–207.

Yinger, J. M. 1970. *The Scientific Study of Religion*. New York: Macmillan.

Yoffee, N. 1995. "The economy of ancient western Asia", in Sasson *et al.* (eds) (1995), 1387–400.

Ziman, J. 1978. *Reliable Knowledge*. Cambridge: Cambridge University Press.

Index